Peace-Making in the Middle East

Peace-Making in the Middle East

Edited by Lester A. Sobel

Contributing editor: Hal Kosut

Facts On File, Inc.
119 West 57th Street, New York, N.Y. 10019

Peace-Making in the Middle East

Published by Facts On File, Inc.,
119 West 57th Street, New York, N.Y. 10019.

Library of Congress Cataloging in Publication Data

Main entry under title:

Peacemaking in the Middle East.

   (Facts On File publication)
   Includes index.
   1. Israel-Arab War, 1973—Peace. 2. Egypt—
Foreign relations—Israel. 3. Israel—Foreign rela-
tions—Egypt. 4. Jordan (Territory under Israeli
occupation, 1967–   ) 5. United Nations—Palestine.
I. Sobel, Leser A.   II. Kosut, Hal.   III. Maidens,
Melinda.
DS128.183.P42   956'.048   80-14441
ISBN 0-87196-267-5

9 8 7 6 5 4 3 2 1
PRINTED IN THE UNITED STATES OF AMERICA

Contents

Reason for Peace Versus Causes of War

A NTAGONISMS SMOLDER AND FREQUENTLY boil over in the Middle East. *Jihad* (the Arabic word for holy war) is no stranger to the Holy Land. For reasons of religion, history, politics and economics, those who dwell in the Middle East are often at each others' throats. For equally valid reasons, the disputes and blood-lettings of the region concern and possibly even endanger most countries of the rest of the world.

The depth and complexity of the problems involved cause many people to doubt that peaceful resolutions can be achieved in the Middle East. Some groups seem to oppose actions to end hostilities there. Some even work to keep the fires of hatred burning. Yet there have always been those who labor for peace. The would-be peacemakers often come from distant countries. They always face frustration and frequently meet with failure. And the factors obstructing accommodation usually seem stronger than those promoting peace.

Toward the end of the 1970s, however, a break-through was recorded in what seems to be the most serious and intractable of the Middle East's problems, the dispute between Israel and the Arabs. With the United States acting as peacemaker, Israel achieved a peace treaty with the most formidable of its hostile neighbors, Egypt.

Ironically, it is said, the Arab-Israeli dispute may be the greatest unifying force in the Middle East, greater even than the pull of pan-Arabism or Islamic unity. Sworn enemies in the Middle East can often sit down in amity to discuss brotherly cooperation in the campaign against Israel.

1

The land now known as Israel, and its immediate neighbors, served throughout history as both highway and battleground for the world's conquerers. The emergence of Islam in the seventh century added another power to the pageant of armies that fought and pillaged their way through the Middle East. But although the conquests of Islam were dramatic and far-flung—from Spain to India and beyond—Islam itself was soon split by antagonistic religious sects. These divisions continue to the present, compounded by ethnic and political rivalries. Although united as Muslims and as foes of Israel, Arab nations do not always find much strength in unity. Their governments seem to live under the constant threat of revolution, religious violence or attack from even an Islamic ally.

Lebanon is the most conspicuous as well as the most tragic example of an Arab country torn by internal discord and inter-Arab conflict. Although Muslims number somewhat more than half of the population, most elements had seemed willing to accept the political myth that fifty-five per cent of Lebanese were Christians. Operating under this fiction and the governing machinery it justified, Lebanon had been peaceful much of the time, and its economy had prospered. This benign but obviously precarious arrangement was ended as a by-product of the Arab-Israeli wars. Lebanon became a haven for a growing number of Palestinian Arab refugees and a base for Palestine Liberation Organization (PLO) attacks on Israel.

The Palestinian presence proved to be a disaster for Lebanon. PLO attacks on Israel brought Israeli military response. And the Lebanese suffered as severely as did the PLO commando groups from Israel's retaliatory strikes. Lebanese factions sprang up in opposition to—or in support of—PLO activities on Lebanese soil. Dormant conflicts were awakened. By mid-1975 the country was in a state of confusing, generalized strife that virtually amounted to all-out civil war.

Despite inter-Arab conflict, Arab-Israeli hostility is considered the chief problem of the Middle East and is the principal target of the outside peacemakers. Arab-Israeli wars have produced more than a million and a half Arab Palestinian refugees, whose plight has aroused the concern of world leaders and fellow Arabs. Although this concern is interpreted sometimes as cynical and is seen as lubricated occasionally by the oil of the Middle East, it does bring many champions of the Palestinians into the arenas at the United Nations and other international forums that comprise the verbal killing ground of the Arab-Israeli wars.

The Arab-Israeli conflict presents the peace-makers with a problem that exists in probably all intractable struggles of this kind.

Neither side can be expected to compromise its objectives unless either it is faced with almost certain destruction or it is offered better terms for peace than it can hope to win through continued fighting. In the case of the Palestinians and the Israelis, the leaders of each side describe the struggle as one of survival as a people. This appears to be a genuine conviction on both sides. As long as it is sincerely held, there can be little or no compromise and, therefore, little or no possibility of realistic bargaining for peace.

Many of Israel's citizens remember the Nazi Holocaust as personal, individual and family tragedies rather than as impersonal history. They invoke this memory as a warning made immanent by past Arab threats to sweep the Israelis "into the sea" and by the reaffirmed Palestinian National Charter (or "Covenant"), whose call for "the liberation of Palestine" and "the elimination of Zionism in Palestine" by "armed struggle" is quite specifically aimed at the extinction of the state of Israel. An oft-repeated reply of Israeli militants is the Holocaust-inspired slogan "Never Again!"

Israel has its "doves," its "moderates" and its "hawks." Israel has suffered greatly in its wars with the Arabs. There is much agitation for peace in war-weary Israel. Yet an overwhelming majority of Israelis appears to support the policy of the government not to make peace on terms that would greatly endanger the continuation of Israel as a Jewish state. The stated Israeli goal amounts to peace under conditions that the Israelis would perceive as offering reasonable security. They concede that their terms are probably not acceptable to their antagonists.

The situation of the Palestinians provides little hope for early agreement. Except for those who live in Israel and the occupied territories (the Israeli-occupied West Bank of the Jordan and the Gaza Strip), almost all Palestinians are either former Arab residents of Palestine who have been embittered in exile for periods of up to thirty years and longer or younger people born in exile and educated to hate Israeli Jews as usurpers who drove their parents from their homeland.

Palestinians seem to feel that they can hope for little through compromise. Israel, it is argued, is not likely to cooperate in its own destruction. But demography, economics and international politics are seen as being all on the side of the Palestinians.

The population growth of the Arabs far exceeds that of the Israeli Jews, and Arab spokesmen predict that the Jewish population must ultimately drown in a human sea of Arabs. The Palestinians hold that the thirst for Middle Eastern oil will make Western and Third World nations more and more fearful of antagonizing the Arab oil producers and increasingly solicitous of Arab desires. The sympathies of Third World nations, moreover, may be further aroused by the charge that Israel is a racist, colonialist outpost of an American imperialism whose destructive rapacity has already caused untold harm to the dark-skinned natives of four continents. This accusation is enthusiastically seconded by the Soviet Union and other Communist nations, from whom Palestinian commandos have reason to expect material as well as propaganda support.

The Palestinians thus may have good cause for feeling that all they have to do to defeat Israel is to keep up the pressure. Israel will finally be overwhelmed by Arab numbers, by the practical requirements of the oil-using economies and by the righteous indignation of an aroused Third World. What value, therefore, can the Palestinians place in peace through compromise?

The Arab nations may have less reason than the Palestinians for fighting Israel, but they do not in every case have strong reasons for making peace with the Jewish state.

Aside from Lebanon, the only Arab nation with strong cause to want peace probably is impoverished Egypt. It was Egypt that bore the brunt of the Arab-Israeli wars; Egypt was the country that sent most men into the fray; Egypt suffered most of the casualties of the wars; Egypt lost most of the land seized by Israel when the Arabs were defeated. And it was Egypt, with its poverty-stricken masses, that paid most for the wars through continued economic underdevelopment despite subsidies from the Arab oil producing countries. Thus, as perhaps could have been expected, it was Egypt that became the first Arab nation to put aside unprofitable hostility and to negotiate a peace treaty with Israel. First, however, Egypt "vindicated" its honor through its October 1973 war with Israel. And by agreeing to peace, Egypt was able to recover captured land that it had been unable to win back by either war or diplomacy.

The other Arab nations probably have good reason to feel that there is little for them to gain through making peace with Israel, even if, unlike the Palestinians, they would have little to lose. Reasons for Arab governments to continue supporting the Palestinians and opposing peace may include such factors as Arab unity, Islamic unity, a conclusion that the Palestinian cause is just, mass religious demand, antagonism toward Western imperialism (of which they claim that Israel is a tool), support for the Soviet Union (a factor that obviously would not influence the more anti-Communist governments) and the diversion of domestic discontent toward an external adversary. Significantly, none of these reasons, even in combination, proved sufficient to keep Egypt from opting for peace. If they are offered sufficient motivation, how many other

Arab nations would abandon confrontation and bargain for peace?

The Western nations have an obvious stake in Middle East peace—oil. War in the Middle East could cause more than temporary disruptions or unconscionable increases in oil prices. If hostilities produced changes in governments or alliances in the Middle East, the new hands at the oil spigot might turn off the flow in directions determined by political considerations. The losers would almost certainly include the West.

But there is an another and equally strong motivation for Western efforts to bring peace to the Middle East. Increasingly, it appears, the local clashes there threaten to embroil the great powers in a conflagration that conceivably may bring devastation to much of the world. It is presumed that the great powers are cautious and sophisticated enough to keep their confrontations from reaching such a level. However, there are no guarantees. The higher the stakes, the greater the risks that may be considered justified. Somebody may make a mistake. In such a situation, there are unlikely to be any real winners.

The Middle East is an area where major American and Soviet interests conflict. U.S. Ambassador-at-Large Alfred L. Atherton, Jr., pointed out in Pittsburgh April 3, 1979, at the Conference on Examination of Vital Interests in the Middle East, that "there are few areas in the world today where so many different and important American interests come together." A partial list includes: "our historic and moral commitment to the security of Israel"; U.S. relations with the Arab nations, a consideration that comprises "access to oil and cooperation in maintaining order in the global economy"; "our humanitarian commitment to those people of the region—above all the homeless Palestinians"; "concern for the dangers which persisting crisis in this region poses for global stability, for superpower confrontation and for the prosperity of the United States and its allies."

Others have described Western—primarily American—interests in Middle East peace more bluntly. The dangers posed by Soviet activities in the area are frequently emphasized. Sen. Jacob K. Javits (R, N.Y.) warned in a 1976 speech that "the Soviet Union has made the Mideast a prime target for expansion and control. . . . The radical socialist forces which have seized control of a number of Arab states have closely aligned themselves internationally with the Soviet Union; and the Soviet Union . . . has placed billions upon billions of rubles worth of sophisticated military equipment in the hands of Arab governments whose avowed aim has been to drive Israel into the sea."

Sen. Charles McC. Mathias, Jr. (R, Md.), provided an equally sharp warning about the perils implicit in continued conflict in the Middle East. "The military explosions that have punctuated Arab-Israeli relations since 1948 have increasingly menaced U.S. interests," he asserted, "for they not only threaten Israel's security but they also enable the U.S.S.R. to seek its own advantage in troubled waters. Soviet involvement on the Arab side and U.S. involvement on the Israeli side have raised the specter of direct great-power confrontation in the area which won't be laid to rest until some settlement is reached."

Even those who suspect Soviet motives, however, do not deny that the U.S.S.R. may prefer to achieve its objectives through methods less dangerous than those of war. Bernard Lewis, professor of the history of the Near and Middle East at the University of London, had discussed Soviet activities in the Middle East in the aftermath of the October 1973 war. Testifying March 8, 1974 before the U.S. Senate Permament Subcommittee on Investigations, Lewis said that the Soviets then were "more concerned with the Chinese than with the Western adversary and therefore inclined to avoid confrontation on matters where the U.S. shows firmness. They are permitting and to some extent encouraging the movement toward peace, but at the same time are taking the routine precaution of laying a political minefield across the way to peace which they can detonate at any time that peace endangers Soviet interests."

IN THE TROUBLED HISTORY OF THE MIDDLE EAST, the goal of peace has never been easy to achieve and has often seemed impossible to attain. Causes of hostility abound in the area, and fresh reasons are not infrequently imported from afar. Over the centuries, reasons to make peace have often seemed less convincing than causes of war. This book is intended to serve as a record of the efforts to make peace in the Middle East since the October 1973 war. To some extent, it can be considered a companion volume to the 1977 FACTS ON FILE book *Palestinian Impasse: Arab Guerrillas & International Terror*. It covers some of the same territory but essentially tells a different part of the story. The material that follows consists principally of the record compiled by FACTS ON FILE in its weekly reports on world affairs. A conscientious effort was made to record all events without bias and to produce a balanced and accurate reference work.

LESTER A. SOBEL

New York, N.Y.
May, 1980

Ending the 1973 Hostilities

Egyptian-Israeli Cease-Fire & Separation of Forces

The fourth war between Israel and its Arab neighbors started Oct. 6, 1973 on Yom Kippur, the Jewish Day of Atonement, with a simultaneous two-front attack on Israel by Egypt and Syria. The all-out fighting was halted after intensive United Nations Security Council sessions and the adoption by the Council of no fewer than three cease-fire resolutions Oct. 22, 23, and 25.

There was no clear cut victor of the 1973 war, and the cease-fire agreement produced no resolution of the basic dispute between the adversaries. Continued minor clashes between the opposing forces posed a threat of a renewal of the war. This threat was largely defused in mid-January 1974 by an Israeli-Egyptian agreement to separate their military forces at the Suez Canal.

Agreement to Disengage. Egypt and Israel Jan. 18, 1974 signed an accord to separate their military forces along the Suez Canal. The agreement had been announced simultaneously Jan. 17 in Jerusalem, Cairo and Washington. The pact had been negotiated through the mediation of U.S. Secretary of State Henry A. Kissinger, who had held separate meetings with Egyptian and Israeli officials, shuttling between Aswan and Jerusalem Jan. 11–17.

The accord was in two parts: one dealt with the actual pullback of troops and establishment of disengagement zones; the other provided for the limitation of troops and arms in the zones. Details of the latter agreement were kept secret. Copies of it were signed by Premier Golda Meir in Jerusalem and by President Anwar Sadat in Aswan. Kissinger attended both ceremonies.

The troop withdrawal treaty was signed at Kilometer 101 on the Suez-Cairo road by the Egyptian and Israeli chiefs of staff—Maj. Gen. Mohammed Abdel el-Gamasy and Lt. Gen. David Elazar. The commander of the United Nations Emergency Force (UNEF), Lt. Gen. Ensio Siilasvuo, presided.

The text of the agreement was accompanied by a map delineating the zones of disengagement. Israel was to abandon its bridgehead on the west bank of the Suez Canal and withdraw its forces on the east bank 14–20 miles from the waterway. In the southern sector the Israelis would be deployed immediately west of the Mitla and Gidi Passes, which controlled the routes into the heart of the Sinai Peninsula. The Egyptians were to remain on the east bank in a 5–7½ mile-wide zone. The Israeli zone was to be of equal size. Both forces were to be separated by a buffer zone 3½–5 miles deep patrolled by UNEF troops.

7

The accord pledged that Israel and Egypt would "scrupulously observe the cease-fire" and stressed that the agreement was only the first step toward a permanent peace.

In his announcement Jan. 17 of the disengagement accord, U.S. President Richard M. Nixon had said that Americans could "be proud of the role that our government has played, and particularly the role that has been played by Secretary Kissinger and his colleagues" in bringing both sides closer together.

While describing the pact as "the first significant step toward a permanent peace in the Middle East," the President stressed "the difficulties that lie ahead" in resolving other aspects of the dispute.

Nixon noted the mediative role the U.S. had conducted in bringing Egypt and Israel "together, to help them narrow differences, working toward a thorough and just settlement for all parties concerned where every nation in that region will be able to live in peace...." The President pledged continued U.S. involvement to that end, saying "I personally shall see that all negotiations, any efforts, which could lead to a permanent peace, not only between Egypt and Israel but between other countries involved, have the full and complete support" of the U.S. government.

Israeli Knesset Approves Pull-Back. The Israeli Knesset (parliament) Jan. 22 approved the Suez troop disengagement agreement by a vote of 76 to 35 following sharp debate in which right-wing Likud Party members denounced the accord as a surrender.

The debate opened with a statement by Premier Golda Meir in which she declared that the object of the agreement was to attain "a permanent peace settlement." The alternative, she warned, "is nothing but the renewal of the war."

Menachem Begin, leader of Likud, assailed the agreement as a unilateral pullback and a violation of the government's mandate, which he said was committed to make peace, not to carry out a withdrawal.

Another Likud member attacking the government's position was Maj. Gen. Ariel Sharon, who had announced his resignation from the army Jan. 18 to protest the disengagement accord.

Sadat tours Arab states. Egyptian President Anwar Sadat toured eight Arab states Jan. 18–23 to rally support for Egypt's troop disengagement agreement with Israel.

At his last stop in Rabat, Morocco Jan. 23, Sadat called his meetings with the Arab leaders a "complete success." Sadat, who had met Jan. 19 with Syrian President Hafez al-Assad in Damascus, disclosed that Syria was willing to meet with Israel to discuss separation of their military forces along the Golan Heights front. Peace talks suspended in Geneva would not resume until that matter was settled, Sadat said.

Sadat said the reopening of the Suez Canal was "purely a matter of Egyptian sovereignty" and was "in no way" linked to the disengagement accord. He said that pact dealt only with military matters and there had been no secret agreement with Israel. The U.S. was no longer following a policy of giving Israel "total and unconditional support," Sadat noted. The U.S., he said, "now says they favor a balance of power in the area."

After meeting with Algerian President Houari Boumedienne in Algiers Jan. 22, Sadat said at a news conference that the Arab oil-producing states should take note of "an evolution" in U.S. policy in the Middle East since Kissinger first visited the area in November 1973. Without mentioning the oil embargo against the U.S., Sadat said "now that the Americans have made a gesture, the Arabs should make one too."

Government-controlled newspapers in Iraq and Libya Jan. 21 condemned the agreement, asserting that it "ushers American penetration and domination into the area." The Iraqi government newspaper Al Jomhouriya urged · that progressive Arab forces prevent other countries from making similar agreements with Israel.

Palestinians at odds over Suez pact— The Palestinian guerrilla movement was reported Jan. 21 to have split over the Egyptian-Israeli troop separation agreement.

Criticism of the accord came from the Palestine Liberation Organization (PLO), which represented the various commando groups. The position taken by its key members was regarded as a challenge to Yasir Arafat, head of the organization's Executive Committee and leader of Al Fatah. President Sadat said Arafat endorsed the agreement.

The Executive Committee denounced the agreement at a meeting Jan. 20 and sent a cable to Sadat expressing its opposition. Arafat disavowed the criticism in a telegram to Sadat Jan. 21. Arafat said the committee meeting at which the statement was drawn up was illegal because he was not in attendance.

A member of the committee said Jan. 21 that the group regarded the Israeli-Egyptian agreement a "surrender to the American plan." He pledged continued war against Israel "until all occupied Palestinian soil is liberated."

A committee member denied a report Jan. 20 in the Egyptian newspaper Al Ahram that the committee had approved establishment of a PLO coordination group with Egypt following Arafat's meeting with Sadat in Aswan Jan. 18. Arafat was present at Sadat's signing of the troop separation agreement.

Suez troop separation begins. Details of the agreement to separate the Israeli and Egyptian forces along the Suez Canal were completed Jan. 24 at a meeting held at Kilometer 101 on the Cairo-Suez road. Participants were the two armies' chiefs of staff—Lt. Gen. David Elazar and Maj. Gen. Mohammed Abdel el-Gamasy.

Military officers of both sides had been meeting since Jan. 20 to work out the technical arrangements that were based on the more general agreement reached by Israel and Egypt Jan. 18. The meetings were presided over by Lt. Gen. Ensio Siilasvuo, commander of the United Nations Emergency Force (UNEF).

The troop withdrawal formally got under way Jan. 25 after Israel had begun moving troops and armor on the canal's west bank eastward to new positions in the Sinai Jan. 23, two days before the deadline. Engineers also had started removing minefields in the area.

Disengagement completed—The separation of forces along the canal was completed March 4, 1974. Israeli troops withdrew to their prescribed Sinai zone after turning over the east bank of the waterway to troops of the United Nations Emergency Force (UNEF). Egyptian troops moved in six hours later and assumed control of both banks of the canal for the first time since the 1967 war.

UNEF troops then completed deployment in their buffer zone between the Israeli and Egyptian sectors.

The U.S. Navy had sent demolition experts to the Suez Canal to advise Egypt on clearing mines and other explosives from the waterway, an American official disclosed Feb. 26. The mission was being undertaken at Egypt's request.

U.S. to sweep Suez mines. The U.S. Navy was authorized to help clear the Suez Canal of mines and unexploded ordnance under a formal agreement reached by Egypt and the U.S. March 18. British naval ships also were to participate in the project.

The State Department said the U.S. also had agreed to provide technical advice and to train Egyptian personnel in clearing explosives from the waterway and its banks.

The Soviet Union was reported March 26 to be pressing Egypt for a role in the canal clearance program. An 11-man Soviet team had arrived in Egypt and started to survey the canal a few days earlier, foreign diplomats in Cairo said. According to the diplomats, Moscow had warned Egypt that leaving the operation exclusively to the Americans and British would pose a serious military security problem since some of the military equipment at the bottom of the canal might include secret weapons that Egypt had received from the Soviet Union.

The Soviet Communist Party newspaper Pravda April 21 voiced opposition to some of Egypt's Middle East policies and was especially critical of the Cairo-approved British and U.S. role in the clearance of mines and explosives from the Suez Canal as it related to the use of Cyprus as a supply base.

Pravda noted that U.S. participation in the project called for its helicopters and ground personnel to be brought to Cyprus. Utilization of British bases on that island to assemble the aircraft established "a dangerous precedent" for a continuing U.S. presence in the region, Pravda said.

The Soviet journal quoted several Cyprus newspapers of April 21 protesting that the U.S. was employing the helicopters to "create a pretext" for setting up a permanent military base on the island.

Syria Urged to Negotiate

Kissinger presses Syria on talks. U.S. Secretary of State Henry A. Kissinger completed a fresh diplomatic tour of the Middle East by flying Jan. 20, 1974 to Damascus, where he called on the Syrians to enter into negotiations with Israel.

After a four-hour meeting with President Hafez al-Assad, Kissinger stopped briefly in Tel Aviv to convey to Israeli officials Syria's latest stand. He said Assad had submitted to him "very constructive suggestions" on disengagement of Israeli and Syrian forces on the Golan Heights and on a final peace settlement. Assad had given him assurances that the Israeli prisoners held by Syria "are being treated in a humane fashion," Kissinger disclosed. The secretary was not given a list of the prisoners demanded by Israel as its condition for negotiating with Syria. But another U.S. official said later that Assad had agreed to turn over the list when Syrian-Israeli discussions started. Damascus had previously insisted that the names of the POWs would not be handed over until after conclusion of the talks.

The Israeli officials apprised of Assad's views by Kissinger were Deputy Prime Minister Yigal Allon, Defense Minister Moshe Dayan and Foreign Minister Abba Eban.

Before flying to Damascus, Kissinger had stopped briefly at Aqaba, Jordan where he conferred Jan. 19–20 with King Hussein and Premier Zaid al-Rifai. Rifai announced after the talks that Israel and Jordan would "shortly" start negotiations. Jordan would insist that "the first item of discussion" be the disengagement

of Israeli and Jordanian forces along the Jordan Valley, the premier said.

Kissinger reports on mission—Kissinger returned to Washington Jan. 21 and he and President Nixon later that day briefed 16 Congressional leaders at a closed meeting on the secretary's latest trip to the Middle East..

A senior State Department official later disclosed the "eight or nine" assurances and understandings that Kissinger had developed with the Israelis and Egyptians in his discussions with them Jan. 11–17. These unwritten principles were in addition to the troop disengagement agreement and the arms limitation accord, still unpublished.

Among the statements:

■ The U.S. had informed Israel that it assumed that after the troop pullback along the Suez Canal Egypt would reopen the waterway to international shipping, including Israel-bound vessels.

■ Cairo told the U.S. that it could inform Israel that after signing of the disengagement accord Egypt would no longer blockade the Bab el Mandeb strait at the entrance to the Red Sea. The blockade actually had been lifted in November 1973 under a secret agreement with the U.S. and Israel.

■ The U.S. assured Israel that it would continue to receive American support for its existence, including military assistance, but there would be no formal commitment to this effect.

■ The U.S. told Israel it believed that the United Nations Emergency Force (UNEF) to be deployed in a buffer zone between the Israeli and Egyptian zones in the Suez Canal area could only be disbanded by the U.N. Security Council. The previous UNEF force had been unilaterally dispersed by Egypt in 1967 without a Council vote.

Kissinger told reporters at a news conference Jan. 22 that he had been given assurances by Arab leaders that when the Israeli-Egyptian disengagement accord was reached, the Arab oil embargo against the U.S. would be lifted. He said failure to do so "in a reasonable time would be highly inappropriate and would raise serious questions of confidence in our minds with respect to the Arab nations with whom we have dealt on this issue."

Kissinger said the U.S. had no formal obligation to act in case the disengagement agreement was violated by either side. However, he foresaw American involvement if Egypt or Israel asked the U.S. for "diplomatic support."

Although the reopening of the Suez Canal would benefit the Soviet Union by permitting its fleet to move more readily from the Mediterranean to the Indian Ocean, the U.S. "can be compensated both by the greater ease with which we can transfer some of our ships to the Indian Ocean and other measures that can be taken of a different nature," Kissinger said.

Syria prodded on pullback accord. The Soviet Union urged Syria Jan. 30 to agree to a military disengagement with Israel, similar to the accord Egypt had reached with Israel.

The Soviet statement, appearing in the Communist Party newspaper Pravda, said, "The issue of disengagement of troops as a first step toward the settlement of the issue" of Arab territories occupied by Israel "directly involves Syria." Damascus' refusal to enter into such an agreement played into the hands of Israel, which was "persistently pursuing a line toward weakening the unity of Arab countries," Pravda said.

Egyptian Foreign Minister Ismail Fahmy had briefed Soviet leaders on the accord with Israel during a visit to Moscow Jan. 21-24.

The Soviet Union endorsed the Israeli-Egyptian agreement in a joint communique Jan. 24. It cautioned, however, that the pact had a "positive significance" only if it was followed by "a radical settlement in the Middle East" that was based on the United Nations Security Council resolutions of 1967 and 1973 calling for Israeli withdrawal from Arab territories.

Egyptian officials said Jan. 27 that the Soviet leaders had promised Fahmy they would exert their influence on Syria to reach agreement with Israel. Egypt was said to be seeking a more active Soviet role in the Geneva conference.

Premier Golda Meir, expressing interest Jan. 30 in negotiations between Israel and Syria on military disengagement, said her country had no intention of retaining Syrian territory captured in the October 1973 war. But she reiterated Israeli opposition to enter into such discussions until Syria provided a list of its Israeli prisoners and permitted International Red Cross officials to visit them. Mrs. Meir also ruled out Israeli negotiations with "Arab terrorist organizations" at the Geneva conference. She said they were "not interested in territorial questions but only in expelling Jews from the land of Israel."

U.S. seeks Israeli-Syrian talks. State Department officials in Washington said Feb. 9 that the U.S. had begun to sound out Syria and Israel on a formula to negotiate an agreement to disengage their troops on the Golan Heights and to have Syria issue a list of Israeli war prisoners they held. Secretary of State Henry A. Kissinger was acting as intermediary.

State Department officials had informed Israel that the Soviet Union would try to use its influence to get Syria to submit the POW list and to permit International Red Cross officials to visit the captives, Foreign Minister Abba Eban disclosed Feb. 10. It was believed Soviet Foreign Minister Andrei A. Gromyko had given Kissinger such assurances in their talks in Washington Feb. 4.

Israeli government sources Feb. 5 had reported the Cabinet's rejection of a U.S. compromise proposal to get talks started with Syria. Under the plan, Syria would meet one of Israel's conditions for agreeing to negotiations by providing a list of prisoners. Syria, however, would not permit Red Cross officials to visit the prisoners, as demanded by Israel, until progress had been made in the talks. Premier Golda Meir was said to have polled her ministers on the U.S. formula Feb. 4 and they rejected it.

Meir had told settlers in the Golan Heights Feb. 8 that Israel considered the Syrian territory taken in 1967 "an inseparable part of Israel." She was quoted as saying that Israel would not withdraw beyond the cease-fire lines that were established in that conflict.

Plans for building a city on the heights were announced by the Israeli government Feb. 10.

President Nixon announced Feb. 19 that Kissinger had again been designated to go to the Middle East in a personal effort to bring about negotiations between Israel and Syria on disengagement of their forces on the Golan Heights.

Nixon made the announcement in the presence of Ismail Fahmy and Omar Saqqaf, the Egyptian and Saudi Arabian foreign ministers, who had conferred with Kissinger Feb. 16–18. They submitted to Kissinger a plan for Syrian-Israeli disengagement drawn up at a summit conference in Algiers Feb. 13–14 of the leaders of Egypt, Syria, Saudi Arabia and Algeria. Kissinger held another meeting with Fahmy Feb. 20 and with Sabah Kabani, Syria's chief diplomat in Washington. The secretary also held separate discussions Feb. 17 and 19 with Simcha Dinitz, Israeli ambassador to Washington.

Neither Kissinger nor the Arab diplomats would disclose what they had discussed, but it was known their meetings dealt with the Arab oil embargo against the U.S. and the Syrian-Israeli negotiations.

A final communique issued at the Algiers summit Feb. 14 did not mention the oil embargo or the proposed Israeli-Syrian talks. The joint statement only reaffirmed the call for withdrawal of Israel from all Arab territories and a guarantee of Palestinian rights. The conferees decided to send Fahmy and Saqqaf on their mission to Washington.

Attending the summit were President Anwar Sadat of Egypt, King Faisal of Saudi Arabia, President Houari Boumedienne of Algeria and President Hafez al-Assad of Syria.

Kissinger meets Assad, Meir—Kissinger flew to Damascus Feb. 26 and conferred with Syrian President Hafez al-Assad to pave the way for Syrian negotiations with Israel. Kissinger was said by officials to have been in possession of the roster of 65 Israeli POWs held by Syria before his arrival in Damascus, but was unable to turn it over to Israel until he was authorized by Assad in their seven hours of talks.

The secretary flew to Jerusalem Feb. 27 and gave the list to Premier Golda Meir. He also gave her Assad's assurances that International Red Cross officials would be permitted to visit the captives starting March 1.

Israeli officials said the release of the prisoner list and the promise of Red Cross visits fulfilled Israel's conditions for holding talks with Syria. A U.S. official said an understanding had been reached that the 65 Israeli prisoners and the 386 Syrians held by Israel would be exchanged as soon as a disengagement accord was arranged.

Syrian-Israeli talks set in U.S. Israeli and Syrian representatives were to continue negotiations on troop disengagement in separate talks with Kissinger in Washington at the end of March, it was announced by U.S. officials March 2.

The announcement was made in the plane carrying Kissinger from Amman to Riyadh, Saudi Arabia, the last leg of his current Middle East peace trip. The decision to continue the disengagement discussions followed Kissinger's latest visit to Damascus March 1 after completing his discussions in Cairo that day with Egyptian President Anwar Sadat. Before going to the Syrian capital, Kissinger visited Israel to receive Premier Golda Meir's proposal on troop separation. He then transmitted the plan to President Hafez al-Assad in Damascus later March 1. Assad found the plan unacceptable and gave Kissinger an undisclosed counterproposal for relay to the Israelis "in order to continue the talks on disengagement of troops," a Damascus official said.

Kissinger left Damascus March 2 and flew to Riyadh and conferred with King Faisal. He left the same day for Amman, where he met with Jordan's King Hussein.

After a stopover in Bonn, West Germany March 3, Kissinger returned to Washington March 4 and reported to President Nixon the following day.

Gromyko visits Syria, Egypt. Soviet Foreign Minister Andrei A. Gromyko visited Syria and Egypt Feb. 27–March 6. His mission followed U.S. Secretary of State Henry A. Kissinger's tour of those two countries earlier in the week.

Kissinger's round of talks in the Egyptian and Syrian capitals had been critically alluded to by the Soviet Communist Party newspaper Pravda Feb. 24. An article warned the Arabs, including Syria, that the main goal of U.S. diplomacy was "not a settlement of the Middle East problem, but the lifting as soon as possible" of the Arab oil embargo against the U.S. "The peoples of Arabic countries are maintaining their vigilance toward any maneuvers directed at infringing upon their legal rights," Pravda said.

Gromyko echoed Pravda's sentiments in a speech in Damascus Feb. 28, one day after arriving in the Syrian capital. He said, "The opponents of a just and lasting peace both in Israel and beyond [an apparent reference to the U.S.] want to retain the Arab lands captured by them. In this they hope by means of various maneuvers and tricks they will manage to split the Arabs and their friends and allies."

After conferring with President Hafez al-Assad and other Syrian officials, Gromyko flew to Cairo March 1, a few hours after Kissinger ended his 24-hour visit to the Egyptian capital. Gromyko met with President Anwar Sadat during his stay until March 5, at which time a joint communique was issued. It stressed that both governments would work closely toward a settlement of the Arab-Israeli conflict.

Gromyko returned to Damascus and held more discussions with President Assad March 5–6. A joint communique March 7 declared that a Syrian-Israeli disengagement agreement should be "an inseparable part" of a final peace settlement—"a first step for full Israeli withdrawal from all occupied territories according to a fixed timetable."

Syria demands total Israeli pullout— President Hafez al-Assad declared March 8 that Syria would continue its state of belligerency against Israel until "all the Arab territory is liberated." Assad told a Damascus rally, "If Israeli leaders think we are tired of fighting or making sacrifices, then they have made another serious mistake." Challenging Israel's claim to the Golan Heights, Assad said Palestine, including the state of Israel, was "a basic part of southern Syria."

For the first time, Assad publicly endorsed Resolution 242 adopted by the United Nations Security Council after the 1967 war. However, the president said his government accepted the resolution as a basis for a political settlement only "if it fulfills there two conditions": total Israeli withdrawal from occupied Arab territories and Israeli recognition of the full "rights" of the Palestinians.

Israel claims Syrian war plan. Premier Golda Meir said March 8 that Israel had received "reliable information from diplomatic sources that Syria had a plan" to renew the war to recapture the territory it had lost to Israel in the October 1973 conflict.

It was believed the U.S. had informed Israel of Syria's alleged plan to renew the fighting. In a television address, Meir said other foreign sources and Israel's own field reports confirmed that the Syrian armed forces were in a high state of alert. She said Israel had urged "foreign governments" to take action to prevent a new outbreak of hostilities.

In response to the Syrian buildup, Israeli troops had been on maximum alert for the past two days. Leaves had been canceled and units on the Golan Heights reinforced. Meir implied that the Soviet Union was contributing to the tension as a result of Foreign Minister Andrei A. Gromyko's late visit to Damascus, which was followed by a joint Soviet-Syrian communique March 7 warning of a possible outbreak of war.

Meir's statement followed an Israeli report of three skirmishes on the Syrian front earlier March 8. Sporadic clashes continued through March 13.

Arab League meets in Tunis. The foreign ministers of the 20-nation Arab League met in Tunis March 25–28, 1974 to discuss prospects for an Israeli-Syrian troop disengagement agreement, a summit meeting of Arab heads of state and other Middle East problems.

The conference was marked by an open clash between Syria and Egypt. Syrian Foreign Minister Abdel Halim Khaddam accused Egypt March 26 of isolating his country by negotiating a separate disengagement agreement with Israel. He said that Cairo's insistence on lifting the Arab oil embargo against the U.S. had encouraged Israel to move slowly on troop pullback on the Golan Heights front.

The Syrian attack prompted Egyptian Foreign Minister Ismail Fahmy to make an unexpected trip to Tunis March 27 to take part in the Arab League meeting. Before meeting that day with Khaddam, Fahmy told newsmen that "Egypt will never abandon Syria." After a final discussion with Khaddam March 28, Fahmy told a news conference, "There is no conflict between Syria and Egypt. We are co-ordinating our positions all the time."

Syria renews truce conditions—Speaking at a news conference in Tunis March 28, Foreign Minister Khaddam reiterated the two principal conditions Israel must accept in exchange for a troop disengagement agreement. He said that when the indirect negotiations on the accord start in Washington, Syria would insist that Israel "must recognize the obligation to withdraw from all the Arab territories it occupies, . . . without exception" and that it "must recognize the legitimate national rights of the Palestinian people."

The Problems of Jerusalem & the West Bank

Vatican changes stand on Jerusalem. The Vatican no longer favored internationalization of Jerusalem and dropped its objections to Israeli control of its holy shrines, a Vatican spokesman said Feb. 5, 1974 in an interview with the Israeli newspaper Haaretz.

The spokesman, Federico Alessandrini, said, "Internationalization of Jerusalem, which the church originally supported is not a realistic solution today. The church wishes free access to holy places for freedom of religion."

Vatican sources had reported Jan. 8 that Pope Paul VI was intensifying his efforts to have a voice in settling the Jerusalem problem. The Vatican had earlier made public a memorandum the pope had written after a pilgrimage to the desire of Catholics for "guardianship over the Holy Places."

Paul urged Roman Catholics April 5 to increase pilgrimages to Jerusalem to strengthen the presence of the church there and in other parts of the Holy Land (Israel).

The pope's plea, contained in an apostolic exhortation, expressed concern that if the Christian presence in Israel were to "cease, the shrines would be without the warmth of this living witness and the Christian holy places of Jerusalem and the Holy Land would become like museums." The statement stressed that the pope's ap-

peal was "intended to have no other significance than a religious and charitable one." This was later confirmed by a Vatican aide, who denied at a news conference that the appeal had any political meaning.

In a specific reference to the status of the holy places in Jerusalem, the pope said that "the continuing existence of situations lacking a clear juridical basis that is internationally recognized and guaranteed" constituted a threat to peace.

In another statement on the status of Christian shrines, the pope told a weekly general audience April 10 that he supported an "appropriate international juridical guardianship for the holy places" in the Middle East and deplored the fact that Jerusalem remained a source of friction. A revised version of the statement issued later by the Vatican press officers raised the question whether the pope had hardened his position and was now advocating internationalization of the city, a move Israel had always rejected. The press spokesmen quoted the pope as having called for "an appropriate statute with international guarantees for the holy city of Jerusalem and a convenient juridical guardianship for the holy places."

Moslems urge Arab restoration. A summit meeting of heads of state and government of 38 Moslem nations, held in Lahore, Pakistan Feb. 22–24, 1974, called for Jerusalem's restoration to the Arabs.*

A conference declaration Feb. 23 recognized the Palestine Liberation Organization as "the sole legitimate representative of the Palestine nation in its just struggle." A PLO delegation headed by Yasir Arafat attended the summit.

A resolution adopted at the Feb. 23 meeting stressed the Arab demand for the return of Old Jerusalem and its shrines to

---

*Participants in the conference: Afghanistan, Algeria, Bahrain, Bangla Desh, Chad, Egypt, Gabon, Gambia, Guinea, Guinea Bissau, India, Indonesia, Iran, Iraq, Jordan, Kuwait, Lebanon, Libya, Malaysia, Mali, Mauritania, Morocco, Niger, Nigeria, Oman, Pakistan, Palestine Liberation Organization, Qatar, Saudi Arabia, Senegal, Somalia, South Yemen, Sudan, Syria, Tunisia, Turkey, Uganda, United Arab Emirates and Yemen.

Among the heads of state attending were King Faisal of Saudi Arabia, and Presidents Anwar Sadat of Egypt, Muammar el-Qaddafi of Libya, Houari Boumedienne of Algeria and Hafez al-Assad of Syria.

the Arabs. "Restoration of the holy city of Jerusalem to Arab sovereignty is a paramount and unchangeable prerequisite for any solution in the Middle East," the statement said. It added: "Any solution which does not restore this position will not be acceptable to the Islamic countries." The resolution rejected any attempt to internationalize the city. The Islamic nations, the resolution said, were "convinced that the military, economic, political and moral support given to Israel by some countries, particularly the United States, enables it to pursue the execution of its policy of aggression and to consolidate its occupation of Arab territories."

Another resolution called for "action in all fields to force Israel to withdraw immediately and unconditionally from all Arab territories occupied since 1967." It "condemned all states that provide Israel with military, economic and human assistance" and urged "an end to this practice immediately."

Sadat sees U.S. policy change— Egyptian President Anwar Sadat, a key figure at the Lahore conference, told a news conference Feb. 24 that as a result of his previous meetings with Secretary of State Henry A. Kissinger, he believed the U.S. was changing its policies on Israel. Sadat said he did not expect Washington to shift its allegiance from Israel to the Arab states, but felt the U.S. would probably now conduct a more evenhanded approach to the Middle East.

King Hussein meets Nixon. King Hussein of Jordan conferred with President Nixon and other U.S. officials in Washington March 12.

The king was assured by Nixon that the U.S. would continue to use its influence to bring about peace between Israel and the Arabs, including Jordan, even if the oil embargo against the U.S. was not lifted at a meeting of the Arab oil producers March 13.

Hussein also met with Secretary of State Henry A. Kissinger and Defense Secretary James Schlesinger to discuss Jordan's need for U.S. military equipment.

In a New York Times interview March 14, Hussein called on Israel to accept his offer of negotiations with his government

through the U.S. The monarch referred to Israel's reluctance to enter into such talks until it came to an agreement with Syria on troop disengagement on the northern front, saying that "no country in the area can afford to sit and wait."

The king confirmed published reports that he had suggested an Israeli-Jordanian troop withdrawal scheme and transmitted the proposal to Israel through Kissinger during their meeting in Jordan Jan. 19. The plan he proposed would require Israeli forces to pull back from the Jordan River to a line on the western edge of the Jordan Valley, with the strip between made into a demilitarized zone. Kissinger was said to have informed Hussein that the Israelis would not accept his proposal but would favor a plan of their own in which they would retain their military positions along the Jordan River and turn over the populated parts of the northern half of the West Bank to Jordanian administration.

Hussein rejected the Israeli counteroffer at a closed meeting of his Parliament Feb. 13. The king said: "For Jordan, separation of forces means the beginning of Israeli withdrawal from the West Bank. It should be all along the front from the Dead Sea to the positions in the north. And it should be as deep as possible."

Oil Pressure

Arabs meet on lifting ban. Petroleum ministers of nine Arab states met in Tripoli, Libya March 13, 1974 to consider lifting the oil ban against the U.S. and restoring the production cuts imposed after the 1973 Arab-Israeli war. According to widespread reports, the conferees agreed to end the ban and were to formalize their decision at a full meeting of the 13-member Organization of Petroleum Exporting Countries to be held in Vienna March 17.

According to an unidentified Libyan official March 13, the ministers agreed to lift the embargo, but wouldn't announce the step in Libya, possibly out of deference to the host country's known opposition to lifting the ban.

Attending the Tripoli meeting were the nations that joined in the embargo and production curtailment: Abu Dhabi, Algeria, Bahrain, Egypt, Kuwait, Libya, Qatar, Saudi Arabia and Syria. A terse communique did not mention action taken on the embargo or the production curbs. It merely said the meeting had discussed the world tours taken by Sheik Ahmed Zaki al-Yamani and Belaid Abdelsalam, Saudi and Algerian petroleum ministers, to apprise other nations of the Arab oil stand. The ministers re-examined earlier decisions "in light of developments in the Middle East situation," the statement said. The communique concluded by announcing the time and place of the OPEC meeting.

The oil conference originally had been scheduled in Cairo March 10 at President Anwar Sadat's invitation. However, it was called off that day after representatives of only six of the nine nations appeared. The absent states were Algeria, Libya and Syria, which were opposed to removing the oil restrictions until there was evidence that progress was being made in forcing Israel to withdraw from the Golan Heights.

The site of the conference also appeared to be a source of friction. In a move to overcome this obstacle, a press statement issued by the ministers of Egypt, Saudi Arabia, Kuwait, Abu Dhabi, Qatar and Bahrain announced that the meeting of all nine countries would be held March 13 in Tripoli, restoring it to the site where it originally was to be held Feb. 14. The statement attributed the first shift from Tripoli to Cairo to logistical reasons but explained that the meeting was changed back to the Libyan capital since those problems had now been overcome.

Soviets back continued oil ban—The Soviet Union called for the continued oil embargo against the U.S. and criticized those Arab states that favored lifting the ban.

One Moscow broadcast monitored in London March 12 said if "some Arab leaders are ready to surrender in the face of American pressure and lift the oil ban before those demands [for Israeli withdrawal] are fulfilled, they are taking a chance by challenging the whole Arab world and the progressive forces of the world, which insist on the continued use of the oil weapon."

Another Soviet broadcast March 5 had said "United States imperialism has hid-

den behind the mask of a friend of the Arabs in order to break up Arab unity."

U.S. officials in Washington March 12 conceded that the Soviet Union was taking the side of the radical Arab states on the oil embargo, but said this was only a reiteration of a standing policy and did not represent a major shift.

7 nations lift ban. Seven of nine Arab petroleum-producing countries agreed at a meeting in Vienna March 18 to lift the oil embargo they had imposed against the U.S.

One of the seven nations, Algeria, said it was removing the ban provisionally until June 1. The Arab producers were to meet again on that date in Cairo to review their decision. The embargo was to remain in effect against the Netherlands and Denmark. The delegates placed Italy and West Germany on the list of "friendly nations," assuring them of larger supplies.

The Arab decision on the embargo, taken at an OPEC meeting, was approved by Algeria, Saudi Arabia, Kuwait, Qatar, Bahrain, Egypt and Abu Dhabi. Libya and Syria refused to join the majority. Iraq boycotted the talks.

The OPEC delegates agreed at the March 17 meeting that oil prices would not be rolled back, despite protests and appeals from consumer nations. A communique said the oil ministers would convene a new meeting if any of the countries asked for one before July "with a view to revising the posted prices" for oil.

Saudi Arabia was the only country which pressed for a lower price for oil.

With the announcement of the agreement to end the oil embargo, Saudi Arabia pledged March 18 an immediate production increase of a million barrels a day for the U.S. market.

A formal statement on the Arab decision did not mention the restoration of production cutbacks. The communique explained that a shift in American policy away from Israel had prompted the producers to terminate the embargo. The new U.S. "dimension, if maintained, will lead America to assume a position which is more compatible with the principle of what is right and just toward the Arab-occupied territories and the legitimate rights of the Palestinian people."

Algerian Petroleum Minister Belaid Abdelsalam said March 18 his country believed the U.S. had shown enough "goodwill" in using its influence to get Israel to carry out military disengagement with Egypt and to agree to contacts with Syria to negotiate a similar pullback to warrant lifting the embargo. Libya and Syria, however, were not convinced of this and decided not to go along with the majority opinion, Abdelsalam said.

Saudi Arabia Petroleum Minister Sheik Ahmed Zaki al-Yamani said March 18 the decision against resuming the flow of Arab oil to the Netherlands and Denmark was taken because these two countries "have not made clear their position on asking for a full [Israeli] withdrawal from occupied territories."

Saudis renew oil shipments to U.S. Saudi Arabia had resumed shipment of oil to the United States, it was reported March 25. The action officially marked the end of the Saudi oil embargo.

Resumption of the oil shipments was coupled with Saudi Arabia's formal notification to the Arabian-American Oil Co. (Aramco) March 21 to increase production by one million barrels a day to approximately the pre-October 1973 level of 8.3 million barrels a day, a company spokesman said March 24.

The first tanker heading for the U.S. had left a Saudi port with 1.5 million barrels of Saudi crude, it was reported March 26.

Nixon for permanent peace. U.S. President Nixon, speaking March 19, 1974 at a convention of the National Association of Broadcasters in Houston, Tex., said that when the Arabs reviewed their oil decision, the U.S. would press for a permanent peace in the Middle East regardless of the oil embargo. The President stressed that "being a friend of one of Israel's neighbors does not make us an enemy of Israel." It was in the long-term interest of all the Mideast countries, he said, that the U.S. "play a constructive and positive role." And while the Soviet and U.S. interest were not always the same in the area, "there cannot be permanent peace in the Mideast if the Soviet Union is against it." Therefore, "our policy of working toward permanent peace with Israel, with her neighbors and working with the Soviet Union where the Soviet Union is willing to work with us, is in the best interests of everybody concerned."

The lifting of the embargo, he said, was in the interest of the countries that imposed it as well as in the U.S. interest. "Inevitably, what happens in one area affects the other, and I am confident that the progress we are going to continue to make on the peace front in the Mideast will be very helpful in seeing to it that an oil embargo is not reimposed."

Sadat meets Tito. Egyptian President Anwar Sadat met with Yugoslav President Tito on the Adriatic island of Brioni March 28–30 and discussed the Middle East situation and their respective policies among the nonaligned nations.

At a news conference before returning to Cairo March 30, Sadat sought to counter Tito's reported objections to his reliance on American mediation efforts and his willingness to end the oil embargo against the U.S. without the consent of Libya and other radical Arab states. Sadat said the U.S. "is one of the two superpowers who guaranteed" U.N. ceasefire resolutions, thus making it "normal" for Egypt to have continued contacts and exchanges with Washington as well as with Moscow.

At a dinner given in Sadat's honor March 28, Tito had warned that Israeli leaders had not renounced their "aggressive thinking," that the Middle East crisis was not over and that a true settlement would not come about until Israel gave up "all occupied Arab lands."

Israel & Syria: Talks & Clashes

Indirect negotiations under way. U.S.-sponsored indirect negotiations to bring about a Syrian-Israeli troop disengagement on the Golan Heights front began March 29, 1974 as Israeli Defense Minister Moshe Dayan submitted an Israeli proposal in talks with Secretary of State Henry A. Kissinger in Washington.

The Israeli plan was not divulged, but Kissinger said March 30 after conclusion of the talks that the proposal Dayan had given him provided "a useful basis" for negotiations of the troop pullback.

Dayan also expressed optimism about a future agreement with Syria and predicted that the sharp fighting on the Syrian front "will not deteriorate into an all-out war."

(The Israeli disengagement formula was known to provide essentially for the withdrawal of Israeli troops from the 150-square-mile Syrian territory seized in the October 1973 war and establishment of a United Nations buffer zone between "thinned-out" areas on the Syrian-Israeli front lines.)

Dayan met with Defense Secretary James Schlesinger April 1 to discuss Israel's need for more U.S. arms. Before departing for Israel that day, Dayan said he had been assured that U.S. aid to Israel would continue.

The defense minister had said March 31 that his country wanted more sophisticated weapons to counter continuing Soviet arms shipments to Syria and Egypt. Speaking on the NBC-TV program "Meet the Press," Dayan said he was generally satisfied with the quality of U.S. weaponry, but noted that the antiaircraft missiles the Soviet Union was sending the Arabs were of "higher quality." He said the Israeli defense force was satisfied with the U.S. antitank missiles.

Clashes on Golan Heights. Israel reinforced and alerted its troops on the Golan Heights front April 2 as defense officials expressed fear that the unabated tank and artillery clashes with Syria presaged a possible all-out war by the Syrians.

United Nations Secretary General Kurt Waldheim told the Security Council April 2 that the situation "remains unstable and potentially dangerous" on the Syrian front. He recommended a six-month extension of the U.N. Emergency Force (UNEF) after its current mandate expired April 24.

The U.S. was reported April 2 to have appealed to Syria and Israel to bring a halt to the fighting. Egypt was said to have expressed similar concern to Damascus.

Two U.N. observers—an American and an Irishman—were captured by the Syrians March 31. Syria claimed the two

men, who were not wearing their uniforms, were mistaken for Israelis. They promised their quick return after Waldheim protested to Syria's U.N. representative April 2.

Syrian Deputy Premier Mohammed Haidar said April 1 that the "fighting is natural" since Syria, but not Israel, had accepted the U.N. Security Council's October cease-fire resolution. Israel, he claimed, had thus far failed to comply with the resolution's requirement that it withdraw from all occupied Arab territory.

Israeli jets attack Syrians. Israeli jets April 6 went into action for the first time since the October 1973 war, striking twice at Syrian forces that crossed the truce line in the Golan Heights.

The air strikes were directed against Syrian units that crossed the ceasefire line on Mount Hermon, in the northwestern sector of the Israeli salient jutting into Syria.

In the air combat April 18, Syria claimed its jets had "dealt concentrated blows to enemy positions and assembly points on Mount Hermon and several other parts of the front, including heavy losses in men and material."

The Israelis denied the extent of the Syrian raids, saying the planes were driven off after negligible attacks. The Tel Aviv command said Israeli planes had bombed Syrian artillery positions, which had been shelling Israeli points on Mount Hermon, as well as Syrian engineering units said to be constructing roads up the slopes.

Israeli and Syrian jets engaged in dogfights April 19 for the first time since the 1973 war, with Syria claiming the destruction of 17 Israeli jets, seven in aerial combat and 10 others by antiaircraft fire. One of the downed planes was an unmanned reconnaissance aircraft. Syria acknowledged the loss of one of its own aircraft. The Tel Aviv command admitted the loss of two of its jets to Syrian ground fire and said Israeli planes had knocked down two Syrian jets.

Syria had claimed destruction of 25 Israeli jets since the fighting on Mount Hermon erupted April 10.

Dayan warns clashes may lead to war—
Israeli Defense Minister Moshe Dayan

warned April 19 that the fighting on the Golan Heights could lead to war, but softened his views the following day.

He said April 19 that when U.S. Secretary of State Henry A. Kissinger arrived in the Middle East at the end of the month to help arrange an Israeli-Syrian disengagement agreement, he might find an "all-out battlefield" rather than "a negotiating table."

Dayan said April 20 that the Syrians were not deploying their full force in the fighting, that the purpose of their attacks was to soften up Israel for the coming disengagement talks and were not a prelude to another full-scale war.

Syria submits disengagement plan. Brig. Gen. Hikmat Khalil al-Shihabi, Syrian military intelligence chief, submitted his country's proposal for troop disengagement with Israel in a meeting with Secretary of State Henry A. Kissinger in Washington April 13. They also discussed the Israeli withdrawal proposal and detailed map Kissinger had received from Israeli Defense Minister Moshe Dayan March 30.

(Kissinger met with Egyptian Foreign Minister Ismail Fahmy later April 13 to appraise him of his discussions with Shihabi.)

Kissinger, acting as go-between, transmitted the Syrian plan and an accompanying map to Israeli Ambassador Simcha Dinitz April 14. Dinitz later told newsmen that Damascus' proposal had "room for give and take" but represented no breakthrough.

Qiryat Shemona attack aimed at blocking peace. While Israel and Syria were engaged in indirect discussions and direct clashes, Palestinian terrorists struck at an Israeli target in what was later described as a move to block peace.

Three armed guerrillas, entering from Lebanon, crossed the border April 11 into the Israeli town of Qiryat Shemona, less than a mile away, stormed a four-story apartment building, forced their way into apartments and began shooting indiscriminately, killing 18 persons, including eight children and five women. Two of the dead were Israeli soldiers who had taken part in the assault on the terrorists after the commandos attacked a second build-

ing in the town. All three infiltrators were killed when explosive-laden knapsacks they were carrying ignited after being hit by Israeli fire, according to Israeli accounts. Sixteen persons were wounded, mostly soldiers.

Credit for the attack was claimed April 11 by the Lebanese-based Marxist Popular Front for the Liberation of Palestine-General Command (PFLP), a small splinter group. The PFLP did not belong to the Palestine Liberation Organization (PLO), the umbrella group for the other commando factions, and opposed peace negotiations with Israel.

A member of the PFLP Politburo, identifying himself as Abdul Abbas, said in Beirut April 12 that "this operation is just the beginning of a campaign of revolutionary violence within Israel that is aimed at blocking an Arab-Israeli peace settlement."

Insisting that the guerrillas had infiltrated from Lebanon, Premier Golda Meir warned April 11 that Israel regarded the Lebanese government and its people "who collaborated with the terrorists, as responsible for these murders."

Lebanese Premier Takieddin Solh April 11 supported the commandos' claim that they had launched their assault against Qiryat Shemona from inside Israel. Solh repeated this view April 12 in a meeting with the ambassadors of the U.S., France, China, Britain and the Soviet Union.

Israelis attack 6 towns in Lebanon—In retaliation for the Qiryat Shemona attack, Israeli forces crossed into southern Lebanon April 12 and raided the villages of Dahira, Yaroun, Muhebab, Blida, Ett Taibe and Aitarun, west and north of Qiryat Shemona. An Israeli communique said buildings in the towns were blown up after their inhabitants were evacuated. The communique said "the action was intended to harm villages whose residents had given assistance to terrorists."

A Lebanese communique said the Israeli raiders had blown up 24 houses and a power station in Ett Taibe, kidnapped 13 civilians and killed two women in blowing up a house in Muhebab.

Defense Minister Moshe Dayan said April 13 that the raid into Lebanon was "political, not military," that it had been purposely limited in size and damage as a warning to the Beirut government that it must prevent commandos from crossing into Israel if it wanted to be spared future Israeli incursions. Dayan said "The Lebanese villagers will have to abandon their homes and flee if the people of Qiryat Shemona cannot live in peace. All of southern Lebanon will not be able to exist."

The Israeli raid, Dayan explained, was part of a new government policy to pressure Lebanon to curb the commandos. "We are trying to explain that we are not the police of Lebanon," that Lebanon was "responsible for what is taking place inside its territory."

Egyptian Foreign Minister Ismail Fahmy told the U.N. April 15 that if Israel continued to escalate retaliation against Syria and Lebanon because of Palestinian commando raids, it risked Egyptian intervention. "We will not stand by and let them strike at Lebanon and Syria," Fahmy said.

U.N. condemns Israel—The United Nations Security Council April 24 approved by a 13–0 vote (with China and Iraq not voting) a resolution condemning Israel for its retaliatory attack on Lebanon.

The resolution criticized Israel for "violation of Lebanon's territorial integrity" and also deplored "all acts of violence" but made no mention of the Qiryat Shemona incident. It called on Israel to return the 13 Lebanese hostages abducted in the raid on Lebanon.

Shortly before the vote, Israeli delegate Yosef Tekoah walked out of the Council chamber, attacking the draft resolution as "another example of the bias and inequity which prevail in Security Council debates on the Middle East." He said Israel "will continue to hold the Lebanese government responsible for any armed attacks organized in or perpetrated from Lebanon."

The resolution had no specific sponsor, but was drafted largely by Britain and France at Lebanon's urging. The Council earlier had defeated by a 7–6 vote (2 abstentions) a U.S. amendment, which would have mentioned the Qiryat Shemona attack.

Kissinger begins new peace mission. U.S. Secretary of State Henry A. Kissinger began his fifth Middle East peace mission,

meeting April 28, 1974 with Soviet, Algerian, Egyptian and Israeli officials in an effort to promote an Israeli-Syrian troop disengagement agreement and to discuss other problems of the region.

Kissinger conferred in Geneva April 28–29 with Soviet Foreign Minister Andrei A. Gromyko to enlist Moscow's aid in achieving an Israeli-Syrian accord and to take up Soviet-U.S. issues. A joint statement April 29 said the two had exchanged views on current moves to get an Israeli-Syrian accord, "expressed themselves in favor of the resumption" of the Geneva peace conference on the Middle East and pledged to coordinate their efforts to attain a general peace settlement in the region.

Before departing Geneva, Kissinger said his two days of talks with Gromyko had left him with the expectation that "we'll have Soviet understanding and, I hope, cooperation" in his forthcoming negotiations with Israel and Syria.

Kissinger flew to Algiers and conferred April 29–30 with Algerian President Houari Boumedienne. The secretary said after the talks that he now had "increased hopes" for the success of disengagement as a result of Boumedienne's "understanding and support." Boumedienne said that in his discussions with Kissinger he had stressed Algeria's "intention of making a positive contribution about the most immediate problem," the separation of Israeli and Syrian forces.

Kissinger's next stop was Alexandria, where he met April 30–May 1 with Egyptian President Anwar Sadat. At a joint news conference May 1, Sadat said he had "full confidence" that Kissinger "will achieve disengagement." Kissinger said he expected his talks with the Syrians and Israelis "to be difficult. This will not be an easy passage." The principal obstacle confronting him, Kissinger said, was "the distrust between the two sides."

Addressing steel workers at a May Day rally in Helwan earlier in the day, Sadat defended his cooperation with the U.S., saying that Arab solidarity and military action in the October 1973 war had forced the Americans to adopt a more balanced position in the Middle East "and that is an Arab victory."

Kissinger formally started his shuttle diplomacy to arrange a Syrian-Israel accord in talks in Jerusalem May 2 with

Premier Golda Meir, Itzhak Rabin, Premier-designate, and other Israeli leaders. On arriving at the Tel Aviv airport, Kissinger had sought to reassure the Israelis that the U.S. was not pressuring them to make concessions to reach an agreement with Damascus. He said: "I come here not to discuss concessions but to discuss security. The issue is not pressure, but a lasting peace."

Information Minister Shimon Peres warned at a news briefing that "meaningful negotiations" could not be conducted as long as fighting continued on the Syrian front.

Syrian Premier Mahmoud Ayoubi said May 2 that his government's talks with Kissinger would be difficult if Israel did not agree to pull its forces out of all Syrian territory. Syria, he said, would continue to attack the Israelis on the Golan Heights "until two conditions are fulfilled: complete Israeli withdrawal and guarantees of the legitimate rights of the Palestinian people."

Kissinger was back at work in Damascus May 3–4. He met with President Hafez al-Assad, then flew to Alexandria May 4 to brief Egyptian President Anwar Sadat, and returned to Jerusalem where he met with Premier Golda Meir and other Israeli officials through May 5 to apprise them of his talks with Assad. Kissinger's aides said they had intelligence information that Syrian shelling on the Golan Heights had slackened in the last 24 hours as a result of Kissinger's talks with Assad. The Israelis, however, insisted there was no letup in the Syrian attacks.

Kissinger flew to Amman, where he briefed King Hussein of Jordan May 5–6 and then returned to Jerusalem for more discussions with the Israelis.

A conference of Kissinger with Foreign Minister Gromyko in Nicosia. Cyprus May 7 produced guarded Soviet support for his peace efforts. Kissinger's aides told newsmen that the Soviet Union now appeared to be acting somewhere between being "not unhelpful and helpful." Gromyko had first held a long meeting with President Assad in Damascus May 5–6. Kissinger reportedly had declined Gromyko's suggestion that they both meet in the Syrian capital, and proposed Cyprus as a neutral site instead.

Kissinger was back in Jerusalem May 7 to receive Israel's new proposals for troop separation. Information Minister Shimon Peres said Premier Meir and other Israeli officials had given the secretary "a shaped opinion of a position" for transmission to the Syrians. He said this was Israel's "complete point of view, including geographic considerations," a reference to a new map that was to be drawn up.

Kissinger shuttled between Jerusalem and Damascus May 8. His top aides insisted that although some progress had been made, the two sides remained far apart and that an agreement was far off.

Saudi Foreign Minister Omar Saqqaf gave Kissinger a strong endorsement for his peace moves following a meeting with the secretary in Riyadh May 9. Kissinger went on to Cairo, where he held a 40-minute meeting with President Sadat, filling him in on the results of his talks with the Israelis and Syrians.

Kissinger's aides reported some progress had been made in his talks, but no definitive agreement appeared in the offing. The crucial issue centered on exactly where the disengagement lines should be drawn, according to U.S. officials. Other problems included establishment of a buffer zone, limitation of forces on both sides of the eventual demarcation line, release of prisoners and the United Nations role in the buffer zone.

Kissinger had told the Israelis and Syrians that they would have to modify the original proposals they had submitted to him in the previous six weeks if an agreement were to be reached.

Israelis oppose concessions—Opposition deputies had called on the Israeli government May 6 to explain its "plans to retreat behind the 1967 ceasefire lines." The demand made at the opening of the summer session of the Knesset (parliament) produced near-pandemonium and forced cancellation of the meeting. Several protest demonstrations and newspaper advertisements in Israeli newspapers May 6 warned of a "Kissinger sellout." Pickets marched before the premier's office in Jerusalem and the U.S. embassy in Tel Aviv.

Opposition Likud leader Menachem Begin warned during a Knesset session May 7 that "if no debate is held today, Kissinger will go to Damascus bearing a

new map, one different from the one
Dayan presented in Washington a month
ago, one which includes withdrawal
beyond the purple line," which demar-
cated the Golan Heights territory captured by the Israelis in the 1967 war.

The crucial issue in the negotiations
centered on how far the Israeli forces
would withdraw. The Israelis had
proposed pulling back 300 square miles
from the Syrian salient captured in the
October 1973 war and returning some of
the 400 square miles of the Golan Heights
taken in the June 1967 war, including the
now uninhabited town of Quneitra. The
Israelis insisted on retaining three
strategic hills near Quneitra because they
overlooked Israeli settlements and because of their military importance in preventing any possible Syrian advances.

A Kissinger aide told newsmen in
Jerusalem May 13 that the U.S. had never
proposed to Israel that it abandon any of
its 17 settlements on the Golan Heights.
He said the U.S. understood, and Syria
tacitly accepted, that it would be
"politically unthinkable" for any Israeli
government to give up any of the settlements.

**Maalot raided, 25 Israelis die, in move
against peace mission.** In an action
described by its planners as an intended
blow against the Kissinger peace mission,
three Palestinian commandos May 15,
1974 attacked the Israeli village of Maalot,
five miles from the Lebanese border.
Twenty-five Israelis, all but four of them
teenaged school children, were slain.

Israeli forces retaliated May 16 with air
strikes against suspected Palestinian guerrilla bases in southern Lebanon.

The violence came as Kissinger intensified his efforts to arrange a Syrian-
Israeli troop disengagement agreement.
He suspended his shuttle diplomacy for
one day after the latest crisis.

The Beirut-based Popular Democratic
Front for the Liberation of Palestine,
headed by Nayef Hawatmeh, took credit
for the attack. The three guerrillas, who
were said by Israel to have infiltrated from
Lebanon, burst into a high school at
Maalot, where about 90 students from
other towns on an excursion were sleep-
ing.

Israeli troops stormed the building after a breakdown in negotiations with the
guerrillas who were seeking the release of
20 commandos imprisoned in Israel in return for the lives of the youths. Sixteen
children were killed immediately and five
of 70 injured students died later. Israel
claimed the children were shot by the
guerrillas, all of whom were slain themselves in the exchange of fire with the
soldiers. One Israeli soldier was killed.

Before taking over the school, the commandos had burst into an apartment in
Maalot and killed a family of three. Police
said that prior to arriving in Maalot, the
guerrillas had killed two Arab women and
wounded several others after firing on a
van carrying workers from a textile plant
in nearby Haifa.

Israeli jet May 16 carried out two
attacks in southern Lebanon, bombing
and strafing Palestinian targets from the
foothills of Mount Hermon to the coastal
city of Saida. Initial casualty figures reported by Lebanese and Palestinian commando authorities said 21 were killed and
134 wounded. It was the heaviest Israeli
air attack ever carried out in Lebanon.

Announcing the raids, an Israeli military spokesman said they had been directed at commando storehouses, work
shops and training camps largely in the
Nabatiyah, Saida and Tyre regions.

Hayef Hawatmeh, head of the Popular
Democratic Front for the Liberation of
Palestine (PDFLP), said in Beirut May 16
that his organization's raid on Maalot
had been directed against Kissinger's
peace mission. He said Kissinger sought a
peace that would "mean the surrender of the Palestinian people and the
liquidation of the Palestinian cause."
The secretary did not recognize "the national rights of the Palestinian people"
and his proposals were "based on American, Israeli and Arab reactionary interests," Hawatmeh said.

The PDFLP leader said he would not
oppose peace talks if they led to "restoration of Palestine" in the West Bank
and the Gaza Strip, now occupied by Israel. He pledged to "establish a Palestinian state on every part of Palestinian
soil liberated by armed combat or diplomacy."

Premier Golda Meir, in a television
broadcast May 15 after the commando
pledged to do everything possible to prevent future attacks.

Mrs. Meir said: "I can't promise they will let us live in peace. But I want to and can promise that the government—any government of Israel—will do everything in its power to cut off the hands that want to harm a child, a grown-up, a settlement, a town or a village."

She said that the raid was by the group whose leader, Nayef Hawatmeh, "wants to lure us into living in a secular democratic state together with him. This is an organization that knows only blood and murder—and of children."

Mrs. Meir thanked the international community for its expressions of sympathy to Israel and said she hoped those nations would "finally recognize who they are who stand at the head of the so-called liberation movements, to what they send their men and to what they educate their people."

Soviets, Libya vow aid to guerrillas—The Soviet Union and Libya announced May 21 that they would provide "every assistance" to the Palestinian guerrilla movement in its struggle against Israel, but no specific measures were mentioned. The pledge was contained in a joint communique based on talks Premier Abdel Salam Jalloud had held in Moscow with Soviet leaders since May 15.

Although the Soviet Union pledged support to the Palestinians, the government newspaper Izvestia May 21 had deplored the Maalot raid. "Terror against peaceful citizens is not the weapon of a just struggle even in the name of the most just cause," the newspaper said.

Kissinger delays mission. The commando attack on Maalot forced Secretary of State Henry A. Kissinger May 15 to suspend his peace efforts for one day.

The secretary, who was in Jerusalem, had been slated to meet that day with Premier Golda Meir and other Israeli officials after a scheduled Cabinet meeting that was to discuss final ideas on troop disengagement to be conveyed by Kissinger to officials in Damascus later May 15. But the Israeli officials were preoccupied with the terrorist crisis and urged Kissinger to delay his departure for the Syrian capital until they could give their full attention to the disengagement problem.

Kissinger had issued a statement earlier May 15 before Israeli troops stormed the Maalot school, assailing the guerrilla assault. He said he was "shocked and outraged" and stated that the U.S. government "strongly condemns this mindless and irrational action and appeals to those holding innocent hostages to release them." The secretary warned that violence of this kind could "undermine the prospects for peace in this area." He called on "all responsible governments to make clear, that whatever their political differences, such unhuman acts must be condemned and those who carry them out be dealt with severely."

After Kissinger renewed his shuttle diplomacy May 17, aides reported in Tel Aviv May 22 that two major issues were delaying a troop separation agreement between Israel and Syria—the size of the proposed United Nations buffer force separating the soldiers of the two countries and the limits to be placed on Israeli and Syrian troops on each side of the U.N. strip. The U.N. neutral zone was to be 1–4 miles wide.

The U.S. officials said Kissinger had already arranged the basic text for the disengagement accord, including the map specifying the location of the new troop-separation lines, the procedure for release of prisoners and the role of the U.N. in supervising the agreement.

The Israelis were insisting on a U.N. force estimated at about 3,000 men, while the Syrians favored a smaller number, reportedly about 300. The U.N. buffer zone would be under Syrian civil administration and would include Quneitra, the Golan Heights town seized by the Israelis in the 1967 war.

Kissinger called on Egypt May 22 to persuade Syria to remove some of the remaining obstacles to an agreement. In compliance with the request, Lt. Gen. Mohammed Abdel Ghany el-Gamasy, Egyptian chief of staff, was reported to have contacted Syrian military authorities.

An apparent breakthrough in Kissinger's efforts to bring about troop separation had followed the secretary's meeting with President Hafez al-Assad in Damascus May 18. The secretary told newsmen before departing for Israel that as a result of his discussions that day "significant progress has been made and the prospects for an agreement have been advanced."

Syria & Israel Agree:
Cease-Fire & Disengagement

Accord reached in Geneva. Israeli and Syrian military officials in Geneva May 31, 1974 signed an agreement providing for a cease-fire, the separation of their forces on the Golan Heights by a United Nations buffer zone and the exchange of prisoners captured in the October 1973 war.

Both countries had agreed to the accord May 30 after 32 days of intensive negotiations conducted by U.S. Secretary of State Henry Kissinger in a series of meetings with Israeli and Syrian leaders in Jerusalem and Damascus. The Israeli Knesset (Parliament) and Syria's ruling Baath Party approved the pact May 30. The pact marked the first formal agreement reached by Syria and Israel since the armistice that had ended the 1948 Israel war of independence.

A generalized text of the agreement, with an accompanying map showing the actual disengagement area, was released May 30. As in the case of the Israeli-Egyptian accord that preceded it, the U.S. had made a number of unpublished statements to either or both sides concerning its understanding on some points in the agreement.

The agreement was signed at U.N. headquarters in Geneva by Israeli Maj. Gen. Herzl Shafir and Syrian Gen. Adnan Wajih Tayara. News media witnesses were barred at the request of Syria. After the signing, the generals were named to the military group that would begin to work out details of the disengagement June 1.

Among the principal points of the agreement:

■ Israel would return to Syria the 300 square mile salient captured in the October 1973 war plus a strip of the Golan Heights seized in the 1967 war, including the town of Quneitra. The Israelis would withdraw about 350 yards from Quneitra but would retain three hills overlooking the town and Israeli settlements.

■ Quneitra would be included in a 1/4 mile-wide U.N. buffer zone that was to be manned by 1,250 armed troops called the United Nations Disengagement Observer Force (UNDOF). All territory east of Israel's demarcation line would be under Syrian administration and Syrian civilians would be permitted to enter this region.

■ The exact delineation of the detailed map and the implementation of the disengagement of forces was to be worked out by the two sides in stages, with the discussions starting 24 hours after signing of the agreement. The pullback of forces was to be completed within 20 days.

■ War prisoners were to be returned within 24 hours after signing of the agreement. The bodies of all dead soldiers held by both sides were to be returned within 10 days.

A separate protocol dealt with Syrian and Israeli agreement on the functions of UNDOF. Its members were to be selected by U.N. Secretary General Kurt Waldheim, with the command vested under the authority of the Security Council. The troops were to be selected from countries who were not permanent members of the Council.

The text of the agreement did not specify the arms and troop limitations in the Syrian and Israeli zones. According to Israeli officials, the "thinning-out zones" would extend on each side of the respective buffer areas for 15 miles, and would be subdivided. Both forces would be limited to 6,000 troops each in the first six miles of the zones. Weapons there would be limited to 36 artillery pieces of 122-mm or the equivalent and 75 tanks. In the second six-mile wide area, each side could have an unlimited number of troops, 450 tanks, and additional medium-range artillery pieces, but no long-range artillery. The last three miles of the zone would be unrestricted except for anti-aircraft missiles, which were barred from the entire 15 miles.

U.S. guarantees pact—The U.S. had agreed to conduct aerial reconnaissance to assure implementation of the disengagement agreement and to support Israeli retaliation for any Palestinian commando attacks. These guarantees were among unpublished understandings in the disengagement agreement disclosed May 30 by Israeli Premier Golda Meir and U.S. officials in Cairo. Speaking to the Knesset, Meir said the U.S. had privately assured Israel it would condone and politically support Israeli actions taken against guerrillas in self-defense. She quoted the following passage from the understanding: "Raids by armed groups or individuals across the demarcation line are contrary to the cease-fire. Israel, in the exercise of its right of self-defense, may act to prevent such actions. The United States will not consider such actions as violations of the cease-fire, and will support them politically."

The premier said the U.S. had reached a number of other understandings with Israel in connection with the troop-separation accord, but she provided no details. Indicating that this involved increased U.S. military aid, Meir said "the consistent aid of the United States to Israel has been assured for the future by the President of the United States."

Nixon announces pact, other reaction— In making the first official announcement of the Syrian-Israeli disengagement agreement, President Nixon described it in a television broadcast May 29 as "a major diplomatic achievement" that would enhance the prospects for a permanent peace in the Middle East. Secretary of State Henry A. Kissinger "deserves enormous credit for the work he has done" in bringing about the accord and "also credit goes to the governments concerned which had great differences to be resolved," the President said.

Nixon said he had sent messages to Premier Golda Meir and President Hafez al-Assad congratulating them for "the statesmanship they have shown" in bridging their differences. He conceded that despite the Israeli-Syrian and Israeli-Egyptian troop withdrawal accords, "there are many difficulties ahead before a permanent settlement is reached." But he expressed confidence that the two pacts would pave the way "for progress" when the peace talks resume in Geneva.

The President pledged continued American "initiatives" in cooperation "with all governments in the area" to arrange a permanent settlement.

An Administration official said Nixon had closely followed Kissinger's progress in the past 32 days and held repeated radio-telephone conversations with the secretary, and with Premier Meir and Egyptian President Anwar Sadat.

Other comments May 29:

The Soviet Union and Syria said the disengagement agreement was only the first step toward an overall settlement. In a joint communique based on talks Soviet Foreign Minister Andrei A. Gromyko had held with Syrian officials in Damascus May 28–29, both nations said "a just and lasting peace" must "be based on complete Israeli withdrawal from all occupied territories and on the restoration of the legitimate rights of the Palestinian people." The statement said Moscow and Damascus would "not permit any third party to jeopardize the strong and friendly relations existing between the Soviet Union and Syria."

Egyptian officials expressed satisfaction over the agreement and lauded Kissinger's diplomatic skills in achieving it.

United Nations Secretary General Kurt Waldheim praised the agreement and said the U.N. had started preparations to send troops to enforce the accord. He said contingents could be detached from the 6,322 men from 11 countries currently serving in the Sinai Desert area between Israel and Egypt.

Kissinger briefs Sadat, returns to U.S.— Secretary Kissinger stopped off briefly in Cairo May 30, before returning to Washington, to brief Egyptian President Anwar Sadat on his successful negotiations. At a joint news conference later, Sadat praised Kissinger for having "done again a miracle; I myself am proud because Kissinger is my friend and brother." Sadat also praised Syrian President Hafez al-Assad for his "wisdom and far-sightedness" in reaching the agreement and also paid tribute to "the leadership of President Nixon."

Golan Heights fighting ends— Israeli and Syrian forces on the Golan Heights reported that fighting there stopped about a half hour after the disengagement agreement was signed in Geneva May 31. There had been militant activity for 81 straight days.

Disengagement pact signed. Syria and Israel signed a provisional accord June 5 setting the precise lines of troop and weapons disengagement and demarcating the United Nations buffer zone. The May 31 cease-fire agreement had specified a June 5 deadline for reaching final determination of a buffer zone and disengagement details.

The buffer zone established by the pact ran from Mount Hermon in the north to the southern end of the Golan Heights, varying in width from 500 yards to six miles. Military sources in Tel Aviv said that Israeli troops were destroying bunkers and other installations as withdrawals began, in an operation believed to be similar to the Israeli pullback from the Suez Canal in January.

The June 5 accord was negotiated and signed at U.N. headquarters in Geneva by Israeli Maj. Gen. Herzl Shafir and Syrian Brig. Gen. Adnan Wajih Tayara, both of whom had signed the May 31 agreement. Lt. Gen. Ensio Siilasvuo, commander of the U.N. Emergency Force in the Middle East, presided at the June 1–4 negotiations, which were held in the framework of the Israeli-Egyptian working group established by the Geneva Middle East peace conference in December 1973. Maj. Gen. Taha el-Magdoub, the group's Egyptian member, attended the Israeli-Syrian talks; the U.S. and Soviet Union were represented by observers.

U.N. troops in buffer zone—The first 500 men of the 1,250-man U.N. Disengagement Observer Force (UNDOF) arrived in the town of Quneitra June 5 to prepare the buffer zone. The first contingents comprised Austrian and Peruvian members of the 7,000-man U.N. Emergency Force (UNEF) stationed along Israeli-Egyptian disengagement lines.

The U.N. Security Council had approved a U.S.-Soviet joint resolution May 31 establishing UNDOF. The vote was 13–0, with China and Iraq not participating. Like UNEF which supervised the Israeli-Egyptian pullback, UNDOF would be subject to renewal every six months. UNDOF was set up under Security Council authority and could not be withdrawn without Council approval.

Tripartite assurances reported—Middle East peace conference sources in Geneva revealed May 31 a number of unpublished U.S., Syrian and Israeli assurances reportedly made as a prelude to the signing of the May 31 cease-fire and disengagement agreement.

Chief among them was a verbal agreement said to have been given to U.S. Secretary of State Henry A. Kissinger by Syrian President Hafez al-Assad that Palestinian guerrillas would not infiltrate into Israel across the Syrian border. It was understood that Assad's assurance represented a vital breakthrough in reaching the final pact. Informed of the Syrian statement, Israel reportedly dropped its demand for formal guarantees that Damascus halt guerrilla activities from Syrian territory.

Conference sources also said that Washington had offered assurances to Syria, including pledges that the U.S. would not recognize the disengagement lines as legal frontiers and that it would help negotiate with the Palestinians to enable them to join the Geneva peace conference. However, in a Washington press conference June 6, Kissinger declined to enunciate U.S. policy on the question of Palestinian participation at the next Geneva session, saying the issue had not yet arisen. He also denied reports that economic aid had been promised to Syria, although he did confirm a May 30 statement by Israeli Premier Golda Meir concerning U.S. guarantees to support Israel against guerrilla incursions.

The Lebanese publication Arab World reported June 3 that Israel had agreed that the buffer zone placed under U.N. control would eventually revert to Syrian sovereignty. It also said that the U.S. would conduct aerial and satellite reconnaissance of cease-fire lines and that at Syria's request the Soviet Union could undertake similar reconnaissance.

War prisoners returned—Israel and Syria exchanged their prisoners of war June 1 and 6. Israel received 68 servicemen and Syria received 392 Syrian soldiers, 10 Iraqis and six Moroccans.

The prisoner exchange began June 1 when Red Cross airplanes returned 12 wounded Israelis to Tel Aviv and 25 wounded Syrians and one wounded

Moroccan to Damascus. The remaining prisoners were exchanged five days later, after Israeli and Syrian representatives in Geneva signed a procedural accord on disengagement of their forces on the Golan Heights.

Syria: U.S. attitude changed—In a major statement June 5, the Syrian government declared that the U.S. understood Syrian attitudes and that its friendship would be cultivated as a means of weakening Israel.

A long article in the official government newspaper Al Thawrah stated Syria had achieved "during the disengagement talks a great success with regard to changing the attitude of the United States. This attitude has changed and has become an attitude of understanding of our situation."

Syria claimed that "in the disengagement agreement we dictated our will ... We have liberated parts of the territory occupied in the June, 1967 war, thus breaking the will of the enemy who was insisting on not withdrawing."

The new U.S. attitude, Syria claimed, was "an implicit recognition that will soon take another aspect, namely, that Israel has to withdraw from all Arab territory. Every step in that direction serves our firm and basic line of struggle. We have to preserve friendship and we have to endeavor to weaken the friendship that Israel maintains with others in order to obtain the friendship of these others for us and for our cause."

Syria claimed that as a result of the October 1973 war and the disengagement agreement, "signs of internal dissension" had begun to appear in Israel. "We must accelerate methods to increase these signs and to expand them," the article asserted.

Israelis complete troop pullback. Israeli forces June 23 completed withdrawal from the Syrian salient captured in the October 1973 war. They also pulled out June 25 from the town of Quneitra and the Rafid salient seized in the 1967 war and from three peaks on Mount Hermon taken in the October fighting. The pullout had started June 7 under terms of the Syrian-Israeli disengagement agreement.

The salient was turned over to the Syrians, while to the west of the salient the United Nations Disengagement Observer Force (UNDOF) established a buffer zone separating the Israeli and Syrian troops.

A three-mile strip of Golan Heights territory relinquished by the Israelis June 23 was part of the UNDOF buffer zone and was not turned over to the Syrian military. Instead, a Syrian civilian team established a local administration there June 24. Israel June 23 also turned over to UNDOF a military cemetery deeper inside Syria on the Khan el Arnabeh road, that contained the bodies of 780 Syrian soldiers killed in the war.

Rabin approved as premier. The Israeli Knesset approved Yitzhak Rabin to succeed Golda Meir as premier June 3 by a 61–51 vote with 5 abstentions. The vote of confidence, the closest ever registered for a new Israeli Cabinet, followed an eight-hour debate centered on war and peace with the Arabs and the disengagement agreements signed with Egypt and Syria.

Outlining his government's policy, Rabin said Israel would "strive for arrangements which will create conditions under which we shall be able to test the intentions of each Arab state, whether it is really bound for peace or not." He reiterated the outgoing government's opposition to establishment of a separate Palestinian state on the West Bank of the Jordan River and to negotiations with the Palestinian commando groups.

Israel would seek "a peace treaty with Jordan which will be founded on the existence of two independent states: Israel with united Jerusalem as its capital and an Arab state to the east of Israel," Rabin said. He insisted that his government "will not conduct negotiations with terrorist organizations whose declared goal is the destruction of the state of Israel." Rabin's associates later explained that this left open the possibility that the Palestinians could be represented at the Geneva peace conference by a delegation, preferably within the Jordananian delegation, that had no connections with the commando groups.

Rabin repeated another policy of the outgoing government, pledging that Israel would not return—"even within the context of a peace treaty" with Jordan, Egypt and Syria—to the borders it had before the 1967 war.

U.S. Aid to Peace

Kissinger: U.S. aid 'essential' to peace.
U.S. Secretary of State Henry Kissinger
said June 4, 1974 that U.S. economic assistance programs to Middle East nations
were "essential instruments as we seek
to shape a cooperative international order that reflects our interests."

Kissinger spoke before the U.S. House
of Representatives Foreign Affairs Committee, where he defended the Nixon Administration's $4.2 billion foreign aid
request. Committee Chairman Thomas E.
Morgan (D, Pa.) said committee members
had "severe" reservations about the request.

Kissinger disclosed that a $100 million
request for a "Special Requirements
Fund" might be earmarked for reconstruction in Syrian territory evacuated
by Israeli forces. He stressed that no
commitments had been made on this issue
during the negotiations for a disengagement of Syrian and Israeli forces, but he
said: "We would look favorably on a request for economic reconstruction" by
Syria.

The potential for U.S. aid was believed
to have strengthened Kissinger's hand
during the disengagement talks, although
U.S. officials denied that financial incentives had any effect in softening negotiating positions, the Washington Post
reported June 5.

In addition to the projected aid for
Syria, the Administration aid request included $350 million in grants and credits
for Israel, $207 million to Jordan and
$250 million to Egypt.

Kissinger's contention that U.S. aid was
essential to peace in the Middle East was
supported by Defense Secretary James R.
Schlesinger in testimony before the House
Foreign Affairs Committee June 5.

The projected aid to Syria was attacked
June 5 by Sen. Barry M. Goldwater (R,
Ariz.). In a time of economic difficulty
for the U.S., Goldwater asked, "How can
anyone suggest that for 'openers' we hand
out $100 million to a country we have
never attacked, never been particularly
friendly to, and whose aid we have never
particularly sought?"

U.S. nuclear aid to Egypt. An accord
signed in Cairo June 14, 1974 by Presidents Nixon and Anwar Sadat, the U.S.
agreed to provide Egypt with nuclear technology for peaceful purposes. The agreement was part of a wide-ranging declaration of friendship and political and
economic cooperation signed by the two
leaders at the end of a three-day visit by
Nixon to Egypt, first leg of a seven-day
tour of the Middle East.

The accord on nuclear energy was contained in a four-section joint statement. It
said both governments would start negotiations soon on "an agreement for cooperation in the field of nuclear energy
under agreed safeguards. Upon conclusion of such an agreement, the United
States is prepared to sell nuclear reactors
and fuel to Egypt." Meanwhile, a provisional pact was to be worked out at the
end of June to enable Egypt to purchase
nuclear fuel to produce electricity for industrial purposes.

White House Press Secretary Ronald
Ziegler said the agreement would not enable Egypt to develop military nuclear
capability.

Officials of the U.S. State Department
and the Atomic Energy Commission expressed confidence that the nuclear assistance to Egypt would not lead to that
country's possession of nuclear weapons.
On the basis of an AEC briefing, Rep.
Melvin Price (D, Ill.) said Egypt had
pledged that it would not use the fissionable materials for peaceful nuclear explosions.

The U.S. had similar cooperative atomic
agreements with about 35 countries, including Israel.

The other three sections of the joint
statement outlined general principles of bilateral relations, stressing cooperation to
attain a peaceful resolution of the Arab-Israeli dispute, and established a Joint
Cooperation Commission and working
groups to implement the commission's objectives in the economic, scientific and cultural fields.

The document said "A just and durable
peace based on full implementation" of
United Nations Security Council Resolution 242 of November 1967, "should take
into account the legitimate interest of all
peoples in the Middle East, including the
Palestinian people, and the right of existence of all states in the area." It cited
Council Resolution 338 of Oct. 22, 1973,
ending the last Arab-Israeli war, and the
Geneva peace conference on the Middle

East as added instruments to be employed in attaining a permanent settlement.

"In recognition of these principles," both nations pledged a joint effort to "enhance" the cause of peace in the Middle East and in the rest of the world by strengthening "their bilateral cooperation" on the diplomatic level.

To strengthen U.S.-Egyptian friendship, the statement said, both governments would seek greater bilateral trade, cultural and scientific exchanges, increased tourism and more contacts between government agencies and officials.

On arriving in Cairo June 12, Nixon was greeted at the airport by President Sadat. Both men rode in a motorcade to the Egyptian leader's residence in the center of the city as thousands of persons lined the 10-mile route.

In a welcoming speech, Sadat said: "The role of the United States leadership of President Nixon is vital to promote peace and tranquility in the area. It is a challenge but I am convinced that with goodwill and determination, statesmen of the stature of President Nixon are apt to meet it."

Nixon responded: "It has been too long that our two nations have been through a period of misunderstanding and non-cooperation." His current meeting with Sadat, Nixon said, meant that "we cement the foundation of new relationship between two great peoples."

Later the two leaders held intensive discussions on the Middle East, followed by a state dinner given for Nixon. In toasts that followed, Sadat praised Nixon's "personal strategy" in the approach to the Middle East problem. But Sadat stressed that "the political solution and the respect of the national aspirations of the Palestinians are the crux of the whole problem" and warned that peace could not be achieved without meeting Palestinian Arab demands. But this "does not mean liquidation of Israel, contrary to what the Israelis claim to justify their expansionist plans," Sadat said.

Nixon announced June 13 that he and Sadat had agreed on further steps to resolve the Arab-Israeli dispute. Prior to the next session of the Geneva peace conference, there would be a series of bilateral meetings of the Arab countries, the U.S. and the Soviet Union to facilitate the next round of the Geneva talks, according to the U.S.-Egyptian proposal. "What is needed is the step-by-step approach, not because we want to go slow, but because we want to get there," Nixon said. The President added: These talks would be held "nation by nation, first with Egypt, then with Syria, taking up each problem as it is timely to take it up in a quiet confidential way, like President Sadat and I have talked to each other in complete confidence, . . ."

The two leaders disclosed their plans to newsmen on a train taking them from Cairo to Alexandria. Thousands of persons lined the route and thousands more greeted Nixon as he arrived in the port city.

Further achievements—President Nixon continued his five-nation tour of the Mid-East with visits to Saudi Arabia, Syria, Israel and Jordan June 14–18. The remainder of the President's one-week visit to the region was highlighted by a joint announcement in Damascus June 16 by Nixon and President Hafez al-Assad of resumption of U.S.-Syrian diplomatic relations, and by Nixon's pledge in Jerusalem June 17 of long-term military and economic aid to Israel and the promise to that country of nuclear technology for peaceful purposes.

Highlights of the President's tour:

Saudi Arabia—After concluding a three-day visit to Egypt, Nixon flew to Jidda, where he conferred June 14–15 with King Faisal and other Saudi Arabian officials. Faisal warned Nixon at a banquet June 14 that "there will never be a real and lasting peace in the area unless Jerusalem is liberated and returned to Arab sovereignty, unless liberation of all the occupied Arab territories is achieved and unless Arab people of Palestine regain their rights and return to their homes and the right of self-determination."

Nixon did not reply directly to Faisal's warning. He assured him of U.S. interest in "a lasting peace" in the Middle East.

Faisal June 15 expressed confidence that Nixon would end all differences between the U.S. and the Arab world. "But what is very important, is that our friends in the United States themselves be wise enough to stand behind you, . . . in your noble efforts, . . . aimed at securing peace and justice in the world," Faisal said.

In reply, Nixon lauded the growing cooperation between the U.S. and the Arab states and noted the American military aid promised Saudi Arabia was part of the new "partnership" with the Arab world. In pledging the military assistance, the President said if Saudi Arabia was "strong and secure, as it will be, it will enhance the chances for peace."

Syria—In their joint statement June 16 announcing resumption of U.S.-Syrian relations, broken by Syria in 1967, Presidents Nixon and Assad described the move as a first step toward establishing a lasting peace in the Middle East. The accord, announced by the two leaders after a two-hour meeting in Damascus, was to be followed by the appointment of ambassadors within two weeks and the resumption of cultural and educational exchanges.

Assad said his country was ready to pursue "sincere, constructive cooperation" with the U.S. to establish peace in the Middle East. He thanked the U.S. for helping Syria achieve a troop disengagement agreement with Israel.

Nixon had received a warm welcome on arriving in Damascus June 15. At a dinner later in the day, Assad stressed the need to satisfy Palestinian demands to bring about a "lasting and durable peace." Nixon said that although he did not bring "any instant solution" to the Middle East, the U.S. "is committed irrevocably to working for a just and equitable solution."

Israel—President Nixon was greeted by Premier Yitzhak Rabin and President Ephraim Katzir as he arrived in Israel June 16.

At a state banquet later in the day, Nixon called on the Israeli government to pursue "the way of statesmanship, not the way of the politician alone," in seeking peace with its Arab neighbors because "continuous war in this area is not a solution for Israel's survival."

A comprehensive communique issued June 17 before Nixon's departure said Israel and the U.S. would soon negotiate an agreement in the field of "nuclear energy, technology, and the supply of [nuclear] fuel from the United States under agreed safeguards," similar to the pact concluded with Egypt June 14.

According to the communique, Nixon also "affirmed the long-term nature of

military supply relationship between the two countries," as well as continued U.S. economic assistance to Israel, including the assurance of the supply of oil and other essential raw materials to Israel on "a continuous basis."

The pledge to provide Israel with military equipment on a long-term basis represented a new departure. Heretofore, Israel had to negotiate each military and economic assistance package on a contract-by-contract basis, encountering delays and resistance.

(The Israeli Knesset by a 60–50 vote June 19 defeated an opposition Likud no-confidence motion in Premier Rabin's government for its "irresponsible and light-hearted" response to the U.S.-Egyptian nuclear agreement. Rabin said he had expressed anxieties about the accord to Nixon because of its possible military implications for Israel.

(Foreign Minister Yigal Allon had said June 15 he was "not happy" over the U.S.-Egyptian nuclear accord. He expressed disappointment that the U.S. did not inform Israel in advance of such an offer to Cairo.)

Jordan—President Nixon was given a state dinner by King Hussein after arriving in Amman, Jordan June 17, the last leg of his Middle East tour.

Both leaders announced after a meeting June 18 agreement on creation of a joint Jordanian-U.S. commission to review on a regular basis cooperation between the two countries in the field of economic development, military assistance and supply, trade and investment, and scientific, social and cultural relations.

A joint statement issued by the two leaders said Nixon had submitted to the U.S. Congress legislation for a big increase in economic and military aid to Jordan. It also said the U.S. had offered to help in any negotiations between Jordan and Israel and that King Hussein had been invited to Washington "to hold further talks on the strategy of future efforts to achieve peace."

Nixon reports on trip—President Nixon declared at his White House welcome June 19 that as a result of intensified U.S. involvement in the Middle East "there is now hope" for peace there. He added:

"Where there was hostility for America, there is now friendship. While we did have the opportunity to meet new friends in Egypt and Syria, we were able to reassure old friends in Israel, Saudi Arabia and Jordan."

Nixon cautioned against expecting "instant peace as the result of one series of negotiations or just one very long trip. But what it does mean is that we are on the way."

His visit, the President observed, pointed up the desire of people in the Middle East for peace and progress, and their trust, respect and affection for the U.S. Asserting that "we must not let these people down," Nixon pledged that the U.S. would "play a crucial role in continuing the progress" toward peace in the Middle East.

Nixon briefed Congressional leaders on his Middle East trip June 20. He assured them he had not reached any secret agreements or understandings with the Arabs or Israel and sought to ease any Congressional apprehension about the U.S. nuclear aid agreements with Egypt and Israel. Sen. Robert C. Byrd (D, W. Va.) later told newsmen that he was "concerned about possible misuse" of nuclear reactors the U.S. would provide under the accords. The President justified this assistance on the ground that it would encourage Egypt to work with the U.S. toward peaceful relations with Israel, Byrd said.

Palestinian answer: a raid—Four Palestinian terrorists were killed after slaying three women in a raid June 13 on the northern Israeli kibbutz of Shamir. Israeli artillery the same day shelled three Lebanese villages on the eastern slopes of Mount Hermon.

The Popular Front for the Liberation of Palestine-General Command claimed credit for the attack on Shamir. An organization statement issued in Beirut said the raid was "our reaction to the Nixon visit to the Arab world."

Israeli planes June 18–20 raided suspected Palestinian guerrilla bases in Lebanon in retaliation for the attack on Shamir and other terrorist strikes.

The reprisal strikes had been delayed until President Nixon left the Middle East. Information Minister Aharon Yariv had acknowledged June 17 that Nixon's presence in Israel that day was a factor in Israel refraining from an immediate response.

The raids, the heaviest on Lebanon since the October 1973 war, were directed against commando installations near Mount Hermon and other Palestinian targets to the west, including at least a dozen refugee camps and settlements

The Israeli Foreign Ministry said June 20 that Israel would continue attacking Palestinian groups responsible for "the murder of Israeli civilians," while continuing to seek peace.

Israel had informed the United Nations Security Council June 18 that it would take all necessary measures to defend itself against guerrilla attacks from Lebanon.

Egyptian Foreign Minister Ismail Fahmy charged June 18 that the Israeli raids undermined peace and warned that Egypt would not stand by while the attacks continued.

Palestine Liberation Organization (PLO) chairman Yasir Arafat sent a message to Arab leaders June 20, charging that the Israeli-U.S. communique issued after President Nixon had left Israel June 17 "has given the green light for Israel" to continue its attacks against the Palestinians. Arafat appealed to the Arab governments to supply his forces with antiaircraft weapons.

The U.S. State Department June 20 declared the U.S. "had not given a green light to anybody" for attacks across the Lebanese-Israeli frontier, and deplored "the continuing action-reaction cycle of violence."

Israeli troops June 24 killed three Palestinian commandos after the guerrillas had slain three civilians in a raid on an apartment house in Nahariya, four miles south of Lebanon. An Israeli soldier was killed and five were wounded in the clash. The dead civilians were a woman and her two children.

Al Fatah claimed credit for the attack on Nahariya in a statement issued in Baghdad June 25. It was believed to be the first time that Al Fatah, regarded as one of the more moderate Palestinian commando groups, publicly acknowledged responsibility for such a mission.

According to Israeli accounts, the terrorists apparently reached Nahariya by water from Lebanon.

The Israelis retaliated for the Nahariya raid by firing artillery shells at Palestinian targets in southern Lebanon June 25.

Israel filed a complaint with the United Nations Security Council June 25, charging that Lebanon must be held responsible for the attack on Nahariya because it continued to permit the terror groups to operate freely on its territory.

Egyptian President Anwar Sadat called on President Nixon June 21 to take "a firm stand against Israel's repeated aggressions against Lebanon." It was reported that Nixon had replied to Sadat, saying his message had been received with "due attention."

Lebanese Premier Takieddin Solh had said that his country had no intention to curb the Palestinians, that Israeli attempts to divide the Palestinians and the Lebanese were bound to fail.

Defense Minister Peres asserted June 23 that recent Arab threats against Israel conflicted with their professed desire to conclude peace with his country. Israeli Premier Yitzhak Rabin said June 24 that Israel had "entered an epoch of perpetual war against terrorists. Our army will do everything within its power to seal off the border hermetically."

President Sadat informed Lebanese President Suleiman Franjieh June 24 that Egypt was prepared "to supply Lebanon with weapons and men, if necessary, to defend Lebanon against Israeli attacks."

Libyan leader Col. Muammar el-Qaddafi cabled PLO leader Yasir Arafat June 24 that Libya "places all its capabilities at your disposal."

Premier Rabin said in the Knesset June 25 that Palestinian terrorist attacks against Israel were aimed at disrupting peace developments, particularly the Israeli troop disengagement agreements with Egypt and Syria. Rabin disputed the claim that there were moderates among the PLO, arguing that these factions were as dedicated as the extremists to the destruction of Israel.

Israel Information Minister Aharon Yariv said June 25 there was an increased coordination between the so-called moderates and the militant wing of the PLO. He assailed the Arab governments for failing to control or influence the guerrillas, charging that this inaction "means whatever they declare and whatever they sign is not sincere. It means any set-tlement to which we shall agree would not be valid because it would be upset by what the Palestinians will later do."

U.S.-Saudi economic, military pact. The U.S. and Saudi Arabia agreed to wide-ranging economic and military cooperation under an accord signed in Washington June 8, 1974 by Kissinger and Prince Fahd Ibn Abdel Aziz, second deputy premier and King Faisal's half-brother.

Fahd, who had arrived in Washington June 6 for the negotiations, said the pact was "an excellent opening in a new and glorious chapter in relations" between the two countries. Kissinger called the agreement "a milestone in our relations with Saudi Arabia and with Arab countries in general."

The agreement established two joint commissions on economic cooperation and on Saudi Arabia's military requirements.

U.S. bars arms to Egypt, Syria. Secretary of State Henry A. Kissinger assured Israeli Ambassador Simcha Dinitz June 21 that the U.S. had no intentions to sell arms to Egypt or Syria.

A State Department statement June 22 said Dinitz had informed Kissinger of Israel's apprehension stemming from the U.S. decision to negotiate the sale of a nuclear reactor to Egypt and a disclosure that a team of American military officers was going to Cairo at the invitation of the Egyptian Defense Ministry.

The Defense and State Departments had said earlier that the military mission was not authorized to negotiate the sale of military equipment. In his talks with Dinitz, Kissinger reaffirmed that the military mission had nothing to do with arms for Egypt.

U.S. to aid Israeli air force. Nixon Administration officials disclosed June 29 that they had advised Israel that the U.S. would provide it with a new generation of fighter-bombers if necessary to help modernize its air force.

The assurances had been conveyed to Israeli Defense Minister Shimon Peres during his talks in Washington June 24–26 with Secretary of State Henry A. Kissinger and Defense Secretary James R. Schlesinger. The Israelis were said to be seeking $1.5 billion annually in U.S. military aid over a five-year period, much of it in grants because of Israel's heavy indebtedness. The Israelis said they were interested in advance fighter jets, such as the F-14 and F-15, as well as the lighter weight prototypes of the F-16 and F-17.

Peres had said at a Washington news conference June 25 that Israel did not have tactical nuclear weapons. Asked whether his country had a chemical processing plant to handle plutonium for atomic weapons, Peres said "to the best of my knowledge, Israel is just in the scientific part of this program."

In denying that Israel had atomic weapons, Peres was discounting a statement made by Egyptian President Anwar Sadat the previous week that Cairo had obtained intelligence information indicating that Israel was in possession of these nuclear arms. Sadat's statement was "not a real description of the Israeli situation," Peres said.

Nixon waives part of Israeli debt— President Nixon June 29 waived repayment of $500 million in credits to Israel for replacing military equipment after the October 1973 war. The debt was part of a $2.2 billion emergency package of equipment approved by Congress in December 1973, most of which already had been delivered to Israel. Congress had given Nixon authority to transform as much as $1.5 billion of that total into grants. In April the President had decided to declare only $1 billion in grants. His latest action extended his waiver to the full amount permitted.

Peace Politics & Arms Politics

Palestinian Political Gains

The Palestinian Arab cause and the Palestine Liberation Organization (PLO), regarded by its supporters as the authentic voice of the Arab Palestinians but by its foes as a terrorist group, made consistent international political advances in the period following the October 1973 war. A high point in its political progress was reached in November 1974 when PLO leader Yasir Arafat was invited to deliver the opening address at a session of the United Nations General Assembly. As was usual in events involving this controversial group, there was a sharp cleavage of option as to whether Arafat had taken a stride toward peace or had struck a blow against conciliation.

Palestinians discuss future state. The Central Council of the Palestine Liberation Organization met in Damascus, Syria Feb. 16, 1974 to discuss the possible establishment of a Palestinian state in territory then held by Israel and whether to attend the Geneva peace conference when it resumed.

A working paper drawn up at the conference called for the right of Palestinians to "establish a national authority on any lands that can be wrested from Zionist occupation." This was the first time the commando groups agreed to consider accepting control of any territory then held by Israel. Previously they had insisted that all territories occupied by Israel, including Israel itself, be taken over by the Palestinians for establishment of a secular state of Moslems, Christians and Jews.

The areas specifically referred to in the document were the West Bank, the Gaza Strip and the El Hamma region south of the Golan Heights on the Jordanian border. El Hamma was included in a Palestinian state that was to have been established in 1948. It was captured by the Syrians in the 1948–49 Arab-Israeli war and was taken by Israel in the 1967 war.

The working paper was drawn up by Al Fatah and was also endorsed by As Saiqa and the Marxist Popular Democratic Front for the Liberation of Palestine. Two other commando groups, the Popular Front for the Liberation of Palestine (PFLP) and the Arab Liberation Front, rejected the proposal.

The PFLP submitted its own working paper, which rejected the Middle East peace settlement, the Geneva conference and establishment of a Palestinian state in the West Bank and Gaza Strip.

The conference came to no decision on whether the Palestinians should attend the Geneva conference.

Hussein backs Palestinian role. In a major policy shift, King Hussein of Jordan agreed May 1 to the presence of a separate PLO delegation by Geneva and recognized the PLO as the exclusive representative of the Palestinian people.

Hussein had previously insisted that the Palestinians be part of the Jordanian delegation at the conference. In his latest statement, he said the Palestinians, when in Geneva, should "discuss all that lies beyond the scope of our specific powers and responsibilities within the framework of United Nations Security Council Resolution 242," which called for the withdrawal of Israeli forces from Arab territories taken in the 1967 war. Arab diplomats in Beirut interpreted the king's remarks to mean that he retained the right to ask that the Israeli-occupied West Bank be returned to Jordan.

Hussein had discussed the Palestinian question with Egyptian President Anwar Sadat in Alexandria April 4–6. A joint communique issued after the talks said the two men would maintain contacts on that issue and other problems.

PLO plans future moves. The Palestinian National Council met in Cairo June 1–9 to press demands to be represented at the Geneva peace conference and to map plans for a future Palestinian state. The 150-member council served as the PLO's parliament.

Among the major actions taken by the council at the nine-day conference:
■ The Executive Committee (cabinet) was enlarged to 14 members by adding four independent moderates recently expelled by the Israelis from the West Bank and by giving one seat to the extremist splinter group, the Popular Front for the Liberation of Palestine-General Command, responsible for the April 11 attack on the Israeli town of Qiryat Shemona.
■ The Palestinian leadership was to seek representation at the Geneva conference but was instructed to obtain a change in terms of reference at the meeting so as to make "the national rights of the Palestinian people" a topic of discussion. "National rights" meant minimally the right of the Palestinians to establish a "national Palestinian authority" on any part of the West Bank or Gaza Strip that might be evacuated by Israel. The Palestinian radical wing regarded the phrase to mean the displacement of the state of Israel by a "secular democratic state" in all of

Palestine in which Moslems and Jews would have equal rights.
■ The Palestinian leadership was barred from attending any conference based on U.N. Security Council resolution 242 of November 1967 which referred to the Palestinian "refugee problem" but not to the Palestinian nationalist movement.
■ The PLO was to increase its military operations "inside occupied lands," meaning Israel proper and the Arab territory occupied by Israel.

Nayef Hawatmeh, leader of the Popular Front for the Liberation of Palestine, said after a ceremonial closing of the conference June 9 that the meeting had given the Executive Committee "the freedom to maneuver" for a solution to the Palestinian problem "by all means, armed and unarmed."

At a meeting with Arafat and other members of the Executive Committee June 10, Egyptian President Anwar Sadat promised that he would seek concessions from Jordan to permit the Palestinians to participate in the Geneva talks. Sadat said he would take up the matter at a future meeting with Syrian President Hafez al-Assad and then seek a four-way meeting with Jordanian King Hussein, Arafat, Assad and himself. Addressing the Palestinian delegation, Sadat said: "To sum up, we—Egypt and Syria—will try to coordinate with Jordan but we are committed to you."

Palestinians rebuff Sadat & Hussein— After three days of talks in Cairo, Sadat and Hussein July 18 issued a joint statement recognizing Hussein as the representative of Palestinians in Jordan and the PLO as the representative of Palestinians elsewhere.

The statement, representing a concession on Hussein's part, was immediately rejected by leaders of the PLO's five guerrilla groups, though not by PLO Chairman Yasir Arafat. The reaction was a blow to Sadat's avowed plan to arrange a meeting in the near future with Hussein, Arafat and Syrian President Hafez al-Assad.

Sadat had said July 15, before Hussein's arrival in Egypt, that he was confident he could arrange such a meeting within a few weeks, and sources quoted by the New York Times July 16 said he had Arafat's support. However, PLO Foreign Minister Farouk Kaddoumi said July 19, after the Sadat-Hussein communique was released, that the meeting was out of the question.

The statement by the two Arab leaders declared the PLO the legitimate representative of all Palestinians living outside the "Hashemite Kingdom of Jordan," and asserted the PLO should have a separate delegation at the recessed Middle East peace talks in Geneva. The statement did not specify who represented the Palestinians living in the Israeli-occupied West Bank area of the Jordan River.

The communique also called for troop disengagement on the Jordanian-Israeli front, a long-standing demand of Hussein's which the Palestinians opposed for fear the evacuated areas would revert to Jordanian rather than Palestinian control.

The Palestinian news agency WAFA rejected the communique July 19, asserting the PLO was the only legitimate representative of the Palestinian people "wherever they may be." It charged Egypt and Jordan were trying to divide the Palestinians and prevent them from forming their own state. After denouncing the communique individually, leaders of the major PLO groups met in Beirut July 21 and issued a collective rejection of it.

Israeli reaction to the communique was mixed, according to reports July 19. Officials interpreted it as supporting their position that a settlement should be negotiated with Jordan, and not the PLO.

Israeli Premier Yitzhak Rabin and his Cabinet July 21 reaffirmed their opposition to talks with the PLO and to establishment of a Palestinian state outside Jordan. Peace in the Middle East would be "founded on the existence of two independent states only, Israel with a united Jerusalem as her capital and a Jordanian-Palestinian Arab state east of Israel, with borders to be determined in negotiations between Israel and Jordan," the Cabinet declared.

In an apparent reversal of Sadat's agreement with Hussein, Egyptian Foreign Minister Ismail Fahmy was quoted by the Cairo newspaper Al Ahram Aug. 5 as having recently told a PLO official, Zaid Kamal, that "Egypt is committed to the principle that the West Bank should not be returned to Jordanian civil and military authorities for this is the land of the Palestinian people." Fahmy called for the establishment of a "national Palestinian authority on [West Bank] territory evacuated by Israel either through negotiations in Geneva or through military action."

Jordan Aug. 6 denounced Fahmy's statement and called on Cairo for an official explanation.

Faisal visits Sadat. The dispute between Jordan and the Palestinians over the future of the West Bank was one of the principal topics of discussion in Cairo July 30–Aug. 7 between King Faisal of Saudi Arabia and Egyptian President Anwar Sadat.

A joint communique issued Aug. 7 announced that Faisal would give $300 million to Egypt to finance the cost of reconstruction and the needs of the Egyptians. The statement noted a need to strengthen the PLO.

A statement by Faisal praising Sadat for his July 18 agreement with King Hussein of Jordan recognizing the PLO as the representative of all Palestinians outside Jordan drew a sharp rebuke Aug. 5 from Saleh Khalef, deputy commander of the PLO's Al Fatah. Asserting that the Hussein-Sadat accord was "dividing the Palestinian people," Khalef declared, "We tell Faisal 'no' as strongly as we told it to Sadat."

Khalef also criticized Saudi Arabia for not providing enough money to the PLO while it was "pouring millions" into Egypt.

Hussein confers in U.S. King Hussein conferred with U.S. President Gerald Ford, Secretary of State Kissinger and other U.S. officials in August 1974 and then briefed reporters Aug. 17.

The king warned that his government would boycott the resumption of the Geneva peace conference unless Israel withdrew from at least part of the West Bank or if the PLO got "the responsibility at the outset to negotiate for the return of lost territories." Israel's unofficial offer to turn over some populated areas of the West Bank, such as Jericho, was termed by Hussein as "almost impossible to accept." Jordan had been pressing for an Israeli pullback of six to seven miles from the Jordan River.

The king also insisted that "under no condition" would his country negotiate with Israel for the return of the West Bank only to turn it over to the PLO. Hussein rejected Egypt's view that the West Bank was only under Jordanian trust as the Israeli-occupied Gaza Strip, once part of Egypt, was in Egypt's trust. Hussein's main argument was that there was "a difference between Gaza and the West Bank" because the West Bank Palestinians held Jordanian citizenship during its occupation by Jordan between 1949 and 1967, while the Gaza Palestinians did not hold Egyptian citizenship.

Egypt, Syria back PLO. Following a two-day meeting in Cairo Sept. 21, Egypt, Syria and the PLO said the PLO was "the sole representative of the Palestinian people." The endorsement of the PLO and the conferees' invitation to Jordan to join the three parties at a meeting in Cairo to adopt a common stand on further negotiations with Israel were rejected by King Hussein Sept. 22.

The Cairo communique drawn up by Foreign Ministers Ismail Fahmy of Egypt and Abdel Halim Khaddam of Syria and Farouk Khaddoumy of the PLO said Cairo and Damascus had agreed to coordinate their policies in consultations to be held on a regular monthly basis. Both countries also would be in periodic contact with the PLO and with other Arab nations, the statement said. The communique rejected partial political settlements, saying "the Arab cause is one cause."

The invitation extended to Jordan by Foreign Minister Khaddam who visited Amman Sept. 22 was rejected by Hussein because the Cairo conference endorsement of the PLO was considered a reversal of Egypt's support of Jordan's position in July that Amman represented the interests of the Palestinian people in Jordan. "Jordan considers the tripartite statement issued by Egypt, Syria and the PLO . . . a serious development that leaves Jordan no option but to take this stand," a Jordanian spokesman said. An Amman broadcast said as a result of the Cairo decision Jordan had "frozen" participation in the Geneva conference on the Middle East, but intended to raise the issue at the Arab summit conference in Morocco in October.

Israeli Foreign Minister Yigal Allon said Sept. 22 that the PLO backing by Syria and Egypt was a step toward obtaining a United Nations General Assembly resolution that would accord "legitimization of terrorist activities." He said the PLO's aim in initiating a debate at the Assembly on the Palestine issue was to undermine the Geneva conference.

Egyptian President Anwar Sadat Sept. 28 reaffirmed his support of the Palestinians, declaring that his government and Syria would reject any peace settlement that did not restore their rights. "We are ready to use all possible means to reach a political settlement, but it is imperative that the Israelis withdraw from every inch of occupied Arab territory," Sadat said in an address to a joint session of the National Assembly and the Arab Socialist Union commemorating the fourth anniversary of the death of President Gamal Abdel Nasser.

Militant group quits PLO. The militant Popular Front for the Liberation of Palestine (PFLP) announced its withdrawal Sept. 26, 1974 from the PLO's Executive Committee.

In making the announcement in Beirut, Ahmed Yamani, PFLP representative in the Executive Committee, accused the PLO of "deviation from the revolutionary course" by joining in U.S.-sponsored moves for political settlement of the Arab-Israeli conflict. He said he had "accurate information" of PLO contacts with the U.S. through a third party. Denouncing the PLO policy of seeking to establish a Palestinian state in the West Bank and Gaza Strip if and when those territories were given up by Israel, Yamani asserted that the PFLP would continue the struggle until all of Palestine was "liberated," Israel destroyed and King Hussein overthrown in Jordan.

Yamani disclosed that two other PLO factions supporting the PFLP's decision, the Popular Front for the Liberation of Palestine-General Command and the Iraqi-sponsored Arab Liberation Front, had also decided to withdraw from the Executive Committee.

Arab leaders back PLO. Twenty Arab heads of state, at a summit meeting held in Rabat, Morocco Oct. 26–28, 1974, voted unanimously to recognize the PLO as "the sole legitimate representative of the Palestinian people." The resolution called for creation of an independent Palestinian state "on any Palestinian land that is liberated" from Israeli occupation, meaning the West Bank and the Gaza Strip.

The seventh summit conference of the Arab League since 1964, called to map a coordinated Arab strategy for the immediate future toward Israel, also agreed to a multi-billion dollar program of financial assistance to the three Arab countries bordering Israel—Egypt, Jordan and Syria—and the PLO.

The deputy secretary general of the Arab League, Sayed Nofal, who read the text of the declaration to newsmen at the conclusion of the meeting, said King Hussein of Jordan, at odds with the PLO as to who would administer any West Bank territories relinquished by Israel, accepted the summit decision "without any reservations."

Although Hussein endorsed the declaration, members of his delegation disclosed Oct. 29 that the king was still standing by his repeated refusal to enter into any further Middle East peace negotiations if the PLO was recognized as the sole representative of the Palestinians.

Yasir Arafat said at the last session of the conference: "Today is the turning point in the history of the Palestinian people and Arab nation. I vow to continue the struggle until we meet together in Jerusalem with the same smiling faces we see here tonight. Victory is close at hand ... This enemy, this military gang, is a pack of wounded wolves. They are preparing for a fifth war, and we must get ready for it." As a result of the summit decisions, U.S. Secretary of State Henry Kissinger's "policy is in ruins," Arafat said.

The financial program agreed to by the conference was to be provided by Saudi Arabia, Kuwait and other Arab oil-producers, excluding Iraq and Libya. According to conference sources, Egypt and Syria were to receive $1 billion annually over a four-year period, Jordan $300 million a year and the PLO $5 million annually. Southern Yemen was to receive $150 million for a 99-year Arab League lease of strategic Perim Island in the Bab al Mandeb, the strait at the southern end of the Red Sea.

The groundwork for the summit conference had been prepared by a meeting of Arab League foreign ministers in Rabat Oct. 22-25, which recommended to the full conference that the PLO rather than Jordan take future control of the West Bank.

A spokesman for the Jordanian delegation, Hashem Abu Amara, told newsmen after the Oct. 25 meeting that his country rejected PLO claims to the West Bank because Amman had been informed by "big powers" that this would wreck all chances of peace. Israel, he said, would consider an agreement with Jordan, but would refuse to surrender any territory to the Palestinians.

U.S., Arab, Israeli reaction—Secretary of State Kissinger said Oct. 30 that despite the Arab summit recognition of the PLO, he did not "believe that the door to all negotiations in the Middle East is closed, but in what framework there can be negotiations—that will have to be seen."

In a broadcast Oct. 30, King Hussein hailed the Arab summit decision as "a triumph of the Arab nation's will," saying it was made "in a climate of serenity, brotherliness and frankness." He assured the Palestinians of the West Bank that Jordan would continue to provide them with aid and services until their status was changed. Jordan had been paying the

---

Text of Arab Resolution

The seventh Arab summit has decided:

1. To affirm the rights of the Palestinian people to return to their homeland and to self-determination.

2. To affirm the rights of the Palestinian people to establish an independent national authority, under Palestine Liberation Organization leadership, as the sole legitimate representative of the Palestinian people on any liberated Palestinian territory. The Arab states must support this authority when set up in all fields and at all levels.

3. To support the Palestine Liberation Organization in the exercise of its responsibilities in the national and international fields in the framework of Arab commitments.

4. To invite Jordan, Egypt, Syria and the Palestine Liberation Organization to work out a formula governing their relations in the light of these decisions and in order to implement them.

5. To affirm the undertaking of all the Arab states to safeguard Palestinian national unity and not to interfere in internal affairs regarding Palestinian action.

salaries of Jordanian administrative officials of the West Bank and had been providing aid to its municipalities despite Israel's occupation of the territory since the 1967 war.

In an assessment of the Arab summit, Moroccan King Hassan said Oct. 30 that "the Palestinians do not exclude King Hussein from negotiating a [West Bank] disengagement [with Israel] if one can be obtained." Hassan urged the U.S. and Israel to accept the Arab decision to help the PLO establish a Palestinian state or risk defeat in a new war. "In this arms race, we are going to win, since we are the richer ones," Hassan said.

At a separate news conference in Rabat Oct. 30, Arafat said he would meet with the heads of state of Egypt, Syria and Jordan in Amman to coordinate Arab strategy on "the military, economic and political level." The meetings would be held within the framework of talks as specified by the summit resolutions, Arafat said.

Four militant Palestinian groups issued a joint statement in Beirut Oct. 30 which protested the decisions of the Arab summit and denounced Arafat for his apparent reconciliation with King Hussein. The declaration of the Popular Front for the Liberation of Palestine, the Arab Liberation Front, the Popular Struggle Front and the Popular Front for the Liberation of Palestine-General Command called the Rabat resolutions a reversal of the PLO program, particularly of the anti-Hussein stand it had taken since the monarch's suppression of the guerrilla forces in his country in 1970. The four groups instead renewed their call for a war to destroy Israel and to gain control of all of Palestine.

Israeli Premier Yitzhak Rabin said Oct. 30 that the Arab summit decisions "bode no good" for Israel and "may possibly call for significant conclusions regarding our policy." Rabin made the statement in Parliament, where a debate was to start on the Rabat summit but was postponed for one week at Rabin's request. He said he expected to have details of the summit meeting at that time. Rabin reiterated his government's decision "not to negotiate with terrorist organizations whose avowed aim is Israel's destruction."

Rabin's view was reaffirmed by Defense Minister Shimon Peres, who also said the only difference between Arab moderates and extremists was timing. The extremists wanted to destroy Israel in one blow, while the moderates were prepared to do it in stages, he said.

In further comment on the Arab summit, Rabin said Oct. 31 that the central question remained whether Egypt would continue its separate movement toward peace with Israel.

If the Arabs barred Jordan from participation in peace talks, there would be no one to talk to about Israel's eastern frontier, the premier said. In expressing his opposition to negotiating with "the terrorist organizations," Rabin also warned against their appearance at the peace table "in Husseini masks." This was an apparent allusion to the idea that King Hussein would take part in talks on disposition of the West Bank, with the PLO later taking over any part of the territory Israel agreed to relinquish.

Rabin Nov. 5 repeated his stand that Israel could not accept the Arab summit decision to recognize the PLO as the sole representative of the Palestinian people. Speaking during Knesset debate, the premier said his government was willing to discuss the territorial question with the Arabs on the basis of compromise but not with the Palestinian guerrilla groups.

Rabin denounced the Arab summit for supporting the aim of a group "that would negate our existence as a state and resorts to violence and terror to destroy our state."

Hussein says peace up to Israel—King Hussein said in an interview in the Nov. 11 issue of Newsweek that the Arab summit decision supporting the PLO left the question of war or peace "entirely Israel's choice." The king added: If Israel was willing to negotiate the return of the West Bank "with Jordan on behalf of the PLO, why then shouldn't it negotiate directly with the PLO?"

"The threat of war becomes very real" unless negotiations resumed soon on "the basis of complete Israeli withdrawal from all occupied territories," Hussein said.

As a first step toward implementing the decisions taken at the Rabat summit,

Jordan planned to rewrite its Constitution and to reorganize its Cabinet and Parliament to remove Palestinians in the West Bank from the Amman government, Hussein said in a New York Times interview Nov. 4. He explained that as a result of the summit decisions, "the situation has altered very basically. A new reality exists and Jordan must adjust to it. The West Bank is no longer Jordan, and we have no place in the negotiations over its future."

The king expressed hope of close cooperation with the PLO, but ruled out use of his territory by the guerrillas for attacks on Israel.

Hussein said he foresaw no possibility that Jordan and a Palestinian state in the West Bank might confederate into a loose union. He chided Israel for having been "terribly slow over the very many years that have passed in terms of moving toward peace."

Jordan's Parliament Nov. 5 approved an amendment permitting King Hussein to reorganize the government to exclude Palestinian representation from the Israeli-occupied territory.

PLO aide predicts war. A PLO official said Nov. 2, 1974 that the Arabs must prepare for a new war being planned by Israel.

Yasir Abed Rabbo, a member of the PLO's Executive Committee, said in Beirut that Israel was "preparing a fifth Middle East war with the support of the United States to dictate their peace terms to the Arabs. The primary duty of the Arab states at this stage is to prepare themselves militarily and economically to face the new war."

Reporting on the Oct. 26–28 Arab summit meeting in Rabat, Rabbo said the conference had rejected a four-point peace plan proposed by U.S. Secretary of State Henry Kissinger. He said it called for: a limited Israeli troop pullback from the Sinai Peninsula in exchange for an Egyptian declaration on non-belligerency that "would end the state of war permanently between the two countries"; an Israeli agreement with Jordan that would give Hussein administrative control of the principal towns of the West Bank "except Jerusalem," while Israel maintained control of the West Bank countryside; a minor Israeli withdrawal from the Golan

Heights in the Quneitra area but continued Israeli occupation of the strategic highlands; and a unanimous agreement by Arab oil-producing states to reduce their prices.

Rabbo said that in its forthcoming talks with Egypt, Jordan and Syria, the PLO would insist on the right to resume military operations against Israeli forces in the West Bank from Jordan.

PLO leader Yasir Arafat also had predicted an early war in the Middle East. In a Time magazine (Nov. 11 issue) interview in Rabat, Arafat told correspondent Wilton Wynn that "a catastrophe is coming to this area" unless the United Nations "brings pressure to bear" on Israel. He said the Israelis were using the energy crisis as "blackmail" by attempting to "convince the West that they can be the spearhead of what is called the military solution" in the Middle East. The Israelis were preparing to launch "a pre-emptive strike" in six months, the PLO leader charged. Warning the U.S. against military intervention to protect the Middle East oil fields, Arafat said it would "be an extremely misleading calculation if the Americans think other superpowers will not act."

Arafat said that his reconciliation with King Hussein at the Rabat conference was "an agreement only on principles," but was "a new starting point."

Kissinger renews peace talks. U.S. Secretary of State Henry A. Kissinger revisited five Middle East capitals Nov. 5–7, 1974 in continuation of his step-by-step approach to peace between Israel and the Arabs and to discuss the actions taken by the Arabs at their summit meeting in Rabat Oct. 26–28. The secretary's mission was further complicated by the summit decision to support the PLO, with which Israel refused to negotiate.

Kissinger conferred with President Anwar Sadat in Cairo Nov. 5–6 and received the Egyptian leader's endorsement for a "second stage" of discussions with Israel on the further withdrawal of its forces from the Sinai Peninsula despite the Arab backing of the PLO. "I can't see all that the Rabat conference has put any block" in the Kissinger formula for peace, Sadat told a new conference. He was said to have told Kissinger, however, that

Egypt could not meet Israel's request for a statement of nonbelligerency in exchange for relinquishment of more Sinai territory because that would seem too much like a peace accord. Cairo would not agree to such a pact until Israel withdrew from all Arab territories, Sadat said.

Kissinger received similar backing for his peace efforts from King Faisal at a meeting with the Saudi Arabian monarch in Riyadh later Nov. 6. The king also assured Kissinger that he would seek stable oil prices. Speaking for Faisal, Foreign Minister Omar Saqqaf said the Saudi policy was "to keep the oil prices as they are and to try to reach a reduction, albeit a symbolic reduction, or if we can, a greater reduction."

The secretary flew to Amman Nov. 7 and met with Jordanian King Hussein, who reportedly informed him that the Arab summit decision giving the PLO sole authority over any part of the West Bank given up by Israel left his country with no political role in negotiations over the territory. Before departing for Damascus, Kissinger conceded in an airport statement that the Rabat decisions "had complicated the problem" of finding a Middle East solution.

Syrian President Hafez al-Assad was said to have informed Kissinger at their meeting Nov. 7 that the Rabat talks gave the Palestine problem first priority in steps toward peace. Kissinger replied that giving the PLO authority over West Bank territories in effect ruled out Arab recovery of the area because of Israel's refusal to deal with the guerrilla organization.

On arriving in Tel Aviv later Nov. 7 for the start of a two-day visit, Kissinger assured the Israelis in an airport statement that "since I have been here last, there has been no change in American policy on any of the issues before us." (The statement was in apparent reference to a remark made by President Ford at a news conference Oct. 29 in which he advocated talks between "Israel and Jordan or the PLO" as well as between Israel and Egypt,. Jordan and Syria.)

On returning to Washington Nov. 9, Kissinger said he believed that an "impasse had been averted" in the Middle East as a result of his talks with Arab and Israeli leaders.

Israel vs. French-PLO tie. French Foreign Minister Jean Sauvagnargues conferred with Israeli officials in Jerusalem Oct. 30–Nov. 2 and encountered criticism for his meeting with PLO leader Yasir Arafat in Beirut Oct. 21.

Foreign Minister Yigal Allon declared at a state dinner honoring Sauvagnargues Oct. 31 that French policy in the Middle East, including its contacts with the PLO, "damages the prospects of peace and increases the danger of conflagration in the area." He said it was time to encourage moderates in the Middle East who were "prepared for negotiations."

The French minister replied that Israel's security depended "not on conquered territory" but on complying with United Nations decisions and entering "a whole series of peace undertakings and guarantees."

Sauvagnargues told newsmen in Cairo Dec. 23 that the Arab states must recognize Israel's right to exist and that Israel must also recognize the right of the Palestinians to have a national home. According to French diplomats, the foreign minister was saying in effect that no member of the world community would sacrifice Israel no matter how strongly it supported the Arab cause. Sauvagnargues, who was visiting Egypt, had made a similar declaration in a televised address to a meeting of the Arab League headquarters attended by a PLO delegation.

Troubles Re West Bank

Aside from the desire of the Palestinian Arabs to end the Israeli occupation of the West Bank, a cause of friction was the claim of many Israeli Jews that Israel had a right to sovereignty over the area, which they referred to by the Biblical names of Samaria (for the territory to the north) and Judea (the area to the south). The Israeli government policy provided for Jewish settlement in some limited West Bank areas but clashed with Jews who tried to establish settlements on West Bank land from which the government had barred them.

Israel evicts West Bank squatters. Israeli troops July 29, 1974 evicted 150 Jews from an area they were attempting to settle near Nablus in the occupied West Bank. The squatters and several hundred supporters were taken in buses to Jerusalem and escorted by soldiers.

The squatters had moved into the unauthorized area July 25. They belonged to a movement that maintained that all of the Jewish ancestral homeland, including the entire West Bank, must be opened to Jewish settlement.

The Cabinet had ruled unanimously July 26 to remove the would-be settlers. National Religious Party Deputy Yehuda Ben-Meir defended the settlers, asserting that the "government's position outlawing settlement in Samaria is untenable."

The government had designated specific areas in the West Bank for Jewish settlement. They were for the most part in sparsely inhabited sections.

Troops and police Oct. 9 blocked another attempt by about 5,000 young Israelis to establish unauthorized Jewish settlements in the West Bank.

After gathering at rendezvous points throughout the country Oct. 8, the would-be settlers had moved in buses and automobile convoys on several points in the West Bank near Nablus, Ramallah and Jericho, north and south of Jerusalem. Security forces anticipating the intrusion had set up barricades to block the move. About 500 demonstrators managed to break through the lines near Ramallah and were forcibly evicted by soldiers.

Several leaders of the demonstration said they had acted in anticipation of U.S. Secretary of State Henry A. Kissinger's scheduled arrival in Jerusalem to underscore their opposition to Israeli withdrawal from any part of the West Bank. One spokesman said: "We wanted to establish a Jewish presence in Jericho because we have seen that in these Kissinger negotiations the line is drawn just east of the forwardmost settlements." This was in reference to the 18 government-approved Israeli settlements already on the West Bank, mostly in the Jordan Valley and near the pre-1967 border.

Participants in a counterdemonstration held outside Premier Yitzhak Rabin's office Oct. 9 charged that the settlers were attempting to undermine Kissinger's peace mission. Rabin also criticized the action in a Knesset speech.

Troops sealed off an area near Jericho Oct. 10 and rounded up several hundred squatters who had eluded army roadblocks to penetrate the West Bank.

Government forces Oct. 15 ousted about 100 would-be settlers at Tel Shilo, north of Jerusalem, and 160 others Oct. 16 near Tulkarm, 25 miles northeast of Tel Aviv.

The Mapam Party in Premier Yitzhak Rabin's coalition regime threatened Oct. 10 to vote against the entry of the National Religious Party (NRP) into the ruling alignment unless the governing Labor Party took sterner measures against the squatters and forced the NRP to halt its support of the illegal occupiers. The NRP replied that although it supported the squatters in principle, it opposed their establishment of unauthorized settlements on the West Bank.

More than 100 followers of the left-wing Moked Party demonstrated in front of Premier Rabin's office Oct. 10 in opposition to the squatters. The Mapai Party issued a statement that day saying that the action by the West Bank intruders "strikes at the very basis of democracy in Israel."

Israel plans West Bank projects—Israel announced Nov. 24 it planned to construct a major new industrial center and housing for its workers in the occupied West Bank between Jerusalem and Jericho and several smaller projects on the eastern outskirts of Jerusalem.

Information Minister Aharon Yariv announced the decision after it was adopted at a Cabinet meeting. He said the timing of the move was "coincidental," implying that it was not related to the resolution of the United Nations General Assembly declaring that the Palestinian people had the right to independence and sovereignty and to return to their former homes in the West Bank and in other parts of Israel.

Plans for the West Bank project, Yariv said, had "been in the works for a couple of years."

The industrial development was to go up at Mishor Haedomim, eight miles east of Jerusalem, on 1,500 acres of a 20,000-acre site originally set aside by the government in 1972. The other new projects included an area for automotive garages and small workshops in Anatot, on the northeastern edge of Jerusalem, and new housing for poor Arabs of East Jerusalem in Azaria, just east of the city.

Yariv conceded that the government's decision could harm Israel's ties with Jordan and further alienate its relations with the Palestinians.

Israel bars West Bank referendum. The Israeli Knesset Aug. 15, 1974 rejected by 53–42 vote an opposition Likud bill calling for a national referendum on the future of the West Bank. The Likud maintained that the West Bank, captured from Jordan in 1967, was part of a historic Jewish homeland and could not be surrendered. The party held that a majority of Israelis were opposed to giving up any part of that territory.

Despite defeat of the bill, the government remained committed to holding new elections before concluding any treaty with Jordan that would involve ceding West Bank areas.

Rabin on partial withdrawal. Israeli Premier Yitzhak Rabin asserted in a TV interview Oct. 1, 1974 that his government would consider a partial withdrawal from the West Bank in exchange for a Jordanian declaration of non-belligerency. He repeated his previous offer to Egypt of returning the bulk of the Sinai for a peace treaty but less territory for a mere non-belligerency pact.

The Israeli opposition Likud Party assailed Rabin and Foreign Minister Yigal Allon for proposing the return of occupied land. Saying that Rabin's offer on the West Bank was "irresponsible," Likud spokesmen contended Oct. 2 that the government was bound by a Knesset (Parliament) resolution declaring that the rights of the Jewish people to the land of Israel (including the West Bank) were irrevocable. Likud denounced Allon's remarks Oct. 6.

Palestinian terror unit emerges. The emergence of a Palestinian terror group seriously resisting Israeli rule in the West Bank for the first time since Israel's occupation of the area was reported by the New York Times Aug. 22, 1974.

The new movement, known as the Palestinian National Front (PNF), had surfaced since the October 1973 war and launched a terror campaign in the West Bank in March, it was reported. According to Israeli government officials, 896 West Bank Arabs had been arrested recently on security charges. Of the total, 549 had been tried and were serving jail terms; 314 were awaiting trial; and 33 were being held under administrative detention.

Israeli officials said the core of the PNF was the Jordanian Communist Party, outlawed by King Hussein. They said the PNF had decided to embark on a terror campaign before the October war, when the Soviet Union began to improve its ties with the Palestine Liberation Organization (PLO). The PNF's objective was to assume the leading resistance role on the West Bank and thus place itself in the forefront in any future negotiations on the territory, according to the Israelis.

Israelis oust 4 West Bank activists—Israeli authorities Nov. 4 banished four Palestinian activitists from the West Bank to Lebanon on charges of having solicited support for the PLO and of involvement in terrorism against Israelis and Arab moderates.

The men were identified as Ali Mahmud al-Khatib, editor of Al Shaab, a Jerusalem newspaper; Mustafa Hasan Milhim, deputy mayor of Halhul; Isam Bakr Fatah and Daoud Arikat.

The four were said to have been active in the Palestinian National Front.

The suspects "were found to have incited the populace against the Israeli authorities and to have tried to disrupt public order, law and security," according to the official announcement.

West Bank riots intensify. Arabs staged violent demonstrations in West Bank towns Nov. 16–19 in an intensified campaign of opposition to the Israeli occupation and in support of the PLO.

Thousands of Arab students rioted Nov. 16 in Jenin, Nablus, Halhul and Hebron, hurling stones at Israeli policemen. A 16-year old girl was killed in Jenin. Scores were injured and at least 50 were arrested in the three towns.

Police arrested 33 persons during rioting in Hebron and Jenin Nov. 17 and closed schools in the towns indefinitely.

Israeli riot police and soldiers battled young Arab rioters in East Jerusalem and on its outskirts Nov. 18, while similar violence broke out in the nearby towns of Ramallah and Al Birah.

Israel authorities contended that the West Bank rioting had been precipitated by PLO leader Yasir Arafat's address to the United Nations General Assembly Nov. 13. Arafat urged West Bank Arabs Nov. 18 to "continue and escalate your resistance and sacrifices" in their drive against Israeli occupation. Speaking at a news conference in Algiers, Arafat said: "We are with you and you have our complete support."

War Scare

Mobilization & troop moves. A threat of a major war in the Middle East emerged following Israel's mobilization Nov. 14, 1974 of part of its armed reserves and the shifting of its troops up to the Syrian and Lebanese borders in response to what it said were Syrian maneuvers near the Golan Heights. The danger of a possible flareup subsided Nov. 17 after the U.S. informed Israel that Syria had no intention of attacking. The assurances were conveyed Nov. 16 by Secretary of State Henry A. Kissinger to Israeli Ambassador Simcha Dinitz in Washington. Despite the easing of tensions, Syrian and Israeli forces remained on alert.

Kissinger was said to have sent cables Nov. 15 to the heads of state of Syria, Egypt and Saudi Arabia. The Syrians and Egyptians quickly cabled back that they had no plans to launch a war against Israel. King Faisal of Saudi Arabia said he would use his influence to calm the situation.

The Israeli embassy in Washington was said to have informed the State Department Nov. 14 that Israel had mobilized "several thousand troops," reportedly one-third of its reserve force, following Israeli intelligence reports of a Syrian massing of artillery and tanks near the Golan Heights, and the arrival of large shipments of Soviet arms in the Syrian port of Latakia. The Israeli decision was "precautionary," aimed at guarding against a surprise Syrian attack and was not offensive in nature, the State Department was told.

Israeli concern had been further heightened by speculation that Syria might not agree to extension of the mandate of the United Nations Disengagement Observer Force (UNDOF) on the Golan Heights when its current term expired Nov. 30.

Israeli Premier Yitzhak Rabin had disclosed the Soviet arms shipments Nov. 15, saying that more than 20 ships were unloading weapons at Latakia "at this very moment." Asserting that "this intervention will not contribute to peace in the Middle East," Rabin cautioned that Moscow "had better consider her actions in good time and wisely." (The State Department Nov. 19 disputed Rabin's report. It acknowledged the presence of 20–25 Soviet and East European Communist bloc ships in Latakia, but noted that this number was about the "normal" level, and that "only a small number of the total" was believed unloading military materiel.)

The first public confirmation of the Israeli mobilization came Nov. 16 from Defense Minister Moshe Peres, who said the massing of his country's forces and movements in the Golan Heights were in response to "unexplained movements" by Syrian troops in the region. Recalling that Israel had been taken by surprise in the October 1973 war, Peres said "it's better to err by superfluous mobilization than by ignoring signs or question marks."

Commenting on reports about new Middle East tensions, Secretary Kissinger hold told a Washington news conference Nov. 15, "I do not think that war is likely. We are not in a situation of imminent conflict. We cannot believe that any of the parties would resort to war in these circumstances." The Administration, Kissinger said, had been in touch with Moscow about the situation and "there is no evidence that the Soviet Union is encouraging war." The secretary said he had met with President Ford and Defense Secretary James R. Schlesinger earlier in the day to routinely review "contingencies and mechanisms to put into effect in the event of an emergency."

Syrian Foreign Minister Abdel Halim Khaddam asserted Nov. 16 that Israel's charges of a Syrian buildup were "aimed at misleading world public opinion and covering up its aggressive designs." He said his country was committed to the cease-fire with Israel, but was prepared to repulse Israeli "aggression."

Peres had warned July 26 that his government had "information that the Arabs were preparing to attack Israel in a matter of months—six, nine or 12 months." He said the evidence gathered was "based mainly on Syria," accusing it of being "extremist, impatient and overflowing with armaments." Syria's air force was already stronger than Egypt's, "while its patience is far shorter," Peres said.

Peres renewed charges Aug. 6 that Syria was preparing for war against Israel. Speaking to the Knesset (parliament), the defense minister said, "The stepped-up arms supplies, the accelerated training of their troops, the constant threats, the stated deadlines—all these have led us to express publicly what is apparent in fact: Syria has indeed harnessed her horses of war." As a result of Soviet arms shipments, Syria's air force was 25% stronger than it had been on the eve of the October 1973 war and its antiaircraft missile defense system was about 20% stronger, Peres said. He noted that the Soviet Union had "increased Syria's arsenal of heavy guns, including long-range 180-mm. pieces, and supplied her with Scud ground-to-ground missiles."

To prepare Israel for a possible outbreak of war, Peres said, the armed forces had begun to take a series of combat-readiness steps: younger regular army officers were being promoted into key positions left vacant by casualties of the October war; new weapons systems were being introduced; more reservists were being trained; and several thousand key reservists had been called up to repair vehicles and weapons damaged in the last conflict.

Egyptian Foreign Minister Ismail Fahmy, on an official visit to Paris, accused Israel Aug. 7 of "saber-rattling" by carrying out "such provocative acts as mobilization exercises and massing of troops on the Syrian border." Fahmy declared that Israel was introducing new tensions into the area and warned that if "the Arab world sees these moves as warlike, we will react in the same way."

Diplomatic sources in Cairo reporteᴅ Aug. 8 that Egypt had called up some military reservists, but the extent of the move was not certain.

Syria charges Israeli war plans—Syria had accused Israel Aug. 14 of planning a new war with an attack on Syria. The Syrian regime cited reports that "Israel has mobilized its reservists and moved tanks and heavy arms toward the Syrian and Lebanese borders."

The Damascus allegation followed Arab press reports for four days that Israel was massing troops and arms along the Syrian, Lebanese and Egyptian frontiers.

Israel had announced Aug. 11 that it planned to conduct a one-day, nationwide call-up of military reservists "to test the efficiency of the method" of mobilization in the event of war.

Israeli military sources Aug. 13 accused Syria of violating the disengagement agreement by moving heavy mortars into the limited forces zone on the Golan Heights, bringing about 100 troops into the demilitarized city of Quneitra and sending planes into the air space of the United Nations buffer zone separating the two armies. In retaliation, Israel had refused to permit Syrian engineers to clear mines from the U.N. buffer strip until it removed the mortars from its zone and the troops from Quneitra.

Israel bars war of attrition. Israeli Foreign Minister Yigal Allon said Oct. 4 his country would not permit itself to be drawn into a war of attrition if the Arabs attacked Israel. In an interview shortly before he left for home after a 10-day visit to the U.S., the minister said Israel would not allow the Arabs to determine "the type of war" to be fought but would counterattack with all its military power.

Allon expressed confidence Israel would triumph if attacked, but said "it is not correct that the military balance is sufficient to deter Arabs from attacking." Emphasizing that his country must be better equipped to avoid a conflict with the Arabs who had numerical superiority, Allon said that "since we cannot hope for quantitative parity, we must aim at a qualitative balance."

While being prepared for possible war, Israel was pledged to continue its pursuit of peace with the Arabs, the minister said. "Now is the best chance to get a political settlement in the Middle East. War is behind us and the fear of another war is in front of us."

Discussing the political aspects of the dispute, Allon said Israel might agree to a federation between a future Palestinian state and Jordan.

Syrian war warning—Syrian President Hafez al-Assad warned in an interview published Dec. 19 that if a new war broke out in the Middle East, Syria "shall see to it that it is a long war. It will expand both qualitatively and quantitatively. We can fight longer than Israel can, and this means the outcome will not be in Israel's favor. Israel will not be able to get us out of the battle."

Guerrillas raid Beit Shean. Three Palestinian guerrillas Nov. 19, 1974 invaded an apartment building in the northern Israeli town of Beit Shean, five miles from the Jordan border, and killed four civilians, including two women, before they were shot dead by an Israeli assault squad. Nineteen others were injured, most of them by leaping from windows to escape the terrorists.

Israeli authorities said leaflets in the possession of the terrorists showed they were members of the Popular Democratic Front for the Liberation of Palestine (PDFLP) and had probably crossed into Israel from Jordan after setting out from Syria.

Defense Minister Shimon Peres, who flew to the scene, warned that Israel would continue its attacks on the terrorists "in their centers in Lebanon and in their roots on both sides of the border."

A PDFLP communique issued in Damascus claimed credit for the attack.

The PDFLP's chief of operations, Abou Leila, said in Damascus that the group's operations, including the one against Beit Shean, were "authorized by the PLO Executive Committee." He contended that the town was a "military target" because some of its residents were officers in the Israeli army who were engaged in security missions against Palestinian resistance on the West Bank. Leila warned that the raids would continue until Israel agreed to negotiate with the PLO.

The PLO's chief spokesman at U.N. headquarters in New York, Shefiq al-Hout, said Nov. 19 that "we don't feel any embarrassment" over the Beit Shean raid. "This operation is an example of a negotiation on an equal level," he said.

Israelis shell Lebanon—Israeli artillery struck Palestinian targets eight miles inside Lebanon Nov. 14, while Israeli troops crossed the border to attack other guerrilla centers in the country.

A Lebanese Defense Ministry report said four persons were killed in the artillery strike on Nabatiye and two others died in the shelling of three villages to the east.

The ministry said about 100 Israeli soldiers landed in helicopters near Verubin, two miles from the border, and blew up three houses.

The two Israeli raids followed an Israeli Defense Ministry announcement of guerrilla shelling Nov. 13 of the northern towns of Qiryat Shemona and Safed. The Palestinian press agency claimed their attacks had caused "serious casualties."

Israeli gunboats Nov. 18 shelled a Palestinian refugee camp near Tyre, killing three persons, according to the Palestinian news agency.

UNDOF mandate extended. The United Nations Security Council Nov. 29 approved by a 13-0 vote (with China and Iraq not participating) a resolution extending the mandate of the United Nations Disengagement Observer Force (UNDOF) on the Golan Heights for six months through May 31, 1975.

Secretary General Kurt Waldheim had said in a report to the Security Council Nov. 27 that the continued presence of UNDOF between Israeli and Syrian forces on the Golan Heights "is essential not only for the maintenance of the present quiet in the area, but also to assist any further efforts toward establishment of a just and durable peace in the Middle East."

Washington diplomatic sources reported Nov. 30 that President Assad had suggested renewal of UNDOF in a Nov. 20 telephone conversation with U.S. Secretary of State Henry A. Kissinger, who was in Tokyo with President Ford at the time. Kissinger then relayed the proposal to the Israeli government. At the same time, the U.S. informed Waldheim that an effort to extend the life of UNDOF was under way, which caused the secretary general to delay his scheduled visit to Damascus by 24 hours.

Waldheim had received Syria's assent to prolong UNDOF at a meeting with

President Hafez al-Assad in Damascus
Nov. 25. The secretary general's visit to
the Syrian capital was part of a three-
nation Middle East tour aimed at easing
tension in the area and securing approval
of the continuation of the Golan Heights
peace force. He conferred with Premier
Yitzhak Rabin and other Israeli officials
in Jerusalem Nov. 26 and with Egyptian
President Anwar Sadat and Foreign
Minister Ismail Fahmy in Cairo Nov. 27.

Before leaving for New York Nov. 28,
Waldheim said in a Cairo interview that
his trip had helped avert a new round of
fighting in the Middle East, but expressed
fear that war could break out by the
spring or summer of 1975 unless a
breakthrough in peace negotiations was
achieved.

Negotiators Active

U.S. holds pre-Geneva talks. U.S.
officials in Washington opened an intensive month of negotiations with Israeli and
Arab leaders in August 1974 in hope of
progress toward a Middle East settlement
as a forerunner to resumption of the Geneva peace talks.

Israeli Foreign Minister Yigal Allon
met Aug. 1 with Secretary of State Henry
A. Kissinger, Defense Secretary James R.
Schlesinger and Vice President Gerald
Ford. Allon informed Kissinger that Israel was prepared to negotiate with either
Jordan or Egypt in the next stage of peace
discussions. The minister told newsmen
later in the day that the Israeli-Jordanian
frontier could be negotiated "in such a
way to satisfy the Arabs politically and Israel strategically." Allon reiterated his
government's position that any accord
with Jordan on the disposition of the Israeli-occupied West Bank would have to
be ratified by a national referendum in Israel.

Allon stressed the importance of the
Palestinians, saying that Israel "does not
ignore the problem of a Palestinian
identity. I would refuse any settlement
without a settlement of the Palestinian
question." Any agreement, however, must
be reached in the context of a settlement
with Jordan, he added.

Kissinger conferred with Jordanian
Premier Zaid al-Rifai Aug. 6–7. At the
Aug. 7 meeting, Rifai arranged for King
Hussein to visit Washington the following
week to discuss his demands for Israeli
withdrawal from the West Bank.

Israeli-Jordanian meeting denied—Several press reports that former Premier
Golda Meir and former Defense Minister
Moshe Dayan had met secretly May 27
with King Hussein were denied by the Israeli government Aug. 4. The meeting was
said to have been arranged by Kissinger
during his visits to Jerusalem and Amman
in May. Meir and Dayan were reported to
have met Hussein shortly before they left
office. They were said to have discussed
the general outlines of an agreement but
not the details. Hussein reportedly had
stressed the need for Israeli withdrawal
from the West Bank, while Meir and
Dayan proposed the return of Jordanian
civilian administration in the occupied territory.

The purported Israeli-Jordanian
meeting was again denied Aug. 6 by Premier Yitzhak Rabin. Speaking in the
Knesset, Rabin said Israel was prepared
to make contacts with Jordan to discuss
an agreement, "as openly as possible," or
"without publicity should the opposite
side so desire for its own reasons."

U.S.-Arab talks—President Ford and
Kissinger met in Washington with Jor-
dan's Hussein and Egyptian Foreign
Minister Ismail Fahmy.

Fahmy arrived in Washington Aug. 11.
After a week of talks with Ford and Kissinger, Fahmy and the secretary signed a
joint communique Aug. 19 that was coupled with a separate Administration announcement that the U.S. had agreed to
provide Egypt with 100,000 tons of wheat
before Oct. 1.

The communique noted that the talks
"were a constructive contribution to the
consultations now under way looking
toward the next stage of negotiations,"
but the following phase was not clarified.

The communique said the two sides
"agreed that the Geneva peace conference
on the Middle East should resume its
work as soon as possible . . . with the question of other participants from the Middle East area to be discussed at the con-

ference." This meant that the role of the Palestinians would not be taken up beforehand.

King Hussein's meeting Aug. 16–18 with Ford, Kissinger and Defense Secretary James R. Schlesinger concentrated on Jordan's demand for disengagement of Israeli and Jordanian troops along the Jordan River as the next stage in Middle East peace moves. A joint statement issued by Ford and Hussein Aug. 18 announced agreement to work for such an accord, with Ford reaffirming "his commitment that the United States would continue its determined efforts to help bring about a peace settlement in the Middle East."

The communique said the Middle East "consultations will continue with a view of addressing at an appropriate early date the issues of particular concern of Jordan, including a Jordanian-Israeli disengagement agreement."

Hussein had said Aug. 17 that although he had been "reassured" in his talks with American officials of their sympathy for his cause, he had received no commitment that the U.S. would press for Jordanian-Israeli disengagement talks as the next phase of Middle East peace negotiations.

Israel vs Jordan River pullout—Israeli representatives called on the State Department Aug. 19 to provide clarification of the U.S.-Jordan communique, questioning whether it constituted American endorsement of Jordan's proposal that Israeli forces pull back six-seven miles from the Jordan River as part of a disengagement agreement. The Israelis had in the past informed Kissinger of their opposition to any accord with Amman that called for an Israeli troop withdrawal from the river.

Kissinger said at a news conference Aug. 19 that the Ford-Hussein communique did not commit the U.S. to any specific accord. He provided a more detailed clarification in a message sent later Aug. 19 to Israeli Foreign Minister Yigal Allon.

U.S.-Syrian talks—Kissinger conferred with Syrian Foreign Minister Abdel Halim Khaddam in Washington Aug. 22–24. President Ford joined the talks Aug. 23.

The meetings were extended for an extra day. The failure to issue a communique at the conclusion of the discussions and their one-day extension did not mean that the meetings were deadlocked, U.S. officials said.

At a dinner for Khaddam Aug. 23, Kissinger had described negotiating with the Syrians as a "difficult process," but said Khaddam's visit had made a major contribution toward restoring good relations between Syria and the U.S.

Israeli premier visits U.S. Israeli Premier Yitzhak Rabin conferred in Washington Sept. 10–13 with President Ford, Secretary of State Henry A. Kissinger and Defense Secretary James R. Schlesinger. The U.S. officials sought to obtain from Rabin a strong commitment to continue negotiations toward a Middle East peace settlement and to determine whether those talks should be between Israel and Egypt, or Isarel and Jordan.

At the conclusion of the discussions, Rabin said Sept. 13 that he and the U.S. leaders had "reached an understanding on our ongoing military relationship in a concrete way with concrete results," an apparent reference to Israel's request for arms. Israeli officials said Ford had given Rabin assurances that most of Israel's arms needs would be met.

Rabin said that in the diplomatic phase of the discussions "we have reached an understanding on the need to continue the search for peace." He did not elaborate, but suggested that the U.S. and Israel were concentrating on new talks between Egypt and Israel as a fruitful follow-up to the troop separation accords that Israel had reached with Egypt and Syria.

In exchange for relinquishing Egyptian territory in the Sinai, Israel wanted a state of "non-belligerency" with Cairo, the premier said. Appearing on NBC-TV's Meet the Press Sept. 15, Rabin explained this to mean an end to all Egyptian military, diplomatic and economic action against Israel.

President Ford had greeted Rabin at the White House Sept. 10 with a declaration that the U.S. remained "committed to Israel's survival and security."

Kissinger resumes travels. Kissinger visited seven major capitals of the Middle East Oct. 9–15 in an effort to create a framework for resumption of Arab-Israeli peace negotiations and to discuss high petroleum prices with oil-producers of the region.

On returning to Washington Oct. 15, Kissinger said he had "found a general receptivity to a step-by-step approach" to peace talks.

The secretary's first stop was Cairo, where he conferred Oct. 9–10 with President Anwar Sadat. Kissinger later told newsmen that he and the Egyptian leader had discussed the "modalities" of the next stage of talks, but he declined to give details.

Egyptian sources reported Oct. 12 that Sadat had informed Kissinger that Egypt would refuse to grant any political concessions in exchange for a new partial Israeli withdrawal from the Sinai. Any agreement on additional Israeli pullbacks would be an extension of the January military disengagement agreements and not an interim political accord, as the Israelis reportedly have suggested, according to the sources.

Kissinger held meetings in Damascus Oct. 11 with Syrian President Hafez al-Assad and Foreign Minister Abdel Halim Khaddam. The secretary then flew to Jordan and conferred with King Hussein in Amman later Oct. 11 and in Aqaba Oct. 12. In a brief statement before leaving for Israel, Kissinger said he had reaffirmed the U.S. desire to bring about talks not only between Egypt and Israel but between Jordan and Israel as well.

The secretary's arrival in Israel Oct. 12 coincided with a demonstration in Jerusalem by about 8,000 persons chanting anti-Kissinger slogans outside the office of Premier Yitzhak Rabin. Most of the demonstrators were members of right-wing religious parties opposed to any return of the West Bank. Similar demonstrations were held throughout Kissinger's stay.

Before departing Israel Oct. 13, Kissinger announced he had reached agreement with Israeli leaders on "the principles and procedures" that might be followed in the next round of Arab-Israeli talks. Correspondents aboard Kissinger's jet were later told that the principles would essentially provide that any agreement between Israel and Egypt and Israel and Jordan would have to include further Israeli territorial concessions in

exchange for Arab moves that would improve Israel's security.

In talks with Kissinger in Riyadh Oct. 13, Saudi Arabian King Faisal acknowledged that high oil prices could wreck the world's economy and pledged to help bring them down.

Kissinger returned to Cairo and Damascus Oct. 14 to inform Presidents Sadat and Assad of his discussions with the Israelis and the Jordanians. The secretary flew to Algiers later Oct. 14 to take up the oil situation with Algerian President Housari Boumedienne.

Before returning to Washington Oct. 15, Kissinger visited Rabat and met with King Hassan of Morocco.

Gromyko conciliatory. Soviet Foreign Minister Andrei Gromyko, addressing the U.N. General Assembly Sept. 24, 1974, delivered an unusually moderate speech. Gromyko offered to resume Soviet diplomatic relations with Israel when genuine progress was made toward peace in the Middle East. However, he warned Israel against trying to "freeze" the Middle East situation by holding occupied Arab territory, and said "militarist intoxication" could lead to a new outbreak of war. He also called for an early resumption of the Middle East peace conference in Geneva and urged that Palestinians be allowed to take their "rightful place" at the conference table.

Gromyko denied that the Soviet position was "one-sided and only serving the interests of the Arab states." Moscow did support "the legitimate demands of the Arabs" and oppose retention of occupied territories by aggressors, but it also stood "in favor of Israel existing and developing as an independent sovereign state," Gromyko said.

"Real, not illusory, progress toward a Middle East settlement will create prerequisites for the development of relations between the Soviet Union and all the states of the Middle East, including Israel," he asserted.

U.S.-Soviet plan reported. Arab diplomatic sources in Beirut reported Nov. 28, 1974 that U.S. President Gerald Ford and Soviet Communist Party General Secretary Leonid Brezhnev had reached an agreement at a Vladivostok summit meeting Nov. 23–24 on a formula to break the Middle East diplomatic impasse. Israel expressed doubt Nov. 29 that such a plan had been broached, and the U.S. government issued a denial.

Under the reported plan, the Soviet Union would attempt to persuade Palestine Liberation Organization leader Yasir Arafat to recognize the right of Israel to exist as an independent state, while the U.S. would try to persuade Israel to drop its refusal to negotiate with the PLO. The proposed move to bring the two adversaries to the negotiating table constituted an extension of the U.S.-Soviet detente to the Middle East as a means of preventing an outbreak of war in the region, according to the Arab sources.

Israeli Premier Yitzhak Rabin said Nov. 29 he saw no sign of detente in the Middle East, asserting that the policies of the U.S. and the Soviet Union were in conflict there. Rabin pointed out that Brezhnev's scheduled visit to Cairo Jan. 15, 1975 was tantamount to an Egyptian warning to the U.S. that time was running short for Washington to bring about separate Egyptian-Israeli negotiations for a limited settlement. The premier said the Soviet Union and the Arab extremists were opposed to this kind of formula and preferred instead the reconvening of the Geneva conference, where, he noted, they could muster a united Arab front to demand Israeli withdrawal from occupied Arab territories and the establishment of a PLO-governed Palestinian state in the West Bank and the Gaza Strip. The Soviet Union and the Arabs believed this stand would receive nearly worldwide support and force the U.S. to change its policies, Rabin said.

In an Israeli newspaper interview published Dec. 3, the premier suggested that Israel may forgo its demand for a formal Egyptian declaration of non-belligerency in exchange for a further Israeli troop withdrawal in the Sinai Peninsula. Instead, Israel might have to accept a private Egyptian pledge of non-belligerency given to the U.S., Rabin said.

The premier said that in future negotiations Israel would insist that Egyptian forces stay out of areas evacuated by Israeli troops, and that Israel retain the strategic Mitla and Gidi passes in the Sinai.

Egyptian diplomatic sources said Dec. 4 that Cairo would not accept a second-stage Israeli withdrawal unless the strategic passes were given up, as well as the Abu Rudeis oil fields, occupied by Israel since the 1967 war.

Israeli Foreign Minister Yigal Allon said Dec. 3 that in an unpublished part of the January disengagement agreement, Egypt had promised to permit Israeli cargo to pass through the Suez Canal once the waterway was cleared for shipping. Egypt also had agreed to permit ships flying the Israeli flag to use the canal after a further peace step had been achieved, but he did not disclose that step.

U.S.-Israeli talks. Israeli Foreign Minister Yigal Allon conferred in Washington Dec. 9 with President Ford and Secretary of State Henry Kissinger to review the possible next step in Middle East peace negotiations, including a second round of Israeli-Egyptian talks on further disengagement of Israeli troops from the Sinai Peninsula.

A spokesman who had participated in the discussions said Allon and Kissinger had drawn up general principles that would be conveyed by the U.S. to Egypt and other Arab countries. Allon said the talks did not center on a possible pact with Egypt alone "but with the entire Middle East because each one of the countries there are candidates for political progress."

Addressing newsmen in Washington Dec. 11, Allon reiterated his government's refusal to conduct negotiations with the Palestine Liberation Organization, saying Israel would use its veto power to prevent the PLO from participating in the Geneva conference, if it ever was reconvened. Allon based that position on the U.S. contention that the question of inviting new parties to Geneva must be decided by unanimous vote of the participants (the U.S., the Soviet Union, Israel, Syria, Egypt and Jordan), thereby giving each of them a veto.

The foreign minister discounted the Dec. 10 proposal of the Trilateral Commission, a nongovernmental group of influential citizens of West Europe, the U.S. and Japan, calling for a joint U.S.-Soviet guarantee of peace. There was no substitute for a peace treaty, Allon said.

Egyptian Foreign Minister Ismail Fahmy had said Cairo relied on the U.S. and the Soviet Union to press for a peace accord, according to an interview published Dec. 9. It was in Egypt's "national interest that the Soviet Union should play a greater role in the peace-making effort," while the U.S. was the only country that "can force Israel to withdraw" from Arab territories, he said. Fahmy called the Soviet Union Egypt's "principal arms supplier."

Rabin defends peace terms remarks—Israel's opposition Likud Party criticized Premier Yitzhak Rabin Dec. 9 for the Dec. 3 newspaper interview in which he was interpreted as softening his stand in regard to a pullback in the Sinai.

Opposition spokesmen accused Rabin of "political retreats that jeopardize Israel's security" and of revealing the government's hand in advance of Allon's meetings in Washington. Some members of Rabin's own government accused him of "excessive frankness" in the interview.

Egypt demands Israel immigration ban. Egypt called on Israel Dec. 13 to "freeze" its population and suspend immigration for the next 50 years as a condition for peace in the Middle East.

The demand, by Egyptian Foreign Minister Fahmy, was made after U.S. Ambassador Hermann F. Eilts had informed President Sadat of Kissinger's talks Dec. 9 with Israeli Foreign Minister Allon. Cairo was reported to consider the results of the Kissinger-Allon talks "disappointing."

Fahmy's statement was in response to remarks made by Israeli Premier Yitzhak Rabin in a television interview Dec. 12 in which he said Israel wanted to avoid a new war but was capable of inflicting 10 times more destruction on Arab cities than the Arabs could carry out against Israeli civilian targets.

Fahmy said Rabin "fails to understand the situation in the Middle East. Sooner or later, Israel has no alternative but to recognize the PLO as representative of the Palestinian people, or face expulsion" from the U.N.

Fahmy said Israel must also pay compensation for the destruction resulting from the "aggressive wars" it had conducted against the Arabs in the past 26 years and for its "exploitation of raw materials, including oil from Sinai." He said Israel must accept the PLO proposal for a secular state in Palestine or accept partition with the Arabs along the lines of the 1947 U.N. partition plan.

Premier Rabin said Dec. 15 that Fahmy's proposal raised doubts about Egypt's serious intentions to resume peace negotiations with Israel. Foreign Minister Allon called the Fahmy proposal "absurd."

Sadat's peace desire. Egyptian President Anwar Sadat, in remarks broadcast on U.S. TV Dec. 19, 1974, expressed interest in a peace agreement with Israel. Israeli Premier Rabin replied Dec. 20 with a call for Sadat to meet with him personally to discuss prospects for peace.

Sadat had warned publicly Dec. 15 that the Middle East was ready to explode into war unless "the momentum of the progress of peace continued." The Egyptian leader said he welcomed any success in Secretary Kissinger's "step-by-step" formula to achieve peace. If this approach failed, Egypt favored resumption of the Geneva conference, Sadat said. He said he was in contact with Kissinger and President Ford "and we shall see in the near future what will be the result and after that we shall decide."

Sadat said he believed Israel now had atomic weapons. But "we [the Egyptians] shall not be scared or intimidated" and "we shall also find a way of having atomic weapons," he warned.

A month later Sadat issued a warning that unless Israel withdrew from the Sinai, the Golan Heights and the West Bank within three months, Cairo would abandon Kissinger's step-by-step moves to peace and would seek a meeting of the Geneva conference and "explode everything there."

In a Beirut newspaper (Al Nahar) interview published Jan. 16, Sadat said an Israeli pullout from the occupied Arab territories must be simultaneous. "When the Geneva peace conference materializes, it will be final and conclusive, and not merely [to discuss] a few kilometers under disengagement," he said.

Arafat visits Moscow. Palestine Liberation Organization (PLO) leader Yasir

Arafat conferred with Soviet officials in Moscow Nov. 25–26, 1974. The PLO had appointed a representative to the Soviet Union and would soon open an office in Moscow, Palestinian sources reported.

In a communique issued after Arafat's departure from Moscow, the Soviet government pledged to support the Palestinian people's "inalienable right to self-determination and creation of their own national home."

Arafat flew to Belgrade and conferred Nov. 30–Dec. 3 with President Tito and other Yugoslav officials.

India gives PLO political status—India granted the PLO diplomatic status Jan. 9, 1975. The accreditation of the PLO representative in New Delhi, Fathi Abdulhamid, was contained in an exchange of notes between PLO leader Yasir Arafat and S.K. Singh, Indian ambassador to Lebanon. The PLO office in New Delhi had previously operated under the auspices of the Arab League.

Brezhnev cancels Middle East visit. Soviet Communist Party General Secretary Leonid I. Brezhnev indefinitely called off a January visit to Egypt, Syria and Iraq, it was announced in Moscow Dec. 30, 1974. No official reason was given; speculation ranged from Brezhnev's ill health to serious diplomatic differences between Moscow and Cairo over a common approach to resolving the Middle East problem.

The announcement was made by the Soviet press agency Tass at the end of a three-day visit to Moscow by Egyptian Foreign Minister Ismail Fahmy and Gen. Mohammed Abdel Ghany el-Gamasy, war minister. A joint communique issued at the conclusion of the discussions Dec. 30 said both countries "firmly come out for the Geneva conference to resume at an early date with the participation of all interested sides, including the Palestine Liberation Organization as the representative of the Arab people, and will exert every effort in that direction." Discussions between Brezhnev and other Soviet officials and the Egyptians were said by the communique to have been conducted "in an atmosphere characteristic of the firm friendship between the two states and peoples" and "produced positive results."

Brezhnev had told Fahmy that ill health forced him to postpone his visit to the Middle East, Cairo diplomatic sources reported Dec. 31 as Fahmy and Gamasy returned home to report to President Anwar Sadat. The diplomats said Brezhnev had received the Egyptian delegation in a sanatorium outside Moscow and not in a government villa, as originally reported.

Sadat sent a New Year's eve message to Brezhnev and other Soviet officials Dec. 31, expressing hope that "the ties of friendship and cooperation" between their two countries would grow.

U.S. and other Western diplomatic sources speculated that Moscow had decided to drop Brezhnev's planned trip because of Egypt's refusal to support strongly enough the U.S.S.R.'s call for resumption of the Geneva conference, where the Soviets would have a direct role in a peace settlement. The Russians were believed displeased with Egypt's insistence on backing U.S. Secretary of State Henry A. Kissinger's step-by-step approach in negotiations between Egypt and Israel.

The visit to Moscow by Fahmy and Gamasy was unexpected, having been arranged suddenly after Sadat had received an urgent message from Brezhnev Dec. 24, foreign diplomatic sources in Cairo reported. The sources attributed the decision to dispatch the Egyptian delegation to Moscow to a loss of momentum in U.S. efforts to mediate between Israel and Egypt.

Gromyko visits Syria, Egypt. Soviet Foreign Minister Andrei A. Gromyko visited Syria Feb. 1–3, 1975 and Egypt Feb. 3–5.

Following Gromyko's talks with President Hafez al-Assad in Damascus, a joint communique was issued Feb. 3 reiterating the U.S.S.R's commitment to "consolidate Syria's defense power" and stressed Syria's "legitimate right to use all means to liberate its occupied territories." The communique also called for reconvening the Geneva conference on the Middle East "in February or early March at the latest."

Gromyko also held a separate meeting in Damascus Feb. 2 with Palestine Liberation Organization leader Yasir Arafat.

Gromyko met with Egyptian President Anwar Sadat in Cairo and announced to newsmen after the Feb. 4 discussions that Communist Party General Secretary Leonid I. Brezhnev would tour the Middle East shortly.

Appearing with Gromyko at the same news conference, Sadat said that as a result of their talks, both countries were "turning a new leaf" in their relations and had "come to an understanding and reached decisions on some matters." However, the settlement of "other outstanding issues" would have to await Brezhnev's visit, Sadat said.

A joint communique issued after Gromyko's departure Feb. 5 called for "immediate" resumption of the Geneva conference, but did not stipulate a date. Other Cairo officials participating in the talks said Egypt opposed setting a date to give U.S. Secretary of State Henry A. Kissinger time to negotiate another step-by-step agreement between Israel and Egypt.

Other Egyptian officials said Feb. 5 that Gromyko had given Sadat partial satisfaction on his request for Soviet arms but that total settlement of this problem would have to be taken up when Brezhnev visited Cairo.

Sadat assails Soviets—Sadat criticized Soviet behavior toward Egypt since 1967 and disclosed further details about his expulsion of Soviet technicians from Egypt in 1972, according to an interview published Sept. 9 in the Kuwaiti newspaper As-Siyasah.

The Soviets had been dissatisfied with him since his assumption of power and "want another president," Sadat said. Despite this attitude, the president said he would continue to seek to improve relations with Moscow.

Sadat said Israel "is an established fact" and the threat of "throwing Israel into the sea and the destruction of Israel is mere talk that does not represent the truth." Sadat said he was "not one of those people" who "want to bury their head in the sand" about this matter.

Turning to the Israeli-Egyptian interim agreement, Sadat said he had "the right to repatriate" the U.S. technicians who were to operate the early-warning system in the Sinai. The statement contradicted terms of the agreement, which stated only that

"if both parties . . . request the United States to conclude its role . . . the United States will consider such requests conclusive."

PLO-Arab talks. The foreign ministers of Jordan, Syria and Egypt and a representative of the Palestine Liberation Organization met in Cairo Jan. 3–4, 1975 to settle differences between the PLO and the Jordanian government and to coordinate military and political strategy toward Israel. The meeting had been ordered by the Arab summit conference in Rabat Oct. 26–28, 1974.

A communique released Jan. 4 announced that Jordanian Premier Zaid al-Rifai, who also served as his country's foreign minister, and Farouk Kaddoumi, head of the PLO's political department, had agreed that their sides would hold periodic meetings to discuss the issues dividing them. The three foreign ministers and the PLO planned similar meetings.

Kaddoumi pledged the PLO would cease propaganda attacks against Jordanian King Hussein, while Rifai vowed that Amman would respect the "vested rights" of the nearly one million Palestinians in Jordan.

The others attending the conference were Egyptian Foreign Minister Ismail Fahmy, Syrian Foreign Minister Abdel Halim Khaddam and Arab League Secretary General Mamoud Riad, who presided.

Rifai said after the meeting Jan. 4 that Jordan may withdraw from the "confrontation states," which also included Egypt and Syria, now that the PLO had been acknowledged by the Rabat conference as the sole representative of the Palestinian people. "There is no reason following Rabat why we cannot adopt the same status in the second line as Kuwait and Libya," Rifai said.

PLO information chief Yasir Abd Rabbou charged Jan. 7 that Jordan had rejected discussion of "essential military and political issues" and the restationing of guerrilla forces in Jordan at the Cairo conference. Rabbou said that conference had failed because of those who "propagate Jordanian-Israeli disengagement and the American-inspired partial resolutions" to the Middle East dispute.

PLO leader Yasir Arafat alluded to a reported Israeli-Jordanian disengagement plan, according to an interview published in the French newspaper Le Monde Jan. 7. Arafat said, "We have the painful impression that, despite appearances, King Hussein has not renounced his ambitions to speak in the name of the Palestinians" at the Geneva conference. Arafat construed the reported plan as a denial of the Rabat decision designating the PLO as the sole representative of the Palestinians in the West Bank.

The U.S. and Israel had denied Palestinian claims that secret proposals on an Israeli-Jordanian troop disengagement had been submitted to Cairo and Amman.

U.S.-Israeli talks. Israeli Foreign Minister Yigal Allon met with President Ford, Secretary of State Henry A. Kissinger and other U.S. officials in Washington Jan. 15–17, 1975 to discuss approaches to possible negotiations for a second-stage disengagement agreement with Egypt.

Following Allon's meeting with Ford Jan. 16, the White House said the President had stressed "the seriousness" of the Middle East situation and "repeated his commitment" to assist Israel and the Arabs in reaching a settlement.

Premier Yitzhak Rabin had said that Israel was willing to return "most of the Sinai," including the Abu Rudeis oil fields and the strategic Mitla and Gidi passes, according to an interview with Rabin published in the French newspaper Le Figaro Jan. 8. Israel, however, would have to retain Sharm el Sheik at the tip of the Sinai peninsula, Rabin said.

Two Lebanese newspapers had reported from Cairo Jan. 9 that Shah Mohammed Riza Pahlevi of Iran had proposed that if Israel returned the Abu Rudeis oil fields to Egypt, Iran would compensate Israel for the oil loss. Abu Rudeis provided Israel with half its oil requirements; Iran supplied Israel with the remainder.

Sadat demands passes, oil fields—President Sadat repeated his insistence on regaining possession of the strategic Sinai passes and the oil fields in an interview published in the French newspaper Le Monde Jan. 22. The Egyptian leader also further explained his Jan. 16 statement in which he had warned that Israel must withdraw from the occupied lands of Egypt, Syria and Jordan simultaneously

within three months or Cairo would seek a reconvening of the Geneva conference. Sadat told Le Monde that he was "disposed to accept if need be successive " pullbacks by Israel. His immediate demands, he said, were for Israel to pull out of the passes and the oil fields.

Sadat repeated Egypt's obligation to aid Syria if it came under attack by Israel. But he said this commitment did not apply to Lebanon, even if Israel attempted to occupy the southern part of that country in its fight with the Palestinian guerrillas based there. Lebanon's defense was a "collective responsibility" of the Arab countries, Sadat said.

Oil Linked to Peace & War

Saudi ties price cut to peace. Saudi Arabia Petroleum Minister Sheik Ahmed Zaki al-Yamani told newsmen in Washington Oct. 2, 1974 that oil prices would fall if a political solution were found to the Arab-Israeli conflict. He warned, however, that if the Israelis did not withdraw from occupied Arab territories, "this would produce a war" that would "have a very dangerous effect on prices, as well as on the supply of oil." "Any solution that will stop the fighting," he said, "is in the hands of the American government."

Asked why he was linking a political solution of the Middle East situation with a cut in oil prices, Yamani said, "If you give them [the Arabs] an incentive, they will be on your side."

Saudis pressured U.S. on Israel. Saudi Arabia had used U.S. oil companies in May 1973 in an attempt to pressure the U.S. government to change its pro-Israel policy, according to testimony released Aug. 6, 1974 by the Senate Foreign Relations Subcommittee on Multinational Corporations. The subcommittee had been investigating the Arabian American Oil Co. (Aramco) and its four U.S. shareholders, Exxon, Mobil, Texaco and the Standard Oil Co. of California.

Subcommittee Chairman Frank Church (D, Ida.) said the seven-month probe showed "the extent to which the companies that are hostages of the Saudis are forced to operate at their beck and call. The companies followed these instructions and reported on their activities to the king [Faisal]. The capstone of their efforts" was a joint memorandum to President Nixon sent by the chief executives of the owner companies Oct. 12, 1973, warning Nixon "that any actions of the U.S. government at this time in terms of increased military aid to Israel will have a critical and adverse effect on relations with the moderate Arab producing states." The memo was sent six days after Egypt and Syria had attacked Israel.

Company memorandums portrayed Faisal as warning the firms' executives that they would "lose everything" unless they intensified their efforts on behalf of the Arabs.

Subcommittee chief counsel Jerome Levinson said that although the U.S. had become friendlier to the Arabs, there was no evidence that this change in policy had been brought about by the companies' efforts.

One document supporting the subcommittee's charges was a cable sent to Aramco owning companies shortly after the outbreak of the war by Frank Jungers, Aramco's chairman and chief executive. It said that James E. Akins, U.S. ambassador to Saudi Arabia, through an Aramco official had "urged that industry leaders in the USA use their contacts at highest levels of USG [U.S. government] to hammer home point that oil restrictions are not going to be lifted unless political struggle is settled in manner satisfactory to Arabs."

According to another aspect of the investigation record, Saudi Arabia, after it realized it could not administer the oil embargo against the U.S. smoothly, called on Aramco and its owners to run the embargo for them. Sen. Church said the Saudis received total compliance with their wishes, "including the operations of a primary and secondary embargo aimed at the U.S. military." Jungers had cabled the owning companies Oct. 21, 1973 of the Saudis' intention of "looking to Aramco to police" the embargo and reported the embargo on shipments to the U.S. armed forces.

U.S. hints military move over oil. Secretary of State Henry A. Kissinger warned that the U.S. might use military force in the Middle East "to prevent the strangulation of the industrialized world" by the Arab oil producers. Kissinger made the statement in an interview with Business Week in the Jan. 13, 1975 issue (made public Jan. 2).

Kissinger said the use of force would be "considered only in the gravest emergency." "We should have learned from Vietnam that it is easier to get into a war than to get out of it," he said. "I am not saying that there's no circumstances where we would not use force. But it is one thing to use it in the case of a dispute over [oil] price; it's another where there is some actual strangulation of the industrialized world."

As for possible counteraction by the U.S.S.R., Kissinger said, "Any President who would resort to military action in the Middle East without worrying about the Soviets would have to be reckless. The question is to what extent he would let himself be deterred by it. But you cannot say you would not consider what the Soviets would do."

Kissinger said "the only chance to bring oil prices down immediately would be massive political warfare against countries like Saudi Arabia and Iran to make them risk their political stability and maybe their security if they did not cooperate." He ruled out this action, however, as being too risky since it entailed the possible destruction of those countries' systems and their take-over by extremists, which would defeat the "economic objectives" of the West.

Kissinger discounted reports of a possible outbreak of war in the Middle East as "exaggerated." If there were such a conflict, it is not certain the Arabs would impose an oil embargo as they did in 1973, Kissinger said. "It would now be a much more serious decision than it was the last time."

The secretary expressed displeasure with the failure of Western European nations to support U.S. policy on the Middle East. He attributed their stand to "an enormous feeling of insecurity. They recognized that their safety depends on the United States, their economic well-being depends on the United States, . . . So the sense of impotence, the inability to do domestically what they know to be right, produces a certain peevishness which also stops short of policy action."

Kissinger reiterated his call for cooperation among the oil-consuming nations of the West to make them "less vulnerable to the threat of embargo and to the danger of financial collapse."

Commenting on statements made in December by Shah Mohammed Riza Pahlevi that Iran would side with the Arabs in any future war, Kissinger said this was indicative of "the trends in the Moslem world" toward "the direction of greater solidarity."

The shah had asserted in a Cairo newspaper interview published Dec. 27 that Iran would not enter into any future war in the Middle East, although its sympathies would be with the Arabs. Al Ahram quoted the shah as saying: "Of course Iran is not thinking of participating in the fighting. You are aware of geographical and other obstacles. But our sentiment will certainly be on your side." He called for "close regional cooperation" between Iran and the Arab states to remove "the military presence of the great powers" in the Middle East. The shah said he had been misinterpreted by a Beirut magazine which reported Dec. 12 that he hinted of a possible Iranian military alignment with the Arabs in the event of any new war with Israel. The magazine Hawadess had quoted the shah as saying: "All Islamic countries would be involved in a new war with Israel. Of course, we would have no choice this time. The war would be ours."

Questioned by newsmen about the interview, Kissinger Jan. 2 restated his belief that the use of U.S. military force in the Middle East was unlikely and that the circumstances that would warrant it were extremely remote. He expressed confidence that "the oil problem would be dealt with by other methods," but, repeating his remarks to Business Week, Kissinger declared that he was not saying "there's no circumstances where we would not use force."

The secretary repeated his assurances to newsmen Jan. 3 and said his statements in the interview reflected the views of President Ford. "I do not make a major statement on foreign policy on which I do not reflect his views," he said.

Ford's press secretary Ron Nessen Jan. 4 confirmed that Kissinger's statement on the possible employment of military action "did reflect the President's views."

Nessen had said Jan. 3 that Ford regarded Kissinger's statement on the possible use of military action "a highly qualified answer on a hypothetical situation involving only the gravest kind of emergency with the industrialized world."

The use of military force in the Middle East as a possible "option" was said to have been discussed by Ford's energy advisers at a meeting Dec. 14–15, 1974 to prepare policy recommendations for the President. A Ford spokesman said Jan. 3 that the President "knew of no plan for military action" discussed at the meeting. However, Ford conceded that such contingency plans might exist in the Defense Department or in other branches of government, the spokesman said.

Arab and other reaction—Iranian Premier Amir Abbas Hoveida warned that the use of force against the oil-producer states by one superpower would result in military intervention by the other superpower and cause "a catastrophe," according to an interview published Jan. 4 in the Egyptian newspaper Al Ahram.

Algerian President Houari Boumedienne said Jan. 6 that "occupation of one Arab state would be regarded as an occupation of the entire Arab world." U.S. military action, he predicted, would destroy the oil fields.

Egypt endorsed Boumedienne's position in a statement released Jan. 7 by Information Minister Ahmed Kamal Abul Magd. He asserted that Kissinger's declaration "did not serve the cause of American-Arab relations or the cause of peace in the area."

Kuwait Oil Minister Abdel Rahman Atiki reacted to the Kissinger warning Jan. 4 by telling other Arab oil producers that "any excessive reduction [of oil output] affecting or threatening world interests means placing ourselves in international trouble." A production cutback, he said, could precipitate "a possible war launched against us by the advanced industrial countries."

Egyptian President Sadat said Jan. 9 that the Arabs would blow up their oil wells if the U.S. attempted to take them over by force. Describing Kissinger's remarks as "very regrettable," Sadat said, "We will not need armies, because it is much easier to blow up oil wells than to carry out an invasion."

The Soviet press and television Jan. 6 carried a summary of critical reaction to Kissinger's remarks by newspapers in Asia, Africa and Europe. These comments, the press agency Tass said, showed "that the times of gunboat diplomacy and intimidation are gone."

The Soviet Communist Party newspaper Pravda charged Jan. 7 that "defenders of monopoly interests" in the West were employing "military blackmail" against the Arab oil producers in an effort to bring oil prices into line.

West German government officials and the press expressed anxiety about Kissinger's statement on force, it was reported Jan. 5. A government spokesman said: "I don't see the danger of [industrial] 'strangulation' at the moment. We are not interested in any kind of confrontation with the oil countries, but rather in cooperation...."

North Atlantic Treaty Organization (NATO) Secretary General Joseph Luns said Jan. 12 that any nation "faced with strangulation" was apt "to consider the use of force. That applies to the European countries as well as to the Arabs or to the Soviets."

Ford restates possible use of force. President Ford reaffirmed his support of Secretary of State Henry Kissinger's warning about possible use of U.S. force against the Middle East oil countries to prevent "economic strangulation." The President made the statement in an interview in the Jan. 20 issue of Time magazine (made public Jan. 12).

Ford said the key word was "strangulation. If you read his [Kissinger's] answer to a very hypothetical question, he didn't say that force would be used to bring a price change" in oil exported from the Middle East. "His language said he wouldn't rule out force if the free world or industrialized world would be strangled. I would reaffirm my support of that position as he answered that hypothetical question."

Asked to define his definition of the term "strangle," Ford replied "Strangulation, if you translate it into terms of a human being, means that you are just about on your back."

On other aspects of the Middle East situation, Ford said the prospects for war were "very serious" and that the opportu-

nities for peace diminished every day the dispute remained unresolved.

Ford said he would not rule out a U.S. guarantee for Israel's security "under some circumstances," but insisted that there must be more progress toward a settlement "before that step would be taken." "In the final analysis" the U.S. would act in its own "national interest above any and all considerations," Ford said.

U.S. Defense Secretary James R. Schlesinger Jan. 14 acknowledged that the use of American force in the Middle East would "indeed be feasible to conduct ... if the necessity should arise." However, such action would be taken "only in the gravest emergency," a situation which the U.S. did not consider "likely to arise," Schlesinger said.

Arms & Middle East Peace

The Middle East is a major arms importing area. Even Israel, the only country of the region with a substantial armaments industry, imports a large proportion of its arms. The exporting of weapons to Middle Eastern countries had obvious implications on the outcome of the Arab-Israeli conflict and on the prospects of peace or continued war.

Arms producing countries ship weapons to (or withhold them from) nations in the Middle East (or elsewhere) on the basis of political or economic considerations or a combination of the two. The Soviet Union is a major supplier of arms to some Arab nations because it considers that its political interests in the area are served by supporting the Arab cause. The U.S. is the chief exporter of weapons to Israel because of its commitment to Israel's existence. But the U.S. also sells arms to Arab nations to support them against a perceived Soviet plan of penetrating the area. The U.S. also does so to maintain friendly relations with Arab oil exporting nations. Other Western nations have similar reasons for arms deals with both Israel and the Arab countries.

Egypt to end reliance on Soviet arms. President Anwar Sadat said April 18, 1974 that Egypt would end its dependence on the Soviet Union as its main supplier of arms and that it would seek the military equipment from other countries. The Soviet Union had become Egypt's sole provider of weapons in 1955 when the late President Gamal Abdel Nasser negotiated a deal for arms that were first delivered through Czechoslovakia.

Addressing a joint session of the People's Assembly and the Arab Socialist Union, Sadat said he had made the decision after Soviet Communist Party Chairman Leonid I. Brezhnev had ignored four of his requests in the past six months for arms delivery. "It is inconceivable that our requests should remain under study for six months—including the crucial month of November when Israeli forces held a part of the west bank of the Suez Canal," Sadat said.

Sadat did not name the countries he hoped would sell Egypt arms, but it was believed Arab oil-producing states would be of assistance. Sadat said that Saudi Arabia had put $100 million at his government's disposal in recent days, presumably for the purchase of military equipment. Kuwait was said to have set aside a similar amount for Egypt. Kuwait and Saudi Arabia, which had recently contracted for Western arms, reportedly said they were free to make the new weapons available to other Arab countries.

In his address, Sadat also said Egypt intended to retain its policy of nonalignment and "positive neutrality." He praised the U.S. for its peace efforts in the Middle East, but said Cairo "does not want to be friendly with the United States at the Soviet Union's expense or vice versa."

Sadat had previously alluded to disaffection with the Soviet Union over its arms policy in a statement to students April 16. He declared that he had come close to renouncing the 1971 Egyptian-Soviet friendship treaty but said that he had decided not to do so at the last moment. In reporting Sadat's remarks April 17, Egyptian newspapers did not say what reason the president had given for his intentions to end the accord, but he was known to have complained on previous occasions about the Soviet failure to supply Egypt with an adequate supply of arms during and after the October 1973 war.

Sadat also reaffirmed his intentions to work through the U.S. for a peace settlement. He said that his meetings with Secretary of State Henry A. Kissinger had convinced him that the U.S. had become "the basic factor" in negotiations.

Sadat said April 21 Egypt had decided to end its exclusive reliance on the Soviet Union for arms because Moscow had been using the supply of its equipment as an "instrument of policy leverage" to influence Cairo's actions.

In a further explanation of the arms policy he had first announced April 18, Sadat said he was prepared to continue to purchase weapons from the Soviet Union, but "If the United States is ready to sell me arms, I shall be very happy." The president again complained of the Soviet failure to respond to his arms requests for six months since the October war, saying that such delays had been frequent in Cairo-Moscow relations since Egypt first started buying arms from the Soviet Union in 1955. "Therefore, from now on I'm going to vary the source of my military equipment," he said.

Despite the deterioration in Soviet-Egyptian ties, Communist Party General Secretary Leonid I. Brezhnev was reported to have sent Sadat a conciliatory note April 23, assuring him that Moscow remained interested in a stable peace in the Middle East and was playing an active and positive role to achieve it.

Sadat again complained that the Soviet Union had refused to replace all the Egyptian arms lost in the October 1973 war and had failed to reschedule Cairo's estimated $4 billion debt, according to an interview published in the Beirut newspaper Al Anwar Jan. 8, 1975.

Sadat disclosed that the Soviet decision on the arms and the debt had been made at a meeting with Egyptian Foreign Minister Ismail Fahmy and Gen. Mohammed Abdel Ghany el-Gamasy in Moscow Dec. 28–30, 1974. "Our request for complete replacement and for new weapons developed since the October war has not been met," Sadat said. He added: "I want every Arab throughout the Arab world to know that since the cease-fire of October 1973, up to this moment, Egypt has received from the Soviet Union only some weapons bought and paid for by [Algerian President Houari] Boumedienne and small quantities of ammunition and spare parts. There has been no Soviet replenishment and no fundamental arms received up to this moment."

Sadat noted that the Soviet Union had replaced Syrian war losses and the U.S. has "not only compensated Israel for her losses, but has also provided her with new sophisticated weapons."

Egypt sought a delay on repayment of the debt to the Soviet Union because of economic hardships stemming from the war, but the Russians had rejected Egypt's request to send an economic team to Moscow along with Fahmy and Gamasy to discuss the matter, Sadat indicated.

Soviets renew arms flow to Egypt—The Soviet Union had renewed the shipments of arms to Egypt, including MiG-23 fighter planes, for the first time since the 1973 war, Foreign Minister Fahmy confirmed Feb. 18, 1975. Before a foreign relations committee of Parliament, Fahmy implied that Cairo did not consider the military equipment as a replacement for the losses it had incurred during the war since the latest deliveries were part of deals made earlier in 1973 and in 1972. Fahmy said Egypt would not return to the Geneva conference until those losses were replaced.

East European and Lebanese press sources reported Feb. 19 that the latest Soviet supplies had been arranged by Fahmy and Lt. Gen. Mohammed Abdel Ghany el-Gamasy, commander in chief, in Moscow Dec. 28–30, 1974. Under a six-month supply program, which had started in January, the Soviet Union was to send Egypt 50 MiG-23s, ground-to-ground missiles, more surface missiles and 500 tanks, according to the sources. The Russians were said to have rejected Cairo's request for the more advanced MiG-25s, which Egypt wanted to balance future deliveries to Israel of the U.S.-made F-14 and F-15. The Soviet leaders also were said to have turned down Gamasy's demand for 120 MiG-23s, the number of jets lost by Egypt in the 1973 war.

The recent arrival in Egypt of six MiG-23s aboard a Soviet freighter was confirmed by the U.S. State Department Feb. 19. The Egyptian Air Force was already equipped with 200 of the less-advanced MiG-21s.

Soviet planes & Cubans in Syria. Israeli Defense Minister Moshe Dayan March 31,

1974 revealed Israeli intelligence reports of Soviet ships unloading planes in Syria, apparently the advanced MiG-23 (Flogger). The jet was more sophisticated than 200 MiG-21s already in Syria and, according to Dayan, would have an important effect on the balance of power in the Middle East. The MiG-23s were part of a general strengthening of Arab forces, Dayan said. He reported that the buildup also included the deployment of about 3,-000 Cuban troops in Syria. The London Times confirmed the Cuban presence April 2 and reported the unit was believed to have about 110 tanks.

The U.S. Defense Department April 2 confirmed the presence of Cubans in Syria, but said they only numbered 100–500 men believed serving as replacements in a Syrian armored brigade. A department spokesman said he did not know what functions they were performing in the unit. He said the Cubans had been in Syria "for some months."

Israel's radio military commentator, Gen. Haim Herzog, had said in a broadcast April 1 that the Cuban force was probably in Syria at the Soviet Union's instigation. The presence of the Cubans was believed to have been known by Israel for some time, but newsmen were not permitted to mention them.

The Soviet Union promised to give Syria more military aid following a visit to Moscow by President Hafez al-Assad April 11–13.

A joint statement issued in Moscow and Damascus April 16 signed by Assad and Soviet Communist Party General Secretary Leonid I. Brezhnev said both countries had "discussed and outlined steps for further strengthening the defense capacity of the Syrians." It affirmed Syria's "inalienable right to use all effective means for liberation of her occupied lands" and emphasized "the importance of the Soviet Union's participation in all the stages and areas" of a peace settlement in the Middle East.

On prospects for the separation of Syrian and Israeli forces, the statement said "any agreement on troop disengagement must be part and parcel of an overall settlement of the Middle East problem, a step on the way to a fundamental and all-encompassing settlement."

In a critical reference to the Egyptian-Israeli disengagement accord negotiated by U.S. Secretary of State Henry A. Kissinger, the joint statement said "partial steps that are now being taken do not cover the main, key elements of a settlement."

Brezhnev had warned April 11 that the U.S. and Israel might attempt to substitute a disengagement agreement with Syria for a genuine peace settlement. Speaking at a dinner for Assad, Brezhnev said these "ersatz plans" for troop separation would result in "replacing an overall settlement with partial agreements of a different kind."

Assad and Brezhnev had signed a long-term agreement April 13 on economic and technical cooperation, a cultural and scientific accord and a protocol on trade for 1974.

Israeli Defense Minister Shimon Peres filed a complaint Aug. 1 with the United Nations Emergency Force (UNEF) charging that Soviet helicopters in late July had repeatedly violated Israeli airspace over the southern Sinai Peninsula. The helicopters, based on an aircraft carrier, were involved in mine-clearing operations in the Red Sea and the Gulf of Suez. Peres reported to the Cabinet Aug. 2 that the Soviet aircraft had attempted to photograph Israeli warships but fled when Israeli fighters appeared on the scene. The Soviet Union denied the charge Aug. 2.

Peres said the Syrians had installed 160-mm. mortars in the limited forces zone on the Golan Heights in violation of the disengagement accord.

Denying press reports that the Syrians were disbanding Palestinian groups, Peres said Damascus was still arming the terrorists in Lebanon. The defense minister expressed concern that Syria had taken no steps to restore civilian life in the areas evacuated by Israel and appeared to be concentrating on military preparations.

Peres said Dec. 17 that Soviet soldiers in Syria were manning Syrian missile batteries in Damascus "as well as various electronic systems all over" the country.

Peres said he was not certain how many Soviet soldiers were in Syrian military positions, but estimated that the force totaled about 3,000 men.

Since the 1973 October war, the Soviet Union had supplied Syria with more than 1,000 tanks, more than 300 jet fighters, ground and air missiles, hundreds of armored troop carriers and hundreds of artillery pieces and anti-tank guns, Peres said.

U.S.-Saudi military agreement. Riyadh radio announced April 14, 1974 that the U.S. had agreed to develop and modernize the Saudi Arabian national guard under an accord signed by U.S. Ambassador James E. Akins and Prince Abdul Ben Abdul Aziz, the guard commander. The U.S. was to provide the weapons and training valued at $335 million. The broadcast said the arms would include armored vehicles, antitank weapons and artillery.

The signing of the pact followed an announcement in Riyadh and Washington April 5 that the countries had agreed to strengthen their cooperation in the economic, industrial and military areas. Negotiations were to be held to set up the mechanism for bilateral exchanges.

According to an accompanying State Department statement, "Despite the strain that arose during the oil embargo, we remained in close touch with our Saudi friends." The U.S.' aim was "to broaden and deepen the entire range of Saudi-American relations in ways that will enhance stability in the Middle East."

The Saudi Arabian government later had agreed to purchase 60 F-5 jet fighters at a cost of $750 million, it was announced simultaneously in Washington and Riyadh Jan. 9, 1975. The deal included spare parts, training and ground equipment and barred transfer of the aircraft to another country without U.S. permission.

The State Department said the sale, the largest by the U.S. to the Saudi government in more than 20 years, would contribute to "the legitimate self-defense needs" of Saudi Arabia and would "contribute to stability" in the Persian Gulf area.

The Saudis had ordered $582 million in arms and training from the U.S. in the fiscal year ended June 30, 1974.

Soviets arm Palestinians. Israeli Defense Minister Shimon Peres said July 30, 1974 that the Soviet Union was supplying the Palestinian guerrillas with arms and equipment from ships unloading in ports in Algeria, Iraq and Syria. He added that the guerrillas were also receiving military assistance from other Soviet-bloc nations "with the knowledge, encouragement and mediation of the Russians."

Palestinians get Syrian arms—PLO leader Yasir Arafat said Syria had shipped "sophisticated weapons" to his forces in Lebanon in recent weeks and would continue to send the arms, the Beirut newspaper Al-Yom reported July 10. Western intelligence sources in Beirut had reported July 4 that the Syrians had sent the guerrillas shoulder-launched Strela SA-7 missiles.

France ends embargo. France announced Aug. 28, 1974 that it was lifting the arms embargo it had imposed on the Middle East belligerents in 1967.

A government statement said arms sales to Israel and Egypt, Syria, Jordan and other Arab countries "could henceforth be considered on a case-by-case basis."

An Israeli Defense Ministry spokesman said the removal of the French arms ban would have "no effect on Israel at this point."

France was reported in the process of delivering $250 million worth of weapons ordered by Saudi Arabia, Libya, Iraq, Kuwait, Abu Dhabi, Qatar and Lebanon.

French Foreign Minister Michel Jobert had visited the Middle East Jan. 24–29 to offer French arms for oil.

In his meetings with Saudi Arabian King Faisal Jan. 24–26, Jobert discussed a proposed 20-year agreement in which France would receive 800 million tons of oil in return for sophisticated arms and industrial equipment.

Jobert was said to have sought a similar oil-arms agreement in his discussions in Kuwait Jan. 27–28. Kuwait government sources reported Jan. 28 that France was ready to supply fighter planes, tanks and anti-aircraft missiles without political conditions.

The French foreign minister conferred in Damascus Jan. 29 with Syrian President Hafez al-Assad and Foreign Minister Abdel Halim Khaddam. Jobert criticized the exclusion of European states from the Geneva conference on the Middle East.

On his return to Paris Jan. 30, Jobert said the U.S. had made some "spectacular initiatives" in the Middle East but with "perhaps less spectacular results."

Jobert had defended his government's policy of bilateral arms-oil agreements with Arab countries Jan. 21. He charged that this policy was being criticized in some quarters "because France might take someone else's place or ask that a little room be made for her."

France April 16 announced its agreement to sell an undisclosed number of Mirage F-1 fighter planes to Kuwait.

It was reported that the accord called for providing Kuwait with 32 of the aircraft with spare parts as well as construction of a radar network and early-warning system at a cost of $300 million. The aircraft were to be equipped with air-to-air and air-to-ground missiles, with delivery starting at the end of 1974. No conditions had been imposed.

Saudi Arabia had bought $800 million worth of weapons from France under an agreement signed in Riyadh, Defense Minister Prince Sultan ibn Abdel Aziz announced Dec. 3.

Aziz said the shipments would include anti-aircraft missiles and anti-tank weapons. The deal also was said to involve 200 AMX-30 tanks, 250 armored cars and machine-gun carriers and 38 Mirage III planes. The defense minister said the arms would be purchased with cash over a period of four years.

Kuwait sources reported Dec. 4 that states in the Persian Gulf area regarded the arms contract as a demonstration of Saudi Arabia's determination to match the $3 billion worth of U.S. and British military equipment recently purchased by Iran, whose neighbors were said to be concerned that it was seeking to establish strategic control in the region.

France agreed to sell Mirages to Egypt under an arrangement worked out by President Anwar Sadat in talks with President Valery Giscard d'Estaing in Paris Jan. 27–29, 1975. A communique made general reference to the arms sale, stating that "France would provide certain military material to compensate for part of Egypt's losses" in the October 1973 war with Israel.

Speaking at a news conference later Jan. 29, Sadat would not disclose the number of planes contracted for, but said they were "very much less" than the 120 aircraft Egypt reportedly had lost in the conflict. "Delivery will be in years to come," he added. (According to U.S. and

French sources in Paris, France had agreed to sell 44 Mirages to Egypt—22 F-1E M53s, still in the development stage, and 22 F-1 9K50s.)

The joint Sadat-Giscard communiqué further recognized "the right of all states in the area to live in peace with secure, recognized and guaranteed frontiers" as one of the three agreed "fundamental conditions" for peace. The other two were Israeli withdrawal from occupied Arab territories and the right of the Palestinians to a homeland.

U.S. sees Israeli arms gains. U.S. intelligence officials and Middle East specialists estimated that Israel was in a stronger military position in relation to Egypt and Syria than before the outbreak of the 1973 war, according to a private national security study memo made public by the New York Times Oct. 2, 1974. The study had been requested by Secretary of State Henry A. Kissinger as a guide to President Ford in making decisions on new Israel arms requests.

The study had been given in some form to the Israelis and was limited to Israel and the "confrontation countries," Egypt and Syria. Its principal points: If there were no progress in political negotiations soon, prospects for a new war would be heightened; if the fighting resumed, the scale of combat would be more intense because of the huge amount of firepower possessed by both sides; and both sides had developed extremely sensitive military readiness as a consequence of the surprise attacks in 1956, 1967 and 1973.

The study attributed Israel's relative improvement in military capability to more and better equipment, an increased training program and improved mobilization techniques. It noted that Israel's equipment losses in the 1973 conflict were not as extensive as first estimated, that many damaged tanks and other armored vehicles had been repaired. The new equipment was the advanced weaponry Israel had received from the U.S. during and after the war, including television-guided "smart bombs" and anti-tank missiles.

The study also took note of the substantial amount of Soviet arms shipped to the Middle East, estimating that the Syrians had a bigger arsenal of weapons than before the war and that the Egyptians had about the same amount as a year ago.

Israel's A-arms capability. Israeli President Ephraim Katzir said Dec. 1, 1974 that Israel "possessed the potential to produce atomic weapons" and "if we need it we will do it." In the past Israel had denied reports that it already possessed atom bombs.

Speaking to an international science reporters' group in Jerusalem, Katzir said: "It has always been our intention to provide the potential for nuclear weapons development. We now have that potential. We will defend this country with all possible means at hand. We have to develop more powerful and new arms to protect ourselves."

The president, however, reiterated Israel's previous pledges that it would "not be the first to introduce atomic weapons into the area."

Arab diplomatic sources in Beirut reported Dec. 4 that Syria, Egypt, Iraq and Algeria had received assurances from the Soviet Union that it would provide them with nuclear devices if it became known that Israel was armed with atomic weapons. The Arab statement, in direct response to Katzir's declaration, also said that Egyptians and Syrians had received training in arming Soviet-made missiles with nuclear warheads.

Israel unveils its own jet. An Israeli-designed and manufactured jet fighter was publicly displayed April 14, 1975.

The aircraft, named the Kfir (Lion Cub), was similar in design to the French Mirage-5 but was powered by General Electric J-79 engines used in the U.S. Phantom F-4. Built at a cost of $4 million, the Kfir had a top speed of more than twice the speed of sound and was regarded by foreign air attaches in Israel in a class with the latest versions of the Soviet MiG-21, which was used by the Egyptian and Syrian air forces.

Israel to buy 200 U.S. missiles. The U.S. was to sell Israel about 200 Lance missiles, which were capable of carrying nuclear warheads, the Defense Department said Jan. 23, 1975. Israel's plans, however, called for using the weapon with a conventional warhead, particularly for attacking antiaircraft missile sites, the department said.

76 Senators oppose reduced aid to Israel.
Seventy-six members of the Senate sent a letter to President Ford May 21 opposing any Administration attempts to reduce military and economic assistance to Israel. "Within the next several weeks," the letter said, "the Congress expects to receive your foreign aid requests for fiscal 1976. We trust that your recommendations will be responsive to Israel's urgent military and economic needs. We urge you to make it clear, as we do, that the United States acting in its own national interests stands firmly with Israel in the search for peace in future negotiations, and this premise is the basis for the current reassessment of U.S. policy in the Middle East."

In their letter, the senators also indicated their support for Israel's insistence on "secure and recognized boundaries that are defensible."

"We believe that a strong Israel constitutes the most reliable barrier to domination of the area by outside parties. Given the recent heavy flow of Soviet weaponry to Arab states, it is imperative that we not permit the military balance to shift against Israel."

Israel had been pressing for purchase of the Lance for nearly four years. Its sale would be the first time that the U.S. had supplied the missile to the Middle East.

Lebanon receives U.S. arms. The U.S. was providing Lebanon with anti-tank missiles for the first time and it had been urged by Beirut to send rapid-fire antiaircraft guns for protection against Israeli air attacks, the Washington Post reported from the Lebanese capital Jan. 16, 1975. The report said that several of the tube-launched, optically tracked, wire-guided (TOW) anti-tank missiles had already arrived in Lebanon, and U.S. forces were training a few Lebanese soldiers in their use outside Lebanon.

The U.S. Defense Department confirmed Jan. 17 that the Lebanese were getting 18 launchers and several more missiles. U.S. officials said the shipments were aimed at providing the small Lebanese army with psychological support in dealing with pressure from Syria.

U.S. seeks Persian Gulf area base. The U.S. had asked Britain for landing rights at its air base on Masira Island off the east coast of Oman, the Defense Department and British Foreign Office said Jan. 20, 1975. The sultan of Oman, Qabus bin Said, had conferred with U.S. officials in Washington about the base two weeks earlier and was reported to have said he was amenable to granting the Americans the use of Masira if the British raised no objections.

Shortly after the sultan had left Washington, it was confirmed that the U.S. had sold a "small number" of antitank missiles to Oman.

Acquisition of Masira's landing rights would enable U.S. naval reconnaissance planes to operate in areas previously available only through mid-flight refueling. The base was 400 miles south of the strategic Strait of Hormuz at the entrance to the Persian Gulf and its use would permit the U.S. to counter growing Soviet air power in the area, reported to be operating from in Iraq and Somalia.

U.S. firm to train Saudi troops. A private American firm was to hire former U.S. special forces soldiers and other retired Vietnam veterans to train Saudi Arabian troops to protect oil fields, the company announced Feb. 8, 1975. The U.S. Defense Department confirmed this Feb. 10.

The program was to be carried out over a three-year period starting in July in Saudi Arabia under a $77 million Defense Department contract awarded Jan. 8 to the Vinnell Corp. of Los Angeles. The firm was to recruit 1,000 men to train the 26,000-man Saudi National Guard in the use of artillery and other weapons. The guard's primary role was to protect the country's oil fields and related facilities. The force also provided the key bodyguards for Saudi Arabia's royal family and served as a backup for the country's 36,000-man regular force. The U.S. Army Material Command would establish an office in Saudi Arabia to administer the contract, with Vinnell reporting to the command.

The U.S. government was to provide the equipment and modernization program under a $335 million contract signed in April 1974.

In confirming the report on the project, the Defense Department Feb. 10 insisted that the Saudis would be trained only in the use of weapons and in maintaining internal security, not in field tactics. The department emphasized that other American firms had provided similar services in Saudi Arabia, citing Northrop Corp. instruction of Saudi pilots in flying F-5 fighters and Raytheon Corp. training of Saudis in the use of Hawk antiaircraft missiles.

U.S. to sell Jordan missiles. The State Department said May 5, 1975 that the U.S. would sell Hawk surface-to-air missiles to Jordan at an estimated cost of $100 million over a period of years. A department spokesman said the agreement on the weapons had been reached "in principle" during Secretary of State Henry A. Kissinger's visit to Jordan in November 1974.

The disclosure on the missiles was made following Hussein's talks in Washington with President Ford April 29 and with Kissinger April 30. After the Kissinger discussions, Hussein told newsmen there was no truth to the accounts of the previous week that Jordan had established a joint military command with Syria.

The decision on the Hawks later ran into Congressional trouble, and the deal was suspended temporarily. But objections were finally overcome.

The Administration had informed Congress July 28 that it was deferring the sale. By then the Administration was describing the equipment as a modern air-defense system of 14 Hawk batteries costing $260 million and 8 batteries of Vulcan antiaircraft guns costing $90 million. The transaction involved at least 500 Hawk missiles (including spares): a Hawk battery has six mobile launchers, each with three Hawks and radar equipment.

Congress members warned that this much military equipment would exceed Jordan's defensive requirements and that it would have the effect of destabilizing the military balance in the Middle East. Some critics also warned against the sale because the missiles might fall into the hands of the Soviet Union, thereby permitting the Soviets to develop countermeasures to the weapon.

Hussein warned that he would seek the arms elsewhere if the U.S. failed to provide his full requests for Hawks.

Hussein insisted in a statement published July 23 that his country would not "accept any reduction in any quantity of arms" it had "lately concluded agreements to obtain from the United States. Jordan is unswervingly determined not to leave its airspace open for Israeli warplanes."

Hussein indicated Aug. 7 that he would seek to purchase weapons from the Soviet Union if the U.S. refused to sell him the 14 Hawk batteries. If the request to Washington were not fully met, Hussein said, Jordan must "find a compatible option." This "compatible option," he pointed out, "does not exist in Europe and this means we will probably have to go to our friends in the Soviet Union."

Assurances from Ford Sept. 17 that the arms sought by Jordan would not be used for offensive purposes against Israel overcame U.S. congressional disapproval of the deal. Jordan at first objected to conditions imposed by the President but later agreed to terms of the sale.

Under a compromise plan worked out by the Ford Administration and key members of Congress, the Jordanians would be permitted to purchase the Hawks, including a reserve supply of 532 missiles, in return for a guarantee that they would be fixed in place and not be mobile, it was reported Sept. 10. The delivery would be stretched over a period of several years: one battery each in October, November and December of 1976, three more in January-March 1978 and the eight remaining over a period extending into 1979.

In his letter to Congress Sept. 17, Ford said the missiles would not be permitted to come under a binational or multinational force and would be permanently installed in the Amman-Zerka area and at airbases and radar stations to the east and south of Amman. The reference to the binational force was an allusion to the growing Jordanian-Syrian military ties but was also a routine condition attached to any sale of American weapons to a foreign country.

Sen. Clifford P. Case (R, N.J.), the leading Senate critic of the deal, said Sept. 17 that he accepted Ford's assurances. Rep. Jonathan Bingham (D, N.Y.), who headed the opposition in the House of Representatives, said he would no longer seek to block the sale, but said he was "still very unhappy over the deal."

Jordanian Premier Zaid al-Rifai Sept. 18 said his government rejected the conditions for the missile sale, asserting they were "unique and insulting to Jordan's national dignity." Any American weapons sold to Jordan "should become Jordanian once they reach the kingdom," he said in complaining about the delivery schedule. Rifai repeated King Hussein's warning that if Jordan could not buy the missiles from the U.S., it would "seek antiaircraft defenses elsewhere."

The withdrawal of Jordan's objections to the missile transaction was announced by the State Department Sept. 19. "Misunderstandings" that had developed had been "cleared up," the statement said. Department officials explained that, while Hussein had approved the substance of Ford's letter to Congress Sept. 17, he was embarrassed by the publicity given the compromise plan and the specific conditions under which the missiles were to be sold to Amman. The king's first statement rejecting the deal might have been issued to counter possible Arab criticism that he was yielding to Israeli pressure, according to department officials.

Soviet-Libyan arms deal. The Soviet Union and Libya concluded a major agreement under which the U.S.S.R. would significantly increase its arms sales to Libya, it was reported May 23, 1975. The accord was apparently negotiated during a visit May 12–14 to Libya by Soviet Premier Alexei N. Kosygin, who had held extensive talks with Libyan leader Col. Muammar el-Qaddafi.

As first reported in a Beirut dispatch by the Egyptian newspaper Al Ahram, the arms deal was believed to involve the supply of $4 billion in military equipment in exchange for permission to establish, land, sea and air bases on Libyan territory. Soviet sources in Cairo, however, asserted that Moscow had agreed to sell Libya $800 million worth of military equipment, including planes and missiles, "but not in exchange for Soviet bases." The Kremlin official denied the Egyptian report May 27, assailing Al Ahram for publishing such a "crude fabrication."

In an interview with the Los Angeles Times, published May 28, Egyptian President Anwar Sadat insisted that the arms deal was worth 4 billion Libyan pounds ($12 billion) and charged that Moscow had refused to sell such modern equipment to either Egypt or Syria.

U.S. intelligence officials in Washington May 28 said the Soviet Union had agreed to sell Libya more than $1 billion in modern military equipment, but apparently did not obtain permanent bases.

U.S. bars Libya planes, training. The U.S. had barred 56 Libyan air force men from training in the U.S. and blocked the export of eight cargo planes to Libya because of that country's bellicose attitude toward a Middle East peace settlement, Rep. Les Aspin (D, Wis.) disclosed Aug. 26, 1975.

Aspin had protested a Lockheed Aircraft Corp. application to train the Libyans in the U.S. in the maintenance of C-130 cargo planes. A State Department letter sent to Aspin informing him of the rejection of the application said the department shared his "concern about the Libyan attitude toward our efforts to reach a Middle East peace settlement."

The U.N. & Mideast Peace

Arafat at the U.N.

The Palestine Liberation Organization was elevated to a new pinnacle of prestige in November 1974 when the United Nations General Assembly accorded PLO leader Yasir Arafat the treatment of a chief of state and gave him the further honor of serving as the session's initial orator. The world body, dominated by the majority votes of "third world," Islamic and Communist nations, repeatedly supported the PLO cause in PLO-Israeli confrontations.

Choice offered: olive branch or freedom fighter's gun. The U.N. General Assembly Nov. 13, 1974 opened a debate on "the Question of Palestine." Yasir Arafat, leader of the Palestine Liberation Organization (PLO), delivered the opening address, declaring that his group's goal remained the creation of a Palestinian state that would include Moslems, Christians and Jews.

Israel's delegate Yosef Tekoah denounced Arafat's speech in rebuttal, asserting that his proposal would mean the destruction of Israel and its replacement by an Arab state. He reiterated his government's policy of refusing to permit the PLO to take over any territory relinquished by Israel.

In his speech, Arafat outlined the historical reasons for the Palestine problem, attributing it to a "Zionist scheme" to bring Jewish immigrants into the country as part of a wave of colonialism in Africa. The Israelis had launched four wars of aggression against the Arabs and were planning a fifth conflict, he said. Arafat warned that the "only alternative open before our Arab nations, chiefly Egypt and Syria, was to expend exhaustive efforts in preparing forcefully to resist this barbarous invasion, and this in order to liberate Arab lands and to restore the rights of the Palestinian people."

In calling for a secular state of Palestine, Arafat declared that "when we speak of our common hopes for the Palestine of tomorrow we include in our perspective all Jews now living in Palestine who choose to live with us there in peace and without discrimination." He called on Jews "to turn away from the illusory promises made to them by Zionist ideology and Israli leadership. Those offer Jews perpetual bloodshed, endless war and continuous thralldom."

Arafat appealed to the Assembly "to aid our people in its struggle to attain its right to self-determination." Concluding his address, the PLO chief said: "I have come bearing an olive branch and a freedom fighter's gun. Do not let the olive branch fall from my hand."

In his speech, Tekoah denounced the Arab states "who are in the vanguard of a fanatical assault on the Jewish people."

Assailing the Assembly's decision to invite Arafat to address the body, the Israeli delegate characterized it as a virtual capitulation "to a murder organization which aims at the destruction of a state member of the United Nations."

The Arab states, Tekoah charged, had exploited the Palestinian question as "a weapon of Arab belligerency against Israel." He quoted King Hussein of Jordan as having said of the Arab leaders: "They have used the Palestine people for selfish political purposes."

Citing the Palestinian terrorists as "murderers of athletes in the Olympic Games in Munich, the butchers of children in Maalot, [and] the assassins of diplomats in Khartoum," Tekoah said "Israel will not permit the establishment of PLO authority in any part of Palestine. The PLO will not be forced on the Palestinian Arabs. It will not be tolerated by the Jews of Israel." No resolution "can establish the authority of an organization which has no authority, . . . which has no foothold in any part of the territories it seeks," Tekoah said. Repeating his government's view that the Palestinians already had a country called Jordan Tekoah recalled the decision taken by Israel July 21, when it declared "that it would work toward negotiating a peace agreement with Jordan and that in the Jordanian-Palestinian Arab state east of Israel the specific identity of the Jordanians and Palestinians will find expression in peace and good-neighborliness with Israel."

(Both Arafat and Tekoah were absent from the Assembly chamber during each other's speeches. On instructions of Assembly President Abdelaziz Bouteflika of Algeria, Arafat was accorded the honor of chief of state, being seated in an armchair, a U.N. status symbol for such dignitaries. U.S. Ambassador John Scali expressed displeasure with Arafat's treatment. Arafat had made his appearance on the rostrum wearing a holster that a U.N. guard said contained a gun. A PLO spokesman, however, said the holster was empty.)

Assembly limits debate—At its Nov. 14 session, the General Assembly voted 75–23 (18 abstentions) to limit each nation to one major speech in the current debate on Palestine. The restriction was believed to be the first of its kind in U.N. history. The

decision was opposed by the U.S. and Israel. U.S. Ambassador Scali called it a "deeply disturbing trend." Tekoah denounced it as a move to "muzzle Israel's freedom to speak." The Assembly rules still permitted Israel the right to reply, but Tekoah noted that these responses were customarily limited to 10 minutes and depended on the discretion of the Assembly president. The new ruling affected Israel more than the others since there were 20 potential Arab speakers, while Israel alone spoke for its case in the debate, Tekoah said.

The dispute over the speaking privileges had emerged earlier in the day when Tekoah called a news conference to announce that his name had been dropped from the Assembly list of speakers. He said he had protested to Secretary General Kurt Waldheim, asserting that "this is one more act of bias on the part" of Assembly President Bouteflika. Another example of Bouteflika's alleged discrimination cited by Tekoah was his decision to receive Arafat with the honor usually reserved for a chief of state.

In the continued debate on the Palestine problem, Lebanese President Suleiman Franjieh lauded the Assembly for having granted the PLO the right to present its case. He added, however, that "the recognition of the Palestinian people and its representatives is only an accession to a half-truth. We will decide to the entire truth by helping these poeple to recover fully their national rights." Franjieh said the Rabat summit meeting in October had designated him to represent all 20 Arab League countries in the Assembly debate.

West Bank Arabs support PLO—Palestinian demonstrations were held Nov. 13 in the Israeli-occupied West Bank in support of Arafat and the PLO to coincide with Arafat's appearance before the U.N. General Assembly.

The largest outpouring occurred in Nablus, where Arabs staged a general strike, closing their shops, and hundreds of school children marched to the town square. Israeli soldiers and police scattered the demonstrators, but no serious injuries were reported. Similar but smaller demonstrations were held in other West Bank towns.

Thousands of Palestinians took part in rallies in Beirut Nov. 13. Some praised

Arafat's appearance before the U.N., while others condemned it. His opponents carried banners denouncing a "partial settlement with Israel."

In an apparent gesture supporting Arafat's address to the U.N., King Hussein of Jordan Nov. 13 decreed an amnesty for about 100 political prisoners, most of whom were Palestinian guerrillas and members of Arafat's Al Fatah.

Arafat laid claim to Jordan, as well as to the West Bank and all of Israel, according to a letter he had sent to the Jordanian Student Congress in Baghdad, Iraq, it was reported Nov. 11. He was quoted as saying: "Jordan is ours; Palestine is ours, and we shall build our national entity on the whole of this land after having freed it of both the Zionist presence and the reactionary-traitor presence."

Arafat had said in a New York Times interview in Beirut Nov. 8 that there would be no peace in the Middle East until the U.S. recognized the right of the Palestinian people to statehood and stopped "the flow of arms to Israel and the economic, diplomatic and political" support for Israel's "expansive and aggressive ambitions."

He said a Palestinian government in exile would soon be formed as a step toward establishment of Palestinian sovereignty over the Israeli-occupied West Bank and Gaza Strip, which, he said, would serve as a "nucleus" of a future Palestinian state that would absorb Israel.

U.S. congressmen meet with PLO—A group of 13 U.S. senators and representatives held an informal meeting at U.N. headquarters Nov. 14 with members of the PLO to discuss the group's aims.

One of the participants, Sen. Frank E. Moss (D, Utah), said later that the PLO appeared to be interested in an "interim accommodation" in creating a state alongside Israel, but emphasized its ultimate goal was to establish a state of Moslems, Christians and Jews that would do away with Israel.

A PLO spokesman expressed annoyance at the line of questioning by the the U.S. congressmen, saying they had shown concern "not for the victims but for the victimizers."

The meeting had been arranged by Sen. James G. Abourezk (D, S.D.) and Clovis

Maksoud, a Lebanese writer and representative of the Arab League.

(The Soviet Union for the first time had called for establishment of a separate Palestinian state as a condition for peace in the Middle East. Foreign Minister Andrei A. Gromyko said Nov. 6: "No one can deny the Arabs of Palestine their lawful right of self-determination, including their own statehood." Heretofore, Moscow had spoken only vaguely of the legitimate rights of the Palestinians.)

U.S. assures Israel on PLO—The U.S. sought to reassure Israel that its policy was not shifting toward recognition of the PLO.

Israeli fears of a U.S. movement in the direction of the Palestinian group were raised after Undersecretary of State Joseph Sisco said in an NBC television interview Nov. 18 that "we regard the PLO as the overall umbrella organization of the Palestinians."

Sisco qualified his statement Nov. 20, explaining that he had meant that "the Arabs consider the PLO as the umbrella organization" and that the Administration had not recognized the group as a party to Middle East negotiations. Sisco also said he had found "no openings" for negotiations in PLO leader Yasir Arafat's address to the U.N. General Assembly Nov. 13.

President Ford also appeared to retreat from a statement he had made Oct. 29 that he advocated talks between Israel and Egypt, Syria and "Jordan or the PLO." Speaking at a news conference in Phoenix, Ariz. Nov. 14, the President denied that he favored negotiations between Israel and the PLO. That question, he said, was "the responsibility of the parties involved. Our plans are aimed at trying to get Israel to negotiate a settlement, or an additional settlement, with Egypt and the other Arab nations."

U.S. opposes talks with PLO. Secretary of State Henry A. Kissinger said in an interview published in the Dec. 30 issue of Newsweek that it would be "impossible" for the U.S. to pressure Israel to negotiate with the Palestine Liberation Organization "until the PLO accepts the existence of Israel as a legitimate state." Kissinger added that "as long as the PLO proposals envisage, in one form or another, the destruction of Israel, we don't see much hope for negotiating with the PLO."

Asserting that "the survival of Israel is essential," Kissinger emphasized that neither the U.S. nor Western Europe would negotiate the right of Israel to exist as a state. His statement was in response to a question on how Arab oil policy would affect Western support of Israel.

Based on his talks with Israeli leaders, Kissinger said he believed they would not undertake a pre-emptive military strike against the Arabs. The Israelis were "genuinely interested in moving toward peace" and would not "deliberately engage in such a reckless course," Kissinger said.

The secretary discounted reports that the U.S. military arsenal had been depleted of some of its equipment in the U.S. military resupply of Israel during and after the 1973 war.

Resolution grants Palestinians sovereign right. The United Nations General Assembly concluded its debate on the Palestine question Nov. 22 by approving two resolutions declaring that the Palestinian people had the right to independence and sovereignty, and granting the PLO observer status in U.N. affairs.

The resolution on rights was adopted by an 89–8 vote, with 37 abstentions. The negative ballots were cast by Israel, the U.S., Norway, Iceland, Bolivia, Chile, Costa Rica and Nicaragua. The resolution on PLO status was passed by a 95–17 vote, with 19 abstentions. Most Western European countries joined the U.S., Canada and Israel in voting against the second resolution. France, Japan and some Latin American countries abstained.

The resolution on sovereignty stated that the Palestinian people were entitled to self-determination without external interference and to national independence. It affirmed "the inalienable rights of the Palestinians to return to their homes and property from which they have been displaced and uprooted." The resolution did not mention Israel. It was co-sponsored by 38 states, including all the Arab nations, several third-world countries and Cuba.

Before the voting started, Barbados delegate Waldo Waldron-Ramsey asked, "What does the resolution mean by Palestine?" The Saudi Arabian and Jordanian delegates replied that Palestine means "what has at this moment been replaced by Israel and the Israeli occupation of the West Bank and Gaza Strip."

Israeli delegate Yosef Tekoah denounced the Assembly vote, asserting that the U.N. "has plunged into an abyss from which there is no exit." The world organization, he said, was "trampling to dust its own charter by submitting itself to violence and savagery, by hailing lawlessness, inhumanity and hypocrisy."

PLO delegate Nabil Shaath told a news conference that the U.N. decision meant "We are entitled to use political and diplomatic, as well as military means to continue our struggle."

In previous Assembly debate, U.S. chief delegate John A. Scali Nov. 21 reaffirmed that "Israel has a right to exist as a sovereign, independent state within secure and recognized boundaries." Scali called on all sides to support U.N. Security Council resolutions 242 of November 1967 and 338 of October 1973 "to help establish an international climate in which the parties will be encouraged to maintain momentum of peace." He reiterated the call by Secretary of State Henry A. Kissinger for a step-by-step approach to negotiations, saying "the legitimate rights of the Palestinian people" could be enhanced in such talks. Scali warned against the danger of another war in the Middle East, and condemned terrorism.

The delegates of France, Britain and Italy had urged in debate Nov. 20 that any Middle East peace settlement must guarantee Israel's right to exist. The statements represented a common position worked out by the nine countries of the European Economic Community. Their position had first been presented by the West German delegate in the Nov. 19 Assembly session.

French delegate Louis de Guirngaud said in his statement Nov. 20 that Israel's permanent borders should be those of June 4, 1967, just before the Six-Day War, except for "minor rectifications."

Israel Under Pressure

Assembly equates Zionism, racism. An Arab-inspired resolution defining Zionism as "a form of racism and racial discrimination" was passed by a 72–35 U.N. General Assembly vote Nov. 10, 1975 with 32 abstentions and three delegations absent.

The vote was immediately denounced by Israel, the U.S. and France, among other nations. It was assailed Nov. 11 by the Assembly's president, Gaston Thorn of Luxembourg, who asserted the resolution had "destroyed" a climate of conciliation which had developed at the U.N. in recent months.

The Assembly approved two other resolutions Nov. 10 favoring the Palestine Liberation Organization (PLO). The first, sponsored by Egypt and Syria and passed 101–8 with 25 abstentions, called for inclusion of the PLO as an equal partner in any Middle East peace talks, including the suspended Geneva conference. The second resolution, drafted by the PLO and approved 93–18 with 27 abstentions, established a 20-nation U.N. Committee on the Exercise of the Inalienable Rights of the Palestinian People, which would promote creation of an independent Palestinian state. Both resolutions were denounced by Israel as "totally unacceptable."

The anti-Zionist resolution was passed after the two PLO resolutions and

U.N. Resolutions on Palestinian Rights and PLO Status

On Palestinian Rights

The General Assembly,

Having considered the question of Palestine,

Having heard the statement of the Palestine Liberation Organization, the representative of the people of Palestine,

Having also heard other statements made during the debate,

Deeply concerned that no just solution to the problem of Palestine has yet been achieved and recognizing that the problem of Palestine continues to endanger international peace and security,

Recognizing that the Palestinian people is entitled to self-determination in accordance with the Charter of the United Nations,

Expressing its grave concern that the Palestinian people has been prevented from enjoying its inalienable rights, and in particular its right to self-determination,

Guided by the purposes and principles of the Charter,

Recalling its relevant resolutions which affirm the right of the Palestinian people to self-determination,

1. Reaffirms the inalienable rights of the Palestinian people in Palestine, including:

(a) The right to self-determination without external interference;

(b) The right to national independence and sovereignty;

2. Reaffirms also the inalienable right of the Palestinians to return to their homes and property from which they have been displaced and uprooted, and calls for their return;

3. Emphasizes that full respect for and the realization of these inalienable rights of the Palestinian people are indispensable for the solution of the question of Palestine;

4. Recognizes that the Palestinian people is a principal party in the establishment of a just and durable peace in the Middle East;

5. Further recognizes the right of the Palestinian people to regain its rights by all means in accordance with the purposes and principles of the Charter of the United Nations;

6. Appeals to all states and international organizations to extend their support to the Palestinian people

in its struggle to restore its rights, in accordance with the Charter;

7. Requests the Secretary General to establish contacts with the Palestine Liberation Organization on all matters concerning the question of Palestine;

8. Requests the Secretary General to report to the General Assembly at its 30th session on the implementation of the present resolution;

9. Decides to include the item entitled "Question of Palestine" in the provisional agenda of its 30th session.

On Observer Status

The General Assembly,

Having considered the question of Palestine,

Taking into consideration the universality of the United Nations prescribed in the Charter,

Recalling its resolution 3103 (XXVIII) of 12 December 1973,

Taking into account Economic and Social Council resolutions 1835 (LVI) of 17 May 1974 and 1840 (LVI) of 20 May 1974,

Noting that the Diplomatic Conference on the Reaffirmation and Development of International Humanitarian Law Applicable in Armed Conflicts, the World Population Conference and the World Food Conference have in effect invited the Palestine Liberation Organization to participate in their respective deliberations,

Noting also that the Third United Nations Conference on the Law of the Sea has invited the Palestine Liberation Organization to participate in its deliberation as an observer,

1. Invites the Palestine Liberation Organization to participate in the sessions and the work of the General Assembly in the capacity of observer;

2. Invites the Palestine Liberation Organization to participate in the sessions and the work of all international conferences convened under the auspices of the General Assembly in the capacity of observer;

3. Considers that the Palestine Liberation Organization is entitled to participate as an observer in the sessions and the work of all international conferences convened under the auspices of other organs of the United Nations;

4. Requests the Secretary General to take the necessary steps for the implementation of the present resolution.

following the defeat of efforts by Western delegates to put off a vote until 1976. It was supported by Arab and other Islamic countries, Brazil, Mexico and many Asian and African nations, and opposed by the U.S., Canada, the nine members of the European Economic Community and other countries in Western and Northern Europe, Israel, Australia, New Zealand and several Latin American and African nations.

Israeli Ambassador Chaim Herzog charged immediately before the vote on the anti-Zionist resolution that the U.N. was becoming "the world center of anti-Semitism." The issue in the vote was "not Israel or Zionism," he said. "The issue is the continued existence of this organization, which has been dragged to its lowest point of discredit by a coalition of despotisms and racists."

It was fitting that the vote on the resolution should come on Nov. 10, Herzog asserted. "This was the night—on Nov. 10, 1938—when Hitler's Nazi storm troopers launched a coordinated attack on the Jewish community in Germany, burned the synagogues in all its cities, destroyed Jewish holy books and attacked Jewish homes," he declared.

Earlier, during debate on the resolution, Herzog had noted that Zionism was a national, not racial movement, asserting it was to the Jewish people "what the liberation movements of Africa and Asia have been to their own people." The "wicked" resolution against Zionism had divided the world into "good and bad, decent and evil, human and debase," he asserted.

Speaking in favor of the resolution, delegate Abdallah al-Sayegh of Kuwait noted that Article I of the U.N.'s Declaration on the Elimination of all Forms of Racial Discrimination included under the term "racial discrimination" any "distinction, exclusion, restriction or preference based on . . . national or ethnic origin." Zionism, he continued, was "a concrete political ideology" manifested in "concrete practices which have the effect of excluding some people on the basis of their being non-Jews and including others on the basis of their being Jews—Jewishness being defined officially as an ethnic and not strictly religious definition."

Denouncing the resolution after its passage, U.S. Ambassador Daniel P.

Moynihan declared that the U.S. "does not acknowledge, it will not abide by, it will never acquiesce in this infamous act." The French ambassador, Louis de Guiringaud, changed his country's votes on the PLO resolutions from favorable to abstaining in a protest against the anti-Zionist measure.

(Chile, which had voted in favor of the anti-Zionist resolution in the Assembly's Social, Humanitarian and Cultural Committee, abstained from voting Nov. 10, following a claim by President Augusto Pinochet Oct. 29 that he had not approved the first vote. The U.S. had applied strong pressure to Chile to vote against the resolution, according to press reports.)

The anti-Zionist vote followed a weeklong Assembly debate on the question of Palestine. Opening the debate Nov. 3, PLO delegate Farouk Kaddoumi accused the U.S. of moving nuclear weapons into Israel and asserted, "We are closer to war than to peace" in the Middle East. "The Soviet Union," Kaddoumi noted, "has consistently endorsed the rights of our Palestinian people and the struggle of our Arab nation for freedom and progress."

Kaddoumi called on the U.N. to consider expelling Israel and he sharply criticized the recent Egyptian-Israeli disengagement accord in the Sinai, which he described as conducive to war.

Replying for Israel, Ambassador Herzog asserted the influence of the PLO in the Middle East was "declining in inverse ratio to the noise that it was creating abroad." He rejected any direct negotiations between Israel and the PLO but pledged Israeli efforts to achieve a "solution of the Palestine Arab problem on a basis of growing understanding."

Entering the debate Nov. 7, Ambassador Moynihan said the U.S. supported a Mideast settlement which accounted for the "legitimate interests" of the Palestinian people, but he rejected participation of the PLO in peace talks unless the PLO recognized Israel's right to exist.

Committee action—Less than a month earlier, in an action leading to the General Assembly vote, the Assembly's Social, Humanitarian & Cultural Committee Oct. 17 had recommended that the Assembly declare Zionism a form of racism and racial discrimination The proposal was adopted by 70–29 vote with 27 abstentions over the protests of the U.S. and Israel, which denounced it as an attempt by Arab nations to revive and spread anti-Semitism.

Following the vote, a movement developed among delegations to block the resolution in the General Assembly, it was reported Oct. 23. Ambassador Waldo Waldron-Ramsey of Barbados said Oct. 22 that he would introduce an amendment to delete the anti-Zionist passage in the resolution, which also dealt with racism in South Africa and Rhodesia.

Moynihan declared Oct. 21 that the vote in itself was not against Zionism but against Israel, "and not the state of Israel nearly so much as the significance of Israel as one of the very few places outside Western Europe and North America and a few offshore islands where Western democratic principles survive, and of all such places, the most exposed." Almost all of the world's democracies had voted against the resolution, Moynihan asserted.

The resolution split the black African countries, two of which voted against and 13 of which abstained. Western European nations and some Latin American delegations joined the U.S. and Israel in voting against, while Asian, black African, Communist and five Latin American countries joined the Arab states in supporting the resolution.

The Latin nations were Cuba, Mexico, Guyana, Brazil and Chile. U.S. sources charged Oct. 18 that Chile had "sold its vote to the Arabs" in exchange for support against charges that Chile tortured political prisoners and committed other abuses of human rights.

U.S., Israel score U.N. action—The U.S. and Israel were in the forefront of nations assailing the United Nations General Assembly resolution equating Zionism and racism.

The White House quoted President Ford as saying after a meeting with a nine-member Israeli parliamentary delegation Nov. 11 that the U.N. move was "a wholly unjustified action." A later White House statement said President Ford "reaffirmed that the United States deplores ... and [believed] that the adoption of this resolution undermines the principles on which the United Nations is based," but that Ford "will not consider [U.S.] withdrawal" from the world organization.

The Senate Nov. 11 unanimously adopted a resolution condemning the U.N. vote and calling for immediate hearings to "reassess the United States' further participation in the United Nations." The resolution also opposed U.S. participation in the U.N.'s anti-racism program and demanded reconsideration of the General Assembly vote on Zionism.

The House of Representatives Nov. 11 unanimously adopted a similar resolution, but deleted the call for reappraisal of U.S. participation in the U.N.

President Ford said Nov. 12 that he would be "reviewing the implication of the [U.N.] vote and considering possible courses of action" but would not change his requests for aid to Egypt and other Arab countries.

A number of former U.S. representatives to the U.N. Nov. 11 deplored the General Assembly vote on Zionism. Henry Cabot Lodge said, "From a psychological point of view it is very serious and very bad, most deplorable." Ernest Gross said, "Disgusting and discouraging action like this confounds the friends of the United Nations and confirms its enemies." George W. Ball called the vote "a very stupid action on the part of the Arab-African bloc, and it will prejudice rather than help their position."

Secretary of State Henry A. Kissinger said after a speech in Pittsburgh Nov. 11 that the U.S. would "ignore" the U.N. vote. The U.N. "will damage itself if it continues in this way," he said.

Kissinger was again critical of the U.N. resolution at a news conference in Pittsburgh Nov. 12, but he cautioned against any American action that involved ending support for the world body or reducing economic relations with "third world" countries that voted for the resolution. The U.N.'s "moral condemnation" of Israel, he said, "smacks of some practices that it would be better for mankind to forget." Asserting that "we have to see the United Nations in some perspective," Kissinger warned that "we must not now swing to the extreme of not realizing some of the benefits that the United Nations with all its failings still has for the United States."

Israeli Premier Rabin said Nov. 11 that the Assembly vote had excluded the U.N. as a possible factor in bringing peace to the Middle East. He noted that the delegates who voted for the anti-Zionism resolution were from countries that suppressed democracy, freedom and human rights and practiced "a lot of discrimination against religious minorities."

The Israeli Parliament Nov. 11 adopted a policy resolution (with only Communists and other extreme leftists opposed) rejecting the U.N. vote. The statement also opposed further Israeli participation in any Geneva talks on the Middle East if the PLO were invited to participate. This proposal was made in a response to the General Assembly's resolution calling for Palestinian participation in all Middle East peace efforts. The Israeli Parliament also opposed recognition of a General Asembly-approved committee that would give the Palestinians a voice to press their demands at the U.N.

Israeli Foreign Minister Yigal Allon, visiting the Netherlands Nov. 11, called the U.N. resolution "a heavy blow against the chances of peace in the Middle East." Dutch Foreign Minister Max van der Stoel, who appeared at a news conference with Allon, said his country would no longer participate in the U.N. program to combat racism.

Moslems ask Israel ouster from U.N. A resolution adopted July 16, 1975 at the end of a four-day conference of 40 Islamic nations in Jidda, Saudi Arabia called on all members of the grouping to "sever their political, cultural and economic relations with Israel and work to expel Israel from the United Nations" and all other international bodies.

The conference also adopted a resolution recognizing the Palestine Liberation Organization as the sole legitimate representative of the rights of the Palestinian people to establish an "independent national authority" in territories occupied by Israel.

The meeting established a 13-member committee, including a PLO delegate, to carry out a worldwide diplomatic campaign to establish Moslem religious and political rights in Jerusalem as part of a Palestinian state. King Khalid of Saudi Arabia told the July 16 session that Jerusalem must "once again be Arab, free,

pure and dedicated to Allah and the Moslem faith."

The conference was attended by foreign ministers of African, Asian and Middle Eastern countries and a PLO delegation.

Israeli Foreign Minister Yigal Allon July 23 urged "enlightened" members of the U.N. to block any move to suspend Israel from the U.N. General Assembly.

Israel scored on occupation. Ending a five-day debate, the General Assembly Dec. 5, 1975 voted to condemn Israel's "continued occupation of Arab territories," and urged all countries to refuse military and economic aid to Israel as long as it continued the occupation and continued to "deny the inalienable" national rights of the Palestinians. The vote was 84-17, with 27 abstentions; the U.S., West Germany, Belgium, the Netherlands and France were among those abstaining.

UNDOF extended, PLO invited. The United Nations Security Council, by a 13–0 vote (China and Iraq abstaining), approved Nov. 30 a six-month extension of the U.N. Disengagement Observer Force separating Israeli and Syrian troops on the Golan Heights, and accepted a Syrian demand that the Palestine Liberation Organization be invited to future Council debate on the Middle East, a condition denounced by Israel.

A preamble to the resolution said the Council, which had opened debate on the U.N. force Nov. 28, would meet again Jan. 12, 1976 "to continue the debate on the Middle East problem, including the Palestine question, taking into account all relevant United Nations resolutions."

A separate statement read by Council President Yakov Malik of the Soviet Union said it was "the understanding of the majority" of the body that "the representatives of the Palestine Liberation Organization will be invited to participate in the debate" when it resumed in January.

Israeli delegate Chaim Herzog denounced the resolution "as a surrender to Syrian blackmail and Soviet dictates."

U.S. Ambassador Daniel P. Moynihan said before the vote that the U.S. considered "relevant" to the Middle East situation only resolutions adopted by the Security Council, an apparent disavowal of any interpretation that the document extending the mandate of UNDOF was linked with the General Assembly resolutions on the PLO. He also said the Council resolution had no bearing on the Geneva conference on the Middle East.

Moynihan said after the vote that the U.S. did not support Council President Malik's statement that the PLO should be invited to future talks on the Middle East.

Israel Dec. 1 approved in principle the extension of the U.N. force but declared it would boycott Security Council debate on the Middle East in protest against the PLO's proposed presence. The decision was announced by the cabinet, which declared in a communique that the Council had "yielded to Syrian pressure to create a linkage between the renewal of the U.N. force . . . with foreign elements which have nothing whatsoever to do with the separation of the forces agreement between Israel and Syria." The resolution, the statement added, "is likely to disturb progress toward peace in the area through negotiations between the parties without prior conditions."

Israeli government officials, newspapers and the public were incensed at the U.S. for its approval of the Council decision. Government officials said they had urged the U.S. to veto the resolution, but Washington had refused because it feared Syria might not agree to extension of the Golan peace force.

The State Department announced Dec. 1 that the U.S. would participate in the Council debate along with the PLO but insisted that this did not mean that Washington had shifted its policy of refusing to deal with the Palestinian organization.

Israeli officials said they had received an explanatory message from Secretary of State Henry A. Kissinger Dec. 1 assuring them that the U.S. would veto any resolution in the Council's January debate that would be harmful to Israel's interests.

Premier Yitzhak Rabin Dec. 2 reiterated Israel's distress with American support of the Council resolution, asserting that "any attempt to bind progress toward peace to negotiations with the terrorist organizations will end in failure." The resolution, he said, "does not fit in with . . . the declared policy of the United States." The premier's statement was made in a report delivered to the Parliament's Defense and Foreign

Affairs Committee on contacts he had made with the U.S. over the issue.

The Israeli radio reported Dec. 2 that a government committee had approved a plan to build four more settlements in the Israeli-occupied sector of the Golan Heights in response to the pro-Syrian U.N. resolution. Israel already had 18 such settlements in the area.

The PLO Dec. 1 hailed the Council decision as "a triumph for the Palestinian cause over the schemes of the United States and Israel."

U.S. opposes boycott by Israel. U.S. State Secretary Henry Kissinger called on Israel Dec. 5, 1975 to give up its planned boycott of the United Nations Security Council when it reconvened in January 1976 to debate the Middle East situation with Palestine Liberation Organization participation, it was reported Dec. 8 by U.S. Administration officials and diplomatic sources.

Kissinger's request, sent to Foreign Minister Yigal Allon, was rejected by the Israeli government Dec. 7. Kissinger was said to have cited the need to coordinate U.S.-Israeli positions in the Council debate and said it would be helpful to both countries if Israel attended. The secretary also had repeated Washington's refusal to recognize the PLO until it extended recognition of Israel and accepted Council resolutions 242 and 338, the basis for Middle East negotiations.

President Ford was said to have sent a separate note to Premier Yitzhak Rabin, again reassuring him of American support for Israel and the refusal to recognize the PLO. But Ford also stressed that the U.S. was interested in diplomatic progress.

Israel's refusal to negotiate with the PLO had been restated by Rabin in an interview with the Israeli newspaper Maariv Dec. 5. He said: "It is imperative that the whole solution of the Palestine issue should be tied to Jordan. Israel should oppose any tendency to establish a third state in the area between it and Jordan. Any Israeli agreement for political negotiations with a Palestinian faction necessarily lays the groundwork for such a possibility." The premier warned that "the establishment of such a state would lead to an 'Arafatist' state whose whole purpose is the destruction of Israel."

Foreign Minister Allon Dec. 9 indicated a possible shift on the Israeli position boycotting the Council debate, saying that although his government held to that stand, "there are many days" remaining before the Council convened, during which "circumstances may change." The boycott, he explained, was not a question of principle, but "a form of political warfare."

Before the session U.S. Secretary of State Henry Kissinger had assured Israeli Foreign Minister Yigal Allon in talks in Washington Jan. 7–9 that the U.S. would veto any Security Council resolution that provided for PLO participation in the resumed Geneva conference or that established new conditions for an overall settlement of the Middle East dispute. Assistant Secretary of State Alfred L. Atherton Jr. had also apprised Arab leaders of this stand in visits to Egypt, Syria, Jordan and Saudi Arabia in December 1975. Atherton also visited Israel. American ambassadors to these five countries had been briefed in Washingon the week of January 4 and returned to their posts to reaffirm the American position, it was reported.

The U.S. opposed any change in the deliberate ambiguity of Resolution 242, which called for a "just and lasting peace," Israeli withdrawal from "territories" captured in the 1967 war, and "secure" borders for Israel. Although acknowledging that the Palestinian question was at the core of the Arab-Israeli dispute, the U.S. also threatened to veto any alteration of the section of 242 that referred indirectly to the "refugee problem" of the Palestinians. The Arabs sought inclusion of the phrase Palestinian "national rights" in an attempt to politicize the cause of the Palestinians.

Kissinger had said after his first meeting with Allon Jan. 7 that, "as far as the United States is concerned, any peace negotiations must be based on Security Council Resolutions 242 and 338 [a reaffirmation of 242], and we consider those the only relevant U.N. resolutions."

Allon confirmed after his meeting with Kissinger Jan. 9 that there had been "full agreement" between Israel and the U.S. on: maintaining the Geneva conference as the framework for peace negotiations; opposing any changes in Resolutions 242 and 338; and opposing any Security Council resolutions that contained any "element of imposition" on the parties, such as admitting the PLO to Geneva.

The divergent views of the opposing parties had been reflected in earlier statements made by Israeli and Egyptian officials. Premier Yitzhak Rabin warned Jan. 4 that the Security Council would "stalemate" peace moves if it attempted to intervene in Arab-Israeli negotiations. He predicted "serious developments might result" from Council debate, adding that Israel had "sufficient military strength to provide it with room for political maneuver, but possibly we will have to give expression to this sooner than we may think."

Rabin renewed his warning against Security Council replacement of Geneva as the arena for peace talks, according to a West German film interview broadcast Jan. 11. The premier said: "If the Syrian and the so-called PLO attempt to change the basis that has been accepted by all parties to bring about peace and if they succeed in shifting the handling of the Middle East from the Geneva conference to the Security Council, this will create a totally new situation that might lead to total chaos and practically break any accepted basis for the peace-making process."

Egyptian government statements also advocated resumption of the Geneva talks, but veered sharply from the Israeli position by pressing for PLO attendance. Foreign Minister Ismail Fahmy told Parliament Jan. 5 that the Geneva talks "should be reconvened before the end of the first half of this year, now that the climate is propitious for PLO participation on an equal footing with the other parties." Although Cairo favored dealing with the Palestine issue strictly as a political matter, Fahmy said Egypt would avoid taking any steps in Security Council debate to amend Resolutions 242 and 338.

President Anwar Sadat said Jan. 13 Egypt would be willing to attend the Geneva talks initially without the PLO, but would press hard for the organization's eventual role in the talks on an equal footing with the other parties. Although he was urging the "start of a dialogue between the United States and the Palestinians, we shall be ready to go to Geneva as we already did in December 1973," Sadat said. He reaffirmed Cairo's intention to regard Resolution 242 as the basis for peace in the Middle East.

U.N. Secretary General Kurt Waldheim said Jan. 9 that "the time has come for the Palestinians to get recognition for their political status," and added that the forthcoming Security Council debate "should" adopt a resolution to that effect.

U.S. vetoes pro-Palestinian proposal—

The Security Council debate ended Jan. 26 with U.S. veto of a pro-Palestinian resolution that had been backed by 9–1 vote. Voting approval were France, the Soviet Union, Japan and the resolution's six sponsors—Pakistan, Tanzania, Rumania, Panama, Guyana and Benin. Britain, Italy and Sweden abstained. China and Libya did not participate, having preferred an earlier resolution that made no suggestion that Israel had a right to exist.

Asserting that "the question of Palestine is the core of the conflict in the Middle East," the resolution stated that: (a) the Palestinian people were entitled "to exercise its inalienable national right of self-determination, including the right to establish an independent state in Palestine"; (b) the Palestinian refugees had the right "to return to their homes and . . . those choosing not to return [had the right] to receive compensation for their property"; (c) "Israel should withdraw from all the Arab territories occupied since 1967"; and (d) all states in the region should be guaranteed their "sovereignty, territorial integrity and political independence . . . and their right to live in peace within secure and recognized boundaries."

The vote followed Council rejection of a British amendment aimed at softening the resolution by saying that nothing in its texts was aimed at countervening Council resolutions 242 and 338. The vote was 4–2, with 9 abstentions.

The final Council resolution was a compromise of previous Arab drafts, including a Syrian-sponsored one which called for an independent state in Palestine and total Israeli withdrawal from all Arab territories to the original 1947 Palestine partition lines, and made no allusion to the right of Israel to exist.

In casting the veto, the U.S.' 13th, American Ambassador Daniel P. Moynihan said the resolution changed the existing negotiating framework in resolutions 242 and 338, imperiling "the future of the peacemaking process."

The U.S. State Department similarly said that "with this resolution the Council would have blocked the surer and tested way to a settlement in favor of one that would not have worked." The U.S., the State Department added, "is firmly and irrevocably committed to progress in the negotiation of a settlement."

Syrian delegate Mowaffak Allaf asked in a speech after the vote, "Who is really conducting the foreign policy of the U.S.? Is it President Ford" or Israeli Premier Yitzhak Rabin? The veto, Allaf asserted, proved that the U.S. "lacks any quality of fairness, any quality which would make it a neutral and acceptable mediator in the Middle East crisis."

Jordanian delegate Sherif Abdul Hamid Sharaf complained that the veto was contrary to the U.S. call "to preserve the process of peace" and instead was creating a "stalemate."

An Egyptian official in Cairo said the U.S. "position has become not only isolated but also untenable." He also blamed "theatrical" extremist tactics by Syria and the Palestine Liberation Organization for the Security Council's failure to act on the Middle East crisis.

Attack on occupation. The U.N. Commission on Human Rights in Geneva Feb. 13, 1976 accused Israel of having committed "war crimes and an affront to humanity" by its "continued grave violations" of international law in the occupied Arab territories. The vote was 23–1, with the U.S. casting the lone dissenting ballot. Eight nations abstained: Britain, France, Italy, West Germany, Austria, Canada, Costa Rica and Uruguay. The resolution had been inspired by the Arab members of the 32-nation commission, with India, Cuba, Pakistan, Yugoslavia, Cyprus, Senegal and Upper Volta sponsoring the document.

One of the principal sections of the resolution condemned Israel's "mass arrests, administrative detention of the Arab population," moves to annex parts of the occupied territories, destruction of Arab houses, confiscation of Arab property, interfering with religious freedom and impeding "the exercise by the population of the occupied territories of their rights to national education and cultural life."

U.S. vetoes occupation resolutions. The U.S. March 25, 1976 vetoed a Security Council resolution assailing allegedly oppresive Israeli occupation policies against the Arab population of the Old City of Jerusalem and the West Bank. Fourteen Council members voted for the document. The Council had been called into session March 22 at the request of Pakistan and Libya to consider the anti-Israel unrest in the Old City and West Bank.

Israel, which had stayed away from Council debates in December 1975 and January because of the presence of the Palestine Liberation Organization representatives, ended its boycott and participated in the debate alongside the PLO delegates for the first time.

The resolution deplored "Israel's failure to put a stop to actions and policies tending to change the status of the city of Jerusalem." It urged Israel, "pending speedy termination of its occupation, to refrain from all measures against the Arab inhabitants of the occupied territories" and called on Israel "to respect and uphold the inviolability of the Holy Places . . . and to desist from the expropriation of or encroachment upon Arab lands and property or the establishment of Israeli settlements in the occupied Arab territories and to desist" from changing the legal status of Jerusalem.

Explaining March 24 why he planned to veto the resolution, U.S. Ambassador William R. Scranton said it did not correspond to the realities of the Israeli occupation and that it was untrue that Israel was attempting to alter the religious character of Jerusalem. "Quite to the contrary, we think Israel's administration of the holy places in Jerusalem has literally and actively minimized tensions."

Israeli delegate Chaim Herzog lauded the U.S. veto, saying it was an effort "to stem attempts to convert the United Nations into an instrument of intransigent despotism."

Scranton had aroused Israeli anger in a statement made at the March 23 Council session, in which he criticized Israel's occupation policies. He called Israeli settlements in Arab territory "an obstacle to the success for a just and final peace" and said that Israel's annexation of East Jerusalem "cannot be considered other than interim and provisional."

Israeli Ambassador Simcha Dinitz protested Scranton's remarks in a telephone call March 24 to Secretary of State Henry A. Kissinger. Israeli political leaders and newspapers assailed Scranton's statement, but the government made no public comment. One official said privately that the U.S. ambassador had "collected passages from speeches made over the years" and the "aggregate created a momentum that was not there before."

The State Department said March 24 that there was nothing new in Scranton's position, that previous U.S. ambassadors at the U.N. had made similar statements. Noting that Scranton "was restating a long-standing position," the department assured Israel that the U.S. still ruled out American talks with the PLO until it recognized Israel and accepted Security Council resolutiohs calling for a peaceful settlement.

Israeli Foreign Minister Yigal Allon called in U.S. Ambassador Malcolm Toon March 26 to complain about the Scranton statement. Allon told newsmen later that "without the veto there certainly would have been a big crisis" in U.S.-Israeli relations. The American rejection of the U.N. attack on Israel, he said, averted such a break.

Israeli's ambassador to London, Gideon Rafael, lodged a protest March 27 with Britain, one of the 14 Council members that had voted for the resolution.

Egypt's chief U.N. delegate, Ahmed Esmat Abdel Meguid, said March 26 that despite the U.S. veto the "fact remains that the world community deplored Israeli practices in the occupied territories." Noting that 14 Council members had voted for the resolution, Zehdi Labib Terzi, the permanent observer of the Palestine Liberation Organization at the U.N., said, "Our people at home got the feeling they are not alone, cut off from the world."

The Security Council May 26 adopted a statement deploring the establishment of Israeli settlements in occupied areas.

The statement was presented as the majority view of the council. The council had decided to devise a consensus that would be accepted without a vote by the Arab countries and the U.S. The U.S., however, dissociated itself from the majority position during private negotiations May 25.

The document read by Council President Louis de Guiringaud of France deplored Israeli measures to change the status of occupied Arab territories, "particularly the establishment of settlements," and stated that such actions "constitute an obstacle to peace." It also urged Israel to abide by the Geneva Convention dealing with the protection of civilians in occupied territories.

U.S. Ambassador William R. Scranton objected to the text because it lacked "balance" by failing to recognize the "many areas in which the Israeli occupation has been responsible and just." At the same time, Scranton warned Israel that it "would be a mistake to dismiss all the points contained in the council statement as products of blind partisanship." He specifically endorsed the council's views on the Geneva Convention and on Israeli settlements. Israel's settlement policy, he said, was "increasingly a matter of concern and distress to its friends, and not helpful to the process of peace."

Israeli Ambassador Chaim Herzog told the council after Scranton's remarks that "Any attempt to point the finger at Israel's actions and to characterize them as obstacles to peace is nothing but a cynical falsification of history . . . We reject it out of hand."

The U.S. June 29 vetoed a Security Council resolution calling on Israel to withdraw from occupied Arab lands. The vote was 10 to 1, with Britain, France, Italy and Sweden abstaining. The text was approved by Benin, China, Guyana, Japan, Libya, Pakistan, Panama, Rumania, Tanzania and the Soviet Union. The resolution supported the recommendations adopted May 19 by the U.N. Committee on the Exercise of the Inalienable Rights of the Palestinian People. It called for Israeli withdrawal from the Arab territories by June 1, 1977 and for the U.N. to hand over the evacuated land to the Palestine Liberation Organization.

After casting the 16th U.S. veto in the Council, delegate Albert W. Sherer Jr. said the resolution was "totally devoid of balance." He said, "The political interests of the Palestinians and their role in a final Middle East settlement constitute, . . . a matter that must be negotiated between the parties before it can be defined in resolutions of this Council."

Israel had been boycotting the Council debate since it had started June 9. Chaim Herzog, Israel's chief delegate, assailed the resolution June 29 as another example "of miserable behavior of the U.N. under Arab instigation engaging in its paranoiac obsession with Israel while ignoring the human tragedy of Lebanon. . . ."

The council Nov. 11 unanimously passed a consensus statement condemning Israeli policy in occupied territory. It was the first time the U.S. had joined in council action critical of Israel.

The statement called on Israel "to insure the safety, welfare and security of the inhabitants of [the occupied] territories and to facilitate the return of those inhabitants who have fled the areas since the outbreak" of war in 1967. Israel was urged to "refrain from adopting any measure" that would violate international law. This was softer than the council's May 26 statement calling on Israel to "refrain and rescind" any such measure.

The council statement "deplored" Israeli actions in the territories that "alter their demographic composition and administrative measures, which have no legal validity" and threaten the peace. It cited particularly Israel's establishment of settlements in these areas.

On the question of Jerusalem, the council said that any moves taken by Israel "which tend to change the legal status" of the city, including legislative and administrative measures and expropriation of land and properties, "are invalid and cannot change that status."

In a concluding remark, the council noted that "profanation of the holy places, religious buildings and sites . . . may seriously endanger international peace and security." This was a reference to interference in Jewish holy places as well as Christian and Moslem sites.

Chaim Herzog, Israel's chief delegate, assailed the council statement for displaying "biased selectivity, one-sidedness and political expediency." He accused the U.N. of embarking on a "modern international expression of anti-Semitism" and said that Israel would "not agree to any solution proposed here."

U.S. diplomats held that the consensus statement was "fully consistent" with previous council resolutions in which the U.S.

had joined. During negotiations before adoption of the statement, the U.S. had resisted attempts by the Soviet Union to call for an immediate end to the Israeli occupation and by Libya to have the entire occupation called "illegal."

The council had begun debate Nov. 1 on a complaint filed by Egypt. The council then gave the PLO the right to participate as an observer in the debate. The vote was 11-1, with the U.S. opposing. Britain, France and Italy abstained.

Zehdi Labib Terzi, the PLO observer, assailed Israel's occupation policy in his address to the council. Israeli delegate Herzog had been invited to participate in the debate, but walked out as soon as Terzi started to speak.

Palestinians' return backed. The new U.N. Committee on the Exercise of the Inalienable Rights of the Palestinian People met at U.N. headquarters in New York Feb. 26–May 19, 1976 and adopted recommendations May 19 supporting the Palestinians' "right to return" to their homeland.

The text was adopted by consensus without vote. It provided for the immediate return of all Palestinians displaced during and following the 1967 war. This was to be followed by the return of the Palestinians displaced between 1948 (when Israel was established) and 1967.

A Palestine Liberation Organization Observer attended the committee meeting but was not permitted to vote.

Israel Feb. 26 had restated its decision to boycott the committee meetings. Chief delegate Chaim Herzog assailed the body as "an instrument in the hands of the extreme Arab elements, who are unwilling to acknowledge the Jewish people's right to national sovereignty, and whose purpose is to block the road toward peace in the Middle East."

Assembly approves proposals—In an action supporting the committee's proposals, the Assembly Nov. 24 approved 90-16 with 30 abstentions, a resolution calling for the right of the Palestinians to establish their own state and to reclaim their former homes and properties in what was now the state of Israel.

Citing the "legitimate and inalienable rights of the Palestinian people," the committee report declared that they had the right "to return to their homes and property and to achieve self-determination, national independence and sovereignty."

The resolution endorsed the committee's call for the refugees displaced by the 1967 war to reclaim their homes immediately. As for the Palestinians displaced between 1948, when Israel was established, and 1967, the assembly urged the U.N. to carry out "necessary arrangements" with the Palestine Liberation Organization and the states involved to allow for the return of those refugees. Those who chose not to go back "should be paid just and equitable compensation."

The committee called for Israeli withdrawal from all occupied Arab territory by June 1, 1977, without making any references to previous Security Council resolutions calling for Israeli-Arab negotiations to bring about such a pullback.

During two weeks of debate, Israel had criticized PLO participation in drawing up the committee's report and noted that only four of its 20 member states maintained diplomatic relations with Israel.

Mediation & Negotiations

Kissinger's Peace Efforts

The "honest broker" may sometimes play a vital role in international peacemaking. Negotiators for contending parties often meet, bargain and come to agreement without the intervention of third parties. Frequently, however, the process is aided, accelerated—or simply made possible—by disinterested conciliators. An outsider, disinterested or otherwise, may carry messages between warring sides, may arrange for them to meet, may assist the presentation of each side's viewpoints and proposals, may suggest compromises, may make pledges and may actually be the deciding factor in forging an acceptable peace accord. In the mid-1970s, Henry A. Kissinger was the outstanding mediator in the Arab-Israeli dispute.

Kissinger plans Mideast trip. U.S. Secretary of State Henry A. Kissinger announced plans Jan. 28, 1975 to visit the Middle East again to determine "the real possibilities of a solution" to the Arab-Israeli problem.

The secretary told a news conference that the trip would be "exploratory" and would not be "designed to settle anything or to generate shuttle diplomacy." Previously, Kissinger had said he would not return to the region unless he was certain of making progress. He now changed his tactics, he said, "at the request of all the parties and based on the belief that the urgency of the situation requires that this step be taken."

Kissinger expressed confidence in working out a second-stage disengagement agreement between Egypt and Israel, saying that their differences over the transfer of territory in exchange for progress toward peace "can be reconciled."

Israeli, Egyptian policy statements— Israeli Premier Yitzhak Rabin Jan. 23 had rejected any deadlines for an agreement for the withdrawal of Israeli forces from occupied Arab territories as proposed by Egyptian President Anwar Sadat in recent public pronouncements. Sadat's assertion that the Geneva conference must be reconvened if an accord on Israeli withdrawal were not reached in three months "has no validity whatsoever for Israel," Rabin said. Israel had "nothing to fear" from the Geneva talks, but lack of preparations for them, he warned, could lead to a political stalemate and possible war. The Israeli leader said his government was prepared to continue negotiations with Egypt on the Sinai "that will have political meaning as well as military meaning, with the purpose of advancing" peace in the area.

Rabin declared in another statement Jan. 25 that if the Arabs entered into peace talks with Israel, "they'll find us more generous than they think." He acknowledged that withdrawal from occupied Arab territories as part of a peace agreement posed risks to Israel's security, but said he was determined to propose such concessions despite domestic criticism.

Rabin called on the Soviet Union Jan. 27 to resume diplomatic relations with Israel, severed in 1967, if it wanted "to play a meaningful role in the Middle East." While the Soviets had contacts with Egypt and Syria, "they have to learn from the Americans that they cannot have an influence in the area unless they are able to talk to both sides in the Middle East conflict," Rabin said.

Sadat pledged Jan. 23 that Egypt "will never start war unless Israel attacks us." He said that Egypt aligned itself militarily and politically with Syria and that Cairo would not make a separate peace with Israel because it would not "dissociate itself from the other Arab fronts."

In an interview published in the French newspaper Le Figaro Jan. 24, Sadat predicted that the U.S. would soon recognize the Palestine Liberation Organization (PLO). "The U.S. can play a big role" in getting Israel to realize that "the PLO is responsible for the Palestinians, their future, their land," he said.

The U.S. State Department said Jan. 24 that the U.S. had no plans to recognize the PLO under present circumstances. The department said that Washington still adhered to the policy outlined by Secretary Kissinger in December 1974: The U.S. could not recommend negotiations with the PLO as long as it refused to recognize the existence of Israel as a legitimate state.

Kissinger in Middle East. Henry Kissinger visited five Middle East countries Feb. 10–15 on what was described as a preliminary mission to determine the possibility of negotiating a further interim troop disengagement agreement between Israel and Egypt.

In addition to meeting with Israeli and Egyptian officials in Jerusalem and Cairo, the secretary also visited with Syrian, Jordanian and Saudi Arabian officials to brief them on his peace efforts, held similar discussions with Soviet Foreign Minister

Andrei A. Gromyko in Geneva Feb. 16–17 and conferred with Shah Mohammed Riza Pahlevi of Iran in Zurich Feb. 18.

Kissinger's discussions in Jerusalem and Cairo centered on efforts to reconcile Egyptian-Israeli differences over conditions for further Israeli troop withdrawal in the Sinai. Israel was said to insist on an Egyptian commitment not to resume fighting for at least three to five years in exchange for another limited troop pullback. President Anwar Sadat refused to make such a commitment publicly and demanded extensive Israeli withdrawals from the Mitla and Gidi passes and the Abu Rudeis oilfields.

Kissinger conferred in Jerusalem Feb. 10–11 with Premier Yitzhak Rabin, Foreign Minister Yigal Allon and other Israeli officials. During the discussions Feb. 11, Lt. Gen. Mordechai Gur, Israel's chief of staff, gave a detailed report on the strategic value of the passes.

Addressing the Knesset after Kissinger's departure for Egypt, Premier Rabin said Feb. 12 that Israel would not relinquish the passes and the oilfields "as long as Egypt does not withdraw from the war."

Kissinger conferred with Sadat in Cairo Feb. 12–13. Before he left, the secretary and Foreign Minister Ismail Fahmy had signed an agreement under which the U.S. was to provide Egypt with an $80 million loan for essential imports from the U.S., largely agricultural and industrial machinery and spare parts.

Kissinger stopped off in Damascus later Feb. 13 to brief Syrian President Hafez al-Assad and returned to Jerusalem the same day to present Israeli officials with Sadat's views on a proposed agreement.

Kissinger and Sadat expressed confidence that progress was being made in the preliminary negotiations, a view not shared by an unidentified senior Israeli official Feb. 14. The official said, "Neither the Egyptians nor we really conceded anything in this opening round. The hard bargaining remains to be done."

Kissinger flew to Aqaba, Jordan Feb. 14 and met with King Hussein, who expressed support for the secretary's efforts to achieve a new Israeli-Egyptian agreement. Hussein reiterated Jordan's refusal to return to a reconvened Geneva conference as long as the Palestine Liberation Organization had sole responsibility for recovering the West Bank from Israel.

The secretary's meeting with Saudi King Faisal in Riyadh Feb. 15 was said to have dealt with the U.S. plan for long-term oil agreements between producers and consumers at lower prices than the current world price of $10–$11 a barrel.

Kissinger meets Gromyko—U.S.-Soviet differences over the Middle East were discussed by Kissinger and Foreign Minister Gromyko in Geneva Feb. 16–17. A communique issued after the talks did not reflect a reported rift in which Gromyko accused the U.S. of excluding Moscow from diplomatic efforts to help resolve the Arab-Israeli dispute. The joint statement merely said that both sides "believe that the Geneva conference should play an important part" in establishing peace and "should resume its work at an early date."

At a joint news conference Feb. 17, Gromyko was asked whether critical remarks on Middle East peace moves made Feb. 14 by Soviet Communist Party Secretary General Leonid Brezhnev were an allusion to Kissinger's diplomatic efforts. Gromyko said Brezhnev had no one in particular in mind. (The Soviet leader had said that "certain persons apparently would like to offer the Arab peoples something like a soporific, hoping that they will be lulled and will forget their demands for restoration of justice and full liquidation of the consequences of aggression.")

Shah on oil to Israel—Following his talks with Kissinger in Zurich, Switzerland Feb. 18, Shah Mohammed Riza Pahlevi indicated at a news conference that Iran would send Israel additional oil if it returned the Abu Redeis oilfields as part of a peace settlement with Egypt. The shah said: "Our policy is to sell oil to those who buy it. Once the tankers are loaded, where it goes is of no importance to us . . . because it is a purely commercial transaction for my country."

The shah also pledged not to join any Arab oil embargo against the West, asserting that "we have never boycotted any one."

Arriving in Paris on the last stop of his 10-day tour, Kissinger conferred with French Foreign Minister Jean Sauvanargues Feb. 18 and with President Valery Giscard d'Estaing Feb. 19. The secretary flew back to Washington later Feb. 19 and said in an airport statement that he believed he had "made some progress for establishing a framework for negotiations."

Shuttle resumed. Henry Kissinger was back in the Middle East in March 1975, shuttling between Aswan, Egypt and Jerusalem March 8–13, conferring with President Anwar Sadat and Premier Yitzhak Rabin and their aides and conveying their proposals to each other.

Kissinger sought to remove the chief stumbling block to an agreement, which remained Israel's reluctance to return the Abu Rudeis oilfields and the strategic Mitla and Gidi passes, Egypt's minimum demands, unless Egypt gave Israel an unequivocal pledge of nonbelligerency.

Kissinger had made a side trip to Damascus March 9 on the way from Aswan to Jerusalem to confer with Syrian President Hafez al-Assad. With Kissinger at his side, Assad said at a news conference before their talks started that he remained opposed to "separate, partial agreements." This was in reference to Assad's repeated objections to Sadat's willingness to negotiate separately with Israel. Assad said he would support limited accords such as Kissinger was currently arranging if progress could be made on all three fronts—Sinai, the Golan Heights and the West Bank.

Assad indicated that unless the Palestine Liberation Organization was represented at the reconvened Geneva conference, Syria would absent itself from the meeting. (Assad had proposed March 7 "to form a unified Syrian-Palestinian" military and political command "if this meets with the requirements of consolidating the Palestinian struggle." He said he was not proposing a specific plan but was showing "how far we are willing to go in the interest of the Palestinian struggle.")

Talks suspended—Kissinger March 22 announced suspension of his latest efforts to achieve a second Israeli-Egyptian troop disengagement agreement in the Sinai Peninsula because the differences between both sides "on a number of key issues have proven irreconcilable." The secretary's statement was issued in Jerusalem.

As a result of the deadlock, Kissinger said, "a period of reassessment is needed so that all concerned can consider how best to proceed toward a just and lasting peace."

A parallel statement issued by the White House said President Ford regretted the suspension of the talks and reaffirmed the U.S. commitment to continue its efforts to help both sides reach a settlement.

In a farewell statement before returning to Washington later March 23, Kissinger said this was "a sad day for America, which has invested much hope and faith, and we know it is a sad day also for Israel, which needs and wants peace so badly." Despite the failure of the negotiations, Kissinger said, "the search for peace must continue, although we will now have to look for different methods and new forums."

Israel and Egypt blamed each other for the breakdown in the talks. The focus of the problem centered on Sadat's demand that Israel withdraw from the Sinai's strategic Mitla and Gidi passes and the Abu Rudeis oilfield, and Israel's refusal to do so without a pledge of nonbelligerency from Egypt.

A New York Times report March 23 gave this account of the final stages of the negotiations that lead to the impasse:

Jerusalem, in a softening of its demands, proposed that Israel would accept less-sweeping political concessions than a nonbelligerency pledge in exchange for a lesser withdrawal in which Israel would relinquish only the western side of the passes and Egypt would operate the oilfield in an enclave within Israeli-controlled territory. Kissinger conveyed this proposal to Sadat March 20 and the Egyptian leader rejected it March 22. Sadat insisted on complete and unrestricted access to the passes and the oilfield in his reply to Kissinger.

An Egyptian counterproposal rejected by Israel included a statement on the matter of nonbelligerency in which Cairo would say that disputes should be settled by negotiation and not by force; a promise there would be no recourse to force during the life of the agreement; a reaffirmation of the cease-fire; renewal of the United Nations peace force on a yearly basis rather than the current six-month term, with an extension of its mandate every 12 months without opposition.

In rejecting the Egyptian offer, Israel said the proposal did not merit giving up the passes and the oilfield.

Two maps based on Israel's and Egypt's Sinai withdrawal plans were made public by Simcha Dinitz, Israel's ambassador to the U.S., it was reported March 26. The Israeli version showed a north-to-south line running through the middle of the passes and ending north of the town of Sudr on the Gulf of Suez. Egyptian forces would be allowed to move eastward to the current Israeli truce line and a new U.N. separation area would be established on the western approach to the passes. In a further compromise, Israel offered the Egyptians land as well as sea access to the projected Abu Rudeis enclave by permitting them use of a U.N.-supervised road that would run from Egyptian territory through the Israeli-held sector to the oilfield.

The Egyptian map showed a north-south line running as far south as El Tur on the Gulf of Suez, in addition to Egyptian reoccupation of the passes and the oilfield. The Israelis opposed the line running south to El Tur as a threat to their positions in Sharm el-Sheikh.

Egyptian, other Arab reaction— Egyptian Foreign Minister Ismail Fahmy charged March 22 that because of its "intransigence" Israel "bears the sole responsibility" for the failure of Secretary Kissinger's mediation. Speaking to newsmen in Aswan, Fahmy said that Israel's insistence on an immediate Egyptian pledge of nonbelligerency led to the deadlock. As a result, Egypt would now ask the U.S. and the Soviet Union to reconvene the Geneva peace conference, he said.

Fahmy disclosed that from the start of the talks Egypt had made it clear that Israel could get a formal nonbelligerence vow only as part of an overall peace agreement and that such an accord must fulfill "the rights of the Palestinians." These' views, Fahmy said, were submitted to Kissinger "formally and in writing." Sadat also had informed Kissinger that Egypt would not be bound by a peace agreement with Israel if Israel attacked Syria, that Cairo's armed forces would "automatically fulfill Egypt's obligations toward Syria" and come to its assistance.

Fahmy said March 23 that as far as Egypt was concerned "this was the end," there could be no renewal of Kissinger's step-by-step approach to peace. Fahmy did not rule out possible Egyptian military action as a result of the negotiation breakdown.

Syria and the Palestine Liberation Organization welcomed the collapse of the Kissinger mission in statements made in Damascus March 23. The PLO's Executive Committee met and a spokesman later attributed the failure of the talks to Israel's intransigence to "American political and military support."

In reporting the suspension of Kissinger's mediation efforts, the official Syrian radio called for an early resumption of the Geneva conference. The secretary general of the Syrian Arab Socialist Union Party, Fawzi Kayyali, sent a telegram to Sadat praising his position on the talks as "very wise" and "a service to Arab solidarity."

Israelis back Rabin stand—Premier Rabin's refusal to cede the Sinai passes and the Abu Rudeis oilfields without an Egyptian offer of nonbelligerency during the negotiations was praised March 23 by the Israeli press, the coalition parties of the government and the right-wing opposition Likud bloc.

Speaking to a news conference shortly after Kissinger's departure for Washington, Rabin reviewed the offer his side had made to Egypt. The premier acknowledged that Sadat had made a few concessions but he said they did not amount to "the beginnings of the peacemaking process" and were, therefore, unacceptable.

Rabin expressed hope that the suspended talks could be resumed "under circumstances that will protect Israel's security." He said Israel was willing to attend a reconvened Geneva conference "if conditions emerge that make it possible."

Rabin asserted that Israeli press accounts of a letter President Ford was said to have sent to the premier toward the close of the negotiations were "exaggerated and irrelevant." The message reportedly had called on Israel to make concessions in order to reach an agreement. Rabin confirmed receipt of the letter but declined to disclose its contents. Israeli sources later confirmed that Ford had urged the Israelis to exert

every effort to reach an accord but denied that the President had spelled out "conditions, threats or anything close to an ultimatum."

U.S. announces policy reassessment. The Ford Administration announced March 24 it was undertaking a total reassessment of its Middle East policy following the breakdown of Secretary of State Kissinger's negotiations. The review would cover "all aspects and all countries," according to White House and State Department announcements. A reassessment of policy toward Israel in the event of an impasse in the talks reportedly had been mentioned by President Ford in his last-minute message to Israeli Premier Yitzhak Rabin to promote an accord.

Congressional support for Kissinger's role in the talks was evident at an Administration briefing of 21 Congressional leaders March 24. Ford and Kissinger were accorded a standing ovation when they entered the room. Kissinger was reported to have stressed to the group that neither Egypt nor Israel should be blamed for the breakdown and that the internal political situation in each country made impossible the concessions necessary for an accord.

Kissinger gave assurance later March 24 that reassessment was not a matter "of cutting off any aid." "Reassessment," he said, "means that we are facing a new situation of some peril" and it was "inevitable in such a situation that the President order a review to see what is the best policy for the United States to follow."

Kissinger was firm in his public statements about not blaming either side for the impasse, although there were reports that he had privately indicated disappointment that Israel had not been more flexible, especially in view of the more complex negotiations in the offing.

Kissinger, in testifying March 25 before the House Foreign Affairs Committee, said both sides in the negotiations had made a "serious" effort but "the problem was balancing tangible positions on the ground against less tangible assurances which have symbolic meanings and importance," a reference to the demands for an Israeli troop withdrawal and Egyptian declaration of nonbelligerency.

The U.S. announcement that American policy in the Middle East would have to be reassessed in view of the failure of Kissinger's mediation efforts precipitated bitter comments among Israeli leaders March 24. One unidentified official was quoted as interpreting Washington's statement to mean that Israel was "being blamed for the breakdown when in fact it was Egypt that refused to alter its opening position in the talks."

Meanwhile, Rabin reported on the talks March 24 to a special session of Parliament and received a 92–4 vote of confidence in his handling of the negotiations. Only the Communist deputies, including two Arabs, voted against the premier. The parliamentary resolution held Egypt "responsible for the suspension of negotiations" and pledged that Israel would "continue to strive for a just and durable peace with each of its neighbors."

Rabin conceded in his statement that the break-off in talks had caused a deterioration in the Middle East situation but he insisted that war was not inevitable. He added: "Consideration for the attitude of the United States is a central factor" in Israel's policy "but it is we who have to take the decisions on matters that determine our fate and we must do so as a result of our own sober and independent judgment."

Kissinger cites gravity of events—At a televised news conference March 26, Kissinger stressed the gravity of the situation and urged moderation on all sides, including "outside powers." He said the U.S. was prepared to go to the Geneva peace conference and would "be in touch with the co-chairman of the conference, the U.S.S.R., in the near future." The "dangers" in the Middle East "are still with us," he said, and the U.S. was "determined to continue the search for peace."

He said "with the end of the step-by-step approach, the United States faces a period of more complicated international diplomacy. Consequently, a reassessment of policy is essential."

The assessment of U.S. policy, he said, was "not directed against Israel" and "not designed to induce Israel to alter any particular policy. It is designed to develop a position that the United States can take in order to prevent an increasing radical-

ization in the area and in increasing tension and, above all, in order to avoid a war in which inevitably the United States would be involved at least indirectly given the international circumstances."

As part of the policy review, Kissinger had called on a group of prominent public figures, most of them former high government officials, to seek their advice on any new approach toward a Middle East settlement. His first meetings with the group were held March 31 and April 2. The advisers included former Secretary of State Dean Rusk, former Defense Secretary Robert S. McNamara, former Undersecretary of State George Ball, former Treasury Secretary C. Douglas Dillon and W. Averell Harriman, former ambassador to the Soviet Union.

Ford charges Israeli inflexibility. President Ford asserted in an interview made public March 27 that chances for peace in the Middle East would have been improved if Israel had displayed more flexibility in the negotiations with Egypt, suspended March 22. The interview had been conducted March 24 by publisher William Randolph Hearst Jr. and others from the Hearst newspaper chain.

Asked whether Israel "should be prepared to take greater risks for peace in the long-term interests of its survival," Ford replied: "If they had been a bit more flexible ... I think in the longer run it would have been the best insurance for peace."

As a result of the collapse of the Kissinger mission, the President said, "the potential volatility in the area has increased." That was why, he pointed out, it was necessary for the U.S. to reassess its entire Middle East policy.

Ford said the failure of the U.S. Congress to meet his requests for arms for Cambodia and South Vietnam "undoubtedly had some impact in the Middle East. It is my impression that some of the news media in Israel have indicated that was a factor."

Defense Secretary James R. Schlesinger said March 31 that any future U.S. military assistance to Israel must be held in abeyance until Washington completed the review of its Middle East position. He noted that the U.S. had agreed to supply Israel with a substantial amount of arms by April 1, and most of it had been received. "Israel wanted a much longer term commitment with respect to security supplies, but such a matter will have to wait," Schlesinger said.

But Schlesinger assured Israel April 22 that the Ford Administration's reassessment of its Middle East policies would have no bearing on continued American support Israel's security. He said this in a meeting with Israeli Ambassador Simcha Dinitz.

President Ford was noncommittal when questioned later April 22 about continued "favored-nation treatment of Israel." Replying to Walter Cronkite on a CBS-TV interview, the President said "the possibility of war is certainly a serious one." Since a new conflict in the Middle East could bring another oil embargo, "I think we have to be very cautious in our process of reassessment," Ford said.

Contacts, Proposals & Irenic Activity

The March 1975 breakdown in the Egyptian-Israeli negotiations conducted by Kissinger was followed by a variety of contacts, proposals and other actions that indicated a desire by Egypt and Israel to maintain some momentum toward peace.

Egypt Requests New Geneva Conference. Egyptian Foreign Minister Ismail Fahmy formally called on the Soviet Union March 31 and the U.S. April 1 to reconvene the Geneva peace conference on the Middle East. Both nations were co-chairmen of the conference.

Fahmy submitted Cairo's request to Ambassadors Vladimir Polyakov and Hermann F. Eilts without specifying a date. The foreign minister was said to have insisted that the Palestine Liberation Organization be represented at the parley.

Israeli sources said April 1 that major differences in the Middle East must be settled before the Geneva conference was reconvened. The discussions in Geneva "should be well-prepared" because "a rash move to Geneva that leads to a deadlock would only play into the hands of the Soviets," the Israeli officials were quoted as saying. The sources added: "If nothing is decided before Geneva, Geneva will be a dead end. We will not go there to formalize an impasse."

The Soviet Union had sent its reply to Egypt's formal request for reopening the Geneva conference, it was reported April 5. Although the contents of the message received by President Anwar Sadat from Communist Party General Secretary Leonid I. Brezhnev were not divulged, it was believed to have called for a thorough preparation in advance. This was publicly stressed by Soviet Premier Aleksei N. Kosygin in a warning to Arab nations April 14. He said the Arab countries should "be more united in their anti-imperialist struggle" to avoid being at a disadvantage in dealing with Israel and the U.S. at the conference. Kosygin made the statement at a Moscow dinner honoring Saddam Hussein, vice president of Iraq's ruling Revolutionary Command Council.

Soviets contact Israelis. Israeli officials reported April 11, 1975 that two Soviet representatives had held two days of separate discussions in Jerusalem the previous week with Premier Yitzhak Rabin, Defense Minister Shimon Peres and Foreign Minister Yigal Allon. The high-level visit, the first of its kind between the two countries since December 1973, dealt with possible resumption of the Geneva peace conference and the Middle East situation in general, Israeli officials said.

The Israelis said they believed the Soviet representatives sought to take advantage of the strain in U.S.-Israeli relations following the breakdown in Secretary of State Henry A. Kissinger's shuttle diplomacy and to assert Moscow's role as co-chairman of the Geneva conference. The visit had been preceded by at least one unpublicized meeting in Washington between Simcha Dinitz and Anatoly F. Dobrynin, the Israeli and Soviet ambassadors to the U.S., the officials said.

The U.S. State Department said April 11 it had been informed of the Israeli-Soviet meeting in Jerusalem "after it happened" but "had no objection to it." A department official said "if Israel wants to go back to the 1967 borders with a Soviet guarantee, this is the way to do it."

The Soviet Union April 23 offered to guarantee Israel's existence as an independent state if it withdrew from occupied Arab lands.

The proposal was made by Foreign Minister Andrei A. Gromyko at a dinner given for visiting Syrian Foreign Minister

Abdel Halim Khaddam. His suggestion was delivered within the framework of proposed subjects for discussions at a reconvened Geneva conference. The parley's principal task, Gromyko said, should be: "first, agreement on the liberation of all Arab lands from foreign occupation; second, agreement to insure the legitimate rights of the Arab people of Palestine up to the establishment of their own state; third, agreement to insure and guarantee the right of all states in the Middle East, including the state of Israel, to independent existence and development."

Sadat asks U.S. to pressure Israel. President Anwar Sadat suggested April 12 that the U.S. pressure Israel to withdraw from Arab-occupied territories and go back to its pre-1967 borders.

The Egyptian leader said in a New York Times interview: "It is time for the United States to declare to the whole world and not only to Israel whether it is protecting Israel within its borders or whether it is protecting Israel's occupation of the land of other states as well." The U.S. now had "more leverage" with Israel, having "saved" it "in the October war," he added.

Sadat asserted that Israel had "humiliated the United States in the area" during Secretary of State Henry A. Kissinger's last round of shuttle diplomacy in Cairo and Jerusalem. A Middle East settlement would be reached when Israel was "ready to make peace," Sadat said. He claimed that Egypt's peaceful intentions was evidenced by its decision to reopen the Suez Canal, rebuild its destroyed cities along the waterway and abide by the United Nations Security Council Resolution 242, which called for Israeli withdrawal from occupied Arab areas and the recognition of sovereignty of all states in the area. Sadat denied Israeli contentions that a secret agreement in the 1974 Sinai disengagement pact obliged Egypt to reopen the canal and permit Israeli-bound cargo to go through. Any action taken in regard to the canal, he said, would "be Egypt's decision alone because we are sovereign."

Israeli Foreign Minister Yigal Allon acknowledged the next day that American officials had been pressuring Israel to make further concessions to reach an interim accord with Cairo, but insisted/that there was no "crisis" between Washington and Jerusalem. Defense Minister Shimon Peres April 12 had defended Israel's decision not to bow to Egypt's demands, citing the collapse of U.S. guarantees to South Vietnam. "In a world going up in flames with so many guarantees toppling like stacks of cards . . . I am convinced that our decision was the right one," Peres said.

Sadat tours Arab states. President Anwar Sadat visited Kuwait, Iraq, Jordan and Syria May 12–18 to create what Egyptian officials said was "a consensus among Arab leaders on what they want from the United States during the coming stage of the Arab-Israeli conflict," a reference to the possible reconvening of the Geneva conference. Winding up his tour, Sadat said in Damascus May 18 that he had received a mandate from the Arab leaders to represent their interests at his scheduled meeting with President Ford in Salzburg, Austria June 1–2.

During his trip, Sadat conferred May 12–14 with Emir Sabah al-Salem al-Sabah, ruler of Kuwait, with Iraqi officials in Baghdad May 14–16, with King Hussein of Jordan in Amman May 16–17 and with Syrian President Hafez al-Assad in Damascus May 17–18. Before leaving Baghdad May 16, Sadat disclosed that the Iraqi officials continued their refusal to cooperate with Egyptian efforts to settle the Arab dispute with Israel by diplomatic means, and had no intentions of becoming involved in negotiations with Israel. Sadat did receive an Iraqi pledge of large quantities of oil and promises from Kuwait for substantial financial assistance.

In addition to his meetings with Assad in Damascus, Sadat also met with Palestine Liberation Organization leader Yasir Arafat.

Suez Canal reopened. Egypt reopened the Suez Canal June 5, 1976, eight years after its closure during the 1967 Arab-Israeli war. President Anwar Sadat gave a formal address at Port Said, then boarded an Egyptian destroyer and stood on its bridge in admiral's uniform as the ship led a ceremonial convoy south through the canal. The first commercial ships followed two hours later.

In his formal address Sadat declared: "Egypt presents this step as a gift to the world in order to help the lives of all friendly and peace-loving peoples. While making this initiative as a contribution to peace, Egypt reminds friendly nations that parts of its dear soil are still under foreign occupation and that an entire people are still suffering the consequences of suppression and homelessness. Egypt reiterates its determination to do its holy duty toward its own and other Arab lands—in the Golan Heights, Sinai and Palestine— and toward usurped Arab rights."

Sadat boarded the destroyer Sixth of October, named for the day in 1973 when Egyptian forces crossed the canal and broke through the Israeli defense line. The ceremonial convoy of four Egyptian vessels was joined by the U.S. cruiser Little Rock, flagship of the 6th Fleet in the Mediterranean, in a gesture believed designed to emphasize the prominent role taken by the U.S. in helping clear the canal of obstacles to shipping.

As the destroyer sailed toward the Gulf of Suez, the Egyptian leader praised Israel's partial withdrawal of troops and equipment from the canal's east bank but said this "must be followed by a main step." He left unanswered a question from newsmen whether Israeli cargo would be allowed to pass through the canal in non-Israeli ships. Instead, Sadat described himself as "still hopeful, and I am more hopeful since my talks with President Ford. The question of cargoes is no real problem. The real question is: Are we going to continue the peace process or not?"

The decision to reopen the canal had been announced by Sadat March 29 in an address to the Egyptian National Assembly.

Sadat's decision was a reversal of previous policy, which had called for keeping the canal closed unless Israeli forces pulled out of the strategic passes and oilfields. Sadat said he had set the June 5 reopening date on the assumption that U.S. Secretary of State Henry A. Kissinger would bring about a second-stage Israeli withdrawal in the Sinai.

Egyptian officials said March 30 that Israeli-bound cargo aboard ships of other nations as well as Israeli vessels would be barred from using the Suez Canal when it reopened. They said that one of the principal aims of putting the canal back in operation was to "isolate Israel diplomatically" and to refute Israeli charges that Egypt was not interested in peace.

Israeli-bound cargo would be permitted to pass through the canal only if an agreement was reached leading to an Israeli withdrawal from the positions they held 10–15 miles from the waterway, Egyptian officials said March 31.

Israeli Premier Yitzhak Rabin said April 1 that Egypt's reopening of the Suez Canal "contributes nothing of benefit to Israel" and was no "contribution to the promotion of relations between Egypt and Israel." The canal, Rabin said, benefitted Egypt, "for whom it ensures a source of sorely needed revenue" and Europe and the Soviet Union.

Sadat met with U.S. President Ford in Salzburg, Austria June 1–2 while the latter was in Europe for NATO summit talks. In the June 6 issue of the New York Times, correspondent Bernard Gwertzman said in his account of the Ford-Sadat meeting, in which Kissinger participated: "Under the January 1975 disengagement agreement... Mr. Sadat told Mr. Kissinger privately, Israeli-bound cargoes would be permitted to enter once the canal was reopened." In the same issue of The Times, correspondent Terence Smith reported from Israel that Sadat had made a similar pledge in a secret letter to President Nixon dated Jan. 18, 1974.

Israel thins Canal force—In what was officially described as a response to Egypt's reopening of the Suez Canal, the Israeli government June 2 said it was ordering the partial withdrawal of some of the Israeli military personnel and equipment deployed in the limited-force zone of the Suez Canal area. The move was completed June 4.

The pullback, understood to have gained the full support of the Israeli cabinet earlier in the day, was announced at a news conference by Premier Yitzhak Rabin as a measure designed to show "the world and Egypt that Israel really wants and intends to progress toward peace either by an over-all or interim agreement."

Rabin said Israel was reducing by half the number of its tanks and troops allowed in the limited-force zone under terms of the 1974 disengagement of forces agreement and was withdrawing artillery and missiles to points farther east of the zone. He said Israel would deploy 15 tanks, instead of the 30 allowed by the agreement, in its limited-force zone, an area 12–18 miles wide running parallel to the canal. Half the permitted 7,000 Israeli troops were to be pulled out of the zone. All artillery would be moved to a point two miles east of the zone and all missiles except antitank weapons were to be moved seven miles east of the zone. The agreement had allowed Israel six batteries of artillery within its limited-force area.

Rabin declared the reopening of the canal to international shipping was an "important and constructive development in concordance with the [1974] disengagement of forces agreement between Israel and Egypt."

Israel's partial Suez withdrawal was welcomed June 2 by Sadat as a "step toward peace."

Rabin meets U. S. officials. Israeli Premier Yitzhak Rabin conferred with President Ford and Secretary of State Henry A. Kissinger in Washington June 11–12 on the possibility of reviving the negotiations with Egypt. The premier also discussed the matter in separate talks with Kissinger June 12–13 and 15.

Rabin and Ford agreed at the conclusion of their discussions on the advantages of renewing efforts to negotiate another limited Israeli-Egyptian accord in the Sinai. Rabin said at a news conference later in the day that he believed there was a basis for such negotiations but that he was still awaiting "answers" to determine whether Egypt was prepared to compromise. Israel expected Egypt to make some concessions on the duration of any agreement and on easing the Arab economic boycott against Israel, Rabin said.

Rabin also said Ford showed "great understanding" for Israel's request for $2.5 billion in economic and military assistance.

Rabin and Kissinger concurred after meeting in New York June 15 that further U. S. diplomatic contacts with Israel and Egypt in the next few weeks would have to be taken to determine whether the Ford Administration would undertake new peace initiatives. Kissinger said he would conduct another phase of shuttle diplomacy "only when the chances of success are more clearly established."

Appearing on the CBS-TV program "Face the Nation" after meeting with Kissinger, Rabin urged the secretary not to press his peace mission until "everything is known in a very precise way." Otherwise, false hopes would be raised, Rabin said.

Rabin said on returning to Israel June 16 that "there is now an understanding by the United States government that there must be changes in the positions of both sides."

Israel proposes new Sinai plan. Israel proposed a new Sinai disengagement agreement with Egypt, Israeli officials disclosed June 24, 1975. The plan, transmitted by U. S. Ambassador Hermann F. Eilts to Egyptian President Anwar Sadat in Cairo June 23, represented a modification of an earlier Israeli position discussed by Secretary of State Henry A. Kissinger in March.

Among the major points of the new Israeli proposal:

■ The agreement must last three to four years. Israel would withdraw from the western parts of the Mitla and Gidi passes in the Sinai but would retain the eastern parts and access to electronic surveillance stations it maintained in the Gidi Pass.

■ Egypt would be given back the Abu Rudeis oilfield and would have access to it along a corridor on the western Sinai coast between the town of Suez and the oilfield; Israeli vehicles would be permitted to patrol the road under United Nations supervision.

■ The new line to which Israel would withdraw would extend south from Lake Bardawil on the Mediterranean coast, through the middle of the passes and down to the narrow coastal strip along the Gulf of Suez to a point south of Abu Rudeis.

■ Most of the area to be evacuated by Israel would be demilitarized and incorporated into the current U.N. buffer zone; Egyptian forces would be permitted to move several miles deeper into Sinai.

Under any new agreement, Israeli officials said, Israel would seek a series of understandings with the U. S. that would provide for assurance of full military and economic aid, including compensation for the loss of the Abu Rudeis oil.

Details of the new Israeli offer had been approved in principle by the Israeli cabinet June 17, finalized by Premier Yitzhak Rabin and his key aides June 18 and taken to Washington the following day by Rabin's military aide, Brig. Gen. Ephraim Poran, who reportedly carried a Sinai map delineating the new lines.

The State Department was critical June 25 of the Israeli report of its new Sinai offer. Asserting that the accompanying maps were "inaccurate and highly misleading," department spokesman Robert Anderson, reading a statement in the name of President Ford, said, "We would caution anyone from drawing any conclusions from these press accounts. Finally, competitive leaks of confidential diplomatic exchanges make negotiations extremely difficult."

Israeli Foreign Minister Yigal Allon sent a note to Kissinger June 26, denying the charges that Israel was deliberately leaking confidential information. The note also expressed Israel's determination that the dispute over the alleged leaks should not hinder negotiations.

Israeli-Egyptian peace exchanges. With the U.S. acting as mediator, Israel and Egypt continued to exchange proposals and counterproposals in June and July on plans for a new interim disengagement agreement in the Sinai but no early accord was indicated. The principal topic of discussion remained Egypt's demand for the return of the strategic Mitla and Gidi passes and the Abu Rudeis oilfields and the location of a new cease-fire line.

As the secret negotiations continued, the United Nations Security Council July 24 approved a three-month extension of the United Nations Emergency Force (UNEF) in the Sinai, whose mandate was to expire that day. Egypt at first had opposed renewal of the peace-keeping mission but later withdrew its objections after a Council appeal.

In the ongoing exchange of peace plans Israeli officials said July 24 that an Egyptian proposal, including a map, they had received that day from Washington was "serious and well considered" but important differences remained to be overcome on several issues.

Virtually no information was being released as to specific proposals. However, newsmen traveling with Secretary of State

Henry A. Kissinger from Bonn to London July 12 were informed that the U.S. was considering the possibility of having American technicians operate electronic surveillance stations in the Sinai passes as a means of facilitating an agreement. This was disclosed after Kissinger had conferred earlier July 12 with Israeli Premier Yitzhak Rabin.

The previous round of U.S. contacts with the principal parties to the dispute included Kissinger's meetings with Israeli Ambassador Simcha Dinitz July 1-2, 7, 17-18 and 23. U.S. Ambassador Hermann F. Eilts met with President Anwar Sadat in Cairo July 22 to convey the latest suggestions by Israel. Eilts had briefed Sadat June 23 on the results of talks President Ford and Kissinger had held with Rabin in Washington June 11-13.

Kissinger had advised Israel July 5 to make concession and "take a chance on making progress toward peace, because any other approach is going to lead to a war sooner or later which is going to have serious consequences, above all for the people of Israel." Kissinger assured the Israelis, however, that the U.S. "will stand behind them in conditions which we can reasonably say to our people that progress is being made."

Premier Rabin declared July 23 that any new Israeli-Egyptian agreement must be finalized by "face-to-face negotiations" between the delegations of the two countries. Speaking in Jerusalem, Rabin warned Egypt that negotiations would take time and that any accord must include a pledge to refrain from the use of force "as a means of solving disputes between the two countries."

(Israeli officials explained that Rabin's suggestion for direct talks with Egypt did not constitute new conditions for an agreement. They said the premier was referring to the kind of direct technical discussions that had preceded the signing of the disengagement pacts with Egypt and Syria in 1974.)

Rabin also was critical of President Anwar Sadat for his reference to Israel in a speech July 22 as "a dagger pointed at Egypt and the Arab world." Rabin said Sadat's remark "put a disturbing question mark over the possibility of advancing toward an interim agreement... If that is the way he really sees Israel, then it is doubtful whether his aim is peace."

A senior Egyptian official July 23 denounced Rabin's call for direct talks and said it "has cut the ground from under the American mediation efforts." President Sadat ruled out face-to-face meetings with the Israelis in a speech July 23 to the Arab Socialist Union, Egypt's only political party. He said: "The current negotiations are conducted through a third party, the United States. At the Geneva conference we shall all sit and discuss the problem just as we sit at the United Nations. Let it be known here that there is no question of direct talks."

Israel rejects Egyptian proposal. Israeli Premier Yitzhak Rabin stated July 25 that Egypt's latest unspecified proposal for a new disengagement agreement in the Sinai was still "substantially not acceptable" to Israel. Cairo's offer, however, was better than the one proposed in March.

Taking issue with charges in Israel that his government was being asked to make all the concessions, Rabin noted that the territory being discussed was 25–31 miles east of the Suez Canal and 169 miles west of the pre-1967 borders. "So we are discussing territories closer to the heartland of Egypt than to Israel's prewar borders," he said.

Rabin observed that the current negotiations differed from the discussions in 1974, when both sides were solely concerned with disengaging their military forces in the Sinai. Now "we are dealing with changing the realities in the relationship between Egypt and Israel." The premier repeated his demand that any new pact between the two countries would have to be completed in direct talks, signed by the parties and made public.

Israeli Defense Minister Shimon Peres said July 28 that Israel's latest proposal to Egypt transmitted by the U.S. was Israel's final offer. He said: "We have gone far, very far, and we have made it clear that our suggestions are final. It is hard to believe that we shall be able to concede any more."

In a speech ending a four-day congress of the Arab Socialist Union, Egypt's only political party, President Anwar Sadat July 25 alluded to the current negotiations with Israel. He said: "It does not matter to us at all whether a certain step succeeds or fails. Our armed forces are ready."

Sadat had conferred earlier July 25 with United Nations Secretary General Kurt Waldheim. Waldheim later told a news conference that it would be a mistake to "underestimate" the significance of Egypt's threat made the previous week to end the mandate of the United Nations Emergency Force in the Sinai. The next three months of UNEF's mandate would be crucial and failure to achieve "a breakthrough toward peace" during that period could result in serious consequences, Waldheim said.

2d Sinai Withdrawal Pact

As the climate of agreement between Egypt and Israel improved, Henry Kissinger returned to the Middle East in August 1975 for a fresh round of shuttle diplomacy. The negotiations produced agreement on a second Israeli withdrawal in the Sinai and on the stationing of American civilians there to monitor observance of the agreement.

Kissinger resumes shuttle diplomacy. U.S. Secretary of State Henry A. Kissinger arrived in Israel Aug. 21 to start a new round of shuttle diplomacy in an effort to bring about a second interim Israeli-Egyptian troop disengagement agreement in the Sinai.

Kissinger's arrival in Israel was marked by nationwide demonstrations against his method of diplomacy and the projected agreement. The protesters expressed fear that under the reported terms of the pact Israel would concede too much territory to Egypt without balanced political concessions from Cairo. Kissinger was trapped with Premier Yitzhak Rabin and most members of the Israeli cabinet for more than hour in the Parliament building in Jerusalem when demonstrators blocked all exits. Earlier the demonstrators had tried to prevent the secretary and his party from reaching the Knesset but were driven off by police. A counter-demonstration of about 70 carloads of Israelis drove to Jerusalem to express support for the secretary's mediation efforts.

On arriving at Tel Aviv's Ben-Gurion airport, Kissinger had noted in a statement that he had returned to the U.S. in March with "a heavy heart" after the failure of his diplomatic efforts then. But now, he said, "the gap in the negotiations has been substantially narrowed by concessions on both sides."

Newsmen on the plane with Kissinger had been told that the major obstructions to an agreement had been overcome but that some "crucial specifics" remained to be resolved. They included: The exact lines of an Israeli pullback to the east of the Mitla and Gidi passes and a parallel Egyptian advance eastward; a projected Egyptian road to the Abu Rudeis oilfields, to be given up by Israel in exchange for U.S.-guaranteed compensatory oil supplies and an Israeli road in that area; and the specific role the U.S. was to play in the operation of electronic surveillance systems in the Sinai.

The resumption of Kissinger's mission had been officially authorized Aug. 17 by President Ford after conferring with the secretary at his vacation retreat in Vail, Colo. Israel and Egypt gave their formal approval that day. Kissinger emphasized after his talks with the President that the anticipated new accord "of course, is not a peace agreement." But if it succeeded, it would be "an interim step toward peace between Egypt and Israel," he added.

Preliminary negotiations paving the way for the resumption of shuttle diplomacy had been conducted earlier in August, with Israeli diplomats, including Ambassador Simcha Dinitz, conferring with Kissinger and other U.S. officials in Washington and with U.S. Ambassador to Egypt Hermann F. Eilts transmitting Israeli and Egyptian proposals between Cairo and Washington.

U.S. diplomats in Washington disclosed Aug. 19 that Egypt, Israel and the U.S. had agreed to support the establishment of an independent peacekeeping force in the Sinai if the United Nations Security Council should refuse to renew the mandate of the current United Nations Emergency Force during the three-year term of the projected Israeli-Egyptian accord. Israel had asked for the U.S. to guarantee such a substitute force if for some reasons the Soviet Union or China vetoed the Security Council's extension of UNEF's term.

Israelis approve, debate mission—The Israeli cabinet Aug. 17 had formallly endorsed the government's negotiating stand on a Sinai accord, thus paving the way for Secretary Kissinger to resume his direct mediation.

Addressing a special session of the Knesset (parliament) called by the opposition Likud bloc, Premier Rabin acknowledged Aug. 18 that while progress had been made "there are also clauses of great importance on which agreement has not yet been reached." He assured the deputies that his government would "sign an interim agreement only if we are convinced that it will be to the benefit of Israel."

Rabin spoke in reply to a Likud motion calling for full debate on the negotiations. The Knesset deferred action on the motion after the premier, Likud leader Menachem Begin and other deputies had voiced their views. In his speech, Begin accused the government of yielding too much to Egypt and of gradually withdrawing its previous demands for an Egyptian declaration ending the state of war and of dropping its insistence on retaining the Abu Rudeis oilfields. Israel was softening its position because of American pressure, which would only lead to further demands for Israeli concessions, Begin said.

Palestinians warn against pact—Palestinian leaders assailed the impending Sinai agreement as a threat to their struggle with Israel, it was reported Aug. 18.

Zuhair Mohsen, head of the Palestine Liberation Organization's (PLO) military department, said, "This American agreement ... poses the greatest danger to the nationalist cause—that is, the Arab struggle with Zionism—since the June 1967 war."

The head of the Popular Democratic Front for the Liberation of Palestine, Nayef Hawatmeh, had charged in a speech in Saida, Lebanon Aug. 17 that the U.S. was attempting "to wrest the key to the area by getting Egypt out of the Arab region and in addition wants to land American troops" in the Mitla and Gidi passes in the Sinai. The U.S. also hoped to get Syria to agree to a troop disengagement with Israel, "which would strike at the heart of the commando movement," Hawatmeh asserted.

The head of the PLO's political department, Farouk Kaddoumi, called on Palestinians Aug. 20 to employ violence to disrupt Secretary of State Kissinger's projected visits to Arab countries during his current diplomatic tour. Kaddoumi charged that the purpose of the Kissinger mission was to carry out "another conspiracy against the Palestinians."

Abu Maher, a spokesman for PLO leader Yasir Arafat, had warned the previous week that the Palestinians "will foil this agreement with their own guns." Maher said, "The people who carried arms, will not be able to achieve liberation except through their arms."

Arafat said in an interview published in Le Monde Aug. 20 that Israel planned to launch a preventive war on other Arab states after concluding an interim agreement with Egypt.

Negotiators work on draft. Egyptian and Israeli negotiators in late August 1975 concentrated on the final disagreements in the language of the draft accord on the second interim troop disengagement in the Sinai. Henry Kissinger continued to shuttle between Israel (Tel Aviv and Jerusalem) and Alexandria.

He also made a side trip to Syria Aug. 23 to inform President Hafez al-Assad that the U.S. would be willing to act as mediator on any Israeli-Syrian negotiations following a Sinai agreement, even though Israeli Premier Yitzhak Rabin Aug. 22 had said the chance for an interim agreement with Syria was "limited."

Kissinger's visit to Israel had been marked by four days of violent demonstrations that culminated Aug. 24 as police wielding clubs broke up rightwing demonstrations in and around Tel Aviv and Jerusalem.

The cause of the demonstrations was criticism expressed by the right-wing leadership, headed by Likud Party leader Menachem Begin, and Zevulun Hammer and Yehuda Meir of the National Religious Party. Joining them was former Defense Minister Moshe Dayan.

The Egyptians for their part also had a public relations problem, but unlike the situation in Israel, President Anwar Sadat was faced with selling the projected pact to his Arab allies, reported the Washington Post Aug. 25. Said President Sadat's spokesman, Tashin Bashir, "We don't want to make difficulties for ourselves—or for the enemy we are negotiating with."

Both Israel and Egypt continued to characterize the negotiations as military agreements solely. The Palestinian leadership had indicated, in contrast to reports of their continuing opposition, that it would accept a Mideast pact only if it were military in nature, the Financial Times of London reported Aug. 20.

Using the same basic texts, the Egyptians, Israelis, and Americans worked feverishly Aug. 27 to finish the documents as Kissinger flew to Israel for the fourth time since his arrival Aug. 21.

Among issues that surfaced anew on Kissinger's arrival were use of the Suez Canal by Israeli-bound ships; freedom of the seas for Israeli vessels; $3 billion in aid to Israel and Egypt with $2.4 billion going to Israel; and an arrangement for the U.S. to come to Israel's aid in the event of a Soviet attack.

Israel & Egypt sign accord. Israel and Egypt in Geneva Sept. 4 signed a U.S.-mediated interim agreement providing for a further Israeli troop withdrawal in the Sinai Peninsula and the stationing of U.S. civilians in the region to monitor the accord. Israel in turn was to receive a number of Egyptian concessions and a pledge of increased American economic, military and political assistance. Egypt was also promised U.S. economic aid. The establishment of the American presence in the Sinai was subject to U.S. congressional approval; Israel said it would not implement the agreement unless that endorsement was given.

Among the major points of the agreement:

■ Israel would pull its troops back on a front varying from 12 to 26 miles, yielding control of the Mitla and Gidi passes and returning the Abu Rudeis oilfield to Egypt. Israel would share a road to the area of the oilfield with the Egyptians. The U.S. pledged to compensate Israel for the loss of the oil.

■ Egypt agreed publicly to permit non-military cargoes to pass through the Suez Canal to and from Israel and promised not to blockade Bab el Mandeb, the strait providing access to the Red Sea. (Egypt had privately agreed to allow Israel use of the canal under terms of the 1974 disengagement agreement but continued the maritime ban after the waterway's reopening in June.)

■ Both sides pledged not to resort to the use of force during the three years of the agreement and to employ peaceful means to resolve the Middle East dispute. Egypt was pledged to the continuance of the accord until it was superseded by another one.

■ The areas vacated by the Israeli forces would become an expanded new United Nations Emergency Force buffer zone, except for a small strip south of Suez city, where the Egyptian army would move in. UNEF's mandate would be renewed annually. The Israeli and Egyptian zones on each side of the UNEF strip would be limited to 8,000 men, 75 tanks and 60 artillery pieces. There would be a ban on weapons that could reach the other side's lines and a restriction on antiaircraft missiles.

■ A U.S. civilian force of no more than 200 men would have control of the early-warning systems in the Mitla and Gidi passes in the U.N. buffer strip. Israel and Egypt would operate their own observation stations, each manned by no more than 250 men, with U.S. civilians posted there to verify that they were being used only for surveillance purposes. The U.S. technicians also would operate three manned stations and three unmanned ones in the passes to report any movement in the area by armed forces not attached to UNEF. The Americans would be armed with light weapons for self-defense.

■ A joint Israel-Egyptian commission would be established to "consider problems arising" from the agreement and would meet under UNEF sponsorship.

The treaty was composed of three documents with 14 accompanying maps that were made public and a fourth unpublished memorandum of understanding between the U.S. and Israel, which was said to deal largely with American pledges of financial, political and arms aid to Israel and reportedly contained private Egyptian assurances such as UNEF mandate renewals. The three published documents dealt with the Israeli-Egyptian military and political accords, an annex covering the terms of reference for the Israeli-Egyptian working groups that would meet in Geneva five days after signing to arrange for the accord's implementation and a tripartite agreement between Israel, Egypt and the U.S. concerning the American presence in the Sinai.

The accord was signed in Geneva by Mordechai Gazit, Israel's ambassador-designate to France, Major Gen. Herzl Shafir, chief of the Israeli army's general staff branch, Egyptian Maj. Gen. Taha el Magdoub and Ahmed Osman, head of Cairo's delegation to the U.N. office in Geneva.

The part of the pact dealing with the U.S. surveillance group was signed in separate ceremonies by Kissinger and Premier Yitzhak Rabin in Jerusalem and by Kissinger and Egyptian Premier Mamdouh Salem in Alexandria.

As co-chairmen of the Geneva peace conference, the U.S. and the Soviet Union were expected to attend the signing ceremonies but their representatives stayed away. The Soviet boycott reportedly was based on Moscow's annoyance over having been left out of the recent negotiations and its opposition to the stationing of the U.S. technicians in the Sinai. U.S. Assistant Secretary of State Alfred L. Atherton Jr. had arranged to attend the ceremonies but decided to cancel his plans after the Soviet decision, apparently to avoid embarrassing the Russians.

The accord had been previously initialed when first publicly announced Sept. 1, in Jerusalem by Avraham Kidron, director general of Israel's Foreign Ministry, and Gen. Mordechai Gur, chief of staff; and in Alexandria by Gen. Mohammed Aly Fahmy, Egyptian chief of staff, and Ahmed Osman.

Kissinger returned to Washington Sept. 3 after visiting Saudi Arabia, Jordan and Syria Sept. 2–3 to brief their leaders on the agreement. The Saudis gave their endorsement in a meeting with the secretary Sept. 2. Foreign Minister Prince Saud said his government viewed the accord as "a step toward a final settlement." Kissinger was said to have received a cool reception from King Hussein in his meeting with the Jordanian monarch in Amman Sept. 3. Hussein, upset over U.S. congressional refusal to permit him to purchase U.S. missiles, gave his qualified approval, saying he hoped the accord would be followed by similar Israeli agreements with Jordan and Syria. Kissinger stopped off in Damascus later Sept. 3 to confer with Syrian President Hafez al-Assad.

President Gerald R. Ford had hailed the agreement in telephone conversations Sept. 1 with President Sadat and Premier Rabin, and extended congratulations to Kissinger "on a great achievement." Ford assured the two leaders that he would press for congressional approval of the posting of the U.S. monitors in the Sinai. Failure to assign the American technicians there would "have a very serious impact" on efforts to achieve a broad peace agreement, he said.

Sadat scores Russians, Arab critics—President Anwar Sadat Sept. 4 assailed the Soviet Union for absenting itself from the signing of the Israeli-Egyptian pact in Geneva and the Syrians and other Arabs for criticizing his decision to enter into another interim agreement with Israel.

Addressing the National Assembly and the central committee of the Arab Socialist Union, Egypt's only political party, Sadat asserted that the Soviet boycott of the Geneva ceremonies was a "flagrant incitement and an attempt at splitting the ranks of the Arab nation." The president disclosed that Moscow's decision had been transmitted earlier Sept. 4 by its ambassador to Syrian Foreign Minister Abdel Halim Khaddam, who in turn gave him a copy of a statement of the ruling Baath Party terming the agreement an "Arab defeat."

Sadat deplored an anti-Egyptian demonstration in Damascus that followed the Soviet-Syrian exchange. He also complained of a statement issued that day by Iraq's ruling Baath Party charging that Egypt "had clearly expressed its readiness to sign a peace treaty with the enemy." Sadat replied to this by saying, "if we want to conclude a peace treaty with Israel, we have enough courage to face our nation and say so."

Sadat expressed anger at President Hafez, al-Assad's refusal to receive Egyptian Vice President Husni Mubarak when he had flown to Damascus Sept. 2 with all the documents to explain the agreement to the Syrians.

In further defense of the agreement, Sadat declared that during the negotiations Egypt "never for a moment forgot the cause of the people of Palestine and the need to realize a second disengagement on the Syrian front." He said that in his telephone conversation with President Ford [see above] he reminded the President "that there could be no peace at this stage unless a second disengagement on the Syrian front took place and a dialogue started" between the U.S. and the Palestine Liberation Organization.

Israeli Parliament approves pact—The Israeli Parliament Sept. 3 had approved the interim agreement with Egypt by a 70–43 vote after nine hours of debate. Former Defense Minister Moshe Dayan and two other Labor Party deputies and two deputies of the National Religious Party joined the 38-member right-wing opposition Likud bloc in casting negative votes. Dayan said Israel should not have given up the Sinai passes for anything less than a formal Egyptian declaration of nonbelligerency.

The Labor Party had approved the agreement in a special caucus Sept. 2 by a 370–4 vote with four abstentions; Dayan abstained.

Arabs, Russians assail pact—The Israeli-Egyptian agreement was assailed by the Palestinian leadership and other Arabs and sharply criticized by the Soviet Union.

The Soviet Communist Party newspaper Pravda Aug. 30 criticized the projected stationing of American observers in the Sinai as a "new complicating element" when the United Nations already had an "effective monitoring system" in the region. "Why should the system agreed upon be broken and an existing international mechanism be replaced by the unilateral control of only one of the powers, whose pro-Israeli position is no secret to anyone?" the newspaper asked. Pravda also cautioned that the proposed Israeli pullback in the Sinai was "a partial agreement of limited significance that not only does not replace a political settlement in the Middle East but also does not bring one nearer."

Palestine Liberation Organization leader Yasir Arafat Aug. 31 denounced the American role in arranging the accord, charging that its aims "were to divide the Arab ranks and exploit the time for Israel and strike the Palestinian resistance."

Arafat charged Sept. 1 that the agreement was "an imperialist plot to liquidate the Palestine cause" and "would collapse upon the unshaken will of the Palestinian people." He appealed to

Arabs to "fight off the American presence" in the Middle East.

Libyan leader Muammar al-Qaddafi Sept. 1 assailed the agreement and pledged that his government would "give its unlimited support to restore the usurped land to the Palestinians." "The struggle," he said, "never was settled by agreement, and it never will be."

Denouncing the pact as "strange and shameful," Syria's ruling Baath Socialist Party newspaper Sept. 5 accused President Anwar Sadat of "sacrificing the blood of thousands of martyrs" who died in the 1973 Arab-Israeli war. Sadat's willingness to resolve the Middle East conflict by "peaceful means" had resulted in an accord "without attaining any real geographic or political gains." the newspaper said.

The head of the Palestine Liberation Organization's military department, Zahir Mohsen, Sept. 5 called Sadat a "traitor and conspirator" and vowed an all-out drive against his government.

A PLO statement issued in Beirut Sept. 6 scored the agreement as "a plot to liquidate the Palestinian cause" and urged Arabs, particularly in Egypt, to block the pact.

George Habash, leader of the Popular Front for the Liberation of Palestine, warned Syria Sept. 9 against entering into negotiations with Israel over troop disengagement on the Golan Heights. Habash also reiterated his opposition to PLO leader Yasir Arafat's possible intentions to negotiate with Israel on establishment of a Palestinian state in some of the areas occupied by Israel. The PFLP, he said, "will never go to Geneva" to discuss this matter.

Ford seeks quick approval by Congress. President Ford and Secretary Kissinger sought quick sanction of the pact by Congress. The immediate reaction in Congress was, in general, favorable to eventual approval although there was concern, uneasiness even, over the commitment to put Americans in Sinai to monitor the peace.

The most important outright opposition to the agreement came from Senate Democratic leader Mike Mansfield (Mont.), who objected to the U.S. monitoring role. "I don't believe we should act as a buffer which will get us involved in another conflict," he said Aug. 29. "We cannot be the policemen of the world."

The President sent a letter to both houses of Congress Sept. 3 requesting formal approval of the Middle East accord. The next day, 16 leaders from both houses and both parties gathered at the White House for a briefing by the President and Kissinger. Later Sept. 4, Kissinger attended a 2½-hour closed hearing of the Senate Foreign Relations committee.

It was reported that the Administration had requested that Congress approve the stationing of Americans in Sinai within two and a half weeks, that the issue had been linked in the negotiations to withdrawals of Israeli troops from advance positions, and that, therefore, the accord could not go into effect until this were done.

White House press secretary Ron Nessen quoted the President as having told the congressional delegation that the Sinai role for Americans was "a gamble for peace" and "a risk I'm willing to take." He stressed the point that there would be no more than 200 technicians involved, Nessen said, and these would be stationed in the United Nations buffer zone between the two armies. He pointed out, Nessen reported, that the idea for the U.S. presence had originated independently from both sides at different times.

On the aid commitment, Nessen quoted Ford as having told the members, "when you look at the need for stability and the cost of another war, this is a good investment."

Some details of the aid agreement emerged from the congressional hearing. The total was about $3 billion for one year, of which $2.1 billion to $2.3 billion was intended for Israel, of which $1.5 billion would be in military aid; $650 million was intended for Egypt, all of it in economic assistance.

Nessen quoted Kissinger as having assured the members of Congress that the monitoring provision essentially removed the threat of surprise attack and that "we do not guarantee the agreement; we have no role to enforce the agreement."

The American presence drew the most immediate comment from Congress. Sen.

John C. Stennis (D, Miss.), chairman of the Senate Armed Services Committee, said Sept. 3 he was "queasy" about the provision. House Speaker Carl Albert said Sept. 3 it evoked "shadows" of the first U.S. military advisers sent to South Vietnam long ago.

Sen. Henry M. Jackson (D, Wash.), who reserved judgment on the accord, did express concern Sept. 2 that the Russians would demand a parallel role and that that could result in the "stationing of Russian troops and American troops face to face" in circumstances permitting "no flexibility."

Israel, Egypt start Sinai talks. Israeli and Egyptian representatives opened discussions in Geneva Sept. 9 on the technical details of implementing the Sinai troop disengagement agreement signed the previous week. Gen. Ensio Siilasvuo, commander of the United Nations Emergency Force, was serving as chairman of the talks.

Israeli Defense Minister Shimon Peres asserted in Jerusalem Sept. 9 that Israel had begun to dismantle its fortifications in the Sinai and would meet the required five-month deadline for deploying its forces to a new defense line to the east.

Texts of the Sept. 4, 1975 Egyptian Israeli Accord

The texts of the Egyptian-Israeli agreement on disengagement in the Sinai, the United States proposal for an early-warning system in the Sinai, and the annex to the Egyptian-Israeli agreement.

Egyptian-Israeli Accord on Sinai

The Government of the Arab Republic of Egypt and the Government of Israel have agreed that:

ARTICLE I

The conflict between them and in the Middle East shall not be resolved by military force but by peaceful means.

The agreement concluded by the parties Jan. 18, 1974, within the framework of the Geneva peace conference, constituted a first step towards a just and durable peace according to the provisions of Security Council Resolution 338 of Oct. 22, 1973; and they are determined to reach a final and just peace settlement by means of negotiations called for by Security Council Resolution 338, this agreement being a significant step towards that end.

ARTICLE II

The parties hereby undertake not to resort to the threat or use of force or military blockade against each other.

ARTICLE III

(1) The parties shall continue scrupulously to observe the cease-fire on land, sea and air and to refrain from all military or paramilitary actions against each other.

(2) The parties also confirm that the obligations contained in the annex and, when concluded, the protocol, shall be an integral part of this agreement.

ARTICLE IV

A. The military forces of the parties shall be deployed in accordance with the following principles:

(1) All Israeli forces shall be deployed east of the lines designated as lines J and M on the attached map.

(2) All Egyptian forces shall be deployed west of the line designated as line E on the attached map.

(3) The area between the lines designated on the attached map as lines E and F and the area between the lines designated on the attached map as lines J and K shall be limited in armament and forces.

(4) The limitations on armament and forces in the areas described by paragraph (3) above shall be agreed as described in the attached annex.

(5) The zone between the lines designated on the attached map as lines E and J will be a buffer zone. On this zone the United Nations Emergency Force will continue to perform its functions as under the Egyptian-Israeli agreement of Jan. 18, 1974.

(6) In the area south from line E and west from line M, as defined in the attached map, there will be no military forces, as specified in the attached annex.

B. The details concerning the new lines, the redeployment of the forces and its timing, the limitation of armaments and forces, aerial reconnaissance, the operation of the early warning and surveillance installations and the use of the roads, the U.N. functions and other arrangements will all be in accordance with the provisions of the annex and map which are an integral part of this agreement and of the protocol which is to result from negotiations pursuant to the annex and which, when concluded, shall become an integral part of this agreement.

ARTICLE V

The United Nations Emergency Force is essential and shall continue its functions, and its mandate shall be extended annually.

ARTICLE VI

The parties hereby establish a joint commission for the duration of this agreement. It will function under the aegis of the chief coordinator of the United Nations peace-keeping missions in the Middle East in order to consider any problem arising from this agreement and to assist the United Nations Emergency Force in the execution of its mandate. The joint commission shall function in accordance with procedures established in the protocol.

ARTICLE VII

Nonmilitary cargoes destined for or coming from Israel shall be permitted through the Suez Canal.

ARTICLE VIII

(1) This agreement is regarded by the parties as a significant step toward a just and lasting peace. It is not a final peace agreement.

(2) The parties shall continue their efforts to negotiate a final peace agreement within the framework of the Geneva peace conference in accordance with Security Council Resolution 338.

ARTICLE IX

This agreement shall enter into force upon signature of the protocol and remain in force until superseded by a new agreement.

U.S. Proposal for Early-Warning System in Sinai

In connection with the early-warning system referred to in Article IV of the agreement between Egypt and Israel concluded on this date and as an integral part of that agreement (hereafter referred to as the basic agreement), the United States proposes the following:

[1]

The early-warning system to be established in accordance with Article IV in the area shown on the attached map will be entrusted to the United States. It shall have the following elements:

A. There shall be two surveillance stations to provide strategic early warning, one operated by Egyptian and one operated by Israeli personnel. Their locations are shown on the map attached to the basic agreement. Each station shall be manned by not more than 250 technical and administrative personnel. They shall perform the functions of visual and electronic surveillance only within their stations.

B. In support of these stations, to provide tactical early warning and to verify access to them, three watch stations shall be established by the United States in the Mitla and Gidi passes as will be shown on the agreed map.

These stations shall be operated by United States civilian personnel. In support of these stations, there shall be established three unmanned electronic-sensor fields at both ends of each pass and in the general vicinity of each station and the roads leading to and from those stations.

[2]

The United States civilian personnel shall perform the following duties in connection with the operation and maintenance of these stations:

A. At the two surveillance stations described in paragraph 1A, above, United States personnel will verify the nature of the operations of the stations and all movement into and out of each station and will immediately report any detected divergency from its authorized role of visual and electronic surveillance to the parties to the basic agreement and the UNEF.

B. At each watch station described in paragraph 1B above, the United States personnel will immediately report to the parties to the basic agreement and to UNEF any movement of armed forces, other than the UNEF, into either pass and any observed preparations for such movement.

C. The total number of United States civilian personnel assigned to functions under these proposals shall not exceed 200. Only civilian personnel shall be assigned to functions under these proposals.

[3]

No arms shall be maintained at the stations and other facilities covered by these proposals, except for small arms required for their protection.

[4]

The United States personnel serving the early-warning system shall be allowed to move freely within the area of the system.

[5]

The United States and its personnel shall be entitled to have such support facilities as are reasonably necessary to perform their functions.

[6]

The United States personnel shall be immune from local criminal, civil, tax and customs jurisdiction and may be accorded any other specific privileges and immunities provided for in the UNEF agreement of Feb. 13, 1957.

[7]

The United States affirms that it will continue to perform the functions described above for the duration of the basic agreement.

[8]

Notwithstanding any other provision of these proposals, the United States may withdraw its personnel only if it concludes that their safety is jeopardized or that continuation of their role is no longer necessary. In the latter case the parties to the basic agreement will be informed in advance in order to give them the opportunity to make alternative arrangements. If both parties to the basic agreement request the United States to conclude its role under this proposal, the United States will consider such requests conclusive.

[9]

Technical problems including the location of the watch stations will be worked out through consultation with the United States.

Annex to the Sinai Agreement

Within five days after the signature of the Egypt-Israel agreement, representatives of the two parties shall meet in the military working group of the Middle East peace conference at Geneva to begin preparation of a detailed protocol for the implementation of the agreement. In order to facilitate preparation of the protocol and implementation of the agreement, and to assist in maintaining the scrupulous observance of the cease-fire and other elements of the agreement, the two parties have agreed on the following principles, which are an integral part of the agreement, as guidelines for the working group.

1. Definitions of Lines and Areas

The deployment lines, areas of limited forces and armaments, buffer zones, the area south from line E and west from line M, other designated areas, road sections for common use and other features referred to in Article IV of the agreement shall be as indicated on the attached map (1:100,000—U.S. edition).

2. Buffer Zones

(a) Access to the buffer zones shall be controlled by the UNEF, according to procedures to be worked out by the working group and UNEF.

(b) Aircraft of either party will be permitted to fly freely up to the forward line of that party. Reconnaissance aircraft of either party may fly up to the middle line of the buffer zone between E and J on an agreed schedule.

(c) In the buffer zone, between line E and J, there will be established under Article IV of the agreement an early-warning system entrusted to United States civilian personnel as detailed in a separate proposal, which is a part of this agreement.

(d) Authorized personnel shall have access to the buffer zone for transit to and from the early-warning system; the manner in which this is carried out shall be worked out by the working group and UNEF.

3. Area South of Line E
and West of Line M

(a) In this area, the United Nations Emergency Force will assure that there are no military or paramilitary forces of any kind, military fortifications and military installations; it will establish checkpoints and have the freedom of movement necessary to perform this function.

(b) Egyptian civilians and third-country civilian oilfield personnel shall have the right to enter, exit from, work and live in the above-indicated area, except for buffer zones 2A, 2B and the U.N. posts. Egyptian civilian police shall be allowed in the area to perform normal civil police functions among the civilian population in such numbers and with such weapons and equipment as shall be provided for in the protocol.

(c) Entry to and exit from the area, by land, by air or by sea, shall be only through UNEF checkpoints. UNEF shall also establish checkpoints along the road, the dividing line and at other points, with the precise locations and number to be included in the protocol.

(d) Access to the airspace and the coastal area shall be limited to unarmed Egyptian civilian vessels and unarmed civilian helicopters and transport planes involved in the civilian activities of the area, as agreed by the working group.

(e) Israel undertakes to leave intact all currently existing civilian installations and infrastructures.

(f) Procedures for use of the common sections of the coastal road along the Gulf of Suez shall be determined by the working group and detailed in the protocol.

4. Aerial Surveillance

There shall be a continuation of aerial reconnaissance missions by the U.S. over the areas covered by the agreement following the same procedures already in practice. The missions will ordinarily be carried out at a frequency of one mission every seven to 10 days, with either party or UNEF empowered to request an earlier mission. The U.S. will make the mission results available expeditiously to Israel, Egypt and the chief coordinator of the U.N. peacekeeping mission in the Middle East.

5. Limitation of Forces
and Armaments

(a) Within the areas of limited forces and armaments the major limitations shall be as follows:

(1) Eight (8) standard infantry battalions.

(2) Seventy-five (75) tanks.

(3) Sixty (60) artillery pieces, including heavy mortars (i.e., with caliber larger than 120 mm.), whose range shall not exceed twelve (12) km.

(4) The total number of personnel shall not exceed eight thousand (8,000).

(5) Both parties agree not to station or locate in the area weapons which can reach the line of the other side.

(6) Both parties agree that in the areas between lines J and K, and between line A (of the disengagement agreement of Jan. 18, 1974) and line E, they will construct no new fortifications or installations for forces of a size greater than that agreed herein.

(b) The major limitations beyond the areas of limited forces and armament will be:

(1) Neither side will station nor locate any weapon in areas from which they can reach the other line.

(2) The parties will not place antiaircraft missiles within an area of 10 kilometers east of line K and west of line F, respectively.

(c) The U.N. Force will conduct inspections in order to insure the maintenance of the agreed limitations within these areas.

6. Process of Implementation

The detailed implementation and timing of the redeployment of forces, turnover of oil fields and other arrangements called for by the agreement, annex and protocol shall be determined by the working group, which will agree on the stages of this process, including the phased movement of Egyptian troops to line E and Israeli troops to line J. The first phase will be the transfer of the oil fields and installations to Egypt. This process will begin within two weeks from the signature of the protocol with the introduction of the necessary technicians, and it will be completed no later than eight weeks after it begins. The details of the phasing will be worked out in the military working group.

Implementation of the redeployment shall be completed within five months after signature of the protocol.

Additional Documents

Sinai pact documents made public. The U.S. had pledged to provide Israel with military and economic assistance on "an on-going and long-term basis" and promised Egypt that it would press for "further negotiations between Syria and Israel," according to three hitherto secret documents of the Sinai accord made public Sept. 16, 1975.

The U.S. policy position on Israel was contained in a 16-point Memorandum and an Addendum on Arms. In the latter document, the U.S. promised Israel, subject to congressional approval, specific military equipment, including the F-16 fighter plane, and said it would consider "a joint study of high technology and sophisticated items, including the Pershing ground-to-ground missiles with conventional warheads." The third text, Assurances to Egypt, dealing with the projected Israeli-Syrian negotiations, also contained two other points: a pledge of U.S. consultation with Egypt in the event of an Israeli truce violation and a promise of American "technical assistance to Egypt for the Egyptian early-warning system in the Sinai."

Among the other points of the Memorandum: The U.S. and Israel would hold periodic meetings to consider Israel's "long-term military supply needs"; the U.S. was prepared to assist Israel if Israel encountered any difficulties in acquiring alternate oil supplies in view of its relinquishment of the Abu Rudeis oilfields in the Sinai; the U.S. would not expect Israel to implement the agreement until Cairo fulfilled its pledge made in the 1974 disengagement accord and in the present one to permit Israeli cargo to pass through the Suez Canal; the U.S. would consult with Israel on any Egyptian violation of the agreement; in light of the U.S.' longstanding "commitment to the survival and security of Israel," it would "view with particular gravity threats to Israel's security and sovereignty by a world power"; the U.S. regarded the Bab el Mandeb and the Strait of Gibraltar as international waterways and would support Israel's right to their use; and the U.S. and Israel agreed, with Egypt concurring, that the accord would not go into effect until the U.S. Congress approved the stationing of an American surveillance team in the Sinai.

U.S.-Israeli memorandum on Geneva— Another unpublished memorandum between the U.S. and Israel, dealing with the Geneva peace conference, was made public Sept. 17. In the document, signed by Secretary of State Henry A. Kissinger and Foreign Minister Yigal Allon in Israel, the U.S. reaffirmed its refusal to recognize or negotiate with the Palestine Liberation Organization until the PLO recognized Israel's right to exist and accepted United Nations Security Council resolutions 242 and 338 ending the 1967 and 1973 Arab-Israeli wars.

The U.S. pledged to consult with Israel to coordinate joint strategy on future Geneva sessions and to consider the inclusion of additional states at the conference. "It was understood" that the original members of the parley had a veto on future participants, the document said.

The U.S. also pledged "to make every effort" to insure that further talks at Geneva would deal with substantive issues that would advance a negotiated peace between Israel and the Arab states.

Texts of additional documents. These are the texts of hitherto-secret documents relating to the Sinai agreement among the U.S., Egypt and Israel. The first three were made public Sept. 16, the fourth Sept. 17.

Agreement Between U.S. and Israel

The United States recognizes that the Egypt-Israel Agreement initialed on Sept. 1, 1975 (hereinafter referred to as the agreement), entailing the withdrawal from vital areas in Sinai, constitutes an act of great significance on Israel's part in the pursuit of final peace. That agreement has full United States support.

[1]

The United States Government will make every effort to be fully responsive, within the limits of its resources and Congressional authorization and appropriation, on an on-going and long-term basis, to Israel's military equipment and other defense requirements, to its energy requirements and to its economic needs. The needs specified in paragraphs 2, 3 and 4 below shall be deemed eligible for inclusion within the annual total to be requested in FY '76 and later fiscal years.

[2]

Israel's long-term military supply needs from the United States shall be the subject of periodic consultations between representatives of the U.S. and Israeli defense establishments, with agreement reached on specific items to be included in a separate U.S.-Israeli memorandum. To this end, a joint study by military experts will be undertaken within three weeks. In conducting this study, which will include Israel's 1976 needs, the United States will view Israel's requests sympathetically, including its request for advanced and sophisticated weapons.

[3]

Israel will make its own independent arrangements for oil supply to meet its requirements through normal procedures. In the event Israel is unable to secure its needs in this way, the United States Government, upon notification of this fact by the Government of Israel, will act as follows for five years, at the end of which period either side can terminate this arrangement on one year's notice.

(a) If the oil Israel needs to meet all its normal requirements for domestic consumption is unavailable for purchase in circumstances where no quantitative restrictions exist on the ability of the United States to procure oil to meet its normal requirements, the United States Government will promptly make oil available for purchase by Israel to meet all of the aforementioned normal requirements of Israel. If Israel is unable to secure the necessary means to transport such oil to Israel, the United States Government will make every effort to help Israel secure the necessary means of transport.

(b) If the oil Israel needs to meet all of its normal requirements for domestic consumption is unavailable for purchase in circumstances where quantitative restrictions through embargo or otherwise also prevent the United States from procuring oil to meet its normal requirements, the United States Government will promptly make oil available for purchase by Israel in accordance with the International Energy Agency conservation and allocation formula as applied by the United States Government, in order to meet Israel's essential requirements. If Israel is unable to secure the necessary means to transport such oil to Israel, the United States Government will make every effort to help Israel secure the necessary mean of transport.

Israeli and U.S. experts will meet annually or more frequently at the request of either party, to review Israel's continuing oil requirement.

[4]

In order to help Israel meet its energy needs, and as part of the over-all annual figure in paragraph 1 above, the United States agrees:

'(a) In determining the overall annual figure which will be requested from Congress, the United States Government will give special attention to Israel's oil import requirements and, for a period as determined by Article 3 above, will take into account in calculating that figure Israel's additional expenditures for the import of oil to replace that which would have ordinarily come from Abu Rudeis and Ras Sudar (4.5 million tons in 1975).

(b) To ask Congress to make available funds, the amount to be determined by mutual agreement, to the Government of Israel necessary for a project for the construction and stocking of the oil reserves to be stored in Israel, bringing storage reserve capacity and reserve stocks, now standing at approximately six months, up to one year's need at the time of the completion of the project. The project will be implemented within four years. The construction, operation and financing and other relevant questions of the project will be the subject of early and detailed talks between the two Governments.

[5]

The United States Government will not expect Israel to begin to implement the agreement before Egypt fulfills its undertaking under the January, 1974, disengagement agreement to permit passage of all Israeli cargoes to and from Israeli ports through the Suez Canal.

[6]

The United States Government agrees with Israel that the next agreement with Egypt should be a final peace agreement.

[7]

In case of an Egyptian violation of any of the provisions of the agreement, the United States Government is prepared to consult with Israel as to the significance of the violation and possible remedial action by the United States Government.

[8]

The United States Government will vote against any Security Council resolution which in its judgment affects or alters adversely the agreement.

[9]

The United States Government will not join in and will seek to prevent efforts by others to bring about consideration of proposals which it and Israel agree are detrimental to the interests of Israel.

[10]

In view of the long-standing U.S. commitment to the survival and security of Israel, the United States Government will view with particular gravity threats to Israel's security or sovereignty by a world power. In support of this objective, the United States Government will in the event of such threat consult promptly with the Government of Israel with respect to what support diplomatic or otherwise, or assistance it can lend to Israel in accordance with its constitutional practices.

[11]

The United States Government and the Government of Israel will, at the earliest possible time, and if possible within two months after the signature of this document, conclude the contingency plan for a military supply operation to Israel in an emergency situation.

[12]

It is the United States Government's position that Egyptian commitments under the Egypt-Israel agreement, its implementation, validity and duration are not conditional upon any act or developments between the other Arab states and Israel. The United States Government regards the agreement as standing on its own.

[13]

The United States Government shares the Israeli position that under existing political circumstances negotiations with Jordan will be directed toward an over-all peace settlement.

[14]

In accordance with the principle of freedom of navigation on the high seas and free and unimpeded passage through and over straits connecting international waters, the United States Government regards and Straits of Bab el Mandeb and the Strait of Gibraltar as international waterways. It will support Israel's right to free and unimpeded passage through such straits. Similarly, the United States Government recognizes Israel's right to freedom of flights over the Red Sea and such straits and will support diplomatically the exercise of that right.

[15]

In the event that the United Nations Emergency Force or any other United Nations organ is withdrawn without the prior agreement of both parties to the Egypt-Israel agreement and the United States before this agreement is superseded by another agreement, it is the United States view that the agreement shall remain binding in all its parts.

[16]

The United States and Israel agree that signature of the protocol of the Egypt-Israel agreement and its full entry into effect shall not take place before approval by the United States Congress of the U.S. role in connection with the surveillance and observation functions described in the agreement and its annex. The United States has informed the Government of Israel that it has obtained the Government of Egypt agreement to the above.

Addendum on Arms to Israel

On the question of military and economic assistance to Israel, the following conveyed by the U.S. to Israel augments what the memorandum of agreement states.

The United States is resolved to continue to maintain Israel's defensive strength through the supply of advanced types of equipment, such as the F-16 aircraft. The United States Government agrees to an early meeting to undertake a joint study of high technology and sophisticated items, including the Pershing ground-to-ground missiles with conventional warheads, with the view to giving a positive response. The U.S. Administration will submit annually for approval by the U.S. Congress a request for military and economic assistance in order to help meet Israel's economic and military needs.

Assurances
to Egypt

1. The United States intends to make a serious effort to help bring about further negotiations between Syria and Israel, in the first instance through diplomatic channels.

2. In the event of an Israeli violation of the agreement, the United States is prepared to consult with Egypt as to the significance of the violation and possible remedial action by the United States.

3. The United States will provide technical assistance to Egypt for the Egyptian early-warning station.

U.S.-Israel Agreement
on Geneva

The following, released Sept. 17, is a memorandum of agreement between the United States and Israel on the Geneva peace conference.

1. The Geneva peace conference will be reconvened at a time coordinated between the United States and Israel.

2. The United States will continue to adhere to its present policy with respect to the Palestine Liberation Organization, whereby it will not recognize or negotiate with the Palestine Liberation Organization so long as the Palestine Liberation Organization does not recognize Israel's right to exist and does not accept Security Council Resolutions 242 and 338. The United States Government will consult fully and seek to concert its position and strategy at the Geneva peace conference on this issue with the Government of Israel. Similarly, the United States will consult fully and seek to concert its position and strategy with Israel with regard to the participation of any other additional states. It is understood that the participation at a subsequent phase of the conference of any possible additional state, group or organization will require the agreement of all the initial participants.

3. The United States will make every effort to insure at the conference that all the substantive negotiations will be on a bilateral basis.

4. The United States will oppose and, if necessary, vote against any initiative in the Security Council to alter adversely the terms of reference of the Geneva peace conference or to change Resolutions 242 and 338 in ways which are incompatible with their original purpose.

5. The United States will seek to insure that the role of the co-sponsors will be consistent with what was agreed in the memorandum of understanding between the United States Government and the Government of Israel of Dec. 20, 1972.

6. The United States and Israel will concert action to assure that the conference will be conducted in a manner consonant with the objectives of this document and with the declared purpose of the conference, namely the advancement of a negotiated peace between Israel and its neighbors.

'Secret' U.S.-Egyptian agreement. During a visit to Kuwait Feb. 27–29, 1976, Egyptian President Anwar Sadat revealed another three-point "secret agreement"

with the U.S. as part of the Sinai accords signed in September 1975. According to Sadat: The U.S. guaranteed that "Israel will not attack Syria"; the U.S. pledged "to bring about a disengagement similar to the first disengagement on the Syrian front after the conclusion of the second disengagement agreement on the Egyptian front"; and the U.S. promised "to do all it can to insure participation of the Palestinians in any peace settlement."

Sadat did not say whether the alleged accords were written or oral, or how binding they were. He said he was disclosing them for the first time in an obvious effort to refute Syrian charges that the Sinai agreements served only Egypt's interests and that it showed Egypt was withdrawing from the confrontation with Israel.

The reputed American guarantees cited by Sadat had not been aired during the 1975 U.S. Congressional hearings on the U.S. role in the Sinai accord. A state department official March 2 said of Sadat's statement: "All relevant agreements reached in conjunction with the Sinai agreement have been transmitted to committees of Congress concerned. I am unable to go beyond that."

Sadat also had said Feb. 27 that Secretary of State Henry A. Kissinger's step-by-step negotiations in the Middle East were "now over and new solutions must be found." The formula "must be in the presence of the Palestinians ... That is, we must reconvene the Geneva peace conference with the participants of all parties, including the Palestinians." The Geneva talks, Sadat insisted, were the only way of resolving the Middle East crisis because "the Palestinian cause, not the cause of Sinai and Golan, is the heart of the Arab cause."

Implementing the Accord

Israel & Egypt complete discussions. The Israeli-Egyptian talks on implementing the Sinai disengagement agreement ended in Geneva Sept. 23, 1975. Egypt signed but Israel initialed the protocol. The Israeli action thus delayed putting the accord into effect. The Israeli cabinet had decided Sept. 21 to postpone signing the protocol until the U.S. Congress voted to station American civilian technicians between the Egyptians and Israelis in the Sinai, as provided by Clause 16 of the memorandum of agreement between the U.S. and Israel.

The Israelis also had said they would not start enforcing the agreement until Egypt fulfilled its pledge to permit Israeli cargo to pass through the Suez Canal. A canal-bound Greek freighter carrying a Rumanian cargo of cement for Israel had been diverted to the Israeli port of Haifa instead, the Israeli radio had reported Sept. 19. Israeli newspapers said the U.S. had asked Israel to delay the test in order not to embarrass Egyptian President Anwar Sadat while he was still facing Arab criticism for his acceptance of the agreement with Israel.

Meanwhile, Israeli forces in the Sinai were reported Sept. 18 to be in an "advanced stage of evacuation" from their current lines even though the agreement requiring their pullback to new positions to the east was not yet official.

Israel signs protocol—Israel signed the protocol of the Sinai disengagement agreement with Egypt in ceremonies in Jerusalem Oct. 10. U.S. congressional approval that day of the stationing of 200 American technicians in the Sinai to operate the early-warning systems paved the way for formal Israeli approval of the documents implementing the accord.

At the Jerusalem ceremonies, held at the headquarters of Lt. Gen. Ensio Siilasvuo, chief coordinator of the United Nations peace-keeping forces in the Middle East, the protocol was signed by Avraham Kidron, director general of the Israeli Foreign Ministry, and Maj. Gen. Herzl Shafir, chief of the Israeli General Staff, operations branch. Siilasvuo signed as a witness.

A similar ceremony, with a U.N. representative in attendance, was held seven hours later at Ras Sudr in the Sinai, in which Israel signed a document turning over oil facilities there to the Egyptians, under terms of their agreement. Three American technicians from the Mobil Oil Corp., who were maintaining the facilities under contract to the Egyptian government, signed for Egypt.

The transfer of the Ras Sudr field, north of the larger field at Abu Rudeis, was among the 32 separate steps before the Israeli pullback to new lines by Feb. 22, 1976 was completed. Among other provisions of the protocol: Israeli troops were to withdraw from the Ras Sudr region by Nov. 15 and turn it over to the United Nations Emergency Force; subsequent Israeli withdrawals and the takeovers by UNEF or the Egyptians were to be staggered over a three-month period; the Israelis were to leave the Abu Rudeis field Nov. 30, and the Egyptians were to take control Dec. 1; civilian and military personnel were to have access to evacuated areas; Israel and Egypt were to use certain roads along the Gulf of Suez; and about 700 Egyptian civilian policemen were to be stationed along the gulf coast.

U.S. observers in Sinai approved. President Ford Oct. 13 signed a U.S. Congressional resolution authorizing the stationing of up to 200 U.S. civilian technicians in the Sinai Desert to monitor the Israeli-Egyptian disengagement accord.

In signing the resolution, Ford called the agreement between Israel and Egypt "a significant step toward an overall settlement in the Middle East," but he added that none of the nations involved saw the accord "as an end in itself." There remained, the President said, "a pressing need for a just settlement of the problems which underlie the tension and instability in that part of the world." Toward that end, the U.S. must continue its diplomatic efforts to "sustain the momentum toward peace generated by the Sinai agreement," Ford stated.

The Senate had approved the resolution Oct. 9 on a vote of 70–18. Identical to that endorsed by the House Oct. 8, the resolution required that the technicians be withdrawn in the event of renewed Israeli-Egyptian hostilities or if Congress determined that their safety was endangered. The President was required to submit to Congress a report every six months on the prospect for ending or reducing the presence of the technicians.

A major opponent of the measure, Majority Leader Mike Mansfield (D, Mont.), warned colleagues supporting the resolution that they might be making the same "mistake" he said they made in 1964 when they endorsed the Gulf of Tonkin Resolution approving U.S. military action in Vietnam.

Israelis, Egyptians meet in Sinai. The joint Israeli-Egyptian commission for carrying out the Sinai agreement held its first session Oct. 22, 1975. On Egypt's insistence, only military members of the commission met. The Israeli delegation headed by Maj. Gen. Herzl Shafir and the Egyptian group led by Maj. Gen. Taha el Magdoub met for five hours at United Nations Post 512 in the U.N. buffer zone in the northern Sinai to start discussions on preparations for an Israeli pullback to new lines. The meeting was under the chairmanship of Gen. Ensio Siilasvuo, coordinator of the U.N. forces in the Middle East.

Israel gives up oilfields. Israel completed evacuation of the oilfield at Ras Sudr in the Sinai and turned it over to the United Nations Emergency Force Nov. 14, 1975. Israel then surrendered the Abu Rudeis oilfield Nov. 30. This action completed the Israeli withdrawal from a 90-mile-long coastal strip on the gulf. United Nations officers and Italian technicians representing the Egyptian owners took over the oilfield. The Egyptians moved into the installations Dec. 1.

Disengagement completed. The final phase of the disengagement accord was implemented Feb. 22, 1976 as U.N. Emergency Forces handed over to the Egyptians the last 89 square miles of Sinai territory they were entitled to under terms of the pact. The action moved Egyptians eastward to an average of little less than 10 miles from the Suez Canal, along a line parallel to the waterway; Cairo also took military and civilian control of a narrow 95-mile strip along the east coast of the Gulf of Suez from Sudr to the Abu Rudeis oilfield.

The Israelis had completed their final pullback Feb. 20–21, following a series of other withdrawals earlier in February. UNEF men had moved into evacuated Israeli territory from a 100-mile strip one to three miles wide to a new zone ranging in width from 10–25 miles. A force of 250 Israelis remained west of their new lines to operate a radar station at Umm Khisheib, near the western end of the Gidi Pass, while the Egyptians were to build a similar facility near the eastern end of the pass.

The American surveillance posts in the Sinai became operational Feb. 21. They consisted of three manned watch stations and electronic-sensor stations at each end of the Mitla and Gidi passes.

Israeli Defense Minister Shimon Peres, who had visited the Sinai Feb. 19, hailed the final implementation of the pact as "the single most important step leading to the pacification of the area taken in the past 10 years."

Stations where Americans were to monitor Israeli-Egyptian Sinai pact.

Israeli cargo sails through canal. The Greek freighter Olympus bearing the first Israel-bound cargo to sail through the

Suez Canal since 1959 reached Israel's port of Eilat Nov. 3, 1975. The passage of the ship's cargo, 8,500 tons of cement from Rumania, was in conformity with the Israeli-Egyptian Sinai agreement that permitted nonstrategic cargo bound to and from Israel to pass through the waterway aboard ships of a third nation.

Egypt had opened the canal to Israeli cargo in 1952–53 and in 1957–59. The first ban had been dropped following United Nations approval of a resolution demanding freedom of passage in the canal to ships of all nations. Following the 1956 Sinai campaign, Israel had conditioned its withdrawal on permission to send its cargo through the waterway.

Soviet, Israeli ministers meet. Foreign Ministers Andrei Gromyko of the Soviet Union and Yigal Allon of Israel met for three hours at the Soviet Mission to the U.N. in New York Sept. 25, 1975. It was the highest-level contact between the two countries since Gromyko met Abba Eban, then foreign minister, in Geneva in December 1973.

An Israeli spokesman said Gromyko and Allon had discussed the Middle East as well as other topics. Their meeting had been arranged by Chaim Herzog, Israeli ambassador to the U.N., who suggested it to Soviet officials.

Another Israeli official said that Gromyko and Eban had agreed at their Geneva talks to hold similar meetings at "international occasions."

U.S. reaffirms Middle East role. Secretary of State Kissinger told representatives of 19 Arab countries Sept. 29, 1975 that the U.S. role in promoting a peace settlement and economic progress in the Middle East was "irrevocable" and "irreversible." Speaking at a dinner at the U.S. Mission to the United Nations in New York, Kissinger said, "The American people are conscious of this new approach and support it." He assured the Arabs that the U.S. Congress would ultimately approve the Ford Administration's proposal for nearly $3 billion in military and economic assistance to Egypt and Israel as an adjunct to the Sinai pact.

Although the U.S. was still involved in a step-by-step approach to peace, Kissinger expressed confidence that "at some point" this method "would merge with discussion of an over-all settlement."

Kissinger's diplomatic methods had come in for criticism Sept. 27 by Syrian President Hafez al-Assad. He charged that American foreign policy had three goals: "To strengthen Israel, to weaken the Arab nation and to divide it and to weaken or eliminate Soviet influence in the Middle East." This policy, Assad stressed, made "it difficult if not impossible to accomplish a just and lasting peace in the area."

Jordan urges Syrian support for accord. King Hussein of Jordan was said Sept. 28 to be interceding with Syrian President Assad to obtain his support for the Sinai agreement. Hussein was said to have visited Amman the previous week and urged Assad to accept the accord and concentrate on negotiations with Israel for the return of Arab lands occupied since 1967.

Jordan was said to have qualms about the Sinai pact and was particularly concerned about the possible sale of Pershing missiles to Israel. Information Minister Salah Abu Zeid was quoted as saying: "These weapons would put Israel in a position to dominate and threaten the whole area by remote control without actually conquering the territory."

An Arab League statement issued in New York Sept. 27 assailed the U.S. for promising to provide Israel with "a supply of further offensive weapons." This would "lead to consolidation of Israel's continued occupation of Arab territories and her continued denial of the national rights of the Palestinian people."

The league's permanent observer at the United Nations, Amin Hilmy of Egypt, said the U.S. could display its good faith and "evenhandedness" in the Middle East by supplying the Arabs "with the same weapons that it would send to Israel."

Arms Race Continues

U.S. ends Israel arms ban. Israeli government sources said Sept. 6, 1975 that, with the signing of the Sinai agreement, the U.S. had lifted its ban on long-term arms sales to Israel. The embargo had been imposed after U.S. failure to achieve a similar accord in March.

Following cancellation of the ban, the U.S. and Israel had resumed negotiations, with Israel particularly interested in the purchase of F-15 jet fighter planes, the Lance ground-to-ground missiles and laser-guided bombs.

Israel presses for U.S. missiles—Israel called on the U.S. Sept. 17 to provide it with Lance and Pershing missiles with the promise that it would arm the weapons with conventional, not nuclear warheads. The statement was made by Defense Minister Shimon Peres, who arrived in Washington for talks with Secretary of State Kissinger and Defense Secretary James R. Schlesinger on Israel's defense needs.

Speaking at the National Press Club, Peres said Israel needed the missiles to offset similar weapons the Soviet Union was providing Egypt, Syria and Libya. Israel, he said, was seeking only "a very small and limited number" of Pershings, and "I emphasize, without nuclear warheads, to create the necessary balance of deterrence to maintain peace in our area." (The Pershing had a 450-mile range, the Lance 60 miles.)

Secretary Kissinger emphasized at a news conference in Cincinnati Sept. 17 that in the U.S.-Israeli Memorandum disclosed the previous day the U.S. had not specifically commited itself to supply Israel with the Pershings, that it only agreed "to study the problem." At any rate, neither the Pershing nor the Lance missiles could "be delivered before the late '70s early '80s, and we're talking here about a long-term relationship and not about something that is going to happen tomorrow," Kissinger said.

Kissinger also warned that the U.S. would oppose any Soviet attempt to thwart the Israeli-Egyptian Sinai accord. He said the U.S. "seeks no special advantage in the Middle East" and was "prepared to consult all countries, including the Soviet Union, about the timing and substance of a reconvened Geneva conference."

Pentagon spokesman Joseph Laitin told a news briefing Sept. 19 that the State Department had not consulted the Pentagon beforehand about the secret U.S. assurances to Israel accompanying the Sinai disengagement agreement.

Kissinger Sept. 20 denied that he had failed to give the Pentagon prior notice about the proposed missile deal and said the department had known that Israel had submitted the request for the weapon and other arms in August 1974 during Premier Yitzhak Rabin's visit to Washington. Speaking to newsmen with Peres at his side, Kissinger said "the basic Israeli [arms] requirements" had been under consideration since August 1974 and "included all the essential items that are now under review, including the Pershing missiles." The secretary insisted that the missile was "not a new item submitted to us during negotiations" leading to the Sinai accord, and "its discussion should not be considered a payment [to Israel] for the negotiations."

The arms asked for by Israel in August 1974 "should be considered as part of a continuing relationship between Israel and the United States and not geared to any particular negotiations," Kissinger said.

Kissinger confirmed that as a result of talks he and Schlesinger had held with Peres earlier in the week agreement had been reached on lifting the American embargo of arms to Israel that had been in effect during the U.S.' reassessment of the Middle East situation. He did not specify the arms but they were known to include F-15 jets, Lance missiles and laser-guided bombs.

Schlesinger indicated Sept. 21 difficulties in meeting Israel's request for the Pershings. He said the production line for the Pershing-1a had closed down in June, and that "the cost of reopening the line would be greater than the benefits." Even if production were resumed soon, the missile could not be ready for delivery until 1978, the secretary said. He said he did not favor stripping Pershings from current U.S. inventories for delivery to Israel. A current model, the Pershing 2, was still under development.

Sadat warns U.S. on arms to Israel. Egyptian President Anwar Sadat warned the U.S. Oct. 18 against providing Israel with certain sophisticated weapons, saying that "this policy does not fit the new American role in the Middle East." This was a reference to the U.S. pledge to consider Israel's request for Pershing missiles.

Speaking to the opening fall session of the People's Assembly, Sadat said "escalation [of an arms buildup] by the other side will be met by escalation from our side, and the consequences of this must be obvious to all."

Defending Egypt's acceptance of the Sinai agreement with Israel, Sadat assured his Arab critics that his policy remained to get Israel to give up all occupied Arab territory and he renewed Cairo's pledge to obtain recognition of the Palestinians' "legitimate rights."

Sadat again cited what he called President Ford's pledge that the U.S. would "seek a second disengagement agreement on the Syrian front and take a step toward recognition of the rights of the Palestinians."

Israel to buy F-15s. The U.S. Defense Department informed Congress Dec. 10, 1975 that Israel would purchase F-15 jet fighters from the U.S. The number and price were not officially disclosed at Israel's request, but Congressional sources said the deal involved 25 of the advanced interceptors at a cost of $600 million.

Israel claimed it needed the F-15 to supplement the F-4 Phantom, the mainstay of its air force, to offset the Soviet MiG-23s in the Syrian and Egyptian air forces and the MiG-24 interceptors and reconnaissance aircraft flown by Soviet pilots in Syria; both MiGs were said to be superior to the F-4.

The F-15s were still in the production stage and would not be ready for delivery until 1977.

U.S. considers selling arms to Egypt. The U.S. was considering the sale of arms to Egypt to help President Anwar Sadat end his dependence on Soviet weapons, it was implied in statements made by President Ford Sept. 20, 1975 and the White House Sept. 26.

In a Los Angeles Times interview Sept. 20, Ford said the U.S. would "discuss with the Egyptians certain arms assistance for them. Our aid to them is under discussion and I would say there is to some extent an implied commitment." Sadat had taken "a very strong position"

that Egypt's national security would be threatened if Cairo did not get quick access to Western sources of arms, according to Ford.

The U.S. had imposed a virtual arms embargo on Egypt since 1950 because it was Israel's principal military adversary in four wars.

The White House statement Sept. 26 reaffirmed Ford's disclosure that the U.S. was considering Egypt's request to buy American arms, but said that no firm commitment had been made. Press secretary Ron Nessen said the U.S. had informed Sadat that supplying it arms would be "difficult so long as a state of war existed" in the Middle East, but that Washington would weigh his request "to increase Egypt's confidence in its course" of diversifying arms supplies as part of the American peace effort in the Middle East.

The American pledge to give sympathetic consideration to Israel's request for long-range Pershing missiles without telling Egypt beforehand left some Egyptian officials disillusioned with the Sinai pact, it was reported Sept. 26. One politician, National Assembly Speaker Sayed Marei, was reported as saying that the U.S. could improve the damage done to its relations with Cairo by providing Egypt with similarly powerful American weapons and greater financial and technological aid than planned.

Israel wary of U.S. arms to Egypt—Israeli Ambassador to the U.S. Simcha Dinitz was reported to have conveyed to Secretary of State Kissinger in Washington Oct. 17 his country's concern about possible U.S. arms shipments to Egypt. Kissinger reportedly assured Dinitz that although President Ford would discuss the matter with President Sadat when the Egyptian leader arrived in the U.S. Oct. 25 for a 10-day visit, no decision on the military sales would be made until the end of the current fiscal year, Oct. 1, 1976.

Egypt seeks British arms. President Anwar Sadat conferred with Prime Minister Wilson and other British officials in London Nov. 5–8, 1975 in a request for British arms, including the Anglo-French Jaguar supersonic jet fighter. Sadat told a news conference Nov. 8 that he was "completely satisfied" with his arms mission, but gave no specifics. He pointed out that Egypt's negotiations for British military supplies, which had started in 1974, were a continuing matter.

British officials confirmed that Foreign Minister James Callaghan had virtually assured Sadat that Britain had dropped its ban on fighter-bombers to Cairo. The embargo had been imposed for fear of upsetting the military balance in the Middle East. Sadat reportedly was seeking 200 Jaguars at an estimated cost of $1.2 billion.

Israeli Foreign Minister Yigal Allon warned Nov. 18 that Britain's proposed sale of Jaguars to Egypt would be an "irresponsible act by a friendly country." Arriving from a European tour, Allon said Israel would regard the deal as upsetting the balance of arms in the region, prompting Israel to make further weapons purchases to redress the balance.

Premier Yitzhak Rabin had said at a cabinet meeting Nov. 16 that his government was seeking clarification from Washington of reports that the U.S. was exerting pressure on Britain to sell the Jaguars to Cairo. Israel's ambassador to Britain, Gideon Raphael, had called on Prime Minister Wilson the previous week not to go through with the sale. Wilson replied that Secretary of State Henry A. Kissinger had urged the deal on him.

French-Egyptian arms talks. France agreed to help build up Egypt's arms industry and provide it with economic assistance following talks held by French President Valery Giscard d'Estaing with Anwar Sadat in Cairo Dec. 10–14, 1975.

A joint communique issued after the final round of discussions Dec. 14 said Sadat expressed hope that France would contribute to the military industrialization of other Arab countries as well.

France sells jets to Egypt—A French government spokesman said Jan. 12, 1977 that France had agreed to sell to Egypt 200 Mirage F-1 advanced fighter jets at a cost of $1.6 billion and to grant Egypt technical aid to build up its defense system. The accord also provided for eventual Egyptian production of the F-1s for sale to other Arab countries. The first few F-1 models would be delivered to Egypt ready-built, with the remainder of the aircraft to be assembled under license in Egypt starting in late 1979 or 1980, the spokesman said.

Final terms of the agreement apparently had been worked out with the Egyptians by French Defense Minister Yvon Bourges, who had completed a five-day visit to Cairo Jan. 9. Bourges said before departing that France would provide technical aid in establishing an Arab arms industry. Egypt, Saudi Arabia, Qatar and the United Arab Emirates had set up an Arab Authority for Military Industry May 10, 1975, but Western sources said the group thus far had produced little.

China, Egypt sign arms pact. Egypt and China signed a military protocol in Peking April 21, 1976. China reportedly agreed to provide Cairo with spare parts for its Soviet-supplied MiG-17 jet fighters. The U.S.S.R. had refused to ship these parts and other military equipment to Egypt.

The protocol was signed by Egyptian State Minister for War Production Gamaleddin Sedki and Chinese Deputy Chief of Staff Chang Tsai-chien. Sedki was part of a delegation headed by Egyptian Vice President Husni Mubarak that had arrived in Peking April 18. Mubarak had met with Communist Party Chairman Mao Tse-tung April 20 and with Premier Hua Kuo-feng April 21.

Hua said in a farewell dinner for Mubarak April 21 that Egypt's struggle against aggression and hegemony (Peking's term for Soviet expansionism) had "met with sympathy and wide support from the people of the world."

Envoys of the Soviet Union, Poland, Czechoslovakia, Mongolia, Hungary, East Germany and Bulgaria had boycotted a welcoming banquet for Mubarak April 19. Addressing the banquet in his first public speech since his appointment as premier, Hua assailed the Soviet Union for "resorting by hook or by crook to all kinds of criminal schemes, including divisive tactics, subversion and sabotage to retaliate against Egypt."

U.S. view of jet deal—China would apparently supply spare parts for Egypt's MiG-21s as well as its MiG-17s, U.S. Air Force officials said April 21. The agreement, however, would probably not include any spare parts for Egypt's more advanced MiG-23 jets since the Chinese did not have this version of the plane, the sources said.

India had confirmed March 17 its rejection of an Egyptian request for spare parts for MiG-21 jet fighters, which New Delhi manufactured under license from the Soviet Union. Egyptian President Anwar Sadat had disclosed the Indian decision in a speech made March 14. The Indian announcement said New Delhi had informed Cairo that it could not "supply the spare parts in view of our contractual commitments" with the Soviet Union, which barred sale of the equipment to third countries.

Kuwait buys British tanks. Kuwait had contracted to purchase more than 150 Centurion tanks from Britain to complement the 100 British tanks it already had, Defense Undersecretary Abdul Razzq al-Hamis said Feb. 16, 1976. Hamis did not disclose the cost of the deal, which was reported to be more than $200 million for the tanks, spare parts, ammunition and training for Kuwaiti crews.

U.S.-Jordan missile problem. The U.S. State Department said April 14, 1976 that negotiations were still in progress to sell Jordan $356 million worth of Hawk missiles even though financial arrangements had "become more complicated and time-consuming than originally contemplated."

The U.S. statement was in response to Jordanian Premier Zaid al-Rifai's statement that the deal had been canceled. In a London Times interview published April 14, Rifai said that the transaction had been dropped because the delays in U.S. congressional approval had almost doubled its cost. Saudi Arabia, he said, "did not find it possible to finance the whole deal at the new prices, and therefore we consider the deal with the United States as off. The only other source which could supply an air defense system at reasonably moderate prices and within acceptable delivery schedule was the Soviet Union."

King Hussein, who had made an official visit to Washington March 30–31, had said before leaving April 4 that the missile deal had foundered because Saudi Arabia apparently could not help finance it.

The U.S. Defense Department disclosed April 15 that Raytheon Corp. had received an order in March to halt work on the missiles. Despite the order, the formal agreement to sell the weapons to Jordan and the contract remained in effect, officials said.

Egyptian Policy

Anwar Sadat had sharply reversed Egyptian policy from a general reliance on Soviet support and acceptance of the anti-Western positions of the Communist and "third world" nations. In October 1975 Sadat visited the U.S. in what appeared to be a reaffirmation of a pro-Western shift and a willingness to risk the opposition of other Arab nations by seeking a path toward accommodation with Israel. The latter step was accompanied by bitter anti-Zionist pronouncements from Sadat and loud calls by Sadat for support of the Palestine Liberation Organization.

Sadat visits U.S. Egyptian President Anwar Sadat began a 10-day visit to the U.S. Oct. 26, 1975 to seek economic and military aid for Egypt and to explain his policies to the American people.

Sadat told President Ford Oct. 27 that he was there "to put the relationship between our two countries in proper position and to thank you . . . personally for what you have done since last June up until this moment, which could be a turning point in the history of the Arab-Israeli conflict."

Ford and Sadat then held a private meeting, with Secretary of State Henry A. Kissinger attending. Press secretary Ron Nessen said afterwards that both men had discussed how to maintain the momentum toward an overall Middle East peace settlement, with Ford reiterating his determination not to "tolerate stagnation or stalemate."

In an appearance later Oct 27 before the National Press Club, Sadat assailed Zionism, asserting it had "brought to the area bitterness, violence, hatred and pain, and we should be against this." Sadat insisted that "we are not against Jews but we are against Zionism." Sadat said "all" of Egypt's "economy was in the hands of the Jews" before 1952.

Sadat also asserted that if the Palestinians were "accorded their rights, they will become a force for peace in the area." He urged that the Palestine Liberation Organization be invited to any future Geneva peace conference as a means of assuring that "reasonable justice" was achieved.

Other points made by Sadat: a new Israeli-Syrian accord on the Golan Heights was an "urgent" matter that could lead to a new Geneva conference; the U.S. "held 99% of the cards" in Middle East diplomacy; Egypt's economy "is really suffering" and Cairo was hoping for U.S. economic aid to refinance its short-term debts into long-term ones; and Soviet refusal to supply Egypt with military aid since 1973 and grant it a grace period on the repayment of its debts to Moscow left Soviet-Egyptian relations either frozen "or in a state of misunderstanding."

At another meeting with Ford Oct. 28, Sadat renewed his appeal to have the U.S. end its diplomatic boycott of the PLO and accept its participation in a future Geneva conference to pave the way for any eventual peace settlement.

Sadat expressed displeasure Oct. 31 with the U.S.' Middle East package unveiled by President Ford the previous day. The totals included $1.5 billion in military aid and $750 million in economic assistance for Israel; Egypt was to receive $750 million in economic aid but no military help.

Sadat also said he accepted the Palestine Liberation Organization formula for a secular democratic state to replace Israel. "What the Palestinians ask I endorse 100 per cent," he said.

In a taped television interview Nov. 2, Ford reaffirmed American opposition to the PLO. He said the Palestinians "have refused to recognize the state of Israel and we, of course, strongly back the state of Israel in its attitude that there must be recognition before there can be any contact or any participation by the Palestinians in any negotiations."

Sadat said Nov. 3 that he did not interpret Ford's remarks as a rebuff of his proposal that Washington extend recognition of the PLO.

Sadat addresses U.N.—President Sadat formally called on the United Nations to help reconvene the Geneva conference on the Middle East in an address to the General Assembly in New York Oct. 29. Asserting that the time was propitious for reaching a peaceful settlement, Sadat urged the U.S., the Soviet Union and Secretary General Kurt Waldheim to immediately start consultations with all interested parties, "including the Palestine Liberation Organization," for an early resumption of the Geneva parley.

The Sinai agreement with Israel, the Egyptian leader said, was "limited in scope and effect," and represented "no intrinsic solution." He warned that if the U.N. did not seize the "unique opportunity for peace" that now existed, "there will be no alternative for safeguarding our sacred rights either in relation to the liberation of the occupied territories or in relation to regaining the legitimate rights of the Palestine people to establish their independent state."

Address to Congress—Sadat ended his visit to the U.S. after addressing a joint session of the U.S. Congress Nov. 5.

Repeating the theme stressed during his entire 10-day visit, Sadat urged American recognition of the Palestinian cause and warned that failure to do so would be "an open invitation to violence, negativism and extremism." He noted that "of almost all nations, the United States remains as the sole dissenter in the long overdue trend to establishing contacts with the Palestinians." American sympathy "towards the aspirations of the Palestinians and their right to establish their own state shall contribute greatly to a speedy solution of the problem," Sadat said.

The president said Egypt expected the U.S. to play a "more important" role in the Middle East, "not to condone expansion or tolerate aggression," and to "refrain from spurring the arms race in the area, for this would certainly lead to the renewal of armed conflict."

Before Sadat's address, a formal announcement had been made that an agreement had been reached in principle on selling Egypt two U.S. nuclear power reactors for use in desalting sea water. The estimated cost was about $1.2 billion. The accord was initialed by Secretary of State Henry A. Kissinger and Foreign Minister Ismail Fahmy.

U.S.S.R. assails Egyptian policy. The Soviet Union charged Oct. 25, 1975 that Egypt's adoption of a new pro-Western policy was a betrayal of Moscow's long-standing alliance with Cairo.

An article in the Communist Party newspaper Pravda stressed the history of Soviet support for Egypt, noting that "at all stages of their freedom and independence, the Soviet Union has invariably supported this just struggle." On Soviet military aid, Pravda recalled that in 1955 Egypt's armed forces were strengthened with modern equipment and training, in 1967 after Israel's victory, Moscow replenished Egypt's arsenal, and in the 1973 war there had been an "uninterrupted flow by sea and air of Soviet arms and ammunition to Egypt and Syria."

In previous attacks on Egypt's policies, Pravda Oct. 15 had assailed Cairo for its willingness to accept Western investments and for its shift toward capitalism. The Soviet press Oct. 20 held that President Sadat's attempt to balance his relationship with the Soviet Union and the U.S. was tantamount to hostility toward Moscow and friendship toward Washington.

Sadat ends Soviet pact—Sadat moved March 14, 1976 to end the five-year-old Soviet-Egyptian Treaty of Friendship & Cooperation. He presented legislation to that effect to the People's Assembly, which approved it March 15 by a 307-2 vote.

Sadat made the proposal in a speech in the assembly dealing with a wide range of internal as well as foreign issues.

He said the 1971 pact had become "only a scrap of paper," largely because of the Soviet's refusal to resupply Egypt with arms, following the 1973 war with Israel, and the Soviet refusal to reschedule Egypt's debts. Sadat cited in particular the recent Soviet action to prevent India from supplying Egypt with airplane parts from the Soviet-licensed MiG plant in India. The Egyptian planes would be "nothing but scrap" without spare parts, Sadat told the Assembly. "They wanted to exert pressure and to bring me to my knees," he said, "but I don't go down on my knees except before God Almighty."

Sadat paid tribute to the U.S. peace effort in the Middle East by saying "the United States holds 99% of the cards" in the search for peace. "These are the facts, whether the Soviets like them or not," he said.

The official Soviet reaction carried by the government press agency Tass March 15 was a warning that Sadat was pursuing an "unfriendly policy" towards the Soviet Union and "the responsibility for the consequences ... rests entirely with the Egyptian side."

Tass amplified its criticism March 22. It said that Sadat's move "draws Egypt into the Western orbit and is only playing into the hands of the forces of imperialism, Zionism and reaction, i.e., forces deeply hostile to the interests of the Arabs."

The Communist Party newspaper Pravda quoted Arab newspapers as saying that Sadat had decided to abrogate the accord as a condition for financial aid from the U.S. and "reactionary regimes of the Arabian peninsula," notably Saudi Arabia. Another Soviet publication, the farming newspaper Selskaya Zhizn, said "the decision to terminate the Soviet-Egyptian treaty was taken by Sadat after Washington promised to give Egypt $695 million in economic aid this year and shortly after Sadat made a trip to Saudi Arabia, where he was given a subsidy of $300 million."

President Ford March 19 had hailed Sadat's decision to annul the treaty with the Soviet Union as a victory for American foreign policy. He told members of the National Newspaper Association at the White House that Cairo's action would "be responded to by the U.S. economically and otherwise."

Sadat tours Europe. President Sadat visited Western Europe and Yugoslavia March 29–April 12, 1976, seeking arms, economic assistance and political support.

Sadat visited Bonn March 29–April 2, meeting with Chancellor Helmut Schmidt, President Walter Scheel, Foreign Minister Hans-Dietrich Genscher and other West German officials. Members of Sadat's delegation signed an agreement March 30 under which West Germany would provide Cairo with $90 million in capital material assistance. West German sources said March 30 that Bonn "will not and cannot" prevent Egypt from purchasing 120 French-West German jet bombers from France. Sadat had sought the planes despite West Germany's ban on arms sales to the Middle East.

In his visit to Paris April 3–5, Sadat was assured that France would help Egypt build up its own arms industry and provide for Egypt's other economic requirements. In discussing foreign affairs, Sadat disclosed April 4 that he had canceled the right of the Soviet Navy to use the Egyptian ports of Alexandria, Port Said and Matruh.

Also on April 4, Sadat expressed fears that Moscow might be planning to establish military bases in neighboring Libya. Sadat claimed that Libyan President Muammar el-Qaddafi had ordered $11 billion in arms from the Soviet Union. "If the Soviet Union gets a base in Libya, it will be very dangerous and I will have to revise all my calculations," Sadat said.

(France was prepared to become Cairo's long-time supplier of arms, it had been announced March 26 by Defense Minister Yvon Bourges following a week-long visit to Paris by Egyptian War Minister Mohammed Abdel Ghany Gamasy.)

Sadat arrived in Rome April 5 and ended his visit April 8 by issuing a joint communique with Italian Premier Aldo Moro. Both men confirmed the need for a lasting peace in the Middle East based on Israeli withdrawal from all Arab territories occupied since 1967, the right of all states in the region to live in peace and the recognition of the "national rights" of the Palestinians.

Sadat affirmed at a news conference before leaving Rome April 8 that he would like to get more arms from the U.S. than the six C-130 transports that the Ford Administration already had agreed to sell to Egypt.

(The U.S. Congress gave tacit approval to the plane deal when it went into recess April 14 without acting on President Ford's request to sell Egypt the transports. Congress had 20 days to approve or reject the $65 million arms deal, but let the deadline, also April 14, pass. The sale initially had aroused some Congressional opposition, but many legislators agreed to it after Secretary of State Henry A. Kissinger assured them that there would be no further arms sales to Egypt in 1976.)

Sadat also told the Rome news conference that if reports that Israel had atomic weapons were true, "we shall not be scared at all." Egypt, he said, "would not be the first to introduce atomic weapons into the area."

Sadat conferred with Yugoslav President Tito on arrival in Belgrade April 8. Tito and Sadat held further meetings April 9, discussing possible Yugoslav arms to Egypt, the Middle East situation and the summit conference of non-aligned nations to be held in Sri Lanka in August.

Preventing Peace

Most Palestinian activists and leaders of most Arab nations continued to profess adamant opposition to any steps toward peace with Israel. Many actions by Palestinians or other Arabs were announced or perceived efforts to block such peace.

PFLP seeks to provoke war. The leader of the Popular Front for the Liberation of Palestine, a splinter group opposed to political accommodation with Israel, vowed that the organization would seek to provoke a Middle East war to prevent a peaceful settlement. In an interview published in a Beirut newspaper Feb. 11, 1975, George Habash warned that new conflict would "be a grave threat to Israel's existence and U.S. imperialist interests."

Habash said that the Marxist PFLP, which had withdrawn from the Palestine Liberation Organization in September 1974, would not rejoin the PLO unless it rejected a political settlement with Israel.

The PFLP had offered Feb. 4 to rejoin the Executive Committee of the PLO if Arafat agreed to spurn a negotiated settlement that would recognize Israel. George Habash asserted that U.S. policy was aimed at getting the Palestinian guerrillas and Arab countries to recognize Israel.

Discontent with the policy of Arab nations also had been voiced Jan. 28 by Nayef Hawatmeh, leader of the Popular Democratic Front for Palestine, a militant faction of the PLO also opposed to a peaceful settlement with Israel. Hawatmeh charged that Egypt and Saudi Arabia had reversed their positions and now wanted Jordan, not the PLO, to negotiate an agreement with Israel for disengagement on the West Bank. He said Egyptian President Anwar Sadat had urged the PLO leadership in December 1974 to permit King Hussein of Jordan to seek an accord because the U.S. wanted the Palestine situation settled within "the context of the Jordan-Israel situation."

A PLO official, Zahir Mohsen, charged Feb. 11 that the principal objective of U.S Secretary of State Henry A. Kissinger's current tour of the Middle East was "to gain time for Israel and the United States."

Mohsen said in Beirut Feb. 27, 1976 that the Geneva conference would never be held, "despite the fuss made by Anwar Sadat and the clowning of the Egyptian information media," because the PLO, Syria and Jordan planned to boycott the parley.

Tel Aviv raid an attack on peace. Eighteen people were killed when eight Palestinian guerrillas attacked a Tel Aviv hotel March 5, 1975 after landing in two boats on a beach. Israeli soldiers killed seven of the guerrillas, and the eighth was captured. Three Israeli soldiers and eight civilians were killed.

The Beirut press March 7 quoted a high Palestinian source as saying the raid was part of a plan of Al Fatah, which took credit for the raid, to intensify military action against Israel. Plans for the assault were said to have been worked out at recent Al Fatah meetings to review Middle East developments in view of Secretary of State Henry A. Kissinger's resumed diplomatic mission.

The only survivor of the raid, captive Moussa Gumah, told a Tel Aviv news conference March 8 that he and the seven others had trained in Syria and set out on their mission from Lebanon. Gumah said his group had been ordered to say they had sailed from Port Said, Egypt if captured "so we can make it less smooth between Israel and Egypt."

PLO accepts joint Syrian command. The Palestine Liberation Organization March 21, 1975 accepted President Hafaz al-Assad's plan to form joint political and military commands with Syria.

The plan was approved by the Central Council of the Palestine National Assembly. The 39-member council served as a link between the assembly, a parliament in exile, and the PLO's Executive Committee. Khaled al-Fahoum, chairman of the assembly, and Executive Committee members said this merger was necessary because of Egyptian President Anwar Sadat's "individual" actions to achieve a separate agreement with Israel. "If this comes about, it will weaken Syria and the Palestinians in their demands for a full withdrawal from the territories occupied by Israel," Fahoum said.

Executive Committee member Zuheir Mohsen said the joint Syrian-PLO commands should provide Syrian protection of all Palestinian refugee camps and guerrilla groups in Lebanon and Syria against Israeli raids. "If the Israelis attack a Palestinian camp anywhere, this will be regarded as an attack on Syria and there will be a response," Mohsen said.

Israel disputes U.S. on PLO. The Israeli cabinet Nov. 16, 1975 disputed a U.S. State Department policy statement on the Palestine Liberation Organization as containing "numerous inaccuracies and distortions."

The statement, delivered Nov. 12 to the House International Relations Committee by Harold H. Saunders, deputy assistant secretary of state for Near Eastern Affairs, indicated that the PLO was a major element to be dealt with on the Palestine problem. The Israeli cabinet said this contradicted previous U.S. policy, which had stated that the matter must be negotiated by Israel and Jordan.

The Israelis also took issue with Saunders' remark that the aim of the Palestinian organizations was to "establish a binational secular state, but there are some indications that coexistence between separate Palestinian and Israeli states might be considered."

According to the Israeli cabinet response, the PLO had never broached the idea of a "binational" state but only a secular one, to replace Israel, and had never mentioned "coexistence" with Israel.

Secretary of State Kissinger was said to have assured Israel that Saunders' statement did not indicate a shift in U.S. policy on the PLO. Kissinger reaffirmed this policy after meeting with United Nations Secretary General Kurt Waldheim at U.N. headquarters in New York Nov. 18.

Israeli group backs Palestine state—A group of prominent Israelis formed an organization Dec. 10 to have the government change its policy and negotiate for the establishment of a Palestinians state alongside Israel on the basis of mutual recognition. The group, Israel Council for Peace between Israel and Palestine, claimed the Palestine Liberation Organization had changed its views as a result of PLO-council contacts abroad, and that the Palestinians were now ready to coexist with Israel. It proposed a dialogue "with every Palestinian sector" which recognized Israel.

Among the council's leaders were former Knesset member Eliyahu Elichar, a member of the first Knesset (parliament), honorary president, and Gen. Mattiyahu Peled, provisional chairman.

Pope backs Palestinian rights—Pope Paul VI called on Israel Dec. 27 to recognize the rights of the Palestinians. The pope said in his annual Christmas message: "Even if we are well aware of the tragedies not so long ago that have compelled the Jewish people to seek a secure and protected garrison in a sovereign and independent state of their own ... we would like to invite the children of this people to recognize the rights and legitimate aspirations of another people which also has suffered for a long time, the people of Palestine."

Arab nations seek unity. Egypt and Syria had agreed to establish a joint committee to assist in unifying military, political and diplomatic strategy against Israel, Presidents Anwar Sadat and Hafez al-Assad announced April 23, 1975.

The accord followed a conference between the two leaders in Riyadh, Saudi Arabia April 21–22 in which King Khalid participated. The joint committee was to consist of Egyptian Vice President Husni Mubarak and Syrian Premier Mahmoud Ayoubi. The conference was the first top-level Arab move to coordinate policy in the wake of the collapse of Secretary

Henry A. Kissinger's shuttle diplomacy in March.

Syria and Jordan had agreed in March to establish joint military commands, it was reported April 24. The accord was said to have been arranged under the sponsorship of the Soviet Union, whose Foreign Ministry official, Vladimir M. Vinogradov, reportedly concluded the pact with King Hussein in Amman, placing Jordan in the group of Middle East countries that relied on Moscow for military and political support. Under the alleged plan, Jordan initially was to get Soviet surface-to-air missiles to protect its airspace, while Syrian units were to move into Amman shortly to establish the joint commands.

U.S. and Israeli officials April 24–25 expressed doubt that Syria and Jordan had agreed to establish joint military commands for their land and air forces. A Jordanian spokesman in Washington April 25 denied the report, although he said Syria and Jordan had been cooperating on a political level. A Syrian official, however, said the report was true but refused to give details.

Syria and Jordan June 12 announced a plan to establish a Joint High Commission whose function would be to coordinate their military, political, economic and cultural policies. The agreement was reached after three days of talks held in Amman by Syrian President Hafez al-Assad and King Hussein.

The commission would be composed of military and civilians and would be headed by the premiers of the two countries. It would meet every two months. Jordanian officials said the formation of the commission fell short of establishing a formal joint military command.

Israeli Defense Minister Shimon Peres assailed the Amman agreement June 13 as an attempt by Syria to create "an aggressive alignment" against Israel. In addition to Syria and Jordan, the anti-Israeli front would eventually include the P.L.O. and possibly Lebanon, Peres charged.

In a further step, Syria and Jordan announced Aug. 22 the establishment of a supreme command to carry out political and military action against Israel. Formation of the body, which was not an actual joint military command, was contained in a joint communique issued at the end of five days of talks King Hussein had held in Damascus with al-Assad.

Hussein and Assad were to head the command, which would coordinate the armed forces of their countries along Israel's entire eastern frontier and would meet every three months or whenever the situation required.

The impetus for the unified Syrian-Jordanian effort was the fear that Israel and Egypt might agree to further Israeli troop pull-backs in the Sinai without similar Israeli withdrawals on the Syrian and Jordanian fronts. This was pointed up by a statement in the communique, which said: "Any attempt by the enemy to evade the facts through a division of the position along the confrontation lines, and consequently dividing the problem in order to avoid the original issue, mainly that of Palestine, would make the situation more dangerous."

Egypt had withdrawn its air units from Syria following condemnation by Damascus of its foreign policy, particularly the Sinai agreement with Israel, Cairo's Middle East News Agency reported Oct. 17. The criticism had been expressed by Syrian air force commander Nadj Jamil before the Egyptian airmen at their base at Qatanah near Damascus.

Diplomatic sources in Beirut Oct. 19 attributed the Egyptian pullout decision to reluctance by Cairo to get involved in a Syrian-Israeli confrontation on the Golan Heights, where tensions had increased in the past week.

The Egyptian force consisted of 24 MiG-19s and MiG-21s and of about 200 pilots and maintenance crew. They had been sent to Syria shortly before the outbreak of the 1973 war with Israel and took part in the fighting.

In a related development, intelligence officials in Washington and Israel reported Nov. 17 that the Soviet Union had recently shipped MiG-25 reconnaissance jets to Syria. It was believed that as many as 20 of the advanced supersonic jets would be sent altogether.

A small force of MiG-25s and their Soviet pilots had been stationed in Egypt, with their principal function to track U.S. naval activity in the eastern Mediterranean.

Syria and Egypt met in Riyadh, Saudi Arabia June 23–24, 1976 in an effort to restore political and military cooperation.

A communique issued at the conclusion of the talks made no mention of the two principal obstacles to reconciliation—Syria's objections to the 1975 Egyptian-Israeli Sinai agreement and Egypt's opposition to Syria's intervention in the Lebanese civil war. The communique said that a joint committee would make recommendations to Presidents Anwar Sadat of Egypt and Hafez al-Assad of Syria for a possible summit meeting of the two leaders.

Egypt and Syria also agreed to create a military-political committee, headed by their foreign ministers, to study ways to carry out the recommendations of the 1974 Rabat conference, at which Arab states agreed to establish a common front against Israel. Syria had charged that Egypt had violated the accord by agreeing to the Sinai pact. The committee would be charged with working out military strategy for "liberation" of Arab lands occupied by Israel and with formulating political action toward "liberation" and the "achievement of a just and permanent settlement in the Middle East." The committee would seek to restore "the national rights of the Palestinian people."

The Riyadh conference, arranged by Saudi Arabia and Kuwait, was attended by Premiers Mahmoud al-Ayubi of Syria and Mamdouh Salem of Egypt, Egyptian Foreign Minister Ismail Fahmy and various Saudi and Kuwaiti officials.

Ayubi, Salem and ranking officials of Saudi Arabia and Kuwait had been meeting for a month to prepare for the Riyadh talks. Plans for an earlier Syrian-Egyptian meeting had collapsed just as the session was about to start May 19.

Syria and Jordan Dec. 8 announced plans for a union of the two countries. The proposal was disclosed in a joint statement issued after a two-day meeting in Amman of al-Assad and Hussein.

Two weeks later Egypt and Syria announced Dec. 21 that they planned to establish a "unified political command" to "develop and strengthen steps toward" a union of the two countries. The two nations said it was possible that other Arab states would join the union at a later date.

The statement was contained in a communique issued simultaneously in Cairo and Damascus. It followed talks held in Cairo Dec. 18–21 by Presidents Sadat and al-Assad. The decision was regarded as an attempt to bolster the Arab position at the expected resumption of the Geneva peace talks on the Middle East in 1977.

Egyptian Foreign Minister Ismail Fahmy told a news conference that joint committees would be formed to study the process of unification in such areas as constitutional problems, defense, foreign policy, finance and economy.

Fahmy said that the Cairo accord did not mean the two countries accepted the formula of a single unified Arab delegation, including Palestinians, at the Geneva talks. Assad and Sadat had agreed that the Palestine Liberation Organization would have its own delegation at the parley, Fahmy said.

Egypt and Syria Feb. 4, 1977 announced the creation of a unified political command. Sadat and Assad issued orders naming their representatives to a 10-man body that would coordinate policy for the two countries. The body consisted of the two presidents, their deputies, premiers, foreign ministers and defense ministers.

Sudan Feb. 28 joined the Syrian-Egyptian political command. It acted during a Feb. 27–28 meeting in Khartoum of Sudanese President Gafaar al-Nimeiry with Sadat and Assad.

The political command had been formed to map common strategy against Israel. Sudan's decision to join had less to do with its involvement in the Arab-Israeli dispute than with its desire to get Syrian and Egyptian support to help to cope with a tense situation along its borders. This was evidenced in a communique signed by the three leaders that called for peace in the Red Sea area and expressed concern about instability allegedly fomented in the region by foreign interests. This was an apparent reference to Sudanese fears of Libyan and Soviet influence on Sudan's eastern frontier, particularly in Ethiopia, where the Khartoum government was supporting the Eritrean rebels. Sudan in turn was threatened by the Ansars, the rightist Moslem sect operating inside the Ethiopian frontier with Soviet arms reportedly financed by Libya.

PLO aide bars Israel recognition. A Palestine Liberation Organization official said Feb. 15, 1976 that the PLO was unequivocally opposed to recognizing Israel and was prepared to join with progressive forces in the Arab world "for a decisive battle with Israel." The statement was made in a speech in Beirut by Saleh Khalef (also known as Abu Iyad),

second in command of Al Fatah, which was headed by Yasir Arafat. Recognition of Israel in exchange for the establishment of a Palestinian state in the West Bank and Gaza Strip was a "high price" the PLO refused to pay, he said. Khalef added: "There is something the world must know. Let us all die, let us all be assassinated, but we will not recognize Israel."

Khalef accused the U.S. of attempting to undermine Palestinian influence by supporting Jordanian King Hussein's 1972 plan to merge Jordan and the West Bank into a federated united kingdom after the West Bank was recovered from Israel, a proposal rejected by the Palestinians and other Arab states.

West Bank Complications, Israeli Arab Problems

Arabs vs. self-rule plan. Israeli troops subdued demonstrations by Arabs in the West Bank town of Ramallah Nov. 8–10, 1975 as Arabs reacted in violent protest against Israeli occupation of the West Bank and an Israeli government plan for limited self-rule for residents of the area.

Dozens of students were arrested and several hospitalized after Israeli soldiers broke into the walled court of a girls' high school in Ramallah and dispersed the demonstrating students. Most of them were later released.

The students opposed the autonomy plan on the ground that it would undermine the influence and standing of the Palestine Liberation Organization, which they and other West Bank residents favored. Ramallah was a center of strong pro-PLO sentiment.

The plan to encourage self-rule had been outlined by Defense Minister Shimon Peres Oct. 21. In discussions held with local Arab leaders in the town of Beit Jalla, Peres proposed expansion of the authority of mayors in the West Bank as well as in the Gaza Strip, giving them charge of agriculture, education, municipal administration and other internal affairs, with Israel retaining military control. Peres told the mayors there was no alternative to the plan since Jordan had decided not to represent the Palestinians and Israel would not deal with the PLO.

West Bank Arabs oppose settlers. Israeli civilians clashed Dec. 4, 1975 with West Bank Arabs protesting the creation of an illegal Jewish settlement at biblical Sebastia, near Nablus. The Arabs erected a roadblock at Anabata, a village west of Sebastia, and stoned a convoy of a bus and two cars carrying about 100 sympathizers on their way to join the 1,500 settlers. Several bus windows were broken but no one was hurt. The obstruction was cleared after a passenger alighted and fired a burst of machinegun into the air.

Arabs in Nablus staged a riotous demonstration against the Sebastia settlement Dec. 8. Israeli security forces moved in and fired shots in the air and used water canon to break up the crowds of protesting high school students.

It was the eighth attempt by members of the religious Gush Emunim (Fidelity Bloc) to establish a settlement in the West Bank in areas other than those prescribed by the government. The aim of the organization was to demonstrate that Jews had the right to settle anywhere in biblical Palestine.

Israelis start Golan settlements. A group of Israelis Jan. 9, 1975 moved into the third of four newly approved settlements on the Golan Heights.

The four settlements had been established in response to the United Nations Security Council's decision Nov. 30, 1975 to invite the Palestine Liberation Organization to participate in Middle East debate. The four settlements increased to 25 the number of outposts set up on the Golan Heights since its seizure by Israel in the 1967 war.

Israel to remove West Bank settlers. The Israeli Cabinet May 9 ordered the removal of about 130 ultranationalist Jewish settlers from the Camp Kadum army base near Nablus in the West Bank. Their presence had aroused strong opposition from Arabs in the area as well as from other Israelis. [See 1975, p. 928C3]

The settlers were permitted to stay for a few weeks until a new site was selected for them by the government. The action was contained in a Cabinet resolution that banned illegal settlements in the West Bank. The resolution stressed, however, that the government would continue to establish new settlements in areas of its own choice.

A New York Times dispatch from Jerusalem May 10 said that the Cabinet meeting had mapped plans for setting up a large number of settlements in the next few years in the Golan Heights, the Jordan Valley and other parts of the West Bank, and the Rafah area of the Gaza Strip.

The Cabinet decision had drawn mixed reaction May 9 from political leaders. Foreign Minister Yigal Allon said it left open "good options for territorial compromise on the West Bank if the negotiating opportunity [with the Arabs] arises."

More than 25,000 persons had attended a rally in Tel Aviv May 8 to protest the unauthorized Kadum settlement and to urge the government to evict its occupants, by force if necessary. The demonstrators warned that Israeli democracy would not survive unless the government took prompt action against both the Kadum squatters and the rightist Gush Emunim, which had initiated the settlement.

Moslems win re Temple Mount. Israel Feb. 28, 1976 assured Jerusalem's Moslem Arabs that the government would respect their exclusive prayer rights on the Temple Mount in the Old City. Police Minister Shlomo Hillel warned that Jews caught praying on the mount would be arrested.

When the Israelis had captured the Old City in the 1967 war, the government ruled that access to the mount would be guaranteed to all religions, but that Jews would be barred from conducting organized prayers there in deference to the feelings of Moslems living in Israel. A January court ruling on the mount dispute which cleared eight Jewish youths of staging religious services in the area and which was being challenged by the Israeli government had sparked widespread demonstrations among Arabs in the Old City and the West Bank. Demonstrators clashed with Israeli security forces in Nablus, Jenin and Tulkarm Feb. 19 and 200 Arab women staged a prayer protest at Al Aksa Mosque on the mount. Violent clashes also erupted in Al-Bireh, Ramallah, Nablus and Bir-Zeit and Bethlehem schools were closed by a student boycott. More than 200 students were arrested in Nablus.

In a move to curb the unrest, Israeli authorities threatened to impose heavy fines on communities and individuals involved in the protest movement. Residents of Ramallah, Al-Bireh and Nablus, whose communities were warned about such penalties, were forbidden to cross the Jordan River bridges into Israel proper or to export goods across the river until the situation returned to normal.

The Arab Chamber of Commerce in Jerusalem and the Nablus town council called on the Israeli government Feb. 17 to state unequivocally that it would not permit Jews to hold public prayers near the Al Aksa Mosque. The Moslem Supreme Council in Jerusalem charged that Israel's failure to make such a declaration was responsible for the violence in the West Bank.

Israel upholds Temple Mount ban—The Israeli Supreme Court March 21 upheld a 1970 lower court ruling banning Jewish prayer on the Temple Mount. The decision followed a request by an Israeli Jew for an order requiring the police minister to permit him to visit the mount to pray.

The District Court in Jerusalem June 30 nullified the January court decision clearing the eight Jewish youths who had sought to pray publicly on the mount. The higher tribunal held that the youths were guilty of disturbing the peace.

State Attorney Gavriel Bach said the District Court's decision reaffirmed that prayer by Jews on the mount was illegal and that the police therefore had the right to ban it.

West Bank Arabs riot. Arabs staged violent demonstrations and strikes throughout the West Bank March 7-23 in the worst outbreak of unrest since the territory came under Israeli occupation after the 1967 war. One of the principal causes of the disturbances was the Moslem-Jewish religious controversy over the Temple Mount in Jerusalem. But the outbursts were also linked to opposition to a Jewish settlement near Nablus and to the Israeli occupation of the West Bank in general, and to tension arising from local elections scheduled to be held in the West Bank April 12.

The crisis was further aggravated by the resignation March 8, 10, 18 and 20 of the mayors and town councils of Nablus, Ramallah, Bir Zeit, El Bireh, Beit Sahur (near Bethlehem) and Hebron in protest against alleged brutality by Israeli troops in quelling the disturbances. In the first incident, the Israeli forces had reacted after being stoned by student demonstrators in Nablus March 7. The local officials of Ramallah, Bir Zeit and El Bireh resigned in protest after Israeli soldiers broke up a demonstration of Bir Zeit College students March 10. A joint statement by the mayors and council members accused the Israelis of "brutal attacks." Hebron Mayor Sheik Mohammed Ali Jabari announced his resignation March 20 after Israeli soldiers forced their way into the city hall to break up a disturbance. Jabari withdrew his resignation March 22 and said he would remain in office until the April elections.

Violent street demonstrations in Ramallah March 15 prompted Israeli authorities to impose an indefinite 24-hour curfew on the town and on nearby El Bireh. Baton-wielding soldiers clashed with rock-throwing students outside most of the schools in Ramallah during the day. Karim Khalaf, who resigned as mayor of Ramallah, said the majority of its residents supported the Palestine Liberation Organization and favored creation of "an independent Palestinian national authority."

Violence broke out for the first time March 15 in Bethlehem, where university students barricaded themselves in their school and hurled stones at policemen and passersby.

The violence spread March 16 to the Old City of Jerusalem, where 200 Arab youths marched to the Temple Mount shouting anti-Israeli slogans. Israeli police scattered the marchers and arrested 11

Police fired tear gas to quell a second day of rioting in the Old City March 17. A curfew was imposed in Halhoul, south of Jerusalem. Israeli soldiers opened fire on a crowd of Arabs besieging an Israeli car outside Jerusalem, wounding three. One of the victims, an 11-year old boy, died of his wounds March 22.

Old City merchants closed their shops March 18 to protest the shooting of the three Arabs, while demonstrations continued at the Temple Mount, where police arrested another 50 young Arabs, bringing the total number of arrests there to 160.

Israeli paratroopers March 18 reinforced border police in Hebron, where civilian guards accompanying a rabbi had fired shots into the air the previous day after Jewish settlers in nearby Kiryat Arba were attacked as they were marching to a Jewish shrine in Hebron.

Israeli reinforcements were moved into the West Bank March 18. A large number of Israeli soldiers was dispatched to the Old City March 19, cutting it off from the West Bank to block an expected mass demonstration called by Arab guerrilla groups and Moslem leaders.

Militants win West Bank elections. Palestinian militants and Arab radicals scored heavily in elections held April 12, 1976 for West Bank mayors and municipal councils.

Communists, Syrian Baathists and candidates sympathetic to the Palestine Liberation Organization and running on the National Bloc ticket won power in many of the 24 major towns and villages. National Bloc candidates won most of the municipal seats in Hebron, Nablus, Ramallah, Tulkarm, Jericho, Beit Jala and Beit Sahur. Among the candidates in those towns were a number affiliated with the outlawed West Bank Communist Party. Bethlehem resisted the radical tide, reelecting Christian Mayor Elias Frej and putting six members of his slate on the 11-member council. Among the others elected to the council, however, were a Communist and two militant nationalists. Hebron Mayor Sheik Mohammed Ali Jabari was replaced by Fahad Kawasma, a PLO sympathizer.

Commenting on the results, Israeli Defense Minister Shimon Peres said April 13 that "this is not a day of mourning for Israel."

"I see it as a national challenge with which we will now have to grapple," Peres said. He warned the newly elected officials not to use their offices to promote Palestinian politics. "That's not what they were elected for," he said.

Other Israeli leaders expressed alarm at the results of the election. Social Welfare Minister Zevulun Hammer, a leader of the right-wing National Religious Party, said the election "proves

that if we return the West Bank to Jordan or so-called moderates, it will pass immediately—in a matter of hours—into the hands of the PLO."

Study of Arab grievances. The Israeli Cabinet May 23, 1976 approved the formation of three committees to take up the grievances of Arabs living in Israel and to help reconcile the differences between the Jewish and Arab communities in the country.

The committees were a joint council of Jewish and Arab community leaders, a permanent ministerial committee headed by Premier Yitzhak Rabin, and a body comprised of high officials of all government ministries. Shmuel Toledano, Rabin's adviser on Arab affairs, said, "It is the first time that Arabs in Israel will become partners in shaping their destiny."

Premier Rabin May 24 told local Arab leaders that the Israeli government was firm in its determination to preserve Israel as "a country with a Jewish destiny, a country in which Jewish aspirations will be fulfilled."

Proposals & Negotiations

Soviets urge Geneva conference resumption. The Soviet Union called on the U.S. Nov. 9, 1975 to reconvene the Geneva conference on the Middle East with full participation of the Palestine Liberation Organization. In a message delivered by Ambassador Anatoly Dobrynin to Secretary of State Henry A. Kissinger, Moscow was critical of the secretary's shuttle diplomacy in the Middle East, saying "the road of partial measures, carried out on a separate basis, does not lead to a resolution of the problem."

Asked by Kissinger to respond to the Soviet suggestion, the Israeli government said Nov. 16 it would accept the proposal for resumption of the Geneva parley if Syria agreed first to renewal of the mandate of the United Nations Disengagement Observer Force on the Golan Heights, which would expire Nov. 30. Israel, however, rejected the call for PLO participation in the talks.

The U.S. suggested to the U.S.S.R. Dec. 1 that both nations, as co-chairmen of the Geneva conference, call a preliminary meeting in that city to fix the agenda and procedures for a full-scale parley and to decide whether to invite the Palestine Liberation Organization. The American plan, released Dec. 2, was in reply to the Soviet message of Nov. 9.

According to Washington's note, the preliminary meeting would discuss PLO role in future talks only if all the parties agreed to it and then only on the basis of the key U.N. Security Council resolutions 242 and 338. The U.S. said it also was prepared to conduct bilateral talks with the Soviet Union on the Middle East.

Moscow reacted negatively to Washington's proposal, with Foreign Minister Andrei A. Gromyko asserting Dec. 2 that the projected preliminary meeting "cannot be qualified as anything but an evasion of convening the [Geneva] conference." Gromyko insisted that the PLO take part in any meeting and said that convening a preliminary conference would not resolve the issue of its participation.

The U.S.S.R. Dec. 18 formally rejected the U.S. plan to convene a preparatory Middle East peace conference in Geneva that would exclude the Palestine Liberation Organization. However, in a note handed by Dobrynin to Kissinger, Moscow agreed to hold bilateral talks on resumption of the conference.

The U.S.S.R., calling April 28, 1976 for resumption of the Geneva talks, proposed that they be held in two phases.

"All the organizational questions that may arise" could be resolved during the first stage of the conference before the delegates took up the substantive issues in the second stage, the Moscow statement said. The Soviet Union repeated its demand that the Palestinians participate in both sessions.

The Middle East stalemate, the Soviet statement said, carried the danger of "a new military explosion," and "a radical political settlement" was therefore required. The statement charged: "The preservation of the present situation in the Middle East accords with the long-term plans of certain forces establishing their control over the Middle East area, over its tremendous oil resources and important strategic positions."

Moscow criticized Kissinger's shuttle diplomacy of 1975: Although Israel's return of some territory to Egypt "did create in some quarters the illusion of a calming down in the Middle East, now everybody sees that these deals, which sidestepped cardinal questions on a Middle East settlement, not only failed to defuse the situation, but further aggravated it."

The Soviet Union also assailed the U.S. for its military aid to Israel. It said "a potential danger to peace is posed" by American shipment to Israel of "various modern arms, including rockets capable of carrying both conventional and nuclear warheads," and also by reports that Israel "is creating or has already created its own nuclear warheads."

Moscow Oct. 1 renewed its call for a resumption of the Geneva talks. Tass said the call had gone to the governments of the U.S., Israel, Egypt, Jordan and Syria, and to the Palestine Liberation Organization.

The plan called for the withdrawal of Israeli troops from Arab lands occupied in the 1967 war, the creation of a Palestinian state, international guarantees for the independence of Israel and its Arab neighbors and the ending of the state of war between Israel and the Arab states.

Rabin-Hussein meeting reported. The Christian Science Monitor reported Jan. 12, 1976 that for four months Israel and Jordan had been conducting high-level negotiations that were marked on one occasion by face-to-face discussions between Premier Yitzhak Rabin and King Hussein. The bilateral talks were said to be continuing.

According to the newspaper's account, which quoted a usually reliable source, King Hussein had said he would sever his commitment to the Palestine Liberation Organization if Israel returned all of the West Bank and Jerusalem area it had captured from Jordan in the 1967 war. Hussein was said to be willing to accept only minor border adjustments in Israel's favor but offered to demilitarize all areas Israel would turn over to Jordan.

Jordan denies West Bank plans—Jordanian Premier Zaid al-Rifai declared Feb. 9 that his country continued to respect the Arab summit meeting decision that designated the PLO as the sole representative of the Palestinian people in the Israeli-occupied West Bank. In making this assertion, Rifai denied suggestions from Israeli sources that Amman was considering negotiations or joint arrangements with Israel regarding the territory and he refuted Israeli and Palestinian allegations that Jordan planned to reassert its influence over the West Bank.

Rifai accused Israel of carrying out a "systematic propaganda campaign of fabrications" to give the false impression of Jordanian receptivity to Israeli overtures to settle the West Bank problem bilaterally. "Any discussions about the West Bank must take place between Israel and the PLO," Rafai insisted. By avoiding this step, Rifai said, Jerusalem was "attempting to relieve the pressure on peace." The U.S. would be remiss "if it failed to recognize Israeli intransigence and failed to realize that new armed conflict will become unavoidable unless some movement is generated."

Rabin in U.S. Israeli Premier Yitzhak Rabin visited Washington Jan. 27–29, 1976 to discuss Middle East strategy for peace with American leaders and to press for continued financial and military assistance for his country.

Greeting Rabin at a White House reception, President Ford Jan. 27 pledged no letup in U.S. assistance to Israel, but urged that further steps be taken to advance peace negotiations. The President stressed this theme again in a 90-minute discussion with the premier. The White House later said that Ford had emphasized "the importance of these talks for developing ideas on how next to move as part of our over-all consultations with the parties involved. He repeated his determination to avoid a hiatus in negotiations."

At a luncheon given by Secretary of State Henry A. Kissinger later Jan. 27, Rabin alluded to the Ford Administration's decision to ask Congress for reduced military and economic aid to Israel (the request was for $1.8 billion, $500 million less than the current fiscal year). Rabin said: "You cannot achieve peace but from the standpoint of strength. It cannot be done from a standpoint of weakness. With a weak Israel no one will negotiate."

Rabin addressed a joint session of Congress Jan. 28 and said his government was ready to negotiate with any Arab state, but he expressed continued opposition to meeting with the PLO. Noting that the PLO sought the destruction of Israel, Rabin said this was "the heart and core of the Arab-Israeli conflict" and "no honest being can blame us for refusing to cooperate in our own suicide." Conceding that the Palestinian issue must "be solved in the context of a final peace," Rabin nevertheless argued that the matter was "not the obstacle to peace as some would suggest."

The premier called on Arab states to shift "from aggressive confrontation to harmonious reconciliation" if there was to be peace.

Rabin repeated his concern about possible American aid reduction to Israel, asserting that "weakness is no prescription for negotiations. If it be perceived that Israel is not so weak, so shall our neighbors perceive the wisdom of mutual compromise, recognition and peace."

Rabin and Ford ended their discussions Jan. 29 with a reported understanding on a common approach to the PLO question. Israeli officials said that both sides ruled out the organization's participation in a resumed Geneva peace conference and concluded that such a conference was unlikely in view of Syrian and Soviet insistence that the Palestinians attend. The U.S. would inform key Arab states and the Soviet Union of the American-supported Israeli position on the PLO, according to the Israeli officials.

A White House statement said: "We have the impression that Israel remains committed to peace efforts."

Rabin then reported on his return to Israel Feb. 6 that he had reached agreement with American officials on a common approach to peace. Israel and the U.S. concurred that the long-range goal should be "peace or its approximation" based on overall settlements with the Arab states, he said. The Americans, Rabin pointed out, had accepted Israel's formula that negotiations with Jordan should be the basis for peace on Israel's eastern borders, and that Washington supported Israel's opposition to the Palestine Liberation Organization and to the establishment of a third state between Israel and Jordan.

Israel backs U.S. peace moves—The Israeli cabinet Feb. 22 empowered the

U.S. to consult with Egypt, Jordan and Syria about the possibility of negotiating an "end to the state of war" between Israel and the Arabs states instead of formal peace accords. The action was in response to suggestions made to Rabin by American officials in Washington.

Rabin had told the U.S. leaders that Israel was prepared to make further territorial concessions to the Arabs, pulling back in the Sinai to a line between El Arish and Ras Muhammad and to make some withdrawals in the Golan Heights, in exchange for Arab acceptance of "peace or something close to it." The cabinet's latest decision in effect endorsed Rabin's interpretation of "something close to it" as "an end to the state of war."

Israeli 'dove' joins government. The Israeli cabinet Feb. 15 approved the appointment of Professor Shlomo Avineri, a critic of Premier Yitzhak Rabin's Palestinian policies, as director general of the foreign ministry. Foreign Minister Yigal Allon's appointment of Avineri, dean of social sciences at Hebrew University in Jerusalem, alarmed hard-liners on the Palestinian issue who feared it might herald a shift in the government's policy of refusing to negotiate with the Palestine Liberation Organization and of opposing the establishment of a Palestinian state between Israel and Jordan, a stand previously favored by Avineri.

Rabin said after the cabinet decision that Avineri's appointment did not indicate a change in the direction of the government's foreign policy.

Israel to get new U.S. arms. The U.S. had agreed to lift the ban on sales to Israel of some sophisticated weapons and to hasten the delivery of equipment already approved, President Ford announced Oct. 11, 1976.

Ford made the announcement during a White House meeting with Israeli Foreign Minister Yigal Allon, who expressed thanks for "the new items." Ford replied that "it was the right thing to do so there would be no question about the support, in order to prevent circumstances we want to avoid."

Arafat proposes peace plan. Palestine Liberation Organization leader Yasir

Arafat had proposed that Israel create two United Nations buffer zones in the occupied West Bank and Gaza Strip as an initial step toward a Middle East peace conference and recognition of Israel's right to exist, U.S. Sen. Adlai E. Stevenson (D, Ill.) reported Feb. 28, 1975. Stevenson had returned from a 16-day trip to the Middle East, where he conferred with Arafat and officials of Israel, Egypt, Syria, Lebanon, Saudi Arabia, Iraq and Iran.

Stevenson said Israeli leaders had expressed little interest in Arafat's plan, which he described as "an offer," not a "hard proposal."

Among Stevenson's other observations:

Syrian President Hafez al-Assad remained adamant about total Israeli withdrawal from occupied Arab lands as a precondition for negotiations.

Officials in all Arab states, except Iraq, "acknowledged privately the right of Israel to exist."

Israeli troop pullback plan. An Israeli peace plan that called for Israeli withdrawal from most of the Arab territory occupied since the 1967 war was proposed by Foreign Minister Yigal Allon in an article in the October 1976 issue of the magazine Foreign Affairs, made public Sept. 17.

The article carried a map of the proposed changes. They called for creation of a joint Jordanian-Palestinian entity in demilitarized zones of the West Bank, which would be slightly reduced from its current size. Israel would retain Jerusalem and the arid areas immediately west of the Jordan River, except for a corridor that would link the remaining section of the West Bank with the East Bank of the Jordan at Jericho.

The city of Gaza would be under Arab control, but the rest of the Gaza Strip would be part of the joint Jordanian-Palestinian entity, with guaranteed road access to the West Bank.

In the Sinai, Israel would keep the territory east of a newly drawn demarcation line that would stretch from El Arish on the Mediterranean Sea, along a line roughly parallel to the traditional Egyptian-Israeli border, to the area around Elath on the Gulf of Aqaba. From there, it would run southwest parallelling the gulf coast, and provide Israel with control of Sharm el-Sheikh at the southern tip of the Sinai Peninsula.

Israel would retain territory in the Golan Heights just west of the 1967 truce lines to enable it to protect Galilee from shelling or invasion.

The territory that Israel would retain would give it an "essential minimum of strategic depth" to defend itself, Allon said. It would enable the Israeli army, Allon explained, to hold back any Arab invader until civilian reserves could be mobilized.

Allon complained in a message to Foreign Affairs Sept. 17 that he had not seen or approved the map accompanying the article and that it did not accurately reflect his views. William P. Bundy, editor of the magazine, said that the map had originated with the publication and "was intended only to be illustrative of the outlines of Allon's proposals."

An Israeli spokesman defended the article as part of Israel's efforts to offset Arab propaganda.

A Washington Post report from Cairo Sept. 21 said that Allon's plan had evoked no response from the Egyptian government. The only official response came from Egypt's United Nations mission, which rejected the proposal.

PLO seeks Palestinian state. The Central Council, the leadership body of the Palestine Liberation Organization, called Dec. 14, 1976 for the creation an independent Palestinian state as one of the "legitimate rights" of the Palestinian people. The council declaration, issued at the conclusion of a meeting that had started in Damascus Dec. 12, also listed self-determination and repatriation as being part of the "rights of the Palestinian Arab people." These rights, the statement added, were recognized by the world community "with the exception of the Zionist enemy and its ally, the United States."

Although the council's announcement stopped short of proposing a Palestinian state or defining its borders, conference sources said the territories referred to were the West Bank and the Gaza Strip, now occupied by Israel. It was the first time the term "Palestinian state" had been used in an official PLO declaration, the sources said.

Sadat backs Palestine-Jordan link. Egyptian President Anwar Sadat said he supported a formal link between any Palestinian state that was created and Jordan, according to an interview given to a Washington Post writer Dec. 29, 1976. This type of relationship between the two states had long been advocated by Israel but opposed by the Palestine Liberation Organization.

Sadat recalled that he and King Hussein of Jordan had previously backed such a plan in a joint declaration in 1974, but "I was attacked vehemently by the Palestinians at the time." Sadat said he still favored this tie between the Palestinians and Jordan.

Sadat said that Israel would have to evacuate quickly the West Bank and Gaza Strip, the area in which he had called for establishment of a Palestinian state, as well as other Arab territories occupied by Israel. The evacuation, Sadat said, should not be over a phased period as suggested by the Jerusalem government.

King Hussein visits Moscow. King Hussein of Jordan visited Moscow June 17–28, 1976 to discuss with Soviet leaders the Middle East crisis and possible purchase of Soviet arms. Jordan was seeking an antiaircraft missile system from the Soviet Union after negotiations to buy a similar system from the U.S. had broken down.

No mention was made of an arms sale in a Soviet-Jordanian communique issued June 28. The joint statement said that a peace settlement was "possible only with the participation of all immediately interested sides, including the Palestine Liberation Organization, as the representatives of the Arab people of Palestine."

U.S. to arm Saudis, Jordan. Ford Administration officials said July 31, 1976 that the U.S. had decided to sell Saudi Arabia quantities of a new generation of missiles and of an early version of laser-guided bombs previously sold to Israel. Washington officials announced the same day that Saudi Arabia had agreed to finance the purchase from the U.S. of an air-defense system for Jordan.

Although the proposed Saudi deal was widely reported in U.S. and British newspapers, no figure was given for the number of weapons involved. It was known, however, that the Saudis had asked for 2,-500 Maverick air-to-surface missiles and 1,800 "TOW"—tube-launched, optically-tracked, wire-guided—missiles. The laser-guided bombs, of which 1,000 had been requested, were also known as "smart" bombs.

Soviet, Egyptian ministers talk. Soviet Foreign Minister Andrei A. Gromyko and Ismail Fahmy, his Egyptian counterpart, met in Sofia, Bulgaria Nov. 3–4, 1976 in an effort to improve relations between the two countries.

A final communique called for quick resumption of the Geneva conference on the Middle East and for more Egyptian-Soviet discussions to exchange views on bilateral relations.

The meetings coincided with a call in an Egyptian newspaper Nov. 4 for restoration of good relations with the Soviet Union as a means of countering U.S. President-elect Jimmy Carter's "exaggerated partiality" to Israel.

Egypt gets back 50 Soviet jets—Egyptian President Anwar Sadat disclosed in a U.S. TV interview broadcast Feb. 27, 1977 that the U.S.S.R. had informed him that Egypt would soon receive 50 refurbished Soviet MiG-21 fighter planes. The jets were among the 150 MiG-21s Egypt had sent to the Soviet Union for "complete overhaul" in the previous two years, Sadat said on the ABC-TV show "Issues and Answers."

In the interview, taped the previous week, Sadat said he had been pressing Moscow for more than six months for delivery when "suddenly we were told yesterday that they would be arriving." Sadat's statement was the first high-level acknowledgment by Cairo that despite his frequent complaints of Soviet refusal to continue to supply Egypt with arms, Moscow had not embargoed military aid to Egypt.

The disclosure of the plane shipments followed a sharp exchange between the Soviet Union and Egypt earlier in February over Sadat's memoirs that were being serialized in the Egyptian weekly magazine October. In the articles Sadat criticized the Soviets for inadequate military and financial assistance to Egypt.

The Soviet Communist Party newspaper Pravda Feb. 19 had assailed Sadat's published reminiscences as "lies, slander and falsification" of the Soviet role in Egypt and the Middle East. Accusing Sadat of "political libel" and of disseminating "misinformation on every question," Pravda said the Egyptian leader had distorted Soviet policy on Egypt and a Middle East peace settlement, slandered "the many years of friendly Soviet-Egyptian cooperation" and falsified Egypt's history under the late President Gamal Abdel Nasser, who had invited the Soviets into Egypt in the 1950s.

The Pravda article made a rare admission of the Soviet military role in the Middle East. It noted that the Soviet Union had re-equipped the defeated Egyptian armed forces after the 1967 Arab-Israeli war with "large quantities of modern weapons" and had even "assumed the defense of Egyptian air space." The latter phrase appeared to be further confirmation of reports at the time that Soviet airmen had piloted planes provided to Egypt by Moscow and that Soviet personnel had manned radar and antiaircraft missiles in Egypt.

In the 1973 Arab-Israeli war the Soviet Union delivered to Egypt "additional large quantities" of arms by air and sea and "undertook vigorous political actions" in support of the Arab cause in the United Nations, Pravda said.

Soviets cancel Egyptian arms deals. The Soviet Union had canceled its military contracts with Egypt, and Saudi Arabia had agreed to finance the development of Egypt's armed forces, President Anwar Sadat disclosed July 16, 1977.

Addressing a meeting of the governing Arab Socialist Union, Sadat said the Egyptian-Soviet dispute had come to a head while Foreign Minister Israel Fahmy had visited Moscow June 9–10. The Soviets demanded that Sadat meet with Communist Party Secretary General Leonid I. Brezhnev to sign a new "political agreement, defining the foundation of relations between the two countries," Sadat said. Moscow demanded that the pact be ratified by the Egyptian Parliament, which "would turn it into a treaty," according to Sadat.

As for the arms shipments, Sadat said the Soviets had "canceled all contracts between the two countries, although they have not honored their commitments under some of these contracts." Moscow, he said, insisted that in the future Cairo would have to pay in hard currency, even for spare parts.

The Soviet leaders, Sadat revealed, had presented Fahmy with two "ultimatums," which Cairo rejected. Moscow demanded that it be included in any future Middle East peace settlement and warned Egypt that it was backing Ethiopia against Sudan, which had Egyptian support.

On the matter of Saudi aid, Sadat said the Riyadh regime had pledged in 1976 to finance a five-year program to develop Egypt's armed forces "without us paying a penny."

Sadat's offer to Israel was a continuation of a startling new policy he had begun enunciating in November 1976, when he announced willingness to make peace with Israel.

As for Israel, Sadat said Egypt was prepared to sign an accord that would "end the state of war politically and legally." He added, "For the first time in its history, Israel's legal existence within its borders will be recognized."

Prelude to a Breakthrough

Sadat Calls for
Arab-Israeli Peace,
Other Peace Efforts Continue

In an unprecedented action for an Arab national leader, Egyptian President Anwar Sadat asserted in November 1976 that Arabs were ready for peace with Israel. His peace call was greeted with scepticism by Israelis and was either ignored or ridiculed by Arabs.

Sadat persisted, however. A scant year later he was in Jerusalem, on Israeli invitation, to address the Knesset, and a peace treaty was concluded by Egypt and Israel in March 1979. The Palestinians and other Arab nations, however, refused to follow Sadat's precedent, and the Arab confrontation with Israel continued.

Sadat, denounced by many Arabs as a traitor to the "Arab nation," continued his peace negotiations. He also criticized Israeli actions frequently and repeatedly asserted his loyalty to the Palestinian cause in particular and the Arab nation in general.

Sadat's peace signals. President Anwar Sadat of Egypt told U.S. Congress members in Cairo Nov. 11, 13, 14 and 17, 1976 that the Arabs were prepared to make peace with Israel.

Sadat Nov. 11 asked a 12-member congressional group headed by Rep. Walter Flowers (D, Ala.) to tell Israeli Premier Yitzhak Rabin that Sadat and other Arab leaders were ready to negotiate a peace settlement "on a sound and just basis" without preconditions. Sadat voiced similar views Nov. 13 to a 12-member Senate delegation headed by Abraham Ribicoff (D, Conn.) and Howard Baker (R, Tenn.) and at a meeting Nov. 14 with Sen. James Abourezk (D, S.D.).

In his Nov. 13 statement, Sadat urged that President-elect Jimmy Carter promote peace when he assumed office. "Let Carter take his time, but not for long because the problem of this area is so explosive," Sadat said.

Sadat also appealed for American arms, saying, "It's an obligation. We are friends and you know my policy. I have proved myself to you."

At a meeting Nov. 17 with a congressional group headed by Rep. Lester Wolff (D, N.Y.), Sadat again suggested that Carter take the initiative "in the coming spring with an American proposal for a peace settlement."

Rabin Nov. 11 had asked Ribicoff before he left Israel for Cairo to tell Sadat that Israel wanted to know what the Egyptian leader meant by "the nature of peace" and asked that he "stop talking in generalizations."

After completing his visit to Cairo Nov. 14, Ribicoff told a news conference that he was convinced by his talks with Sadat that "the Arab world is ready to accept that Israel is here to stay, that Israel has a right to exist."

Rabin Nov. 14 expressed further doubt about Sadat's peaceful intentions, saying that his statements were a diplomatic ploy to influence U.S. policy in the Middle East. "Israel is ready for immediate dialogue with Egypt if President Sadat is truly interested in a peace agreement."

Israeli Foreign Minister Yigal Allon and Defense Minister Shimon Peres Nov. 16 also were skeptical. Peres said that Sadat's remarks "lacked the ingredients Israel sees as essential to real peace."

Rabin said Nov. 17 that he hoped the U.S. "would not be fooled by beautiful words of peace from Arab states."

The Senate group headed by Ribicoff was in the Middle East to study the problem of nuclear proliferation in preparation for Senate action on U.S. offers of nuclear power reactors to Israel and Egypt. During their stay in Israel the Israeli Atomic Energy Commission had rejected a request by the senators to tour the nuclear installation at Dimona, Israeli sources reported Nov. 8. Ribicoff confirmed that the request had been made in Washington before his group left, but that the Israelis had refused, saying that no-one had visited the installation since 1969 and that they were opposed to international supervision of their research.

Geneva conference urged. Israeli Premier Rabin Nov. 27, 1976 proposed that the Geneva Conference on Middle East peace be reconvened on the model of the 1975 Helsinki security conference. The theme of such a parley, as at Helsinki, Rabin said, should be dialogue, detente and coexistence and acceptance of the principle that the Arab-Israeli dispute "cannot be solved by war." The premier noted that the statements about peace expressed in recent days by "some voices in the Middle East" had not been "addressed to Israel, directly or indirectly."

In apparent response to Rabin's statement on peace, Egyptian Foreign Minister Ismail Fahmy Dec. 2 urged the U.S. and the Soviet Union, as co-chairmen of the Geneva conference, to call for a renewal of the talks in the first quarter of 1977. "The invitation should be accompanied by definite proposals for achieving an overall settlement," Fahmy said.

He was critical of Rabin's call for a Helsinki-type conference and accused the Israeli leader of attempting to "distort facts and mislead world public opinion." Israel should either agree to become a secular state where Palestinians and Jews would live as equals or it should agree to formation of a separate Palestinian state, Fahmy said.

In an interview appearing Dec. 30 in the Beirut newspaper An Nahar, Sadat said that the Arabs were prepared to go to Geneva for "a final settlement" of the Arab-Israeli conflict.

The U.N. General Assembly Dec. 9 approved, 122–2, an Egyptian resolution to reconvene the Geneva conference by March 1, 1977. The U.S. and Israel were the only nations to vote "no."

The document asked that Secretary General Kurt Waldheim contact "all the parties to the conflict" to prepare for the opening of the Geneva parley not later than March 1.

The assembly also approved a second Egyptian resolution, 91–11 with 29 abstentions, specifically citing the right of the Palestinians to take part in the Geneva talks and demanding that Israel withdraw from occupied Arab lands and permit the establishment of a Palestinian state.

Israel expressed opposition to the first resolution on the ground that the phrase "all the parties to the conflict" implied participation of the Palestinians at Geneva, a move opposed by Israel as well as the U.S. Israel's ambassador, Chaim Herzog, told the assembly that the resolution would "change the ground rules of the Geneva conference and substitute a dictated settlement for direct negotiations between the two parties." This was an apparent reference to the resolution's implied attempt to inject the assembly and the Security Council into the peace efforts that had thus far been the responsibility of the U.S. and the Soviet Union, co-chairmen of the Geneva conference.

William W. Scranton, chief U.S. delegate, said that although the U.S. favored resumption of the Geneva talks, "We do not consider it appropriate to join now in a definition of detailed options or time limits governing the evaluation of this crucial negotiating process." The matter, he said, "obviously is a question which will be addressed" by the new U.S. administration when it assumed office in January 1977.

The Egyptian resolutions had been introduced Dec. 2. An Israeli counterresolution submitted by Herzog Dec. 6 called for reconvening the Geneva conference "without delay" with its original participants—Israel, Jordan, Egypt and Syria—and excluding the Palestinians. This was followed by an Arab-supported amendment to the Israeli draft, introduced by Yugoslavia, India and Sri Lanka, that called for Palestinian participation at Geneva.

In another statement on peace prospects, Sadat said the PLO must be permitted to attend any future Geneva peace conference, otherwise the parley could not be held, according to an interview published Jan. 4, 1977 by the Egyptian newspaper Al Ahram. This was the first time Sadat had implied that the Arabs might boycott Geneva if the Palestinians were excluded.

Speaking to an Arab delegation from the Gaza Strip, Sadat also said the Arab demand for the establishment of a Palestinian state in the Israeli-occupied West Bank and Gaza Strip was a "strategic Egyptian-Syrian decision, and there is no room to back down from it."

Egyptian Foreign Minister Ismail Fahmy warned Jan. 11 that his country might go to war against Israel if the Geneva talks or other peace efforts failed. If the Geneva conference were not reconvened or if peace talks were held and they collapsed, Egypt would then "call for a U.N. Security Council meeting that will have to work out a just solution to the Arab-Israeli conflict," Fahmy said. If this effort also did not succeed, he said, "friends and foes must know that the liberation of Israeli-occupied Arab territories is a sacred cause to us. War will always remain in our calculations."

Sadat and King Hussein of Jordan agreed at an Aswan meeting Jan. 14–15 to back a separate PLO delegation to Geneva.

The discussions were part of a continuing Arab effort to forge a common strategy for their expected peace negotiations with Israel. Hussein and Sadat also agreed to strengthen relations between their two countries. Those ties had become particularly strained in 1976 when Jordan supported Syria's intervention in the Lebanese civil war.

Assessing the Sadat-Hussein stand on the PLO, Israeli Foreign Minister Yigal Allon Jan. 19 reiterated his government's refusal to negotiate with the Palestinian group. Allon called the PLO a "murderous organization" whose aim remained "the destruction of Israel" despite its recent claims of moderation. Israel, Allon said, also would continue to oppose "the sterile idea of a third [Palestinian] state between Israel and Jordan." He insisted that "there is only room for one Arab state" in the area, a Jordanian-Palestinian state whose boundaries should "be determined in free negotiations for peace."

French role? The possibility of France playing an important part in Arab-Israeli negotiations was brought up in meetings at which Saudi Arabia agreed to increase oil exports to France. The discussions took place during a visit by French President Valery Giscard d'Estaing with King Khalid of Saudi Arabia and other Saudi officials in Riyadh Jan. 22–25, 1977.

In an interview with an Agence France-Presse correspondent Jan. 24, the king offered a suggestion that the French should play an "eminent role" in a Middle East peace settlement. He urged France to call on other Western European nations to support the "just cause" of the Palestinians. The monarch insisted that the Palestine Liberation Organization be represented by an "independent" delegation at any resumed Geneva peace conference.

Before his departure Jan. 25, Giscard told a news conference that he and the Saudi leaders had agreed that prior to any Geneva conference there must be thorough preparation "on the basis of substance rather than procedure." The term "procedure" was an apparent reference to the dispute over PLO participation in the Geneva talks.

Waldheim in Mideast. U.N. Secretary General Kurt Waldheim toured six Middle Eastern states Feb. 2–12, 1977 to determine prospects for peace. Before his departure he had said Jan. 30 that "if we are unable to achieve a breakthrough in the negotiating process this year, we will have another Middle East war in two years' time."

On arriving in Cairo Feb. 2, Waldheim said the principle purpose of his diplomatic mission was to remove procedural impediments to renewal of the Geneva peace conference at the earliest possible date and to gather suggestions for an agenda. The secretary general said after a meeting Feb. 3 with Egyptian Foreign Minister Ismail Fahmy that Cairo was flexible on the timing for the Geneva talks but adamant about having the PLO participate.

Waldheim met with Syrian officials in Damascus Feb. 4–5 and then went on to Riyadh, where he conferred with Saudi Arabian leaders. From there he flew to Beirut and met with Lebanese officials and PLO leader Yasir Arafat Feb. 6–7 and then traveled to Amman where he held discussions with King Hussein of Jordan Feb. 8–9.

Waldheim arrived in Israel Feb. 10, meeting with Premier Yitzhak Rabin, Foreign Minister Yigal Allon and Defense Minister Shimon Peres. The Israelis informed Waldheim of their long-standing refusal to enter into peace talks with the PLO as long as it adhered to that part of its founding covenant calling for the replacement of Israel with a "democratic secular" state.

Waldheim assured the Israelis that he had not come as a "mediator" but only to seek commitments from all parties for new peace talks.

Prior to leaving Jerusalem Feb. 11 after a second day of talks with Israeli leaders, Waldheim said he saw "a new, more flexible Palestinian attitude" toward Israel. But Israeli leaders disputed his assessment. Allon said Waldheim had told the Israeli leaders that "the situation was ripe for negotiations." Allon said he had pointed out to Waldheim "that whenever an Arab expresses himself—that he is ready to negotiate—he immediately attaches a long list of preconditions as if he was trying to decide the results of the conference before it begins."

Waldheim's remarks were an apparent response to an Israeli Foreign Ministry statement reported Feb. 6 that Israel favored peace efforts by the U.S., not the U.N., to reach a settlement. Implying that the world body was biased, a senior ministry official was quoted as saying that Israel would oppose "majority tyranny," which he contended was contained in the Dec. 9, 1976 U.N. General Assembly resolution calling for PLO participation in any peace talks.

Foreign Minister Allon had said Feb. 7 that the U.N. was not an "honest broker" in the Arab-Israeli dispute and that his government therefore had "no intention of giving the United Nations any role in peace negotiations in this area."

Waldheim returned to Cairo that day for another round of talks with Egyptian leaders Feb. 11–12.

Waldheim expressed optimism about prospects for peace during a stopover in Vienna Feb. 16. He said Israel and the Palestine Liberation Organization might "mutually recognize each other" at some future peace negotiations. Although Israel had ruled out any PLO participation at a resumed Geneva peace conference, there was "a very clear and visible interest on both sides for negotiation," according to Waldheim. He said Arafat seemed "more flexible." Arafat, he said, represented a relatively modern faction that did not support a "hard-line" wing that demanded the destruction of Israel. The so-called moderates in the PLO, he held, no longer insisted on a "secular state" that would mean elimination of Israel but would settle for a "small" Palestinian state consisting of the West Bank and the Gaza Strip.

Reporting to the Security Council on his mission to the Middle East, Waldheim said Feb. 28 that the principal elements of the Arab-Israeli dispute "remain intractable" and that the Middle East faced dangers unless agreement were reached soon on resuming peace negotiations to resolve these differences.

The secretary acknowledged that he had failed to break the Arab-Israeli impasse over the most immediate obstacle to the reconvening of the Geneva peace conference—the matter of participation by the Palestine Liberation Organization.

Waldheim for the first time provided details of a number of interim procedures he had proposed as a means of getting negotiations started. These included a preparatory U.N. working group to be established under his auspices to maintain discussions with the disputants and with the U.S. and the Soviet Union as co-chairmen of the Geneva conference. But Waldheim said he concluded after his meetings with Arab and Israeli leaders that a number of formulas he had explored were doomed unless there were "changes of attitudes" on both sides. He said this meant the PLO's adamant stand against the existence of Israel and Israel's attitude toward the Palestinians.

In a related development, Austrian Chancellor Bruno Kreisky said Feb. 13 he had received a PLO document that said the Palestinians would accept the establishment of a state in the West Bank and Gaza Strip and that they would agree to "a non-belligerent status" with Israel. Calling this a "a total change of policy," Kreisky said "it is up to the Israelis now to find a way of co-existence with the Palestineans."

But the PLO's chief political officer, Farouk Khaddoumi, declared that his organization's policy remained the ultimate establishment of a secular state in all of Palestine, with the resultant dissolution of the state of Israel, according to an interview published in the March 14 issue of Newsweek.

Khaddoumi said there was no "possibility" that the PLO would revoke its covenant, which called for the dismemberment of Israel. The establishment of a Palestinian state in the West Bank and Gaza Strip "doesn't mean that we are giving up the rest of our." claim to the remainder of Palestine, he said. According to Khaddoumi, his people would take over all of Palestine in three phases: "the first phase to the 1967 lines, and the second to the 1948 lines. . . . The third stage is the democratic state of Palestine."

Palestinians, Jordan & the West Bank Dilemma

Jordan, PLO agree on link. Representatives of Jordan and the Palestine Liberation Organization met in Amman Feb. 22–23, 1977 and agreed "in principle" to form a strong link between Jordan and a proposed Palestinian state in the West Bank and Gaza Strip. President Anwar Sadat of Egypt had made such a proposal in a meeting with U.S. Secretary of State Cyrus Vance in Cairo Feb. 17.

Participating in the discussions were Jordanian Premier Mudar Badran and a PLO delegation headed by Khaled Fahoum, head of the Palestine National Council (the PLO's parliament). The discussions were the first between the two sides since they were involved in heavy fighting in Jordan in 1970.

Israeli party backs land return. Israel's Labor Party Feb. 25, 1977 for the first time agreed on an election platform that called for ceding some of the occupied West Bank to Jordan. Israeli government leaders in the past had favored such territorial concessions and had held exploratory talks with Jordan.

The new formula stated that "political efforts to reach permanent peace in defensible borders with Egypt, Jordan and Syria are to be continued with readiness for territorial compromise with each of them."

Previously, the Labor Party's platforms had merely favored "territorial compromise" to attain peace, but never specified what territory Israel would be willing to return. This was in consideration of Israelis who were opposed to giving back any section of the West Bank, which they regarded as part of the historic Jewish homeland.

A motion by former Defense Minister Moshe Dayan opposing the party plank was defeated by a 659–606 vote. Dayan argued that he was not against returning some land to Jordan, but was opposed to the plank on the ground that it implied Israeli recognition of Jordanian claims to the West Bank. Originally the territory had been designated as part of an Arab state under a United Nations partition plan, but Jordan seized it in fighting with the newly established state of Israel in 1948. As a result, Dayan said, "We shouldn't be the ones to annex it to Jordan."

Another party plank classified the Jordan Valley and the Jerusalem district among occupied areas that would receive priority in Jewish settlements "for security consideration." The party also adopted a clause reiterating its refusal to deal with the Palestine Liberation Organization.

Palestinians unchanged on Israel. The Palestinian leadership reconfirmed its opposition to the existence of Israel at a meeting of the Palestine National Council in Cairo March 12–20, 1977.

A 15-point declaration adopted March 20 by a 194–13 vote called for establishment of a Palestinian state on "national soil" and a continuation of the "armed struggle" against Israel—especially in the Israeli-occupied Arab territories. It rejected recognition of Israel or the signing of any complete peace agreement. The PNC left unaltered its charter, which called for the establishment of a secular, democratic state, a move that would be tantamount to ending Israel.

The council declaration also affirmed the right of the Palestine Liberation Organization "to participate on an independent, equal footing in all international conferences, forums and efforts concerned with the Palestinian question and with the Arab-Israeli conflict." This clause differed from the one adopted at the National Council's 1973 conference, which had called for council approval of any PLO participation in international meetings.

The resolution reiterated Palestinian rejection of United Nations Security Council Resolution 242 as the basis for peace negotiations, but implied acceptance of U.N. General Assembly Resolution 3236 adopted after the 1973 war as the foundation for settlement talks. Resolution 242 referred to the Palestinian question as a refugee problem whereas 3236 referred to the Palestinians' national rights.

Adoption of the resolution represented a victory of the so-called moderate wing of the Palestinian movement over the Rejection Front, whose 13 members voted against. The front was opposed to a negotiated settlement in the Middle East.

Yasir Arafat was reelected chairman of the executive council of the PLO at the end of the session.

Khaled Fahoum, a pro-Syrian, had been reelected president of the National Council March 13, defeating Bahjat Abu Gharbiyah by a vote of 172–69. There were 21 abstentions. Abu Gharbiyah was a member of the Popular Struggle Front, one of four groups belonging to the Rejection Front. His candidacy was sponsored by the Popular Front for the Liberation of Palestine, the most radical group in the front.

Israeli Premier Rabin said March 20 that the meeting showed that when even so-called moderates prevailed, the Palestinians still called for the destruction of Israel. He said the only place Israel could meet the Palestinian guerrillas was on the battlefield.

The U.S. State Department said March 21 that the National Council's decision to continue to oppose Israel's existence would "not contribute" to a Middle East settlement.

Carter Continues U.S. Peace Role

The U.S. administration of President Jimmy Carter took office in January 1977 and assumed a major burden shouldered by previous American governments—the effort to bring peace to the Middle East.

Vance tours Mideast. U.S. Secretary of State Cyrus Vance visited Israel and five Arab states Feb. 15–21, 1977 on a fact-finding mission as part of the continuing American effort to seek a comprehensive settlement of the Middle East dispute. His immediate aim was to help pave the way for reconvening the Geneva peace conference. Vance was particularly concerned about the role of the Palestine Liberation Organization and sought to determine whether it had eased its adamant stand against the existence of Israel. In his meeting with Egyptian President Anwar Sadat Feb. 17, the secretary received a surprise proposal calling for "an official and declared link" between the PLO and Jordan before the Geneva talks were held.

Also during his tour, Vance advised the Israelis of the Carter Administration's decision not to sell the controversial concussion bomb to Israel.

Vance arrived in Jerusalem Feb. 15 on the first leg of his tour and conferred Feb. 16–17 with Premier Yitzhak Rabin, Foreign Minister Yigal Allon, Defense Minister Shimon Peres and other Israeli officials. The secretary stated both days that unless the PLO revised its covenant to accept the right of Israel to exist and as long as it refused to accept U.N. Security Council Resolutions 242 and 338 as the basis for a peace settlement, the U.S. would continue to oppose the participation of the PLO at the Geneva conference.

The announcement on the cancellation of the concussion bomb sale was made simultaneously Feb. 17 in Jerusalem by Vance and in Washington by the White House. The decision reversed a pledge by President Ford in late 1976 to sell the sophisticated weapon to Israel. White House Press Secretary Jody Powell said, "We have no intention of selling these weapons to any country, and we are . . . reassessing the need to retain the weapons in our own inventory." The administration would go ahead with the sale of M60 tanks and 155 mm. artillery pieces to Israel, as promised by the Ford Administration, Powell said.

President Sadat's proposal for a PLO-Jordanian link was made at a Cairo news conference Feb. 17 following a two-hour talk with Vance. Stating that "the Palestinian question is the core of the whole problem," Sadat suggested that "they should participate [at the Geneva conference] if you want to reach a permanent peace as we are trying now. And I say an official and declared link should take place between this Palestinian state and Jordan even before Geneva starts."

The Sadat plan appeared aimed at overcoming Israeli objections to the presence of a separate PLO delegation at Geneva and to the creation of a separate independent Palestinian state on the West Bank and Gaza Strip.

Israel Feb. 18 reacted cautiously to Sadat's proposal. A Foreign Ministry official said the government would not issue a formal response until it received details from the U.S.

Vance lauded the Sadat proposal at a news conference Feb. 18 aboard his plane on his way to Amman, Jordan. He said it showed "more flexibility" existed in the Egyptian position "than I had thought before I had come to Cairo." His talks with Sadat had led him to believe that the Egyptians were pressuring the PLO to amend the anti-Israeli stand in its charter, Vance said.

Vance conferred with King Hussein in Amman Feb. 18–19. The king was reported Feb. 19 to have expressed reluctance about forming a link with the PLO. He told Vance that he still felt bound by the Arab summit decision at Rabat, Morocco in 1974 that gave the PLO full responsibility for negotiating the future of the Palestinians in the West Bank. Sadat's

proposal, the king noted, represented a reversal of that decision.

Hussein also cautioned Vance against becoming too hopeful about achieving a breakthrough in current peace moves. The king expressed fear that the secretary's mission could lead to expectations that might not be realized, thus sparking new tensions in the area.

Vance had stopped off briefly Feb. 18 in Beirut. Authorities there sounded him out on what Washington's reaction would be if Lebanon asked to participate in the Geneva talks.

At his meetings Feb. 19 with Saudi officials in Riyadh, Vance was told the U.S. must recognize the PLO in order to break the political impasse that was barring the way to resumption of the Geneva talks. Crown Prince Fahd, first deputy premier and acting head of state, said the Arabs would be flexible at Geneva but that the U.S. had to pressure Israel to make concessions, including withdrawal from occupied Arab territory and recognition of Palestinian rights.

Vance conferred with President Hafez al-Assad and other Syrian officials on the last leg of his tour in Damascus Feb. 20. A Syrian statement issued after the discussions said Assad had voiced skepticism that Israel would make major concessions that could lead to a Middle East solution. Vance and the president discussed the procedural problems involving a PLO presence at Geneva. The statement repeated the Syrian demand that Israel pull out of all occupied territories and recognize the rights of the Palestinians.

Vance said on his departure for the U.S. Feb. 21 that he found the Arabs and Israelis still "deeply divided" on how to resolve their dispute. He foresaw "a very hard and difficult road ahead," adding that "these are deeply held views and they will be difficult for people to change."

Vance said he found that disagreement among the Arabs themselves on the question of the Palestinian problem posed a further complication.

Carter meets Israeli premier. Israeli Premier Yitzhak Rabin met with President Carter in Washington March 7–8, 1977 to discuss the reconvening of the Geneva conference and other matters.

In greeting Rabin March 7, Carter caused a stir by appearing to support Israel's policy of refusing to return all the Arab land it had captured in the 1967 war. The President March 9 offered a new approach to a settlement by suggesting at his news conference that Israel or an international force maintain a defense line in Arab areas from which Israel would withdraw.

In his welcoming remarks to Rabin, Carter said that in their talks in the next two days the Administration wanted "to explore some common ground for peace so that Israel might have defensible borders and so that the peace commitments might never be violated and so that there could be a sense of security about" Israel.

Israel had always used the phrase "defensible borders" to mean that it would retain enough territory seized from Egypt, Syria and Jordan in the 1967 war to enable it to defend itself. The Arabs had been demanding total Israeli withdrawal. The U.S. in the past had deliberately avoided taking a stand on the territorial question relating to a peace settlement in order not to compromise its impartial mediation efforts.

Administration officials immediately sought to qualify Carter's remarks. Secretary of State Cyrus Vance told reporters "there is no change in [the U.S.] position by the use of the words 'defensible borders.' "

White House Press Secretary Jody Powell said newsmen should "avoid a narrow definition of 'defensible borders' in geographic terms" and instead should note that Carter was speaking "in broad terms, reiterating the intent of the United Nations resolutions about secure borders."

Speaking to newsmen after his concluding round of talks with Carter March 8, Rabin made no claim that the President supported Israel's own definition of "defensible borders." The premier, however, insisted that "legally we have the right to negotiate boundaries" quite apart from the pre-1967 borders, which he called only "demarcation lines."

Rabin also reiterated the Israeli policy of refusing to participate in any Geneva conference that included the Palestine Liberation Organization and of insisting on a "real peace" in which the Arab states had to accept Israel and conduct normal trade, travel and other contacts with it.

Rabin supported Carter's efforts to arrange the Geneva talks in the summer or fall. But privately Israeli officials asserted a total settlement was unattainable and regarded individual step-by-step agreements with Egypt, Syria and Jordan as a more realistic goal.

Jody Powell said Carter still believed that 1977 was "a crucial year of opportunity" and would continue to explore the prospects for peace in meetings in the next two months with leaders of Egypt, Jordan, Syria and Saudi Arabia.

Carter also had informed Rabin that his Administration would carry out the Ford Administration's decision to sell Israel F-16 jets.

Speaking at his news conference March 9, President Carter outlined a set of principles under which Israel ultimately would withdraw from all Arab lands it had taken in the 1967 war, with only "some minor adjustments" in the frontiers that existed before the conflict. The President foresaw this settlement taking as long as eight years to reach through a step-by-step approach. During the interim, he said, Israel could have "defense lines" that "may be extensions of Israeli defense capability beyond the permanent and recognized borders." He said there must be a "distinction" between actual sovereign borders and "the ability of Israel to defend herself by international agreement or by some placement of Israeli forces themselves or by monitoring stations, as has been the case in the Sinai, beyond the actual sovereign borders."

Under further questioning, Carter later broadened his suggestion by saying, "I didn't confine the defense capabilities to the Israeli forces. These might very well be international forces. It might very well be a line that's fairly broad, say 20 kilometers or more, where demilitarization is guaranteed on both sides." Any accord on "permanent and recognized borders must be mutually agreed to by Israel and its Arab neighbors," Carter said.

Carter supported the basic Israeli condition for peace, that the Arabs should recognize its "right to exist, the right to exist in peace, the opening up of borders with free trade, tourist travel [and] cultural exchanges between Israel and her neighbors."

Alluding to Carter's views, Premier Rabin said in an impromptu speech to a luncheon of American Jewish leaders in Washington later March 9 that Israel was prepared to take advice from the U.S. but ultimately it "was up to the parties to the conflict to make final decisions."

Administration officials March 9 reassured Israeli and Arab diplomats in Washington that Carter's views did not constitute a definitive U.S. plan but that they were aimed at encouraging both sides to negotiate. Zbigniew Brzezinski, national security adviser, telephoned Hanan Bar-on, the second-ranking official at the Israeli Embassy, and read him the following portion of the transcript of Carter's news conference, which Brzezinski described as "the crux of the policy": "We are going to mount a major effort in our own government in '77 to bring the parties to Geneva. Obviously any agreement has to be between the parties concerned. We will act as intermediary when our good offices will serve well. But I am not going to predispose our own nation's attitude toward what might be the ultimate details of the agreement that can mean so much to world peace."

Rabin said in a taped televised interview in the U.S. March 13 that he was opposed to the President's call for Israel to withdraw from all Arab territories taken in the 1967 war except for "minor adjustments" in the prewar frontiers. "Without any qualification, Israel will not return to the lines that existed before the 1967 war," the premier said. Carter's remarks March 9 called on Israel to return "more territories" than "we want to give," Rabin said.

On returning to Israel March 13, Rabin defended his meetings with Carter as "positive on the whole," but he said "not everything was to our liking." He insisted that the President had not accepted the Arabs' demand for total Israeli withdrawal, noting that Carter "qualified what he thinks, and he added a new element—the distinction between political boundaries and defensible boundaries."

Reporting to his Cabinet March 14 on his U.S. trip, Rabin rejected claims by some Israeli officials and the Israeli press that Carter's formula for a settlement represented a revival of the plans advanced by Secretary of State William P. Rogers in 1969 and 1970 that had been rejected by Israel. The Rogers scheme had been intended as an imposed solution, while Carter made clear that it was up to both sides themselves to reach an agreement, Rabin pointed out.

Israeli officials said March 15 that as a result of his talks with Carter, Rabin was now inclined to work for a comprehensive peace settlement with the Arabs. This would be a reversal of the former Israeli position of favoring a step-by-step approach on the ground that the Arab states were too far apart for high-level discussions. The Israeli shift, it was said, was based on Carter's support of Jerusalem's basic condition for peace—total Arab acceptance of Israel's right to exist.

One Israeli official said: "It seems like Carter wants to go for the maximum. We prefer that now that we know what the Americans define as peace."

A Palestine Liberation Organization spokesman March 10 had assailed Carter's views, asserting that "this is another confirmation that American foreign policy still supports Israel and denies the rights of the Palestinian people." A PLO source was especially critical of the President's support of "defensible borders for Israel," calling it backing "for Israel's expansionist policies."

Secretary of State Cyrus R. Vance met in Washington March 12 with four Arab ambassadors and said afterward they were convinced that the U.S. had not changed its Middle East policies.

Egypt scores Carter's views—Carter's Middle East views as expressed in his news conference drew sharp criticism from Egyptian officials March 10.

Coming on the heels of his meeting with Premier Rabin, the President's remarks raised Egyptian fears that he had been persuaded by the premier to bring the U.S. position closer to that of Israel. "It sounds as if he has swallowed the old Allon plan," one official said. This was a reference to a plan advanced in 1968 by Foreign Minister Yigal Allon, then labor minister, that called for the establishment of Israeli paramilitary settlements along the west bank of the Jordan River as a buffer zone beyond Israel's 1967 borders.

Criticizing Carter for "juxtaposing borders with defense lines," another Cairo leader said: "In international law, we only know of legal borders and defense arrangements. U.N. Emergency Forces and demilitarized zones are not defense lines, they are security arrangements."

President Anwar Sadat said March 12 that Egypt "will not cede a single inch of

Arab land and that our national territory is not open to bargaining; the Israelis must withdraw from all occupied lands." His statement, made at the opening of the Palestine National Council's conference in Cairo, was in obvious response to a distinction made by Carter March 9 between Israel's future "legal boundaries" and forward "defense lines." The issue of secure borders, Sadat stressed, was "nothing but a fantasy. It is not admissible that anybody should speak of secure boundaries as part of the Israeli conception; it is absolutely unjust and unacceptable."

Carter calls for Palestinian 'homeland.'
President Carter set off another controversy by calling for a Palestinian "homeland" in a speech to a town hall meeting in Clinton, Mass. March 16, 1977.

Discussing the prospects for a Middle East settlement, the President said "the first prerequisite of a lasting peace is the recognition of Israel by her neighbors, ... Israel's right to exist in peace. ... The second one is ... the establishment of permanent borders for Israel. ... And the third ultimate requirement for peace is to deal with the Palestinian problem."

Carter observed that "the Palestinians claim that Israel has no right to be there" and "they have never yet given up their publicly professed commitment to destroy Israel. This has to be overcome."

The President then concluded, "There has to be a homeland for the Palestinian refugees who have suffered for many, many years."

Administration spokesmen later explained that Carter's statement did "not imply that the U.S. takes a position on what form it [the 'homeland'] will take."

Carter told newsmen while flying to New York that his call for a Palestinian "homeland" was "appropriate." He said that "some provision has got to be made for the Palestinians, in the framework of the nation of Jordan or by some other means."

Israel was opposed to the establishment of a third state between it and Jordan. Premier Yitzhak Rabin reiterated this view March 17, stating he was concerned about Carter's suggestion. Rabin said he could endorse the President's formula if the homeland became part of a Jordanian-Palestinian state at peace with Israel. "But I fear Carter did not mean it that way," Rabin said.

PLO leader Yasir Arafat and other delegates attending the Palestine National Council conference in Cairo March 17 welcomed Carter's proposal. Other representatives, however, said it did not go far enough and doubted that the U.S. would try to get the plan implemented. Informed of the Carter remark, Arafat said, "They tell me he mentioned the Palestinian homeland. If he did, ... it is a progressive step because it means he has finally put his hand on the heart of the problem of the Middle East crisis. It helps the whole situation."

In an address to the conference earlier March 17, Arafat had restated PLO policy of working toward the eventual establishment of a secular and democratic state in all of Palestine, an action that would eliminate the state of Israel.

Sadat confers with Carter. Egyptian President Anwar Sadat met with President Carter in Washington April 4–5, 1977 to seek U.S. military and economic assistance and to press his views on a peace settlement for the Middle East. Differences between the two countries on major issues were not resolved, however.

Summing up the conferences, a White House statement April 5 said the Egyptian leader had spoken of his request for military equipment that day with Carter and Defense Secretary Harold E. Brown. Sadat had said in the past that he wanted about 200 F-5E fighter planes, as well as antitank weapons and other equipment. The White House said the military discussions had been "in general terms" and "no commitments or decisions are anticipated" soon.

Sadat reportedly had stressed that the requested American arms were necessary to offset the threat to his country by Soviet influence in neighboring Libya and Ethiopia, and by Moscow's alleged support for the invasion of Zaire.

Sadat had said on being welcomed by Carter April 4 that the Palestinian question was "the core and crux" of the Arab-Israeli dispute and that "no progress whatsoever can be achieved so long as this problem remains unsolved." Recalling Carter's March 16 statement on the need for a Palestinian "homeland," Sadat told the President that he "came very close to the proper remedy. What is needed is the establishment of a political entity where the Palestinians can, at long last, be a community of citizens, not a group of refugees."

Sadat's allusion to a Palestinian "entity" rather than a "state" and alteration of his prepared text to read Palestinian "normal rights" instead of his oft-repeated "national rights" appeared to represent a change in the Egpytian leader's approach to the Palestinian problem.

A communique issued after the April 4 talks said Carter and Sadat had agreed "the time is right for a major effort to resume negotiations, and reaffirmed that they will work toward reconvening the Geneva conference in the second half of 1977."

Discussing his meetings with Carter, Sadat told a Washington news conference April 6 that U.S.-Egyptian differences still existed. He took particular issue with Carter's previous suggestion that Israel be permitted to maintain defense lines beyond its sovereign borders as part of a peace agreement. Sadat said, "Sovereignty is indivisible, and we can't have two borders. There is always one border for any country."

Sadat also said he was seeking "to end the state of belligerency, to give Israel whatever guarantees she asks for . . ., and to solve the Palestinian question by creating the new Palestinian state on the West Bank and Gaza Strip with a corridor between them through Israel, and, for sure, everything will be normalized." Sadat, however, ruled out trade between Egypt and Israel as part of a normalized state of affairs.

Before arriving in Washington, Sadat had said during a stopover in Paris April 3 that all Arab states were in favor of an "official and declared relation between the new Palestinian state" and Jordan.

Sadat defended the decision by the Palestine National Council at its meeting in Cairo March 12-20 not to alter its charter to permit recognition of Israel. Asserting that the council had shown "very great flexibility," Sadat said, "It is not fair to recognize Israel beforehand while Israel has its state, its land and is a member of the United Nations recognized by 140 nations, while the Palestinians have got nothing. . . ."

Carter meets with Jordan's Hussein. President Carter discussed the Middle East situation with Jordanian King Hussein in Washington April 25-26, with emphasis on the Palestinian question.

Carter April 26 cautioned against reconvening the Geneva peace conference prematurely. He said unless there was "a strong possibility of achievements" before the meeting, "then I think it would be better not to have the Geneva conference at all."

The "more agreements that we can reach before going to Geneva, the less argument there is going to be about the form of the Palestinian representation" at the talks, Carter stressed. The Arabs themselves, he noted, must work out "the exact composition" of their delegation to Geneva and the interrelationships among the Arabs.

Hussein echoed Carter's views on Geneva at a news conference. The parley, he warned, "would be a disaster without prior planning and without a realistic appraisal" of the difficult problems that had to be resolved in advance.

The king said prospects for peace were good but he placed the burden of achieving it on Israel. Was Israel, he asked, "willing to withdraw from territories occupied in the 1967 war against [the assurances of] peace for her and for all of us? If she is not, there will be disaster for all of us—and maybe the world."

Hussein told a Washington gathering April 27 that it was up to the Palestinians to decide the type of a "homeland" they wanted. Speaking at a joint meeting of the American-Arab Association for Commerce and Industry and the Middle East Institute, the king said, "If it is not to be a Palestinian state, we accept that, if it is to be affiliated with Jordan, we would welcome the resumption of natural brotherly ties." The monarch reiterated his call to Israel to "have enough historic courage and seek a lasting peace."

Israel cautious on Geneva—Israel April 27 supported the stand of President Carter and King Hussein on reconvening the Geneva conference. A Foreign Ministry spokesman said Israel would "rather

postpone a Geneva conference than go to
a conference that has not been very well
and in detail prepared in advance." It
would be "much more dangerous to have a
failure at Geneva than to postpone a
conference," the spokesman said.

Acting Premier Shimon Peres had said
April 25 that peace talks were still possible in 1977, but he maintained that the
obstacles remained formidable. In his first
major address since he assumed the duties
of the office, Peres said even Arab leaders,
including King Hussein and Egyptian
President Anwar Sadat, "who talk of ending the state of belligerency are not prepared to pay the price." Referring to Arab
demands that Israel withdraw from occupied Arab territories, Peres said "only
Israel is ready for territorial compromise.
There is not one Arab I know who is prepared to accept territorial compromises in
order to put an end to war and bring about
peace."

Speaking to a Cabinet meeting April 24,
Foreign Minister Yigal Allon said that
recent remarks by President Carter and
other American officials pointed to possible U.S.-Israeli differences on means of
reaching a peace settlement. Among the
potential divergences cited was a reported
Carter proposal that mechanical monitoring devices be placed at a distance from
Israel's borders to protect it against Arab
attack. A Cabinet communique quoted
Allon as saying "that no technical means
or other security arrangements could be
considered a substitute for defensible
borders for Israel, but only as supple-
menting them."

Allon also expressed concern about
Carter's use of the term "minor adjustments" in discussing Israeli withdrawal
from Arab territories. U.S. failure to
specify the geographical extent of "minor
adjustments" would create U.S.-Israeli
tensions, Allon warned.

Carter & Syria's Assad meet. President
Carter met May 9, 1977 with Syrian
President Hafez al-Assad in Geneva as
part of the continuing American effort to
sound out Middle East leaders on prospects for resolving the Arab-Israeli
dispute. Carter had traveled to the Swiss
city after attending an international economic conference in London.

Following his three-hour discussion with
the Syrian president, Carter repeated to
reporters the key elements of his Middle
East policy: "a resolution of the Palestine
problem and a homeland for the Palestinians"; "some resolution of border disputes," and "an assurance of permanent
and real peace with guarantees for the future security of these countries, which all
can trust."

Praising Assad as one of the "moderate
leaders" of the Middle East, Carter said
he looked to the Syrian president "for
guidance and advice and support" in the
search for peace. Carter insisted that the
U.S. was prepared to act as an "intermediary," but that accords must be negotiated by the parties directly involved.

Assad warned in a prepared statement
that Israel's continued occupation of Arab
territories captured in the 1967 war, and
the "homelessness" of the Palestinians,
posed a threat of new "wars and tragedies
from which our region has suffered for 30
years."

Reviewing the talks, Zbigniew Brzezinski, the President's national security
adviser, said the two leaders had discussed
the matter of demilitarized zones or
"other security arrangements" to guarantee borders.

(Assad had told a news conference in
Damascus May 5 that he was prepared to
accept demilitarized zones as part of a
Middle East peace settlement. Previously
he had insisted that Israel return to its
pre-1967 borders and that Syria not cede
"an inch" of territory in any settlement,
including in the Golan Heights. In his
latest statement, Assad said: "If a
Mideast settlement requires the establishment of a demilitarized zone, we are free
to discuss the issue provided the zones are
narrow and on both sides of the border.")

Palestine problem stressed—President
Carter's renewed call for a Palestinian
"homeland" was regarded as significant
because of a Soviet report that Palestine
Liberation Organization leader Yasir
Arafat was prepared to accept the
existence of Israel if Israel would endorse
a Palestinian homeland. Soviet Ambassador to the U.S. Anatoly F. Dobrynin
had informed Secretary of State Cyrus R.
Vance the previous week of Arafat's
reputed new stand. In his briefing of
newsmen May 9, however, Brzezinski said

there was no indication "at this stage" that the PLO had adopted a new position on the matter.

President Assad reportedly had submitted to Carter a proposal by Syria, Egypt, Saudi Arabia and the PLO for the creation of a Palestinian state in the Israeli-occupied West Bank and Gaza Strip as part of an overall settlement.

The proposal also was raised May 10 by Crown Prince Fahd, first deputy premier of Saudi Arabia, in an interview with eight American correspondents in Jidda. The "leaders of the Palestinian people will be willing to accept any peaceful solution to the problem" if it included the establishment of the Palestinian state, Fahd said. He warned there would be war if the Arab-Israeli dispute were not settled peacefully in 1977.

PLO officials in Beirut refused to comment on the reported proposal for the Palestinian state. The information had come from Arab press sources who said they had received the news from Arab diplomats and some Palestinians. The informants said Egypt, Syria and Saudi Arabia had insisted that the new state be linked to Jordan in a federation. The PLO, however, was said to have demanded that the state be set up first and that its relationship with Jordan be taken up later.

Zahir Mohsen, head of the PLO's military department, had charged that the U.S. was planning to overthrow Jordanian King Hussein and establish a Palestinian state in Jordan, according to an interview published May 8. He warned that if this alleged plot were successful, a "civil war would break out between Jordanians and Palestinians." Syria, he said, "might then be forced to interfere in Jordan to end the conflict as it has done in Lebanon." The PLO was "well aware of these designs," Mohsen said, and urged the Palestinians not to fall into the "trap."

The PLO May 1 had repeated its conditions for attending a renewed Geneva conference. Farouk Khaddoumi, head of the group's political department, said the U.S. and the Soviet Union, as co-chairmen of the conference, must issue separate invitations to the PLO, which must attend the parley from beginning to end as an active participant, not as a mere observer.

Khaddoumi also insisted that the Palestinian question be discussed as a separate item on the agenda, not within the context of the United Nations Security Council resolution 242 of 1967, which called for Israeli withdrawal from occupied territories and settlement of the Palestinian refugee problem.

Khaddoumi dismissed President Carter's reference to a "homeland for Palestinian refugees" as "insignificant." "As long as [Carter] thinks of the Palestinians as refugees, he is talking about a Palestinian refuge, not a Palestinian state," Khaddoumi added.

U.S. seeks to assure Israel—Secretary of State Cyrus R. Vance May 11 assured Israeli Foreign Minister Yigal Allon at a meeting in London that the U.S. would continue its "special relationship" with Israel and would continue to send the American arms and "advanced technology" needed to guarantee Israel's security. The statement was designed to reassure Israel that recent American actions, including President Carter's repeated references to a Palestinian "homeland" and a proposed new arms policy toward Israel, did not mean the U.S. was softening its support of Israel in preparation for the imposition of a Middle East peace settlement.

Vance, who briefed Allon on Carter's talks with Syrian President Assad, also assured Allon that the U.S. would not make public any American peace proposal before the disputants had had a chance to react to it. The U.S. suggestions were meant to "facilitate" negotiations and were not aimed at imposing a settlement, Vance said.

The secretary reaffirmed the Carter Administration's pledge not to have contacts with the PLO or to recognize it prior to PLO acceptance of relevant United Nations resolutions on the Middle East and recognition of the existence of Israel.

Allon said he regarded the U.S. position as expressed by Vance as "very positive." But he questioned Carter's view that the present Arab leaders were "moderate," saying "there is only one way to show moderation, and that is by proposing moderate policies."

(Vance said later May 11 on a flight to Madrid that he saw "no signs of a real shift in PLO attitude" toward Israel, despite reports to the contrary.)

Israel received further assurances of American support from President Carter May 12. The President pledged that the U.S. had "special security responsibilities" to Israel and that "special treatment" would be given to Israel for the purchase of advanced weapons and for co-producing them. Carter voiced his views at a closed-door White House meeting with congressional supporters of Israel and later at a news conference.

Carter's statement was in effect a reversal of his Administration's plans to limit transfer of advanced weaponry and co-production of such systems to NATO members, Japan, Australia and New Zealand, except in extraordinary circumstances. Although Israel had not been formally covered by a treaty, it considered itself as having a special relationship with the U.S. in regard to the arms program. Adoption of the new plan would have excluded Israel from this special category and would have restricted its ability to receive modern weapons.

The Israeli Embassy in Washington May 12 said it was satisfied with Carter's statement, calling it a reaffirmation of "the historical relationship between the United States and Israel."

Saudis to avoid oil embargo. Crown Prince Fahd of Saudi Arabia assured President Carter during talks in Washington May 24–25 that his country would not impose an oil embargo on the U.S. to force concessions from Israel in order to achieve a Middle East peace settlement. Reports of a possible renewal of such action (previously employed in 1973) had begun to circulate in the Middle East May 22 when Egyptian Foreign Minister Ismail Fahmy was quoted as having said that if the forthcoming right-wing dominated Israeli government made no concessions, "the oil weapon will be used again automatically."

Carter, commenting on his talks with Fahd, said the Saudi leader had told him that the statement attributed to Fahmy "was a completely false report."

Carter also said he and Fahd had "no disturbing differences" about the Middle East situation, but that the Likud victory in Israel's May 17 elections had created "a lot of uncertainty" about future diplomatic efforts to end the Arab-Israeli dispute. The crown prince had asked him to urge the Israelis to keep an open mind on a settlement that would be "just and lasting," the President said. Fahd had "expressed his strong hope that Israel would be reassured about the inclinations of his country toward the protection of their security," Carter said.

In their meeting May 24, Carter and Fahd had agreed that "the major effort should continue toward trying to reconvene the Geneva conference in the second half of 1977," according to a White House statement.

Fahd was the last of several Middle East political figures President Carter had met in the past months as part of his Administration's efforts to sound out prospects for a peace formula in the region.

Carter sees Mideast opportunity. President Carter May 22, 1977 urged a new and broader American foreign policy designed to respond to "a politically awakening world." The President outlined his foreign policy concepts in an address at the commencement exercises of Notre Dame University in South Bend, Ind.

In discussing the Middle East, Carter said, "This may be the most propitious time for a genuine settlement since the beginning of the Arab-Israeli conflict." He warned that "to let this opportunity pass could mean disaster, not only for the Middle East but perhaps for the international political and economic order as well."

In reference to the recent change of government in Israel, Carter stressed that the U.S. expected Israel and its neighbors to remain bound by United Nations resolutions 242 and 338, which demanded as part of a peace settlement the return of territories captured by Israel in the 1967 war.

"The historic friendship between the United States and Israel is not dependent on domestic politics in either nation," Carter said. "Our own policy will not be affected by changes in leadership in any of the countries in the Middle East."

Carter remarks worry Israel. President Carter May 26 restated his suggestions for a Middle East peace settlement. Concerned that the President's latest remarks indicated a further U.S. shift from a pro-Israel stand, Israel's Ambassador to the U.S., Simcha Dinitz, May 28 said that Carter's statements could not be accepted.

At his news conference May 26, Carter appeared to have expanded his previous calls for implementation of United Nations Resolutions 242 and 338. The President said U.S. "binding policies" in the Middle East were based on a number of U.N. resolutions, including "the right of the Palestinians to have a homeland, to be compensated for losses that they have suffered. They do include the withdrawal of Israel from occupied territories from the 1967 war, and they do include an end to belligerency and re-establishment of permanent and secure borders."

A "clarification" later issued by the White House said the idea of a Palestinian homeland had been contained in U.N. General Assembly Resolution 181 of November 1947. This was the so-called "partition" resolution, which had provided for separate Jewish and Arab states in Palestine. The Arabs had rejected the plan. The Israelis had accepted it. The Arabs then launched a war against the new Israeli state in 1948.

The White House statement also said Carter's mention of compensation for the Palestinians had been spelled out in U.N. General Assembly Resolution 194 of December 1948. This endorsed the right of the Palestinians who had been displaced by the war to return to their homes in Israel or be compensated.

Israel had argued that Resolutions 242 and 338 were the only U.N. policy statements applicable to the current Middle East situation. Israel had never accepted Resolution 194.

Ambassador Dinitz raised objections to Carter's statement at a Washington meeting May 28 with Secretary of State Cyrus R. Vance. Dinitz said after the discussions that he had repeated his government's position that Israel accepted Resolutions 242 and 338 as the only basis "for any future negotiations." But neither of these resolutions had mentioned a Palestinian homeland or compensation, Dinitz observed. Reiterating opposition to Resolution 194, Dinitz said if there were to be restitution, "hundreds of thousands of Jews" expelled from Arab states also should be compensated.

Vance and a statement issued later by the State Department upheld Israel's argument that 242 and 338 were the only two resolutions that currently served as the basis for negotiations.

Israeli Foreign Minister Yigal Allon expressed further concern about Carter's remarks at a meeting May 31 with U.S. Ambassador Samuel Lewis.

At a Cabinet meeting May 29, outgoing Premier Yitzhak Rabin and Allon said they were disturbed about the U.S. government's series of statements on the Middle East. Allon said "the sporadic statements voiced by different levels in the U.S. Administration" indicated a totally different American approach, despite Washington's assurances that it had no new plan and had no intention of imposing a solution.

In a related development, Menahem Begin, Israel's prospective premier, had sent a representative to Washington to ease U.S. fears that Begin would pursue a hard-line policy when he assumed office. His emissary, Shmuel Katz, met with newsmen June 2 and said Begin would accept Resolution 242 in "all its parts." He also said Begin would negotiate with the Arab leaders "without prior conditions."

U.S. ties Israeli pullback to peace. The U.S. said June 17, 1977 that any Israeli withdrawal from occupied Arab territories must be coupled with Arab acceptance of "real peace" with Israel. This view was expressed in an address by Vice President Walter F. Mondale. Mondale's statements were later characterized by the White House as the official explanation of the Carter Administration's policy on the Middle East.

Mondale's speech was regarded as an attempt by the Administration to assure American Jewish leaders that the U.S. was not softening its strong support of Israel. Israeli officials, however, said June 19 that their growing concern about U.S. policy was not allayed by Mondale.

Speaking in San Francisco to the World Affairs Council of Northern California, Mondale said Israel's security would best be strengthened if Israel agreed to return to "approximately" the borders that had existed before the 1967 war as part of a peace settlement. The pullback, he said, would be predicated on the understanding that Israel would be protected by special "security lines" "until confidence in a lasting peace can be fully developed."

Mondale warned Israel that "no borders will be secure if neighboring countries do not accept them." Frontiers that provided Israel with maximum military security, he said, "would not be accepted as legitimate" by the Arab states.

Mondale made a distinction between "separate lines of defense" and "recognized borders." He cited United Nations buffer zones in the Golan Heights and the Sinai as "models" of how Israel's security could be improved.

Mondale reiterated the Administration's views on the Palestinians, saying they "should be given a chance to shed their status as homeless refugees." This, he noted, could be achieved through the establishment of a homeland or "entity" associated with Jordan.

An Israeli Foreign Ministry official June 19 said Mondale had merely repeated "well known positions" that had been enunciated by President Carter in recent weeks to the dissatisfaction of the Jerusalem government. "The positions are the positions we know," he said. The Israelis were especially concerned about the repeated U.S. references to Israeli withdrawal with "minor modification." The new Israeli government of Premier Menahem Begin was opposed to giving up the West Bank.

President Carter was said to have assured Israel about his Middle East policies at a White House meeting June 15 with Shlomo Goren, the Ashkenazic chief rabbi of Israel. Goren said Carter had told him that: "He doesn't intend to see a Palestinian homeland established as a separate state. He always intended it should be established through Jordan . . . . He also said that he never suggested Israel had to return to the June 1967 lines."

An American Jewish leader said June 13 that Carter, during his 1976 election campaign, had suggested that Israel retain some of the occupied Arab territories. Rabbi Alexander Schindler, chairman of the Conference of Presidents of Major American Jewish Organizations, had released June 11 the text of a statement Carter had made to a group of American Jewish leaders Jan. 22, 1976. In it Carter was quoted as having said: "If I was premier of Israel, I would not yield control of the Golan Heights to the Syrians, I would not yield control of the Jewish and Christian Holy places" in Jerusalem and elsewhere in the occupied territories.

Israeli Policy & International Pressure

The Likud bloc, described as "right-wing" and "hard-line," came to power in Israel in 1977 through victory in elections in May. Likud leader Menahem Begin, characterized as a "former terrorist" (before Israel won its independence) and "hawk," became premier. Despite their reputations, the new premier and ruling party quickly gave indications of at least some willingness to make compromises for peace.

Israel's Likud eases territory stand. Israel's Likud bloc, which had won a plurality May 17, 1977 in the Knesset (parliament) elections, appeared May 24 to ease its hard-line stand on retention of occupied Arab territories.

The Likud Party submitted proposals to the Democratic Party for Change, which had won 14–15 seats, in an effort to induce the DMC to join it in forming a majority coalition government. Likud said that when it assumed office it would not annex the West Bank and Gaza Strip without first seeking a new mandate in elections. It said that although an Israeli government was permitted to impose its own laws on the occupied territories, a Likud government would not do so as long as Arab-Israeli peace negotiations were possible.

Likud had long advocated retention of the occupied territories; the DMC favored concessions.

In another internal Israeli development, former Defense Minister Moshe Dayan, Labor Party Knesset member, May 25 accepted in principle an offer made by the Likud bloc leader, Menahem Begin, to serve as foreign minister in his government. Dayan's decision was made possible by Likud's reversal of its stand on the occupied Arab territories, it was reported. Although the former defense minister had been opposed to giving up the West Bank, he had considered Likud's demands to incorporate the region into Israel as too extreme.

Begin had called for more Israeli settlements in the West Bank during a visit May 19 to the unauthorized Jewish settlement of Kadum, about 12 miles southwest of the West Bank Arab town of Nablus. "We stand on the land of liberated Israel, settled and made flowering by the wonderful pioneers and workers of the soil," he told a cheering crowd of about 200. Begin said there would be more such settlements in the area.

Begin took issue with U.S. President Carter's recent statements on the Middle East in a U.S. television interview broadcast May 22. Speaking on ABC-TV's "Issues and Answers," Begin rejected Carter's suggestion that Israel return to its pre-1967 borders, ruled out Palestine Liberation Organization (PLO) participation in any Geneva peace talks and opposed the establishment of a Palestinian state on the West Bank.

"I would like to point out that we don't know what he [Carter] means by 'homeland' for the Palestinians," Begin said. The Palestinians, he said, have "a homeland. They live on their places, in their cities."

Reiterating his refusal to sit down with the PLO, Begin asked: "What are we going to negotiate with them? The destruction of the state of Israel? This is absolutely absurd."

Arab reaction to Likud victory—The Voice of Palestine Radio in Cairo May 18 said the Palestinians would rise up against any Likud attempt to create "a Greater Israel." A PLO spokesman in Geneva, Daud Barakat, said the Arabs should now prepare for a fifth war against Israel.

Farouk Khaddoumi, head of the PLO's political department, May 19 charged that the U.S. was "behind" Likud's election win. He said Begin's assumption of power would mean an expansionist Israel. He predicted this would lead to an escalation of Palestinian resistance in the West Bank. Khaddoumi assailed Begin as a terrorist and singled out his role in the slaying of more than 200 Arabs in Deir Yassin in 1948 by the Irgun Zvai Leumi, the Jewish guerrilla group headed by Begin at the time. (Begin had insisted that Deir Yassin was a military target in the battle for Jerusalem and that its civilians had ignored a warning to evacuate the town before the Irgun attack.)

Egyptian President Anwar Sadat May 20 asserted that "it does not really matter who heads the Israeli government." Equating Begin with former Premier Yitzhak Rabin and acting Premier Shimon Peres, Sadat said all Israeli premiers "adopt the same line. There are no hawks or doves." Later Sadat May

29 said that as a part to any agreement with Israel his country would claim $2.1 billion in compensation for the oil Israel had pumped from Egyptian wells during its eight-year occupation of the Sinai. "Every drop they took from my wells in the Sinai, I have put in on my account" and Egypt would raise the matter at any renewed Geneva peace conference, Sadat said.

The Arabs also reacted militarily to the Begin victory, with Syria May 24 announcing army maneuvers "to crush enemy cross-border infiltration attempts," meaning Israeli attacks. PLO leader Yasir Arafat warned of a possible outbreak of fighting between Israelis and Palestinians in southern Lebanon.

Iraq called on Arab governments to give up the negotiating process and prepare for a military confrontation against Israel, Arab diplomatic sources in Beirut reported May 31. The Likud bloc's emergence as Israel's dominant political force made another Middle East war certain, Iraq was quoted as saying.

The Iraqi note reportedly had urged an emergency meeting of Arab chiefs of staff to map plans to revive the so-called eastern front against Israel. The front had consisted of Iraq, Syria, Jordan and the Palestine Liberation Organization. It had been suspended after Iraq withdrew its forces from Syria at the end of the 1973 war in protest against Syria's acceptance of a cease-fire.

Begin becomes premier. Menahem Begin became Israel's sixth premier June 21 after his new coalition government received a vote of confidence from the Knesset (parliament). Begin June 20 had presented his government to President Ephraim Katzir. It consisted of representatives of his Likud bloc and two religious groups—the National Religious Party and the ultra-Orthodox Agudat Israel. Begin had signed the coalition pact with the two religious parties June 19.

The Knesset vote of confidence in Begin's regime was 63 in favor—two more than the bare majority of 61 that was required to govern in the 120-seat body. Fifty-three voted against. The ballot was taken after Begin presented his 12-member Cabinet, which included Likud and NRP members. (Although Agudat Israel had agreed to join the coalition, it was not represented in the Cabinet.) Three Cabinet positions were to be left vacant for a month in the hope that the Democratic Movement for Change would reverse its decision and join. The DMC had thus far refused to enter into a Likud-dominated government because of its disagreement with Likud's hard-line stand on occupied Arab territories.

In a speech to the Knesset, Begin said the prime object of his government was peace. He called on King Hussein of Jordan and Presidents Anwar Sadat of Egypt and Hafez al-Assad of Syria to meet with him to "discuss the establishment of true peace between their countries and Israel." If those three states turned down his offer, "we shall make a note of Arab intransigence," Begin said.

A foreign policy plank adopted by Likud June 17 reaffirmed the bloc's position that "the Jewish people have an eternal historic right to the land of Israel." The statement, however, omitted Begin's election promise that "Judea and Samaria [the West Bank] shall therefore not be relinquished. Between Jordan and the sea there will be Jewish sovereignty only."

The party plank said the government could legally apply Israeli law throughout the occupied territories but that it would not exercise this authority while peace negotiations with the Arabs were in progress.

Likud's apparent softening of its stand on the territories followed Moshe Dayan's request for "clarification" from the party before joining it as foreign minister.

U.S. for Israeli withdrawal. The U.S. June 27, 1977 reaffirmed its stand that Israel must withdraw from all occupied Arab territories and agree to establishment of a Palestinian homeland in return for a peace agreement with the Arabs.

The remarks drew a sharp rejoinder June 28 from the Israeli government. A Foreign Ministry spokesman said there was "no foundation for the assumption implied by the Washington spokesman's statement as though Israel had excluded any territories whatsoever from the framework of the expected discussions with the Arab states."

The statement, issued by the State Department, said the U.S. believed "progress toward a negotiated peace in the Middle East is essential this year if future disaster is to be avoided." It insisted that the U.S. was "not asking for any one-sided concessions from anyone." The Arabs, a department spokesman said, must accept "a kind of peace which produces confidence in its durability." This would include "steps toward normalization of relations with Israel."

The U.S. restated the need for acceptance by both sides of the 1967 United Nations Security Council Resolution 242 as the basis for a negotiated peace. This resolution, the department stressed, "means withdrawal [by Israel] from all three fronts ... Sinai, Golan and West Bank and Gaza—the exact borders and security arrangements being agreed in the negotiations."

Discussions on the territorial question, the department said, "must start without preconditions from any side." In specifically citing the West Bank, the statement said that "to automatically exclude any territories strikes us as contradictory to the principle of negotiations without preconditions."

The statement reflected State Department concern about remarks by Begin and Dayan of reluctance to quit the West Bank and Gaza Strip. It also appeared to lay the groundwork for Begin's scheduled meeting with President Carter in July. (Dayan had said June 22 that Israel wanted peace with the Arabs, but "not on the basis of the territorial partition of the West Bank nor by the splitting of the region in two parts with one area belonging to Israel and one to an Arab country." Dayan said he opposed linking the West Bank or Gaza Strip with Jordan.)

The Israeli Foreign Ministry's June 28 reply also called attention to remarks made by Begin June 23, in which he had said Israel was not "putting forth any ultimatum." The premier was further quoted as having said, "the words 'not negotiable' do not appear in any dictionary of ours."

In the Senate June 27, Sen. Jacob K. Javits (R, N.Y.) scored the Carter Middle East peace formula as "unrealistic." He asserted that there was an "imbalance in what the Israelis and the Arabs are being called on to do." The U.S. was demanding too many specific concessions from the Israelis, while the Arabs were merely being asked for not much more than promises, he said.

In the text of his address (released June 26), Javits took particular issue with Vice President Mondale's June 17 speech, in which he had called for Israeli withdrawal to the 1967 lines. To ask Israel to give up the "territories which it had administered since 1967" would mean virtually depriving Israel of "the totality" of its "bargaining power," Javits declared. Israel's pre-1967 frontier, furthermore, Javits stressed, was "virtually indefensible" and therefore "would be a constant invitation to attack."

The Administration's call for a Palestinian "homeland," Javits noted, "establishes at once a parallelism with the Jewish national home in Israel and exactly contradicts an association with Jordan." He criticized the Administration for failing to speak out on "three of the most critical" aspects of the Middle East dispute: Jerusalem's status as a unified city, the integrity of Lebanon and the future of the Golan Heights.

Javits warned that the Carter proposals might "undercut the possibility of a successful U.S. role as mediator."

Javits' critical appraisal of the Administration's peace plan received support from a number of other senators, including Edward W. Brooke (R, Mass.) Robert Packwood (R, Ore.) and John J. Sparkman (D, Ala.).

Nine Democratic senators sent a letter to President Carter June 29 supporting his "efforts to help Israel and the Arab nations secure a genuine and lasting peace." The letter did not back the Administration's proposals for a Palestinian homeland or its suggestions for Israel's withdrawal to its 1967 borders. The senators endorsed "a commitment to a comprehensive and genuine peace," "the establishment of mutually and accepted secure borders" and "a fair and permanent solution" of the Palestinian problem. Among the signers were Edward M. Kennedy (Mass.), Robert C. Byrd (W. Va.), Hubert H. Humphrey (Minn.), Abraham Ribicoff (Conn.) and John J. Sparkman (Ala.).

King Hussein of Jordan May 31 gave strong backing to President Carter's Middle East peace efforts but expressed fear that the Likud bloc's election victory in Israel May 17 increased the chances of a new war. "Before the Israeli election, the chances of war were rather remote, but now I think there is ground for serious concern," the king said.

Syrian President Hafez al-Assad said his country might not recognize Israel even if it withdrew from all occupied Arab territories as part of a peace settlement, it was reported June 15.

Syria's official newspaper Al Baath June 17 charged that the U.S. was responsible for the hard line being taken by Israel. The Damascus allegation was in apparent response to a statement made by Israel's chief Ashkenazic rabbi, Shlomo Goren, that President Carter had assured him at a meeting June 15 that he never favored establishment of an independent Palestinian state. The White House June 16 had denied that Carter had made such a statement to Goren.

President Assad and Palestinian Liberation Organization leader Yasir Arafat agreed at a meeting in Damascus June 20 to take a tougher stand against Israel in relation to U.S. peace proposals.

Carter assures U.S. Jewish leaders— President Carter July 6 insisted that it was vital that the Arabs establish full diplomatic relations with Israel as part of an overall peace settlement. Meeting with a group of 40 American Jewish leaders at the White House, Carter also was said to have cited the dangers of establishing an independent Palestinian state that was not linked to Jordan.

One participant of the meeting quoted Carter as having said: "We see any kind of Palestinian entity as tied to Jordan. Anything else would be a distinct threat to peace; it could be easily used by [Libyan leader Muammer el-] Qaddafi or the Soviets as a threat to peace. We don't envisage an independent state at all."

The White House conference was called to reassure the American Jewish leaders, as well as Israel, that President Carter's statements in recent months proposing a comprehensive Middle East peace plan did not mean Washington was reversing its support of Israel or was attempting to impose a solution. Many participants at the discussions said at its conclusion that their apprehensions about Carter's policies were reduced but not eliminated.

Carter's comments reversed a decision he had announced at a news conference June 30 to impose a moratorium on further comments by his Administration about details of a Middle East settlement prior to Premier Begin's visit to Washington July 19. The ban was aimed at preventing additional statements that would aggravate the tense relations between

Washington and Jerusalem resulting from Carter's controversial remarks.

At the June 30 conference, Carter also had said, "An overwhelming consideration for us is the preservation of Israel as a free and independent and hopefully peaceful nation. That is pre-eminent."

EC for Palestine 'homeland'—The leaders of the nine nations belonging to the European Community (EC) June 29 declared that any Middle East peace settlement must provide for a Palestinian "homeland" and secure borders for Israel. The EC also called for Palestinian participation in future peace talks "in an appropriate manner to be worked out in consultation between all the parties concerned."

The EC's views were contained in a statement issued after the first day of a two-day summit meeting in London.

Israeli Premier Menahem Begin June 30 assailed the EC stand on the Palestinians. Asserting that Europe was "drenched with Jewish blood," Begin said the Common Market nations "should know better."

Israel & Egypt set for Geneva. Egyptian President Anwar Sadat July 4, 1977 accepted a proposal by Israeli Premier Menahem Begin that Geneva peace talks on the Middle East be resumed in October.

Begin had made the suggestion in talks with visiting U.S. Sen. Jacob K. Javits (R, N.Y.) and in later discussions with reporters. The premier specifically mentioned Oct. 10 as an acceptable date for the start of the conference, noting that it followed the Jewish New Year and Day of Atonement holy days.

Sadat, who was in Libreville, Gabon for the Organization of African Unity summit conference, said: "It is an encouraging sign that Begin announced he will go to Geneva in October. If it happens, we hope the Geneva conference could reconvene on or before October."

Begin July 5 said in reply, "Every positive response by Arab rulers to Israeli statements should be welcomed."

Despite the informal optimistic exchange between the two countries, other Israeli officials reaffirmed the government's refusal to go to Geneva if the Palestine Liberation Organization participated as a separate delegation. They said the Arabs had not changed their demands that the PLO join the original Arab participants at the Geneva talks—Egypt, Syria and Jordan.

Sadat had disclosed that in his meeting with President Carter March 4–5 he had informed the U.S. leader that the Arabs could not accept diplomatic or trade relations with Israel as part of a peace settlement, according to an interview published in a Beirut magazine July 2. It would be impossible "to persuade Moslem or Christian Arabs to open their borders with Israel after 29 years of hatred, four wars, rivers of blood and massacres," Sadat said.

Sadat reiterated the view that a Palestinian state created from the Israeli-occupied West Bank and Gaza Strip and linked with Jordan was "the backbone of peace."

Israel's peace plan. Menahem Begin July 20, 1977 made public Israel's proposal for a peace settlement. He disclosed the plan to newsmen after he had discussed it with President Carter at the White House July 19–20. The President July 20 said his talks with Begin led him to "believe that we have laid the groundwork now" for resumption of the Geneva peace conference between Israel and the Arabs in October.

Begin's formula dealt with procedural matters of the conference itself, and contained no specific views on territorial or political terms Israel might agree to. The premier again insisted that under no conditions would Israel negotiate with the Palestine Liberation Organization and said Israel would oppose the PLO's inclusion in any Arab delegation. Since the PLO's goal was "bluntly and simply to destroy our country," the Palestinian organization "can't be a partner to any negotiations," Begin insisted.

Among other aspects of the Begin plan:

■ The Geneva conference should be called on the basis of United Nations Security Council Resolutions 242 of 1967 and 338 of 1973, which he said were the bases for most diplomatic moves.

■ No prior conditions would be permitted by any participant, and any topic could be submitted for discussion.

■ Israel would conclude separate treaties with Jordan, Syria and Egypt through "mixed-commissions"; a Lebanese-Israeli commission also would be set up if Lebanon agreed to attend.

■ The accords should include an end to the state of war and clauses for diplomatic, economic and other facets of normal relations.

■ The treaties must delineate the final frontiers between Israel and its Arab neighbors.

■ There could be an alternative negotiating approach if the Geneva talks failed to materialize because of Arab insistence on PLO participation. The U.S. could use its good offices to promote talks between Israel and the direct Arab parties to the dispute through bilateral commissions; the talks could be held either in the capitals of the parties concerned, a neutral site or in New York.

Begin reiterated his refusal to accept a Palestinian state in the West Bank. He told newsmen that for Israel to concede this territory to a "so-called Palestinian state" would place Israel in jeopardy. The possession of the West Bank by a Palestinian state would place Israel within range of Soviet-made artillery and Israel could be bisected by tanks in 10 or 15 minutes across its narrowest point only nine miles from the sea, Begin said.

Begin had indicated Israel would be prepared to yield territory in the Sinai and Golan Heights.

After bidding Begin goodby, President Carter told newsmen, "I don't think the meetings with him could have been any better." Carter acknowledged that Arab-Israeli differences over territories and the Palestinian question remained deep, "but we have not found any of them to be so adamant in their positions that they are not eager for accommodation."

The President reaffirmed that Secretary of State Cyrus R. Vance would travel to Israel and the Arab states in August. His mission would be to work out further details on a Geneva conference and apprise the Arabs of Begin's proposals.

In a speech to an Israel fund-raising dinner in New York July 21, Begin conceded that he and Carter "still had divergences of opinion on certain vital issues," but added that "both of us agreed they are not going to cause any rift."

Arabs assail Begin views—Arab opposition to the Begin plan centered on its ex-

clusion of the Palestine Liberation Organization from peace talks and on continued Israeli refusal to withdraw completely from Arab territories.

Cairo radio July 20 said the Israeli proposal "is rejected in form and substance." Foreign Minister Ismail Fahmy was quoted as saying that the PLO was "the sole legitimate representative of the Palestinian people" and therefore must be included in any resolution of the Middle East conflict.

Fahmy said President Anwar Sadat had sent urgent messages to some world leaders emphasizing the seriousness of the Middle East situation and insisting that there could be no "stalling or Israeli maneuvers."

A PLO spokesman in Beirut said, "This is not a peace plan but a war plan, and we reject it from A to Z because it negates the right of the Palestinian people to self-determination and nationhood."

Saudi Arabian newspapers warned that U.S. acceptance of the Begin plan could lead to "inevitable war."

The newspaper of Syria's ruling Baath Party July 21 said the purpose of the Begin plan was to block peace, retain the occupied Arab lands and to avoid "recognizing the rights of the Palestinian people."

The Palestinian press service Wafa charged that some unnamed Arab states, "especially those faithful to Washington," would join the U.S. in supporting "the first Israeli precondition" of barring the PLO from Geneva. The statement warned, "Any solution that does not include the establishment of an independent Palestinian state will ultimately fail, and the Palestinian revolution . . . will keep on fighting the conspiratorial U.S.-Israel solution."

Israeli opposition criticizes plan—The Begin plan also drew criticism from Israel's opposition Labor Party, it was reported July 20. After being shown the proposal in Knesset (parliament) committees July 19, former Premier Yitzhak Rabin and former Foreign Minister Yigal Allon were quoted as having said their party's program of favoring "territorial compromise" was superior to the Begin plan. They claimed the Begin plan advocated "significant" Israeli withdrawal from the Sinai and the Golan Heights, but not the West Bank.

Foreign Minister Moshe Dayan was said to have replied that Begin's formula should not be taken as a hard-and-fast plan but as a basis for Begin's discussions with Carter and as an attempt to pave the way for opening peace talks with the Arabs.

On returning from his U.S. visit July 25, Begin scored some of Rabin's alleged actions. He charged that Rabin and his Labor Party colleagues had made public the details of a secret memorandum Begin gave Carter and which Dayan disclosed to the Knesset Foreign Affairs Committee in strictest confidence. The memorandum reportedly dealt with possible substantial Israeli withdrawals in the Sinai and with some readjustment of the Israeli line in the Golan Heights. Begin said Carter had promised not to publicize that part of the proposal to the Arabs.

In further criticism of Rabin, Begin said the former premier had had a "very serious and sharp confrontation" with President Carter when they had held their meetings that March. Begin attributed this to the Rabin administration's attempt to reach an agreed position with the U.S. prior to the reconvening of the Geneva conference. Begin said Carter at the time had rejected Rabin's proposal for retention of parts of the West Bank, with the remainder returned to Jordan. By contrast, Begin said, his meetings with Carter had ended the U.S.-Israeli confrontation created by his predecessor. The establishment of his deep rapport with Carter was the main achievement of his mission to the U.S., Begin said.

Rabin had warned July 23 that Begin's visit to Washington would bring about Israel's further isolation in a reconvened Geneva conference and lead to a more serious rift with the U.S. later. Rabin objected to Begin's push for a Geneva conference, arguing that efforts to reach further partial agreements were preferable to the impasse he said was certain to result at a full-scale parley at Geneva.

Settlements & Occupied Areas

West Bank settlements legalized. The Israeli regime July 26, 1977 formally approved three existing Jewish settlements in the occupied West Bank that hitherto had been regarded as illegal. The action brought strong condemnation by the U.S.

The ruling was handed down by the Cabinet's Ministerial Committee on Settlements. It reversed a decision by the previous government of Premier Yitzhak Rabin to bar recognition of the settlements of Kadum (Elon Moreh), near Nablus; Ofra, near Ramallah, and Maale Adumim, east of Jerusalem on the road to Jericho. All three were near large Arab population centers. In being granted official status as established communities, the three settlements were now entitled to government funds.

A protest by U.S. Secretary of State Cyrus R. Vance conveyed to Israeli Ambassador Simcha Dinitz said the U.S. was "deeply disappointed" by the Israeli decision, which it said created "an obstacle to the peacemaking process."

President Carter said July 28 he saw the establishment of permanent settlements on the West Bank as an obstacle to peace but "not an insurmountable problem."

In response to several questions at a news conference, Carter said he and Israeli Premier Menahem Begin had discussed the issue during Begin's visit to Washington. But Begin had not given him any commitment about "what he would do" nor "any prior notice" about recognizing the legality of the settlements, Carter said.

Carter said he had discussed with Begin the establishment of new settlements but had not thought about raising the subject of legal recognition of the existing settlements. What he had told Begin, Carter said, was, "I thought it would be easier for us to accept an increase in the population of existing settlements than it would be to accept the establishment of new settlements."

Carter said he though it was "not fair to overly criticize" Begin on the issue. The number of people involved in the settlements was "quite small," he said, and "it would be a mistake to overemphasize or to exaggerate the significance of it."

"And the Israeli government," he added, "have never claimed that these settlements are permanent. What they have done is to say that they are legal at the present time."

Carter thought there was "a good chance to go to Geneva." He urged restraint by the leaders of all sides. The chief stumbling block, he said, was the issue of participation by the Palestinian representatives. The U.S. position, he pointed out, was that the Palestinians "ought to be represented" and that "they forego" their "publicly espoused" commitment that Israel be destroyed.

Carter observed that both sides at this point seemed to have "at least a moderate amount of confidence in us" in the search for peace.

Begin July 27 rejected Washington's criticism of the legalization of the settlements. And the Knesset defeated a motion to bar future Jewish settlements in the West Bank. Following the vote, the Ministerial Committee on Settlements was authorized to decide on "establishment of new settlements."

Begin expressed his government's "deep distress and disappointment" at Vance's remarks. In their talks, the President had asked that Israel refrain from setting up new Jewish communities in the West Bank, Begin said, "But I told him Jews have the inalienable right to live anywhere in the West Bank and the Gaza Strip." (Carter was said to have asked Begin that he defer further action on new settlements until the Geneva conference was reconvened.)

The premier insisted that the three newly authorized settlements did not violate international law. "These settlements," he said, "in no way harm Arabs. We did not evict Arabs for these three settlements.

West Bank, Gaza Arabs get new rights. The Israeli government announced Aug. 14 that it planned to grant Arabs in the occupied West Bank and Gaza Strip "equal rights, the same as those enjoyed by residents" of Israel. The Israeli opposition and Arabs in the affected areas expressed fears that the action could be the forerunner of Israeli annexation of the two territories.

Among the social services that might be extended to the Arabs: health care; construction of hospital buildings; improved labor conditions; maternity grants; a ban on child labor; national insurance; free education; extension of an electric power grid; improved water supply, and automation of telephone service.

The proposed benefits were announced after a Cabinet meeting by Cabinet Secretary Arych Naor.

Naor denied the proposed move was "annexation," arguing that "you can't annex what already belongs to you." This

was a reference to the Begin government's claim that Judea and Samaria (the West Bank) were part of Israel.

Begin Aug. 15 defended his government's action, stating that it was "by no means the beginning of annexation but was motivated solely by a desire to improve the lot of Arabs under Israeli rule."

Defense Minister Ezer Weizman was quoted as saying that the proposed change would not be made without consulting the Arab municipalities involved.

New settlements authorized. The Israeli government Aug. 17, 1977 approved plans for the establishment of three new Jewish settlements on the West Bank. The U.S. and Palestinians denounced the move.

The communities were among 25 that already had been approved by the previous Israeli government. A Cabinet official said the current regime was merely carrying out that decision.

All three settlements were to be within a few miles of Israel's pre-1967 borders. They were north of Latrun on the main Jerusalem-Tel Aviv road, near Qalqilya west of Nablus and on the road between Hebron and Beersheba. The government set no date for constructing the new settlements.

The U.S. State Department Aug. 17 called the Israeli action "an obstacle to progress in the peacemaking process."

Another department statement Aug. 18 reaffirmed that "these illegal, unilateral acts in territory presently under Israeli occupation create obstacles to peace." The department took issue with the government's statement that it was merely carrying out the decision of the previous regime. "No matter whose government policy, it is being implemented by that government and it creates obstacles to peace."

The U.S. had long contended that Israeli settlements in the West Bank were illegal because they contravened a Geneva convention barring civilian settlements in occupied land. Premier Menahem Begin had argued that since the land was part of the state of Israel, the convention did not apply.

President Carter personally protested the Israeli action Aug. 18 in a letter U.S. Ambassador Samuel Lewis delivered in

Jerusalem to Begin and Foreign Minister Moshe Dayan.

The State Department also criticized Israel's Aug. 14 decision to extend social services to Arabs in the West Bank. The "action creates an impression of permanence of Israel's occupation" of the former Arab lands, the statement said.

The Israeli Embassy in Washington Aug. 18 rejected the U.S. protests. It said Israel did not view the proposed settlements as an obstacle to peace, adding that "all subjects are open to negotiations."

United Nations Secretary General Kurt Waldheim Aug. 18 expressed "deep concern" and "regret" over the Israeli decision. Israeli chief U.N. delegate Chaim Herzog replied that Waldheim "seemed so preoccupied with the decisions of the Israeli government that he was impervious to the shedding of Israeli blood by the PLO."

A Reuters report from Beirut Aug. 17 said Palestinian sources condemned the Israeli move as further evidence that Israel planned to annex the West Bank outright.

Egyptian Foreign Minister Ismail Fahmy Aug. 19 charged that Israeli actions regarding the West Bank constitute a "violation of her international obligations and an aggression on Arab rights and legitimacy."

Israeli Foreign Minister Moshe Dayan disclosed Aug. 19 that he had broached a plan for Israel and Jordan to divide administrative functions of the West Bank. Dayan said the formula was gaining support "on the other side," and that the U.S. also was displaying interest. Dayan said U.S. Secretary of State Cyrus R. Vance, during his meeting with Israeli officials in Israel Aug. 9–10, had not ruled out partitioning of the West Bank.

Israel proposes major settlement plan. Israeli Agriculture Minister Ariel Sharon Sept. 2, 1977 revealed a plan to settle about two million Jews by the end of the century in a security belt stretching from the Golan Heights in the north to the tip of the Sinai Peninsula. Sharon drafted the project as chairman of the Ministerial Committee on Settlements. He submitted the plan to Begin and the Cabinet.

The plan provided for new settlements in the Gaza Strip as well as in the West Bank. In the West Bank there would be urban and agricultural communities in areas with relatively sparse Arab population. The sectors to be settled would include the Jordan Valley along the Jordan River and the Nablus and Jerusalem areas.

Government sources had reported Aug. 26 that a paramilitary settlement had been established two weeks earlier at Reichan, northwest of the Arab town of Jenin. Soldiers belonging to a Nahal, a soldier-farmer unit, moved into the outpost. Reichan could be transformed into a totally civilian settlement if the government decided to make the change.

2 settlements blocked. The Israeli government Sept. 28, 1977 barred attempts by followers of the Gush Emunim (Faith Bloc), an ultrareligious Jewish group, to establish two unauthorized settlements in the West Bank near Jericho and Jenin.

The disputing sides negotiated a compromise that would permit the would-be settlers to move into six Israeli military camps in the West Bank in the next three months. The male members of the group would be called up for military reserve duty, while accommodations would be provided for their wives and children. The agreement also allowed the settlers to move into four Gush Emunim communities already established in the West Bank.

Gush Emunim had planned to set up 11 communities in the West Bank Sept. 28 but canceled its action at the last moment because of negotiations with Premier Menahem Begin.

Begin had informed the Gush Emunim at a meeting with its leaders Sept. 25 of his intentions to bar their 11 settlements. He said his opposition was based on their timing. This was an apparent reference to Foreign Minister Moshe Dayan's talks with American officials in the U.S. and the current meeting of the United Nations General Assembly, which was about to debate an Arab motion to censure Israel for its settlement policy.

Arabs map plans against Israel. The foreign ministers of the Arab League met in Cairo Sept. 3–6, 1977 to map common strategy against Israel in preparation for the forthcoming meeting of the United Nations General Assembly.

At the final session Sept. 6 the ministers approved a policy statement declaring Israel's recent actions in the occupied West Bank as "null and void." The conferees also reiterated Arab demands for total Israeli withdrawal from occupied Arab lands as a condition for peace and for the right of the Palestinians to establish an independent state of their own.

The league ministers Sept. 4 adopted an Egyptian proposal to have the U.N. General Assembly condemn Israel's settlement policies.

The Egyptian plan was accepted in preference to a harsher one submitted by Syrian Foreign Minister Abdel Halim Khaddam. He proposed that Arab, Islamic and nonaligned nations push for condemnation of Israel's policies and for its suspension from the U.N. and U.N. agencies. Khaddam also called for diplomatic and economic sanctions against Israel by the Arab states and all U.N. members.

In an opening address Sept. 3, Saudi Foreign Minister Saud al-Faisal had asserted that Israel's moves in the occupied territories were aimed at "changing the geographical, demographical and legal nature" of those areas. He urged concerted action to confront this "flagrant Israeli challenge."

U.N. 'deplores' Israeli settlements. The United Nations General Assembly Oct. 28, 1977 approved an Egyptian resolution that "strongly deplores" Israel's occupation of Arab lands and its establishment of Jewish settlements in those territories. The vote was 131 to 1, with Israel casting the only negative ballot. Seven nations abstained: the U.S., Costa Rica, Fiji, Guatemala, Malawi, Nicaragua and Papua New Guinea.

U.S. Ambassador Andrew Young said that the resolution largely reflected the U.S. policy of opposing Israeli settlements in the West Bank. But the U.S. abstained because it had to maintain strict neutrality as co-chairman of the Geneva peace conference on the Middle East, Young explained.

Mediators, Negotiators & Competing Proposals

Vance starts U.S. mediation mission. U.S. Secretary of State Cyrus R. Vance conferred with Egyptian and Syrian leaders Aug. 1–4, 1977 to promote U.S. efforts to reconvene the Geneva peace conference on the Middle East. Vance's visits to Alexandria and Damascus were the opening phase of a 12-day tour.

Vance's conversations with Presidents Anwar Sadat and Hafez al-Assad centered on resolving the deadlock over the problem of PLO representation.

After his talks with Sadat Aug. 1–2, Vance said he and the Egyptian leader had agreed that the impasse over the PLO made it unlikely that the Geneva conference could be held soon. Instead, he said, he had accepted Sadat's suggestion for a preliminary meeting of the foreign ministers of Israel, Egypt, Syria and Jordan to pave the way for an eventual top-level conference. Vance said he would attempt to persuade the four countries to join a working group to meet under his auspices in Washington and New York in mid-September. The panel would discuss procedural as well as substantive matters "as long as it is useful," Vance said.

Speaking at a joint news conference with Vance, Sadat said he would raise no objections to Egyptian Foreign Minister Ismail Fahmy meeting in the same negotiating room with Israeli Foreign Minister Moshe Dayan, but he ruled out two-sided talks between the two countries.

Sadat also said he was "willing to sign a peace agreement with Israel tomorrow." He said this would imply "automatic recognition" of Israel. But such an accord, Sadat added, must require total Israeli withdrawal from Arab lands captured in the 1967 war.

Egyptian officials later issued a clarification of the working-group proposal. One Cairo source said, "What it means is intensified consultations between the Americans and the Arab foreign ministers on the one hand and the Israeli foreign minister on the other, not a joint meeting." Other Egyptian sources said the working group was not meant to serve as a preliminary conference, but merely a means for Vance to continue his contacts with Arab and Israeli foreign ministers attending opening sessions of the United Nations General Assembly in New York.

President Sadat Aug. 4 sought to reassure PLO head Yasir Arafat on the working-group plan. The president was said to have told the PLO leader in Cairo that Egypt, in proposing the plan, in no way had reversed its stand that the PLO must take part in peace talks. The working group was not meant to be a substitute for Geneva, Sadat said.

Assad opposes pre-Geneva talks—After meeting with Vance Aug. 4, Syrian President Hafez al-Assad told a news conference that he opposed Sadat's suggestion for a preliminary foreign ministers conference. Despite Cairo's clarification of the proposal, Assad said, "Our brothers in Egypt who proposed it saw certain benefits that so far we have not seen."

The Syrian leader warned that if the "working group should fail it would have the same results if a Geneva conference failed." Furthermore, there was danger that the working group "would be looked upon as a competition for Geneva, and none of us would like that," Assad added. Instead, the Syrian leader advocated reconvening the Geneva conference "after thorough preparations."

Assad said that as a result of his talks with Vance the issues remained unresolved and therefore he saw no chance of reconvening the Geneva parley in 1977.

An official Syrian statement on the Vance-Assad meeting reiterated Damascus' conditions for a peace settlement: Israeli withdrawal and "the confirmation of the rights of the Palestinian people."

Israel endorses Sadat proposal—Israeli Premier Menahem Begin Aug. 3 gave his support to the formula of meetings of Arab and Israeli foreign ministers. An aide to the premier quoted him as saying that Begin welcomed Sadat's position "as a very positive development in the Egyptian attitude."

Other Israeli officials discounted the argument, as later voiced by President Assad, that substantive negotiations in the U.S. would undermine the reconvening of the Geneva talks. A Foreign Ministry official said: "Geneva is a concept. It is a framework for negotiations on the basis of Security Council resolutions 242 and 338. The venue does not matter."

Impasse continues. Cyrus Vance ended his Middle East tour Aug. 11 after he had reported little progress in efforts to get Arab and Israeli leaders to agree on the reconvening of the Geneva peace conference.

The secretary had conferred with Jordanian King Hussein in Amman Aug. 5–6. Vance told a news conference Aug. 6, after concluding his talks with the king, that major obstacles remained. Hussein, however, said Aug. 7 before Vance's departure that he was "cautiously optimistic" and that he and the secretary had made "progress on most points."

Vance arrived Aug. 7 in Taif, Saudi Arabia and was informed by officials there Aug. 8 that the PLO might reverse its stand on Israel and recognize the Jewish state.

PLO spokesman Mahmoud Labady issued a statement in Beirut later Aug. 8 confirming that his organization's proposed shift called for revising United Nations Security Council Resolution 242 to include "the legitimate rights of the Palestinians," an allusion to the establishment of a Palestinian state. The resolution, which served as the basis for settling the Middle East dispute, called for Israeli withdrawl from Arab territories occupied since the 1967 war and recognition of all states in the area. The document made no reference to a Palestinian state, but only to a just solution to the Palestinian refugee problem.

Amending the resolution, Labady said, would remove any obstacles to PLO attendance at the Geneva conference. As for PLO recognition of Israel's right to exist, "this can only come out of a series of very long and difficult negotiations," Labady added.

President Carter said Aug. 8 that PLO acceptance of Resolution 242 "would open an avenue" for PLO participation at Geneva. Heretofore, the U.S. had insisted that it would have contacts with the PLO only if it altered its charter, which called for destruction of the Israeli state.

Arriving in Jerusalem after leaving Taif Aug. 9, Vance encountered strong Israeli objections to returning the West Bank and Gaza Strip, to creation of a Palestinian state in the territory or to dealings with the PLO even if it accepted Resolution 242. The secretary was given these views in discussions with Premier Menahem Begin, Foreign Minister Moshe Dayan and other Israeli officials.

Dayan acknowledged to newsmen that the U.S. and Israel did not see "eye to eye" on all issues, but he said Israelis were prepared "to take care of ourselves."

At a dinner in Vance's honor later Aug. 9, Begin read parts of the PLO charter and said, "That organization, the philosophy of which is based on an Arabic 'Mein Kampf' [Adolf Hitler's political testament], is no partner whatsoever and never will be a partner to hold any talks."

(Begin had said in an address Aug. 8 that it would be pointless to get the PLO to peace talks by trying to make the Palestinian organization recognize Israel. He said Israel would use its Geneva conference right to veto participation of any Palestinian group at the parley.)

At a meeting with West Bank Arab leaders Aug. 10, Vance said the U.S. favored turning their territory over to a United Nations trusteeship for an undetermined period as the most reasonable method of resolving the question of a Palestinian homeland.

One group of West Bank Arabs refused to attend the meeting with Vance. Instead they sent a message to his staff in Jerusalem and to the Soviet Union as cochairmen of the Geneva conference. Their statement called the PLO the legitimate voice of the Palestinians and repeated PLO demands for participation at Geneva, recognition of Palestinian national rights and full Israeli pullout from the occupied Arab lands.

Another West Bank Arab group attending the gathering presented Vance with a petition denying that the PLO spoke for West Bank residents. "The people actually living in the area have the right of self-determination so that we won't have here the tragedy of Lebanon," the statement said.

Following another round of talks with Israeli officials Aug. 10 which officially ended his Middle East mission, Vance said both sides remained far apart on the basic issues that had to be resolved before Geneva talks could be held. Reviewing his trip, the secretary said the Arabs and Israelis were given the American "framework for a Geneva conference." Although he provided no details, the proposals were believed to resemble the views previously expressed by President Carter: Israeli withdrawal from all Arab lands taken in the 1967 conflict, with minor adjustments; establishment of a Palestinian homeland on the West Bank with a possible link to Jordan, and Arab agreement to "real peace" with Israel, including diplomatic and trade relations.

Vance Aug. 11 made a quick return visit to Syria, Jordan and Egypt to brief their leaders on his discussions with the Israelis. With Vance at his side, Egyptian President Anwar Sadat told a news conference in Cairo that he remained confident the U.S. would help reconvene the Geneva conference, "despite the fact that there is a very hard Israeli line."

Israeli, Arab reaction—Among Israeli and Arab reaction to the Vance mission:

Israeli Foreign Minister Moshe Dayan Aug. 11 said he was optimistic about reaching peace agreements with Egypt, Jordan and Lebanon, but foresaw a problem in obtaining an accord with Syria. Egyptian President Anwar Sadat was "a good partner for a peace agreement" because of his country's internal problems and because he "really wants peace," Dayan said.

Premier Menahem Begin Aug. 11 did not share Dayan's assessment of Sadat. It was misleading, Begin said, to cast the Egyptian president as the most moderate of the Arab leaders when he espoused views that were extreme as those of Syria. Begin cited Sadat's demand for total Israeli withdrawal and the establishment of a Palestinian state. As for his talks with Vance, Begin discounted reports of gloom because the secretary had failed to narrow Arab-Israeli differences. What mattered was that the momentum was continuing, Begin said.

Syrian President Hafez al-Assad Aug. 12 said he was opposed to the American idea of "proximity talks" between Israeli and Arab foreign ministers at the U.N. in September. "To be more specific," Assad said, "there will not be any such contacts between the Syrian foreign minister and Israeli officials." Assad also said that Syria and Egypt were opposed to "partial or unilateral agreements" with Israel.

A Jordanian official Aug. 14 also came out against any separate agreement with Israel. Abdul Hamid Sharaf, chief of the Royal Court, said Jordan would consider a peace treaty with Israel, but only as part of an overall Arab-Israeli accord.

Carter briefed on mission. Vance Aug. 14 reported to President Carter on his Aug. 1–11 peace mission to the Middle East.

After the closed door-session, Carter announced that he would confer with the foreign ministers of Israel and the Arab states when they visited New York in September to attend the opening of United Nations General Assembly. Carter promised that despite the great differences separating the two sides, the U.S. would "do all that is possible to bring about a settlement."

A White House statement reiterated the Administration's willingness to "use its influence, offer its advice, volunteer its suggestions, and work to bring the parties into fruitful negotiations."

In reviewing Vance's mission, the statement said the principal progress he had made had been in "moving both sides closer to a common concept of mutual obligations of peace, although much remains to be accomplished in this respect." The major unresolved obstacles were Palestinian representation at peace talks, "the definition of secure and recognized borders and the nature of a Palestinian settlement," the statement said. The U.S. was said to be more in agreement with the Arabs than with the Israelis on these issues.

In a televised interview taped for broadcast later Aug. 14, Carter said if Israeli officials "genuinely wanted a peace settlement," they would have to accept new frontiers that "satisfy the minimum requirements of their Arab neighbors and the United Nations resolutions." He said they also would have accept "some solution to the question of the enormous numbers of Palestinian refugees who have been forced out of their homes and who want to have some fair treatment."

U.S. Assistant Secretary of State Alfred Atherton told newsmen Aug. 16 that it was now up to the Palestine Liberation Organization to make the next move in the current peace maneuverings. He said, "the central issue being discussed by the PLO and the Arab governments" was United Nations Security Council Resolution 242. The PLO had indicated that it would endorse the resolution, which would be tantamount to recognizing Israel, if the document were revised to take note of the need for a Palestinian state. Atherton repeated U.S. opposition to "any attempts to amend, modify or supersede" the reso-

lution to make it more acceptable to the PLO. Altering the resolution, he said, would be "a very dangerous course" because it would lead to a U.N. debate that would stress oratory and emotion rather than diplomacy.

PLO opposes U.S. peace efforts. The Central Council of the Palestine Liberation Organization met in Damascus Aug. 25–26, 1977. It rejected U.S. mediation in the Middle East and reaffirmed PLO opposition to United Nations Security Council Resolution 242.

In a four-point statement issued Aug. 26, the PLO again rejected the resolution on the grounds that it ignored "the national rights" of the Palestinians and that it treated the Palestinian question as "a refugee problem." Instead, the PLO called for revision of 242 along the lines of the 1974 U.N. General Assembly Resolution 3236. This document delared that the Palestinian people had the right to independence and sovereignty.

Alluding to a reported American pledge to open talks with the PLO if it recognized Resolution 242, the statement warned against "rushing after the promises of the imperialists and Zionists." It assailed all U.S. and Zionist "maneuvers in ignoring the right of our people to return to self-determination, to establish an independent state on its national soil and to gather under the leadership of the PLO."

(The Central Council served as a liaison between the Palestine National Council [parliament-in-exile] and the PLO executive committee, the 15-member "cabinet" headed by Yasir Arafat.)

Arafat assails U.S. aims—U.S. intentions in the Middle East were assailed Aug. 30 by Yasir Arafat during a meeting in Moscow with Soviet Foreign Minister Andrei A. Gromyko. The Soviet news agency Tass quoted Arafat as having said Vance's mission to the Middle East Aug. 1–11 had "caused an aggravation of the situation" because Vance "tried to disregard fully the Palestinian problem, which is known to be the cornerstone of any Middle East settlement."

The Vance mission, Arafat added, "has shown that the United States has not given up its plans, if not of torpedoing the

Geneva conference, then if possible of emasculating its meaning [by] striving to bar the Soviet Union from participating in the Middle East settlement."

Arafat, who had arrived in Moscow Aug. 30, concluded his talks with Gromyko Aug. 31. A joint communique said the two had agreed that settlement of the Middle East dispute "can be insured only at the Geneva peace conference with the participation of all sides directly concerned, including the Palestine Liberation Organization."

Assad backs peace pact with Israel. Syrian President Hafez al-Assad declared Aug. 26 that he would sign a "peace agreement" ending the state of war with Israel. However, he said he opposed normalizing relations with Israel until it abandoned its "expansionist character."

In an interview with a New York Times correspondent, Assad voiced these views:

■ If the U.S. supported the idea of normal Arab-Israeli ties as a condition for a peace settlement, "it is seeking a coercive relationship in favor of Israel and at the expense of the Arabs."

■ "If Israel were willing to recognize the rights of the Palestinians without talking with them [the PLO] or anyone else, we'd welcome this—but we believe Israel is rejecting the PLO not because of its leadership but because Israel rejects the rights of the Palestinians."

■ The Arab League might serve as a substitute for the PLO at a Geneva conference.

■ The Arabs, including the Palestinians, favored reaching a peaceful solution, "but it is completely rejected by Israel." "The qualitative gap" between Israeli and Arab technology "is closing" in favor of the Arabs. "The future cannot be in favor of Israel."

Another Syrian official, Information Minister Ahmed Iskander, Aug. 28 indicated the Arabs might go to war against Israel if current peace efforts failed. "When all peace efforts are blocked, it is my opinion that the Arabs must use all means at their disposal to impose the resolutions of the United Nations, liberate the lands taken from them in 1967 and restore the rights of the Palestinians," Iskander said.

Israeli premier in Rumania. Israeli Premier Menahem Begin conferred with Rumanian officials Aug. 25–29, 1977 in Bucharest, with the Palestinian question high on the agenda.

An official Bucharest statement Aug. 29 said the talks between Begin and Rumanian officials, including President Nicolae Ceausescu, had improved relations between the two countries, despite their differences over the Middle East. Ceausescu had voiced these views long opposed by Israel: total Israeli withdrawal from occupied Arab lands, the right of the Palestinians to create a state of their own and inclusion of the Palestine Liberation Organization at renewed Geneva talks.

Ceausescu had come out for PLO representation in a toast at a dinner for Begin Aug. 25. According to a Rumanian press official, Begin departed from a prepared speech to say: "Any demand to involve the PLO in Geneva is totally and unequivocally unacceptable to Israel."

The official Rumanian press agency did not carry Begin's reply to Ceausescu.

The Israeli radio had reported Aug. 26 that Begin had accepted Ceausescu's offer to use his good offices to assist in Middle East peace efforts.

U.S. for Palestinian role. The U.S. State Department said Sept. 12, 1977 in a new policy statement on the Middle East that "the Palestinians must be involved in the peacemaking process" to insure a settlement of the Arab-Israeli dispute. Palestinian representatives "will have to be at Geneva for the Palestinian question to be solved," the statement said.

As co-chairman of the Geneva conference, the document continued, the U.S. had been "exploring with the confrontation states and Saudi Arabia a number of alternatives with regard to participation of the Palestinians in the peace negotiations."

The department said its statement was essentially a reaffirmation of Washington's policy on the Middle East, and that the purpose of its release at the current time was to make the Administration's position "extra clear" before "we enter into a new round of discussions."

Arab, Israeli reaction—The U.S. State Department's statement drew praise from Egypt and the PLO Sept. 13. A Cairo official said, "it's a new chance for the PLO to put their trust in the United States peace efforts and we hope they will take the risk."

PLO leader Yasir Arafat called the State Department statement "a positive step confirming an objective fact, namely, that the Palestinian case is the crux of the conflict in the Middle East."

Another PLO official, Khalid al-Hassan, a member of the Central Council, said his organization was "ready to talk to the American government, but we can't accept Resolution 242 without guarantees of our national rights."

Shmuel Katz, Israeli Premier Menahem Begin's public affairs adviser, declared that the American position in the Middle East was based on a misconception. Katz said that President Carter based his policy on a Brookings Institution paper which, the Israeli contended, presumed that the Middle East problem dated from Israel's capture of Arab territories in the 1967 war. "In actual fact the dispute started long before then and results from the unwillingness of the Arab states to accept Israel," Katz said.

U.S. contacts with PLO—The Beirut newspaper Al Anwar had reported July 20 that the U.S. and the Palestine Liberation Organization had been in secret contact since May. One of these contacts included a meeting in London June 24 between Willian W. Scranton, former chief U.S. delegate to the United Nations, and Basil Akl, a member of the PLO's U.N. delegation, the newspaper said.

The exchange had begun with a note to President Carter from PLO leader Yasir Arafat. It had been transmitted by Saudi Arabian Crown Prince Fahd during his May meeting with Carter. The message was said to have contained Arafat's view of the PLO's role in any resumed Geneva peace conference and his formula for a Palestinian state and peace treaties with Israel.

Scranton was said by Al Anwar to have sought some clarification of Arafat's note in his meeting with Akl.

The Carter Administration July 19 confirmed Scranton's meeting with Akl, but denied Scranton was on a mission for the U.S. government or had met with Akl on instructions.

U.S. gets Israeli plan. Israeli Foreign Minister Moshe Dayan Sept. 19, 1977 submitted his country's proposal for a Middle East peace settlement at a White House meeting with President Carter and other U.S. officials. The talks were the start of a new round of American discussions with Israeli and Arab leaders in an attempt to achieve progress toward resumption of the Geneva peace conference.

The Israeli proposal was not made public, but its principal element was a plan to provide Arabs in the Israeli-occupied West Bank with substantial internal autonomy and self-government. Under the proposal, Israel would maintain strategic military positions in the area for security purposes.

A U.S. statement was issued with Dayan's concurrence after his meetings with Carter, Vice President Walter F. Mondale, Secretary of State Cyrus R. Vance and others. It acknowledged that Israel and the U.S. remained far apart on such issues as Palestinian representation at the Geneva talks, possible American dealings with the Palestine Liberation Organization and Israeli settlements on the West Bank. But the statement said the talks had been held in "the open and friendly spirit of relations between our two countries which permits differences to be discussed candidly."

Dayan was urged by Carter and Vance to approve an American formula that would permit Palestinians who accepted the existence of Israel to participate in a unified Arab delegation at the Geneva parley, U.S. officials disclosed. The delegation would consist of geographic committees to negotiate with Israel on the territorial claims of Egypt (Sinai Peninsula), Syria (Golan Heights) and Jordan (the West Bank).

Israel had opposed holding talks with a unified Arab delegation at Geneva. Instead it favored a plan under which Arab states would be represented as individual delegations, with the possible inclusion in the Jordanian delegation of Palestinians not affiliated with the PLO.

Carter and Vance were said to have reacted to Israel's West Bank plan by suggesting to Dayan that the Arabs in that area be given the opportunity for self-determination, either as an independent state or as a homeland linked to Jordan.

Reviewing his talks with Administration officials, Dayan Sept. 20 told newsmen in Washington that he believed "an agreed formula" would be found that would lead to the reconvening of the Geneva talks before the end of 1977. The foreign minister said he based his optimism on the "attitude" of some Arab states who "want negotiations and a peace agreement." He cited Egypt and Jordan.

Dayan was questioned about his secret travels the previous week when he made an unexpected visit to Paris, then returned abruptly to Israel before flying on to the U.S. He would not provide details, except to say that the secrecy was imposed by a "certain personality."

The Voice of Palestine radio in Cairo Sept. 20 said Dayan had met in Europe Sept. 16 with Jordanian Premier Mudar Badran to discuss the Israeli peace plan that he later submitted to Carter.

Dayan had left Israel Sept. 15 and made a scheduled stopover in Brussels, where he conferred with Gen. Alexander M. Haig, supreme commander in Europe of the North Atlantic Treaty Organization. Instead of going on to New York, Dayan apparently changed his plans and arrived in Paris Sept. 16. On returning to Israel Sept. 17, Dayan told newsmen that he was on his way to report to Premier Menahem Begin on a matter related to Dayan's office as foreign minister. Dayan then left for the U.S. the following day.

Israel for U.S. naval base at Haifa—Foreign Minister Dayan Sept. 20 told the House International Relations Committee that his country would be willing to permit the U.S. to establish a naval base in Haifa, Israel's principal Mediterranean port, it was reported Sept. 21.

Dayan's statement was in response to a question by Rep. Paul Findley (R, Ill.), a committee member, about Findley's resolution calling on Israel to relinquish all the Arab lands it had captured in the 1967 war, in exchange for U.S. security guarantees that could include American bases in Israel.

Dayan said Israel did not want American troops stationed in Israel because he did not believe the U.S. would be willing to fight on Israel's side against the Arabs in view of the post-Vietnam atmosphere. Israel, however, would cooperate if the U.S. wanted a naval base in Israel for its own security, Dayan was said to have told the committee members.

Carter meets Egyptian minister—President Carter and Secretary of State Vance Sept. 21 continued their pre-Geneva peace moves with a meeting with Egyptian Foreign Minister Ismail Fahmy.

The minister followed up his discussions Sept. 22 with a statement that the Arab countries were prepared "for the first time to accept Israel as a Middle East country to live in peace in this area, in secure borders" if Israel accepted Arab terms for a settlement. Speaking to newsmen in Washington, Fahmy cited the two principal conditions long opposed by Israel—total withdrawal from occupied Arab lands and agreement to establishment of a Palestinian state.

The Egyptian minister said agreed security arrangements in the region were needed not only by Israel but "far more" by the Arabs because of Israel's "continued aggression" and its stockpile of arms.

U.S. plan on Geneva talks accepted. Israel Sept. 25, 1977 accepted a U.S. plan for reconvening the Geneva peace conference on the Middle East. The three Arab states directly involved in the conflict—Egypt, Jordan and Syria—also approved the U.S. formula, but rejected a number of conditions imposed by Israel. The controversy centered largely on the role the Palestinians would assume at the proposed parley.

Washington's plan called for a single unified Arab delegation, including Palestinians, at the opening session at Geneva. The Israeli Cabinet, which had previously opposed the plan, accepted it Sept. 25 by a 10–1 vote.

Under the conditions sought by Israel, all Arabs attending the Geneva talks would be represented in the pan-Arab delegation at the opening ceremonial session. Palestinian Arabs living in the territories captured by Israel in the 1967 war could be included in the Arab delegation provided they were not known members of the PLO. Israel said Palestinians could participate only as part of a Jordanian delegation. Israel would not enter into negotiations with the unified Arab delegation but would hold talks with each separate group—Egypt, Jordan, and Syria—after the opening ceremonial session.

Israeli Foreign Minister Moshe Dayan, who was visiting the U.S., said Sept. 25

that his government's acceptance of the American plan was no reversal of its refusal to deal with the PLO. Israel, he said, would make no special attempt to determine whether Palestinian representatives at Geneva were also representing the PLO.

Secretary of State Cyrus R. Vance Sept. 26 said the U.S. was pleased with the Israelis' approval of the American proposal, although some of their conditions "do not accurately reflect our views." While he agreed with Israel that "there should be bilateral discussions" with individual Arab delegations at Geneva, the secretary said the discussions should also deal with the Palestinian question if the Palestinians were in attendance. Vance also took issue with the Israeli conditions by noting that the U.S. had not ruled out the presence of some PLO members at Geneva.

Vance made his statement after arriving at U.N. headquarters in New York, where he was to hold two weeks of bilateral meetings with Israeli and Arab foreign ministers. Vance met that day with Foreign Minister Dayan.

Dayan said Sept. 27 that two key Palestinian issues were still blocking peace talks—which Palestinian group would attend and what role it should play in the actual negotiations. In an interview with the New York Times, the foreign minister said the U.S. had informed Israel that it opposed "high-level" PLO officials at Geneva, but that it favored some "low-level" members of the organization. This problem could be resolved, Dayan said, by having the PLO accept West Bank Palestinians as their "representatives."

Arabs oppose Israeli conditions—A PLO spokesman in Beirut Sept. 25 reacted to the conditions proposed by Israel by saying the organization "reiterates that it is the sole legitimate representative of the Palestinian people. Once the PLO gets a formal invitation to Geneva, then it can consider the details of Palestinian representation there."

President Carter conferred separately at the White House Sept. 28 with Syrian Foreign Minister Abdel Halim Khaddam and Abdul Hamid Sharaf, chief of Jordanian King Hussein's royal court. Both officials expressed opposition to the Israeli demand that no talks be held with a unified Arab delegation. They were said to

have told the President that their governments wanted a unified Arab delegation to hold discussions with Israel or that there be a breakdown into smaller "functional" groupings, in which two or more Arab parties would meet with the Israelis.

Khaddam later told newsmen that the Arab and U.S. positions "coincided regarding the possibility of forming a unified Arab delegation, including the PLO." This would represent a reversal of the U.S. position on the PLO. A White House spokesman later refused to say whether Khaddam's description of the American stand was accurate.

Egyptian Foreign Minister Ismail Fahmy Sept. 26 said the proposal for a unified Arab delegation at Geneva was aimed at overcoming Israeli objections to the presence of a separate PLO delegation at Geneva. To convene the conference without the PLO presence, as insisted by Israel, would be a "nonstarter," Fahmy said.

Syrian President Hafez al-Assad said in an interview published Sept. 26 that the pan-Arab delegation would have to include the PLO "on an equal footing" with other Arab members.

Speaking at the United Nations General Assembly Sept. 28, Foreign Minister Fahmy listed conditions Israel would have to meet to attain peace: it would have to abandon its commitment to acquire atomic weapons, accept a limit on conventional arms and end its "open door" immigration policy.

Israeli delegate to the U.N. Chaim Herzog responded by accusing Fahmy of introducing an "atmosphere of unyielding intransigence" while the U.S. was attempting to bring about peace negotiations.

Carter for PLO peace role—President Carter said Sept. 29 he favored participation of the PLO in a Middle East peace settlement, although he did not regard the organization as "the exclusive representatives of the Palestinians."

Carter made the remark at his news conference when asked to clarify the U.S. position on the PLO in the light of the "confusing statements from the White House" and from Middle East leaders on the PLO's possible participation at Geneva peace talks.

The U.S. was "not just an intermediary or mediator" in the Arab-Israeli dispute, the President observed. He added: "We have a vital national interest in the ultimate peace in the Middle East. It's obvious to me there can be no Middle Eastern peace settlement without adequate Palestinian representation."

Carter said he recognized the wide divergence between the Arab states and Israel on the PLO's right to be present at Geneva. The U.S. was attempting to reconcile these differences "about the format of the meeting and also who would be welcomed to the conference to represent the Palestinians."

Carter reaffirmed Washington's refusal to deal or negotiate directly with the PLO until it accepted United Nations Security Council Resolution 242, which included a statement on the right of Israel to exist. If it did approve the resolution, "then we will begin discussions" with the organization's leaders, Carter stated. But the President said he had "no inclination to give the PLO assurances other than we will begin to meet with them and search for some accommodation and some approach to their problem" if they accepted the U.N. resolution.

The President acknowledged that the PLO "represents certainly a substantial part of the Palestinians." But he conceded that they were not the Palestinians' sole representatives, citing local Arab leaders in the West Bank, who "may or may not be members of the PLO."

Carter lauded the Arabs and the Israelis for having "come a long way" to settle their dispute. "They are genuinely searching for a formula by which they can meet" and "they want peace," the President said

U.S.-Soviet Geneva plan. The U.S. and the Soviet Union Oct. 1, 1977 issued a joint declaration suggesting that a Middle East peace conference at Geneva guarantee "the legitimate rights of the Palestinian people" and establish "normal peaceful relations" in the region. Both nations drew up the statement as co-chairmen of the Geneva parley, which had recessed after a brief session in December 1973. The declaration was issued in New York by Secretary of State Cyrus R. Vance and in Moscow by Foreign Minister Andrei A. Gromyko. The two had discussed the matter Sept. 30 at U.N. headquarters in New York.

Their three-point document outlined the principles and objectives to govern the Geneva conference and was aimed at expediting efforts to reconvene the meeting. Both nations pledged to get the conference started no later than December.

In discussing the Palestinian question, the statement did not mention the Palestine Liberation Organization by name, nor did it specify what it meant by Palestinian "rights." Newsmen at the U.N., where the document was released in New York, were told that the U.S. believed that these "rights" and the question of who was to represent the Palestinians at Geneva were still open to negotiation.

A State Department spokesman said the Palestinians' "rights cannot be achieved separately from ending belligerency" in the Middle East. Nor can these rights "be purchased at the expense of Israel," he said.

Other aspects of the joint U.S.-Soviet statement called for: "insuring the security of borders between Israel and the neighboring Arab states"; "withdrawal of Israeli armed forces from territories occupied in the 1967 conflict"; participation at Geneva of "the representatives of all the parties involved in the conflict, including the Palestinians," and Soviet-American willingness to participate in the "international guarantees" of secure borders in the region.

Israel rejects statement—The Israeli government Oct. 2 rejected the joint U.S.-Soviet statement as "unacceptable." Finance Minister Simcha Ehrlich, acting premier, said after a Cabinet meeting: "We can go to Geneva but without the PLO. If the PLO is in the representation we can't take part in this Geneva conference."

Ehrlich said the declaration contained three implied aspects that his government had long opposed: The indication of an imposed solution, establishment of a Palestinian state and recognition of the PLO.

The Israeli government also objected to the document's call for the withdrawal of Israel's forces to the pre-1967 borders, which Jerusalem contended contravened the meaning of U.N. Security Council Resolution 242; the failure to mention the concept of "a peace treaty" between the Arabs and Israel, and the lack of reference to Resolutions 242 and 338, which Israel insisted were the sole basis for reconvening the Geneva conference.

The government said the issuance of the document was ill-timed and could not fail "to harden the position of the Arab states."

Israeli opposition figures also expressed criticism. Labor Party leader Shimon Peres said the U.S. position as outlined in the document placed Israel in an unprecedented state of international isolation. Former Foreign Minister Yigal Allon warned the statement "may block the reconvening of the peace conference."

The U.S.-Soviet document was denounced in the U.S. Oct. 2 by influential members of Congress, labor officials and leaders of the American Jewish community. Sen. Henry M. Jackson (D, Wash.) called the statement "a step in the wrong direction." Sen. Robert J. Dole (R, Kan.) described it as an "abdication of Mideast leadership by President Carter." The chairman of the Conference of Presidents of Major American Jewish Organizations, Rabbi Alexander M. Schindler, said "on its face," the docu-

ment "represents an abandonment of America's historic commitment to the security and survival of Israel."

The Anti-Defamation League of B'nai Brith Oct. 3 called the statement "a shocking about-face" in American policy. It also took issue with the Soviet Union's renewed involvement in the Middle East, a region the league said "was comparatively well rid of it." Sen. Daniel Patrick Moynihan (D, N.Y.) said, "Past history and current developments make it clear that the Soviets share no interest in a true peace in the Middle East."

The U.S. sought to allay Israeli fears that the Carter Administration was reneging on the American commitment to Israel. Zbigniew Brzezinski, presidential adviser on national security, Oct. 2 assured Israel that if it was "mortally threatened, especially by an external power, the United States, even now without a security treaty, would certainly go to its aid."

Secretary of State Vance Oct. 3 voiced concern over Israel's reaction. He repeated the State Department's contention, expressed Oct. 1 when the document

---

Text of Joint U.S.-Soviet Statement on Geneva Parley

The text of the joint U.S.-Soviet statement on reconvening the Geneva peace conference on the Middle East, as released Oct. 1 by the U.S. State Department:

Having exchanged views regarding the unsafe situation which remains in the Middle East, United States Secretary of State Cyrus Vance and member of the Politburo of the Central Committee of the Communist Party of the Soviet Union, Minister for Foreign Affairs of the U.S.S.R. A. A. Gromyko, have the following statement to make on behalf of their countries which are co-chairmen of the Geneva Peace Conference on the Middle East:

1. Both governments are convinced that vital interests of the peoples of this area as well as the interests of strengthening peace and international security in general urgently dictate the necessity of achieving as soon as possible a just and lasting settlement of the Arab-Israeli conflict. This settlement should be comprehensive, incorporating all parties concerned and all questions.

The United States and the Soviet Union believe that, within the framework of a comprehensive settlement of the Middle East problem, all specific questions of the settlement should be resolved, including such key issues as withdrawal of Israeli armed forces from territories occupied in the 1967 conflict; the resolution of the Palestinian question including insuring the legitimate rights of the Palestinian people; termination of the state of war and establishment of normal peaceful relations on the basis of mutual recognition of the principles of sovereignty, territorial integrity and political independence.

The two governments believe that, in addition to such measures for insuring the security of the borders

within Israel and the neighboring Arab states as the establishment of demilitarized zones and the agreed stationing in them of U.N. troops or observers, international guarantees of such borders as well as of the observance of the terms of the settlement can also be established, should the contracting parties so desire. The United States and the Soviet Union are ready to participate in these guarantees subject to their constitutional processes.

2. The United States and the Soviet Union believe that the only right and effective way for achieving a fundamental solution to all aspects of the Middle East problem in its entirety is negotiating within the framework of the Geneva Peace Conference, specially convened for these purposes, with participation in its work of the representatives of all the parties involved in the conflict including those of the Palestinian people, and legal and contractual formalization of the decisions reached at the conference.

In their capacity as co-chairmen of the Geneva conference, the U.S. and the U.S.S.R. affirm their intention through joint efforts and in their contacts with the parties concerned to facilitate in every way the resumption of the work of the conference not later than December 1977. The co-chairmen note that there still exist several questions of a procedural and organizational nature which remain to be agreed upon by the participants to the conference.

3. Guided by the goal of achieving a just political settlement in the Middle East and of eliminating the explosive situation in this area of the world, the U.S. and the U.S.S.R. appeal to all the parties in the conflict to understand the necessity for careful consideration of each other's legitimate rights and interests and to demonstrate mutual readiness to act accordingly.

was released, that it represented a compromise that did not damage Israel's interests, despite its acceptance of the "legitimate rights" of the Palestinians. Vance cited the importance of the document's "definition of peace," which he explained was "not merely the end of belligerency but is, in addition, the establishment of normal relations," a condition sought by Israel.

Arabs weigh U.S.-Soviet stand—A statement issued in Beirut Oct. 2 by the PLO said the U.S.-Soviet declaration "gives rise to the feeling that a genuine effort has been made to insure a just and permanent peace in the Middle East." The PLO was especially pleased with the recognition by Washington and Moscow of the "legitimate rights of the Palestinian people" and their call for Palestinian representation at Geneva.

The first negative reaction from the Arabs came Oct. 3 from Iraq, which was opposed to any negotiations with Israel. A government-controlled newspaper said the Soviet-U.S. declaration brought about no basic change in favor of the Palestinian people.

Libyan leader Muammer el-Qaddafi Oct. 8 assailed U.S. efforts to convene a Geneva conference and called on Israel's Arab neighbors to open their frontiers to permit Palestinian forces to attack Israel. Qaddafi criticized some of the Arab states, stating that while they "drown in the illusions of negotiations, conferences and how to form delegations, the Zionist enemy prepares to carry out his expansionist ideas."

U.S., Israel agree on Geneva talks. The U.S. announced Oct. 5 that it had reached an agreement with Israel on procedures for a Middle East peace parley that improved chances for reconvening the Geneva conference by the end of 1977.

The reported accord followed the issuance Oct. 1 of the joint U.S.-Soviet statement suggesting a set of guidelines for proposed Arab-Israeli negotiations. The document was denounced by Israel and by Israel's American backers, who claimed it indicated a tilt by Washington toward the Palestine Liberation Organization, an erosion of traditional U.S. support of Israel, injection of the Soviet Union in the peace process and imposition of a settlement.

The U.S.-Israeli agreement was reached in talks held in New York between President Carter and Foreign Minister Moshe Dayan. Their discussions had started the night of Oct. 4 and a joint statement was completed and released the morning of Oct. 5 by Dayan, Secretary of State Cyrus R. Vance and their aides. A working paper containing details of the arrangement was not disclosed. It was to be submitted later to the Arab states and Moscow for their approval.

The joint statement said Israel and the U.S. agreed that U.N. Security Council Resolutions 242 and 338 "remain the agreed basis for resumption of the Geneva conference. . . . " Among other things, the resolutions guaranteed the existence of the state of Israel, and according to Israel's interpretation, did not require it to withdraw from all the territories it had captured in the 1967 war.

Israeli fears had been aroused by the failure of the U.S. and the Soviet Union to mention the two resolutions in their document.

The U.S.-Israel pronouncement also stressed that "acceptance of the joint U.S.-U.S.S.R. statement . . . by the parties is not a prerequisite for the reconvening and conduct of the Geneva conference."

Israeli officials Oct. 5 greeted the results of the Carter-Dayan talks as a welcome assurance of Washington's concurrence with Jerusalem's position on peace negotiations.

In an interview telecast in Israel, Dayan Oct. 5 urged the Cabinet to approve the understanding he had reached with Carter. Dayan noted that according to the agreement, "the Palestinians do not appear in any way as a separate entity independent from the others. The PLO is not mentioned at all in the working paper."

Israel approves Geneva plan. The Israeli Cabinet Oct. 11, 1977 unanimously approved a working paper on procedures for reconvening the Geneva conference on the Middle East. The secret agreement had been reached Oct. 5 by Foreign Minister Moshe Dayan and U.S. President Carter. In a surprise move, Dayan disclosed its contents Oct. 13.

The U.S. State Department Oct. 11 welcomed Israel's acceptance of the plan, but noted that "it may require further negotiation after the Arab governments have given their views on it."

The text of the working paper as divulged by Dayan Oct. 13:

1. The Arab parties will be represented by a unified Arab delegation, which will include Palestinian Arabs. After the opening sessions, the conference will split into working groups.

2. The working groups for the negotiation and conclusion of peace treaties will be formed as follows:
   A. Egypt-Israel.
   B. Jordan-Israel.
   C. Syria-Israel.
   D. Lebanon-Israel. (All the parties agree that Lebanon may join the conference when it so requests.)

3. The West Bank and Gaza issues will be discussed in a working group to consist of Israel, Jordan, Egypt, and the Palestinian Arabs.

4. The solution of the problem of the Arab refugees will be discussed in accordance with terms to be agreed upon.

5. The agreed bases for the negotiations at the Geneva peace conference on the Middle East are U.N. Security Council Resolutions 242 and 338.

6. All the initial terms of reference of the Geneva peace conference remain in force, except as may be agreed by the parties.

In announcing acceptance of the working paper, a Cabinet spokesman had refused to publicly release the document on the ground that "without publication we promote better the chances of resumption of the Geneva conference."

Dayan read the secret document at a public session of the Knesset (parliament), which had convened to debate the plan. He was said to have decided on this action because distortions of it had been leaked in Jerusalem and because the essential elements of the paper already had been published in the past several days.

The decision to publicly reveal the contents of the working paper also was based on a series of leaks in the U.S., Israeli government officials said privately. They also were said to have been angered by a leaked article appearing Oct. 13 in an Israeli English-language newspaper, The Jerusalem Post. The article said Washington feared that if the Arabs rejected the plan it would be the result of four major changes that were made in the original draft before Dayan gave his approval. The altered text reportedly had deleted a clause calling for low-level participation at Geneva of PLO members; removed mention of placing the question of a Palestinian entity on the agenda; omitted a statement that the opening plenary session at Geneva would remain in session throughout the conference, and substituted the word "discuss" for the word "negotiate" regarding the talks on

the Israeli-occupied West Bank and Gaza Strip.

Although U.S. officials were reportedly annoyed at Dayan's disclosure of the working paper, Secretary of State Cyrus R. Vance said Oct. 11 that he did not believe it would harm U.S. peace efforts.

Dayan raises new issues—Before returning to Israel from the U.S., Foreign Minister Dayan Oct. 10 had delivered an address to the United Nations General Assembly in which he cited four points as Israeli conditions for peace. He listed them as follows:

Israel must retain "defensible borders," a reference to the Arab territory it had captured in the 1967 war; Israel must have free navigational use of the Suez Canal, the Strait of Tiran and the Bab el-Mandeb passageway at the entrance to the Red Sea; Syria must be barred from further attempts to divert waters of the Jordan River and its tributary, the Yarmuk River, both vital for Israel's needs, and there would have to be "full coexistence" between Israelis and Palestinian Arabs in the Gaza Strip and the West Bank, a reference to Israeli Jewish settlements in those two areas.

In reply to Dayan, PLO official Farouk Khaddoumi told the General Assembly Oct. 11 that the Israeli foreign minister's remarks proved that Israel "would never give up one inch of territory. Our armed struggle will continue because we are witnessing a voracious Israeli territorial appetite."

The U.S. and Israeli delegations had objected to Khaddoumi's addressing the Assembly on the ground that only representatives of states were qualified to do so.

PLO demands peace role—The PLO Oct. 16 in effect rejected the U.S.-Israeli working paper. Following a meeting in Beirut, Al Fatah, the largest guerrilla group in the PLO, announced that: "The PLO is the sole legitimate representative of the Palestinian people and therefore has the right to represent this people at all international conferences, rejecting all attempts and maneuvers aimed at bypassing this right."

The PLO stand had received strong support Oct. 10 from Syrian Foreign Minister Abdel Halim Khaddam. Syria, he said, "will never go to Geneva without the PLO." Khaddam called for an Iraqi-Syrian-Palestinian alliance to confront Israel.

Meanwhile, the U.S. and Israel were in apparent disagreement on the interpretation of one facet of their working paper. Israeli Foreign Minister Moshe Dayan Oct. 13 insisted that both countries were in "full agreement" that "no member of the PLO will participate" at Geneva. However, the U.S. State Department Oct. 14 said "the working paper doesn't foreclose anything."

A State Department spokesman had confirmed the accuracy of the six points in the working paper divulged by Dayan Oct. 13. There were no conditions or secret additions to the document, the spokesman said.

Egypt for PLO at Geneva—Egypt was asking that the U.S.-Israeli working paper on reconvening the Geneva conference be amended to specifically provide for the attendance of the Palestine Liberation Organization, Egyptian Foreign Minister Ismail Fahmy said Oct. 19.

Fahmy said the proposed alteration was among the other changes suggested by President Anwar Sadat in a letter he had sent that day to President Carter.

Fahmy asserted that "the PLO alone had the competence, in accordance with the Rabat conference resolution, to speak in the name of the Palestinians or to send representatives to Geneva."

Fahmy's announcement followed talks in Cairo Oct. 18-19 between PLO leader Yasir Arafat and Sadat and other Egyptian officials. The foreign minister said that Egypt had agreed after these discussions that "the PLO should be mentioned by name" in the working paper.

Sadat was reported Nov. 4 to have proposed a working committee prior to the conference to arrange an agenda. The committee would be made up of the U.S., the Soviet Union, Egypt, Jordan, Syria, Israel, Lebanon and the Palestinians. Egypt, Sadat warned, "will not attend the Geneva conference without real preparations."

Sadat's proposal was quoted by an Arab press delegation that accompanied him on a six-day trip to Rumania, Iran and Saudi Arabia. Sadat returned to Cairo Nov. 3.

Israel Nov. 6 rejected Sadat's proposal for preliminary talks. Such a plan, a

Cabinet spokesman said, would only complicate matters and could impede peace efforts.

Syria rejects paper—Syria Oct. 21 rejected the U.S.-Israeli working paper.

Syria's opposition was stated in a letter President Hafez al-Assad had transmitted to President Carter. Assad opposed a provision that called for conducting the principal peace negotiations in separate bilateral committees grouping Israel with the Arab parties to the dispute—Egypt, Syria, Jordan and Lebanon.

Instead Assad reiterated Damascus' demand that the discussions be held through multilateral committees that should be established to negotiate on broad issues, such as Israeli withdrawal from occupied Arab lands, Palestinian rights and peace guarantees.

Begin rejects Brzezinski's West Bank plan. Menahem Begin Nov. 6, 1977 rejected a proposal by Zbigniew Brzezinski, President Carter's national security adviser.

In an interview in the New York Times Nov. 5, Brzezinski had proposed that Israel relinquish sovereignty over the West Bank and permit its transformation into an autonomous demilitarized zone in return for withdrawal of Arab demands that the area be set aside for a Palestinian state. The West Bank would be politically part of Jordan and would have economic links with Israel, under the Brzezinski proposal.

American Jews briefed on policies—Secretary of State Cyrus R. Vance met with American Jewish leaders in Washington Oct. 26 to brief them on U.S. policy in the Middle East. A State Department spokesman described the off-the-record discussions as "useful," but some of the participants charged that the Carter Administration was adopting an anti-Israel position.

According to participants at the briefing, concern was expressed to Vance about the Administration's purported tilt toward recognizing the Palestine Liberation Organization and its seeming acceptance of the PLO at the Geneva peace conference. Vance denied any Administration drift toward the PLO.

Sadat's Visit to Israel & Aftermath

Sadat Offers to Talk in Israel

The major breakthrough in Arab-Israeli relations was Egyptian President Anwar Sadat's visit to Israel in November 1977 to discuss a peace settlement. He was the first Arab leader to go to Israel—and at the end of the decade was still the only one to do so. Sadat's visit, on the invitation of Israeli Premier Menahem Begin, followed the Egyptian president's assertion that he was so anxious for peace that he was prepared to discuss the issue with the Israeli parliament [the Knesset].

Sadat 'ready' to go to Israel. Egyptian President Anwar Sadat Nov. 9, 1977 urged an all-out drive to reconvene the Geneva peace conference and called on other Arab states to support the move.

In an address to parliament, Sadat expressed impatience with what he said was Israel's raising of inconsequential procedural issues. These actions, he contended, were blocking peace talks. Sadat said he was so determined to have peace that "I am ready to go to the Israeli parliament itself to discuss it with them."

Once at Geneva, he said, he would demand "total Israeli withdrawal from Arab lands and the recovery of the Palestinians' rights, including their right to set up an independent state."

Sadat charged that the Israeli-U.S. working paper of Oct. 5 outlining procedures for Geneva talks was actually an earlier American document that Israel changed by removing all references to the Palestinians and the Palestine Liberation Organization.

Carter also for Geneva—Escalating conflict in Lebanon prompted U.S. President Carter Nov. 10 to urge a reconvening of the Geneva conference.

Speaking at a news conference, Carter said he was gratified that Israel had accepted U.S. proposals for Geneva procedures and was "pleased with the statement yesterday" by Sadat. Carter praised Sadat for saying that he was prepared "to go to Geneva or anywhere else and begin to consult directly with Israel and with other Arab nations without quibbling any more about the detailed wording of the procedures." Carter added: "That is our position."

The President expressed "hope that Jordan, Syria and Lebanon very quickly will make a similar response to us" and "we can then reconvene the Geneva conference."

While deploring the mounting violence in Lebanon, Carter appeared to justify Israel's Nov. 9 reprisal air strikes against Palestinian positions in that country. "The retaliatory measures taken by nations who were attacked by terrorists have been a part of the picture in the Middle East for years," the President said. If Israel's border villages continued to come under terrorist raids, "some retaliation is required," Carter added.

The Middle East, Carter warned, "is just sitting and teetering on another outbreak of even more major violence and I think that at this time, a condemnation of people is probably inappropriate."

Sadat accepts invitation to Israel. Sadat Nov. 17 accepted an invitation from Israeli Premier Menachem Begin to come to Israel to discuss the Arab-Israeli dispute. Sadat said there were no conditions attached to his acceptance of the premier's invitation. "The only condition is that I want to discuss the whole situation and put the full picture and details of the situation from our point of view," Sadat said. "There has never been a [more] suitable moment in the Arab world to reach genuine peace. . . ," the Egyptian leader added.

Israel's formal invitation Nov. 15 was given to U.S. Ambassador Samuel Lewis for transmission to the American ambassador in Cairo, Hermann F. Eilts. Eilts delivered the document to Egyptian authorities, a copy of which was handed later Nov. 15 to U.S. Secretary of State Cyrus R. Vance in Washington by Israel's ambassador to the U.S., Simcha Dinitz.

The Knesset Nov. 15 endorsed the Sadat trip. Addressing the body, Begin said that his government also was asking King Hussein of Jordan, President Hafez al-Assad of Syria and President Elias Sarkis of Lebanon to come to Israel for diplomatic discussions. Later, Begin told newsmen that for the moment these invitations were not being formally transmitted through any other channel.

Sadat's projected visit was the result of an informal Egyptian-Israeli dialogue that had begun with Sadat's Nov. 9 avowal of readiness to speak to the Knesset.

Begin responded Nov. 11, urging the "citizens of Egypt" to join Israel in "a silent oath" of "no more wars, no more bloodshed, and no more threats." The premier said he welcomed Sadat's proposal, and that "I, for my part, will, of course, come to your capital, Cairo, for the same purpose: no more wars—peace, a real peace and forever."

Begin Nov. 12 repeated his bid, saying "I hereby invite President Sadat to come to Jerusalem to conduct talks about permanent peace between Israel and Egypt."

In an interview Nov. 14 with CBS-TV newsman Walter Cronkite, Sadat reiterated his readiness to address the Knesset and said he awaited a formal call.

In another interview, also televised Nov. 14, Begin told Cronkite that like Egypt, Israel had no precondition. Therefore, he said, "let us sit together around the table and talk peace and everybody will bring his position."

A Begin aide disclosed Nov. 16 that Rumanian President Nicolae Ceausescu had acted as a go-between in arranging the Begin-Sadat talks. Begin, the aide said, had raised the question of meeting with Sadat during a five-day visit with Ceausescu in Bucharest in August. Rumania had diplomatic ties with both Israel and the Arab states.

U.S., Arab, Soviet reaction—The U.S. government Nov. 15 strongly endorsed President Sadat's projected visit to Israel. Statements by the White House and State Department indicated that the development came as a surprise and that the Carter Administration had not been apprised beforehand of Sadat's proposal to go to Israel and of Premier Begin's invitation to the Egyptian president. Government officials expressed hope that the future Egyptian-Israeli talks would enhance prospects for reconvening the Geneva conference and not serve as a substitute for it.

President Carter called Sadat's decision "very courageous," "unprecedented," "constructive" and "a step in the right direction."

The Soviet Union Nov. 15 was critical of Sadat's upcoming visit. An Arabic-language statement broadcast by Moscow radio charged that Premier Menahem Begin and other Israeli leaders "see in a separate dialogue with Sadat an opportunity to make greater inroads into the Arab front."

Libya, Iraq and radical Palestinian groups Nov. 16 denounced Sadat's decision to travel to Israel. However, most other Arab countries thus far expressed no opinion publicly.

Tripoli radio reported that an emergency meeting of the Libyan Congress the previous day had expressed concern for "the regrettable and dramatic collapse of Arab confrontation against the

Zionist enemy." Libyan leader Col. Muammer el-Qaddafi had sent special envoys to Cairo and Damascus Nov. 15 with messages voicing his country's concern.

Iraq's ruling Baath Party condemned Sadat's forthcoming visit as "a serious deviation" from Arab nationalism and urged Arab "masses" to forestall Cairo's defection.

While the Palestine Liberation Organization refrained from official comment, some groups connected with it assailed Cairo. A spokesman for the radical Popular Front for the Liberation of Palestine scored the projected visit as part of "an imperialist, Zionist and reactionary conspiracy to liquidate the Palestinian people's cause." A PFLP spokesman called on Arabs to reject the Sadat move and "violently confront this course of surrender."

A spokesman for the largest group in the PLO, Al Fatah, called Egypt's "unilateral course" "a flagrant defiance of Arab popular and official will."

An authoritative Palestinian source was quoted as saying that "the only way for Sadat's projected visit to be a success would be to win major concessions from the Israelis, namely the recognition of an independent and sovereign Palestinian state on the West Bank and Gaza Strip and the repatriation of Palestinian refugees."

Arab League ministers meet in Tunis. Foreign ministers of the Arab League met in Tunis Nov. 12–14 to map strategy on a common approach to the problem of reconvening the Geneva conference.

A communique issued at the end of the conference Nov. 14 assailed Israel's air raids into southern Lebanon earlier in November and called on the U.S. and the Soviet Union to take "all necessary measures" to stop what it called Israel's "aggressive acts." The statement also implied criticism of the Palestine Liberation Organization for its refusal thus far to withdraw its forces in southern Lebanon. The communique urged "immediate implementation" of all agreements aimed at pacifying the situation by removing Palestinian forces from the border area and replacing them with a reconstituted Lebanese army.

The league decided to take no action on the Geneva conference, in part because of Egyptian President Anwar Sadat's scheduled meeting Nov. 16 with Syrian President Hafez al-Assad.

The proposed Geneva talks also figured in a conference decision to postpone until Feb. 15, 1978 a summit meeting of the Arab heads of state. Egypt had asked for the delay to give President Sadat more time to bring about the Geneva negotiations. Other league members had wanted an earlier meeting of the heads of state.

Sadat confers with Syrian leader— President Sadat arrived in Damascus Nov. 16 for discussions with President Assad. Although he denied Nov. 15 that the visit had any connection with his forthcoming trip to Israel, it later became known that this was an important part of his discussions with the Syrian president. Sadat said Assad "cannot impose anything on me as I cannot impose anything on him."

Sadat in Israel

Sadat favors peace & recognition. Visiting Israel Nov. 19–21, 1977, Egyptian President Anwar Sadat suggested that he was ready to offer peace and recognition to Israel if the latter agreed to an acceptable settlement with the Palestinians. This visit to Israel was the first by an Arab leader to the Jewish state since it was established in 1948.

Landing at Ben Gurion International Airport at 8:03 p.m. Nov. 19, Sadat received all the honors of a visiting head of state, including an honor guard, a 21-gun salute and a red carpet—despite the fact that Israel and Egypt did not have diplomatic relations and were still technically in a state of war.

Sadat was greeted as he stepped off the plane by Israeli Premier Menahem Begin and President Ephraim Katzir. As they walked down the reception line at the airport, Sadat shook hands with a number of his major adversaries during the history of Arab-Israeli hostilities—Foreign Minister Moshe Dayan, former Premiers Golda Meir and Yitzhak Rabin and Gen. Ariel Sharon. Then he and President Katzir were driven to Jerusalem's King David Hotel, where he held preliminary talks with Begin, Dayan and Deputy Premier Yigael Yadin. Upon emerging from the talks, Begin commented to reporters, "I have already had a private discussion with [Sadat] and I can say that we like each other."

Sadat spent the first half of Nov. 20 touring Jerusalem's holy places. The visit was considered remarkable since it indirectly acknowledged Israeli sovereignty over the city. Foreign dignitaries who had visited Israel previously had sometimes shunned the city for that reason.

Sadat started his visit with a service at the Al Aksa Mosque in the Old City, which was built on the site where the Prophet Mohammed was believed to have ascended to heaven and was one of the holiest of Moslem sites. Sadat then went to the Church of the Holy Sepulcher, built over the site where Jesus was believed to have been buried. Afterwards he visited Yad Vashem, the memorial to the six million Jewish victims of the Nazis.

The highlight of Sadat's visit was his address that afternoon to the Israeli Knesset (parliament). (In a surprise gesture, Sadat placed a wreath at the Knesset memorial to Israeli war dead before going in to speak.)

While Sadat's speech and the responding speech by Begin did not indicate any new positions on the Middle East issues, they struck a noticeably milder tone than heard previously.

During his one-hour speech in Arabic, Sadat held out the promise of Arab recognition of the Israeli state. He said he had come "to deliver a message," not to arrange a separate Egyptian settlement with Israel. "If you want to live with us in this part of the world, in sincerity I tell you that we welcome you among us with all security and safety," he told the Knesset.

He warned his audience, however, "that there can be no peace without the Palestinians." He added that a settlement must be "based on justice and not on the occupation of the land of others. . . . You have to give up once and for all the dreams of conquest and the belief that force is the best method of dealing with Arabs."

Although he indicated that he would stand firm on the return of all Arab lands occupied by Israel after the 1967 war, he made no specific mention of the Palestine

Liberation Organization, which Israel refused to recognize.

Begin's reply, delivered in Hebrew, avoided a direct response to Sadat's offer of recognition. Begin omitted any explicit refusal to withdraw from the West Bank or to consider a Palestinian state, but he warned the Egyptian leader that Israel "will not be put within range of fire for annihilation." He praised Sadat's "courage" in visiting Israel and invited the Syrian, Jordanian and Lebanese leaders to Jerusalem. He promised that any Egyptian who wished would be free to visit Israel and expressed the hope that he would be able to confer with Sadat in Cairo.

After Begin, opposition Labor Party leader Shimon Peres spoke. He mentioned the Palestinian problem and added that "the identity of the Palestinians must be found without endangering the security of Israel."

Sadat, Begin hold news conference— Before leaving Israel Nov. 21, Sadat held a joint press conference with Begin. (Sadat had returned to the Knesset that morning for informal talks with Israeli legislators and had revisited President Katzir.)

At the news conference, both Sadat and Begin expressed a desire for peace and hope that the Geneva conference on a Middle East peace settlement would be reconvened in the near future. Sadat said the chief accomplishment of his visit had been "to get rid of the psychological barrier, which in my idea was more than 70% of the whole conflict, and the other 30% is substance."

Contrary to expectations, Sadat did not extend to Begin a formal invitation to come to Cairo. He explained that the premier "has got the full right to come and address our parliament . . . but for certain reasons that we discussed we have found that we must postpone this issue for the future." Begin remarked that "I do understand the reasons why at this stage such an invitation was not issued. I would like to say I do hope to visit Cairo. . . ."

Begin stressed that Sadat's visit was the start of a dialogue and did not mean that specific agreements had been reached. "The key word is continuation," he told the reporters. "We agreed we are going to continue our dialogue, and ultimately out of it will come peace." He added that "a momentous agreement was achieved already—no more war, no more bloodshed, no more attacks . . . ," and he praised Sadat's visit as "a great moral achievement. . . ."

Sadat's assessment of the accomplishments of his trip was more reserved than Begin's. He said he and the Israeli leader had "agreed upon the principle of security, but the meaning of security, we differ on it. I think through Geneva we can reach an agreement. . . ." He added, "I am really deeply grateful for the very warm welcome" he had received in Israel.

On the question of Palestinian representation at Geneva, Begin stated that "a proper representation of the Arabs will take place." Sadat said "the Palestinians should decide among themselves" about representation. Both men indicated little change in their views on a Palestinian homeland and the return of occupied lands. "Our land is sacred," Sadat said in answer to a question, and Begin repeated the remark in the context of his own reply.

On the subject of Arab and Soviet disapproval of his Israeli visit, Sadat expressed little concern. He acknowledged that "my relations with the Soviets are strained, and it appears whatever I do isn't to their liking. . . . I fear that the same attitude could be adopted in Geneva. . . ." He assured listeners that "whenever we the parties concerned reach an agreement no one, big power or small power, can prevent us from fulfilling it. . . ."

"My people are 100% behind me," Sadat added. "They don't want any war. . . ." He urged that "whatever happens between [Israel and Egypt] we should solve it through talk rather than going to war." "I'm sure of the fact that the process that we started through my visit here will enable us to solve all the problems," he concluded.

Final communique—The final communique released after the news conference was labeled an agreed communique, not a joint communique, since it was issued by the Israelis rather than worked on jointly by Sadat and Begin.

In response to the sincere and courageous move by President Sadat, and believing in the need to continue the dialogue along the lines proposed by both sides during their exchanges and the presentation of their positions in their historic meeting in Jerusalem, and in order to enhance the prospect of a fruitful consummation of this significant visit, the government of Israel, expressing the will of the people of Israel, proposes that this hopeful step be further pursued through dialogue between the two countries concerned, thereby paving the way toward successful negotiations leading to the signing of peace treaties in Geneva with all the neighboring Arab states.

Sadat hailed upon return—Sadat received a triumphal welcome in Cairo upon his return from Israel Nov. 21. Crowds lined the 20-mile route from the airport and chanted his praises. (According to observers, the outcry in the Arab world over Sadat's visit had only served to rally the Egyptian people more closely around their leader.)

A government statement on the trip said: "We can now say that 30 years of hostilities have been eliminated in 30 hours." It added that the main purpose of the trip was to prepare for the Geneva conference and that Sadat had accomplished his mission.

In other developments concerning Sadat's trip:

While Sadat visited the Suez Canal city of Ismailia Nov. 18, an advance party of 60 Egyptian officials arrived in Israel to help with preparations for Sadat's arrival. The Egyptian contingent provided copies of the Egyptian national anthem for the Israeli military band that was to greet Sadat and brought a load of Egyptian flags.

A telephone link between Israel and Egypt was operated Nov. 19-22 for the first time in Middle East history. Journalists were able to make direct calls from Jerusalem and Tel Aviv to Cairo, but the line was cut Nov. 22 without explanation.

Egyptian foreign minister resigns—Egyptian Foreign Minister Ismail Fahmy resigned Nov. 17, apparently over Sadat's trip to Israel. Fahmy said he could "no longer share in shouldering responsibilities in these conditions." (He was quoted the next day in a Kuwaiti newspaper as saying he "could not continue to support such ill-considered political moves.")

Hours after Fahmy's resignation, Mohammed Riad, Fahmy's deputy and replacement as foreign minister, announced his own resignation. Sadat then named Butros Ghali, a minister of state, to serve as foreign minister. (Sama el-Baz, Fahmy's chief adviser, resigned Nov. 18.)

However, Sadat received strong support Nov. 19 from Gen. Mohammed

Abdel Ghany el-Gamasy, defense minister and commander-in-chief of the armed forces.

In an interview published Dec. 3, Fahmy again assailed Sadat's policies.

The Paris-based Arab publication Al Mustakbal quoted Fahmy as saying that Syria, Jordan, the PLO and Egypt had agreed "on the formulation of a single Arab delegation" that would have cleared away the procedural obstacles to reconvening the Geneva conference. Israel, he claimed, "was about to agree, too." But Sadat's visit to Jerusalem "meant that the conference has now been torpedoed," Fahmy said. He said the Geneva talks were to have started the last week of December.

Fahmy also disclosed that Libyan leader Col. Muammer el-Qaddafi had promised to send Egypt 500 tanks to strengthen Cairo's bargaining position at Geneva. "Now, in my opinion, everything is finished."

Libya reacted the most strongly to Sadat's trip, calling Nov. 18 for Egypt's expulsion from the Arab League. Libyan diplomats at the Libyan mission to the United Nations burned their country's flag Nov. 19 and requested that the Libyan flag not fly outside the U.N. headquarters. (The Libyan, Egyptian and Syrian flags were similar to each other.) That day, Libya announced it had ended diplomatic relations with Egypt.

Saudi Arabia expressed criticism Nov. 18, saying it was "surprised" by Sadat's move and warning that "any move with regard to a settlement must be within the framework of Arab unity."

Iraq registered its protest Nov. 19 as did the United Arab Emirates. Official criticism was withheld in Jordan and Kuwait, but newspapers in those countries expressed disapproval. The only Arab support for Sadat came from Tunisia, Morocco, Sudan and Oman. (Sudanese President Gaafar el-Nimeiry Nov. 22 visited Sadat in Cairo and called his trip "a big victory" for the Arabs.)

After Sadat's speech to the Knesset, attacks against him mounted. The Palestine Liberation Organization Nov. 20 called Begin's stance "conditions for surrender" and called for "maximum sanctions and complete isolation" of the Egyptian president. As Saiqa, a Syrian-backed PLO faction, called for Sadat's overthrow. However, the Jordanian Cabinet that day

urged Arabs to "stop pouring oil on the fire" of anti-Sadat criticism until the complete results of his trip were known.

The Jordanian government had not made any official statement on the trip, but Information Minister Adnan Abu Odeh Nov. 22 said "the visit has broken the ice and removed the psychological barrier and brought fresh hope for resuming the Geneva peace conference. . . ."

(Jordan apparently was making an effort to prevent the Syrian-Egyptian breach from widening. Jordanian Premier Mudar Badran flew to Damascus Nov. 22, reportedly to urge President Assad to put aside plans to form a rejectionist Arab union against Sadat. Syrian and PLO officials that day met to coordinate policy against the Egyptian leader. Libyan government representatives were reported visiting Syria, Iraq, Algeria and South Yemen to discuss the formation of a united front against Sadat. The major obstacle to such a front was long-standing Syrian-Iraqi hostility.)

Egyptian walks out on Syria at U.N.— The Egyptian chief delegate to the United Nations Nov. 22 walked out on a speech by the Syrian delegate at the start of the annual General Assembly debate on the Middle East. The unprecedented move occurred as Mouaffak el-Allaf, the Syrian delegate, opened the debate by denouncing Egyptian President Sadat's visit to Israel as a "stab in the back of the Arab people."

The walkout by Ahmed Esmat Abdel Meguid, the Egyptian delegate, was the first by one Arab delegate against another. Meguid told reporters that he had walked out "more in sorrow than in anger," and he criticized the Syrian delegate for violating an Arab agreement not to quarrel publicly.

Arab reactions to Sadat's trip—The Arab world in general reacted negatively to Sadat's decision to go to Israel, interpreting the move as a threat to Arab unity. There was fear that Sadat might negotiate a separate peace settlement with Israel and abandon the Palestinians, as well as a feeling after Sadat's return that the Egyptian leader had received nothing from the Israeli government in return for his gesture.

Syrian President Hafez al-Assad Nov. 17 called the visit "very dangerous to the Arab cause." He had met with Sadat the day before to discuss the Israeli trip. Upon leaving Syria Nov. 17, Sadat acknowledged Assad's disapproval, adding "he has the right to form his ideas as anyone else." Hours after Sadat's departure, several bombs exploded at the Egyptian Embassy in Damascus. Syria declared a day of mourning Nov. 19, the day of Sadat's arrival in Israel.

Al Fatah, the Palestinian guerrilla organization led by Yasir Arafat, Nov. 17 condemned the proposed visit and urged Sadat to cancel his plans. Palestinian students in Athens, Greece Nov. 18 stormed the Egyptian Embassy but were beaten back by gunfire from embassy guards. Eight students were reported injured and 17 arrested.

Violence also was reported in Beirut, Lebanon, where a rocket attack Nov. 18 on the Egyptian Embassy left one guard dead and two passers-by wounded. A bomb had exploded earlier in the day at the Air Egypt office in the city, and Palestinians held protest marches in the Moslem quarter.

U.S., Soviet reactions—U.S. President Carter Nov. 20 called Sadat's arrival in Jerusalem "a great occasion" and added that "the people were ready for" the visit "and it was just the reluctance of leaders to take this momentous step that was an obstacle."

Carter had spoken to the Egyptian and Israeli leaders before Sadat left for Israel. In a telephone conversation with Begin Nov. 17, he reportedly stressed to the Israeli leader the importance of a positive outcome for the trip. Carter spoke to Sadat Nov. 18, telling him, "The eyes of the world are upon you" and expressing hope that the visit would be successful.

In a policy speech evaluating the trip Nov. 22, Deputy Secretary of State Warren Christopher called for "evidence of tangible progress toward peace" from leaders in the Middle East to continue the progress resulting from Sadat's trip. He said Sadat and Begin "have taken action to prove their determination to work for an overall settlement."

Christopher repeated the Administration stand that "we cannot avoid the Palestinian question—not if we want a real chance for peace." He indirectly criticized the U.S.S.R.'s reaction to Sadat's visit, saying Moscow had "a constructive role

or a troublesome role" to play in a Middle East settlement.

The negative Soviet reaction to Sadat's visit had irked the U.S. Carter met with Soviet Ambassador Anatoly Dobrynin Nov. 18, reportedly to receive a personal message from Soviet President Leonid Brezhnev. The message was not about the Middle East, but Carter reportedly took the opportunity of meeting with Dobrynin to express U.S. dissatisfaction with Soviet criticism of Sadat.

The U.S.S.R. Nov. 19 continued its denunciation of the visit. The Soviet news agency Tass said Sadat's trip was "largely determined by the U.S. and some other bourgeois non-Arab countries that were doing everything to edge Cairo on to separate talks behind the backs of Arabs." Tass added that the visit would "undermine the united front of Arab states in the struggle to liquidate the consequences of Israeli aggression and to achieve a just settlement of the Mideast crisis."

EC backs Sadat despite France—The nine members of the European Community Nov. 22 adopted a resolution praising Sadat's visit to Israel. The resolution was voted after initial objections by France, whose government had vetoed a similar resolution several days before. According to EC officials, France had opposed the resolution because the idea had come from the U.S. and because it feared the consequences of supporting Sadat in the face of Arab condemnation of his trip.

The resolution praised "the courageous initiative of President Sadat" and expressed "hope that the Geneva conference will be reconvened in the near future."

Begin thanks Rumania—Israeli Premier Begin Nov. 18 sent a message of thanks to Rumanian President Nicolae Ceausescu for his help in arranging Sadat's trip to Israel. Rumania was the only Eastern European country that had diplomatic relations with both Egypt and Israel, and Ceausescu had been instrumental as a go-between in bringing the two leaders face to face.

Texts of Sadat & Begin Speeches to Knesset Nov. 20, 1977

Following are texts of the addresses by Egyptian President Anwar Sadat and Israeli Premier Menahem Begin before the Israeli Knesset Nov. 20. Sadat's address, in Arabic, was translated by a parliamentary interpreter. Begin's speech, in Hebrew, was translated in New York for ABC News:

Sadat's Address

In the name of God, Mr. Speaker of the Knesset, ladies and gentlemen, allow me first to thank deeply the Speaker of the Knesset for affording me this opportunity to address you.

As I begin my address I wish to say, peace and the mercy of God Almighty be upon you and may peace be with us all, God willing. Peace for us all, of the Arab lands and in Israel, as well as in every part of this big world, which is so beset by conflicts, perturbed by its deep contradictions, menaced now and then by destructive wars launched by man to annihilate his fellow men.

Finally, amidst the ruins of what man has built among the remains of the victims of mankind there emerges neither victor nor vanquished. The only vanquished remains always a man, God's most sublime creation. Man, whom God has created, as Gandhi, the apostle of peace puts it, to forge ahead, to mold the way of life and to worship God Almighty.

I come to you today on solid ground to shape a new life and to establish peace. We all love this land, the land of God, we all, Moslems, Christians and Jews, all worship God.

Under God, God's teachings and commandments are: love, sincerity, security and peace.

I do not blame all those who received my decision when I announced it to the entire world before the Egyptian People's Assembly. I do not blame all those who received my decision with surprise and even with amazement—some gripped even by violent surprise. Still others interpreted it as political, to camouflage my intentions of launching a new war.

I would go so far as to tell you that one of my aides at the presidential office contacted me at a late hour following my return home from the People's Assembly and sounded worried as he asked me: "Mr. President, what would be our reaction if Israel actually extended an invitation to you?"

I replied calmly: "I would accept it immediately. I have declared that I would go to the end of the earth. I would go to Israel, for I want to put before the people of Israel all the facts."

I can see the faces of all those who were astounded by my decision and had doubts as to the sincerity of the intentions behind the declaration of my decision. No one could have ever conceived that the president of the biggest Arab state, · which bears the heaviest burden and the main responsibility pertaining to the cause of war and peace in the Middle East, should declare his readiness to go to the land of the adversary while we were still in a state of war.

We all still bear the consequences of four fierce wars waged within 30 years. All this at the time when the families of the 1973 October war are still mourning under the cruel pain of bereavement of father, son, husband and brother.

As I have already declared, I have not consulted as far as this decision is concerned with any of my colleagues or brothers, the Arab heads of state or the confrontation states.

Most of those who contacted me following the declaration of this decision expressed their objection because of the feeling of utter suspicion and absolute lack of confidence between the Arab states and the Palestine people on the one hand and Israel on the other that still surges in us all.

Many months in which peace could have been brought about have been wasted over differences and fruitless discussions on the procedure of convening the Geneva conference. All have shared suspicion and absolute lack of confidence.

But to be absolutely frank with you, I took this decision after long thought, knowing that it constitutes a great risk, for God Almighty has made it my fate to assume responsibility on behalf of the Egyptian people, to share in the responsibility of the Arab nation, the main duty of which, dictated by responsibility, is to exploit all and every means in a bid to save my Egyptian Arab people and the pan-Arab nation from the horrors of new suffering and destructive wars, the dimensions of which are foreseen only by God Himself.

After long thinking, I was convinced that the obligation of responsibility before God and before the people make it incumbent upon me that I should go to the far corners of the world—even to Jerusalem to address members of the Knesset and acquaint them with all the facts surging in me, then I would let you decide for yourselves.

Following this, may God Almighty determine our fate.

Ladies and gentlemen, there are moments in the lives of nations and peoples when it is incumbent upon those known for their wisdom and clarity of vision to survey the problem, with all its complexities and vain memories, in a bold drive towards new horizons.

Those who like us are shouldering the same responsibilities entrusted to us are the first who should have the courage to make determining decisions that are consonant with the magnitude of the circumstances. We must all rise above all forms of obsolete theories of superiority, and the most important thing is never to forget that infallibility is the prerogative of God alone.

If I said that I wanted to avert from all the Arab people the horrors of shocking and destructive wars I must sincerely declare before you that I have the same feelings and bear the same responsibility towards all and every man on earth, and certainly toward the Israeli people.

Any life that is lost in war is a human life, be it that of an Arab or an Israeli. A wife who becomes a widow is a human being entitled to a happy family life, whether she be an Arab or an Israeli.

Innocent children who are deprived of the care and compassion of their parents are ours. They are ours, be they living on Arab or Israeli land.

They command our full responsibility to afford them a comfortable life today and tomorrow.

For the sake of them all, for the sake of the lives of all our sons and brothers, for the sake of affording our communities the opportunity to work for the progress and happiness of man, feeling secure and with the right to a dignified life, for the generations to come, for a smile on the face of every child born in our land—for all that I have taken my decision to come to you, despite all the hazards, to deliver my address.

Efforts to find peace

I have shouldered the prerequisites of the historic responsibility and therefore I declared on Feb. 4, 1971, that I was willing to sign a peace agreement with Israel. This was the first declaration made by a responsible Arab official since the outbreak of the Arab-Israeli conflict. Motivated by all these factors dictated by the responsibilities of leadership, on Oct. 16, 1973, before the Egyptian People's Assembly, I called for an international conference to establish permanent peace based on justice. I was not heard.

I was in the position of man pleading for peace or asking for a cease-fire, motivated by the duties of history and leadership, I signed the first disengagement agreement, followed by the second disengagement agreement in Sinai.

Then we proceeded, trying both open and closed doors in a bid to find a certain road leading to a durable and just peace.

We opened our heart to the peoples of the entire world to make them understand our motivations and objectives and actually to convince them of the fact that we are advocates of justice and peacemakers. Motivated by all these factors, I also decided to come to you with an open mind and an open heart and with a conscious determination so that we might establish permanent peace based on justice.

It is so fated that my trip to you, which is a journey of peace, coincided with the Islamic feast, the holy Feast of the Sacrifice when Abraham—peace be upon him—forefather of the Arabs and Jews, submitted to God, I say, when God Almighty ordered him, not out of weakness, but through a giant spiritual force and by free will to sacrifice his very own son, personified a firm and unshakeable belief in ideals that had for mankind a profound significance.

Ladies and gentlemen, let us be frank with each other. Using straightforward words and a clear conception with no ambiguity, let us be frank with each other today while the entire world, both East and West, follows these unparalleled moments, which could prove to be a radical turning point in the history of this part of the world if not in the history of the world as a whole.

'Let us be frank . . .'

Let us be frank with each other, let us be frank with each other as we answer this important question:

How can we achieve permanent peace based on justice? Well, I have come to you carrying my clear and frank answer to this big question, so that the people in Israel as well as the entire world may hear it. All those devoted prayers ring in my ears, pleading to God Almighty that this historic meeting may eventually lead to the result aspired to by millions.

Before I proclaim my answer, I wish to assure you that in my clear and frank answer I am availing myself of a number of facts that no one can deny.

The first fact is that no one can build this happiness at the expense of the misery of others.

The second fact: never have I spoken, nor will I ever speak, with two tongues; never have I adopted, nor will I ever adopt, two policies. I never deal with anyone except in one tongue, one policy and with one face.

The third fact: direct confrontation is the nearest and most successful method to reach a clear objective.

The fourth fact: the call for permanent and just peace based on respect for United Nations resolutions has now become the call of the entire world. It has become the expression of the will of the international community, whether in official capitals where policies are made and decisions taken, or at the level of the world public opinion, which influences policymaking and decision-taking.

The fifth fact, and this is probably the clearest and most prominent, is that the Arab nation, in its drive for permanent peace based on justice, does not proceed from a position of weakness. On the contrary, it has the power and stability for a sincere will for peace.

The Arab declared intention stems from an awareness prompted by a heritage of civilization, that to avoid an inevitable disaster that will befall us, you and the whole world, there is no alternative to the establishment of permanent peace based on justice, peace that is not swayed by suspicion or jeopardized by ill intentions.

In the light of these facts, which I meant to place before you the way I see them, I would also wish to warn you, in all sincerity I warn you, against some thoughts that could cross your minds.

Frankness makes it incumbent upon me to tell you the following:

No separate agreement

First, I have not come here for a separate agreement between Egypt and Israel. This is not part of the policy of Egypt. The problem is not that of Egypt and Israel.

An interim peace between Egypt and Israel, or between any Arab confrontation state and Israel, will not bring permanent peace based on justice in the entire region.

Rather, even if peace between all the confrontation states and Israel were achieved in the absence of a just solution of the Palestinian problem, never will there be that durable and just peace upon which the entire world insists.

Second, I have not come to you to seek a partial peace, namely to terminate the state of belligerency at this stage and put off the entire problem to a subsequent stage. This is not the radical solution that would steer us to permanent peace.

Equally, I have not come to you for a third disengagement agreement in Sinai or in Golan or the West Bank.

For this would mean that we are merely delaying the ignition of the fuse. I would also mean that we are lacking the courage to face peace, that we are too weak to shoulder the burdens and responsibilities of a durable peace based upon justice.

I have come to you so that together we should build a durable peace based on justice to avoid the shedding of one single drop of blood by both sides. It is for this reason that I have proclaimed my readiness to go to the farthest corner of the earth.

Here I would go back to the big question:

How can we achieve a durable peace based on justice? In my opinion, and I declare it to the whole world, from this forum, the answer is neither difficult nor is it impossible despite long years of feuds, blood, faction, strife, hatreds and deep-rooted animosity.

The answer is not difficult, nor is it impossible, if we sincerely and faithfully follow a straight line.

You want to live with us, in this part of the world.

In all sincerity I tell you we welcome you among us with full security and safety. This in itself is a tremendous turning point, one of the landmarks of a decisive historical change. We used to reject you. We had our reasons and our fears, yes.

We refused to meet with you, anywhere, yes.

We were together in international conferences and organizations and our representatives did not, and still do not, exchange greetings with you. Yes. This has happened and is still happening.

It is also true that we used to set as a precondition for any negotiations with you a mediator who would meet separately with each party.

Yes. Through this procedure, the talks of the first and second disengagement agreements took place.

Our delegates met in the first Geneva conference without exchanging a direct word, yes, this has happened.

Yet today I tell you, and I declare it to the whole world, that we accept to live with you in permanent peace based on justice. We do not want to encircle you or be encircled ourselves by destructive missiles ready for launching, nor by the shells of grudges and hatreds.

I have announced on more than one occasion that Israel has become a fait accompli, recognized by the world, and that the two superpowers have undertaken the responsibility for its existence. As we really and truly seek peace we really and truly welcome you to live among us in peace and security.

There was a huge wall between us that you tried to build up over a quarter of a century but it was destroyed in 1973. It was the wall of an implacable and escalating psychological warfare.

It was a wall of the fear of the force that could sweep the entire Arab nation. It was a wall of propaganda that we were a nation reduced to immobility. Some of you have gone as far as to say that even for 50 years to come, the Arabs will not regain their strength. It was a wall that always threatened with a long arm that could reach and strike anywhere. It was a wall that warned us of extermination and annihilation if we tried to use our legitimate rights to liberate the occupied territories.

Together we have to admit that that wall fell and collapsed in 1973. Yet, there remains another wall. This wall constitutes a psychological barrier between us, a barrier of suspicion, a barrier of rejection; a barrier of fear, of deception, a barrier of hallucination without any action, deed or decision.

A barrier of distorted and eroded interpretation of every event and statement. It is this psychological barrier that I described in official statements as constituting 70 percent of the whole problem.

Today, through my visit to you, I ask why don't we stretch out our hands with faith and sincerity so that together we might destroy this barrier? Why shouldn't our and your will meet with faith and sincerity so that together we might remove all suspicion of fear, betrayal and bad intentions?

Why don't we stand together with the courage of men and the boldness of heroes who dedicate themselves to a sublime aim? Why don't we stand together with the same courage and daring to erect a huge edifice of peace?

An edifice that builds and does not destroy. An edifice that serves as a beacon for generations to come with the human message for construction, development and the dignity of man.

Why should we bequeath to the coming generations the plight of bloodshed, yes, orphans, widowhood, family disintegration and the wailing of victims?

Why don't we believe in the wisdom of God conveyed to us by the wisdom of the proverbs of Solomon. [Sadat went on to quote extensively from the proverbs.]

Peace must be based on justice

Ladies and gentlemen, to tell you the truth, peace cannot be worth its name unless it is based on justice and not on the occupation of the land of others. It would not be right for you to demand for yourselves what you deny to others. With all frankness and in the spirit that has prompted me to come to you today, I tell you you have to give up once and for all the dreams of conquest and give up the belief that force is the best method for dealing with the Arabs.

You should clearly understand the lesson of confrontation between you and us. Expansion does not pay. To speak frankly, our land does not yield itself to bargaining, it is not even open to argument. To us, the nation's soil is equal to the holy valley where God Almighty spoke to Moses. Peace be upon him.

We cannot accept any attempt to take away or accept or to seek one inch of it nor can we accept the principle of debating or bargaining over it.

I sincerely tell you also that before us today lies the appropriate chance for peace. If we are really serious in our endeavor for peace, it is a chance that may never come again. It is a chance that if lost or wasted, the resulting slaughter would bear the curse of humanity and of history.

What is peace for Israel? It means that Israel lives in the region with her Arab neighbors in security and safety. Is that logical? I say yes. It means that Israel lives within its borders, secure against any aggression. Is that logical? And I say yes. It means that Israel obtains all kinds of guarantees that will ensure these two factors. To this demand, I say yes.

Beyond that we declare that we accept all the international guarantees you envisage and accept. We declare that we accept all the guarantees you want from the two superpowers or from either of them or from the Big Five or from some of them. Once again, I declare clearly and unequivocally that we agree to any guarantees you accept, because in return we shall receive the same guarantees.

In short then, when we ask what is peace for Israel, the answer would be that Israel lives within her borders, among her Arab neighbors in safety and security, within the framework of all the guarantees she accepts and that are offered to her.

But, how can this be achieved? How can we reach this conclusion that would lead us to permanent peace based on justice? There are facts that should be faced with courage and clarity. There are Arab territories that Israel has occupied and still occupies by force. We insist on complete withdrawal from these territories, including Arab Jerusalem.

I have come to Jerusalem, the city of peace, which will always remain as a living embodiment of coexistence among believers of the three religions. It is inadmissible that anyone should conceive the special status of the city of Jerusalem within the framework of annexation or expansionism. It should be a free and open city for all believers.

Above all, this city should not be severed from those who have made it their abode for centuries. Instead of reviving the precedent of the Crusades, we should revive the spirit of Omar Emil Khtab and Saladin, namely the spirit of tolerance and respect for right.

The holy shrines of Islam and Christianity are not only places of worship but a living testimony of our interrupted presence here. Politically, spiritually and intellectually, here let us make no mistake about the importance and reverence we Christians and Moslems attach to Jerusalem.

Let me tell you without the slightest hesitation that I have not come to you under this roof to make a request that your troops evacuate the occupied territories. Complete withdrawal from the Arab territories occupied after 1967 is a logical and undisputed fact. Nobody should plead for that. Any talk about permanent peace based on justice and any move to ensure our coexistence in peace and security in this part of the world would become meaningless while you occupy Arab territories by force of arms.

For there is no peace that could be built on the occupation of the land of others, otherwise it would not be a serious peace. Yet this is a foregone conclusion that is not open to the passion of debate if intentions are sincere or if endeavors to establish a just and durable peace for our and for generations to come are genuine.

Palestine: the crux of the problem

As for the Palestine cause—nobody could deny that it is the crux of the entire problem. Nobody in the world could accept today slogans propagated here in Israel, ignoring the existence of a Palestinian people and questioning even their whereabouts. Because the Palestine people and their legitimate rights are no longer denied today by anybody; that is nobody who has the ability of judgment can deny or ignore it.

It is an acknowledged fact, perceived by the world community, both in the East and in the West, with support and recognition in international documents and official statements. It is of no use to anybody to turn deaf ears to its resounding voice, which is being heard day and night, or to overlook its historical reality.

Even the United States of America, your first ally, which is absolutely committed to safeguard Israel's security and existence and which offered and still offers Israel every moral, material and military support—I say, even the United States has opted to face up to reality and admit that the Palestinian people are entitled to legitimate rights and that the Palestine problem is the cause and essence of the conflict and that so long as it continues to be unresolved, the conflict will continue to aggravate, reaching new dimension.

In all sincerity I tell you that there can be no peace without the Palestinians. It is a grave error of unpredictable consequences to overlook or brush aside this cause.

I shall not indulge in past events such as the Balfour Declaration 60 years ago. You are well acquainted with the relevant text. If you have found the moral and legal justification to set up a national home on a land that did not all belong to you, it is incumbent upon you to show understanding of the insistence of the people of Palestine for establishment once again of a state on their land. When some extremists ask the Palestinians to give up this sublime objective, this in fact means asking them to renounce their identity and every hope for the future.

I hail the Israeli voices that called for the recognition of the Palestinian people's right to achieve and safeguard peace.

Here I tell you, ladies and gentlemen, that it is no use to refrain from recognizing the Palestinian people and their right to statehood as their right of return. We, the Arabs, have faced this experience before, with you. And with the reality of the Israeli existence, the struggle that took us from war to war, from victims to more victims, until you and we have today reached the edge of a horrible abyss and a terrifying disaster unless, together, we seize this opportunity today of a durable peace based on justice.

You have to face reality bravely, as I have done. There can never be any solution to a problem by evading it or turning a deaf ear to it. Peace cannot last if attempts are made to impose fantasy concepts on which the world has turned its back and announced its unanimous call for the respect of rights and facts.

There is no need to enter a vicious circle as to Palestinian rights. It is useless to create obstacles, otherwise the march of peace will be impeded or peace will be blown up. As I have told you, there is no happiness [based on] the detriment of others.

Direct confrontation and straightforwardness are the shortcuts and the most successful way to reach a clear objective. Direct confrontation concerning the Palestinian problem and tackling it in one single language with a view to achieving a durable and just peace lie in the establishment of that peace. With all the guarantees you demand, there should be no fear of a newly born state that needs the assistance of all countries of the world.

When the bells of peace ring there will be no hands to beat the drums of war. Even if they existed, they would be stilled.

Terms for peace

Conceive with me a peace agreement in Geneva that we would herald to a world thirsting for peace. A peace agreement based on the following points:

Ending the occupation of the Arab territories occupied in 1967.

Achievement of the fundamental rights of the Palestinian people and their right to self-determination, including their right to establish their own state.

The right of all states in the area to live in peace within their boundaries, their secure boundaries, which will be secured and guaranteed through procedures to be agreed upon, which will provide appropriate security to international boundaries in addition to appropriate international guarantees.

Commitment of all states in the region to administer the relations among them in accordance with the objectives and principles of the United Nations Charter. Particularly the principles concerning the nonuse of force and a solution of differences among them by peaceful means.

Ending the state of belligerence in the region.

Ladies and gentlemen, peace is not a mere endorsement of written lines. Rather it is a rewriting of history. Peace is not a game of calling for peace to defend certain whims or hide certain admissions. Peace in its essence is a dire struggle against all and every ambition and whim.

Perhaps the example taken and experienced, taken from ancient and modern history, teaches that missiles, warships and nuclear weapons cannot establish security. Instead they destroy what peace and security build.

For the sake of our peoples and for the sake of the civilization made by man, we have to defend man everywhere against rule by the force of arms so that we may endow the rule of humanity with all the power of the values and principles that further the sublime position of mankind.

Allow me to address my call from this rostrum to the people of Israel. I pledge myself with true and sincere words to every man, woman and child in Israel. I tell them, from the Egyptian people who bless this sacred mission of peace, I convey to you the message of peace of the Egyptian people, who do not harbor fanaticism and whose sons, Moslems, Christians and Jews, live together in a state of cordiality, love and tolerance.

Entrusted with a sacred message

This is Egypt, whose people have entrusted me with their sacred message. A message of security, safety and peace to every man, woman and child in Israel, I say, encourage your leadership to struggle for peace. Let all endeavors be channeled towards building a huge stronghold for peace instead of building destructive rockets.

Introduce to the entire world the image of the new man in this area so that he might set an example to the man of our age, the man of peace everywhere. Ring the bells for your sons. Tell them that those wars were the last of wars and the end of sorrows. Tell them that we are entering upon a new beginning, a new life, a life of love, prosperity, freedom and peace.

You, sorrowing mother, you, widowed wife, you, the son who lost a brother or a father, all the victims of wars, fill the air and space with recitals of peace, fill bosoms and hearts with the aspirations of peace. Make a reality that blossoms and lives. Make hope a code of conduct and endeavor.

The will of peoples is part of the will of God. Ladies and gentlemen, before I came to this place, with every beat of my heart and with every sentiment, I prayed to God Almighty. While performing the prayers at the Al Aksa mosque and while visiting the Holy Sepulcher I asked the Almighty to give me strength and to confirm my belief that this visit may achieve the objective I look forward to for a happy present and a happier future.

I have chosen to set aside all precedents and traditions known by warring countries. In spite of the fact that occupation of Arab territories is still there, the declaration of my readiness to proceed to Israel came as a great surprise that stirred many feelings and confounded many minds. Some of them even doubted its intent.

Despite all that, the decision was inspired by all the clarity and purity of belief and with all the true passions of my people's will and intentions and I have chosen this road, considered by many to be the most difficult road.

I have chosen to come to you with an open heart and an open mind. I have chosen to give this great impetus to all international efforts exerted for peace. I have chosen to present to you, in your own home, the realities, devoid of any scheme or whim. Not to maneuver, or win a round, but for us to win together, the most dangerous of rounds embattled in modern history, the battle of permanent peace based on justice.

It is not my battle alone. Nor is it the battle of the leadership in Israel alone. It is the battle of all and every citizen in all our territories, whose right it is to live in peace. It is the commitment of conscience and responsibility in the hearts of millions.

When I put forward this initiative, many asked what is it that I conceived as possible to achieve during this visit and what my expectations were. And as I answer the questions, I announce before you that I have not thought of carrying out this initiative from the precepts of what could be achieved during this visit. And I have come here to deliver a message. I have delivered the message and may God be my witness.

I repeat with Zachariah: Love, right and justice. From the holy Koran I quote the following verses: "We believe in God and in what has been revealed to us and what was revealed to Abraham, Ishmael, Isaac, Jacob and the 13 Jewish tribes. And in the books given to Moses and Jesus and the prophets from their Lord, who made no distinction between them." So we agree, Salam Aleikum—peace be upon you.

Begin's Address

Mr. President of Egypt, ladies and gentlemen, members of the Knesset.

Our blessing is sent to the President and to all members of the Islamic faith, in our land and everywhere, on the occasion of this special Holiday of the Sacrifice.

This holiday reminds us of the sacrifice. This was the first test that the Lord, the Lord of the Lord, placed upon our father, our joint father, in his faith and Abraham passed this test.

From the point of view of the advancement of mankind, this was forbidden to sacrifice a human being. Our ancient tradition had taught this forbidden practice and to the nations around us, who were in the habit of sacrificing human beings to their gods, and so the nation of Israel and the nation of the Arabs contributed to the advancement of mankind and so do we continue to contribute to human culture until this day.

I bless the President of Egypt and his coming to our country and to his participation in this meeting of the Knesset.

The time of the flight between Cairo and Jerusalem is short. But the distance between them was, until yesterday, quite large.

President Sadat passed this great distance with courage, heartfelt courage. We, the Jews, know how to appreciate this courage of heart and know how to assess it with our guest. For with a courageous heart we were created and with a courageous heart we will live.

Mr. Chairman, this small nation, the remnants of the destruction of the Jewish nation that has returned to our historical homeland, always wanted peace.

And when we thought of our redemption, and independence arose, on the 15th of May, 1948, with the proclamation of independence and our state of independence, said Mr. Ben-Gurion:

"We stretch out a hand of peace to our neighbors and to all the nations that are our neighbors and to the English, and call upon them to cooperate in joint mutual cooperation with the independent Jewish nation in our land.

"A year before that, in the days of the underground, when we stood in the battle for the redemption of the country and of the nation, we showed our neighbors and made clear to them in this tone of language: In this land we shall live together and we shall progress together. For lives of freedom and wealth, our Arab neighbors, don't turn down this hand that is stretched to you in peace."

But it is my obligation, Mr. Chairman, not only my privilege, to decide today and to declare today, according to the truth, our hand that was stretched out for peace was not accepted.

And one day after the arrival of our independence, according to our right that cannot be denied or cannot be discussed, we were attacked on three fronts.

Understand, almost without reference, a few against the many, weak against the strong, that we stood in this test, one day after the proclamation of independence, to choke and destroy the birth and to call an end to the last hope of the Jewish nation in the century of destruction and of redemption.

No, we do not believe in might and we never based our relationship for the Arab nation on strength. The opposite, the strength worked against us.

In all the days of this generation we did not stop in order to stand against the strength that was stretched out to destroy us and destroy our independence in order to destroy our rights.

We defended ourselves—correct. We fought and protected our right, our honor, our women and children against a repeated test to bring against us the strength, not only on one front, but two.

With the help of the Lord, we succeeded in overcoming the attacking forces and we guaranteed the independence of our nation not only for this generation but also for coming generations.

We do not believe in might. We believe in right—only in right. And, therefore, our hope from the depths of our heart, from then and always, and to this very day, it is for peace.

Mr. President. Mr. President of Egypt, in this democratic house sit the commanders of all of the Jewish underground that fought, and they were required to fight against a worldwide power. And sit here, the electors of ours, despite the fact that forces were raised against them because they defended the
. . . .

They belong to various parties, they have different viewpoints. But I am sure, Mr. President, that I will express the viewpoint of all of them, without any exceptions, that we have one hope belonging in our heart, one will in our spirit—in our soul.

And all of us are united in this one hope and longing to have peace—peace for our nation that has not known peace even one day from the time we started to come back to Zion.

And peace for our neighbors, that we wish them all good and we believe that if we do make peace, a true peace, we shall be able to help one another in order to enrich life and to open a new epic period in the history of the Middle East. A period of growth, of development. Growth as it was in days of old.

Therefore permit me today to indicate what is the schedule for peace according to our understanding.

We seek peace, a full peace, true peace, with true reconciliation between the Jewish nation and the Arab nation.

Not to remember about the . . . what has happened in the past. There was much blood spilled. Many wonderful, young members of the generation fell on both sides. We, all our days, shall remember our heroes who sacrificed their lives in order that the day may arrive, and this day shall arrive. And we honor the courageousness, and we give honor to all members of the younger generation that they too fell.

Not to remember the past even if they are difficult but to be concerned with the future, to our children, to our joint future, because we shall live in this region all together for generations to come. The great Arab nation in its states and its lands and the Jewish nation in its land, Herod's Israel.

'Let us continue a dialogue'

Therefore one has to establish what is the schedule for peace. Let us continue a dialogue and negotiations, Mr. President, on a treaty of peace and with the help of God, so we believe with the true faith, the day will come and we shall achieve this with joint mutual respect. And then we shall know that instead of the wars we have stretched out a hand, one to another and we shall grasp the hand of one another. The future will be bright for all nations of this region.

The first wisdom in the schedule of peace is the ending of the state of war. I agree, Mr. President, that you didn't come and we didn't invite you in order, as it was accepted in the past few days, in order to establish a treaty with the nations of the Arabs.

Israel does not wish to rule and does not want to disturb or divide. We are looking for peace with all our neighbors, with Egypt, with Jordan, with Syria, with Lebanon.

We wish to have negotiations for a peace treaty.

And there is no reason to distinguish between a treaty of peace and end of belligerency. We do not suggest this. On the contrary, the first paragraph in a peace treaty is the cessation of hostilities.

We wish to establish normal relations between us, as they exist between all the nations, even after many wars.

We learned from the history, Mr. President, that war can be prevented. Peace does not have to be prevented. Many nations have had wars between them, and even on occasion have used terms such as eternal enemies. There are no such things as eternal enemies. After every war comes the peace.

And therefore we seek to establish in a treaty of peace diplomatic relations between the nations. Today, two flags are flying in Jerusalem—the Egyptian flag and the Israeli flag—and we saw together, Mr. President, our small children who were carrying both flags.

Let us sign a treaty of peace and establish such a situation forever also in Jerusalem and also in Cairo. And I hope and pray that the day will come when the Egyptian children will also be waving the Israeli and Egyptian flags as the children of Israel were waving in Jerusalem these two flags today.

And you, Mr. President, will have an ambassador in our capital and we will have an ambassador in Cairo. And we will even have differences between us. We will discuss them like cultured nations through our accredited representatives.

Joint economic cooperation

We propose joint economic cooperation to develop our countries. In the Middle East there are many wonderful countries. The Lord so created them. There are oases and deserts, and it is possible to change the deserts. Let us cooperate together in this area. Let us develop our countries. Let us abolish poverty. Let us raise our nations to the high level of a developed country and let the world not call us developing countries.

And with all respect I am prepared to endorse the words of His Excellency, the King of Morocco, who said publicly that when the peace will come to the Middle East, the cooperation of the Arab genius and the Jewish genius together will change this region into a Garden of Eden.

Let us open our countries to free passage. Come you to us and we shall visit with you. I am prepared to announce, Mr. Chairman, today that our country is open for all citizens of Egypt. And I do not have this depend on any condition. I think it is only right that there should be a joint announcement in this case. That just as there are Egyptian flags in our area, and today an honored delegation in our capital and in our country, may the visitors be many. Our borders will be open in front of them. And all other borders, we wish, in the north and in the south and in the east.

Invitation to Syrian president

And, therefore, I renew my invitation to the President of Syria to follow in your footsteps, Mr. President, to come to us in order to open negotiations for purposes of peace between Israel and Syria and the signing of a peace agreement between them.

I'm sorry to say there is no justification for the poison that comes from our northern border. Let us change and have such visits and such ties. And visits and events such as that can take place, there can be days of happiness, days of raising the spirit for all nations.

I invite King Hussein to visit us and to discuss with us on all the problems that require discussions between him and us.

And also the legitimate spokesmen of the Arabs of Israel, I invite them to come and meet with us for discussions on our joint policies, on justice, on social justice, on peace, on joint mutual respect.

And if they invite us to come to their capitals, we shall answer their invitations. And if they invite us to open negotiations in Damascus and in Amman and in Beirut, in any one of these capitals, we shall go to any of these capitals in order to discuss with them.

We do not want to separate or divide. We want a true peace with all of our neighbors, to be expressed in treaties of peace, on all of the points that I just mentioned.

Mr. Chairman, it is my obligation today to tell our guest, and the ears of all those nations who are watching and listening to us today, of our ties between our Jewish nation and this land. The President referred to the Balfour Declaration. No, my Mr. President, we did not take strange land, we returned to our homeland. The tie between our nation and this land is eternal.

It began in the dim days of ancient history. It has never been cut. In this land we created our culture, here our prophets prophesied, as you briefly heard.

Here the kings of Judah and Israel ruled. Here we became a nation. Here we established our kingdoms. And when we were exiled from our land because of the force that was applied against us, and when we were thrust far from our land we never forgot this land, even for one day. We prayed for her. We longed for her.

We believe in our return from the day on which the words were said, in the words of the Psalmist: When the Lord returned the captivity of Zion, we were as dreamers. Then will our lips be filled with song. And that song applied to all of our exiles and of all of our travels— the consolation of returning to Zion that would come.

This right was recognized in the Balfour Declaration and was embodied in the League of Nations mandate. And the introduction to that international document read:

"Whereas recognition has thereby been given to the historical connection of the Jewish people with Palestine, and to the grounds for reconstituting their national home in that country."

The historical connection between the Jewish nation and Palestine known in Hebrew as "Eretz Israel" has been renewed again.

In 1912, 1919, we also received the recognition of the spokesman of the Arab nation. And in an agreement in January 1919, that was signed by Emir Faisal and Dr. Chaim Weizmann, it was said:

"Mindful of the racial kinship and ancient bonds existing between the Arabs and the Jewish people, and realizing that the surest means of working out the consummation of their national aspirations is the closest possible collaboration in the development of the Arab state and of Palestine."

And afterward come all of the paragraphs relating to cooperation between the Jewish nation . . . between the Arab nation and Eretz Israel, this is our right.

What happened to us when our homeland was taken from us?

We went this morning, Mr. President, to Yad Vashem. With your own eyes you saw what has happened to our nation when this, its homeland, had been taken from it.

We have both agreed, Mr. President, that he who has not seen with his own eyes all that exists in Yad Vashem cannot understand what has happened to this nation when it was detached from its homeland. And the two of us read a document of Jan. 30, 1939, with the word of destruction: If war will break out, the Jewish race in Europe will be destroyed.

Then it was also said: Don't pay attention. The entire world heard. No one came to ours . . . to save us.

The many months since the time of that declaration that had never been heard before, since the time that the Lord created man and man created the devil, and in those six years when millions of our people including one and a half million small Jewish children were destroyed, no one came to their saving—not from the East and not from the West.

And, therefore, we have sworn an eternal vow, this entire generation—the generation of destruction and rebirths: We shall never again place our nation in such a danger.

We shall never expose our women and children—our responsibility is to defend them, even if necessary at the cost of our lives—we shall never permit them to be in a destruction.

Since then our responsibility for generations is to remember the specific things said against our nation. We shall take them in the full seriousness. And it is forbidden for us, for the future of our nation, to take any advice that it is not necessary to take such words seriously.

President Sadat knows, and knew from us before he came to Jerusalem, that we have a different position than his with regard to borders between us and our neighbors.

However, I call to the President of Egypt, and to all of our neighbors, do not say that we will not have discussions on anything.

I propose, according to the accepted majority of this Parliament, that everything is open to negotiation.

A serious responsibility is taken by anyone who says that in negotiations between the Arab nation and the Jewish nation there are things that must be taken out of the negotiations. Everything is given to negotiation. No side can say the reverse. No side can offer conditions. It is a pleasure, an honor, to have negotiations if there are differences between us. There is nothing that can be excluded.

He who has learned the history of wars and the history of making peace knows that all negotiations on a peace treaty began with differences between the nations. And through the negotiations they arrived at an agreement that made it possible to sign treaties of peace. And this is the way we propose to go.

And let us conduct the negotiations as equals. There are no victors, there are no losers.

All nations of the region are equal. And each one will have to relate to one another with honor and in the spirit of openness, of readiness to listen one to another to the facts and to the points and to the explanations.

With all of the accepted ability to convince one another, let us conduct the negotiations, as I ask and propose, to continue until we arrive at the hour of signing a treaty of peace between us.

We are not only prepared to sit with the representatives of Egypt but with the representatives of Jordan and Syria and Lebanon in a peace conference in Geneva. We have suggested to reconstitute the Geneva conference on the basis of the two decisions of the Security Council—242 and 338.

If there are differences between us relating to the organization of the Geneva conference, let us discuss and negotiate them today and tomorrow.

And if the President of Egypt wishes to receive us in Cairo, or in a neutral place, there is no objection. In every place, let us together clarify, even before the reconvening of the Geneva conference, the problems that may be related to the reconvening of this conference.

Our eyes shall be open, our ears shall be open to listen to every proposal—to every proposal.

Permit me to say a word about Jerusalem. Mr. President, you prayed this morning at the newly reconstituted mosque and then you went to the Church of the Holy Sepulcher. You realized that from time immemorial this is the city that has been joined together. There is a full freedom—

[Momentary loss of audio from Jerusalem. Mr. Begin was saying there is freedom of movement to and from Jerusalem.]

. . . Moslem world and for the Christian world and all nations, that forever there shall be free access and travel to holy places.

We shall defend the right of free entry. For in this we believe: equal rights of all citizens and with honor and with full face—with full face.

Mr. Chairman, this a very special day to our Parliament. And undoubtedly for many years this day will be long remembered in the history of our nation and in the history of the Egyptian nation and perhaps in the history of the various nations of the world.

And this day, with your permission ladies and gentlemen, members of the Knesset, we shall raise a prayer that the God of our fathers, our joint fathers, will give us the wisdom of the heart that is necessary in order to overcome difficulties and pitfalls, to overcome the words of Satan, and the words of evil. And with the help of the Lord we shall achieve, we shall reach that day for which our entire nation is praying—a day of peace. For verily that day—the sweet singer of Israel, King David, wrote about the day—when justice and peace embraced. And in the words of the prophet Zachariah, peace and justice embraced.

Peace Efforts Continue as Opposition Mounts

Sadat seeks pre-Geneva talks. Egyptian President Anwar Sadat Nov. 26, 1977 invited all parties in the Middle East conflict to attend a preparatory meeting in Cairo to arrange a Geneva conference on a Middle East peace settlement. In a speech to the Egyptian parliament, Sadat indicated determination to press ahead with the peace campaign he had begun by going to Israel.

Sadat said the Cairo meeting would seek to resolve the procedural difficulties connected with a Geneva conference "so that we do not go to the Geneva conference and discuss matters for years." He extended the invitation to all Middle Eastern countries including Israel, to the U.S. and the U.S.S.R., as co-chairmen of the Geneva conference, and to the United Nations.

In his speech, Sadat assured the Egyptian public that he had not yielded on the basic Arab demands for a peace settlement with Israel—the withdrawal from lands occupied by Israel since 1967 and the establishment of a Palestinian homeland. He said the Arab nations that had denounced his trip were "ungrateful" considering the sacrifices Egypt had made during the history of Arab-Israeli hostilities.

Sadat revealed to the parliament that a potential Egyptian-Israeli military clash had been headed off two weeks before his visit to Jerusalem. He explained that an Egyptian military buildup in the Sinai had been ordered in response to Israeli maneuvers in the area. He said he discussed the incident with Israeli Defense Minister Ezer Weizman during his visit.

Sadat also revealed that there had been three secret agreements with the U.S. in connection with the 1975 disengagement agreement with Israel: a U.S. commitment that Israel would not attack Egypt, the promise of an Israeli-Syrian disengagement on the Golan Heights and a U.S. pledge not to work out an overall peace settlement without taking into account the Palestinian demand for a homeland.

Formal Egyptian invitations to the Cairo conference were issued Nov. 27 to all parties but the PLO. The Syrian government immediately rejected the invitation and announced instead plans to convene a meeting in Tripoli, Libya of Arab leaders who rejected Sadat's overtures to Israel.

Sadat appeared unconcerned over the Syrian rejection and the possibility that other Arab nations would follow Syria's lead. "If no one is coming, okay, I shall deal with whoever comes," Sadat told a CBS-TV interviewer. He added that his position would be the same toward a Geneva conference. If Egypt were the only Arab nation to attend a Geneva parley, he said, he would negotiate a comprehensive Middle East agreement and submit it for Arab approval afterwards. He ruled out a separate Egyptian settlement with Israel under any circumstances.

Syrian President Hafez al-Assad Nov. 28 repeated Syria's rejection of Sadat's course of action, but he adopted a less virulent tone against the Egyptian president than previously. While ruling out cooperation with Sadat, Assad said Syria did not seek to isolate him. "There are divergences over the methods of working for peace, over procedures," he said. He added that Sadat had "created a new obstacle to peace and lessened the prospects of a Geneva conference" by his actions.

Syrian Information Minister Ahmed Iskandar had said Nov. 25 that Sadat had ruined chances for a Geneva conference, but he added that Syria was not entirely on the side of the rejectionists who had abandoned a negotiated Middle East settlement. He explained that Sadat's visit had divided the Arab world and therefore Arab participation at Geneva was not possible.

The PLO Nov. 27 said it would participate in the rejectionist meeting in Tripoli and would shun the Cairo meeting. (Egypt Nov. 23 had expelled three PLO officials from Cairo, apparently because of Palestinian criticism of Sadat's trip.)

Jordan, without committing itself officially to the rejectionists or to Sadat, Nov. 28 effectively barred participation in either conference. A government statement said Jordan would attend the conferences only if each was attended by all the Arab parties to the Middle East conflict. King Hussein that day declared that while Sadat's trip was "courageous," it had split the Arab would and therefore was dangerous.

Israel accepts Sadat invitation—Immediately following Sadat's speech to the Egyptian parliament, Israel Nov. 26 announced that it would accept a formal invitation to attend the Cairo conference. The invitation was presented the next day to the Israeli ambassador to the United Nations by Egypt's U.N. ambassador, in the first Egyptian-Israeli face-to-face meeting at the world body.

(The meeting took place "at the home of a mutual friend," according to Israeli Ambassador Chaim Herzog and Egyptian Ambassador Ahmed Esmat Abdel Meguid.)

Israeli Premier Menahem Begin Nov. 28 designated Eliahu Ben-Elissar and Meir Rosenne as Israel's envoys to the Cairo conference. Ben-Elissar was director general of the premier's office, and Rosenne was a legal adviser at the Foreign Ministry.

Begin announced the appointments at the start of a parliamentary debate on Sadat's trip to Israel. He called the Cairo conference "negotiations we have always wanted, face to face, between ourselves and our neighbors," and he denied that Israel intended to sign a separate peace treaty with Egypt. Contrary to expectations, Begin's speech did not contain any changes in Israeli policy toward a Middle East settlement.

In the aftermath of Sadat's visit, a number of prominent Israelis had urged the government to rethink its policy on a peace settlement. Foreign Minister Moshe Dayan Nov. 23 said it was imperative that Israel "make decisions on how far we are ready to go" in meeting Arab demands for a return of the lands seized after the 1967 war.

In a televised interview, Dayan said Egypt had shown "readiness ... to make peace on terms which may be unacceptable to us, but which should bring us nevertheless to the crucial stage of making decisions on the price we are willing to pay in return

for peace." He added that immediate Israeli concessions on territory as a goodwill gesture to Sadat would hurt Sadat's standing and further divide the Arab world by reinforcing suspicions that the Egyptian president was considering a separate peace.

U.S. hesitates, then accepts—After three days of indecision, the U.S. Nov. 29 formally accepted Sadat's invitation to participate in the Cairo conference. The U.S. announcement called the conference "an invitation we believe we should support,..."

The appointment of a U.S. representative was announced Nov. 30. In a televised news conference, President Carter said Alfred L. Atherton Jr., assistant secretary of state for Near Eastern and South Asian affairs, would represent the U.S.

U.S.S.R. rejects Cairo conference—The Soviet Union Nov. 29 announced that it would not participate in the Cairo talks on arranging a Geneva conference. In Moscow's first official statement on Sadat's invitation, Foreign Minister Andrei Gromyko called the Egyptian initiative an attempt at "exploding" the Geneva conference "possibly even before it is convened." Gromyko made his remarks at a luncheon in honor of visiting Syrian Foreign Minister Abdel Halim Khaddam.

Moscow issued another statement Nov. 30 saying the Cairo meeting was "a cover for a separate deal between Egypt and Israel."

U.N. suggests second conference—U.N. Secretary General Kurt Waldheim Nov. 29 proposed that another Geneva preparatory conference be held under U.N. auspices after the Cairo meeting. Although Waldheim accepted Sadat's invitation to Cairo, he said the meeting would have "only limited participation" and therefore a U.N.-sponsored meeting, which would bring all the parties together, was important "if we want a Geneva conference...."

Israel Nov. 30 rejected Waldheim's proposal, saying "no purpose will be served by an additional preparatory conference." (According to reports, Israel opposed U.N. sponsorship of a Middle East conference because such a conference would include the PLO, which the U.N. recognized as the official spokesman of the Palestinians. Israel also opposed a central U.N. role because it feared this would increase Soviet influence in a Middle East settlement.)

Lebanon rejects Cairo invitation—Lebanon Dec. 1 formally rejected President Sadat's invitation to attend the Cairo conference to prepare for the Geneva talks.

Foreign Minister Fuad Butros said his government's refusal was based on its long-standing policy that it would participate at Geneva only in the final phase, when Israel and the other Arab states were prepared to conclude a final peace pact.

Lebanese Christian and ·Moslem leaders had been urging Lebanese "impartiality" in the latest intra-Arab dispute. Nevertheless, Lebanese Christians and Shiite Moslems in southern Lebanon had given their support to Sadat's initiatives.

West Bank mayors refuse Geneva role— A group of mayors in the West Bank criticized President Sadat's visit to Jerusalem and said they would refuse to attend the Geneva conference because they supported the PLO, it was disclosed Dec. 5.

The statement was contained in a memorandum signed by 18 mayors and two deputy mayors and dozens of "notables" and associations in the Israeli-occupied territory. It had been distributed to all foreign consulates in Jerusalem.

The mayors frequently had been mentioned as possible standins for the PLO, whose presence at the Geneva talks was opposed by Israel. Their memorandum insisted that they would not serve as substitutes for the PLO, and it opposed "any voice or anybody who is planning to find leadership to replace the PLO."

One of the signatories, Mayor Karim Khalaf of Ramallah, said he would not go to Geneva even if requested by the PLO. "I am not the representative of the PLO. The PLO is our representative."

Anti-Sadat meeting provokes Egyptian break with Arab & Communist nations. Following a meeting in Tripoli, Libya Dec. 2–5, 1977 of Egyptian President Sadat's Arab critics, Egypt Dec. 5 severed diplomatic relations with Syria, Iraq, Algeria and South Yemen.

At the Arab summit meeting in·Tripoli, Sadat's critics had sought to·forge a new front opposed to the Egyptian leader's dialogue with Israel and to impede any separate Egyptian-Israeli meeting that might emerge from a conference of the two states, the U.S. and the U.N. that was scheduled to start in Cairo Dec. 14.

The hard-liners' parley, which was also attended by the Palestine Liberation Organization, issued a Tripoli Declaration setting up a new Arab "front for resistance and confrontation" to oppose what it called the "high treason" of Egypt's peace initiatives. Although the final communique strongly condemned Sadat, it avoided mention of outright rejection of a negotiated peace settlement in the Middle East and left the door open for eventual reconciliation with Egypt. This relatively mild stand was apparently influenced by Syrian President Hafez al-Assad. who favored a cautious approach.

Iraq, which advocated a stronger stand, walked out of the meeting in protest hours before it formally closed. Baghdad's chief delegate, Taha Yassin Jezrawi, a member of Iraq's ruling Revolutionary Council, explained that his country had insisted on sterner measures.

The Soviet Union's support of the five Arab hard-line states prompted Cairo Dec. 7 to order the closing in Egypt of the cultural centers and some consulates of the U.S.S.R. and four of its European Communist allies—Czechoslovakia, Hungary, East Germany and Poland.

Jezrawi charged later at a news conference that Syrian President Assad "showed he still believes in a policy of peaceful surrender and negotiations." It was apparent that the conference "was going to be transformed into an umbrella for those who seek capitulationist settlements, and so we pulled out," Jezrawi added.

Among the other points of the Tripoli Declaration:

■ The four Arab states and the PLO would "freeze" diplomatic relations with Egypt but would not completely break ties with Cairo, as demanded by Libya.

■ Aggression against any member of the new front would be considered aggression against all members. (No specific commitments were made public.)

The other representatives at the Tripoli conference were Presidents Houari Boumedienne of Algeria and Salem Rubayi Ali of South Yemen, Libyan leader Col. Muammer el-Qaddafi and PLO chairman

Yasir Arafat. Also attending was Arafat's rival, George Habash, head of the radical Popular Front for the Liberation of Palestine.

Egypt's break with Syria, Algeria, Iraq, Libya and South Yemen had been preceded by Cairo's recall of its ambassadors from those countries, as well as from the Soviet Union, it was disclosed Dec. 4.

Sadat scores Soviet, Arab critics— Egypt's moves against the Soviet Union and its allies had been foreshadowed in remarks by President Sadat Dec. 6. He accused Moscow of using the Palestinians and the Syrians as "agents" to undermine his peace efforts. In an interview with the New York Times, Sadat hinted at the retaliatory measures by saying he had another "surprise" to be announced the following day that would "teach the Soviets a lesson."

Sadat assailed the Soviet Union for its opposition to his peace overtures to Israel. The Soviets "never played a constructive role" in the Middle East, Sadat complained. "They didn't want us to make any settlement in this part of the world and they don't want this problem to be settled now." Citing an example of what he called Soviet "hypocrisy," Sadat disclosed that the Soviet ambassador to Lebanon had given PLO leader Yasir Arafat a false document on Egypt's secret agreement involving the 1975 Egyptian-Israeli disengagement in the Sinai in an attempt to prevent his signing the accords the following day. But Sadat signed.

Sadat also revealed that during his visit to Moscow in March 1971, Premier Aleksei N. Kosygin had proposed that Sadat meet with Golda Meir, then Israel's premier, in the Soviet Asian city of Tashkent. "Now they condemn my visit when the whole world reacted to it as a genuine move for peace," Sadat said.

Turning to the Arabs, the Egyptian president said he would conduct negotiations "through to the end" with Israel alone even if the other Arab states refused to participate either at the Cairo conference or at Geneva. He called the break in diplomatic relations with the five Arab states "provisional" and said he was prepared to restore ties "whenever they are polite."

Sadat praised U.S. President Carter's peace initiatives, although he had not informed Carter beforehand of his intention

to go to Jerusalem. Sadat disclosed, however, that he had been in "very close contact" with Carter before and after his meetings with Israeli officials in Jerusalem.

Sadat scored the Tripoli meeting threat to impose sanctions on Egypt, calling it "black propaganda to deceive the Arab people."

At an organized mass rally in Cairo supporting his peace drive, President Sadat Dec. 8 assailed his Arab critics who charged that he had sold out to Israel by visiting Jerusalem in November. "We are not asking for peace at any price, and those [Arab] dwarfs and ignoramuses who are casting doubt on what is happening, I wish they had listened to what I said to the Israelis in their very homes," Sadat said.

The Egyptian leader repeated his conditions for a "just peace": Israeli withdrawal from occupied Arab lands and restoration of "Palestinian rights."

Sadat later went from the rally to the airport to greet Jordanian King Hussein, who was on a mediation mission aimed at healing the Arab rift caused by Sadat's personal contacts with the Israelis. After more than two hours of talks, Hussein praised Sadat's actions.

On the first leg of his tour, the monarch had conferred in Damascus Dec. 7 with Syrian President Hafez al-Assad. Results of those discussions were not disclosed. In Damascus, Hussein criticized Sadat for not consulting other Arabs, thus "setting us all back."

Soviet-bloc centers shut—The action taken against the Soviet-bloc facilities in Egypt was announced Dec. 7 to the Egyptian parliament by Premier Mamdouh Salem. He claimed that the cultural centers operated in Cairo by the Soviet Union, East Germany, Hungary and Czechoslovakia were closed because they had disseminated Marxist propaganda in violation of their pledge not to interfere in Egypt's internal affairs. The government also was closing the Soviet, Czechoslovak, East German and Polish consulates in Alexandria, the Soviet and Polish consulates in Port Said and the Soviet consulate in Aswan. The Soviet-bloc consulates in Cairo would be allowed to remain open because Egypt maintained its consulates in their capitals, Salem explained.

The five Arab states with whom Egypt had severed ties, Salem said, were "loyal to the Soviet Union," which he accused of obstructing peace.

U.S. criticizes Soviet stand—The Soviet Union's continued attacks on President Sadat's peace initiatives brought a sharp rebuke Dec. 6 from U.S. Secretary of State Cyrus R. Vance.

The Soviet statements, Vance said, "have not been helpful" to the cause of peace and "raised questions about what their ultimate objectives are" in the Middle East. As co-chairman with the U.S.S.R. of the Geneva peace conference, the U.S. "still believed that their [the Soviets] ultimate objective is to see a comprehensive settlement," Vance said.

A Tass news agency statement Dec. 5 accused Sadat of selling out the PLO in collusion with the U.S. and Israel. The Egyptian leader's contention that he was seeking a comprehensive settlement was "a deliberate lie, dictated by a desire to whitewash his separate deal with the aggressors," Tass said.

Israeli premier visits London. Israeli Premier Menahem Begin visited London Dec. 2–7 to seek a more even-handed British approach to the problems of an Israeli-Arab peace settlement.

Before departing from London Dec. 7, Begin indicated at a news conference that Israel was prepared to sign a separate peace treaty with Egypt, but he observed that such an accord should be regarded only as the initial step toward a comprehensive Middle East settlement with other Arab states.

While assailing the Soviet Union for its "destructive role" in the Middle East, Begin urged Moscow, as co-chairman of the Geneva conference, to adopt a more positive stance in peace efforts.

Israel also was prepared to offer concessions to Jordan on the question of the Israeli-occupied West Bank, Begin hinted. "When we talk to King Hussein we shall have many offers to make," he said.

Begin had reiterated his opposition to the establishment of a separate Palestinian state in the West Bank during discussions Dec. 4 with Prime Minister James Callaghan.

Syria seeks Arab aid against Egypt. Syrian President Hafez al-Assad Dec. 8–11 met with officials of Saudi Arabia, Kuwait, Bahrain, Qatar and the United Arab Emirates to seek their support against Egyptian President Anwar Sadat's peace moves.

Saudi officials said that during Assad's talks in Riyadh Dec. 8–9 he had been urged by his hosts to moderate his views toward Sadat. A Saudi Information Ministry statement issued after Assad ended his visit affirmed the need for Arab unity and merely reported that Assad and King Khalid and other Saudi officials had "discussed Arab issues, especially recent developments" in the Arab world.

(Saudi Crown Prince Fahd was quoted in the Saudi press Dec. 10 as saying that even if Sadat achieved a Middle East peace settlement, Saudi Arabia would still not recognize Israel.)

Assad flew to Kuwait Dec. 9 and conferred with the country's ruler, Sheik Sabah al-Salem al-Sabah. Sabah was said to have expressed sorrow for the rift in Arab unity that resulted from Sadat's contacts with the Israelis. Sabah, however, reportedly wanted to maintain a "balanced position" and would not publicly criticize Sadat or exert economic pressure against Cairo.

Kuwait offered to mediate the Syrian-Egyptian feud, but Assad Dec. 10 told the ruler of Bahrain, Sheik Isa bin Sulman al-Khalifa, that he had rejected the bid.

Assad concluded his diplomatic mission with visits Dec. 11 to Qatar and the United Arab Emirates.

U.S. seeks Arab support for peace moves. U.S. Secretary of State Cyrus R. Vance visited six Mideastern nations Dec. 9–14, 1977 to display American support for the Cairo conference and to persuade Syria, Jordan and Lebanon to join the direct Egyptian-Israeli negotiations. He traveled to Egypt, Israel, Jordan, Lebanon, Syria and Saudi Arabia.

Vance arrived Dec. 9 in the Egyptian capital, where he received a pledge the following day from President Anwar Sadat that the Cairo talks would serve as the opening phase of an overall settlement and not as a forum for reaching a separate Egyptian-Israeli pact. Vance agreed at a news conference that a reconvened Geneva conference "would be the ultimate meeting" at which to achieve a settlement, with the Cairo talks being "a step in the way."

Sadat was ambiguous when questioned about his views on the possible role of the

Palestinians in a settlement. He disclosed that in his talks with visiting Jordanian King Hussein Dec. 8–9, both had agreed with the 1974 Arab summit decision taken at Rabat, Morocco designating the PLO as the sole legitimate representative of the Palestinian people. But this decision was negated by the Dec. 2–7 meeting in Tripoli of the Arab hard-liners, who opposed Sadat's current peace initiatives, he added. Nevertheless, Sadat insisted that despite the Tripoli conference, "we are sticking to the Rabat decisions."

Vance and Israeli Premier Menahem Begin expressed optimism about prospects for peace at a joint news conference Dec. 11 in Jerusalem, at the conclusion of two days of talks.

(President Carter Dec. 9 had urged Israel to display "courage" in response to President Sadat's peace initiatives. Speaking to a group of editors, the President said that Sadat's visit to Jerusalem Nov. 19 "has broken through what seemed to be insurmountable obstacles . . . I believe Sadat showed a great deal of courage, my hope and expectation is that the Israelis will respond accordingly.")

Vance conferred with King Hussein in Amman Dec. 12 and received the monarch's assurance that he supported Sadat's approach to Israel as "a final gesture made with sincerity and the greatest proof that we could offer the world of our good will."

Vance conferred Dec. 13 in Damascus with Syrian President Hafez al-Assad, who expressed continued objection to the Cairo conference and even voiced reservations about attending a follow-up Geneva meeting. His indignation at Sadat was reflected in an official statement issued after his talks with Vance. Assad had told the secretary that Sadat's visit to Israel had "created a new situation in the Middle East, . . . that has brought a chronic disease. . . . Syria cannot depart in its policies on the basis of Sadat's visit to Israel and the results of this trip," the document said. The Syrian leader was further quoted as saying that Sadat's peace moves "have torpedoed all chances of making peace because what he is doing is to surrender and not to make peace."

Vance had met with Lebanese officials in Beirut earlier Dec. 13. Lebanese officials were said to fear that a separate Egyptian-Israeli pact would not resolve the problem of the 400,000 Palestinians in Lebanon.

(Vance's visit to Beirut was believed to have sparked a general strike in the city Dec. 12 by Lebanon's main Christian political organizations. The protest, shutting down businesses in the Christian sector of the city, was aimed at calling to Vance's attention Christian concern with the continued presence of the Palestinians in Lebanon. It also was meant to serve notice on Lebanese and Syrian authorities that the Christians would not tolerate the revival of the PLO's influence that had existed in Lebanon before the civil war. Syria's alliance with the PLO against President Sadat's peace dialogue could mean that "the Syrians will give the green light to the Palestinians" to resume their conflict with the Christians in southern Lebanon, a Christian spokesman said.)

Vance met with Saudi officials in Riyadh Dec. 14 on the last leg of his mission. The secretary was said to have received assurances from King Khalid, Crown Prince Fahd and Prince Saud al-Faisal, foreign minister, of their country's willingness to "pursue the peace process now" through the Cairo conference and to work toward an overall settlement at some unspecified time in the future.

Vance reports to Carter—Secretary Vance gave President Carter an optimistic report on his mission on returning to Washington Dec. 15.

Vance told the President that Israel was "rethinking" its strongly held position on retaining complete control of the West Bank. Saudi Arabia and Jordan indicated that privately they would support President Sadat's peace initiatives, although they would continue to retain a neutral stance in public, Vance said.

Vance told Carter that "there is real momentum in the Middle East" peace process and that the U.S. "must do everything we can to keep the momentum going forward."

Cairo conference. A meeting opened in Cairo Dec. 14, 1977 on procedures for the projected reconvening of the Geneva conference on Middle East peace. Participants were Egypt, Israel, the U.S. and the United Nations, which attended as an observer. After the ceremonial opening session, the negotiators met behind closed doors Dec. 15.

The five other parties invited to attend—Syria, Lebanon, Jordan, the Soviet Union and the Palestine Liberation Organization—stayed away.

The head of the Egyptian delegation, Ahmed Esmat Abdel Meguid, said in his address that the world "hopes that Egypt's genuine desire to establish a just and lasting peace be reciprocated" by Israel. "Tangible and concrete results are expected and should be forthcoming without delay" as a result of the current negotiations, Meguid said.

Israel's chief representative, Eliahu Ben-Elissar, said in return that his government regretted the absence of the other invited Arab parties. "I declare this because the goal of Israel is a comprehensive agreement and not a separate agreement," Ben-Elissar said. "Let us resolve," he declared, that the absence of Syria, Lebanon and Jordan "from these talks will not be permitted to frustrate our sacred common efforts for peace."

Stressing the fact of Israel's existence, Ben-Elissar said that "no future war can possibly change the permanent sovereign reality of our existence."

The conference's Dec. 15 secret session was reported by Israeli, Egyptian and U.N. spokesmen to have made encouraging progress. An Egyptian-Israeli subcommittee of legal advisers had started work on what was described officially as "procedures and the basis for discussions of the Cairo conference."

Other official delegates at the conference were Meir Rosenne and Maj. Gen. Avraham Tamir of Israel; Osama el-Baz and Maj. Gen. Taha el-Magdoub of Egypt, and Michael Sterner and George Sherman of the U.S.

Carter vs. PLO stand. President Carter said Dec. 15, 1977 that the PLO had removed itself from "serious consideration" for a role in Middle East peace talks by its adamant refusal to accept the existence of Israel. The President, however, held that resolution of the Palestinian problem remained vital to achieve an overall settlement.

Speaking at a news conference, the President complained that the PLO had been "completely negative" and uncooperative "in spite of my own direct invitations to them and the direct invita-

tions" by President Anwar Sadat of Egypt, President Hafez al-Assad of Syria, King Hussein of Jordan and Kind Khalid of Saudi Arabia.

Carter expressed hope that Jordan, Syria, Lebanon and Saudi Arabia would accept "any peace move made by Egypt and Israel" at their conference in Cairo. As a result of his meetings with Assad in Washington in May, Carter said there were "good indications" that the Syrian leader "wants to resolve the differences" in the Arab-Israeli dispute.

The President discussed the arrival in the U.S. Dec. 14 of Israeli Premier Menachem Begin. He said that if Begin's ideas seemed to lead "in the right direction and would be acceptable to President Sadat, then I would certainly" tell Begin this. However, should Begin's formula fall far short of what Sadat could accept "without very serious political consequences . . . , I would have no reticence about telling Begin privately I just don't think this goes far enough," Carter said.

As for the U.S.S.R.'s role in the Middle East, Carter said it could "have been much more constructive." He cited as an example Moscow's refusal to attend the Cairo conference. On the other hand, the Soviet Union had "not been nearly as much an obstacle as they apparently were in the past," Carter added.

Begin, Sadat at impasse. Israeli Premier Menahem Begin and Egyptian President Anwar Sadat held a meeting in Ismailia in Egypt Dec. 25–26, 1977 to draft guidelines for establishing peace in the Middle East. The two leaders concluded their talks without reaching agreement on the basic issues discussed—terms for Israeli withdrawal from the Sinai, the West Bank, the Gaza Strip and East Jerusalem.

An Israeli peace plan submitted to Sadat was made public by Begin to the Israeli Knesset (parliament) Dec. 28. It barred the establishment of a Palestinian state in the West Bank and Gaza Strip, reaffirmed Israel's claim to the sovereignty over the two territories and provided for greater autonomy for the Arab residents of the area. Sadat rejected the plan.

On conclusion of their talks Dec. 26, Begin and Sadat did not issue a joint declaration of principles for a Middle East settlement, underscoring their basic differences. Instead they issued separate statements and then spoke at a joint news conference.

In his statement, Sadat disclosed that he and Begin had agreed to upgrade the current Cairo conference (whose purpose was to prepare procedures for a future international parley) to the level of foreign ministers. Two standing Egyptian-Israeli committees would be created—a military committee to be headed by Defense Minister Ezer Weizman of Israel and War Minister Mohammed Abdel Ghany el-Gamasy of Egypt, and a political committee headed by Foreign Ministers Moshe Dayan of Israel and Mohammed Ibrahim Kamel of Egypt.

Starting work in January 1978, the military committee would meet in Cairo and the political committee would convene in Jerusalem.

Sadat conceded that he and Begin had made some progress on the question of Israeli troop withdrawal, but not on the matter of Egypt's demands for the establishment of a Palestinian state. At the joint news conference, Sadat said "the Palestinian question is the crux of the whole problem." He also said that Israel must relinquish East Jerusalem, which Israel occupied after the 1967 war.

In his statement, Begin sounded a more optimistic note, saying that his talks with Sadat had been "successful." He pledged to "continue with the momentum of the peace-making process."

Groundwork for the Ismailia summit had been prepared in talks Defense Minister Weizman held in Egypt Dec. 20-21 with Sadat and Gamasy.

Before meeting with Weizman Dec. 21 for the second time, Sadat reiterated his objection to the continued presence of Israeli troops on the West Bank as part of an overall settlement. Prior to his departure to Israel, Weizman flew to Cairo, where he briefed the Israeli delegation to the Cairo conference (recessed Dec. 22) on his talks with Sadat and Gamasy. After returning to Israel, Weizman said the road to peace was "not going to be a smooth ride."

Begin wins Knesset approval of peace plan—Begin Dec. 28 presented to the Israeli Knesset the 26-point peace plan for the West Bank and Gaza Strip that he had submitted to President Sadat at their Ismailia summit. After 11 hours of debate,

the Knesset approved the proposal by a vote of 64 to eight. There were 40 abstentions, mostly from the opposition Labor Party members, who said they would not vote against the formula but preferred to submit one of their own.

Among the major points of the proposal: Israel would abolish its military administrations in the territories and Arab administrative units would take their place to govern internal affairs; Arab residents would elect an 11-member administrative council that would serve a four-year term and oversee the needs of the Arab inhabitants; Israeli forces would remain in the West Bank and Gaza Strip to maintain security and public order; Arabs in both territories would have a choice of Israeli or Jordanian citizenship; Israelis would be permitted to purchase land and settle in the Arab territories, while the Arabs who chose Israeli citizenship would be allowed to buy land in Israel and settle there, and arrangements would be made for Palestinian immigration to the West Bank and Gaza Strip.

While Israel maintained its claim to sovereignty over the West Bank and Gaza Strip, Begin proposed that in the "knowledge that other claims exist" and "for the sake of agreement and the peace, that question of sovereignty in these areas be left open."

As for the status of Jerusalem, Begin said freedom of access to holy shrines in the city would be guaranteed for members of the Jewish, Christian and Moslem faiths.

Begin also unveiled the following proposal for restoring Egyptian sovereignty over the Israeli-occupied Sinai Peninsula: the area east of the Gidi and Mitla passes would be demilitarized and the forces between the Suez Canal and the line of the passes would be administered by Israel and protected by Israeli forces; Israeli forces would remain on a defense line in the central Sinai for "a number of years" and air bases and early-warning systems would remain during that period "until the withdrawal of our forces to the international boundary," and freedom of navigation in the Strait of Tiran, leading to the Gulf of Aqaba, would be internationally guaranteed "either by a United Nations force which cannot be withdrawn except with the agreement of both countries and by unanimous decision of the U.N. Security Council," or by a joint Egyptian-Israeli patrol. This guarantee would assure Israel's shipping lanes to its southern port of Elath.

During his address to the Knesset, Begin disclosed that his talks with Sadat had nearly broken down on two occasions because of Egyptian proposals that were totally unacceptable to Israel. The premier did not disclose the nature of these proposals, but said it was members of the Egyptian Foreign Ministry, not Sadat, who were responsible for blocking efforts to draft a joint Israeli-Egyptian statement at the end of the summit.

Begin said Israel had made its "contribution" at the summit talks and "it is now the turn of the other side."

During the debate, Labor Party leader Shimon Peres had criticized the Begin plan, asserting that it offered too many concessions on the Sinai too early in the negotiations. He called for the immediate involvement of Jordan in the plan for civil rule in the West Bank and Gaza Strip because otherwise the Begin plan would be unworkable.

Begin gave Carter peace plan—Premier Begin had conveyed his West Bank-Gaza plan to President Carter at a White House meeting Dec. 16 and received Carter's evaluation of the plan Dec. 17.

Appearing on the CBS-TV program "Face the Nation" Dec. 18, Begin said the President had praised his plan, calling it "a fair basis for negotiations." Begin said he did not ask for nor did he receive from Carter an endorsement of it. He said other U.S. officials had told him the previous day that the plan was "constructive" and showed new "flexibility" on Israel's part.

President Carter Dec. 28 lauded the proposal for more autonomy for Arabs in the West Bank and Gaza Strip and reaffirmed his opposition to establishment of an independent Palestinian state in the territories. The President's remarks evoked criticism from President Sadat and the PLO and praise from Israel.

Speaking in a year-end televised interview, Carter said Begin's plan was "a long step forward" and was "certainly a realistic negotiating position." As for his opposition to a Palestinian state, the President reiterated his Administration's preference that there not be "a fairly radical, new independent nation in the heart of the Middle East."

Sadat Dec. 29 said he was "disappointed" and "embarrassed" by Carter's remarks, adding that the President was "making my job very difficult" in negotiating with Israel. "What surprises me most," Sadat said, "was the fact that Carter was "ignoring the importance of the Palestine issue—the core and crux of the whole problem."

The PLO Dec. 29 denounced Carter's opposition to a Palestinian state. The U.S. "has lost its role as a neutral arbiter in the Middle East with its support for Israeli occupation and expansion against Palestinian self-determination," an organization spokesman said.

Administration officials explained Dec. 29 that Carter's praise of the Begin plan was part of an Administration campaign to convince the Israeli leader and President Sadat that despite their disagreement over the Palestinian issue there was still an opportunity to work out an equitable arrangement. Secretary of State Cyrus Vance emphasized that although the U.S. regarded Begin's plan as an appropriate start for continued negotiations, it had not endorsed the proposal.

Carter came in for a sharper attack from the PLO Dec. 31 when its leader Yasir Arafat charged that the President's statement meant that the U.S. was tied with "the enemy—Israel—in a plan to eliminate the Palestinian movement." Speaking to a rally in Damur, Lebanon, Arafat warned Carter to "listen to this. There will be no peace, no surrender. We will keep fighting until victory."

Carter's Dec. 15 charge that the PLO was inflexible had drawn a sharp rebuke from the organization the following day. Farouk Khaddoumi, head of the PLO's political department, accused the President of reverting to former Secretary of State Henry A. Kissinger's policy of "dividing the Arab countries" and "using secret diplomacy" on behalf of Israel. He accused the U.S. of reneging on its Oct. 1 pledge with the Soviet Union, calling for recognition of the legitimate rights of the Palestinians.

Egyptian plan—Carter's statement was said to have prompted the Egyptians Dec. 31 to disclose a counterproposal to Begin's plan earlier than had been anticipated. The formula was made public by Foreign Minister Mohammed Ibrahim Kamel,

Text of Israeli Plan for West Bank and Gaza Strip

Following is the text of the Israeli plan for the West Bank and Gaza Strip that Premier Begin submitted to President Sadat at their summit meeting Dec. 25–26 and to the Israeli Knesset Dec. 28.

[1]
The administration of the military government in Judea, Samaria and the Gaza district will be abolished.

[2]
In Judea, Samaria and the Gaza district, administrative autonomy of the residents, by and for them, will be established.

[3]
The residents of Judea, Samaria and the Gaza district will elect an administrative council composed of 11 members. The administrative council will operate in accordance with the principles laid down in this paper.

[4]
Any resident, 18 years old and above, without distinction of citizenship, or if stateless, is entitled to vote in the elections to the administrative council.

[5]
Any resident whose name is included in the list of candidates for the administrative council and who, on the day the list is submitted, is 25 years old or above, is entitled to be elected to the council.

[6]
The administrative council will be elected by general, direct, personal, equal and secret ballot.

[7]
The period of office of the administrative council will be four years from the day of its election.

[8]
The administrative council will sit in Bethlehem.

[9]
All the administrative affairs relating to the Arab residents of the areas of Judea, Samaria and the Gaza district will be under the direction and within the competence of the administrative council.

[10]
The administrative council will operate the following departments: education, religious affairs, finance, transportation, construction and housing industry, commerce and tourism, agriculture, health, labor and social welfare, rehabilitation of refugees, and the department for the administration of justice and the supervision of the local police forces, and promulgate regulations relating to the operations of these departments.

[11]
Security and public order in the areas of Judea, Samaria and the Gaza district will be the responsibility of the Israeli authorities.

[12]
The administrative council will elect its own chairman.

[13]
The first session of the administrative council will be convened 30 days after the publication of the election results.

[14]
Residents of Judea, Samaria and the Gaza district, without distinction of citizenship, or if stateless, will be granted free choice (option) of either Israeli or Jordanian citizenship.

[15]
A resident of the areas of Judea, Samaria and the Gaza district who requests Israeli citizenship will be granted such citizenship in accordance with the citizenship law of the state.

[16]
Residents of Judea, Samaria and the Gaza district who, in accordance with the right of free option, choose Israeli citizenship, will be entitled to vote for, and be elected to the Knesset in accordance with the election law.

[17]
Residents of Judea, Samaria and the Gaza district who are citizens of Jordan or who, in accordance with the right of free option will become citizens of Jordan, will elect and be eligible for election to the Parliament of the Hashemite Kingdom of Jordan in accordance with the election law of that country.

[18]
Questions arising from the vote to the Jordanian Parliament by residents of Judea, Samaria and the Gaza district will be clarified in negotiations between Israel and Jordan.

[19]
A committee will be established of representatives of Israel, Jordan and the administrative council to examine existing legislation in Judea, Samaria and the Gaza district and to determine which legislation will continue in force, which will be abolished and what will be the competence of the administrative council to promulgate regulations. The rulings of the committee will be adopted by unanimous decisions.

[20]
Residents of Israel will be entitled to acquire land and settle in the areas of Judea, Samaria and the Gaza district. Arabs, residents of Judea, Samaria and the Gaza district who, in accordance with the free options granted them, will become Israeli citizens, will be entitled to acquire land and settle in Israel.

[21]
A committee will be established of representatives of Israel, Jordan and the administrative council to determine norms of immigration to the areas of Judea, Samaria and the Gaza district. The committee will determine the norms whereby Arab refugees residing outside Judea, Samaria and the Gaza district will be permitted to immigrate to these areas in reasonable numbers. The ruling of the committee will be adopted by unanimous decision.

[22]
Residents of Israel and residents of Judea, Samaria and the Gaza district will be assured of movement and freedom of economic activity in Israel, Judea, Samaria and the Gaza district.

[23]
The administrative council will appoint one of its members to represent the council before the government of Israel for deliberation on matters of common interest; and one of its members to represent the council before the government of Jordan for deliberation on matters of common interest.

[24]
Israel stands by its right and its claim of sovereignty to Judea, Samaria and the Gaza district. In the knowledge that other claims exist, it proposes for the sake of the agreement and the peace, that the question of sovereignty be left open.

[25]
With regard to the administration of the holy places of the three religions in Jerusalem, a special proposal will be drawn up and submitted that will include the guarantee of freedom of access to members of all faiths to the shrines holy to them.

[26]
These principles will be subject to review after a five-year period.

who handed it to U.S. Ambassador Hermann F. Eilts in Cairo. The statement said that Israel must accept the principle of total withdrawal from the West Bank and Gaza Strip, that it must recognize the "inalienable" rights of the Arab residents in the areas to self-determination and that it must agree to "the liquidation of Israeli settlements" in those territories.

The statement also said that in further Israeli-Egyptian negotiations "the question of security arrangements among the parties concerned" must be considered. This view was regarded as a reaffirmation of Cairo's position that Israel would be compensated by foolproof security arrangements if it accepted the principles of withdrawal and Palestinian self-determination.

Arabs assail Israel, Egypt moves—Most Arab states and the Palestine Liberation Organization assailed the Israeli-Egyptian peace initiatives before and after the Begin-Sadat summit in Ismailia.

Saudi officials Dec. 25 were noncommittal on the summit meeting, saying only they hoped it would lead to peace. A Syrian government newspaper described the summit talks as "a complete failure" and called on the Sadat government to resign. Libya and Iraq denounced the Begin-Sadat talks, with Tripoli radio charging that Sadat "will sign everything our enemy Israel wants him to."

The PLO charged Dec. 26 after a two-day meeting of its executive committee in Beirut that Sadat had abandoned the cause of the Palestinians in his meeting with Begin. The PLO was determined to block "the United States-Zionist settlement which is being executed by Sadat's regime at the expense of the Palestinian cause and the national interests of the Egyptian people," the statement said.

The statement said the PLO would "liquidate" any Arab who cooperated with the Israeli occupiers, and a PLO spokesman said this had already been done in one instance earlier Dec. 26. Hamdi Kadi, deputy director of education in the West Bank town of Ramallah, near Jerusalem, was shot to death from a passing car as he left his home for work. The PLO said he was assassinated because of his "collaboration" with the Israelis and because of his "suspect relations" with the director of Israeli intelligence.

The PLO struck again Dec. 29, this time inside Israel, where a bomb explosion killed two persons in the coastal town of Natanya. The Democratic Front for the Liberation of Palestine issued a statement in Beirut claiming responsibility, saying the blast was a reply to Begin's proposals.

The Jordanian government Dec. 28 denounced the Begin plan as an "attempt to consolidate and legitimize Israeli occupation of Palestinian territory." The government, the statement added, "completely rejects cooperation in implementing such a settlement calling for the surrender of Arab territories to Israel. . . ."

West Bank mayors Dec. 29 generally reacted negatively to Begin's plan for their territory. They noted that a similar proposal had been rejected by the Arabs in 1967. The mayors also reiterated their contention that the PLO was the sole representative of the Palestinian people.

West Bank Arabs and the PLO had voiced concern earlier in December when parts of Begin's plan for the West Bank had been leaked. A PLO spokesman Dec. 19 said Sadat and King Hussein of Jordan would not accept the plan because it was essentially the same as the one offered by Hussein in 1975 and rejected. "What is new about Begin's plan is that he is trying to win legitimacy from the Palestinians, Arabs and world opinion for the continuation of Israeli occupation of Arab territories, but we will not give him any legitimacy," a PLO spokesman said.

Israeli settlers oppose Begin plan— Begin's proposals came in for criticism Dec. 27 from Israeli settlers in the West Bank, the Golan Heights, the Sinai and Gaza. Several hundred gathered in the West Bank settlement of Ofar to voice their opposition. Begin was accused of abandoning his Likud Party's principle of claiming Israeli sovereignty over the West Bank and Gaza.

U.S.S.R. scores summit talks—The Soviet Union assailed the Begin-Sadat summit talks in statements issued Dec. 25 and 26.

The Communist Party newspaper Pravda Dec. 25 said that Moscow would not attend a Geneva conference to ratify agreements resulting from the Ismailia talks. A Geneva parley held for that purpose, Pravda contended, would merely be "a screen covering separate deals to the detriment of a general Middle East peace settlement."

The government newspaper Izvestia Dec. 26 charged that the real purpose of the summit talks was to draw up a separate Egyptian-Israeli agreement, and did not represent the first step toward an overall Middle East settlement as claimed by Sadat. Izvestia also charged that Sadat's agreement to send his foreign minister to Jerusalem in January for further negotiations was tantamount to Cairo's recognition of the city as Israel's capital.

Shah Backs Sadat's Peace Moves. Shah Mohammed Riza Pahlevi of Iran endorsed President Anwar Sadat's Middle East peace initiatives in a meeting with the Egyptian leader in Aswan Jan. 9, 1978.

The shah said he believed that Egypt was "doing precisely what we believe is right," which he described as carrying out United Nations Security Council Resolutions 242 and 338.

The shah also told newsmen that the Middle East was Iran's "area. We are involved in the Middle East."

After leaving Aswan Jan. 10, the Iranian leader flew to Riyadh, where he briefed Saudi Arabian officials on his talks with Sadat.

U.S.' West Bank-Gaza plan. President Carter Jan. 6, 1978 disclosed a U.S. plan for the West Bank and the Gaza Strip to be either aligned with Jordan or placed under joint Israeli-Arab administration. At a later date the Arab residents of the two areas would vote to decide which arrangement they preferred. The President, however, continued to oppose the creation of an independent Palestinian state on the ground that it would serve as a base for subversion.

Carter suggested that the joint administration be made up of Israel, Jordan, the Palestinians and possibly the United Nations.

The plan had been submitted privately by Secretary of State Cyrus Vance in his meetings with Middle East leaders in August 1977. Israeli Premier Menahem Begin had rejected it.

Israeli-Egyptian Military Panel Meets. The Israeli-Egyptian Military Committee convened in Cairo Jan. 11 to discuss Is-

raeli withdrawal from the Sinai as part of a peace settlement.

The Military Committee, whose delegations were headed by War Minister Mohammed Abdel Ghany el-Gamasy of Egypt and Defense Minister Ezer Weizman of Israel, originally was scheduled to meet Jan. 16. But the Egyptians had the date advanced to sound out Israeli views on the growing controversy over Israeli settlements in the Sinai prior to the parallel talks of the Political Committee, which were scheduled to start in Jerusalem the following week.

Before entering the committee session, Weizman flew to Aswan, where he conferred with Sadat. The discussions were said to have dealt with the Sinai settlements and the forum in which they should be taken up.

At their second session Jan. 12, the conferees submitted their respective positions for Israeli withdrawal from the Sinai and for a system of security guarantees for both countries. Lt. Gen. Mordechai Gur, Israeli chief of staff, was said to have argued that the Israeli settlements in northern Sinai and three desert airfields were essential to Israel's security.

Military Committee Talks Recess—The Israeli-Egyptian Military Committee meeting in Cairo recessed Jan. 13.

Israel's Weizman said Jan. 13 that a general understanding had been reached on an Israeli proposal to divide the Sinai into three zones—a United Nations buffer strip, a demilitarized zone and one containing a limited number of Egyptian troops.

Egypt's Gamasy reported Jan. 13 that there had been no agreement on the related issue of the proposed demilitarized zone and a thinning out of Egyptian and Israeli military forces in the Sinai. Gamasy renewed Egypt's demand for sovereignty over Sharm el Sheikh at the southern tip of the Sinai.

Commenting on the Military Committee talks, President Sadat said Jan. 13 that the disputants' differences over Israeli settlements in the Sinai and self-determination for the Palestinians had "endangered" the negotiations.

In an interview with the Cairo magazine October, Sadat Jan. 12 had said he had "absolutely no hope" that the forthcoming

Political Committee talks would succeed. In his statement, made public Jan. 14, Sadat assailed the Israelis as "stiff-necked" and "clever merchants" who refused to compromise. The president charged that "Begin gave me nothing. It was I who gave him everything. I gave him security and legitimacy and got nothing in return."

Israeli Minister Confers with Pope. Israeli Foreign Minister Moshe Dayan Jan. 12 discussed the Middle East with Pope Paul VI at the Vatican. The hour-long conversation dealt with the Pope's concern for Roman Catholic and other Christian shrines in Jerusalem and with current peace negotiations.

After the meeting the Pope renewed his call for international guarantees of access to Jerusalem's religious shrines. Dayan said later at a news conference that Pope Paul had not requested any special status for the city. The foreign minister noted that Israel already was guaranteeing open access to holy places in Jerusalem and in other territories under its control.

Dayan's meeting with the Pope came on the last day of a four-day meeting with Italian government and political leaders.

Basic Issues Unresolved. The Israeli-Egyptian Political Committee opened talks in Jerusalem Jan. 17, 1978, but they were abruptly suspended Jan. 18 when President Anwar Sadat recalled the Egyptian delegation. Cairo said Sadat acted after it had become clear that the Israelis "all aim at deadlocking the situation and submitting partial solutions" that would not lead to a lasting peace in the Middle East. The convening of the conference had been delayed by one day.

The U.S., which had been represented at the talks by Secretary of State Cyrus Vance, exhorted Egypt to resume the negotiations.

The breakdown had been indicated beforehand in an exchange of sharp statements made by Foreign Minister Mohammed Ibrahim Kamel, head of the Egyptian delegation, and Israeli Premier Menahem Begin. On his arrival in Jerusalem Jan. 15, Kamel repeated earlier assertions by Sadat that there could be no peace without Israeli withdrawal from occupied Arab territories and self-determination for the Palestinians.

Speaking at a dinner Jan. 17 honoring Kamel and Vance, Begin admonished the foreign minister for having "told us on arrival under what circumstances peace can be established." Then Begin reiterated his longstanding position that there could be no peace if Israel were required to return to the "aggression-provoking lines" that existed prior to the 1967 war or if Israel had to agree to a division of Jerusalem. As for Arab demands for self-determination for the Palestinians, Begin said, "We recognize and rejoice in the right of self-determination in 21 Arab states." But he insisted that the principle of self-determination could not apply to a proposed Palestinian state in the West Bank and Gaza Strip.

Kamel, in reply, criticized Begin for having "brought the negotiations" to the reception. He said, "I can only repeat that we believe that the basic elements of a lasting peace, . . . are what I declared this morning to the Political Committee." These conflicting positions should be discussed at those sessions, Kamel said, adding, "I shall keep my views to that meeting."

At a news conference earlier Jan. 17 after the first session of the Political Committee, Israeli Foreign Minister Moshe Dayan confirmed that the opposing sides remained in basic disagreement on such key issues as the size of Israeli withdrawals from occupied territory and the Palestinian question. Dayan also was critical of statements made in recent days by Sadat and other Egyptians. "Any attempt to solve our problems and differences by ultimatums would miss the whole point, destroy the very purpose of the peace talks," Dayan warned.

Following a 15-minute session of the Political Committee Jan. 18, Kamel held an hour-long meeting with Begin. The foreign minister told reporters on emerging that "the atmosphere which surrounded the meeting of the Political Committee—and public statements and things like that—had something to do with my recall now to report" to President Sadat.

Before leaving his hotel for the airport, Kamel denied the talks had broken down, adding that his recall to Cairo was "a very natural thing."

Israeli Cabinet Assails Sadat Move —The Israeli Cabinet Jan. 18 called Sadat's decision to suspend the conference an "extreme" move that proved "the Egyptian government [had] deceived itself that Israel will submit to demands it has never considered feasible."

The Cabinet statement, issued after an emergency session, denounced Kamel's demands at the Political Committee meetings calling for Israeli withdrawal from the Old City of Jerusalem, the West Bank and Gaza Strip and agreement to the establishment of a Palestinian state in those two areas. Such demands, the Cabinet said, "would have removed every prospects of peace and endangered the very existence of the Jewish state."

Premier Begin Jan. 19 disclosed that at their final session the previous day Egypt and Israel had agreed to five of seven paragraphs in a statement of principles proposed by Secretary of State Vance as a compromise document.

(Three points of the U.S. proposal reported to have been accepted by both sides had been made public by Israel Jan. 17. They were: "1. A declaration of principles which would govern the negotiations of a comprehensive peace settlement in the Middle East; 2. The guidelines for negotiations relating to the issues of the West Bank and Gaza Strip; 3. Elements of peace treaties between Israel and its neighbors in accordance with the principles of United Nations Security Council Resolution 242.")

In his meeting with Begin, Vance received "clarifications" on the peace issues in the hope of persuading President Sadat to agree to a resumption of the talks.

U.S. Appeals to Sadat—President Carter Jan. 18 telephoned President Sadat urging him to continue the negotiations with Israel despite his decision to recall his delegation from Jerusalem.

Sadat agreed to Carter's request to permit the Israeli-Egyptian Military Committee, which had recessed Jan. 13, to resume negotiations in Cairo the following week as scheduled, the officials said.

Secretary Vance, who was scheduled to discuss the latest crisis with Sadat in Cairo Jan. 21, also phoned the Egyptian leader Jan. 18 in an effort to keep the diplomatic movement alive. Vance said he had "stressed to him [Sadat] the importance of continuing the process for peace and he agrees on that."

Political Talks Had Been Delayed—The opening meeting of the Israeli-Egyptian Political Committee had been scheduled to start Jan. 16 but was postponed because of a dispute over the agenda. A U.S. compromise submitted Jan. 15 broke the deadlock, enabling the conference to start Jan. 17. The impasse had forced Secretary of State Vance to delay his departure date for Jerusalem from Jan. 14 until the following day.

According to American officials, the disagreement had emerged at the Begin-Sadat summit at Ismailia Dec. 25-26, 1977. Egypt had insisted that the agenda contain specific reference to the "Palestinian question." Israel argued that this item be listed as "the question of the Palestinian Arabs in Judea, Samaria and Gaza." Judea and Samaria were the Biblical names for the West Bank referred to by Israel to support its claims to the area. Egypt opposed the Israeli version on the grounds that the language "would be nothing but the Menahem Begin proposal," which called only for self-rule for the Arab residents of the area.

The U.S. compromise agreed to by both parties Jan. 15 provided for "neutral language" to describe the Palestinian issue. A State Department official that day said the reference to the topic was now broad enough so that "it does not exclude either side from putting forward its own position."

A spokesman for the Egyptian delegation Jan. 15 disclosed that the Palestinian question was not the only source of disagreement. He said the subject of Israeli settlements in the Sinai "was one of the leading reasons" for the agenda dispute.

Sadat Explains Negotiating Stand—President Sadat convened the People's National Assembly (parliament) Jan. 21 to explain his decision to suspend the Political Committee talks. He accused Israeli negotiators of stalling in order "to take us into circles so that we would find ourselves back at the starting point." He further charged that Israel was exploiting his recognition of Israel's "need for security" to justify its continued control over Arab territories.

Sadat disclosed that in his talks with Vance the previous day he had asked the secretary to inform President Carter that he wanted the U.S. "to arm Egypt with all the arms Israel has got and I will pay for it." Sadat implied that Begin's alleged intransigence was the result of the military equipment Israel had received from the U.S. He said that he wanted similar materiel, not to attack Israel, but to serve as a counterbalance in negotiations.

Israel Bars Military Talks. Israel Jan. 22 spurned American efforts to persuade it to return to the Military Committee talks, which had been scheduled to resume in Cairo that day.

Premier Begin told newsmen that the Cabinet had decided to delay Israeli participation in the discussions because Egypt had launched "a campaign of grave vilification" against Israel. "Egyptian newspapers even used notorious anti-Semitic expressions," Begin said. Sadat's address Jan. 21 was an "extremist, aggressive speech and [it] addressed to Israel ultimative demands that are totally unacceptable to Israel," Begin added.

In a speech to the Knesset (parliament) Jan. 23, Begin said "it would be useless and humiliating" for Israel's delegation to return to the Military Committee meetings while Egypt created "an atmosphere of hatred against the Jewish people and the Jewish state." The premier cited nine instances of language he regarded as objectionable in the Egyptian press in recent days. He mentioned one article that referred to him as "Shylock the usurer who wanted a pound of flesh from his debtor." Another article appearing in the semi-official newspaper Al Ahram said, "the Jew will bargain even with the Angel of Death," Begin asserted.

Discussing negotiating differences with Egypt, Begin said that he and the Egyptian president had agreed in their negotiations that a settlement of the matter of Israel's withdrawal from the Sinai would include an agreement that the Egyptian army would not move east of the Gidi and Mitla passes. In later meetings of the Military Committee, Begin said, the Egyptians proposed a line only 40 kilometers (25 miles) from Israel's 1967 frontier. Begin insisted on "the complete demilitarization of the Sinai from the Gidi and Mitla passes to the international boundary." He called on Sadat "to instruct his military staff to abide by his undertaking."

In his speech to the Knesset, Begin disclosed points on which the two sides had already agreed: acceptance of United Nations Security Council Resolutions 242 and 338, which would serve as the framework for working out a Middle East solution; establishment of freedom of navigation through the Gulf of Aqaba, and agreement to press efforts to solve the Palestinian refugee problem.

In an interview published in a French magazine Jan. 21, Begin said Egypt had walked out of the Political Committee talks in Jerusalem "to dramatize the situation, to create a climate of tension" and "to give the impression that there are pressures from Europe and America."

Egyptian Press Denies Insults—While Egypt's government ignored Begin's charges of anti-Semitism, its press Jan. 24 continued to attack the Israeli premier while it denied using racial or religious insults.

A caricature of Begin appearing in Al Ahram, one of the sharpest critics of the premier, carried a caption that read: "Don't make excuses. We are not anti-Semitic. We are anti-you."

The English-language Egyptian Gazette conceded that Begin's role in negotiations had been described in harsh language. But it was never anti-Semitic, the newspaper said. The press campaign against the Israeli leader had been sparked by his "unnecessarily tough statements" on maintaining Israeli settlements in the Sinai, the Gazette claimed.

Mustafa Amin, a columnist for the newspaper Al Akhbar, scoffed at Begin's criticism of the Egyptian press, saying that he too was opposed to discrimination, "especially anything of a religious nature."

In an article Dec. 31, 1977, Amin had criticized the results of the Begin-Sadat summit talks in Ismailia, saying "the meetings were not with the delegates of the state of Israel but with Shylock, the Jewish usurer [in Shakespeare's *Merchant of Venice*] who sought a pound of flesh from his debtor's body." Amin said Begin's proposal to Sadat was not a peace offer "but a bill by a Jewish usurer to his debtor, which, he, the usurer, burdened with compound interest, expenses, fines and profits."

Arab Hardliners Assail Sadat—Arab radical states opposed to President Sadat's peace initiatives assailed the Egyptian leader Jan. 22 for not completely abandoning his dialogue with Israel. At the same time, Arab moderates took issue with U.S. policies, urging Washington to take a stronger stand against Israel.

Syria's ruling Baath Party newspaper was critical of Sadat for his insistence on keeping the peace process going despite the deadlock with Israel. The government newspaper Tichrin charged that "all that Sadat is after now is to increase American influence in the Middle East by demanding weapons from the U.S. not to fight Israel, but to fight the liberation movements in Africa."

A Saudi newspaper said it was up to the U.S. to respond to Sadat's appeal for the pressure of world opinion against Israel. If the U.S. wanted to befriend countries in the Middle East that were not "influenced by Russia, then it must break the hand [Israel] that insists on aggression . . . , using American-supplied rifles," the newspaper said.

A Kuwait newspaper urged other Arab states to use their oil as a weapon, "now that it is confirmed that Israel and America want a peace that would enslave the Arabs."

The most strident criticism of Sadat's decision to suspend the Political Committee talks with Israel had emanated from Syria Jan. 19. A government newspaper said Sadat's move was an attempt to fool "Arab public opinion so as to later justify a separate deal with Israel." Damascus radio said that Sadat had bowed to pressure by President Carter and agreed to a resumption of military talks with Israel.

Other Arab states, particularly Saudi Arabia, welcomed Sadat's decision to suspend talks with Israel as an opportunity to heal the rift in the Arab world that had been precipitated by Sadat's peace moves.

U.S. Mediates. The U.S., which had been seeking to bring the disputants back to the conference table, announced Jan. 26 that Israel and Egypt were near agreement on principles for an overall settlement.

Egyptian President Anwar Sadat had confirmed Jan. 25 that Israel and Egypt were holding private "serious negotiations" despite suspension of their formal talks.

U.S. mediation efforts were being pressed by Secretary of State Cyrus

Vance and Assistant Secretary of State Alfred L. Atherton Jr. Atherton had stayed behind in Jerusalem to meet with Israeli leaders after Vance left the city following the halt in negotiations.

Vance went on to Cairo Jan. 20 to persuade him to reconsider his decision to suspend the talks with Israel. Sadat refused, but he said "the door to peace is not closed." The Egyptian leader stated his terms for reentering the negotiations. He called for Israeli acceptance beforehand of two main principles—Israeli withdrawal from Arab lands occupied since 1967 and the right of self-determination for the Palestinians.

Vance's meeting with Sadat was followed by a sharp public exchange between the Egyptian leader and Israeli Premier Menahem Begin. Each blamed the other for the collapse of the talks. In addition, Begin accused the Egyptian press of waging an anti-Semitic campaign against Israel. The remarks caused Israel to delay participation in further Military Committee meetings.

Atherton Feb. 1 ended two weeks of efforts to get Israel and Egypt to agree to a declaration of principles that would pave the way for an overall Middle East settlement. After spending most of that time in Jerusalem meeting with Israeli officials, Atherton flew to Cairo Jan. 30. He conferred Jan. 31 and Feb. 1 with President Anwar Sadat and Foreign Minister Mohammed Ibrahim Kamel, transmitting Israel's proposals for a working draft of a declaration of principles and receiving an Egyptian plan in return.

(Atherton had briefly interrupted his stay in Jerusalem with a visit to Amman, Jordan Jan. 27–28. He met with King Hussein to transmit a message from President Carter detailing U.S. views on Middle East developments.)

Military Committee Talks Resume. The Egyptian-Israeli Military Committee resumed discussions in Cairo Jan. 31–Feb. 1 on arranging a technical agreement for Israel's return of the Sinai Peninsula to Egypt. The talks were recessed without any formal announcement. It was the first official contact between the two countries since their Political Committee talks broke down in Jerusalem Jan. 18.

The Israeli Cabinet had agreed Jan. 29 to resume participation in the Military Committee sessions. The government had refused earlier in the month to take part to protest what it regarded as an anti-Semitic campaign waged by the Egyptian press against Israel.

Sadat Appeals to American Jews. A U.S. newspaper Jan. 29 published an appeal by Egyptian President Anwar Sadat to American Jews to support his peace initiatives.

In an "Open Letter to American Jews," printed in The Miami Herald, Sadat said a peace settlement was being impeded by Israeli "annexation" of Arab territory; Israel's "suppression of the rights of the Palestinian people to live in peace in their homeland," and Israeli claims that "territorial expansion is more important than the establishment of peace."

One of the American Jewish leaders who responded to the article, Rabbi Joseph P. Sternstein, lauded Sadat's plea for peace. But Sadat, in addressing his "appeal to American Jews to pressure Israel to give in to his demands proves again that he is not of a mind to negotiate seriously with Israel for a just and durable peace," said Sternstein, who was president of the Zionist Organization of America.

The Miami Herald had invited Sadat to write the letter.

Arab Radical States Meet in Algiers. Leaders of Syria, Libya, Algeria, South Yemen and the Palestine Liberation Organization met in Algiers Feb. 2–4, 1978 to map strategy against Sadat's peace initiatives in the Middle East. Iraq boycotted the gathering, which was a follow-up to a similar high-level conference of the Arab radical states in Tripoli, Libya in December 1977.

The Algiers summit did not announce any new steps against Sadat. Algerian Foreign Minister Abdelaziz Bouteflika said Feb. 5, "All that can be made public has been announced." Other decisions taken by the conferees could not "by their very nature" be made public, he added.

A Palestinian representative said Bouteflika was referring to a secret agreement to permit the PLO to reopen military bases in Syria that were closed during the Lebanese civil war in 1976. Sources at the Algiers conference said Feb. 1 that the decision had been made the previous week to bolster efforts by the hardline Arab states to frustrate Sadat's policies.

Syrian President Hafez al-Assad said Feb. 5 before leaving Algiers that the summit had "achieved great results." He said the conference states, which had established a "front for resistance and confrontation" at the Tripoli meeting, would maintain contacts and "continue to resist any defeatist line that tries to impose its domination on our region."

Algerian President Houari Boumedienne said in an address to the opening session Feb. 2 that the "Palestinians are a main member of this front, and we give unconditional and full support to their opposition to Cairo's policy."

Libyan leader Muammer el-Qaddafi, who arrived at the summit one day later, said on landing at Algiers airport Feb. 3 that any peace settlement that ignored the Palestinians could only be "war in abeyance."

Iraq boycotted the summit because it regarded the stand of the other Arab radical states on Sadat's policies as not strong enough.

Sadat Presses Peace Drive in U.S. Egyptian President Sadat visited the U.S. Feb. 3–8, 1978 to urge American officials to pressure Israel to be more amenable to his peace proposals. Sadat also asked for American arms assistance.

Sadat conferred with President Carter on arriving in Washington Feb. 3. The two leaders held further discussions Feb. 4–5 at Camp David, Md. and met again at the White House before Sadat's departure Feb. 8.

A White House statement issued shortly after the Egyptian leader left said the U.S. would adhere to its "historical commitments to the security of Israel" and that it would press for a "comprehensive" peace treaty providing for "normal peaceful relations between Israel and its neighbors."

The statement stressed the need for a "resolution of the Palestinian problem" if there were to be a peace settlement. It then reaffirmed the U.S. commitment to the formula agreed to by Sadat and Carter in Aswan, Egypt Jan. 4. The formula called for "recognition of the legitimate rights of the Palestinian people" and their participation "in the determination of their own future."

The U.S. restated its opposition to new Israeli settlements in occupied territories, asserting that such "activity would be inconsistent with the effort to reach a peace settlement," according to the statement.

On his arrival at the White House Feb. 3, Sadat had urged the U.S. to become the "arbiter" in the Arab-Israeli dispute—a role that would give Washington the power to decide the conflict. In reply, Carter struck a neutral note, saying "it is up to all of us—President Sadat, Premier Begin, other interested leaders, and also the people of the United States, to rededicate efforts" to bring about a peace settlement.

Camp David Discussions—In addition to holding private discussions at Camp David Feb. 4-5, Carter and Sadat also held larger meetings with their aides at the presidential retreat.

A White House statement issued after the conclusion of the talks Feb. 5 said both leaders had vowed to do all they could to achieve "tangible results and broadening" of the Israeli-Egyptian negotiations. It was agreed that Assistant Secretary of State Alfred L. Atherton Jr. would resume his shuttle diplomacy to Israel and Egypt in an attempt to get both sides to accept a "declaration of principles" on a settlement.

As a result of his talks with the Egyptian leader, the statement said, Carter had "a better understanding of President Sadat's concern" about the slow pace of the Israeli-Egyptian negotiations. Apparently rejecting Sadat's suggestion that the U.S. act as arbiter, the statement implied that the Carter Administration would continue its role as mediator. The U.S. regarded itself as a "friend of both sides," the statement said.

In an NBC television interview broadcast later Feb. 5, Sadat said he had told Carter why he severed diplomatic talks with Israel in Jerusalem Jan. 18. The major obstacle, he said, was Israeli settlements in the Sinai. Sadat said he had decided to send his delegation to Jerusalem only after receiving assurances from Carter that Secretary of State Cyrus R. Vance would join the talks.

Sadat Charges Israeli Intransigence—Speaking to the National Press Club in Washington Feb. 6, President Sadat accused Israel of intransigence in its negotiations with Egypt.

Sadat said, "I have given Israel everything" in concessions, but the "Is-raeli position is hardening rather than softening as we go along." He said it was up to the U.S. to alter Israel's course. Appealing for American support, Sadat observed that Israel "relies heavily on your country, militarily, financially and politically. On the other hand, you have global interests. That puts you in a unique position to exert your influence and good offices for the sake of peace and tranquility."

Sadat asserted that Israeli Premier Begin had misstated the Egyptian president's position in their discussions. He denied Begin's charge that he had reneged on an offer not to deploy Egyptian forces east of the Mitla and Gidi passes in the Sinai Peninsula. Sadat insisted that his position remained unchanged, saying that the Israelis wanted the Egyptian forces kept west of the passes "even though it is my land."

At a meeting later Feb. 6 with journalists, Sadat accused Begin of "damaging the spirit" of Sadat's peace initiatives by demanding that Israel maintain its settlements in the northern Sinai.

Sadat spurned Begin's plan for autonomy for Arabs in the West Bank and Gaza Strip and insisted instead on establishment of "a complete, independent Palestinian state" in those territories. In his earlier speech to the press club, Sadat appeared to have taken a softer stand on the issue, suggesting that a Palestinian entity be linked to Jordan.

Sadat also met with leading American Jewish figures, including Philip Klutznick, head of the World Jewish Congress. Sadat had invited leaders of the Conference of Presidents of Major Jewish Organizations to the talks, but they declined. At a meeting Feb. 1 in New York the Jewish group said it had decided to reject Sadat's invitation "lest our community be interpreted as seeking to take part in the negotiations and lest such a meeting be construed as a surrogate for direct Egyptian-Israeli talks."

Sadat Asks U.S. Congressmen for Arms—President Sadat Feb. 7 appealed for U.S. arms for Egypt in separate closed-door appearances before the U.S. House International Relations Committee and the Senate Foreign Relations Committee.

Sen. Henry Jackson (D, Wash.) said after the meeting of the Foreign Relations

Committee that Sadat had made "a very good case for arms, going beyond his country, into the situation in Africa." Sadat had been telling congressmen since his arrival in Washington that he wanted F-5E fighter planes to counter a possible threat posed by Soviet involvement in Ethiopia and Libya, and not for use against Israel.

Sadat had told reporters Feb. 6 that in addition to the F-5Es, Egypt also wanted the advanced U.S. F-15 and F-16 jets. Sadat was said to have asked for 120 F-5Es in his meetings with President Carter in April 1977.

Begin Opposes U.S. Arms to Egypt— Premier Begin warned Feb. 8 that any new American arms shipments to Egypt would increase the threat of war.

Begin said the Egyptian request for U.S. planes constituted another form of Egyptian pressure on Israel. He added: "But of course, we cannot submit to any ultimatum, since these threats are still being issued, and if offensive weapons are being sold it will feed that threat and will be a very negative development in the midst of peace negotiations."

Begin made the remark in Geneva, where he was discussing fund raising and support for Israel with leaders of the European Jewish community.

Sadat Seeks European Backing. After leaving the U.S., Sadat toured Europe Feb. 9–13 to gain support for his Middle East peace initiatives.

Among the highlights of his trip:

Britain—Sadat held a brief meeting at a London airport Feb. 9 with British Prime Minister James Callaghan and Foreign Secretary David Owen. Addressing the House of Commons after Sadat's departure, Callaghan disclosed that he and the Egyptian leader had discussed a possible European role in peace moves. He also said that he would inform Israeli Premier Menahem Begin of Sadat's sincerity in trying to assure Israel of its security.

West Germany—Sadat conferred in Hamburg Feb. 9 with West German Chancellor Helmut Schmidt. Schmidt said he felt the European Community could make a contribution toward maintaining the peace momentum. However, he said he didn't think it would be a good idea for that body or "an individual member to intervene in a spectacularly public way."

Sadat lauded West Germany for supporting the Palestinian cause and for opposing the establishment of Israeli settlements in occupied Arab territories.

Austria—After departing West Germany Feb. 10, Sadat arrived Feb. 11 in Salzburg, where he conferred with Shimon Peres, leader of the Israeli opposition Labor Party. Later at a joint news conference, Sadat said his meeting with Peres was not intended to divide the Israelis. He pledged to continue his peace efforts "even if it is my last mission for me as president."

Peres said he had no message from Premier Begin for Sadat and that he had no mandate to negotiate with the Egyptian president. Begin had been informed of his planned meeting with Sadat, Peres said.

Peres was in Europe to attend a conference of the Socialist International. His talks with Sadat had been arranged by Austrian Chancellor Bruno Kreisky, who also conferred with Sadat in Salzburg.

Rumania—Sadat met in Bucharest Feb. 12 with Rumanian President Nicolae Ceausescu, a key intermediary in the preliminary phase of the Israeli-Egyptian peace dialogue. A brief statement issued later said Ceausescu had agreed with Sadat's views.

France—After meeting with French President Valery Giscard d'Estaing in Paris Feb. 12, Sadat said the following day that he had not discussed Egypt's quest for arms. However, French officials disclosed Feb. 13 that Cairo was discussing the possible purchase of additional French Mirage F-1 fighter planes. Egypt already had ordered 66 such aircraft.

Italy—Before returning to Cairo Feb. 13, Sadat conferred in Rome that day with Italian officials, including Premier Giulio Andreotti, and visited Pope Paul VI at the Vatican. The Pope praised Sadat for "working so intensively for peace." The pontiff called for establishment in Jerusalem of conditions that would eliminate "strife between the parties."

Israeli Settlements
& Occupied Areas

Israel Bars New Settlements in Sinai.
Israel's Cabinet Jan. 8, 1978 barred the
creation of new Israeli settlements in the
Sinai, but approved the expansion of the
20 existing ones and urged more Israelis to
move there.

The decision applied to 17 settlements
in the northern Sinai in the Rafah salient,
just south of the Gaza Strip, and to three
at the southern tip of the peninsula near
Sharm el Sheikh on the Red Sea. It was
not disclosed by how much the communities would be enlarged either in area or
in population. The Cabinet action laid to
rest unconfirmed reports of the previous
week that plans were underway for major
new settlements in the Rafah region.

The Cabinet decision on expanding the
Sinai settlements was not unanimous, as
the Democratic Party for Change, a
member of Premier Menahem Begin's
coalition government, voted against the
plan on the ground that it would undermine current Israeli-Egyptian peace
negotiations.

In statements Jan. 8 and 9, Begin
criticized what he called Egyptian President Anwar Sadat's "hard-line" stand
against the presence of Israeli settlements
in the Sinai after the conclusion of an Israeli-Egyptian peace agreement. Begin
warned that if Sadat rejected Israel's proposals for returning the Sinai to Egypt, Israel might withdraw the plan entirely or
modify it.

Sadat had said Jan. 7 that while Egypt
and Israel were in complete agreement on
the principle of total Israeli withdrawal
from the Sinai, Cairo remained opposed to
the continued presence of Israelis in the
region. Sadat said: "I do not agree to the
presence of a single Jewish settlement on
my land. Let them destroy them. Neither
do I allow a single Israeli civilian or soldier
to remain."

Sadat denied reports that Egypt might
be willing to lease Sharm el Sheikh to Israel. He also disclosed that during his
summit talks with Begin in Ismailia Dec.
25–26, 1977, the Israelis had raised the
question of their air bases in the Sinai.
Sadat said he had replied: "Burn them
down before you leave."

**U.S. Questions New Israeli Settle-
ments.** The establishment of four new Israeli settlements in the West Bank was
reported Jan. 29 and 31, 1978. The U.S.
expressed concern that the action might
be a violation of Israel's reputed pledge to
defer the establishment of new communities in the occupied territory.

The Israeli Knesset's Foreign Affairs
& Security Committee Jan. 10, by 14–9
vote, had approved three new West Bank
settlements and retroactively endorsed
a fourth that had been established in the
region several weeks earlier.

President Carter was reported Jan. 29
to have sent a personal message to Israeli
Premier Menahem Begin the previous
week in which he expressed "regret" over
"the effort to establish another illegal settlement" near the biblical site of Shiloh,
north of Jerusalem. The President,
however, said he was confident that the Israeli leader would "honor the commitment personally made to me and thus will
not permit this settlement to go forward."

Speaking at a news conference Jan. 30,
Carter said he thought the Israeli government "has not authorized the Shiloh settlement other than as an archeological ex-
ploration project." The President added
that he had "information that this is the
policy of the Israeli government, that this
is not an authorized settlement." He said
he understood Israeli policy to be that "no
new settlements would be authorized by
the government, that any increase in settlers would be an expansion of existing settlements as much as possible within the
aegis of the military."

The President reiterated U.S. opposition to the nearly 80 Israeli settlements already in existence in occupied Arab areas.

The Shiloh settlement was occupied by
25 families affiliated with the ultrareligious Gush Emunim. Some of the group's
followers were quoted as saying that the
explanation that the project was for
archeological purposes was a "cover."
They planned to create a permanent community on the site, the followers said.

The three other new settlements
reported under construction by the Israeli
press Jan. 31 were at Tapuach, about nine
kilometers (six miles) from the Arab town
of Nablus; at Silt-a-Dahar, north of
Nablus, and at Tel Kharis, in the western
part of the West Bank. According to the
reports, the government had approved
construction of the three sites Jan. 3 as

military outposts, but civilian settlers, mostly from Gush Emunim, were prepared to take over the centers in March.

Premier Begin discussed the controversial settlements with U.S. Ambassador Samuel W. Lewis Feb. 1. Lewis later told newsmen that he and Begin had clarified the question of the Shiloh settlement. Begin was said to have repeated to Lewis that the three new settlements near Nablus were military camps and that civilians would move in.

Dayan Denies Pledge to Carter— Foreign Minister Moshe Dayan denied Feb. 1 that in his meeting with Carter in September 1977 he had pledged that Israel would refrain from building settlements in the West Bank.

In an address to the Knesset (parliament), Dayan said he had informed the President that all Israeli governments were committed to establishing Jewish settlements in the area. But as long as Arab-Israeli peace talks were in progress, "new settlements in the coming months will be in the framework of military camps," Dayan said he had told Carter.

A U.S. government official Jan. 30 said Dayan had assured Carter that Israel would not set up any civilian communities in the West Bank for a year. Israel later clarified this to mean that its promise applied only for the year 1977, or for only four months after it had first been given. U.S. officials recalled that Dayan informed them of an Israeli commitment only to permit Israelis to move into existing civilian settlements in the West Bank or into eight designated military camps under Israeli army control.

Labor Party Opposes Settlements— The opposition Israeli Labor Party Feb. 2 objected to Premier Begin's policy on settlements. Specifically referring to Shiloh, the party said the government would "fool nobody" with its explanation that Israeli civilians were only there for archeological explorations. Begin's position, the party contended, "only projects Israel as deceptive."

The Israeli press also questioned the government's policy on Shiloh. The independent newspaper Haartez said Feb. 3 that the affair "does not add honor to the government of Israel" and raised questions about the regime's "credibility."

Premier Begin Feb. 3 denied Washington's assertions that Israel had given the U.S. a pledge that "there would not be more settlements."

The Israeli Cabinet Feb. 5 insisted that the activity at Shiloh, once the capital of ancient Israel, was an "archeological dig" and not a new settlement. A spokesman said the Cabinet issued the statement to counter unfounded foreign and domestic press reports that Israel was building a new civilian community on the site. Civilians had been given "a license only for archeological digging ... to find this ancient town but not to build a new one," the spokesman said.

The English-language Jerusalem Post commented Feb. 5 that the government's "decision to bow to Gush Emunim pressure ... had only served to trigger an unnecessary argument with Washington and cause damage to Israel's cause in American public opinion, ..."

U.S., Israel Feud Over Settlements. The U.S. Feb. 7 reiterated its opposition to the establishment of Israeli settlements in occupied Arab lands. The Carter Administration underscored its objections by releasing the text of a six-point chronology of events relating to the issue of the settlements. The document included information on an exchange of letters in January between the President and Israeli Premier Begin and Foreign Minister Dayan.

Carter's messages stressed his concern over Israeli plans to create new communities in the West Bank.

The American side said it had issued the chronology to counter a published report Feb. 7 by syndicated columnist Joseph Kraft that the U.S. was aware of Israeli plans for construction of four new settlements in the West Bank and raised no objections. The U.S. contended that the Israeli settlements were illegal and an impediment to peace.

State Secretary Cyrus Vance Feb. 9 restated American opposition to Israeli settlements in the northern Sinai Peninsula. The secretary's remarks brought a sharp response from Israel and added more fuel to existing U.S.-Israeli differences over the issue.

Speaking at a news conference, Vance linked the Sinai settlements with the status of the Israeli-occupied West Bank and Gaza Strip "and the intertwined Palestinian question," calling them the main obstacles to peace. "These two problems must be overcome if we are going to make progress" in Israeli-Egyptian negotiations, Vance said. "The continued settlements activity by Israel creates an obstacle to peace...."

Vance called on Israel to halt further work on the Sinai settlements, which he said "should not exist" because they violated international law. Vance also said he suspected that the Israeli archeological dig at Shiloh on the West Bank was actually a cover for a new settlement.

The Israeli Cabinet and Premier Menahem Begin Feb. 12 protested Vance's remarks. A statement issued by Begin after a Cabinet meeting said that Vance's utterances contradicted President Carter's statements made to Begin during their meeting in Washington Dec. 16–17, 1977, in which the premier presented his government's peace plan.

The Begin statement said the plan included "a specific reference to the continuous existence of the [Sinai] settlements within a United Nations zone and an Israeli defense contingent for their protection." During the Israeli-U.S. exchange at the time, "not only was there no [U.S.] reservation whatsoever made with regard to this reference, but the plan as a whole was received with a positive reaction," according to the Cabinet's version of the events.

Begin said U.S. criticism of Israel's settlement policies meant that the U.S. was "taking sides" in the peace negotiations.

A U.S. Administration official Feb. 12 denied Israel's inference that Carter had endorsed Begin's peace plan. "All we said to Begin" was that "the plan might be the basis for negotiations."

A State Department official Feb. 12 said Vance's remarks represented "no departure in policy for the United States."

Israeli Foreign Minister Moshe Dayan, who was in the U.S. on a tour to gather support for his government's position, Feb. 12 questioned the U.S. role as as neutral mediator in light of Vance's statement. If the secretary's remarks represented Administration policy, "you can't expect the Arabs to be more moderate than the Americans...," Dayan said during a stay in New York.

In a new rejoinder, the U.S. Administration issued a statement Feb. 13 saying Israeli settlements in all occupied Arab territories were an "obstacle to peace and contrary to international law." In endorsing Vance's stand, the White House said, "We also believe that prospects for a just and lasting peace in the Middle East will be enhanced if such settlement activity is stopped."

While calling Vance's statement "painful," Premier Begin Feb. 13 said U.S.-

---

Text of U.S. Statement on Israeli Settlements

Following is the text of the U.S. State Department chronology on the issue of Israeli settlements in occupied Arab territory:

With reference to the allegation that the United States did not object seriously to the latest Israeli settlements, the chronology is as follows:

1. On Jan. 5, 1978, Prime Minister [Menahem] Begin and Foreign Minister [Moshe] Dayan informed the U.S. ambassador in Israel of Israeli settlement plans in the Sinai and the West Bank.

2. On Jan. 6, the Administration sent a strong reply to Prime Minister Begin's and Dayan's Jan. 5 information. The reply expressed our concern about new settlement reports, particularly those of the Sinai. This reply was in the form of a personal message from the President—dispatched from Air Force One.

3. On Jan. 9, Prime Minister Begin informed the President of his government's decisions concerning Israeli settlement activities in the Sinai and the authorization for new settlements in military sites in the West Bank.

4. On Jan. 10, the President sent a letter to Prime Minister Begin responding to his letter of the 9th, restating our concern about the settlements and the effect they would have on the peace process.

5. On Jan. 23, a number of Gush Emunim settlers declared that a permanent civilian settlement would be erected at Shiloh.

6. On Jan. 27, the President sent a short message to Prime Minister Begin regarding the Shiloh settlement and restating the U.S. position.

Israeli friendship "will continue and will not be affected by this incident." Vance's position, Begin said, "did not affect our positive response" to renewed mediation efforts by Assistant Secretary of State Alfred L. Atherton Jr.

Israel Halts New Sinai Settlement Work.
Israeli Defense Minister Ezer Weizman had ordered a halt to work on new settlements in the northern Sinai, it was reported Feb. 13. A Defense Ministry spokesman said the stoppage was temporary.

Weizman was said to have issued the directive Jan. 31 just before he departed for Cairo for renewed negotiations with the Egyptians on the military aspects of a peace accord. Ministry sources said Weizman regarded work on the new projects as politically harmful.

Agriculture Minister Ariel Sharon, who was in charge of establishing new settlements, said in a newspaper interview published Feb. 13 that he was surprised by Weizman's order since it had not been cleared by the Cabinet. Although Weizman had not sought specific Cabinet approval of his decision, he had invoked authority that had previously been entrusted to him, another Cabinet source said.

While work on new settlements was suspended, expansion of existing ones and road-building in the Sinai were continuing as of Feb. 12, according to visitors to the region.

Israel Retains Settlement Policy.
The Israeli Cabinet Feb. 26 decided to retain its limited policy of establishing settlements in the Sinai Peninsula and the West Bank.

The decision specifically gave formal approval to the building of three new West Bank settlements—at Tel Kharis, Tapuach and Silt-a-Dahar. All three were near Israeli military camps. Tel Kharis already had been transformed into a civilian settlement. The two others were to assume similar status by the end of March.

Work had resumed on an Israeli settlement in the West Bank, Deputy Defense Minister Mordechai Zipori confirmed April 17. He said that ground leveling of the site at Nebi Salah, near Nablus, had started April 17. The project had been approved in January, but work was suspended in March pending Defense Minister Ezer Weizman's discussions in Washington on Israel's request for U.S. arms.

The Israeli Supreme Court May 25, however, ordered a temporary halt to work on the Nebi Salah settlement pending an appeal by Arab village leaders and landowners.

Weizman May 17 had submitted the plan for Nebi Salah and for expanding five other of Israel's West Bank settlements—Efrat, Maale Adumin, Givon, Kharas and Karnei Shomron. Under the proposal, the six settlements would be developed into urban centers and would be the last to be built by Israel in the West Bank.

The Defense Ministry hoped that 38,-000 families would eventually move into the six sites. There were currently 4,500 Israeli civilians in nearly three dozen small communities in the West Bank.

Bethlehem Mayor Elias Freij had charged May 23 that Israel was planning to take over West Bank property owned by Arabs living abroad by enlarging Jewish settlements in the occupied area. Freij said he had been officially informed April 12 that about 80,000 acres around Bethlehem would be turned over to the Israeli Custodian of Absentee Property, which in effect, would make Israel the owner. The property, according to Freij, belonged to Arabs residing in the U.S., Canada and Latin America.

The Israeli Lands Administration, which was responsible for the office of the Custodian, May 23 said its only plan for the absentee-owned lands was to tighten control to prevent any fraudulent transactions. Defense Minister Weizman denied that the government intended to seize West Bank land belonging to Arabs living abroad to expand the six settlements.

Carter Meets Begin, Impasse Remains.
U.S.-Israeli differences on a common approach to a Middle East peace settlement remained unresolved following talks in Washington March 21–22, 1978 between President Carter and Premier Menahem Begin.

The impasse was underscored by conflicting comments issued by the two leaders at the end of their discussions. The deadlock was further emphasized by Secretary of State Cyrus Vance, who said after meeting Begin at the State Department March 22, "I can't say that we've reduced the differences at this point."

In a farewell statement to Begin, Carter said that Israeli withdrawal from occupied Arab lands was necessary "if the peace negotiations are to succeed." This was a reaffirmation of the President's support of U.N. Security Council Resolution 242.

In his talks with Carter, Begin was said to have restated his unwillingness to concede that Resolution 242 necessarily required Israel to give up at least part of the West Bank.

Begin reviewed the negotiations he had conducted with Egyptian President Anwar Sadat and expressed hope they would be resumed.

In their talks Carter and Begin also remained in disagreement over Israeli settlements in occupied Arab territories, with Begin vowing the construction of more settlements in the West Bank.

Begin was said to have faced critical questioning March 21 in separate appearances before the Senate Foreign Relations Committee and the House International Relations Committee. One of the participants, Sen. Charles Percy (R, Ill.), said afterward that Begin had been told by the Senate committee that Israel's insistence on keeping its settlements "has divided Israel, divided the American Jewish community and caused an erosion of support for Israel" in the U.S.

Carter told the Senate Foreign Relations Committee March 23 that his talks with Begin had brought the diplomatic process "to a halt."

Carter said he was unable to change Begin's position on these three major points, the first and third of which represented compromise proposals drawn up by the President:

■ Refusal to relinquish Israeli settlements in the Sinai Peninsula as a condition for peace with Egypt or to accept the Carter plan for permitting Israeli settlers to remain under Egyptian or United Nations control rather than Israel's.

■ Refusal to acknowledge the proposition that Resolution 242 required Israeli withdrawal from at least part of the West Bank and Gaza Strip.

■ Objection to Carter's plan for a five-year interim international arrangement for the West Bank and Gaza Strip, after which Arab residents there would decide whether to join Israel or Jordan or remain under international control.

Before departing Washington March 23, Begin made an appeal for support of his policies in a speech and news conference at the National Press Club.

Begin restated his position in detail and expressed "deep sorrow" that the Carter Administration rejected it after having described his proposals in December 1977 as a "step forward." The premier attributed the reversal of the U.S. views to Egyptian influence.

On returning to Israel March 24, Begin said his talks with Carter had been "difficult" and that "we faced several demands which we could not accept."

Speaking at an airport interview, Begin said: "To everyone else, including the United States, the problems on the agenda are of policy . . . To us they are problems of life, of existence and of making sure of our future."

Begin Wins Support—The Israeli Cabinet March 26 unanimously endorsed Begin's proposals, and the Knesset March 29 approved them by 64–32 vote.

After Begin's meeting with his ministers, in which he reviewed his talks with Carter, the Cabinet issued a communique saying that it "reemphasizes its efforts to reach a full and comprehensive peace in the Middle East."

Begin's peace plan submitted to the Egyptians in the now stalled peace talks constituted "a fair basis for negotiating with the Arab states," the communique added.

During the debate, opposition critics led by the Labor Party supported President Carter's stand against Begin's interpretation of United Nations Security Council Resolution 242.

Most opposition members, however, supported the government's refusal to accept the U.S. demand for a referendum of Arabs in the West Bank and Gaza Strip to determine their future. They also backed the government's opposition to American insistence on dismantling Israeli settlements in the West Bank and Sinai Peninsula.

Coalition Government Urged—Defense Minister Ezer Weizman called for a "national peace government" that would include the opposition Labor Party in order to present the U.S. with a united front on a peace settlement, according to an interview published March 24 in the Israeli newspaper Maariv. Weizman's proposal was made amid opposition demands that Begin be replaced because of what it regarded as his disastrous meeting with Carter.

In his interview, however, Weizman supported the stand Begin had taken in his talks with Carter. "To portray this sharp clash between our concept and the American demands as a confrontation between Premier Begin and President Carter is unfair to the premier and politically harmful," the defense minister said.

Weizman said a "national government" should conduct negotiations directly with Egypt and not through the U.S. He charged that the Cairo-Jerusalem shuttle diplomacy of U.S. Assistant Secretary of State Alfred L. Atherton Jr. in February and early March had "obstructed the peace process."

Sadat-Weizman Talks Fail. Israeli Defense Minister Weizman conferred with Egyptian President Sadat in Cairo March 30–31 in an unsuccessful effort to revive Egyptian-Israeli peace talks.

Egypt refused to revive negotiations of the joint Israeli and Egyptian Political and Military committees as requested by the Jerusalem government. Sadat said after Weizman left Cairo March 31 that their countries remained deadlocked, "mainly in the field of solving the Palestinian question."

An Egyptian government spokesman said formal talks could not start again "unless Israel changes its position." This was a reference to Cairo's demand that Israel agree beforehand to a declaration of principles committing itself to granting self-determination to the Palestinians in the West Bank and Gaza Strip and to total withdrawal from occupied Arab lands.

Weizman, who also conferred in Cairo with Egyptian War Minister Mohammed Abdel Ghany el-Gamasy, briefed the Israeli Cabinet March 31 and April 2 on his talks. A Cabinet communique released later April 2 expressed regret that Egypt had refused Israel's offer to resume talks. It urged Cairo to "reexamine the positive Israeli proposals aimed at the renewal of peace negotiations."

Weizman's mission to Egypt had been initiated by Israel and was announced by Jerusalem March 29. Premier Menahem Begin had disclosed the previous day that he had sent a letter to Sadat through U.S. diplomatic channels urging revival of peace discussions. The message, in response to a recent communication from the Egyptian leader, suggested that Sadat submit counter-proposals to Israel's peace plan.

Sadat April 5 called on Begin to "be more flexible" in peace negotiations. He said Weizman was welcome to return for further talks "whenever there are new ideas."

Lauding U.S. diplomatic efforts in the Middle East, Sadat said, "the American role is very important because America and President Carter are no more mediators. He is a full partner. He has agreed on this conception and for me this is very satisfying."

Demands in the Egyptian Parliament April 13 that Cairo drop all efforts to resume peace discussions with Israel brought a sharp rebuff from the government.

Deputy Foreign Minister Ghali Butros said there would be "negotiations and more negotiations" and that the peace drive was still "at the beginning of the road." American pressure on Israel to soften its position, Ghali said, "has begun and will increase in the coming weeks and months."

Atherton Resumes Mission—U.S. special Middle East envoy Alfred L. Atherton Jr. conferred with government officials in Egypt April 21–25 to press the Carter Administration's efforts for reviving the peace talks.

Atherton said on his arrival in Cairo that he was not bringing any new American proposals to break the deadlock between Egypt and Israel. He said he was only "looking for new ideas, new ways to move the peace process forward."

Following talks with President Anwar Sadat April 23, Atherton said they had reached "a much clearer understanding" on possible means of resuming the stalled negotiations. Atherton said he thought Sadat was waiting for a change in Israeli policy before renewing the talks.

Israelis Stage Anti-Begin Rally. About 4,000 Israelis April 26, 1978 rallied protesting the West Bank policies of Premier Menahem Begin. The demonstrators marched along a 15-mile (24-kilometer) stretch of highway leading from Tel Aviv to Jerusalem, carrying placards that urged Begin to make territorial concessions in Israeli-occupied Arab lands to achieve a peace ; settlement.

The rally was an offshoot of a "Peace Now" campaign launched earlier in April by 300 Israeli military reservists. It ended when a scroll and postcards bearing 60,-000 signatures were handed to Begin's office in Jerusalem. The postcards carried a message urging Begin to refrain from establishing any more Israeli settlements in occupied Arab lands.

The "Peace Now" campaign had received support in a petition signed by 360 professors and intellectuals and published in a Tel Aviv newspaper April 25. The statement charged that "the government's policy is not leading to compromise, but to the loss of friends and the increasing of Israel's isolation."

A counterdemonstration supporting Begin had been held in Tel Aviv April 15 by a group calling itself "Secure Peace."

U.S., Israel Seek Peace Talks Renewal. Israeli Foreign Minister Moshe Dayan and U.S. Secretary of State Cyrus Vance met in Washington April 26–27 to discuss prospects for resuming the stalled peace talks between Egypt and Israel.

Both men sought to reconcile their countries' differences over the language for a declaration of principles that would serve as a guideline for an overall Middle East peace settlement.

At the conclusion of their talks, Dayan said in an interview that he and Vance had concentrated on the problem of the West Bank and Gaza Strip and the future of the one million Arab inhabitants of the Israeli-occupied territory.

Carter Opposes Independent Palestinian State. In a New York Times Special Features interview circulated April 30, President Carter supported many Israeli peace goals.

The President reaffirmed his opposition to "an independent Palestinian state on the West Bank" and said a permanent peace settlement should not "call for a complete Israeli withdrawal from occupied [Arab] territories." The President again said he favored a peace agreement

"based substantially upon the home-rule proposal" offered by Premier Begin in December 1977.

Expressions of concern over Carter's remarks voiced by Egyptian Foreign Minister Mohammed Ibrahim Kamel, brought reassurances from the Carter Administration, Kamel disclosed May 1. He said that U.S. Ambassador Hermann F. Eilts had told him that the U.S. did not consider Begin's plan for the West Bank as "a true basis for a Middle East settlement because it does not allow the Palestinians to participate in determining their future."

A White House spokesman May 1 confirmed that the remarks in the interview attributed to Carter were basically accurate. A State Department official April 30 had said that Egypt was aware of Carter's position but always complained when the President's views were aired publicly, since Cairo officially endorsed the possibility of an independent Palestinian state. President Anwar Sadat had agreed with Carter that a Palestinian state be linked to Jordan.

Carter & Israel—Carter reaffirmed U.S. support for Israel May 1 in welcoming Premier Menahem Begin at the White House. Begin had arrived in the U.S. the previous day for a week of celebrations marking Israel's 30th anniversary of independence and to continue talks with U.S. officials in further efforts to end the impasse in Middle East peace negotiations.

Greeting Begin, Carter said: "For 30 years we have stood at the side of . . . Israel. I can say without reservation . . . that we will continue to do so not just for another 30 years, but forever."

Begin's discussions with Carter and Secretary of State Cyrus Vance were a follow-up to similar talks Foreign Minister Moshe Dayan had held in Washington April 26-27.

In a press briefing after the meeting, a White House spokesman said Carter had reaffirmed American support for Israel's integrity and security, and also had stressed the importance of the U.S. maintaining and bolstering ties with moderate Arab states. Begin and Carter "made it quite clear that we do have differences but that it is possible for friends to have differences," the spokesman said.

During a plane flight to Los Angeles later May 1 Begin told reporters of a possible breakthrough in peace negotiations because "of the change of atmosphere in relations between the United States and Israel." Israeli officials aboard the plane noted that the change was more of atmosphere than of substance. However, they acknowledged that the easing of the strained U.S.-Israeli ties that had prevailed six weeks earlier was of major importance.

Israeli General's Remarks Disputed. Israeli Chief of Staff Lt. Gen. Rafael Eitan created a political controversy when he said May 11 that he questioned the sincerity of Egypt's peace initiatives. He also said Israel could not defend itself unless it retained the West Bank and Golan Heights.

In a television interview, Eitan said, "The basic intention of the Arabs had not changed. They want to obliterate us." He described the Arabs' current diplomatic moves as "other means" of destroying Israel. "Until they make a truthful declaration that they no longer want the liquidation of Israel, we must treat them as if they wish to destroy us," Eitan said.

Eitan's right to express his views was upheld at a regular Cabinet meeting May 14. By a vote of 14-3, the ministers cut off debate on the issue, which had been raised at the meeting by Defense Minister Ezer Weizman. Weizman had earlier supported Eitan, saying his remarks had been military, not political, in nature.

Sadat's War Threat. For a second time in two days, President Anwar Sadat June 7 warned that Egypt would resort to war to "liberate our lands if Israel continues its attitude and misunderstanding of the spirit of the [Egyptian] peace initiative." Sadat made the statement in an address to Egyptian troops at Suez City.

In his address, Sadat also disclosed that in his meetings with Ezer Weizman in March, the Israeli defense minister had proposed returning all of the Sinai to Egypt in exchange for a separate Israeli-Egyptian peace agreement. Sadat said he had rejected the plan because it would not have brought peace unless other Arab states were brought into an accord.

Premier Menahem Begin charged June 8 that Sadat's remarks about renewing a Middle East conflict violated the pledge of no war he had made during his visit to Jerusalem in November 1977.

Israel Defers Move on West Bank, Gaza. The Israeli Cabinet June 18 adopted a policy in support of Premier Menahem Begin's hard line stand on the future of the occupied West Bank and Gaza Strip.

A vaguely worded statement by the ministers was issued in response to a request by the U.S. for an Israeli commitment to negotiate "the permanent status" of the two territories after a five-year period of autonomy for the Arab residents of the regions, as proposed by Begin in his December 1977 peace plan.

The Carter Administration also had asked whether Israel would permit West Bank and Gaza Arabs to decide their future by plebiscite or some other means. The U.S. pressured Israel for a clear-cut position on the occupied territories in an effort to help resumption of the stalled Israeli-Egyptian peace talks.

The Cabinet statement, which was endorsed by the Knesset (parliament) June 19, said that on expiration of the five-year autonomy period, "the nature of the future relations between the parties will be considered and agreed upon" by Israel and the elected representatives of the West Bank and Gaza Strip. This phrase was regarded as a willingness by Israel to reconsider the form of goverment for the two occupied areas in contrast to Begin's original proposal, which said that details of the autonomy plan would merely be reexamined.

Fourteen of the 19 Cabinet members voted for the statement. The five dissenters were Defense Minister Ezer Weizman and four members of the Democratic Movement for Change, which belonged to the coalition government.

The Knesset approved the Cabinet stand by a 59-37 vote. Ten deputies abstained—Deputy Premier Yigal Yadin and nine other members of his Democratic Movement for Change.

The Knesset voted down five opposition alternative proposals, one of which was a Labor Party plan calling on the government to agree to territorial concessions in the occupied areas without giving them up entirely.

In Knesset debate, Labor Party leader Shimon Peres called the Cabinet stand "a

paper barrier of very clever formulation."
He warned that it would only "deepen the
rift" between Israel and the U.S. and
would impede negotiations with Egypt.

In defending the policy, Foreign
Minister Dayan told the Knesset that
there was no need now for the government
to decide on the status of the West Bank
and Gaza Strip.

U.S. Reaction—The U.S., in private
statements made June 20, rejected the Israeli formula as an inadequate response to
American peace proposals. The officials,
however, said the Administration would
avoid a confrontation with Israel and
instead would press ahead with efforts for
a negotiated settlement.

In its first official reaction, the State
Department June 21 expressed "regret
that the Israelis did not fully respond to
our questions."

The department disclosed that the U.S.
had been discussing with Egypt ideas on
the West Bank-Gaza problem and would
now be contacting both Israel and Egypt
about further steps in negotiations.

Israel's policy came in for sharp
criticism June 22 from one of its strongest
supporters in Congress, Sen. Jacob K. Javits (R, N.Y.). Addressing the Senate, Javits called Israel's statement "a disappointment," saying that the U.S. "is correct in its expectations of a more positive
reply from Israel." He urged Israel to be
more forthcoming "to assist the United
States in its role as mediator. . . ."

Egyptian Reaction—Egyptian President
Anwar Sadat said June 20 that Israel's
"response to the American questions was
loose and not positive." Despite
Jerusalem's decision, Sadat said he was
"optimistic" about his peace initiative and
was prepared to discuss "directly any new
plans that Israel will submit" to help bring
about a renewal of their deadlocked talks.

Sadat repeated his demands for Israeli
return of all Arab lands captured in the
1967 war and for resolution of "all aspects
of the Palestinian question."

Egyptian Foreign Minister Mohammed
Ibrahim Kamel had denounced what he
called the Israeli Cabinet's "intransigence" in a meeting June 19 with
Hermann F. Eilts, U.S. ambassador to
Cairo. Nevertheless, Egypt would
continue to cooperate with the U.S. effort
to revive the stalled peace initiative,
Kamel said.

Israel Rejects Egyptian Plan. The Israeli
Cabinet June 25 rejected an Egyptian proposal on Israeli-occupied territory before
it formally received the plan. The
Egyptian formula called for Israel to
return the West Bank and the Gaza
Strip to Egypt, and for Egypt and
Jordan to negotiate with Israel for security arrangements and for some autonomy for the Arabs in the two territories. President Anwar Sadat had suggested the plan informally in interviews in
May as an alternative to negotiating with
Israel for the creation of an independent
Palestinian state.

Egyptian Foreign Minister Mohammed
Ibrahim Kamel had announced June 24
that the Sadat proposal was being drafted
and that it would be submitted later in the
week to the U.S. for transmission to Israel.

In rejecting the plan, an Israel Cabinet
spokesman said, "As broadcast from
Cairo, Sadat's statements constitute a
prior condition. If what Egypt wants to
present constitutes a prior condition, then
it is unacceptable. We insist that there be
negotiations without prior conditions."

Foreign Minister Kamel said June 26
that Egypt would formally submit the proposal despite Israel's rejection of it. The
Israeli Cabinet's dismissal of the formula
was surprising since "it took them some
two months to answer the questions the
United States asked them" concerning
the future of the West Bank and Gaza
Strip, Kamel said.

A statement issued by the Egyptian
Foreign Ministry June 26 said it was
"strange that Israel rushes to reject proposals which are still being drafted in
Egypt and which Israel does not know of."
The Israel action created "obstacles to
peace," the ministry said.

Israeli Premier Menahem Begin June
27 took issue with President Carter's
statement of the previous day that the Israeli Cabinet had "rejected an Egyptian
proposal that had not yet been made."
Begin reiterated his government's position
that, "To this day Egypt has not presented
a peace plan and therefore no such plan
has been rejected by Israel."

What the Cabinet had spurned was
President Sadat's demand, broadcast by
Cairo radio, that Israel relinquish the
West Bank to Jordan and the Gaza Strip
to Egypt as a condition prior to negotia-
tions, Begin said.

Weizman, Begin Dispute Policies—
Defense Minister Ezer Weizman's opposition to Premier Begin's policies on occupied Arab territories also was discussed
at the June 25 Cabinet meeting,
reportedly focusing on purportedly dis-
paraging remarks made by Weizman
about Begin and Foreign Minister Moshe
Dayan. Weizman was among four
ministers who had voted against a statement adopted by the Cabinet June 18 in
support of Begin's stand to defer any move
for the present on the West Bank and
Gaza Strip.

Weizman reportedly had stormed out of
the Cabinet meeting, saying he had to
prepare Israel "for the next war."

Weizman's office denied reports that he
had declared in a corridor outside the
premier's office that Begin and Dayan
"have been lying to us for months. They
are leading the nation to war."

Weizman's alleged statement was said
to have prompted some Cabinet members
to demand his resignation.

In his first public comment on the controversy, Weizman said June 23 that he
intended to remain in the Cabinet and
fight for his principles. He said that President Sadat's mild rejection June 20 of the
Cabinet statement "just proves I'm
right," that Sadat "is sincere" in his
desire for peace.

Egypt, Israel Maintain Contacts—The
June 25 Cabinet meeting that rejected the
Egyptian proposal also authorized Israeli
Defense Minister Ezer Weizman to renew
his meetings with Egyptian War Minister
Mohammed Abdel Ghany el-Gamasy in
an attempt to resume the stalled
Egyptian-Israeli peace talks, it was
reported June 27.

An Israeli Knesset (parliament)
member had said June 21 that Weizman
had been in telephone contact with Gamasy and that the two defense aides had
been conferring every three or four days.

Opposition Labor Party leader Shimon
Peres said June 21 that he was maintaining contacts with President Sadat through
intermediaries.

Egypt Details Peace Plan. Egypt formally made public its plan for peace in the
Middle East in a document made public by
the U.S. July 5. The formula was in
response to one drawn up by Israeli
Premier Menahem Begin in December

1977, which had been rejected by Egypt.
Cairo's proposal had first been handed to
U.S. Vice President Walter Mondale by
President Anwar Sadat during Mondale's
brief stopover in Alexandria July 3, follow-
ing his four-day visit to Israel.

Under the Egyptian plan, Israel would
withdraw from the West Bank, East
Jerusalem and the Gaza Strip in a five-
year period and turn over transitional
sovereignty to Jordan and Egypt. Israel
would be required to immediately abandon
its settlements and military rule in the occupied territories. Israel, Egypt, Jordan,
the United Nations and "representatives
of the Palestinian people" would negotiate
details of the Israeli withdrawal and transitional rule of Egypt and Jordan. After
expiration of the five-year period, the
Arab residents of the West Bank and
Gaza Strip "will be able to determine their
own future."

The Egyptian document did not refer to
the Palestine Liberation Organization,
with which Israel refused to negotiate, or
the Israeli occupation of Syria's Golan
Heights.

Israel Formally Rejects Plan—The Egyptian peace plan, calling for Israel's withdrawal from the West Bank and Gaza
Strip, was formally rejected by the Israeli
Cabinet July 9.

The Cabinet also accepted an American
proposal for a meeting of the Israeli and
Egyptian foreign ministers and U.S.
Secretary of State Cyrus Vance in London
July 18-19.

A Cabinet communique described the
Egyptian formula as "unacceptable to Israel" and one that could not "lead to the
establishment of peace in the Middle East
and the conclusion of peace treaties with
Israel."

A Cabinet spokesman said there was
still only one peace plan on the table, that
of Premier Menahem Begin. "The
Egyptian proposals are proposals for
withdrawal," the spokesman said, adding
that it represented "extreme decisions,
the likes of which we haven't seen since
1967."

A detailed analysis of Israel's reasons
for turning down Cairo's plan was given to
newsmen July 11 by Meir Rosenne, legal
adviser of the Foreign Ministry.

The following points were made by
Rosenne:

■ Egypt called for Israeli withdrawals
but made no mention of peace treaties.

■ Egypt's failure to mention United Nations resolutions 242 and 338, the suggested framework for peace, was a "distortion" since those documents did not call for total Israeli withdrawal from occupied Arab territories, while Cairo's latest plan did.

■ The Egyptian plan was tougher than the formula worked out by Presidents Anwar Sadat and Jimmy Carter at Aswan, Egypt Jan. 4. The formula, opposed by Israel, urged Palestinian participation with the other parties in resolving their problems. Egypt's latest proposal spoke of Palestinians determining their own future without the participation of others.

■ Egypt's plan referred to Palestinian refugees but not to Jewish refugees who fled to Israel from Arab lands.

■ United Nations involvement in peace talks would mean a U.N. role in expediting Israeli withdrawals without providing Israel with security guarantees.

■ Cairo called for Israeli abandonment of East Jerusalem, which had not been discussed at the Egyptian–Israeli talks at Ismailia in December 1977.

■ The failure of the Egyptian plan to mention the demands of the Palestine Liberation Organization was not a positive step because the proposal contained "nothing contrary to the philosophy of the PLO."

Sadat Disappointed—Egyptian President Anwar Sadat July 10 expressed "keen disappointment" over Israel's rejection of his proposal.

Sadat also said he was "not particularly optimistic" about the outcome of the forthcoming foreign minister's conference in London. His latter statement was made to Nahum Goldmann, former president of the World Jewish Congress, who conferred with Sadat in Vienna.

Sadat had discussed peace prospects in the Austrian capital July 9 with Israeli opposition Labor Party leader Shimon Peres. The two men failed to reconcile their divergent views and made no plans to meet again.

The Sadat-Peres talks had been arranged by Austrian Chancellor Bruno Kreisky and former West German Chancellor Willy Brandt, both of whom participated in part of the discussions.

Kreisky and Brandt July 10 made public a plan of their own for a Middle East peace settlement. It called for continued negotiations until peace treaties were con-

---

Text of Egyptian Plan for West Bank and Gaza Strip

Following is the text of the Egyptian plan for the West Bank and Gaza Strip that President Anwar Sadat submitted to U.S. Vice President Mondale in Alexandria July 3 for relay to Israel.

Proposals relative to withdrawal from the West Bank and Gaza and security arrangements.

I

The establishment of a just and lasting peace in the Middle East necessitates a just solution of the Palestinian question in all its aspects on the basis of the legitimate rights of the Palestinian people and taking into consideration the legitimate security concerns of all the parties.

II

In order to insure a peaceful and orderly transfer of authority there shall be a transitional period not exceeding five years at the end of which the Palestinian people will be able to determine their own future.

III

Talks shall take place between Egypt, Jordan, Israel and representatives of the Palestinian people with the participation of the U.N. with a view to agreeing upon:

A. Details of the transitional regime.
B. Timetable for the Israeli withdrawal.
C. Mutual security arrangements for all the parties concerned during and following the transitional period.
D. Modalities for the implementation of relevant U.N. resolutions on Palestinian refugees.
E. Other issues considered appropriate by all parties.

IV

Israel shall withdraw from the West Bank (including Jerusalem) and the Gaza Strip, occupied since June 1967. The Israeli withdrawal applies to the settlements established in the occupied territories.

V

The Israeli military government in the West Bank and the Gaza Strip shall be abolished at the outset of the transitional period. Supervision over the administration of the West Bank shall become the responsibility of Jordan and supervision over the administration of the Gaza Strip shall become the responsibility of Egypt. Jordan and Egypt shall carry out their responsibility in cooperation with freely elected representatives of the Palestinian people who shall exercise direct authority over the administration of the West Bank and Gaza. The U.N. shall supervise and facilitate the Israeli withdrawal and the restoration of Arab authority.

VI

Egypt and Jordan shall guarantee that the security arrangements to be agreed upon will continue to be respected in the West Bank and Gaza.

cluded; a new system of regional relations based on close cooperation as part of any accord; Israeli withdrawal to secure boundaries with provisions for demilitarization and for Israeli security needs, and the right of the Palestinians to participate in the resolution of their problems through their elected representatives.

Peres and Sadat had been shown the plan July 9 before it was made public. Sadat accepted the plan while Peres described it as a "very realistic document, containing many positive points."

Kreisky-Brandt Plan Assailed—Israeli Foreign Minister Moshe Dayan condemned the Kreisky-Brandt formula as worse for Israel than the one developed by Sadat and President Carter in Aswan, it was reported July 13.

Dayan was especially critical of the mention of the Palestinians' "elected representatives," which he said was an obvious reference to the Palestine Liberation Organization.

New Sadat Proposal. Sadat reportedly submitted a new proposal at a meeting with Israeli Defense Minister Weizman near Salzburg, Austria July 13. The discussions, the first between the two men since March 31, were held in response to an urgent invitation sent to Weizman July 12 by Egyptian War Minister Mohammed Abdel Ghany el-Gamasy. Weizman also held separate talks with Gamasy.

Weizman later told newsmen that he had brought new proposals to break the Israeli-Egyptian deadlock, but declined to discuss them. Sadat's plan also remained undisclosed, although it reportedly represented a softening of his previous position. He indicated that he would now accept the presence of Israeli military forces in the West Bank during and after the five-year transition plan as outlined in his original proposal.

Sadat returned to Cairo July 14 from his seven-day visit to Austria, saying that his meetings with Weizman as well as with Israeli opposition Labor Party leader Shimon Peres July 9, had been "more than successful."

The Israeli Cabinet July 16 deferred consideration of the new Sadat proposal pending a scheduled Israeli-Egyptian foreign ministers meeting in England. The Israeli ministers were reportedly dis-pleased with Weizman's apparent by-passing of Premier Menahem Begin to confer with Sadat on his own. They also leveled implied criticism against Peres for his private audience with Sadat.

Begin was said to have cleared Weizman's meeting with Sadat for fear that refusal to do so would have left the premier open to charges that he was not interested in fully exploring peace prospects because of personal pique.

Begin was said to have been further distressed with Weizman's mission to Austria following publication July 16 of a Jerusalem Post interview with Sadat. In the article, Sadat lauded Weizman and Peres and referred to Begin as "hardline," "suspicious" and "bitter." He was quoted as saying that he could speak "the same language" with Weizman and Peres but not with Begin.

A Cabinet spokesman took note of published reports, "which weren't denied," that Sadat "was not willing to maintain a link or have any contact whatsoever with the premier. The government believes that the people of Israel did not give the president of Egypt the authority to determine who will represent the state of Israel."

Begin assailed Peres' meeting with Sadat in Vienna during a sharp exchange with the Labor Party leader in the Knesset July 19.

Peres denied Begin's charges that he sought to negotiate territorial compromises with the Egyptian leader. He said that Sadat had told him he wanted Israel to return all of the Sinai to Egypt but that he was willing to permit Israel to retain some part of the West Bank. Peres called the Begin government's position of holding on to all of occupied Arab territories a "recipe for isolation."

Israeli-Egyptian Talks. The Israeli and Egyptian foreign ministers met in England July 18–19 to discuss their countries' conflicting peace plans for the Israeli-occupied West Bank and Gaza Strip. Both sides held to their positions at the U.S.-sponsored conference.

Secretary of State Cyrus Vance attended the meetings along with Moshe Dayan and Mohammed Ibrahim Kamel. Vance said at the conclusion of the talks July 19 that enough results had been accomplished to warrant a continued U.S. mediation effort.

Vance conceded that "major differences remain between the positions of both sides." But the "mere holding of the meeting here in a sense is progress," the secretary said. "These were the most candid and probing discussions I have heard between the parties," he added.

The Israelis and Egyptians also were divided over whether their meetings constituted direct talks. After the conclusion of the first session July 18, a newsman asked whether the discussions were a continuation of the meeting in Jerusalem in January that had abruptly ended when President Anwar Sadat recalled his delegation. An Israeli spokesman replied that both sides indeed were in "direct negotiations." An Egyptian delegation spokesman challenged this view, saying that his country had agreed to the meeting at the invitation of the U.S., "which is making an effort to get the talks started, and when we find encouraging elements then the direct negotiations will be started again." The current discussions were "preparatory to further talks if there are enough grounds to hold them," the spokesman said.

(The talks had been scheduled to be held at a hotel in London, but the U.S., Israel and Egypt agreed July 16 to shift the discussions to Leeds Castle in Kent. British Prime Minister James Callaghan had requested the transfer July 15 for security reasons.)

Carter Hints Geneva Conference—President Carter had hinted June 30 that the U.S. might press for the reconvening of the Geneva conference if current American efforts to break the Egyptian-Israeli deadlock failed. The President, whose remarks to a press group were released July 1, said that if his Administration's attempts to bring both sides together brought no results, "then, of course, the United Nations has a role to play in the Middle East. . . . And as you know, the Geneva conference is, as a result of the United Nations resolution [that was adopted following the end of the 1973 Arab-Israeli war], the basic framework for peace and that is always a fallback position if we fail as an intermediary or mediator."

Carter said that the Egyptian peace plan, although "a step in the right direction," was "inadequate." Should the London foreign ministers' conference fail

to end the Israeli-Egyptian impasse, then revival of the Geneva conference was called for, the President said.

Israeli officials and a U.S. delegation with Vice President Walter Mondale in Jerusalem expressed surprise at Carter's statement, it was reported July 1. The U.S. mission was said to have voiced disappointment because it regarded the release of Carter's remarks as undermining the purpose of Mondale's visit.

Israeli officials found that Carter's remarks revived their fears that the reconvening of the Geneva conference would lead to invitations to the Soviet Union and the Palestine Liberation Organization, both parties opposed by Israel. The Israelis also lacked confidence in U.N. involvement in the Middle East peace process.

The principal object of Mondale's mission was to present letters from President Carter to the leaders of Israel and Egypt urging a speedy resumption of their deadlocked talks. The vice president also sought to ease the severe strain in U.S.-Israeli relations caused by the two nations' divergent views on a peace settlement.

Mondale reaffirmed the U.S. commitment to Israel at a state dinner given in his honor July 2. But he said the U.S. was "convinced that without eventual withdrawal on all fronts, to boundaries agreed upon in negotiations and safeguarded by effective security arrangements, there can be no lasting peace."

Mondale said after a final private meeting with Begin July 3 that they had agreed on the need for a quick resumption of talks between Israel and Egypt. "The sooner we begin the negotiating process again, the sooner the mood will change from one of desperation . . . to one of hopefulness," Mondale said.

The vice president then flew to Alexandria, where he received the Egyptian peace plan from Sadat and Cairo's acceptance of the American invitation to attend the London conference.

Dayan Softens Stand—Israeli Foreign Minister Moshe Dayan said July 24 that he had offered to soften Israel's stand on the West Bank and Gaza Strip in a private memorandum handed July 18 to U.S. Secretary of State Cyrus Vance at the foreign ministers conference in England. Under the proposal, Israel would discuss the question of sovereignty for the two territories after five years if the Arabs in turn accepted Israel's plan for granting autonomy to the Arab residents of the areas.

The new plan was in contrast to one approved by the Israeli Cabinet June 18. The previous proposal merely stated that after expiration of the five-year autonomy period, "the nature of the future relations between the parties will be considered and agreed upon" by Israel and the West Bank and Gaza leaders.

Dayan submitted the plan to the Knesset (parliament), which approved it by a vote of 69 to 37 along party lines.

Egypt rejected the new Israeli offer July 25 as "nothing new."

Sadat Calls Begin 'Obstacle' to Peace. President Sadat accused Premier Begin July 22 of blocking a peace accord. "If Israel, as it has said for 30 years, is really for peace, there is only one obstacle to peace—Begin," Sadat said. "Peace," he added, "can be established within hours."

Sadat made the remarks in a speech at a political rally on the eve of the anniversary of the 1952 officers' revolution that deposed the Egyptian monarchy.

Sadat offered Israel "peace," "guarantees for both sides," "neighborly co-existence," and "recognition," but no Arab lands. Egypt opposed a separate peace with Israel, but remained "open to any new elements," Sadat declared.

Sadat said Egypt had agreed to attend the foreign ministers conference with Israel in England July 18-19 only at the request of President Carter. Lauding the President's mediation efforts, Sadat said, "If Carter had been in power in 1967, without Arthur Goldberg, the Zionist, we wouldn't have suffered what we are suffering today." (Goldberg was the U.S. ambassador to the United Nations during and after the 1967 war in which Israel occupied the Sinai, Gaza Strip, West Bank and the Golan Heights.)

Israel Bars Return of Sinai Areas—The Israeli Cabinet July 23 rejected a request by President Sadat that Israel make a conciliatory gesture by returning to Egypt Mt. Sinai and the town of El Arish, both on the Sinai Peninsula. The proposal had been given to Israeli Defense Minister Ezer Weizman at his meeting with Sadat in Austria July 13 and was made public by the Cabinet.

Begin told newsmen after the Cabinet meeting that Sadat's proposal was impractical. "Nobody can get anything for nothing and this is going to be the policy of Israel," he said.

The premier expanded on this theme later July 23 in a CBS-TV interview program, *Face the Nation*. Begin said the peace proposal he had offered in December 1977 providing autonomy for Arabs in the West Bank and Gaza Strip represented a "gesture." Insisting on reciprocity, Begin asked, "Why should we give now suddenly El Arish to Sadat without any reply by his side?"

Referring to minutes of the London foreign ministers conference brought back by Moshe Dayan, Begin said the Egyptians had been asked whether they would be willing to compromise on the West Bank and Gaza Strip. "Their reply," the premier said, "was, twice, 'of course not, of course not.'"

Egypt Expels Israeli Mission. Egypt July 26 ordered the expulsion of the Israeli military mission based near Alexandria. The 10 military technicians and communication specialists returned home July 27.

Egyptian officials said the action was taken to avoid further direct contacts with Israel until Jerusalem softened its position in the deadlocked peace talks.

The move came after President Anwar Sadat met with the National Security Council, Egypt's highest policy-making body. Foreign Minister Mohammed Ibrahim Kamel said the Council believed that while Cairo supported the idea of direct negotiations, it felt they would be a "waste of time" unless Israel came forth with radical concessions.

The Israeli mission had stayed behind in Egypt after direct peace talks collapsed in January. The group's function following those meetings was to transmit peace feelers between Cairo and Egypt.

The recall of the Israelis from Alexandria was the culmination of several days of sharp public exchanges between Israel and Egypt in the wake of their foreign ministers' conference in England July 18-19.

The continued impasse was underscored by Premier Menahem Begin in a television interview July 26 in which he disclosed Cairo's decision.

Referring to Sadat's demand for total Israeli withdrawal from the West Bank and from the Gaza Strip, Begin said the Egyptian leader "wants peace with Israel according to his conditions, but his conditions mean the destruction of Israel."

In the past Begin had stressed Israel's biblical links with those territories. In his latest statement, the premier asserted that the territories were vital to Israel's security. A return to the prewar borders, he said, would pose a threat to Israel's population centers.

Begin also assailed the Israeli opposition Labor Party's charges that his refusal to compromise on territories impeded progress toward peace. Begin asserted that the party's criticism was a deception since the Egyptians already had stated they were not interested in territorial compromise but in total Israeli withdrawal.

Egypt Bars New Talks with Israel. Egyptian President Anwar Sadat said July 30, 1978 that he opposed a resumption of direct peace talks with Israel at that time because, he said, "the moves from the Israeli side are negative and backward." Sadat's remark drew a rebuke from the U.S. July 31.

Sadat made his statement following a meeting with Alfred L. Atherton Jr., the U.S. special assistant for the Middle East. Atherton had arrived in Cairo July 28 after conferring with Israeli leaders in Jerusalem July 27–28. The purpose of his mission was to discuss the outcome of the Israeli-Egyptian foreign ministers conference and prospects for further talks.

In rejecting Israel's latest proposal on the West Bank and Gaza Strip, Sadat insisted there could be no "territorial compromise." The return of Israeli-occupied Arab land was not negotiable, he said. The proposal forwarded by Israeli Foreign Minister Moshe Dayan at the Leeds Castle conference, Sadat added, was one of several "new negative elements" introduced by Israel and represented "a step backward." He said only an American peace plan could break the deadlock.

The Egyptian leader assailed Premier Menahem Begin's statement of July 23, which said that the Arabs could not get anything without giving something in return. "This has pushed the whole problem to the climax," Sadat said.

The U.S. said July 31 that it was "very disappointed" that Sadat had decided not to take part in another round of negotiations with Israel. The statement was issued after President Carter had discussed the latest development with his top advisers. One official said the meeting had reflected the Administration's "strong sense" that Sadat had undermined peace hopes by hardening his position.

Premier Begin expressed satisfaction July 31 with the Americans' rebuke of Sadat. He said it was "about time the world began to understand who the truly intransigent party was." Sadat's "unjustified demands represent preconditions and violate the spirit and letter of negotiations," Begin added.

Arabs & Palestinians

Arab League Tries to Settle Rifts. The Arab League held its semiannual council meeting in Cairo March 27–29, 1978 and attempted to resolve internal differences resulting from Egyptian President Anwar Sadat's peace initiatives.

Five member states opposed to Sadat's policies—Syria, Libya, Iraq, Algeria and South Yemen—boycotted the sessions. Only half of the league's 22 members was represented by their foreign ministers or other top-ranking diplomats.

The council announced March 28 agreement on "the necessity of convening an Arab summit conference as soon as possible to confront the Israeli aggressive challenges."

The council also decided "to form a committee of solidarity on the highest level to settle Arab differences and prepare the necessary climate" for the summit.

Egypt Curbs Palestinians. Egypt announced Feb. 27, 1978 its withdrawal of the special privileges granted to the 30,000 Palestinians living in Egypt. The decision was in response to the assassination of Al Ahram editor Youssef el-Sebai by two Palestinian terrorists in Cyprus Feb. 18 and the subsequent killing of 15 Egyptian commandos by Cypriot National Guardsmen in a raid on Larnaca airport.

Cairo's action underscored the widespread bitter Egyptian feeling against the Palestinians, and the Palestine Liberation Organization in particular, in the wake of the incident.

The announcement on the Palestinian curbs was made by Premier Mamdouh Salem to a meeting of the People's Assembly specially convened to consider the Cyprus affair and its aftermath. The government, Salem said, "has decided to consider the Palestinians living in Egypt being just like the citizens of other sister Arab countries." Palestinians had enjoyed the same legal rights and employment and business opportunities as Egyptian citizens. They also had been given preferential admission to universities and institutions.

Despite the curbs, Cairo would continue to espouse the political cause of the Palestinians, Salem vowed. "Egypt can never forget the Palestinian people in the Israeli occupied areas," he said.

Salem assailed the PLO and other Palestinian extremists, pledging that Egypt would not permit the Palestinian people "to remain the victims of conspiracies and machinations by those who trade in their name for personal benefit and gain."

The anti-Palestinian feeling in Egypt was further manifested in an editorial appearing in the Cairo newspaper Al Ahram Feb. 27. Denouncing Yasir Arafat, editor Moussa Sabry recalled that Egypt had held the PLO leader in great esteem, treating him "as head of state." But Arafat had "now changed," wrote Sabry, and had joined with the Arab radical rejectionists who opposed peace negotiations with Israel and with "international communism."

The PLO charged Feb. 28 that Egypt's decision to withdraw special rights of the Palestinians was part of President Anwar Sadat's willingness "to stoop to any level of submissiveness and self-abasement before demands of the enemy [Israel] in order to reach a settlement."

Arafat Feb. 24 had accused Sadat of "poisoning the minds of the Egyptian people against the Palestinians." Arafat's statement and similar views advanced by other PLO officials were said to reflect growing PLO fears that Sadat was preparing to withdraw Egyptian recognition of the organization as the sole legitimate representative of the Palestinian people.

Egypt Smashes Terrorist Group. Egypt confirmed April 26, 1978 that it had uncovered a plot by a Cairo-based foreign terrorist group to attack Israeli and Egyptian peace negotiators in the Egyptian capital in December 1977.

Prosecutor general Ibrahim al-Kalyubi said 24 suspects had been detained—three Swiss, 11 Palestinians, seven Jordanians, an Omani, an Egyptian and a West German. The accused were linked to an extremist splinter wing of the Palestinian Al Fatah (a member group of the Palestine Liberation Organization) headed by Wadi Haddad, who had died in March, and to the Red Brigades in Italy, Kalyubi said.

According to Kalyubi, the terrorists had taken photographs of the Mena House, where the preliminary negotiations were being held, and its approaches.

Other Egyptian officials April 24 said the Palestinian splinter group was headed by Abou Nidal, and that it was responsible for the fatal shooting in January of Said Hammami, the London representative of the PLO, and for the murder in Cyprus in February of Youssef el-Sebai, editor of the Egyptian newspaper Al Ahram.

The smashing of the terrorist group had first been disclosed by Al Ahram April 22. The newspaper said the suspects had made "detailed confessions" about their plans to wage a campaign of assassinations and sabotage in Egypt.

Arafat Asks U.S., Soviet Guarantees. Palestine Liberation Organization leader Arafat said May 1, 1978 that U.S. and Soviet guarantees for Israel and a Palestinian state were "the only possible solution to a Middle East peace settlement."

In an interview with the New York Times in Beirut, Arafat said the Soviet-U.S. declaration of Oct. 1, 1977 could be "a fundamental basis for a realistic settlement." That joint communique had said among other things that the two nations would insure "the legitimate rights of the Palestinian people" and would help guarantee "the security of the borders between Israel and the neighboring Arab states."

Arafat said Israeli fears of an independent Palestinian state on its borders were "groundless." "Would you believe that a state which is going to start from zero for the establishment of its institutions, its economy, culture, social problems—would such a state be able to form any serious threat against Israel?"

Gen. Abu Walid, Arafat's military chief of staff, who was present during part of the interview, interjected, saying that "a guerrilla war [against Israel] could never emerge from a small young state just coming into existence." Israel's expressions of concern about such an attack were "nothing but justification for the permanent Zionist strategy of expansion and denying Palestinians their national rights," he said.

President Carter's latest statement opposing an independent Palestinian state drew sharp criticism from Arafat, who said he was "surprised" and "disappointed" by it. Carter was "trying to form the future of a people the way he likes it," he said.

Iraq Seizes Fatah Arms Plant. Iraqi authorities had seized an Al Fatah arms plant and a facility for making naval vessels, the Palestinian guerrilla group said in Beirut July 17, 1978.

The seizures were said to have resulted from a long-standing dispute between Fatah and Iraq. Iraq considered Fatah leader Yasir Arafat too willing to compromise with Israel. The feud had intensified with the assassination in Kuwait June 15 of Ali Yasin, a representative of the Palestine Liberation Organization. Fatah had accused Iraq and a Palestinian guerrilla leader living in Baghdad, Abou Nidal, of responsibility for the murder.

Fatah also suggested that Iraq was behind the July 9 slaying in London of former Iraqi Premier Abdul Razak al-Naif.

The Fatah statement said the arms plant and the shipbuilding facility were joint Fatah-Iraqi ventures. The naval facility, located at the Iraqi port of Basra, produced small vessels for PLO seaborne raids against israel.

Fatah also accused Iraq of confiscating at some unspecified date a shipment of $50 million worth of arms and medical and other supplies from China, as well as other materiel for the PLO valued at $30 million.

Arms Race

U.S.S.R. Increases Arms Aid to Syria. Syria and the Soviet Union had signed a "new agreement" under which Damascus

would be provided with more Soviet arms aid, the U.S. State Department said Jan. 11, 1978. Moscow was said to have decided to expand its military assistance after Egypt launched its peace dialogue with Israel.

A joint communique issued Feb. 24 said Assad and Soviet President Leonid I. Brezhnev had "discussed and mapped out measures for increasing the level of the military capability" of Syria.

Abdel Salam Jalloud, a member of the ruling secretariat of Libya's People's Congress, was believed to have participated in the top-level Soviet-Syrian discussions. Jalloud, who had briefed Soviet officials on the meeting of Arab radical states in Algiers Feb. 2–4, had stayed on in Moscow five days after the end of his official visit the previous week. Libya was reported to have offered Syria $1 billion to purchase arms.

At a dinner honoring Assad's visit, Brezhnev Feb. 21 assailed the U.S. for supporting direct negotiations between Egypt and Israel. Brezhnev said his government still favored a general Middle East conference under the auspices of the U.S. and the Soviet Union as envisioned in their joint statement issued in October 1977.

Sadat Assails Arms to Syria—Egyptian President Anwar Sadat was critical of the massive Soviet arms shipments to Syria, according to an interview published Feb. 25 in the Eyptian weekly October. Sadat said Syria had an overabundance of arms, while Egypt suffered from a shortage. "Already, in 1972, President Assad told me he did not know where to put the arms Moscow was delivering," Sadat said.

Syrian President Hafez al-Assad visited Moscow Feb. 21–22.

U.S. Arms for Military Balance, Peace. The U.S. government said Feb. 14, 1978 that it planned to sell $4.8 billion worth of jet warplanes to Egypt, Saudi Arabia and Israel. The object of the decision was to maintain the military balance and advance the cause of peace in the region, the Carter Administration asserted.

Saudi Arabia would be permitted to purchase 60 F-15 jets at a cost of $2.5 billion. The plane was described as the most advanced in the U.S. Air Force. Israel would be allowed to buy 15 of the aircraft for $400 million and 75 F-16 fighter-bombers at a cost of $1.5 billion. Egypt would get to buy 50 F-5 fighters for $400 million. The F-5 was less advanced than the F-15 or F-16.

Israel had already bought 25 of the F-15s and would receive the remaining 15 by late 1981. Israel had asked for 25 more F-15s and 150 F-16s, according to Administration officials.

The decision to sell the planes was announced by Secretary of State Cyrus Vance. Anticipating opposition to arming Israel's adversaries, Vance noted that the U.S. commitment to Israel's security "remains firm." But he insisted that Egypt also "must have reasonable assurance of its ability to defend itself if it is to continue the peace negotiations [with Israel] with confidence."

As for Saudi Arabia, Vance said that country was of "immense importance in promoting a course of moderation... , with respect to peacemaking and other regional initiatives and more broadly in world affairs, as in petroleum and financial policy." Saudi Arabia, Vance added, "has a legitimate requirement to modernize its very limited air defense."

In a background briefing, U.S. officials said the F-5s for Egypt could not be used effectively against Israel's more sophisticated planes but could resist threats from neighboring Libya. The Saudis needed the F-15s to counter a rapid buildup of air and ground forces in Iraq, which received its military equipment from the Soviet Union, the officials said. The F-15 and F-16 had strike ranges between 600 and 900 miles, while the F-5 had a combat radius of between 250 and 300 miles.

Initial congressional reaction to the proposed sale of planes to Egypt and Saudi Arabia was negative. A majority of the Senate Foreign Relations Committee had expressed reservations about selling the F-15s to Saudi Arabia. Sen. Daniel P. Moynihan (D, N.Y.) Feb. 14 said the sale of "such potent offensive weapons to the Saudis could in time pose a threat to Israel's security."

Israel Deplores U.S. Decision—The U.S. intention to sell planes to Egypt and Saudi Arabia was deplored by Israeli Premier Menahem Begin Feb. 15.

Speaking in the Knesset (parliament), Begin called on the Carter Administration to reappraise its decision. Claiming that Cairo was threatening war unless Israel complied with its demands, Begin said "the supply of offensive weapons at this time could only nourish that threat."

Providing planes to Saudi Arabia, Begin said, would make that country "a confrontation state" (a term applied to bordering Arab states that had engaged in war against Israel). He said the Saudis had pledged to eventually give their American planes to an Arab country (presumably Egypt) for use against Israel.

The U.S. Feb. 15 rejected Begin's request that it reconsider its decision. A statement issued at a State Department briefing reiterated that the jet sale would be a contribution to peace in the Middle East.

Foreign Minister Moshe Dayan, on a speaking tour in the U.S., Feb. 14 said it was "premature" to provide Cairo with warplanes because it would have "a negative effect on Egypt's willingness to compromise and moderate its position" in peace negotiations.

Dayan warned Feb. 16 that the sale to Saudi Arabia might force Israel to reconsider giving up airfields in the Sinai Peninsula. Dayan made the statement at a Washington press conference after meetings with President Carter and Vance.

Selling the planes to the Saudis, Dayan said, would "have an affect on the entire military picture, our own defensive borders and our military installations." The foreign minister claimed that the Saudis were building an air base at Tebuk, only a few minutes jet flight from the Israeli port of Eilat, at the head of the Gulf of Aqaba.

In a letter sent Feb. 16 to the House International Relations Committee, the State Department said the Saudis had no plans to deploy advanced planes at Tebuk. The Saudis would concentrate instead on protecting their oilfields and other border areas to the east and south, the department said.

Jet Sale a Package Deal—Secretary Vance formally announced Feb. 24 that the proposed sale of American jets to Egypt, Saudi Arabia and Israel was "a package and will be dealt with as a package." Appearing before a House Appropriations subcommittee on foreign operations, Vance warned that if Congress vetoed the sale of the jets to the two Arab countries, the Administration would withdraw the offer to Israel.

Vance rejected the argument by Israeli supporters that the Administration was putting pressure on Israel to make diplomatic concessions by linking its plane request with that of Egypt and Saudi Arabia.

The chairman of the subcommittee, Rep. Clarence D. Long (D, Md.), expressed opposition to the entire package. "There's no way you can convince me you can somehow get peace in a section of the world in which you are pumping vast arms."

Vance Feb. 21 had sought to counter fears by Israel and its congressional backers that Saudi Arabia would transfer the American jets to the Arab states bordering or directly threatening Israel. Appearing before the House International Relations Committee, the secretary said the Administration had made clear to the Saudis that they could not transfer these planes to another country without U.S. permission.

Saudis Insist on Planes—Saudi Arabia had warned the U.S. that if there were a substantial delay in the proposed sale of the F-15 jets, it would try to buy advanced jets elsewhere, Deputy Assistant Secretary of State J. Brian Atwood said March 14.

Atwood said, "a delay is just as bad as a rejection" in the view of the Saudis. A six-month postponement as suggested by some congressional opponents of the sale would actually mean an effective deferment for at least a year because of the adjournment of Congress in the fall, Atwood said.

Egypt Said to Order French Jets—U.S. government sources reported March 1 that Egypt had ordered 46 Mirage F-1 fighter jets from France. A U.S. Senate aide was quoted as saying that the proposed sale "is obviously going to have a bearing" on current U.S. congressional consideration of Administration plans to sell jets to Egypt, Saudi Arabia and Israel. President Anwar Sadat reportedly had discussed the purchase of the Mirages during a visit with French officials in Paris Feb. 12.

U.S. Denies Planes to Libya—The U.S. would deny export licenses for two Boeing transport planes and for spare parts for eight Lockheed C-130 transports ordered by Libya, the State Department announced Feb. 21. The department also would withdraw approval for Lockheed on-site maintenance of the C-130s in Libya.

The department said, "These decisions reflected the United States government's concern with Libya's continuing support for international terrorism."

Israel Seeks U.S. Arms. Israeli Defense Minister Ezer Weizman met with U.S. Defense Secretary Harold Brown in Washington March 9, 1978 on the Israeli request for about $15 billion in American arms over the next 10 years. No specific commitment was forthcoming on the Israeli request, which had been submitted in October 1977.

The discussions between the two officials also dealt with the overall military balance in the Middle East, the status of Israeli-Egyptian negotiations and the Administration's plans to sell jets to Israel, Egypt and Saudi Arabia as a package deal. Weizman reiterated his government's stand against providing the Saudis with advanced F-15s and pressed Brown for more planes for Israel.

Moshe Dayan then met April 27 with six senators to express his government's opposition to the Carter Administration's proposal to sell jet planes to Egypt, Saudi Arabia and Israel as a package deal. Dayan said he was against the sale "at this time because we think it would endanger Israel."

He also objected to "the concept of a package deal" on the ground that "the selling of arms to Israel should be conducted on its merits, . . ." Even if Israel did not get the planes because of its opposition to their acquisition by Egypt and Saudi Arabia, "then we shall accept the punishment but we shall not change our position about it," Dayan said.

France in 4-Nation Arms Pact. France March 14, 1978 signed an agreement with a consortium of four Arab nations that set the basis for future arms production and technical assistance projects. The agreement was signed with the Arab Industries Organization (AIO), a group comprising Egypt, Saudi Arabia, the United Arab Emirates and Qatar.

The pact did not specify what kinds of arms contracts the two sides would conclude. It was similar to agreements signed by the U.S. and Great Britain with the AIO that led to the manufacture of military vehicles, helicopters and missiles by Arab companies under foreign license.

Carter Backs Arms to Arabs. President Carter, rejecting criticism of the proposed sale of military planes to Saudi Arabia and Egypt as well as to Israel, told newsmen that his proposal was in the interests of Israel and of peace.

Carter asserted that the "preeminent consideration" of the U.S. in the Middle East was "the long-range and permanent security and peacefulness for the people of Israel."

Therefore, he said, "to treat the moderate Arabs with fairness and with friendship and to strengthen their commitment to us in return is in the best interests of our own country and of Israel."

As for peace prospects in the region, "every evidence that I have, both publicly and privately known," Carter said, "is that both sides want peace and the progress toward peace is steady."

Senate Approves Jet Sales. The U.S. Senate May 15, 1978, by 54–44 vote, supported the Carter Administration's plan to sell warplanes to Saudi Arabia and Egypt, as well as to Israel.

The proposed sale of the planes to the two Arab nations had set off a sharp debate in Congress.

The Senate vote meant the sales would go through. Under federal law, Congress was not required to approve arms sales, but it did have the power to veto proposed sales. Since both chambers of Congress had to vote against a sale to veto it, the Senate vote removed the possibility of a veto.

In an effort to reduce opposition to the sale of the planes to the Arab countries, Secretary of State Cyrus Vance May 9 informed members of the Senate Foreign Relations Committee that Israel would be permitted to buy 20 additional F-15s later.

There was intense lobbying before the vote. President Carter telephoned "a dozen or more" senators to ask support for the sales over the weekend preceding the vote, White House Press Secretary Jody Powell said May 15.

Opposing the sale to the Arab countries were Jewish groups and a variety of other organizations.

Opponents of the sale said it would imperil the special relationship the U.S. traditionally enjoyed with Israel. Sen. Jacob Javits (R, N.Y.), an opponent of the sale to the Arab countries, asked, "What do we want to do with the Israelis? Sap their vitality? Sap their morale? Cut the legs out from under them? That's what this is about."

Another opponent of the sale, Sen. Clifford Case (R, N.J.), cautioned that the sale would endanger Israel's security. "Will we risk destroying Israel by gradually eroding our support?"

Supporters of the sale made a number of arguments. The sale would strengthen the hand of moderate forces in the Arab countries, they argued, and help to make Arab countries perceive the U.S. as even-handed on questions involving the Middle East. Sen. Howard Baker (R, Tenn.), Senate minority leader and supporter of the sale, said, "Saudi pride and Saudi moderation will receive a stunning blow if a commitment made publicly by the President of the United States is publicly repudiated by the United States Congress."

The Saudis needed the planes because of threats to their security unrelated to Israel, supporters of the sale maintained. Administration officials cited Saudi assurances that the planes would be used for defensive purposes. Defense Secretary Harold Brown wrote May 10 to the Senate Foreign Relations Committee, arguing that "it would be folly to use the F-15 offensively against neighboring countries." Brown continued, "This is particularly so vis-a-vis Israel."

Brown said the Saudis had agreed to several curbs on the use of the F-15s. The Saudis would not seek to have the planes equipped with either auxiliary fuel tanks, which would give the planes greater range, or multiple ejection racks, which would allow a greater bomb load to be carried, Brown said. The Saudis had also promised not to obtain any warplanes from other countries while the F-15s were being delivered, he said.

Before the vote May 15, the Senate held a closed session at which classified information on threats to Saudi national security was presented.

Sen. Thomas Eagleton (D, Mo.), a supporter of the sale, argued that "it would be a catastrophe" if the Saudi oil fields were taken over by a hostile power. "Better that we provide a means for the Saudis to defend that vital resource themselves," Eagleton said, "than face the possibility of some day being forced to commit our own military forces."

Oil—specifically, the impact on the U.S. of the role played by the Saudis in the Organization of Petroleum Exporting Countries—also figured directly in the debate. Sen. Lloyd Bentsen (D, Tex), a supporter of the sale, noted that "for the past five years Saudi Arabia has been a force of moderation within OPEC on the question of oil prices."

Bentsen continued, "The Saudis have steadfastly resisted efforts by some of our friends, Venezuela and Iran in particular, to raise oil prices even higher. In the process they have been branded the lackeys of the United States. To discourage the sale would do incalculable damage to Saudi-American relations."

Sen. Daniel Moynihan (D, N.Y.), an opponent of the sale, viewed the oil link in a different light. U.S. foreign policy, Moynihan said, had become dominated by the need for foreign oil. "The foreign and domestic well-being of the United States," Moynihan said, "is in fact increasingly dependent upon the decisions taken by the royal family of Saudi Arabia. Five years ago, we could not live with Saudi foreign policy; today we cannot live without it."

The split on the vote did not follow either party or philosophical lines. Republicans and Democrats, conservatives and liberals, were found on both sides of the issue. Voting to block the sale were 33 Democrats and 11 Republicans; 28 Democrats and 26 Republicans voted to allow the sale.

The full Senate vote came after the Senate Foreign Relations Committee May 11 split 8–8 on the sales. The tie vote would have allowed the Administration to go ahead with its plans for the sales, but the committee decided unanimously that the controversial issue should be referred to the full Senate. The Administration had hoped to avoid a floor vote.

President Carter May 15 said he was "deeply gratified" by the Senate vote upholding the sales. The action, he said, "reaffirms our historic and unshakeable commitment to the security of Israel."

Carter continued, "At the same time, the Senate vote strengthens our ties with moderate Arab nations who share our goal of peace and stability in the region."

Carter also maintained that the sales would not violate the Administration's policy to limit arms sales.

U.S. Assures Jet Sale Opponents— President Carter and several members of his Administration May 15-16 telephoned American Jewish community leaders and senators who had opposed the jet sale to inform them of Washington's continued support of Israel. Among the other officials who called were Vice President Walter Mondale, Secretary of State Cyrus Vance and national security adviser Zbigniew Brzezinski.

Mondale May 15 also paid a personal visit to the home of Hyman Bookbinder, Washington representative of the American Jewish Committee. Mondale told him that the Administration's decision to sell planes to Egypt and Saudi Arabia along with Israel represented no lessening of U.S. support of Israel or of its determination to seek a peace settlement.

Bookbinder later said he felt "reassured by the very fact that the Administration deemed it advisable and desirable to make these calls and offer these reassurances to friends of Israel."

Israeli, Arab Reaction—In statements issued May 16, Israel deplored the U.S. Senate vote approving the three-nation plane deal, while Egypt and Saudi Arabia praised it.

Israeli Premier Menahem Begin complained that "lumping" the transaction as a package was a U.S. violation of the 1975 Egyptian-Israeli disengagement pact mediated by the U.S. Under terms of the accord, Israel had agreed to a partial withdrawal of its forces from the Sinai Peninsula in exchange for being allowed to purchase sophisticated warplanes from the U.S. and for continued U.S. economic assistance to Israel. "There was no justification whatever to connect it [the sale] with any supply to countries which are in a state of war with Israel," Begin said.

Egypt's Foreign Minister Ibrahim Mohammed Kamel said approval of the jet sale "shows that all the confidence and trust we have in the United States has been reciprocated." The move also "encourages us to continue our peace efforts," Kamel noted. The 50 F-5E interceptor jets destined for Egypt, whose effectiveness had been disparaged by President Anwar Sadat, would be employed strictly for self-defense "against any aggressor," Kamel said.

Sadat himself said the U.S. Senate decision "strengthened Arab confidence in the United States and in its potential role on behalf of peace."

Saudi Arabia said the Senate action was a clear indication that "the Jewish lobby in the United States is weakening." This development, the Saudi statement said, marked "a new era in relations between the United States and Israel, during which Israel will no longer be able to influence United States policy. . . ."

King Khalid of Saudi Arabia had said in a letter to President Carter made public May 13 that his country's "long delayed need for the [F-15] planes has become a matter of pressing urgency because of the continuing and recently stepped-up Communist expansion in the area" surrounding Saudi Arabia. This was reference to Soviet penetration of Ethiopia and to previous Saudi assurances that the planes would be used only for defense against such hostile neighbors as Iraq and South Yemen, both of which were heavily armed by the Soviet Union.

Prince Saud al-Faisal, Saudi Arabia's foreign minister, had implied May 12 that his country opposed U.S. restrictions on the basing of the F-15s. (The U.S. said it had received Saudi assurances that the planes would not be deployed near Israel.)

Camp David: Framework for Peace

Egypt & Israel Agree to Meet in U.S.

The breakthrough for peace in the Middle East was widened in September 1978 when the leaders of Egypt and Israel met with President Jimmy Carter at the U.S. President's Camp David retreat in Maryland. There, with Carter's energetic assistance, Anwar Sadat and Menahem Begin negotiated an agreement on a framework for peace between Israel and its Arab enemies. The meeting was at Carter's invitation.

Sadat & Begin Agree to Meet. The U.S. had arranged for Egyptian President Anwar Sadat and Israeli Premier Menahem Begin to meet with President Carter Sept. 5, 1978 to confer on ways of resolving the Middle East deadlock, the White House announced Aug. 8. The summit meeting would be held at the presidential retreat at Camp David, Md.

Begin and Sadat had accepted Carter's written invitations when they were transmitted by Secretary of State Cyrus Vance during his separate meetings with the two leaders in Jerusalem Aug. 6–7 and in Alexandria Aug. 7–8.

The White House statement said the purpose of the trilateral talks would be "to seek a framework for peace in the Middle East." A White House official said Carter had decided to arrange the meeting

"not because the chances for peace are right now so high, but because the stakes in peace are very high and because the risks, in fact, have risen."

The decision to invite Begin and Sadat to the U.S. had been reached by Carter and his top foreign policy aides July 31. Their meeting was said to have been held in an atmosphere of crisis after Sadat's announcement July 30 of his refusal to resume the foreign ministers talks with Israel until Israel committed itself beforehand to total withdrawal from all occupied Arab territories.

The Carter Administration was said to have been especially concerned about the approaching third anniversary of the September 1975 signing by Israel and Egypt of the Sinai troop disengagement agreement. Sadat had repeatedly implied that if no appreciable diplomatic progress were reached by October, he might take some unilateral action.

Sadat's warnings were underscored by Western intelligence reports that some Egyptian armed forces units had been placed on alert and that Egypt had increased military maneuvers. While this action was said to be directed at Libya, Carter Administration officials believed these moves were a possible cover for a buildup of some military action in the Sinai.

Israeli Foreign Minister Moshe Dayan was said to have expressed his concern to the U.S. about the Egyptian military moves.

221

Sadat said Aug. 8 that he had agreed to go to Camp David because of Washington's commitment to become a "full partner" in negotiations. Sadat had long advocated that the U.S. act as arbiter, rather than mediator, in the peace process.

When questioned about the increased American involvement, Vance said in Alexandria Aug. 8 that the U.S. was "prepared to play a full role in seeking a just and lasting peace." He stressed that Israel and Egypt would "have to reach agreement," but that the U.S. would feel free to make suggestions when it saw "obstacles impeding the road to peace."

Begin disclosed Aug. 8 that he had accepted the summit invitation without having met Egypt's demand for an Israeli commitment to total withdrawal from Arab lands prior to resumption of direct peace negotiations.

The organ of Syria's ruling Baath Party charged Aug. 9 that the summit "is a maneuver, paving the way for a lighting war" by Israel.

The Palestine Liberation Organization said the meeting of the U.S., Israel and Egypt would "serve only the Israeli aim of buying time" and force Egypt to make "other concessions."

Begin said that in his meeting with Vance Aug. 6, the secretary had not asked for any change in Israeli policy.

The ostensible purpose of Vance's visit to Israel and Egypt was to get the two nations to resume their foreign ministers meeting, suspended since the Leeds Castle talks July 18–19.

Before departing for the Middle East, Vance reported on his forthcoming mission to a closed-door meeting of the House International Relations Committee Aug. 4. The secretary was said to have complained that President Sadat was using "shock tactics" to force Israel to make concessions. Citing Sadat's decision in January to cut short Egypt's talks with Israel, Vance said such moves made it more difficult to achieve peace.

Arabs, Soviets Score Talks—Syrian Foreign Minister Abdel Halim Khaddam assailed the Camp David summit Sept. 7 as "a link in a chain of plots against the Arab nation." Khaddam made the statement in Algiers in an effort to rally hardline Arab states opposed to peace with Israel to "make military pacts with the So-

viet Union" if Israel and the U.S. signed a mutual defense treaty.

Algeria was one of the "steadfastness front" states opposed to President Sadat's peace initiatives.

Khaddam said that another meeting of the group, formed in December 1977, was necessary to draw up new strategy in view of the Camp David summit. The other steadfastness states were Syria, South Yemen, Libya and Iraq and the Palestine Liberation Organization.

The Soviet Union denounced the Camp David conference Sept. 6 as an American "trick" to increase its influence in the Middle East rather than as an effort to bring peace to the region. Washington was pursuing "selfish interests of a military character ensuring a strengthening of U.S. control over the Middle East and its oil arteries," the Tass news agency said. Premier Begin was attempting to use the summit to move Israel closer to the North Atlantic Treaty Organization, Tass added.

In a further Soviet criticism of the summit, Foreign Minister Andrei A. Gromyko said Sept. 6 that "separate experiments at the expense of the lawful interests of the Arabs,...do not constitute a road to peace."

Israel Delays Settlements. The Israeli Cabinet decided Aug. 14 to suspend consideration of establishing five new settlements in the West Bank pending the outcome of the Camp David talks.

A Cabinet committee June 28 had endorsed in principle the construction plans (approved by the previous government) but military censorship barred public disclosure of committee actions. After two weeks of rumors and leaked statements about the proposed settlements, the Cabinet publicly announced the plans Aug. 13. Its decision the following day to shelve the project was made to avoid jeopardizing the high-level peace negotiations that Israel, Egypt and the U.S. were scheduled to start Sept. 5.

Deputy Premier Yigal Yadin, who led the Aug. 14 Cabinet session in the absence of vacationing Premier Menahem Begin, said he had blocked the committee's action by requesting that the matter be considered by the full Cabinet.

The U.S. State Department, aware of the Cabinet committee's approval, had complained to Israel. Secretary of State

Cyrus Vance said: "Our position is clear: There should be no settlements."

Vance said Aug. 14 that he was pleased that Israel had delayed final action until after the summit.

U.S. Military Force Hinted.
The Washington Post Aug. 30 quoted Carter Administration officials as saying that the U.S. was considering sending an American military force to the Middle East if such a step were needed to break the Arab-Israeli impasse.

The American presence would include an air base in the Sinai and the deployment of troops in the West Bank, it was said.

When asked to comment on the report, President Carter said Aug. 30 that he would be "reluctant" to dispatch American soldiers to the Middle East "but I'll have to wait and see."

White House Press Secretary Jody Powell said Aug. 30 that while the use of American troops in the region was only a theoretical option at the moment, "the question of a generalized American presence has always been there."

Australia, New Zealand and Canada had indicated a "certain receptiveness" to an American proposal to join an international peacekeeping force in the West Bank and Gaza Strip, the London Times disclosed in a dispatch from Jerusalem Aug. 31.

The newspaper said the account of the reputed proposal was based on an Israeli report from Washington. It said that under the American formula, the international force would not necessarily replace the Israeli military in the West Bank and Gaza Strip during a five-year interim period in which Arab residents of the West Bank would be given self-autonomy. But the U.S. would want the Israelis to withdraw from populated areas of those two regions, it was said.

Israeli Premier Menahem Begin said Aug. 31 that he was opposed to the stationing of American troops in the West Bank or Gaza Strip. While saying he would favor a U.S.-Israeli defense agreement, Begin declared, "We do not want foreign troops to defend our people. We shall defend our people ourselves."

White House Press Secretary Powell Sept. 7 dismissed the report of a proposed U.S. force for the Middle East as "one of the great nonexistent stories of all time." Briefing reporters at the conclusion of the second day of the summit, Powell said the question had arisen as a result of "a chance comment made by way of example in front of some American congressmen. . . ."

Camp David Sessions Produce Framework for Peace

Egypt & Israel Agree to Peace Plan.
President Carter opened meetings at his Camp David, Md. retreat Sept. 6, 1978 with Egyptian President Anwar Sadat and Israeli Premier Menahem Begin. The talks were concluded Sept. 17 with agreement by Begin and Sadat on a framework for Middle East peace. Two documents governing the accords were signed by Sadat and Begin, while Carter signed as a witness.

The documents were made public Sept. 18 when Carter addressed a joint session of the U.S. Congress to disclose the results of the summit.

Under an accord for Egypt and Israel, the two nations were to conclude a peace treaty within three months. Israel would withdraw from the entire Sinai Peninsula and turn it back to Egypt. The area would be demilitarized. The Israeli pullout would occur in phases, with the first one taking place within three to nine months after the signing of the peace treaty. Normal diplomatic relations between Israel and Egypt would then be established. The final Israeli withdrawal would be carried out within two to three years after the peace pact was signed.

Among decisions involving the West Bank and Gaza Strip:

■ Israel, Egypt, Jordan and elected Palestinian representatives would negotiate the key question of sovereignty of the Israeli-occupied territory after a five-year transition period. Israel and Jordan would conclude a peace treaty at the end of that time.

■ Israel would keep troops in specified areas of the West Bank during the five-year period.

■ Israel would dismantle its military government and permit the Palestinians to elect representatives and to decide on a form of local government.

■ New Israeli settlements on the West Bank would be frozen during the peace negotiations.

■ Palestinian police would join Egyptian and Israeli and possibly Jordanian security forces in maintaining public order.

The accord made no mention of Arab demands for control of East Jerusalem, which Israel had annexed in 1967.

The U.S. would be invited to take part in discussions on matters relating to implementation of both agreements.

The President disclosed that Secretary of State Cyrus Vance would leave the following day for Jordan and Saudi Arabia to explain to King Hussein and King Khalid the agreement reached between Egypt and Israel. Vance would try "to secure their support for the realization of the new hopes and dreams of the people of the Middle East," Carter said.

With Sadat and Begin in attendance, Carter lauded "the two men who have made this impossible dream now become a real possibility.... At Camp David we sought peace which is not only of vital importance to their two nations, but to all the people of the Middle East, to all the people of the United States—indeed, to the rest of the world as well."

Citing the "historic importance" of the occasion, the President said, "this is the first time an Arab and an Israeli leader have signed a comprehensive framework for peace."

Carter noted that while the people of the Middle East, especially Egyptians and Israelis, had suffered four wars in 30 years, "the dangers and the costs of the conflict in this region for our nation have been great as well."

Carter, in an address to a joint session of Congress Sept. 18, provided details of the two documents Sadat and Begin had signed the previous day.

Citing the Middle East's strategic location and resources, Carter said the U.S. and its friends "could not be indifferent if a hostile power were to establish dominance there." He warned of the risk of confrontation between the superpowers that could result from local conflicts in the area. For this reason, Carter pointed out, the U.S. had assumed the role of "full partner in the search for peace" in the Middle East.

The President cautioned that the "magnitude of the obstacles that still remain" could not be overlooked. "The summit exceeded our highest expectation—but we know that it left many difficult issues which are still unresolved." Among those issues cited by Carter and not specifically mentioned in the document on the proposed Egyptian-Israeli treaty was the question of the removal of Israeli settlements in the Sinai. The removal of the settlements required approval of the Israeli Knesset (parliament).

Carter said the Egyptians had insisted that removal of the settlements "is a prerequisite to a peace treaty." Israel, he said, held to the position that the issue "should be resolved during the peace negotiations."

Turning to the fighting in Lebanon, the President said, "We must join in an effort to end the conflict and terrible suffering" there.

Carter had briefed the Senate Foreign Relations Committee and the House International Relations Committee on the Camp David summit earlier Sept. 18.

The President reportedly told the congressmen that his meetings with Sadat and Begin faced collapse at a number of points. He said he had deliberately kept the two men apart since their initial discussions Sept. 6–7, which the President described as bitter. Begin and Sadat never formally met together again as Carter arranged the details of the agreement with them separately.

Sadat confirmed in a television interview Sept. 18 that he had threatened to walk out of the summit the previous week.

The key element that broke the impasse was concession by Begin during a meeting with Carter Sept. 15, it was reported. Begin was said to have acceded to the provisions relating to the Palestinian role during a five-year transitional period in the West Bank and to have agreed to permit the Knesset to decide on the future of the Israeli settlements in the Sinai.

Begin conceded Sept. 20 that Israel and the U.S. had different interpretations of the understanding about Israeli settlements on the West Bank.

In an exclusive interview with the Wall Street Journal in New York, Begin said he had pledged to freeze Jewish settlements on the West Bank only for the period during which Israel and Egypt would negotiate their bilateral treaty, which was expected to last three months or less.

U.S. officials insisted that Begin had promised to bar new settlements during the period of negotiations on the disposition of the West Bank. They also said he had promised at the Camp David talks "that the issue of future Israeli settlements will be decided among the negotiating partners." This would mean that the Palestinians, as a party to the West Bank discussions, would have the right to reject any new settlements.

The question of the settlements was one of five highly controversial or technical subjects that had been omitted from the written accords. Begin, Carter and President Sadat had agreed instead to have them covered in an exchange of letters that would outline the details of these subjects. The issuance of the letters, however, was delayed because of the U.S.-Israeli disagreement over the settlements.

Among the other unresolved matters not contained in the text of the accords were the fate of the Israeli-occupied Golan Heights and East Jerusalem. The Arabs wanted both returned to them. Begin told a Jewish group in New York Sept. 20 that he had gained concessions

from Sadat and Carter on these two points by threatening to stalemate the summit unless they yielded.

Sadat and Carter wanted the agreements to include a phrase that could have implied that Israel might eventually give up the Golan Heights and East Jerusalem.

Begin also said that the agreement he signed did not require Israel to give up the West Bank during the five-year transitional period. Begin insisted that Israel would claim sovereignty over the West Bank after the five-year term. If the Palestinians or the Jordanians made the same claim, then the matter would remain unresolved and Israeli troops would stay and the Palestinians would continue to exercise self-rule, Begin said.

Carter's Version of Settlements— President Carter Sept. 27 took direct issue with Premier Begin's version of the Camp David agreement on Israeli settlements on the West Bank.

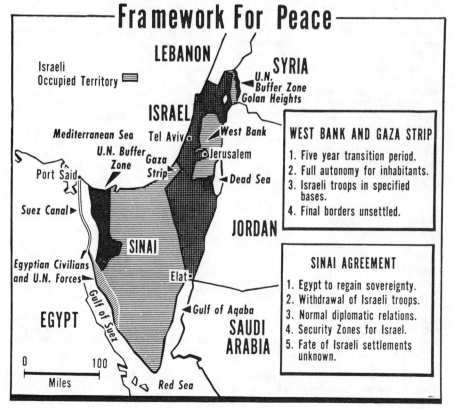

Carter said he had "a very clear understanding" with Begin that the question of establishing new settlements in the territory would be resolved by negotiations during a five-year transitional period during which the final status of the West Bank would be decided.

The President challenged Begin's contention that they had agreed to a freeze on new Israeli settlements on the West Bank only for the period of Israeli-Egyptian negotiations on a bilateral treaty, a process scheduled to take up to three months.

Carter said that he had dropped a demand that existing settlements not be expanded in return for Begin's agreement to an effective five-year moratorium on new West Bank settlements.

Sadat for Comprehensive Pact— President Sadat said Sept. 19 that he favored a comprehensive Middle East peace agreement but implied that he was prepared to pursue a peace initiative on his own if other Arab states refused to join.

Speaking to newsmen in Washington, Sadat said the proposed Egyptian-Israeli accord and the projected West Bank-Gaza pact were "a package deal. The two issues should go parallel. I am not after a separate deal with Israel but a comprehensive deal."

However, if Jordanian King Hussein refused to participate in a West Bank agreement, Sadat said he would negotiate the matter himself, "as I will with Sinai."

Sadat declared Sept. 20 that he would sign a peace treaty with Israel within two months despite opposition from Arab hardliners and reservations from such moderate states as Jordan and Saudi Arabia.

The Cairo newspaper Al Ahram also quoted Sadat as saying that he was ordering a shakeup of the Egyptian government and demobilizing some army units "because the battle of liberating [Israeli-occupied] lands is over."

Kamel Quits; Other Arab Reaction— The Camp David summit agreements drew immediate opposition from within President Sadat's own ranks. His foreign minister, who was involved in the talks, Mohammed Ibrahim Kamel, resigned Sept. 18 in protest against the conference results.

Ashraf Ghorbal, Egypt's ambassador to the U.S., also tendered his resignation for the same reason.

An aide to Kamel in Cairo said Kamel "doesn't want to be remembered by history as the man who drafted a bilaterial agreement [with Israel], abandoning the other Arab states along the way."

Saudi Arabia and Jordan were cautiously critical Sept. 19.

An official Saudi communique said, "What has been reached at the Camp David conference cannot be considered a final acceptable formula for peace." The statement complained of the agreements' failure to mention an Israeli commitment to total withdrawal from Arab lands, a Palestinian right to establish a state and a role for the Palestine Liberation Organization in the peace process.

A Jordanian communique took issue with the proposed Israeli-Egyptian treaty and disavowed any "legal or ethical commitments" to the Camp David accords because Amman was not a party to the pacts.

PLO leader Yasir Arafat denounced the summit agreements as "a dirty deal which the Egyptian people will reject and which does not decide our destiny." Speaking at a guerrilla camp near Beirut, Arafat accused Sadat of having "traded a piece of land in the Sinai desert for Arab Jerusalem." Saying that President Carter would "pay" for the agreements, Arafat hinted that "American interests in the Middle East" would come under guerrilla attack, as well as Israel itself.

Syrian President Hafez al-Assad assailed President Sadat Sept. 20 for having "defected to the enemy" by abandoning "not only Jerusalem but the whole Arab cause."

Assad made the remark to the opening of a meeting in Damascus of the Arab "Steadfastness and Confrontation Front." The group, which opposed negotiations with Israel, convened in emergency session to consider what action to take in light of the Camp David agreements. Besides Syria, the other members were Libya, Iraq, South Yemen, Algeria and the PLO.

Without providing specifics, Assad suggested that Sadat and Begin might be preparing a joint military action against Syria "in the near future."

Lebanon Sept. 20 expressed particular concern with the fact that the Camp David summit made no provision for the creation of a Palestinian "homeland."

This could mean the "establishment of Palestinians outside their homeland," notably in Lebanon, the statement said. About 350,000-450,000 Palestinians resided in Lebanon.

Israeli Reaction—Israeli public and political reaction to the Camp David summit agreements was largely positive, with some opposition stemming from right-wing factions.

The most vehement objection was raised by Gush Emunim, the ultranationalist group that favored unrestricted settlement of the West Bank because of Jewish biblical ties to the area. About 150 members of the organization staked out an illegal claim on a hill near Nablus Sept. 19 as a protest against Premier Begin's acceptance of the peace agreements. The action was in defiance of the accords' provisions imposing a temporary freeze on new settlements on the West Bank.

The squatters were forcibly evicted from the site by Israeli soldiers Sept. 21. The unarmed troops moved in to dismantle prefabricated sheds, water tanks, a generator and about a dozen tents. Fighting broke out during the raid, leaving seven Gush Emunim followers and five soldiers injured, none seriously.

A group of Gush Emunim established another illegal settlement Sept. 21 on the West Bank, atop a hill near Hebron. They vowed to stay until they were forcibly removed by the army.

Moshe Ahrens, a member of Premier Begin's Herut Party, said the accords posed a risk because it was uncertain whether Egypt would sign a separate pact with Israel without resolution of the West Bank-Gaza problem.

Another member of Begin's coalition, Commerce Minister Yigal Hurvitz, said he would find it difficult to support the provision calling for withdrawal of Israeli settlements from the Sinai.

Brezhnev Assails Accords—Soviet President Leonid Brezhnev said Sept. 22 that the U.S., Egypt and Israel at the Camp David summit had come up with an agreement that was a "deal worked out behind the backs of the Arabs."

Brezhnev called the accord "a separate collusion that covers up the surrender of one side and consolidates the fruits of aggression on the other—the aggression of Israel." This kind of an arrangement, he

added, "can only make the situation in the Middle East even more explosive."

Conferees' Letters Released. The White House Sept. 22 released nine letters of understanding exchanged by President Carter with President Sadat and Premier Begin on their interpretations of several controversial issues of the Camp David summit agreements on the Middle East.

The letters dealt with the accord on the Sinai, Israeli settlements there, the dispute over Jerusalem and the resolution of the West Bank-Gaza problem. Other letters still to be released included those dealing with Israeli settlements on the West Bank and a U.S. pledge to build two airbases in Israel to replace three military airfields in the Sinai that Israel was to turn over to Egyptian civilian control.

The most controversial subject of the nine letters was the one concerning Jerusalem. Begin and Sadat agreed that the city should be "undivided." Sadat advocated establishment of a joint Arab-Israeli municipal council, but insisted that East Jerusalem, annexed by Israel after the 1967 war, "should be under Arab sovereignty."

In his letter, Begin called attention to a section of an Israeli law, enacted in July 1967, which stated that "Jerusalem is one city indivisible, the capital of the state of Israel."

President Carter's letter on Jerusalem restated American policy as contained in two statements made at the United Nations. One of them, delivered July 14, 1967, said the status of Jerusalem could not be decided by "unilateral actions" and that the Israeli annexation of East Jerusalem "cannot be considered other than interim and provisional."

On the subject of Israeli settlements in the Sinai, Sadat warned in one of his letters that if Israel failed to withdraw, the "framework" for an Israeli-Egyptian peace treaty "shall be void and invalid."

Vance to Jordan, Arabia, Syria. U.S. Secretary of State Vance visited Amman, Riyadh and Damascus Sept. 21-24 to seek Jordanian, Saudi Arabian and Syrian support for the Camp David accords.

A State Department statement summarizing the reaction of Jordan and Saudi Arabia said both countries had been "vitally interested" in Vance's detailed explanation of the accords and "vitally concerned" about peace negotiations.

Vance's last stopover was in Damascus, where he held inconclusive discussions Sept. 24 with President Hafez al-Assad. A Syrian government communique said Assad had told Vance that "what happened at Camp David works only for the benefit of Israel." The summit talks, the statement added, "gave Israel everything it wanted. It goes against the basic Arab rights, especially the rights of the Palestinians to an independent nation, to sovereignty in their own land."

Texts of Camp David Accords

Following are the texts issued by the White House of the two documents agreed to at the Camp David summit meeting and signed Sept. 17 by the U.S., Israel and Egypt:

"The Framework of Peace in the Middle East"

Mohammed Anwar al-Sadat, president of the Arab Republic of Egypt, and Menahem Begin, premier of Israel, met with Jimmy Carter, President of the United States of America, at Camp David from Sept. 5 to Sept. 17, 1978, and have agreed on the following framework for peace in the Middle East. They invite other parties to the Arab-Israeli conflict to adhere to it:

Preamble:

The search for peace in the Middle East must be guided by the following:

The agreed basis for a peaceful settlement of the conflict between Israel and its neighbors is U.N. Security Council Resolution 242 in all its parts.

After four wars during 30 years, despite intensive humane efforts, the Middle East, which is the cradle of civilization and the birthplace of three great religions, does not yet enjoy the blessings of peace. The people of the Middle East yearn for peace, so that the vast human and natural resources of the region can be turned to the pursuits of peace and so that this area can become a model for coexistence and cooperation among nations.

The historic initiative by President Sadat in visiting Jerusalem and the reception accorded to him by the parliament, government and people of Israel, and the reciprocal visit of Premier Begin to Ismailia, the peace proposals made by both leaders, as well as the warm reception of these missions by the peoples of both countries, have created an unprecedented opportunity for peace which must not be lost if this generation and future generations are to be spared the tragedies of war.

The provisions of the charter of the United Nations and the other accepted norms of international law and legitimacy now provide accepted standards for the conduct of relations between all states.

To achieve a relationship of peace, in the spirit of Article 2 of the U.N. charter, future negotiations between Israel and any neighbor prepared to negotiate peace and security with it, are necessary for the purpose of carrying out all the provisions and principles of resolutions 242 and 338.

Peace requires respect for the sovereignty, territorial integrity and political independence of every state in the area and their right to live in peace within secure and recognized boundaries free from threats or acts of force. Progress toward that goal can accelerate movement toward a new era of reconciliation in the Middle East marked by cooperation in promoting economic development, in maintaining stability and in assuring security.

Security is enhanced by a relationship of peace and by cooperation between nations which enjoy normal relations. In addition, under the terms of peace treaties, the parties can, on the basis of reciprocity, agree to special security arrangements such as demilitarized zones, limited armaments areas, early warning stations, the presence of international forces, liaison, agreed measures for monitoring, and other arrangements that they agree are useful.

Framework:

Taking these factors into account, the parties are determined to reach a just, comprehensive, and durable settlement of the Middle East conflict through the conclusion of peace treaties based on Security Council Resolutions 242 and 338 in all their parts. Their purpose is to achieve peace and good neighborly relations. They recognize that, for peace to endure, it must involve all those who have been most deeply affected by the conflict. They therefore agreed that this framework as appropriate is intended by them to constitute a basis for peace not only between Egypt and Israel, but also between Israel and each of its other neighbors which is prepared to negotiate peace with Israel on this basis. With that objective in mind, they have agreed to proceed as follows:

1. Egypt, Israel, Jordan and the representatives of the Palestinian people should participate in negotiations on the resolution of the Palestinian problem in all its aspects. To achieve that objective, negotiations relating to the West Bank and Gaza should proceed in three stages.

(a) Egypt and Israel agree that, in order to ensure a peaceful and orderly transfer of authority, and taking into account the security concerns of all the parties, there should be transitional arrangements for the West Bank and Gaza for a period not exceeding five years. In order to provide full autonomy to the inhabitants, under these arrangements the Israeli military government and its civilian administration will be withdrawn as soon as self-governing authority has been freely elected by the inhabitants of these areas to replace the existing military government. To negotiate the details of a transitional agreement, the government of Jordan will be invited to join the negotiations on the basis of this framework. These new arrangements should give due consideration to both the principle of self-government by the inhabitants of these territories and to the legitimate security concerns of the parties involved.

(b) Egypt, Israel, and Jordan will agree on the modalities for establishing the elected self-governing authority in the West Bank and Gaza. The delegations of Egypt and Jordan may include Palestinians from the West Bank and Gaza or other Palestinians as mutually agreed. The parties will negotiate an agreement which will define the powers and responsibilities of the self-governing authority to be exercised in the West Bank and Gaza. A withdrawal of Israeli armed forces will take place and there will be a redeployment of the remaining Israeli forces into specified security locations. The agreement will also include arrangements for assuring internal and external security and public order. A strong local police force will be established, which may include Jordanian citizens. In addition, Israeli and Jordanian forces will participate in joint patrols and in the manning of control posts to assure the security of the borders.

(c) When the self-governing authority (administrative council) in the West Bank and Gaza is established and inaugurated, the transitional period of five years will begin. As soon as possible, but not later than the third year after the beginning of the transitional period, negotiations will take place to determine the final status of the West Bank and Gaza and its relationship with its neighbors, and to conclude a peace treaty between Israel and Jordan by the end of the transitional period. These negotiations will be conducted among Egypt, Israel, Jordan, and the elected representatives of the inhabitants of the West Bank and Gaza. Two separate but related committees will be convened, one committee, consisting of representatives of the four parties which will negotiate and agree on the final status of the West Bank and Gaza, and its relationship with its neighbors; and the second committee, consisting of representatives of Israel and representatives of Jordan to be joined by the elected representatives of the inhabitants of the West Bank and Gaza, to negotiate the peace treaty between Israel and Jordan, taking into account the agreement reached on the final status of the West Bank and Gaza. The negotiations shall be based on the provisions and principles of U.N. Security Council Resolution 242. The negotiations will resolve, among other matters, the location of the boundaries and the nature of the security arrangements. The solution from the negotiations must also recognize the legitimate rights of the Palestinian people and their just requirements. In this way, the Palestinians will participate in the determination of their own future through:

A. West Bank and Gaza:

1. The negotiations among Egypt, Israel, Jordan and the representatives of the inhabitants of the West Bank and Gaza to agree on the final status of the West Bank and Gaza and other outstanding issues by the end of the transitional period.

Submitting their agreement to a vote by the elected representatives of the inhabitants of the West Bank and Gaza.

Providing for the elected representatives of the inhabitants of the West Bank and Gaza to decide how they shall govern themselves consistent with the provisions of their agreement.

Participating as stated above in the work of the committee negotiating the peace treaty between Israel and Jordan.

2. All necessary measures will be taken and provisions made to assure the security of Israel and its neighbors during the transitional period and beyond. To assist in providing such security, a strong local police force will be constituted by the self-governing authority. It will be composed of inhabitants of the West Bank and Gaza. The police will maintain continuing liaison on internal security matters with the designated Israeli, Jordanian and Egyptian officers.

3. During the transitional period, the representatives of Egypt, Israel, Jordan and the self-governing authority will constitute a continuing committee to decide by agreement on the modalities of admission of persons displaced from the West Bank and Gaza in 1967, together with necessary measures to prevent disruption and disorder. Other matters of common concern may also be dealt with by this committee.

4. Egypt and Israel will work with each other and with other interested parties to establish agreed procedures for a prompt, just and permanent implementation of the resolution of the refugee problem.

B. Egypt-Israel:

1. Egypt and Israel undertake not to resort to the threat or the use of force to settle disputes. Any disputes shall be settled by peaceful means in accordance with the provisions of Article 33 of the Charter of the United Nations.

2. In order to achieve peace between them, the parties agree to negotiate in good faith with a goal of concluding within three months from the signing of this framework a peace treaty between them, while inviting the other parties to the conflict to proceed simultaneously to negotiate and conclude similar peace treaties with a view to achieving a comprehensive peace in the area. The framework for the conclusion of a peace treaty between Egypt and Israel will govern the peace negotiations between them. The parties will agree on the modalities and the timetable for the implementation of their obligations under the treaty.

Associated Principles:

1. Egypt and Israel state that the principles and provisions described below should apply to peace treaties between Israel and each of its neighbors—Egypt, Jordan, Syria and Lebanon.

2. Signatories shall establish among themselves relationships normal to states at peace with one another. To this end, they should undertake to abide by all the provisions of the charter of the United Nations. Steps to be taken in this respect include:

(a) Full recognition.

(b) Abolishing economic boycotts.

(c) Guaranteeing that under their jurisdiction the citizens of the other parties shall enjoy the protection of the due process of law.

3. Signatories should explore possibilities for economic development in the context of final peace treaties, with the objective of contributing to the atmosphere of peace, cooperation, and friendship which is their common goal.

4. Claims commissions may be established for the mutual settlement of all financial claims.

5. The United States shall be invited to participate in the talks on matters related to the modalities of the implementation of the agreements and working out the timetable for the carrying out of the obligations of the parties.

6. The United Nations Security Council shall be requested to endorse the peace treaties and ensure that their provisions shall not be violated. The permanent members of the Security Council shall be requested to underwrite the peace treaties and ensure respect for their provisions. They shall also be requested to conform their policies and actions with the undertakings contained in this framework.

"Framework for the Conclusion of a Peace Treaty Between Egypt and Israel"

In order to achieve peace between them, Israel and Egypt agree to negotiate in good faith with a goal of concluding within three months of the signing of this framework a peace treaty between them.

It is agreed that:

The site of the negotiations will be under a United Nations flag at a location or locations to be mutually agreed.

All of the principles of U.N. Resolution 242 will apply in this resolution of the dispute between Israel and Egypt.

Unless otherwise mutually agreed, terms of the peace treaty will be implemented between two and three years after the peace treaty is signed.

The following matters are agreed between the parties:

(a) The full exercise of Egyptian sovereignty up to the internationally recognized border between Egypt and mandated Palestine;

(b) The withdrawal of Israeli armed forces from the Sinai;

(c) The use of airfields left by the Israelis near El Arish, Rafan, Ras en Naqb, and Sharm el Sheikh for civilian purposes only, including possible commercial use by all nations;

(d) The right of free passage by ships of Israel through the Gulf of Suez and the Suez Canal on the basis of the Constantinople Convention of 1888 applying to all nations: the Strait of Tiran and the Gulf of Aqaba are international waterways to be open to all nations for unimpeded and nonsuspendable freedom of navigation and overflight;

(e) The construction of a highway between the Sinai and Jordan near Eilat with guaranteed free and peaceful passage by Egypt and Jordan; and

(f) The stationing of military forces listed below.

Stationing of Forces

A. No more than one division (mechanized or infantry) of Egyptian armed forces will be stationed within an area lying approximately 50 kilometers (30 miles) east of the Gulf of Suez and the Suez Canal.

B. Only United Nations forces and civil police equipped with light weapons to perform normal police functions will be stationed within an area lying west of the international border and the Gulf of Aqaba, varying in width from 20 kilometers (12 miles) to 40 kilometers (24 miles).

C. In the area within 3 kilometers (1.8 miles) east of the international border there will be Israeli limited military forces not to exceed four infantry battalions and United Nations observers.

D. Border patrol units, not to exceed three battalions, will supplement the civil police in maintaining order in the area not included above.

The exact demarcation of the above areas will be as decided during the peace negotiations.

Early warning stations may exist to insure compliance with the terms of the agreement.

United Nations forces will be stationed: (a) in part of the area in the Sinai lying within about 20 kilometers of the Mediterranean Sea and adjacent to the international border, and (b) in the Sharm el Sheikh area to ensure freedom of passage through the Strait of Tiran; and these forces will not be removed unless such removal is approved by the Security Council of the United Nations with the unanimous vote of the five permanent members.

After a peace treaty is signed, and after the interim withdrawal is complete, normal relations will be established between Egypt and Israel, including: full recognition, including diplomatic, economic and cultural relations; termination of economic boycotts and barriers to the free movement of goods and people; and mutual protection of citizens by the due process of law.

Interim Withdrawal

Between three months and nine months after the signing of the peace treaty, all Israeli forces will withdraw east of a line extending from a point east of El Arish to Ras Muhammad, the exact locations of this line to be determined by mutual agreement.

Camp David
Adds to Controversy

While Egypt and Israel began steps— halting at times—to implement the Camp David accords, opponents of peace with Israel sought to make the accords ineffective.

Egyptian Cabinet Approves. The Egyptian Cabinet Sept. 19, 1978 unanimously approved the Camp David agreements.

Premier Mamdouh Salem said that despite the protest resignation of Foreign Minister Ibrahim Kamel, "All Egypt is supporting President Sadat and if anybody has a different opinion, this does not change the situation. . . . A minister may be changed, but policy does not change "

Egypt launched a drive Sept. 24 to muster the support of moderate Arab states for the Camp David accords. Deputy Premier Hassan Tuhami was sent to Geneva to confer with King Khalid of Saudi Arabia, who remained cool to the agreements. Other Egyptian emissaries were to be sent out on similar missions.

President Sadat had received a tumultuous welcome on his return to Cairo Sept. 23. Before arriving, the Egyptian leader had stopped off in Rabat, Morocco Sept. 20 to brief King Hassan II on the Camp David talks. Hassan, who had previously supported Sadat's peace initiative, gave no specific backing for the agreements.

Speaking at a news conference in Rabat Sept. 22, Sadat said the summit accords in which Israel agreed to return the Sinai to Egypt could also be applied to the Israeli-occupied Golan Heights. This could only come about if Syria was willing "to sit down with Egypt, Jordan, Israel and the representatives of the Palestinian people to negotiate," Sadat said.

Sadat said all sides at the Camp David conference subscribed to this view, but that it was up to Syria to decide whether to enter the peace process.

Sadat Defends Accords—Sadat Oct. 2 defended his action in coming to agreement with Israel.

Reporting on the talks to the People's Assembly (parliament), Sadat appealed to other Arab states, notably Jordan and Syria, to join the Middle East peace process. He assailed Arab hardline states for opposing his peace initiative. Sadat said: Egypt "constitutes a great danger to all those regimes. They liquidate people in Iraq. They hang people in Libya. Here in Egypt, we have democracy, . . . security, . . . They dread it all."

Sadat invited President Carter to Egypt for the eventual signing of a peace treaty between Egypt and Israel. Sadat later told newsmen that Carter accepted the invitation.

In a parallel development, Sadat issued a decree appointing Mustafa Khalil as premier, replacing Mamdouh Salem, who had resigned earlier in the day. Salem's resignation and other ministerial changes were part of a restructuring of the government from a war footing to a condition of peace in light of the agreements with Israel.

In the other changes made Oct. 3, Sadat removed Gen. Mohammed Abdel Ghany el-Gamasy as war minister and commander in chief, and Lt. Gen. Mohammed Ali Fahmy as chief of staff. Both men, supporters of the Camp David agreements, were to remain as military advisers to Sadat.

Israeli Knesset Endorses Pact. The Israeli Knesset (parliament) Sept. 28 approved the Camp David summit agreements with Egypt and the removal of Jewish settlements in the Sinai. The vote was 84 to 19, with 17 abstentions.

In approving the dismantling of the settlements, the Knesset cleared away the one procedural obstacle to Egyptian-Israeli peace negotiations. The action immediately set in motion the machinery for the start of separate peace talks between the two nations.

One of the Knesset deputies who voted against the pact, Commerce Minister Yigal Hurvitz, resigned from the Cabinet in protest against the decision to accept withdrawal of the settlements as part of the peace agreement with Egypt.

Both issues were combined as a single question after Premier Menahem Begin Sept. 24 had rejected a demand by two Cabinet members—Commerce Minister Hurvitz and Health Minister Eliezer Shostak—for a separate vote on the settlement issue. The Cabinet approved the agreements that day by a vote of 11 to two. Three ministers were absent. The dissenting votes were cast by Hurvitz and Shostak.

Begin warned Sept. 27 that he would resign and form a new Cabinet unless a majority of his coalition's 70 members in the Knesset supported the Camp David agreements. Citing Israeli parliamentary law, Begin said that any Cabinet minister's vote against the peace issue in the Knesset was tantamount to that minister's resignation, requiring the premier to form a new government.

(The opposition Labor Party Sept. 24 approved the Camp David agreements by a 221-16 vote.)

At the start of Knesset debate Sept. 25, Begin urged the legislature to accept President Sadat's prerequisite for abandonment of Jewish settlements in the Sinai or reject peace. Israel had "arrived at the moment when we can, with very difficult sacrifices, sign a peace treaty with an Arab nation [Egypt] with over 40 million people," Begin said.

Hardliners Break with Egypt. Four Arab hardline states and the Palestine Liberation Organization ended a four-day meeting in Damascus Sept. 24, 1978 with an announcement that they were cutting all political and economic relations with Egypt because of its involvement in the Camp David summit meeting.

President Anwar Sadat said Egypt was breaking ties with them in response.

A final statement issued by the leaders of Syria, Algeria, South Yemen, Libya and the PLO pledged the meeting's participants to work for "the fall" of Sadat's peace policies and declared that his signature on the Camp David agreements was null and void. The group, known as the "Steadfastness and Confrontation Front," promised to "reinforce and develop relations with . . . friendly countries [and] the states of the socialist camp led by the Soviet Union. . . ."

Syrian President Hafez al-Assad was "requested to contact the Soviet Union and other friendly states" to press the campaign against Sadat's policies, the statement said.

The participants agreed to establish joint political and military commands, but no further details were provided.

Text of Letters Exchanged at the Camp David Summit

Following are the texts of the letters President Carter exchanged with Premier Begin of Israel and President Sadat of Egypt at the conclusion of the Camp David summit meeting and in the days following. The White House made the texts of the letters public Sept. 22.

A: Letter from Mr. Begin to President Carter (dated September 17):

I have the honor to inform you that during two weeks after my return home I will submit a motion before Israel's parliament (the Knesset) to decide on the following question:

If during the negotiations to conclude a peace treaty between Israel and Egypt all outstanding issues are agreed upon, are you in favor of the removal of Israeli settlers from the northern and southern Sinai areas or are you in favor of keeping the aforementioned settlers in those areas?

The vote, Mr. President, on this issue will be completely free from the usual parliamentary party discipline to the effect that although the coalition is being now supported by 70 members out of 120, every member of the Knesset, as I believe, both on the government and the opposition benches will be enabled to vote in accordance with his own conscience.

B. Letter from President Carter to President Sadat (dated September 22):

I transmit herewith a copy of a letter to me from Prime Minister Begin setting forth how he proposes to present the issue of the Sinai settlements to the Knesset for the latter's decision.

In this connection, I understand from your letter that Knesset approval to withdraw all Israeli settlers from Sinai according to a timetable within the period specified for the implementation of the peace treaty is a prerequisite to any negotiations on a peace treaty between Egypt and Israel.

C. Letter from President Sadat to President Carter (dated September 17):

In connection with the "Framework for a Settlement in Sinai," to be signed tonight, I would like to reaffirm the position of the Arab Republic of Egypt with respect to the settlements:

1. All Israeli settlers must be withdrawn from Sinai according to a timetable within the period specified for the implementation of the peace treaty.

2. Agreement by the Israeli government and its constitutional institutions to this basic principle is therefore a prerequisite to starting peace negotiations for concluding a peace treaty.

3. If Israel fails to meet this commitment, the "framework" shall be void and invalid.

D. Letter from President Carter to Mr. Begin (dated September 22):

I have received your letter of September 17, 1978, describing how you intend to place the question of the future of Israeli settlements in Sinai before the Knesset for its decision.

Enclosed is a copy of President Sadat's letter to me on this subject.

E. Letter from President Sadat to President Carter (dated September 17):

I am writing you to reaffirm the position of the Arab Republic of Egypt with respect to Jerusalem:

1. Arab Jerusalem is an integral part of the West Bank. Legal and historical Arab rights in the city must be respected and restored.

2. Arab Jerusalem should be under Arab sovereignty.

3. The Palestinian inhabitants of Arab Jerusalem are entitled to exercise their legitimate national rights, being part of the Palestinian people in the West Bank.

4. Relevant Security Council resolutions, particularly Resolutions 242 and 267, must be applied with regard to Jerusalem. All the measures taken by Israel to alter the status of the city are null and void and should be rescinded.

5. All peoples must have free access to the city and enjoy the free exercise and the right to visit and transit to the holy places without distinction or discrimination.

6. The holy places of each faith may be placed under the administration and control of their representatives.

7. Essential functions in the city should be undivided and a joint municipal council composed of an equal number of Arabs and Israeli members can supervise the carryout of these functions. In this way, the city should be undivided.

F. Letter from Mr. Begin to President Carter (dated September 17):

I have the honor to inform you, Mr. President, that on June 28, 1967—Israel's parliament (the Knesset) promulgated and adopted a law to the effect: 'The government is empowered by a decree to apply the law, the jurisdiction and administration of the state to any part of Eretz Israel (Land of Israel—Palestine), as stated in that decree.'

On the basis of this law the government of Israel decreed in July 1967, that Jerusalem is one city indivisible, the capital of the state of Israel.

G. Letter from President Carter to President Sadat (dated September 22):

I have received your letter of September 17, 1978, setting forth the Egyptian position on Jerusalem. I am transmitting a copy of that letter to Prime Minister Begin for his information. The position of the United States on Jerusalem remains as stated by Ambassador [Arthur] Goldberg in the United Nations General Assembly on July 14, 1967, and subsequently by Ambassador [Charles] Yost in the United Nations Security Council on July 1, 1969.

H. Letter from President Sadat to President Carter (dated September 17):

In connection with the "Framework for Peace in the Middle East," I am writing you this letter to inform you of the position of the Arab Republic of Egypt, with respect to the implementation of the comprehensive settlement. To ensure the implementation of the provisions related to the West Bank and Gaza and in order to safeguard the legitimate rights of the Palestinian people, Egypt will be prepared to assume the Arab role emanating from those provisions, following consultations with Jordan and the representatives of the Palestinian people.

I. Letter from President Carter to Mr. Begin (dated September 22):

I hereby acknowledge that you have informed me as follows:

(A) In each paragraph of the agreed framework document the expressions 'Palestinians' or 'Palestine people' are being and will be construed and understood by you as 'Palestinian Arabs'.

(B) In each paragraph in which the expression 'West Bank' appears, it is being, and will be, understood by the government of Israel as Judea and Samaria.

The conference called on the Arab League to remove its headquarters from Cairo and suggested that a new league be created if this could not be done.

Libyan leader Muammer el-Qaddafi and PLO leader Yasir Arafat had briefly interrupted their attendance of the Damascus meeting to go to Mafraq in northern Jordan Sept. 22 to confer with King Hussein. Both men, former enemies of the monarch, sought to dissuade him from entering into negotiations with Egypt and Israel, as called for by the Camp David accords.

The meeting was held at Qaddafi's initiative. Hussein said afterward that his four-hour discussion with Qaddafi and Arafat was "very constructive" and produced "very positive results." Hussein said it was up to the Confrontation Front "to coordinate their efforts with us."

In his first public comment on the Camp David summit, Hussein said Sept. 23 that he was "absolutely shattered" by President Sadat's pursuance of his peace initiative in disregard of other Arab states. Hussein warned of "very serious repercussions" if the Egyptian leader signed a separate peace with Israel.

At the same time, Hussein said he would not rule out a role for Jordan in a comprehensive peace settlement. But such an agreement must include the return of East Jerusalem to the Arabs, Palestinian rights and Israeli withdrawal from occupied Arab lands, Hussein said.

Hussein came under further Arab pressure to reject the Camp David accords in a meeting with President Assad in Amman Sept. 26. The king said after the discussions that he and the Syrian leader saw "eye-to-eye" on the need for a "total reexamination" of the U.S.-Egyptian-Israeli agreements. The king also said the U.S. had not come "anywhere near" his demands for a peace accord.

Hussein said Israeli Premier Menahem Begin's recent statements were "not a very helpful factor as far as the impression we are already forming regarding what happened at Camp David." He was alluding to Begin's remarks in which he said Israel would retain East Jerusalem, the West Bank and Israeli settlements on the West Bank.

Speaking on the CBS program *Face the Nation,* Hussein said his conditions for entering the negotiations on the resolution of

the West Bank-Gaza problem depended on how the U.S. answered the following questions: Was East Jerusalem and its environs, which had been annexed by Israel in 1967, considered part of the West Bank?; After the proposed five-year transitional period during which the West Bank Arabs would enjoy autonomy, who would exercise sovereignty?; What would be the status of East Jerusalem after the five-year period?; Would the United Nations or some other international body supervise the agency exercising autonomy during the five-year period?; Would Israeli settlements remain on the West Bank during and after the transitional term?, and What were the plans for the Israeli-occupied Golan Heights (which were not mentioned in the summit accords)?

Hussein insisted that he would continue to avoid the peace talks unless the U.S. assumed the role of an active partner in securing the rights of the Arabs on the West Bank.

Hussein warned Oct. 1 that a separate Egyptian Israeli peace treaty would bring "upheavals" in the Arab world.

U.S. Call to Palestinians. U.S. Secretary of State Cyrus Vance Sept. 29, 1978 called on the Palestinians to join the peace negotiations.

Speaking to the United Nations General Assembly in New York, Vance said the rights of the Palestinians must be central to any long-term settlement. He urged "other interested parties," an apparent reference to Jordan, to enter into the talks with Israel and Egypt and "not to stand still until every last issue is resolved."

After Vance's address, other U.S. officials met with Arab delegates in a U.N. conference room in an attempt to win their approval of the Camp David agreements.

West Bank Arabs for PLO State—A group of 100 West Bank Arab leaders Oct. 1 rejected the Camp David agreements and called for establishment of an independent Palestinian state led by the Palestine Liberation Organization. They urged their followers to boycott elections for an administrative council that would govern the West Bank for five years, as proposed in the Camp David accords.

The West Bank leaders issued their statement at a conference held in the Jerusalem suburb of Beit Hanna. Among those attending were representatives of 19 of the West Bank's 29 municipalities, most of whom were known as supporters of the PLO.

Sadat Criticizes Syria. Egyptian President Anwar Sadat assailed Syria and the Palestinians Oct. 10 for their vehement opposition to his peace agreements with Israel.

Speaking to a meeting of Egypt's Supreme Judiciary Council, Sadat said he had done his "duty" at the Camp David summit conference in agreeing "to the principles governing the Palestinian question and the Golan Heights." The Egyptian leader added: "As for the details, they [the Syrians and Palestinians] will have to go and negotiate them for themselves. I would have liked to do it on their behalf, but their ingratitude and obscenities have gone beyond all limits."

Sadat also was critical of Syria's military role in the Lebanese crisis. He described Syrian attacks on the Christian militia as "murder for murder's sake ... The fate of nations is being played with just as children play with toys ... I shall never put the destiny of Egypt or the Arab cause in the hands of these children, these murderers."

U.S. to Build Israeli Bases. The U.S. promised to help Israel build two new air bases in its southern Negev Desert to replace two similar bases Israel was required to abandon in the Sinai under terms of the Camp David accords, the U.S. disclosed Sept. 29, 1978.

The pledge was contained in a letter (dated Sept. 28) sent by U.S. Defense Secretary Harold Brown to Israeli Defense Minister Ezer Weizman.

Brown said the U.S. was aware of "the special urgency and priority which Israel attaches to preparing the new bases in light of its conviction that it cannot safely leave the Sinai bases until the new ones are operational." In view of this, the secretary suggested that the U.S. and Israel "consult on the scope and costs of the two new air bases as well as on the related forms of assistance" that the U.S. might provide in facilitating construction.

U.S. Defense Department officials estimated that the cost of building the two bases would range from between $150 million and $550 million each.

Syria, Iraq to Join Forces. Syria and Iraq agreed Oct. 24–26, 1978 to resolve their long-standing differences and join military forces to counter "the great dangers looming over the Arab nation" as a result of the Camp David accords.

The agreement was reached in discussions between Syrian President Hafez al-Assad and Ahmed Hassan al-Bakr, Iraqi president and premier. A joint communique said the two men had agreed to establish a bilateral committee of foreign and defense ministers and military chiefs of staff to promote military cooperation. "The committee would draw up a draft joint defense agreement that would serve as the basis for a full military union" between Iraq and Syria, the statement said.

No mention was made in the communique of Iraq's suggestion that it station troops on Syria's Golan Heights to counter Israeli forces and that it set up a $9-billion Arab fund to help the "confrontation states" against Israel.

The communique also was silent about resolving the ideological differences between the ruling Baath parties of Syria and Iraq.

Other Syrian-Iraqi differences concerned the division of oil and water resources and claims and counterclaims of terrorist activity directed by one country against the other.

In a previous act of reconciliation, Syria had reopened its frontier with Iraq Oct. 22. The border had been closed since March to prevent, in Damascus' words, "killers and terrorists crossing from Iraq into Syria to perpetrate terrorist attacks."

Soviets, PLO vs. Camp David Pact. The Camp David agreement between Israel and Egypt was assailed in a joint communique issued in Moscow Nov. 1 by Soviet officials and Palestine Liberation Organization leader Yasir Arafat.

The communique denounced the Camp David settlement "as a collusion at the expense of and behind the backs of the Arabs aimed at helping Israel entrench [itself] on captured Arab land, including

Palestine, and prevent implementation of the Palestinians' inalienable rights." The document urged Arab states of the Middle East to continue to confront "the machinations of imperialism, Zionism, and collusion with the aggressor. . . ."

The joint statement reiterated the Soviet demand for the convening of a Geneva conference of all countries involved in the Middle East dispute. The goal of such a meeting to achieve an overall settlement "requires the collective efforts of all the interested parties with the equal participation in them of the PLO as sole legitimate representative of the Arab people of Palestine," the statement said.

Arafat had conferred with Soviet Foreign Minister Andrei Gromyko Oct. 30 to brief him on the PLO's objectives and its plan for a solution to the Palestinian problem "within the framework of a comprehensive Middle East settlement."

U.N. Role in Palestine State Backed—
Yasir Arafat said in an interview Nov. 19 that he favored the deployment of a United Nations security force inside any new Palestinian state that would be established.

He said he also favored security guarantees for the new state and Israel, including a demilitarized zone.

The remainder of Arafat's interview dealt with the possible repercussions of the Egyptian-Israeli Camp David accords and a treaty between the two nations on the Palestinian movement. He said that if, as a result, Egypt left the Arab ranks, a new alliance would be formed between Syria and Iraq, accompanied by support from the Communist countries, especially the Soviet Union.

Arab Summit in Baghdad. The Arab League concluded a four-day summit meeting in Baghdad Nov. 5, 1978 with the issuance of a communique calling on Egypt not to sign a peace agreement with Israel. The meeting, which had been called by Iraq to counter the Camp David accords, was attended by representatives of 20 of the 21 league members; Egypt was not invited.

The final declaration of the conference, read by Iraqi Foreign Minister Saadun Hammadi, said that the summit regarded the Camp David accords as an infringement on the rights of the Palestinian people and other Arabs. It stressed the need for Arab unity to deal with the "strategic defect" resulting from Egypt's withdrawal from the conflict with Israel.

The declaration reaffirmed the right of the Palestinians to return to their "homeland" and the Palestine Liberation Organization's role as the sole representative of the Palestinian people.

Mahmoud Riad of Egypt, secretary general of the Arab League, disclosed on his return to Cairo Nov. 6 that the league had decided to hold another top-level meeting of the organization to consider moving its headquarters out of Cairo once Egypt signed a peace treaty with Israel. "The Arabs have decided that it would not be logical to keep the league headquarters in Egypt when there will be an Israeli embassy" there, Riad said. According to Riad, Sudan, Morocco and Oman, which had supported President Anwar Sadat's peace initiatives, were the only states at the meeting to question the decision.

Saudi Arabia was said to have successfully blocked a move by such hardliners as Libya and the PLO to blacklist Egypt and impose other penalties on it. Arab diplomatic sources in Beirut, however, said that secret resolutions had been adopted providing for political and economic sanctions against Egypt if it concluded a peace treaty with Israel.

League representatives also were said to have secretly agreed to establish a 10-year, $3.5-billion annual fund to enable front-line states to counter the effects of the Israeli-Egyptian rapprochement. The funds were pledged by Saudi Arabia ($1 billion), Iraq and Libya ($500 million each) and other of the Persian Gulf states for Syria, Jordan and the PLO.

Sadat Shuns Summit Delegation—
Egyptian President Anwar Sadat refused to meet with a four-man delegation of the Baghdad summit that arrived in Cairo Nov. 4 to ask him to reconsider his peace plans with Israel.

Sadat disclosed his action in a speech later Nov. 4 to the opening of a new session of the People's Assembly (parliament). The president, who even refused to let his subordinates meet with the delegation, complained that the four representatives had flown to Cairo "without permission or arrangement" with Egyptian officials. He had only learned about the mission through news agency reports, Sadat said.

Sadat also objected to the relatively low-level status of the delegates. He later told newsmen, "I am not prepared to receive anybody except presidents and kings."

The Baghdad summit delegation was led by Lebanese Premier Selim al-Hoss. The others were Syrian Information Minister Ahmed Iskander, United Arab Emirates Foreign Minister Khalifa al-Sweida and Tarek Aziz, a member of Iraq's ruling Revolutionary Command Council.

Sadat & Begin Win Nobel Prize. The Norwegian Peace Prize Committee Oct. 27 announced that President Anwar Sadat of Egypt and Premier Menahem Begin of Israel had-been named co-winners of the 1978 Nobel Peace Prize.

The committee said it had acted "not only to honor actions already performed in the service of peace [efforts to secure a Middle East accord], but also to encourage further efforts to work out practical solutions which can give reality to those hopes of a lasting peace, as they have been kindled by the framework agreements [Camp David]."

The citation specifically congratulated Sadat for his "historic visit" to Jerusalem in November 1977, which "forced a breach in the psychological wall which for a whole generation had blocked understanding and human contact between Egypt and Israel."

The statement also praised President Carter's "positive initiative" and "great role" in bringing Sadat and Begin together at the Camp David summit. Begin's contributions were not specified.

Sadat Shuns Nobel Award Rites—Israeli and Egyptian differences over the proposed peace pact were underscored in the acceptance of the Nobel Peace prize Dec. 10 by Begin and Sadat. Begin came in person to accept the award in ceremonies in Oslo, Norway, while Sadat stayed away and was represented instead by an aide, Sayed Marei.

Sadat's decision not to attend had been announced in Cairo Nov. 30.

Egypt's ambassador to Norway, Gamal Naguib, said Dec. 2 that "as long as there is no peace, it is meaningless for President Sadat to sit beside Premier Begin's side during the peace prize ceremony."

In his acceptance speech read by Marei, Sadat reiterated his support of the Palestinians. He said the object of the peace process "is to bring security to the peoples of the area, and the Palestinians in particular, restoring to them all their right to a life of liberty and dignity."

Begin said in his address that a U.S.-proposed draft accord accepted by Israel "can serve, if and when signed and ratified, as a good treaty of peace" between Israel and Egypt and "as the first indispensable step along the road towards a comprehensive peace in our region."

Negotiating a Peace Treaty: Hope & Reality in Conflict

Egypt, Israel Open Treaty Talks. Israel and Egypt opened negotiations in Washington Oct. 12, 1978 on drafting a bilateral peace treaty.

After a ceremonial opening of the conference at the White House, the U.S., Egyptian and Israeli delegations moved across the street to Blair House, the site of the actual negotiating sessions.

At the White House ceremonies, speeches were delivered by President Carter and the heads of the Israeli and Egyptian teams—Foreign Minister Moshe Dayan and Defense Minister Kamel Hassan Ali.

Carter said a peace treaty between Israel and Egypt "must be the foundation and the first step toward the larger, even greater, more important result which we all seek—a comprehensive and lasting settlement between Israel and all her neighbors." It should "be complemented by progress toward fulfillment of the provisions of the general framework agreement which was conducted at Camp David dealing with the West Bank and Gaza and the just solution of the Palestinian question in all its aspects," the President said.

Carter repeated his invitation to Jordan and Arabs on the West Bank and Gaza and "others who are ready to seize this opportunity, to join us in the search for peace."

Dayan and Ali thanked Carter for his role in advancing the peace process in the Middle East. All echoed Carter's wish that the two frameworks agreed to at

Camp David "will serve as a solid foundation for a comprehensive peace to be built in good faith by all parties."

At the Oct. 13 session, Secretary of State Cyrus Vance, who headed the American delegation, submitted a draft of a U.S. proposal for a peace treaty, which was accepted by both sides as the basis for negotiations. Details of the document were not disclosed, but a U.S. spokesman said it was "aimed at fleshing out the framework that was reached at Camp David."

President Carter personally intervened in the talks Oct. 17 by holding separate discussions with the Israeli and Egyptian delegations. U.S. spokesmen said the purpose of the President's action was merely to receive a progress report on status of the talks.

However, Foreign Minister Dayan said after meeting with Carter: "We have come up against some difficulties in our negotiations with the Egyptian delegation. The President said to turn to him in such a case, and we have."

After his discussions with Dayan and Egyptian acting Foreign Minister Butros Ghali, Carter told newsmen that there was no "particular problem" or "crisis" that prompted his personal intervention.

In the wake of continuing press speculation about the meaning of Dayan's remarks, the U.S. gave a further reassurance Oct. 18 that "there is no crisis, no deadlock, no emergency" in the negotiations.

Israel, Egypt Get Text of Pact—Egypt and Israel announced Oct. 22 that they had agreed tentatively on the principal points of a peace accord in their talks in Washington. The U.S. State Department said the text of a draft had been sent to both countries.

The discussions had adjourned Oct. 21 after Israel's chief negotiators, Foreign Minister Moshe Dayan and Defense Minister Ezer Weizman, were recalled to Jerusalem for consultations.

Before Dayan and Weizman left, President Carter had personally intervened in the talks that day for the second time in a week. The President held separate talks with both men and with Egyptian acting Foreign Minister Butros Ghali.

The Israeli Cabinet started debate on the draft treaty Oct. 24 and gave final approval the following day, attaching a series of proposed revisions that would have to be negotiated when the Washington talks resumed. The amendments were said to deal with Israel's objections to linking the Israeli-Egyptian treaty with the problem of the West Bank and Gaza Strip. The changes were not specified, but Foreign Minister Dayan said they were "substantial."

The Cabinet vote was 15–0 with two abstentions. In a surprise move, the Cabinet also voted to submit the final draft of the accord for Knesset ratification. The final document also would have to be approved by the Cabinet.

President Anwar Sadat said Oct. 25 that Egypt also would insist on alterations of the draft.

Israeli Outposts Imperil Pact Talks. An announcement by Israel Oct. 25 that it intended to expand existing Jewish settlements in the West Bank and Gaza Strip raised fears of a possible setback to the current Israeli-Egyptian treaty talks in Washington. The proposed move drew a sharp rebuke from the U.S. Oct. 26.

The Israeli stand, proclaimed in the Knesset (parliament) by Premier Menahem Begin, followed Cabinet approval in principle earlier in the day of a draft compromise treaty, whose completion had been announced in Washington Oct. 22.

Begin said Foreign Minister Moshe Dayan would inform U.S. officials in Washington that Israel would embark on a $15-million program to build 300 additional housing units in the West Bank.

The Israeli decision was reported to have been sparked by statements made by U.S. Assistant Secretary of State Harold Saunders in his meetings Oct. 17–19 in Jordan with King Hussein and with Arab notables on the West Bank. Saunders, who later met with Begin in Jerusalem, was said to have infuriated the Israelis by assuring West Bank leaders that Israel eventually would abandon the settlements in the territory and by stating that the U.S. did not agree with Israel's proposal to give the West Bank autonomy for a five-year transitional period.

Saunders also irritated the Israelis for restating the U.S. position that East Jerusalem was Arab territory occupied by Israel and for making unspecified promises to King Hussein. Saunders had provided answers to Hussein's questions about American policy on the West Bank and later explained the answers to Begin.

Begin assured his supporters at a rally in Tel Aviv Oct. 26 that his government would continue to "implement its right to settle anywhere within the occupied West Bank and Gaza Strip." He said he had informed President Carter at the Camp David summit meetings earlier in October that "during the next three months we would be adding hundreds of families to our settlements" in the West Bank. "This we will carry out," Begin added.

Before departing for Washington for a new round of talks with Egypt, Dayan said Oct. 26 that the decision to expand the Israeli settlements did not contradict current Israeli policy or the Camp David agreements, "whether other people like it or not." Dayan added: "Maybe Egypt won't like it, but that's not the point. The [draft] agreement [drawn up by the Israeli Cabinet the previous day] is supposed to express the Israeli interest . . . about what should take place in the [occupied] area."

Dayan denied that Israel had agreed to suspend expansion of existing West Bank settlements during any time period and said Israel never agreed not to construct new settlements "except for the three months during" which Israel and Egypt negotiated a peace treaty.

Dayan confirmed on his arrival in Washington later Oct. 26 that Assistant Secretary of State Saunders' remarks had prompted the Israeli Cabinet to take action "to assure the people [in the settlements] that they could stay—that we do not intend to move" from the West Bank.

Secretary of State Cyrus Vance said Oct. 26 that the U.S. considered Israel's decision a "very serious matter" and was "deeply disturbed by it." President Carter voiced his concern in a message to Premier Begin.

Begin Reaffirms Settlement Plan— Premier Begin Oct. 29 reaffirmed Israel's plans to expand its settlements on the West Bank. The statement was in reply to President Carter's criticism of the program Oct. 26. The Cabinet unanimously approved Begin's response, which was transmitted to Washington.

The contents of Begin's message were not officially disclosed, but Cabinet sources said the premier reminded Carter

that Israel's intentions on the settlements were made clear at the Camp David summit.

Carter was said to have told a news conference in Washington Sept. 27 that the Camp David accords originally prohibited new settlements or expansion of existing ones, but that this section was deleted. Carter was quoted as having said that "we dropped the part on expansion" after accepting Begin's argument that buildings in the existing settlements had to be enlarged to permit the reuniting of families.

Questioned directly as to whether there was a limit on expansion of the settlements, Carter replied, "We had a discussion about this [at Camp David] and the reference was to a very limited expansion plan that would be revealed before the negotiations for the West Bank and Gaza self-government plan would be completed."

Israel-Egypt Pact Delayed. Israel and Egypt resumed talks in Washington Oct. 31 to conclude a bilateral treaty, but their negotiations remained stalled over differences on linking the proposed accord to an overall settlement of the Palestinian problem in the West Bank and Gaza Strip.

Egypt favored wording in the preamble to the text of the pact that would specifically tie the two issues together. Israel wanted a more general reference to the matter rather than a formal, legal link between the two. Other unresolved issues included a military annex to the treaty to set forth details on Israeli withdrawal from the Sinai and oil fields in the Sinai.

Egypt had decided Oct. 27 to recall its delegation from Washington for consultation on the linkage dispute and on Israel's announcement Oct. 25 of plans to expand its settlements in the West Bank. The Egyptians reversed the decision to bring back their representatives to Cairo after President Carter personally appealed to President Anwar Sadat later Oct. 27 to allow his negotiators to remain.

U.S. Secretary of State Cyrus Vance, who had been meeting separately with both sides, said Nov. 3 that "we have resolved almost all the substantive issues." Vance made the optimistic report after meeting in New York Nov. 2 with Israeli Premier Menahem Begin, who stopped off in the city on his way to visit Los Angeles and Canada.

Vance's optimism was tempered on receiving a report Nov. 8 from Israel's two negotiators—Defense Minister Ezer Weizman and Foreign Minister Moshe Dayan—that their government insisted on the elimination from the treaty's preamble of any linkage between the treaty with Egypt and the Palestinian problem. Vance was apprised of the Israeli stand following a briefing Weizman had given to the Cabinet Nov. 5-6. Weizman, who had been recalled to Jerusalem Nov. 2, returned to the Washington talks Nov. 7.

At a meeting with Vance Nov. 9, the Egyptian negotiators said President Sadat wanted some changes in the text of the treaty. An Egyptian official later said that Sadat would prefer stronger language on the linkage problem but added: "We can live with the text if the Israelis can."

Egypt appeared to remain adamant about the linkage problem as reflected in a statement made by President Sadat Nov. 7. He said that his country would not sign a peace treaty with Israel "unless it refers clearly to future upcoming negotiations with representatives of the Palestinian people so they can decide the future of the West Bank and Gaza Strip."

The linkage question had emerged from the Camp David summit in September but its resolution was left to the future Israeli-Egyptian treaty talks. Sadat was determined to connect the Palestinian problem with progress on an accord with Israel to turn aside Arab charges that the Camp David agreement served only to produce a "separate peace" between Egypt and Israel.

Carter Asks End to Linkage Feud—President Carter called on Egypt and Israel Nov. 9 to settle their dispute over the linkage problem.

Speaking at a news conference in Kansas City, the president noted that "one of the premises for the Camp David negotiations was a comprehensive peace settlement, that includes not just an isolated peace treaty between Israel and Egypt, but includes continuation of a solution for the West Bank, Gaza Strip and ultimately for the Golan Heights as well."

The President said he personally endorsed the "presently negotiated language" contained in the preamble, which said "that both nations commit themselves to carry out the comprehensive peace agreement as was agreed at Camp David." Carter said he had "heard Premier Begin say in my presence that he did not desire a separate peace treaty with Egypt" and that President Sadat supported this view.

U.S. Denies Promises to Sadat—The U.S. Nov. 12 denied reports that President Carter had offered President Sadat secret "guarantees" or "commitments" on the future of West Bank-Gaza and East Jerusalem. The denial was in response to remarks by Moroccan King Hassan II Nov. 10 that Carter had made such specific pledges.

In an interview before leaving on a state visit to the U.S., Hassan said Sadat had told him of the American promises. Hassan had met with the Egyptian leader in Rabat Sept. 20 during a stopover on Sadat's way home to Cairo from the Camp David summit.

Hassan asserted that Carter's alleged commitment to Sadat was "the context of my trip to the United States. If President Carter hadn't assured us that Jerusalem would return to the Arabs, . . . if he hadn't reassured the Arabs on the fate of the Palestinians, my trip, . . . it might happen, but in a very different context, or it might have had to be postponed."

Sadat had said at a Rabat news conference Sept. 22 that "the Egyptian and American positions are identical on the question of Jerusalem, as follows: that Arab Jerusalem is a part of the West Bank, and therefore what applies to the West Bank and King Hussein applies to it."

Premier Begin Sept. 25 had reaffirmed Israel's intention to retain East Jerusalem, saying it was "the eternal capital of Israel," and was "indivisible for all the generations and forever and ever."

The U.S. statement refuting Hassan's remarks said the Administration's stand on West Bank-Gaza remained unchanged from the position it had taken at Camp David: the territory's residents should be allowed self-rule and its ultimate future should be decided through negotiations and elections during a five-year period.

As for Jerusalem, the Administration reiterated that the city should no longer be divided, that the Arabs should be granted the right to administer the eastern section and that Israel should relinquish sovereignty over it.

Israel OKs U.S.-Proposed Pact. The Israeli Cabinet Nov. 21, by a 15–2 vote, approved a U.S.-sponsored draft of an Israeli-Egyptian peace treaty that linked the accord to self-determination for Palestinians on the West Bank and Gaza Strip. At the same time, the Cabinet turned down Egypt's demand for a timetable for autonomy for the Palestinians. The Egyptian plan was "inconsistent with the Camp David agreements," the Cabinet said.

Cairo reacted to Israel's rejection of its demands by recalling its chief negotiator from the Washington peace talks, Defense Minister Kamel Hassan Ali.

Premier Menahem Begin said after the Cabinet meeting that his government was "prepared to start negotiations to reach agreement" with Egypt on implementing autonomy for the West Bank and Gaza Strip as stipulated in the Camp David agreements.

Begin said later in the day that he had telephoned President Carter after the Cabinet meeting and that the President had expressed satisfaction with the ministers' decision.

The U.S. proposal, whose terms had not been made public, had been worked out Nov. 12 between Secretary of State Cyrus Vance and Foreign Minister Moshe Dayan, Israel's chief negotiator. The plan had been submitted to Israel and Egypt for consideration.

The American compromise reportedly contained a new sentence in the preamble to the text of the pact committing both nations to implementing the West Bank accord. The plan also provided for an exchange of Egyptian and Israeli letters pledging that the West Bank talks would start soon after ratification of their bilateral treaty.

The American plan was said to require Israel to commit itself to permitting Arabs in the West Bank to vote for local governing councils one year after the signing of the Israeli-Egyptian treaty. The U.S. was said to hope that the balloting would take place before the end of 1979.

Israeli sources said the contents of the American plan reflected Israeli proposals for autonomy for the West Bank and Gaza Strip but excluded specific dates and details as proposed by Egypt.

The new Egyptian proposal asking Israel to agree beforehand to a detailed timetable on giving up military rule in West Bank-Gaza and transferring control to a Palestinian council had been submitted Nov. 9 to Secretary Vance by Acting Egyptian Foreign Minister Butros Ghali. The Israeli delegation was concerned over the new Egyptian demands because they were accompanied by reports from Egypt quoting President Anwar Sadat as saying that he would not be "astonished at all" if the talks collapsed as a result of the dispute over linkage between an Israeli-Egyptian treaty and the West Bank-Gaza question.

In a further demand, President Sadat Nov. 14 called on Israel to turn over the Gaza Strip to Egypt along with the Sinai Peninsula. "If the [Israeli-Egyptian] treaty is not linked to Gaza, then it will not be acceptable to us," Sadat told a meeting of his New Democratic Party.

Sadat had proposed in May the return of the Gaza Strip to Egypt and the West Bank to Jordan pending the creation of a Palestinian state.

Egypt, U.S., Israel Release Texts— Egypt, Israel and the U.S. released their versions of the text of the proposed Israeli-Egyptian treaty.

The semi-official Egyptian newspaper Al Ahram Nov. 24 published what Egyptian sources identified as the U.S.-proposed compromise treaty approved by the Israeli Cabinet Nov. 21. It contained a preamble and nine articles. Plans for its publication were announced Nov. 23.

While the Cairo government did not confirm the authenticity of the released document, an Egyptian source said the preamble proved that "there is linkage within the body of the treaty." This was a reference to linking an Israeli-Egyptian pact to an overall settlement of the West Bank-Gaza problem, an approach opposed by Israel.

Egypt reportedly had permitted publication of the text in order to show Arab critics of President Sadat's peace initiatives that Cairo was not concluding a separate peace treaty with Israel.

U.S. officials Nov. 23 expressed surprise and puzzlement at the Egyptian action. A State Department official speculated that by its move Egypt hoped to prevent any future alteration in the treaty language. Then the Egyptians would attempt to get more specific language incorporated into an accompanying letter dealing with the linkage issue, the official believed.

The Israeli government in turn Nov. 25 released what it described as one of the three annexes to the draft of the treaty. The previous day Israel and the U.S. had released the text of the treaty, without the annexes. The document published by Israel Nov. 25, Annex III, dealt with diplomatic, trade and cultural relations, freedom of movement, transportation and telecommunications, human rights and territorial waters. The other two annexes concerned military and security arrangements.

The U.S. Embassy in Tel Aviv Nov. 25 said it was "astonished" at Israel's release of the document. Foreign Minister Moshe Dayan replied that the U.S. had suggested its publication and he had felt that Annex III was part of the agreement and publishable.

Egypt's released version of the pact was assailed Nov. 25 by Israeli Deputy Premier Yigal Yadin. He charged that Cairo had mutilated the text by omitting a key sentence, which stated that the Egyptian-Israeli treaty would supersede any agreements between Egypt and other nations.

The Israeli newspaper Haaretz Nov. 20 had published what it described as the preamble and the nine articles to the pact, which were similar to the ones carried by Al Ahram.

Talks Stall. The Israeli-Egyptian peace-treaty talks were suspended Nov. 16, 1978, and by early December the U.S. was making intense efforts to restart them.

President Carter warned at a news conference Dec. 7 that failure by the two sides to reach an agreement by Dec. 17, the deadline specified in the Camp David accords, "would have far-reaching, adverse effects."

Carter complained of "unwarranted delays, quibbling over what seems to us to be insignificant language differences and excessive public statements on both sides that have made the negotiating process excessively difficult."

The President had expressed similar disappointment over the slow pace of the negotiations at a news conference Nov. 30 but pledged that the U.S. "was not going to give up on the effort" to help Egypt and Israel reach a final agreement.

The deadlock centered on the following points:

■ The Israeli Cabinet had endorsed the U.S.-drafted preamble, nine articles and three annexes of a treaty package. It rejected an additional "side letter," drafted by Secretary of State Cyrus Vance, which had previously been endorsed by Israel's negotiators in Washington. The letter called on both sides to negotiate an agreement on the holding of elections to establish Palestinian autonomy in the West Bank and Gaza Strip no later than the end of 1979.

Egypt originally insisted on September 1979 as the deadline for autonomy elections, but President Anwar Sadat finally backed the American proposal.

■ Egypt wanted a change in Article 6 of the American proposal (accepted by Israel), which stated that the peace pact should have precedence over any other document Egypt had signed in the past. Egypt reasoned that this appeared to bar it from assisting other Arab states in any future war with Israel. Sadat did not want to give the Arabs the impression that he was giving priority to Israel over the Arabs.

The U.S. communicated this Egyptian stand to Israeli Premier Menahem Begin Nov. 30. Meanwhile, President Sadat's reservations about the U.S.-proposed draft were contained in a letter Egyptian Premier Mustafa Khalil handed President Carter at a White House conference Dec. 1. Vance announced after the meeting that the Israeli-Egyptian negotiations "will continue in fulfillment of the accords reached at Camp David."

Israel Vs. U.S.-Egyptian Proposals— Attempts to break the deadlock received a further setback Dec. 13 when Israel objected to new U.S.-Egyptian proposals.

The new plan had been drafted during Secretary of State Cyrus Vance's meetings with President Anwar Sadat in Cairo Dec. 10-12. Vance, who also met with Israeli officials in Jerusalem, cut short his shuttle mission to return to the U.S. Dec. 15 after being recalled by President Carter.

Among the major points reportedly agreed to by Vance and Sadat:

■ Sadat agreed to drop his proposal to revise Article VI of the pact. This section accepted by Israel, gave the accord precedence over any other treaty. Egypt instead approved a clarifying letter stating its views on making certain that it could come to the assistance of other Arab states that became involved in a war with Israel. Israel was said to regard this interpretation as stripping Article VI of its meaning.

■ The clarifying letter also stated that either side would be permitted to review the security provisions of the treaty after five years.

■ A target date of December 1979 would be set on the holding of elections in the West Bank and Gaza Strip under terms of the autonomy plan for the region as proposed by Israel. Israel opposed any target date for fear that a breakdown of the autonomy plan might negate Israel's separate treaty with Egypt.

■ Egypt would exchange ambassadors with Israel only after Palestinian councils were established following the autonomy elections. Israel also regarded this as a linkage between the treaty's provisions on diplomatic relations and the other accords on the Palestinians reached at Camp David and rejected it.

■ If Jordan's continued lack of cooperation precluded the holding of elections on the West Bank, then the balloting could be held for the Gaza Strip alone. Egypt dropped its insistence on stationing police in Gaza during those elections, and instead agreed to placing liaison officers in the territory.

Vance had met with Pemier Menahem Begin and other Israeli officials in Jerusalem Dec. 11 after the first two days of talks with Sadat in Cairo. Vance concluded his agreement with the Egyptians on his return to Cairo Dec. 12 and went back to Jerusalem, where he held further inconclusive discussions with the Israelis Dec. 13–14. He returned to Cairo later Dec. 14 and departed for Washington the following day.

Carter: Treaty Up to Israel—President Carter said Dec. 14 that it was now up to Israel to accept or reject the proposed peace treaty with Egypt.

In a television interview with Barbara Walters of ABC-TV, Carter ruled out any early reconvening of summit discussions with Egypt and Israel, citing "other pressing international problems" that required his attention as well as that of Vance. "We've really put an extraordinary time and effort in the Mideast and I just cannot neglect other problems in order to accomplish this goal," Carter said.

Nevertheless, Carter pledged that his Administration would continue its peace efforts at a later date.

A State Department spokesman Dec. 14 said "the time has come for a pause, not a breakdown" in U.S. mediation moves.

Carter Dec. 13 had praised President Sadat as having been "very generous" in accepting a "time schedule" for future elections in the West Bank-Gaza Strip, which he said was "basically an original Israeli position." Carter noted that Israeli Foreign Minister Moshe Dayan himself had proposed that the elections be held "by the end of 1979," but pointed out that now the Israelis were objecting to their own proposal.

Israel Reaffirms Stand—The Israeli Knesset Dec. 19 approved a resolution assailing U.S. criticism of Israel's rejection of the latest Egyptian demands.

The Knesset's statement, supporting Premier Begin's position in the negotiations, said "the attitude of the United States charging Israel with responsibility for the failure to sign a peace treaty is one-sided and unjust and does not contribute to the advancement of peace."

During debate, Begin restated Israel's objections to Egypt's insistence that its commitments to other Arab countries had to take precedence over any peace treaty with Israel. The premier argued that this proposed clause would obligate Egypt to come to the aid of an Arab country that said it had been attacked by Israel, and thus nullify the treaty.

Begin also reiterated Israel's opposition to the U.S. proposal, accepted by Egypt, for setting a December 1979 target date for autonomy elections in the West Bank and the Gaza Strip.

The Knesset action followed Israeli Cabinet approval Dec. 15 of Begin's rejection of Egyptian proposals made in talks with Vance earlier in the week.

The Cabinet confirmed that Vance had transmitted the following new demands from Egypt: a delay in exchanging ambassadors until after the autonomy elections, at least in the Gaza Strip; a review of security arrangements in the Sinai five years after the signing of a treaty; recognition of Egypt's obligations to other Arab states, and the December 1979 target date for the autonomy elections.

Egypt Dec. 15 denied Israeli charges that President Anwar Sadat had requested a revision of the projected pact in his talks with Vance. The Foreign Ministry said the

Egyptian proposals conformed "completely in letter and spirit" with the framework accords accepted by Begin and President Carter at the Camp David summit in September.

On returning to Washington Dec. 15, Vance reported on his mission to President Carter but no statement was issued after the briefing. Prior to landing, officials aboard the Vance plane told reporters that Israel had distorted the nature of the proposed revision of the Israeli-Egyptian pact. Vance was described as "saddened" and annoyed by the Israeli Cabinet's decision that day rejecting the plan.

In a further rebuff to the U.S., Israeli Foreign Minister Moshe Dayan said Dec. 18 that Israel would resume negotiations only "if Egypt understands that we do not accept her new demands."

Dayan was quoted as having said that Egypt had stiffened its position because of fear of being isolated by other Arab countries.

In a meeting arranged by the Carter Administration, four American Jewish leaders conferred with Vance Dec. 19 on the latest development in the peace process. After the meeting, one of the participants, Theodore Mann, chairman of the Conference of Presidents of Major American Jewish Organizations, told reporters: "There's a great deal of anguish and concern in the American Jewish community regarding the events of the last 10 days and particularly with the role of the United States."

A group of 33 prominent American Jews, including Nobel Prize winner Saul Bellow, sent a statement to President Carter Dec. 19, asserting that U.S. endorsement of the Egyptian proposals "does serious damage to the prospects of peace."

The same group had issued a statement in April expressing support for the Israeli Peace Now movement, a group favoring greater Israeli flexibility in negotiations.

Israel Halts Pullout of Sinai Gear—As a result of the political impasse with Egypt, Israeli military forces had halted the withdrawal of nonessential military equipment and facilities from the Sinai Peninsula, it was reported Dec. 20.

The pullout of building materials, barbed wire and some unused structures, begun in mid-November, was ordered stopped by Defense Minister Ezer Weizman, according to Israeli Defense Ministry sources.

U.S. Efforts Continue—State Secretary Vance conferred with Egyptian and Israeli representatives in Brussels Dec. 24 in an effort to revive the treaty talks.

After meeting with Egyptian Premier Mustafa Khalil and Israeli Foreign Minister Moshe Dayan, Vance issued an informal statement merely noting that a "useful exchange of views" had taken place and that Egypt and Israel would remain in contact with the U.S. "as to the next steps to be taken."

Privately, U.S. officials emphasized that all three sides had agreed to avoid arguments in public.

Egyptian President Anwar Sadat Dec. 25 complained that refusal of other Arab states to support his peace efforts helped Israeli Premier Menahem Begin block a settlement. "It is in Begin's interest that the Arab countries remain divided to achieve his objectives by creating a greater Israel extending from the Euphrates to the Nile," the Egyptian leader asserted.

Begin said Dec. 26 that he was prepared for resumption of new negotiations with Egypt. But government sources said the premier remained opposed to Egyptian demands for a timetable for Palestinian autonomy in the West Bank and Gaza Strip, one of the principal questions holding up an agreement.

Alfred L. Atherton Jr., U.S. special envoy for the Mideast, met with Israeli officials in Jerusalem Jan. 16–24, 1979 in a renewed U.S. effort to restart the treaty talks. He visited Cairo Jan. 25–27 to convey Israeli views to the Egyptians and get Egyptian proposals. Atherton returned to Washington Jan. 28 without winning agreement on a renewal of the talks.

The Israeli Cabinet Jan. 24 had objected to unspecified compromise proposals worked out by the Israeli and American negotiators led by Atherton. The two sides had expressed confidence Jan. 23 that the Cabinet would endorse the plan after they agreed that day on two of the three aspects under discussion; the third unresolved issue was to be dealt with later at a higher level.

Atherton disclosed after his first meetings with the Egyptians Jan. 25 that one of the basic issues he had discussed with the Israelis was the paragraph of Article VI of the proposed Israeli-Egyptian treaty that gave the accord precedence over any other treaty.

Egypt and Israel blamed each other for the failure of Atherton's mission. Premier Menahem Begin said Jan. 28 that Egypt had "rejected the proposals submitted by Ambassador Atherton following the talks he had with Israeli representatives" in Jerusalem during the previous two weeks. Israel wanted to continue the negotiations and did not regard the talks at a stalemate, Begin said.

Before leaving Cairo Jan. 27, Atherton said "there is still a gap" between Israel's and Egypt's negotiating stands. Egyptian Premier Mustafa Khalil, who had conferred with Atherton Jan. 26 and 27, said the differences were "not insurmountable."

Atherton's mission had been announced by Secretary of State Cyrus Vance Jan. 11. He said that Atherton's task would be to clear away "some of the more minor matters," and that Vance would meet later with the Israeli and Egyptian foreign ministers to take up the other outstanding issues.

Israel Ties Pact to Sinai Oil—Israeli Energy Minister Yitzhak Modai said Jan. 5 that his country would not sign a peace treaty with Egypt unless it was assured of access to oil from the Sinai wells it had developed during the its military occupation of the region. "What is the good of a peace treaty—and a partial one at that—if we don't have our supplies assured?"

While agreeing to Egyptian sovereignty over the oilfields after Israel relinquished the Sinai to Cairo, Modai said Egypt would have to fulfill two conditions before Israel signed a treaty: it would have to sell oil to Israel equal to the amount being produced from Israeli-developed offshore wells, and it would have to permit Israel to take part in oil operations in the Gulf of Suez on an equal basis with American, French and Italian companies.

Modai said Israel's position on the Sinai oilfields had hardened as a result of Iran's suspension of oil shipments to Israel.

Other Problems. The Israeli government announced Jan. 15, 1979 that it planned to establish three new settlements in the West Bank. According to the announcement, all three centers would be military outposts—two on the West Bank, near the Jordan

River, and the third at the southern end of the Gaza Strip.

The government also said that an existing military outpost on the West Bank at the northern end of the Dead Sea would become a kibbutz (a civilian communal settlement) later in the week.

■ About 2,000 Israelis Jan. 13 demonstrated in front of the Jerusalem residence of Premier Menahem Begin, urging him to bar more settlements on the West Bank and to continue efforts to reach a peace agreement with Egypt.

The demonstration was sparked by reports that Begin had acceded to demands by Gush Emunim, the right-wing religious group, for the establishment of a new Jewish settlement near the West Bank Arab town of Nablus. A spokesman for Begin's office told the demonstrators that the premier had made no such commitment.

■ Israeli troops Jan. 1 and 2 blocked the Gush Emunim from gaining a foothold at two proposed settlement sites on the West Bank near Jerusalem.

U.S. Defense Secretary Harold Brown visited Saudi Arabia, Jordan, Israel and Egypt Feb. 10–18 to assure them of the U.S. commitment to the security of their region in the wake of the political and economic upheaval in Iran.

Highlights of the tour:

Saudi Arabia—Brown said on his arrival in Riyadh Feb. 10 that "Arabs have a new role to play in the world, . . . which comes from centuries of Islamic religious tradition . . . We can provide extra strength needed to meet a force from outside the region. We will do so."

Brown informed Saudi officials Feb. 11 that the U.S. was willing to sell jet planes to North Yemen and Sudan, Saudi Arabia's two allies, provided the Saudis agreed to finance the transaction.

Brown handed Crown Prince Fahd a personal letter from President Carter to King Khalid offering periodic consultations between Washington and Riyadh on security matters in the Persian Gulf.

Before leaving for Amman, Jordan Feb. 12, the defense secretary announced that in the next few months the U.S. would take positive measures to defend Saudi Arabia and other friendly nations as a result of new conditions resulting from the radical changeover in Iran. Brown said the cut in

Iranian oil production made other petroleum sources "more important" and underscored the need for "closer ties" betwen the U.S. and Saudi Arabia.

(Brown had suggested the establishment of a U.S. military force in Saudi Arabia, but the Saudis "quickly turned us down," a U.S. Defense Department official disclosed Feb. 26.)

Israel—During his first day in Israel Feb. 13, Brown met with Defense Minister Ezer Weizman and was told that Israel planned a cut of 25% [about $3 billion] in its defense budget in the next 10 years because it expected to sign a peace treaty with Egypt soon.

At the same time, Weizman urged the U.S. to speed up the delivery to Israel by 18 months of the 75 F-16 fighter planes promised over the next few years since Iran had canceled orders for this type of aircraft. The Israelis also asked for the accelerated jet shipment because of a buildup of Soviet MiG-23s in Iraq and Syria. Brown later told Israel that the U.S. would equip its F-16s with air-to-air missiles.

Brown toured the West Bank Feb. 14, becoming the first U.S. Cabinet official to do so. The U.S. Embassy in Tel Aviv had advised him against the visit on the ground that it would appear to endorse Israeli occupation of the area. Brown had decided to go after Secretary of State Cyrus Vance approved the visit in a telephone conversation with the defense secretary Feb. 13.

At a news conference Feb. 15, Brown said U.S plans to increase arms sales to Saudi Arabia and to strengthen its ties with the Riyadh government and other nations in the region "will be made with very careful consideration of Israel's security."

Egypt—In his visit to Cairo Feb. 16–18, Defense Secretary Brown conferred with President Anwar Sadat and other Egyptian officials on their request for U.S. arms and on the prospects for an Egyptian-Israeli peace treaty. The arms list included more than 300 tanks, 2,000 armored personnel carriers, Hawk antiaircraft missiles and advanced jets such as the F-15s or F-16s. Egypt wanted the American arms to replace the Soviet equipment that was wearing out and to bolster its defenses in view of the changed balance of power in the region resulting from the Iranian revolution.

As for the proposed Israeli-Egyptian pact, Sadat told Brown Feb. 17 that Cairo would make no further concessions in the negotiations and that it was "now up to the Israelis."

Egyptian-Israeli Peace Treaty

Treaty Disputes Resolved

In an action unprecedented in relations between any Arab nation and Israel, Egyptian President Anwar Sadat and Israeli Premier Menahem Begin March 26, 1979 signed a treaty of peace ending the 31-year-long state of war between their two nations. A month earlier, however, such an outcome had seemed unlikely because of disputes over important issues. The differences were finally ironed out by U.S. President Jimmy Carter, who visited Sadat and Begin in Cairo and Jerusalem March 8–13 and persuaded them to compromise.

Egypt-Israel Summit in Doubt. The convening of a second Camp David summit by the U.S. to achieve an Israeli-Egyptian peace treaty had appeared in doubt as Sadat and Begin indicated in late February their refusal to attend new talks with Carter.

The President had suggested the high-level meeting Feb. 25 after Secretary of State Cyrus Vance had held preliminary discussions at Camp David Feb. 22–25 with Israeli Foreign Minister Moshe Dayan and Egyptian Premier Mustafa Khalil. In his announcement, Carter disclosed Sadat's decision that day not to attend and said he would be represented by Khalil.

The Israeli Cabinet responded Feb. 27 by refusing to have Begin participate. Israel's action further underscored its growing differences with the U.S. over a peace agreement, leading Carter Feb. 27 to invite Begin to Washington to discuss the matter personally. They conferred March 2–4.

Sadat was said to have declined to take part in the talks with Carter and Begin for fear of being put in the position of being pressured by Carter to make binding commitments while Begin had an out—the premier's requirement for Israeli Cabinet or parliamentary approval of any binding peace agreement.

The Israeli Cabinet decision to withhold Begin's attendance at a Carter-Khalil meeting was approved by a vote of 14 to 2, with Dayan and Defense Minister Ezer Weizman the lone dissenters. A Cabinet communique issued after Dayan submitted a report on his meetings with Khalil and Vance said those discussions had made no progress. The Cabinet said: "On the contrary, a more extreme position was presented by the Egyptian delegation. Under the circumstances, the Cabinet decided that Begin is not in a position to participate in the proposed meeting with Khalil."

Vance and Khalil had reported progress.

While some Israeli politicians complained that Begin had been snubbed by U.S. acceptance of Sadat's refusal to attend, the premier had first indicated Feb.

26 that he would have no objections to meeting Carter without the presence of the Egyptian leader. "I don't think it is a matter of anybody's participation. Why should I be disappointed? It is up to President Sadat to come or not to come."

Dayan had said on his return to Jerusalem Feb. 26, "There is no doubt that Premier Khalil is authorized and qualified to make decisions on behalf of President Sadat."

In a further report on his talks with Vance and Khalil, Dayan told a parliamentary committee Feb. 28 that Israel and Egypt remained deadlocked over the following issues:

■ Egypt insisted on Israeli agreement to establish Palestinian autonomy within a year in the West Bank and Gaza Strip. If Jordan and the Palestinians blocked the West Bank plan, then autonomy for Gaza must be granted within a year.

■ Egypt would establish consular relations with Israel one month after autonomy elections in Gaza, but would not discuss the exchange of ambassadors at the current time.

■ Egypt demanded deletion from the original Camp David agreement of the clause giving an Israeli-Egyptian pact priority over Egypt's treaties with other nations.

■ Egypt would discuss the question of oil supplies with Israel only after other treaty differences had been resolved.

Begin said Feb. 28 before leaving for the U.S. that Israel and Egypt remained far apart and complained that the U.S. was backing Egyptian proposals that were "totally unacceptable to us."

Begin took issue with a statement made by Carter Feb. 27 that "only very small, insignificant things separate" the two sides and "it is just disgusting almost to feel that we are that close and can't quite get" an agreement. On the contrary, Begin said, "grave issues relating first of all to our future security ... now divide the two countries."

Begin said his refusal to meet Khalil had nothing to do with protocol but with remaining broad disagreements between Israel and Egypt.

Begin Accepts U.S. Plan—Arriving in Washington March 1, Begin warned in an airport statement that U.S. proposals would turn the Egyptian-Israeli peace treaty into a "sham document," which "we cannot be pressed into signing."

Israel, the premier said, was being "asked to sign documents attached to this treaty which are contradicting the Camp David peace agreements and would allow our neighbors in the south [Egypt] to declare the treaty null and void and to declare war on us."

In a statement made later in the day at the White House, Begin described Israel as "the only stable ally of the United States and the free world" in the Middle East. Addressing Carter in the presence of reporters, Begin expressed hope that his country's treaty difficulties with Egypt would be resolved in his forthcoming talks with the President.

The compromise was approved by the Israeli Cabinet March 5, and Carter the same day decided to press for quick action by arguing the issues in person that week in Cairo and Jerusalem. A White House statement on Carter's trip said: "There is certainly no guarantee of success, but ... without a major effort such as this, the prospects for failure are almost overwhelming."

During the Begin-Carter discussions March 2–4, however, Begin approved a compromise U.S. proposal that was not to be made public until after it had been fully discussed with Sadat. The proposed change was known to modify the language linking the Egyptian-Israel accord with other agreements reached at Camp David in 1978 on giving self-rule to the Palestinians in the West Bank and Gaza Strip. Also at issue was whether the pact would supersede Egypt's agreements with other Arab states.

Briefing members of the House Foreign Affairs Committee in Washington March 5, Begin said the President's proposals touch "the heart and soul" of the treaty.

On returning to Jerusalem March 8, Premier Begin voiced confidence that a peace treaty would be signed if the Egyptians accepted the American proposals approved by Israel. He warned, however, that if the Egyptians turned them down, "then, of course, we will say no."

Syria Denounces Pact—Syrian President Hafez al-Assad warned March 8 that any U.S.-sponsored treaty between Egypt and Israel would have "achieved nothing because the state of war will continue to prevail" in the Middle East. "What they are signing is not a peace treaty, but a document of war."

Assad denounced President Sadat for preferring "everything foreign to everything Arab" and for having "stabbed the Arabs in the back."

All Issues Resolved. The signing of an Egyptian-Israeli peace treaty was virtually assured as both nations accepted compromise proposals submitted by President Carter at meetings with Sadat and Begin in Cairo and Jerusalem March 8–13. The President returned to the U.S. March 14.

After accepting most aspects of the accord March 12, the Israeli Cabinet March 14 approved by 15–0 the two remaining proposals that blocked an agreement.

On receiving word of the Cabinet's action, Carter said in Washington, "all of the outstanding issues between Egypt and Israel have now been successfully resolved." The U.S., he said, stood ready to assist both nations after a peace treaty was signed.

The Egyptian Cabinet gave its approval to the pact March 15.

The two proposals endorsed by the Israeli Cabinet dealt with Sinai oil and the exchange of ambassadors. Israel accepted an arrangement under which Egypt would sell it 2.5 million tons of oil a year for an "extended period." In addition, the U.S. had agreed with an Israeli request to guarantee Israel's oil supply for 15 years.

On the second point, Israel would submit to Egypt a detailed timetable for withdrawing its forces from the Sinai. The schedule called for the Israelis to pull back halfway across the peninsula nine months after the treaty went into effect, with both countries exchanging ambassadors by the end of the tenth month.

President Carter had attended the March 12 Knesset session, which was marked by sharp criticism of U.S. policy by right-wing and left-wing members and denunciation of Begin for submitting to "American pressure."

Prior to the debate, Carter had addressed the Knesset, criticizing both Israel and Egypt for having thus far failed to "take a chance" for peace. The President said: "We have not yet fully met our challenge. Despite our unflagging determination, despite the extraordinary progress of the past six months, we still fall short."

Vowing continued American support of Israel, Carter said that while there were risks in signing the treaty, the U.S. was prepared "to reduce any risks and to balance them within the bounds of our strength and influence."

Carter also had attended the March 12 Cabinet meeting.

Making a stopover at Cairo airport on his way home, Carter briefed President Sadat March 13 and received the Egyptian leader's acceptance of the American proposals. Carter relayed this development to Begin, who said that the President's telephone message "signified very great progress in the process of the possibility of signing a peace treaty."

Begin then announced his decision to submit the pact to the Knesset, saying that if the legislature rejected the accord, "then it will be the democratic duty of [my] government to resign."

Begin asserted that U.S. government and American news reports criticizing Israel were aimed at forcing Israel to withdraw its objections to the treaty. Begin apparently referred to a briefing given U.S. journalists in Jerusalem March 12 by White House press spokesman Jody Powell, who had said that President Carter had failed to overcome Israeli opposition to the pact and that Carter's mission was on the verge of collapse.

"I think the American commentators should perhaps admit now that they were wrong, that they should apologize to the American people whom they misled," Begin said. "And perhaps it is not the commentators who have to apologize but those who briefed them this way."

Carter Briefs Congressmen—After returning to Washington March 14, Carter briefed a group of about 100 members of the House and Senate, expressing gratitude for their support of his mission.

Carter lauded Sadat and Begin "for their leadership and the courage that they have consistently demonstrated." He voiced pride in the U.S.' efforts "to assist these two longtime adversaries along the path of reconciliation and future cooperation. We stand ready to help the implementation of the peace treaty, in the negotiations that lie ahead on other issues of concern, and in working with these two friends to build a stable and peaceful Middle East."

President Carter was said by Administration officials to have told the congressmen that the treaty would require the U.S. to provide Egypt and Israel with $4 billion more in economic and military aid over the next three years. The funds for Israel would help finance the cost of replacing air bases and civilian settlements in the Sinai that must be abandoned by Israel under terms of the pact.

Arabs Protest—President Carter's Middle East mission was the target of widespread criticism and violent demonstrations by West Bank residents and other Arabs.

Two young Arabs were killed March 15 when Israeli security forces and armed Jewish settlers opened fire on rock-throwing demonstrators in the West Bank town of Halhoul. The Israelis first fired into the air and then into the crowd.

Sporadic violence had occurred in East Jerusalem and other West Bank towns March 13–14. A strike shut down schools and shops in Ramallah and El Bireh.

Hebron Mayor Fahad Kawasmeh March 14 said the Egyptian-Israeli pact was "a separate agreement" that "does nothing to fulfill the legitimate rights of the Palestinian people."

Palestine Liberation Organization leader Yasir Arafat March 13 called for an oil embargo against Egypt if it signed a peace treaty with Israel. Arafat issued the appeal at a meeting in Beirut of the Secretariat of the Arab People's Congress, called by the PLO to discuss means of increasing Arab resistance to Sadat's peace moves. The meeting ended March 14 with calls for strikes and protest demonstrations and with a statement urging Arab leaders to "use the oil weapon in facing American hostile moves and boycott American goods and means of transport."

(The Arab People's Congress had been formed in 1978 after Sadat's trip to Jerusalem in November 1977. The Congress had set up a "People's Court" in Baghdad in January, which condemned Sadat as a traitor.)

In earlier protests, Arafat March 11 sent messages to Arab leaders, with the exception of Sadat, urging them to oppose all peace moves. Carter's visit to Egypt and Israel "constitutes a grave conspiracy against the rights of the Palestinian people and the Arab nation at large," Arafat said in his letters.

A newspaper in Kuwait said Saudi Arabia had informed Sadat that Saudi aid to Egypt would be cut off if Cairo signed a treaty with Israel.

Saudi newspaper editorials addressed to President Carter said the only solution to the Middle East dispute was total Israeli withdrawal from all occupied Arab territory, including East Jerusalem, and the right of Palestinians to have their own state.

Arafat told a rally of 1,000 in Beirut March 12 that the PLO would "burn everything" to prevent a peace between Egypt and Israel.

Hussein, Arafat Join in Protest—King Hussein of Jordan and Palestine Liberation Organization leader Yasir Arafat moved a step closer to reconciliation March 17 with a joint declaration against the Egyptian-Israeli peace treaty. After a four-hour meeting in northern Jordan, both leaders confirmed the decision of the November 1978 Arab summit in Baghdad, Iraq to reject Egypt's decision to negotiate with Israel.

Hussein and Arafat agreed to set up a joint committee to coordinate opposition to the peace treaty. In addition, the monarch permitted the PLO to open offices in Amman, the Jordanian capital. However, Hussein remained opposed to allowing the PLO to reestablish guerrilla bases in Jordan.

Soviets Wary of U.S. Influence—The Soviet Union interpreted the U.S. role in promoting an Egyptian-Israeli peace agreement as a means of extending its military and political influence in the Middle East following the loss of its foothold in Iran, it was reported from Moscow March 15.

The Communist Party newspaper Pravda said Israel and Egypt were being given the roles of gendarmes for Washington. Premier Menahem Begin had offered the U.S. use of the port of Haifa for its warships, and Egypt had suggested that U.S. warships "call more frequently at Egyptian ports" and "patrol more regularly in the Red Sea and in the Indian Ocean," the newspaper said.

The government newspaper Izvestia said the U.S. hoped to reconcile Egypt and Israel "to help create an atmosphere in which the United States can easily inculcate and strengthen its military presence in the area.·... And after the revolution in

Iran, that is precisely the cardinal concern of the American strategists."

U.S. Seeks Saudi, Jordan Support—A high-level U.S. delegation led by national security adviser Zbigniew Brzezinski visited Saudi Arabia and Jordan March 17–18 to gain their support for the Israeli-Egyptian treaty but failed to receive their endorsement.

In announcing President Carter's decision to dispatch the mission, Administration officials had said March 15 that the President was concerned about Arab threats of economic and oil boycotts against Egypt in reprisal for its agreement to sign a peace treaty with Israel.

In his talks with Saudi leaders March 17–18, Brzezinski was told that although Riyadh would not back the treaty, it would not join in any political or economic retaliation against Egypt, an official with the U.S. delegation said March 18.

The Saudis also pledged to shun the Arab "rejection front," which had vowed strong action if President Sadat signed the accord, the official said.

The Saudis had denounced the treaty in their discussions with the Americans as "a separate and bilateral agreement outside the Arab framework," which they described as a "mistake."

The Saudis also had informed Brzezinski that they were particularly distressed with U.S. failure to get a definite treaty commitment from Israel to withdraw from all Arab lands it had occupied since the 1967 war, the American official disclosed.

While the Saudis adopted a cautious approach in their discussions with the American delegation, Saudi government-supported newspapers were more outspoken in editorials appearing March 17–18. They assailed "American weakness" and the peace treaty and called for economic sanctions against Egypt if the accord was signed.

A brief discussion in Amman later March 18 between the Americans and King Hussein and other Jordanian officials was marked by "basic differences of approach" on the main issues, a Jordanian source said.

On arriving in Washington March 19, Brzezinski said at an informal airport news briefing that his mission led him to believe that Saudi Arabia and Jordan would coop-erate with U.S. political peace efforts in the Middle East. "We made it clear throughout that President Carter is dedicated to a comprehensive peace settlement and that the United States supports with its full weight the Egyptian-Israeli peace treaty as the cornerstone of such a settlement," Brzezinski said.

Hussein Criticizes U.S. Mission—King Hussein March 20 charged that the American mission sent to gain his support for the Egyptian-Israeli treaty had used "arm-twisting" tactics.

Speaking to American reporters in Amman, the Jordanian monarch said the U.S. had sought his backing without "taking into consideration the real feeling of the people. It is asking people to acquiesce or support a totally unacceptable situation."

U.S.-Jordanian disagreement over the Cairo-Jerusalem pact had caused a deep estrangement in Washington-Amman relations, the king said. He warned that the pact would also result in the deterioration of U.S. ties with other Arab states "for a long time to come" and in a break in Egypt's relations with its Arab neighbors.

Hussein took issue with Brzezinski's arguments that U.S. and Jordanian interests were threatened by "radicals and Communists." The king implied that "Zionism" posed an equal peril.

Hussein questioned the U.S. role as a fair mediator while it provided Israel with "large amounts of arms and aid."

Alluding to reports that Brzezinski had threatened a cutoff of U.S. arms and other aid to Jordan if it did not support American mediation moves, Hussein said "we will have to look around and see what we can do to line up alternative sources for military equipment."

U.S. officials confirmed that Brzezinski had told Hussein that continued U.S. arms deliveries to his country depended in part on Jordan's attitude toward American peace efforts.

Egyptian-Israeli Military Talks—Defense Ministers Ezer Weizman of Israel and Kamel Hassan Ali of Egypt conferred in Washington under U.S. auspices March 18–19 and agreed on details of Israel's scheduled withdrawal of its forces from the Sinai Peninsula and their redeployment in Israel's Negev. The pullback was a major part of the Israeli-Egyptian peace treaty.

After further meetings of Ali and Weizman with Defense Secretary Harold Brown and other Defense Department officials March 19, the U.S. announced that it would provide Egypt with about $2 billion in arms, and Israel with $3 billion to finance its withdrawal from the Sinai, both subject to expected congressional approval.

The Israeli package, consisting of about $2.2 billion in loans and $800 million in grants, would be in addition to the $1.8 billion it was to receive in U.S. economic and military assistance in 1979.

The $2 billion in arms to be given Egypt would be on top of the $750 million in American economic help it was currently receiving.

The U.S. had agreed with Israel's request for at least 200 tanks, 800 armored personnel carriers and many artillery weapons and air-to-air and air-to-ground missiles, Carter Administration officials disclosed March 20.

Egypt would get planes, tanks and anti-aircraft weapons. The aircraft would include F-4 fighters, and not the more sophisticated F-16s that Egypt had requested.

In his earlier talks with Defense Secretary Brown March 17, Weizman had pressed for speed in the delivery of American weapons in light of Israel's concern that Syria and Iraq would attempt to undermine the Israeli-Egyptian treaty.

Final Israeli Approval—The treaty was approved by Israel's Cabinet March 19 and by the Knesset March 22.

The Cabinet vote was 15 to 2, with Agriculture Minister Ariel Sharon and Transport Minister Chaim Landau casting the only dissenting ballots. Both had been consistent right-wing critics of the pact. (On the eve of the Cabinet decision, the National Religious Party had threatened March 18 to resign from the ruling Likud coalition unless Premier Menahem Begin accepted its demand for continued Israeli control of the West Bank and Gaza Strip. At a meeting with Begin, the NRP called for Israeli refusal to permit the establishment of a Palestinian state in the West Bank; continued Israeli control of public lands and water resources in the West Bank; establishment of new Israeli settlements on the West Bank, and continued Israeli control of the West Bank's internal security and defense.)

Knesset endorsement of the pact March 22 was overwhelming—95 to 18. Despite the wide margin, many of the legislators had expressed reluctant support of the treaty and reservations about future negotiations to reach a comprehensive peace settlement in the Middle East. Particular concern was voiced about implementing the government's proposal for autonomy on the West Bank and Gaza Strip.

In opening Knesset debate March 20, Premier Begin pledged that his country would never permit the establishment of an independent Palestinian state in the West Bank. He said: "We will never agree. We will never make it possible."

Israel, Begin vowed, would refuse to return to the borders of June 1967. He also asserted that Israel would keep East Jerusalem, insisting that the city "will never be divided" again, and that his government would continue to establish Jewish settlements in the West Bank because "they were part of the security setup" of Israel.

Begin's statement was in direct reply to Egyptian Premier Mustafa Khalil, who had said March 17 that the Egyptian-Israeli treaty "will give us back all our lands, Israel will withdraw to the 1967 borders and East Jerusalem will again be part of the West Bank."

Khalil March 20 called Begin's remarks in the Knesset an "inappropriate start" for peace talks between their two countries. "What Begin said contradicts the basis of peace agreed upon at Camp David [in 1978] and spoils the atmosphere which we hoped would prevail at the time of the signing of the agreement," Khalil said.

Khalil insisted that Israel had committed itself to eventual Palestinian independence in the West Bank and Gaza Strip, a contention consistently denied by Israel.

Egyptian President Anwar Sadat March 22 hailed the Knesset's approval of the peace treaty. He attributed the endorsement to "a great ally"—the Israeli mother.

This was a reference to remarks Sadat had made during his visit to Jerusalem in November 1977 that the victims of the four wars fought between Israel and Egypt were the mothers of soldiers of both countries and noted that such women were foremost among Israel's hope for peace.

President Carter March 22 also lauded the Israeli Knesset action, saying that it "spoke with a voice heard around the world today—a voice for peace."

Carter on U.S.-Palestinian Ties—President Carter said March 23 that the U.S. wanted "direct relations" with the Palestinians living in Israeli-occupied lands but acknowledged the difficulties of dealing with the Palestine Liberation Organization. West Bank Palestinians as well as the PLO were opposed to the Israel-Egypt peace treaty.

The President made the remarks in separate interviews taped and broadcast by Egyptian and Israeli television. His appearance was designed to encourage West Bank and Gaza Strip Arabs to participate in the next phase of the negotiations of the treaty, which would deal with the status of their territories.

As for U.S. recognition of the PLO, Carter reaffirmed that his Administration would "start working directly" with the organization if it accepted Israel's right to exist and dropped its opposition to United Nations Security Council Resolution 242, the basis for peace efforts in the Middle East.

Peace Treaty Signed

3 Leaders Vow End to Strife. Egypt and Israel formally ended the state of war that had existed between them for nearly 31 years as President Anwar Sadat and Premier Menahem Begin signed a peace treaty in Washington March 26, 1979. President Carter signed as a witness for the U.S. It was the first such peace pact between Israel and an Arab country.

Also signed later March 26 by Foreign Minister Moshe Dayan and Secretary of State Cyrus Vance were two separate memorandums of agreement between the U.S. and Israel. One dealt with assurances of U.S. military and political assistance to Israel in case Egypt violated its pact with Jerusalem. The other concerned the guarantee of a continued supply of oil to Israel. The text of both documents was released March 28.

A gathering of 1,600 invited guests attended the 45-minute ceremony on the White House lawn. After the signing of three versions of the treaty—in Arabic, Hebrew and English—the three leaders delivered addresses hailing the accord and expressing hope for a lasting peace.

President Carter called the agreements a celebration of "a victory, not of a bloody military campaign, but of an inspiring peace campaign." He praised Begin and Sadat for having "conducted this campaign with all the courage, tenacity, brilliance and inspiration of any generals" leading men into combat.

The President said that although "we have won, at least, the first step of peace," there was "a long and difficult road" ahead. This was a reference to future negotiations on the Palestinian issue.

In his address, President Sadat described the Egyptian-Israeli pact as "a new chapter ... in the history of the co-existence among nations."

Sadat's deepest praise was reserved for President Carter's mediation efforts. The President, he said, "performed the greatest miracle," adding, "without exaggeration, what he did constituted one of the greatest achievements of our time."

The Egyptian leader concluded: "Let there be no more war or bloodshed between Arabs and Israelis. Let there be no more suffering or denial of rights. Let there be no more despair or loss of faith. ..."

Citing biblical prophets, Premier Begin declared in his speech that "the ancient Jewish people gave the new world a vision of eternal peace, of universal disarmament, of abolishing the teaching and learning of war." He called the treaty-signing "a great day in the annals of two ancient nations, Egypt and Israel, whose sons met in battle five times, fighting and falling. ... It is thanks to our fallen heroes, that we could have reached this day."

Like Sadat, Begin gave large credit for the success of their negotiations to President Carter, who had worked "so consistently to achieve this goal. ... A soldier in the service of peace you are."

The signing of the treaty, Begin said, was the third greatest day of his life. The other two, he recalled, were the declaration of Israel's independence in May 1948 and when Jerusalem "became one city" under Israeli rule in June 1967.

Key Elements of the Treaty—The actual treaty package comprised a preamble and nine articles, and three annexes and one appendix dealing with Israeli withdrawal from the Sinai Peninsula and the establishment of United Nations buffer zones in the region.

Among the major points of the accord:

■ Israel would withdraw its military forces and civilian settlements from the Sinai in phases over a three-year period. Two-thirds of the Sinai was to be relinquished to Egypt within nine months of the exchange of instruments of ratification. (The Israeli evacuation started March 27, with supplies being pulled out of a 45-mile strip on the Mediterranean coast, between the U.N. buffer zone and El Arish.)

■ U.N. forces would be deployed in some Israeli-Egyptian border areas to monitor the agreement. The U.S. would assist in bolstering the security arrangements by conducting surveillance flights over the area.

■ After the first nine-month period of Israeli withdrawal from the Sinai, Israel and Egypt would establish normal and friendly relations, and exchange ambassadors 10 months after ratification.

■ Israel would have free right of passage of its ships and cargoes through the Suez Canal.

■ Egypt would end its economic boycott of Israel.

■ Israel would be permitted to purchase oil from the Sinai under normal commercial terms after the fields were returned to Egypt.

■ Israel and Egypt would start negotiations on Palestinian self-rule in the West Bank and the Gaza Strip within a month after the exchange of ratification documents.

Israel's return of the Sinai oilfields was the final issue in the negotiations of the treaty that had been resolved in discussions between Premier Begin and U.S. Secretary of State Cyrus Vance in New York March 24 and between Begin and President Sadat in Washington March 25. Under a compromise plan worked out by Begin and Sadat, the oilfields would be turned over to Egypt seven months after ratification of the treaty. Originally, Israel had asked for a nine-month delay and Egypt wanted the fields returned in six months.

U.S.-Israeli Agreements—Under the separate U.S.-Israeli memorandum of agreement signed March 26, Washington pledged that in the event of Egyptian violation of the treaty with Israel, it would "take such remedial measures as it deemed appropriate, which may include diplomatic, economic and military measures." These steps, the memorandum said, could include "strengthening of the United States presence in the area, providing the emergency supplies to Israel and the exercise of maritime rights in order to put an end" to such breaches of the pact as a naval blockade of Israel or denial of its use of these international waterways: the Suez Canal, the Strait of Tiran and the Gulf of Aqaba.

The U.S. held that the agreement was similar to the one it had signed with Israel in 1975 at the time of the second Sinai disengagement accord between Israel and Egypt.

Egypt denounced the separate U.S.-Israeli agreements in a statement by President Anwar Sadat March 28 and in two protest letters written by Premier Mustafa Khalil to Vance and released that day.

In his first letter, Khalil said he had been shown the text of the U.S.-Israeli memorandum only one day before its signing and that he expressed objections. He said it was "contrary to the spirit existing between our two countries and does not contribute to the strengthening of relations between them."

Khalil also complained that the memorandum "assumes that Egypt is liable to violate its obligations," thus casting doubts on the impartiality of the U.S., which was not supposed "to support the allegations of one side against the other."

Khalil's letter also took issue with the United States' right "to impose a military presence in the region for reasons agreed between Israel and the U.S., a matter which we cannot accept."

In the second letter to Vance, Khalil said Egypt "will not recognize the legality of the memorandum and considers it null and void."

Sadat said the memorandum violated the Israeli-Egyptian accord and that it "could be construed as an eventual alliance" against Egypt.

In a reply to Khalil released March 28, the U.S. State Department assured Cairo that the Israeli memo, and a similar one offered Egypt but refused, "is to facilitate the maintenance of peace in the area." The memo "does not assume that Egypt is likely to violate the treaty," the department said. "On the contrary, we have full confidence that Egypt and Israel are determined to honor their obligations.".

In rejecting the U.S. offer of a similar agreement, Sadat said, "We are not in need for anyone to protect us and we don't want anyone to fight our battles for us. And we don't feel insecure to ask for such measures for us."

Treaty Ratified—The peace treaty was ratified by the Egyptian People's Assembly April 10 by 329–13 vote. One member abstained, and 17 were absent.

The pact also was overwhelmingly approved in a nationwide Egyptian referendum April 19. Officials announced April 20 that 99.95% of the voters endorsed the pact.

In opening Assembly debate on ratification of the treaty, Sadat April 5 had urged the Palestinians to reject the terrorist tactics of the Palestine Liberation Organization and join the autonomy talks.

Sadat also warned Arab radical states against attacks on Egypt, asserting that his country would retaliate. The president scoffed at attempts by other Arab states to isolate Egypt by withdrawing diplomatic relations.

The Israeli Cabinet had approved the treaty in two votes April 1. In the first balloting, Transport Minister Chaim Landau voted against, but he was persuaded to abstain when the pact was voted on a second time.

Text of Egyptian-Israeli Peace Treaty

Following is the official English language text of the Treaty of Peace between the Arab Republic of Egypt and the State of Israel and agreed minutes to certain articles and annexes of the peace treaty, all signed March 26 in Washington:

The Egyptian-Israeli Treaty

The government of the Arab Republic of Egypt and the government of the State of Israel:

Preamble

Convinced of the urgent necessity of the establishment of a just, comprehensive and lasting peace in the Middle East in accordance with Security Council Resolutions 242 and 338:

Reaffirming their adherence to the "framework for Peace in the Middle East Agreed at Camp David," dated Sept. 17, 1978;

Noting that the aforementioned framework as appropriate is intended to constitute a basis for peace not only between Egypt and Israel but also between Israel and each of the other Arab neighbors which is prepared to negotiate peace with it on this basis;

Desiring to bring to an end the state of war between them and to establish a peace in which every state in the area can live in security;

Convinced that the conclusion of a treaty of peace between Egypt and Israel is an important step in the search for comprehensive peace in the area and for the attainment of the settlement of the Arab-Israeli conflict in all its aspects;

Inviting the other Arab parties to this dispute to join the peace process with Israel guided by and based on the principles of the aforementioned framework;

Desiring as well to develop friendly relations and cooperation between themselves in accordance with the United Nations Charter and the principles of international law governing international relations in times of peace:

Agree to the following provisions in the free exercise of their sovereignty, in order to implement the framework for the conclusion of a peace treaty between Egypt and Israel.

Article I

1. The state of war between the parties will be terminated and peace will be established between them upon the exchange of instruments of ratification of this treaty.

2. Israel will withdraw all its armed forces and civilians from the Sinai behind the international boundary between Egypt and mandated Palestine, as provided in the annexed protocol (Annex I), and Egypt will resume the exercise of its full sovereignty over the Sinai.

3. Upon completion of the interim withdrawal provided for in Annex I, the parties will establish normal and friendly relations, in accordance with Article III (3).

Article II

The permanent boundary between Egypt and Israel is the recognized international boundary between Egypt and the former mandated territory of Palestine as shown on the map at Annex II, without prejudice to the issue of the status of the Gaza Strip. The parties recognize this boundary as inviolable. Each will respect the territorial integrity of the other, including their territorial waters and airspace.

Article III

1. The parties will apply between them the provisions of the Charter of the United Nations and the principles of international law governing relations among states in times of peace. In particular:

A. They recognize and will respect each other's sovereignty, territorial integrity and political independence.

B. They recognize and will respect each other's right to live in peace within their secure and recognized boundaries.

C. They will refrain from the threat or use of force, directly or indirectly, against each other and will settle all disputes between them by peaceful means.

2. Each party undertakes to insure that acts or threats of belligerency, hostility or violence do not originate from and are not committed from within its territory, or by any forces subject to its control or by any other forces stationed on its territory, against the population, citizens or property of the other party. Each party also undertakes to refrain from organizing, instigating, inciting, assisting or participating in acts or threats of belligerency, hostility, subversion or violence against the other party, anywhere, and undertakes to insure that perpetrators of such acts are brought to justice.

3. The parties agree that the normal relationship established between them will include full recognition, diplomatic, economic and cultural relations, termination of economic boycotts and discriminatory barriers to the free movement of people and goods, and will guarantee the mutual enjoyment by citizens of the due process of law. The process by which they undertake to achieve such a relationship parallel to the implementation of other provisions of this treaty is set out in the annexed protocol (Annex III).

Article IV

1. In order to provide maximum security for both parties on the basis of reciprocity, agreed security arrangements will be established including limited force zones in Egyptian and Israeli territory, and United Nations forces and observers, described in detail as to nature and timing in Annex I, and other security arrangements the parties may agree upon.

2. The parties agree to the stationing of United Nations personnel in areas described in Annex I, the parties agree not to request withdrawal of the United Nations personnel and that these personnel will not be removed unless such removal is approved by the Security Council of the United Nations, with the affirmative vote of the five permanent members, unless the parties otherwise agree.

3. A joint commission will be established to facilitate the implementation of the treaty, as provided for in Annex I.

4. The security arrangements provided for in paragraphs 1 and 2 of this article may at the request of either party be reviewed and amended by mutual agreement of the parties.

Article V

1. Ships of Israel, and cargoes destined for or coming from Israel, shall enjoy the right of free passage through the Suez Canal and its approaches through the Gulf of Suez and the Mediterranean Sea on the basis of the Constantinople Convention of 1888, applying to all nations. Israeli nationals, vessels and cargoes, as well as persons, vessels and cargoes destined for or coming from Israel, shall be accorded nondiscriminatory treat-

ment in all matters connected with usage of the canal.

2. The parties consider the Strait of Tiran and the Gulf of Aqaba to be international waterways open to all nations for unimpeded and nonsuspendable freedom of navigation and overflight. The parties will respect each other's right to navigation and overflight for access to either country through the Strait of Tiran and the Gulf of Aqaba.

Article VI

1. This treaty does not affect and shall not be interpreted as affecting in any way the rights and obligations of the parties under the Charter of the United Nations.

2. The parties undertake to fulfill in good faith their obligations under this treaty, without regard to action or inaction of any other party and independently of any instrument external to this treaty.

3. They further undertake to take all the necessary measures for the application in their relations of the provisions of the multilateral conventions to which they are parties, including the submission of appropriate notification of the secretary general of the United Nations and other depositories of such conventions.

4. The parties undertake not to enter into any obligation in conflict with this treaty.

5. Subject to Article 103 of the United Nations Charter, in the event of a conflict between the obligations of the parties under the present treaty and any of their other obligations, the obligations under this treaty will be binding and implemented.

Article VII

1. Dispute arising out of the application or interpretation of this treaty shall be resolved by negotiations.

2. Any such disputes which cannot be settled by negotiations shall be resolved by conciliation or submitted to arbitration.

Article VIII

The parties agree to establish a claims commission for the mutual settlement of all financial claims.

Article IX

1. This treaty shall enter into force up on exchange of instruments of ratification.

2. This treaty supersedes that agreement between Egypt and Israel of September 1975.

3. All protocols, annexes and maps attached to this treaty shall be regarded as an integral part hereof.

4. The treaty shall be communicated to the secretary general of the United Nations for registration in accordance with the provisions of Article 102 of the Charter of the United Nations. Done at Washington this 26th day of March 1979, in duplicate in the Arabic, English and Hebrew languages, each text being equally authentic. In case of any divergence of interpretation, the English text shall prevail.

Agreed Minutes

To Articles I, IV, V and VI
and Annexes I and III
of Treaty of Peace

Article I—Egypt's resumption of the exercise of full sovereignty over the Sinai provided for in paragraph 2 of Article I shall occur with regard to each area upon Israel's withdrawal from that area.

Article IV—It is agreed between the parties that the review provided for in Article IV (4) will be undertaken when requested by either party, commencing within three months of such a request, but that any amendment can be made only with the mutual agreement of both parties.

Article V—The second sentence of paragraph 2 of Article V shall not be construed as limiting the first sentence of that paragraph. The foregoing is not to be construed as contravening the second sentence of paragraph 2 of Article V, which reads as follows: "The parties will respect each other's right to navigation and overflight for access to either country through the Strait of Tiran and the Gulf of Aqaba."

Article VI (2)—The provisions of Article VI shall not be construed in contradiction to the provisions of the framework for peace in the Middle East agreed at Camp David. The foregoing is not to be construed as contravening the provisions of Article VI (2) of the treaty, which reads as follows:

"The parties undertake to fulfill in good faith their obligations under this treaty, without regard to action or inaction of any other party and independently of any instrument external to this treaty."

Article VI (5)—It is agreed by the parties that there is no assertion that this treaty prevails over other treaties or agreements or that other treaties or agreements prevail over this treaty. The foregoing is not to be construed as contravening the provisions of Article VI (5) of the treaty, which reads as follows:

"Subject to Article 103 of the United Nations Charter, in the event of a conflict between the obligations of the parties under the present treaty and any of their other obligations, the obligations under this treaty will be binding and implemented."

Annex I—Article VI, paragraph 8 of Annex I provides as follows: "The parties shall agree on the nations from which the United Nations force and observers will be drawn. They will be drawn from nations other than those which are permanent members of the United Nations Security Council."

The parties have agreed as follows: "With respect to the provisions of paragraph 8, Article VI, of Annex I, if no agreement is reached between the parties, they will accept or support a U.S. proposal concerning the composition of the United Nations force and observers."

Annex III—The Treaty of Peace and Annex III thereto provide for establishing normal economic relations between the parties. In accordance therewith, it is agreed that such relations will include normal commercial sales of oil by Egypt to Israel, and that Israel shall be fully entitled to make bids for Egyptian-origin oil not needed for Egyptian domestic oil consumption, and Egypt and its oil concessionaires will entertain bids made by Israel, on the same basis and terms as apply to other bidders for such oil.

---

*Annex II, not appearing in this text, contained three maps depicting Israel's phased military withdrawal from the Sinai Peninsula that were yet to be released for publication.

Memorandums of Agreement Between the U.S. and Israel

Following are the texts of two memorandums of agreement between the U.S. and Israel, one of which provides assurances for Israel in case of Egyptian violations of the Treaty of Peace and the other of which assures Israel of an uninterrupted supply of oil until at least 1990:

Memorandum
Of Agreement
Between the U.S.
And Israel

Recognizing the significance of the conclusion of the Treaty of Peace between Israel and Egypt and considering the importance of full implementation of the Treaty of Peace to Israel's security interests and the contribution of the conclusion of the Treaty of Peace to the security and development of Israel as well as its significance to peace and stability in the region and to the maintenance of international peace and security; and

Recognizing that the withdrawal from Sinai imposes additional heavy security, military and economic burdens on Israel;

The governments of the United States of America and of the State of Israel, subject to their constitutional processes and applicable law, confirm as follows:

1. In the light of the role of the United States in achieving the Treaty of Peace and the parties' desire that the United States continue its supportive efforts, the United States will take appropriate measures to promote full observance of the Treaty of Peace.

2. Should it be demonstrated to the satisfaction of the United States that there has been a violation or threat of violation of the Treaty of Peace, the United States will consult with the parties with regard to measures to halt or prevent the violation, ensure observance of the Treaty of Peace, enhance friendly and peaceful relations between the parties and promote peace in the region, and will take such remedial measures as it deems appropriate, which may include diplomatic, economic and military measures as described below.

3. The United States will provide support it deems appropriate for proper actions taken by Israel in response to such demonstrated violations of the Treaty of Peace. In particular, if a violation of the Treaty of Peace is deemed to threaten the security of Israel, including, inter alia, a blockade of Israel's use of international waterways, a violation of the provisions of the Treaty of Peace concerning limitation of forces or an armed attack against Israel, the United States will be prepared to consider, on an urgent basis, such measures as the strengthening of the United States presence in the area, the providing of emergency supplies to Israel, and the exercise of maritime rights in order to put an end to the violation.

4. The United States will support the parties' rights to navigation and overflight for access to either country through and over the Strait of Tiran and the Gulf of Aqaba pursuant to the Treaty of Peace.

5. The United States will oppose and, if necessary, vote against any action or resolution in the United Nations which in its judgment adversely affects the Treaty of Peace.

6. Subject to congressional authorization and appropriation, the United States will endeavor to take into account and will endeavor to be responsive to military and economic assistance requirements of Israel.

7. The United States will continue to impose restrictions on weapons supplied by it to any country which prohibit their unauthorized transfer to any third party. The United States will not supply or authorize transfer of such weapons for use in an armed attack against Israel, and will take steps to prevent such unauthorized transfer.

8. Existing agreements and assurances between the United States and Israel are not terminated or altered by the conclusion of the Treaty of Peace, except for those contained in Articles V, VI, VII, VIII, XI, XII, XV and XVI of the Memorandum of Agreement between the Government of the United States and the Government of Israel (United States-Israeli Assurances) of September 1, 1975.

9. This Memorandum of Agreement sets forth the full understandings of the United States and Israel with regard to the subject matters covered between them hereby, and shall be carried out in accordance with its terms.

U.S.-Israeli Memorandum Of Agreement On Oil

The oil supply arrangement of September 1, 1975, between the governments of the United States and Israel, annexed hereto, remains in effect. A memorandum of agreement shall be agreed upon and concluded to provide an oil supply arrangement for a total of 15 years, including the 5 years provided in the September 1, 1975, arrangement.

The memorandum of agreement, including the commencement of this arrangement and pricing provisions, will be mutually agreed upon by the parties within 60 days following the entry into force of the Treaty of Peace between Egypt and Israel.

It is the intention of the parties that prices paid by Israel for oil provided by the United States hereunder shall be comparable to world market prices current at the time of transfer, and that in any event the United States will be reimbursed by Israel for the costs incurred by the United States in providing oil to Israel hereunder.

Experts provided for in the September 1, 1975, arrangement will meet on request to discuss matters arising under this relationship.

The United States Administration undertakes to seek promptly additional statutory authorization that may be necessary for full implementation of this arrangement.

Moshe Dayan

Cyrus R. Vance

Annex

Israel will make its own independent arrangements for oil supply to meet its requirements through normal procedures. In the event Israel is unable to secure its needs in this way, the United States Government, upon notification of this fact by the government of Israel, will act as follows for five years, at the end of which period either side can terminate this arrangement on one year's notice.

(a) If the oil Israel needs to meet all its normal requirements for domestic consumption is unavailable for purchase in circumstances where no quantitative restrictions exist on the ability of the United States to procure oil to meet its normal requirements, the United States government will promptly make oil available for purchase by Israel to meet all of the aforementioned normal requirements of Israel. If Israel is unable to secure the necessary means to transport such oil to Israel, the United States government will make every effort to help Israel secure the necessary means of transport.

(b) If the oil Israel needs to meet all of its normal requirements for domestic consumption is unavailable for purchase in circumstances where quantitative restrictions through embargo or otherwise also prevent the United States from procuring oil to meet its normal requirements, the United States government will promptly make oil available for purchase by Israel in accordance with the International Energy Agency conservation and allocation formula, as applied by the United States government, in order to meet Israel's essential requirements. If Israel is unable to secure the necessary means to transport such oil to Israel, the United States government will make every effort to help Israel secure the necessary means of transport.

Israeli and United States experts will meet annually or more frequently at the request of either party, to review Israel's continuing oil requirement.

The maps on the following three pages deal with phased withdrawals of Israeli forces and civilians from the Sinai Peninsula and the final disposition of the region. They constitute Annex II to the Israeli-Egyptian peace treaty signed in Washington March 26.

Map 1 delineates the permanent lines and zones following the total Israeli withdrawal. Zone A would be set aside for the deployment of an Egyptian mechanized division and accompanying military installations and field fortifications. Zone B would contain four battalions of lightly armed Egyptian border units. Zone C would be patrolled by United Nations forces and Egyptian civilian police. The U.N. units would be stationed mainly in camps in the Sharm el Sheikh area to the extreme

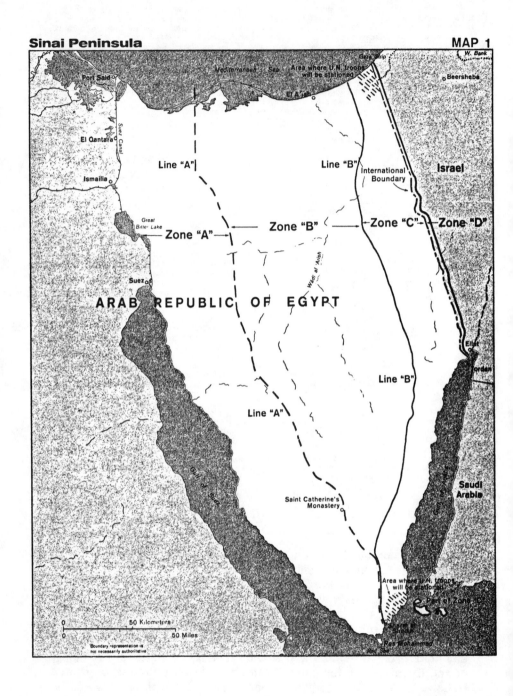

Sinai Peninsula   MAP 1

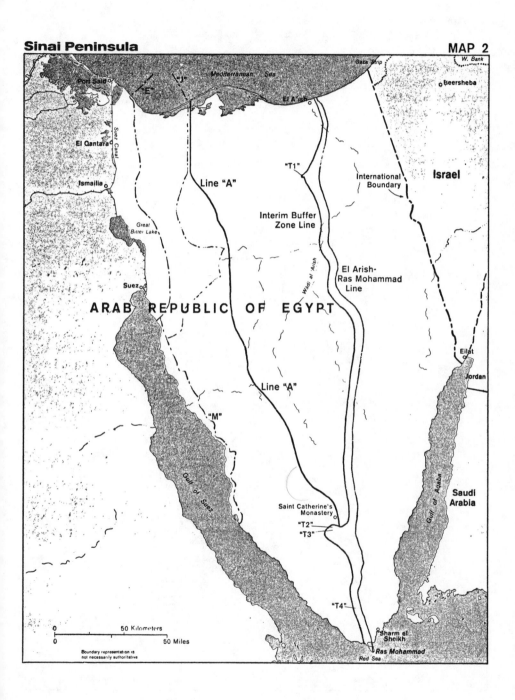

Sinai Peninsula   MAP 2

MAP 3 –
Sub-Phases of Withdrawal to the El Arish-Ras Mohammad Line

······· Israeli Sub-Phase Line
— — Egyptian Sub-Phase Line
U.N. Sub-Phase Buffer Zone

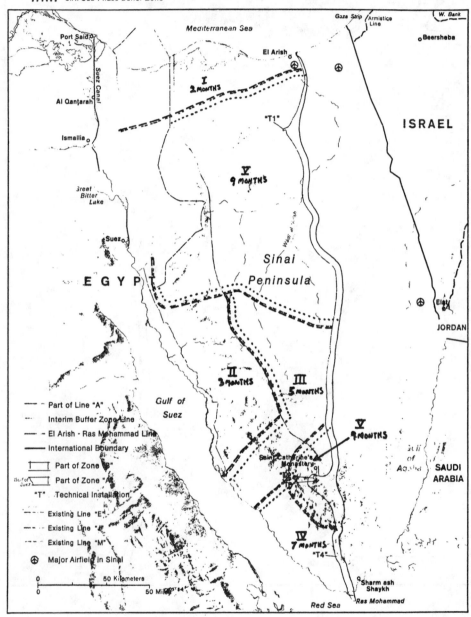

south and near the Gaza Strip in the extreme north. Zone D would be occupied by an Israeli force of four infantry battalions, their military installations and field fortifications, and U.N. observers.

Maps 2 and 3 show the phased withdrawals of the Israeli military from two-thirds of the Sinai Peninsula during a nine-month period. The remainder of the peninsula would be evacuated in three years. Egyptian border units would enter areas in Zones A and B within seven days after the regions had been evacuated by Israeli armed forces. Egyptian civilian police would enter evacuated areas immediately after the U.N. forces to perform normal police functions. The nine-month Israeli pullout to the interim withdrawal lines would be carried out in five subphases: the first subphase within two months; the second subphase within three months; the third subphase within five months; the fourth subphase within seven months, and the fifth subphase within nine months.

Arabs Retaliate, Move to Block Peace

Arabs to Cut Ties with Egypt. The foreign and finance ministers of 18 Arab League countries and a representative of the Palestine Liberation Organization March 31, 1979 adopted resolutions imposing an economic boycott of Egypt and severing diplomatic relations with Cairo in retaliation for its signing of a peace treaty with Israel.

The action was taken at a league meeting that had opened in Baghdad March 27.

The ministers announced an immediate withdrawal of their ambassadors from Cairo, recommended that diplomatic ties with Egypt be cut within a month, suspended Egypt's membership in the Arab League and transferred the league's headquarters temporarily from Cairo to Tunisia.

Iraqi Foreign Minister Saadun Hamadi announced that all the resolutions were binding except the one on cutting ties with Egypt, which, he said, was contingent on "the constitutional procedures prevailing in the respective countries."

Saudi Arabia was said to have suggested a six-month delay in breaking ties with Egypt, but it finally agreed to the one-month deadline.

The conference also condemned American policy in the Middle East, but proposed no specific reprisals against the U.S.

The conferees were said to hope that their punitive measures would isolate Egypt from the rest of the Arab world and lead to a revolt by the Egyptian people that would topple the government of President Anwar Sadat.

The representatives of Syria, Iraq and the PLO had walked out of the March 28 session to protest the league's failure up until then to adopt more drastic measures. PLO leader Yasir Arafat demanded an economic boycott of the U.S. for its sponsorship of the Israeli-Egyptian treaty, and suspension of oil shipments to the U.S. and Egypt.

Saudi Arabia was said to have resisted taking any radical steps, but was reported willing to support the imposition of "minimum sanctions" by boycotting Egyptian companies that did business with Israel. The Saudis also favored suspending Egypt from the Arab League and shifting the league's headquarters from Cairo.

Unable to agree on what action to take, the league suspended its March 29 meeting and reconvened the following day.

Oman and Sudan, which supported Egypt's peace initiative, were absent from the Baghdad meeting.

(Arab League Secretary General Mahmoud Riad of Egypt resigned his post March 22. He said the Israeli-Egyptian pact made it impossible for him to carry out "the league's objective of promoting unity of Arab action.")

A few hours before the Baghdad conference convened March 27, Egypt had announced the "freezing" of its relations with the Arab League. This meant Egypt would not participate in league meetings or pay dues until the other members "respect the league charter."

In another political move, Egypt March 29 withdrew its diplomatic staff from Amman after Jordan had recalled its ambassador from Cairo to protest its treaty with Israel.

Egypt, U.S. Score Moves—The Egyptian Cabinet April 1 called the action taken at the Baghdad meeting "null and void" because Iraq had extended invitations to its participants outside the Arab League and had excluded Egypt, which was a charter member.

The legality of the action was further challenged by Deputy Foreign Minister Butros Ghali, who said that it contravened the Arab League's charter requiring unanimous decisions and barring interference in the internal affairs of member countries.

Ghali said Egypt was prepared to counter "any measures they may take against us," expressing confidence that Egypt "is not isolated diplomatically and economically."

The U.S. April 2 called the Arab League economic boycott of Egypt "negative and unhelpful." The Carter Administration would carefully weigh the intentions of individual Arab countries involved in the decision before reaching conclusions on the potential effects of the boycott on the Middle East peace moves, a State Department spokesman said.

Arab-Egypt Relations Cut. Egypt announced April 7 that it was recalling its ambassadors from Saudi Arabia, Kuwait, the United Arab Emirates, Qatar, Bahrain, Tunisia and Morocco, but retaining the rest of its diplomatic missions there.

Cairo's action was in response to the failure of those nations to "conform to the requirements of Arab solidarity," the Foreign Ministry said.

Premier Mustafa Khalil also told a joint meeting of two parliamentary committees that his government would resist Arab League attempts to move its headquarters out of Cairo. To forestall the shift, the Central Bank of Egypt had already advised local banks not to release the assets of the Arab League or its affiliated agencies, a Cairo newspaper reported.

Denying that the banks were under orders to freeze the organization's assets, Khalil said the institutions were instructed to honor only those powers of attorney on Arab League accounts that had existed prior to the Baghdad meeting.

All seven states involved had already withdrawn their envoys from Cairo.

Two weeks later Kuwait and Saudi Arabia also cut diplomatic relations with Egypt, acting April 22 and 23, respectively. Egypt retaliated April 23 by cutting its ties with those two countries.

Mauritania ended its relations with Egypt April 24, and the United Arab Emirates and Qatar took similar action April 25.

Morocco and Tunisia severed relations with Egypt April 27, bringing to 15 the number of Arab states to cut ties with Cairo.

More Arab Moves vs. Egypt—The Arabs took further retaliatory action against Egypt April 17 by expelling it from the Organization of Arab Petroleum Exporting Countries at a meeting in Kuwait. OAPEC also imposed an oil embargo on Egypt and barred its ships from Bahrain.

Sudan, Somalia and Oman, which supported Egypt's peace initiatives, objected to Cairo's removal from OAPEC.

Cairo was suspended April 18 from the Arab Monetary Fund at a conference in Abu Dhabi and was removed from the Arab Organization of Administrative Sciences at a meeting in Amman, Jordan.

In other anti-Egyptian actions, the Persian Gulf Organization for Development in Egypt had disbanded, Kuwait announced April 27. The organization, which had provided a $2 billion fund for development projects in Egypt, had been financed by Saudi Arabia, Kuwait, Qatar and the United Arab Emirates.

Among other organizations that had expelled Egypt in recent days were the Arab Investment Co., Arab Fund for Economic Development in Africa and the Arab Mining Co., based in Amman, Jordan.

■ PLO leader Yasir Arafat, speaking at a news conference in Beirut March 26, a few hours before the signing of the accord, said he would "finish off American interests in the Middle East," and pledged to "chop off the hands" of President Carter, President

Anwar Sadat and Premier Menahem Begin, the three leaders who had signed the pact in Washington.

■ Palestinians at 15 camps in Lebanon protested the treaty signing March 26 by staging a work stoppage. They were joined by Lebanese Moslems. Similar protests were held that day in the West Bank and Gaza Strip, and a hand grenade exploded in East Jerusalem, wounding five tourists.

■ Demonstrators stormed the Egyptian embassies in Teheran and Kuwait March 25, while the Damascus offices of Egyptair, Egypt's airline, were occupied by protesters.

■ Following a three-day visit to Damascus, Soviet Foreign Minister Andrei A. Gromyko March 26 joined Syrian President Hafez al-Assad in denouncing the Israeli-Egyptian agreement. Their joint statement charged that the pact would not promote stability in the region and was aimed at perpetuating Israel's occupation of Arab lands and East Jerusalem. Gromyko, who also had conferred with Arafat, reached an agreement with Assad and the PLO on dealing with the new Middle East situation resulting from the treaty, the Syrian press agency said.

Egypt Charges Syrian Terror Plot—One of the Arab states that had ended its relations with Cairo, Syria, was accused April 24 of using Palestinians to carry out terrorist attacks against Egypt.

For this purpose, Interior Minister Mohammed Nabawi Ismail told a news conference, Damascus' intelligence service had established a new organization called Eagles of the Palestine Revolution. The group claimed responsibility for a parcel-bomb blast in Cairo April 19 that killed a customs inspector and seriously wounded three others. Ismail also blamed the group for a bomb explosion at a Cairo hotel in January in which four persons were injured.

At the end of the news conference, Ismail had two captured Syrian-trained Palestinians brought in. They had been arrested at the Cairo airport when they tried to enter Egypt with explosives hidden in their luggage.

Sadat Assails Saudis. Egyptian President Anwar Sadat accused Saudi Arabia May 1 of pressuring and "paying other countries to break off diplomatic relations" with Egypt in reprisal for the peace treaty it had signed with Israel.

Speaking at a May Day rally in the Red Sea town of Safaga, Sadat said the retaliatory measures adopted by the Arab states against Egypt would not impede its efforts to make peace with Israel. "We will normalize our relations with Israel; for every step that Israel takes, we will encourage her and take two." Sadat said.

Sadat said some Arab leaders had told him that they had severed ties with Cairo out of courtesy to the Saudis. In rallying other Arab states against Egypt, the Saudis sought to demonstrate to the U.S. that the Riyadh government could be a leader in the area, Sadat contended.

The Egyptian leader minimized the economic aid his country received from Arab states, claiming it amounted to only about $600 million a year. (A Cairo-based Western economist had estimated the 1978 total to be about $950 million, most of it from Saudi Arabia.)

Any financial assistance Arab states withheld from Egypt would be offset by revenues generated by the Suez Canal and by oil sales from the Sinai fields to be returned by Israel, Sadat said.

Saudi Arabia's state-controlled radio responded to Sadat's critical remarks May 2 by calling him "a liar."

Sadat said May 12 that he doubted whether Saudi Arabia would honor its pledge to finance Egypt's purchase of 50 F-5E jet fighter planes from the U.S.

The Egyptian leader said in a New York Times interview that if the Saudis turned him down, he would seek to finance the $525-million deal by appealing to the American people to raise the money by public subscription. He would forego asking the Carter Administration or the U.S. Congress for the funds because he wanted "wider participation" and to show "proof to all the Arabs and to all the world that we intend to continue on our way toward peace," Sadat said.

(Egyptian Defense Minister Kamel Hassan Ali had said in April that Saudi Arabia had made a down payment on the planes, but he did not disclose how much.)

Sadat said the Saudis were going back on their pledge to pay for the F-5Es because they "are scared of Iraq, Iran and Libya."

Arabs to Close Egypt Arms Plant. In another retaliatory move against Cairo, Saudi Arabia announced May 14 the planned termination of the Arab Organization for Industrialization, the multibillion dollar consortium that built arms for Arab states in factories in Egypt. Saudi Defense Minister Prince Sultan said the group would be disbanded July 1 because "the signing by Egypt of the peace treaty [with Israel] contradicted the reason and purpose for which the organization was established."

The consortium had been established in May 1975 by Saudi Arabia, Qatar, the United Arab Emirates and Egypt. Its closing would deal a harsh economic blow to Egypt, which stood to lose 15,000 jobs as a result.

Islamic Group Suspends Egypt. Egypt was suspended from the 43-member Conference of Islamic States May 9 because of its peace treaty with Israel. The Egyptian delegation had been barred from taking its seat at the start of the group's annual meeting in Fez, Morocco May 8.

Militant Arab nations headed by Libya and Iraq had demanded Egypt's outright ouster from the organization. The suspension, excluding Egypt from the conference's activities and assistance funds, would remain in effect until definitive action was decided on.

A statement issued by the Egyptian Foreign Ministry said the decision against "one of the main pillars of Islam in the world [Egypt] can only weaken the Islamic gathering and sabotage the united Islamic path."

Egypt had attempted to forestall its expected condemnation by the Islamic states by suggesting May 3 that the meeting consider the "liberation" of East Jerusalem, annexed by Israel after the 1967 war. A Foreign Ministry statement said the organization should "lay down a line of action" and "take such measures as the leaders of the Islamic countries consider proper and capable of restoring the Islamic rights to occupied Arab Jerusalem."

The ministry said President Anwar Sadat had made such a suggestion in a message to Moroccan King Hassan Dec. 5, 1978.

Israelis Battle Guerrillas. Palestinian guerrillas seeking to undermine the Israeli-Egyptian peace treaty carried out terrorist attacks inside and outside Israel. Israel thwarted some of the raids and also struck back at targets of the Palestine Liberation Organization in Lebanon.

In a major incident, a bomb explosion in a Tel Aviv market April 10 killed one Israeli and wounded 36. The PLO took credit for the blast, the eleventh inside Israel since Jan. 1, bringing the casualty toll to seven killed and 139 wounded.

Several hours later Israeli planes bombed PLO base camps at Damur, just south of Beirut, and in the Tyre area in southern Lebanon. The reprisal raids, the first since Jan. 15, killed four Palestinians and seriously wounded 13, according to PLO sources.

Israeli planes struck Damur and the Tyre area again April 11, while PLO ground forces exchanged fire with Israeli troops and their Lebanese Christian militia allies. PLO targets at Nabatiyeh were heavily shelled. In the exchange PLO gunners fired rockets at the northern Israeli town of Qiryat Shmona and at Israeli coastal areas.

An Israeli army patrol April 15 intercepted and killed four PLO gunmen who crossed the Jordan River into northern Israel. The intruders were spotted close to a kibbutz in the upper Jordan Valley. The PLO said it was responsible for the mission.

An Israeli army communique said it "takes a serious view" that Jordan, which had been quiet for several years, "has begun to serve as an active sector for the terrorists." Jordan would face Israeli reprisals if it assumed a role in the PLO raids against Israel, an Israeli military commander said.

(A Washington Post report from Jerusalem April 15 told of political unrest in Jordan, with King Hussein's brother, Crown Prince Hassan, opposing the monarch's rapprochement with the PLO and the Arab rejectionist states. Two of Hassan's supporters were said to have died under mysterious circumstances in the previous few days.)

Six more PLO guerrillas were killed April 16 by an Israeli patrol just inside northern Israel, south of the Lebanese border. One Israeli soldier was killed and six were wounded.

In Brussels, Israeli security men and Belgian police April 16 thwarted an apparent PLO terrorist attempt to take over an Israeli El Al passenger plane at the city's airport. Barred by security measures from reaching the aircraft, the guerrillas, perhaps numbering four, dropped a small bomb into a crowded arrival lounge, wounding five Belgians. The gunmen wounded seven more Belgians in a nearby restaurant before a shootout with Belgian and Israeli security men. Two of the PLO members were captured, one of whom was wounded. Two others escaped.

Credit for the operation was claimed by a group in Beirut calling itself Black March, after the month in which the Israeli-Egyptian peace pact was signed.

PLO Warned of Attacks—The PLO had warned April 8 that it would block the autonomy plan for the West Bank and Gaza Strip with increased attacks against Israel.

A communique issued by the PLO's central council in Damascus said the group had decided "to step up military activities against the Israelis in the occupied territories." It also said it would "strengthen the resistance of the Arabs in the occupied territories in order to face the conspiracy of the self-administrative rule" in the West Bank and Gaza Strip.

Al Fatah, the largest of the PLO groups, in a meeting in Beirut April 5–6, had adopted measures for "foiling and destroying" Israeli-Egyptian negotiations for the West Bank and Gaza. Undisclosed action would be taken against Israel, Egypt and the U.S., it was reported.

Arab Group Vows Action Against U.S. The Arab People's Congress May 10 called for Arab action against U.S. interests because of Washington's sponsorship of the Egyptian-Israeli peace treaty. The declaration was made at the conclusion of a four-day meeting of the group in Aden, South Yemen.

A document called Aden Declaration urged Arabs "to escalate the struggle to bring down" President Carter, Premier Menahem Begin and President Anwar Sadat. It proposed a boycott of American goods. The declaration appealed to Arabs to support Syria and the Palestine Liberation Organization in their struggle against Israel and suggested an Arab conference to adopt a more radical stand against "U.S. imperialism and Arab reactionaries."

The secretary general of the congress, Omar al-Hamdi, said May 10 that his group considered that President Carter "has declared war on the Arab nation and therefore it is our right and duty to answer with the same means."

The Arab People's Congress had been formed in response to Sadat's visit to Jerusalem in November 1977. Its first meeting was held a month later in Libya. The group represented 150 organizations from 21 Arab League countries and the PLO. Its leadership included representatives of Algeria, Iraq, Libya, South Yemen, Syria, the PLO, the Egyptian National Movement, the Lebanese National Movement and the Federations of Arab Workers, Peasants and Jurists.

Two new members had joined the leadership during the meeting earlier in the week: The National Progressive Force of the Gulf and the Arabian Peninsula, and the Sudanese Communist Party.

The Iraqi delegation had walked out of the Aden meeting in protest against the invitation to the Sudanese Communist Party.

Israeli-Egyptian Relations Following the Treaty

Begin Meets Sadat in Cairo. Israeli Premier Menahem Begin and Egyptian President Anwar Sadat quickened the pace of efforts to normalize relations between their two countries by agreeing to a number of measures in discussions in Cairo April 2–3, 1979.

Begin, the first Israeli leader to visit the Egyptian capital, announced the accords in a report to the Knesset (parliament) April 4. Among the agreements:

■ A hot-line telephone link between Jerusalem and Cairo had opened that day.

■ Israel would return the Sinai town of El Arish to Egypt May 26, several weeks earlier than planned.

■ Begin and Sadat would meet in El Arish May 27 to announce the opening of the Israeli-Egyptian border and the establishment of an airline link between the two countries.

■   El Arish and the Israeli city of Beer-sheba would be the alternate sites of Israeli-Egyptian meetings on Palestinian autonomy in the West Bank and Gaza Strip.

Begin's visit to Egypt had provided a "new momentum for the peace process," Sadat said April 4.

Would Egypt Aid Syria Vs. Israel?

Egyptian Premier Mustafa Khalil, speaking April 9 at a meeting of Egypt's Cabinet, was quoted as saying that "if Syria made an attempt to liberate [the Israeli-occupied] Golan Heights by force, this should be considered a defensive war and the joint Arab defense pact could be invoked," meaning that Egypt would come to the aid of Syria despite its peace treaty with Israel.

Egyptian Foreign Minister Butros Ghali also was quoted as saying that Egypt could provide assistance to the PLO "because Egypt recognizes the PLO and because under the U.N. Charter, the PLO is waging a liberation war."

Demanding an apology from Egypt, an Israeli official said April 10 that even before the exchange of ratification papers, there were "declarations of Egyptian personalities that are interpreted as opposed to the treaty and its spirit."

Egypt April 10 refused to apologize to Israel, explaining that Khalil's remarks were "widely misinterpreted."

Peace Treaty Takes Effect.

The Israeli-Egyptian peace treaty was formally put into effect April 25 as representatives of the two nations exchanged ratification documents at Umm Khisheib, site of a U.S. monitoring station in the Sinai Peninsula.

The ceremony, attended by 400 dignitaries, was delayed for more than two hours by a dispute over the wording of a letter accompanying the treaty. The Israeli representative, Eliahu Ben-Elissar, director-general of Premier Menahem Begin's office, claimed that the Egyptian version of the letter dealing with Palestinian autonomy on the West Bank and Gaza Strip contradicted the agreement by omitting reference to "inhabitants" of the two areas. Israel insisted that the letter should read "full autonomy for the inhabitants of the West Bank and Gaza Strip." Begin had argued throughout the negotiations that

autonomy in the two regions should apply to the people, not to the land. The Palestinians feared that this view meant that Israel would maintain indefinite control of the occupied territories while they would be only granted token self-rule.

According to Egypt's version of the feud, the ceremony was delayed after Cairo insisted that all annexes and interpretive letters dealing with the autonomy question be exchanged at the same time as the treaty and that Israel had accepted the Egyptian demand.

Ben-Elissar said the dispute was settled with a new draft of a letter that satisfied both sides. Details were not disclosed. Two U.S. representatives at the ceremony—Ambassador to Egypt Hermann Eilts and Ambassador to Israel Samuel Lewis—mediated the controversy.

The Egyptian official at the ceremony was Saad Afra, undersecretary in the Foreign Ministry.

The exchange of ratification documents paved the way for negotiations on Palestinian autonomy (to start within a month) and for immediate discussion of Israeli withdrawal from the Sinai.

Israeli Ship Transits Canal.

The cargo ship *Ashdod* sailed through the Suez Canal April 30, 1979, the first Israeli vessel to transit the Egyptian waterway since Israel became a state in 1948. The freighter, bound from Eilat to Haifa, made the trip under terms of the Egyptian-Israeli peace treaty, which provided that Israeli ships "shall enjoy the right of free passage through the Suez Canal."

Israeli Warships Transit Canal—

Three Israeli navy landing craft sailed through the Suez Canal May 29. It was the first peacetime use of the waterway by Israel's armed forces.

With Egyptians along the bank shouting greetings, the three vessels joined an international convoy of 29 ships for the 14-hour trip. The Israeli landing craft had left May 27 from Sharm el Sheik, near the southern tip of the Sinai Peninsula.

Sinai Withdrawal Under Way.

Israeli and Egyptian military officers opened negotiations April 29 to work out the final details of Israel's phased withdrawal from the Sinai Peninsula. The largely ceremonial session was held at a United Nations supply base in the Sinai, 20 miles east of the Suez Canal.

The talks had been preceded by discussions Israeli Defense Minister Ezer Weizman held with President Anwar Sadat, Defense Minister Kamel Hassan Ali and other Egyptian officials in Cairo April 25–27 on the withdrawal and on normalizing relations between the two countries.

Israel started its withdrawal May 25 by handing back the coastal town of El Arish, capital of the Sinai, to Egypt along with a 100-mile coastal strip westward.

Israeli Maj. Gen. Dan Shomron said in the transfer ceremony, "We did not conquer this area [in the 1967 war] out of a desire for expansion [but] rather by the necessity of a war situation which threatened our very survivial."

More than 200 Israeli settlers in the El Arish area had battled with Israeli soldiers May 24 to resist their eviction from nearby farmland.The demonstrators withdrew after the government assured them the matter would be taken up with Egypt.

The settlers were from the outpost of Neot Sinai, just outside El Arish, which was to remain in Israeli hands for three years. A 500-acre area on which they had been raising vegetables was located inside the coastal strip that reverted to Egypt the following day.

Israel returned an additional 2,700 square miles of the Sinai Sept. 25.

Israel Jan. 25, 1980 finished withdrawing from two-thirds of the Sinai. This was followed Jan. 26 by the formal opening of the Israeli-Egyptian border in a further step toward the normalization of relations between the two countries.

A ceremony was held July 25 at Bir Nasseb, an oasis near Abu Rudeis on the Gulf of Suez, in which the Israelis relinquished a 2,500-square-mile tract of desert land populated by 4,000 Bedouins.

Ceremonies marking the Israeli pullback in the Sinai were held at a military airfield near Bir Gafgafa. Under terms of their peace treaty, Israel would not turn over the final eastern third of the territory to Egypt until April 1982.

Israel and Egypt Jan. 24 had agreed to open a single land route between the two countries. The two sides also approved the establishment of policing guidelines for the interim buffer zone separating them in the Sinai. The agreement was announced at the end of a three-day visit to Cairo by Israeli Defense Minister Ezer Weizman.

UNEF Mandate Expires—The United Nations Security Council July 24, 1979 had refused to extend the mandate of the United Nations Emergency Force (UNEF) separating Egyptian and Israeli forces in the Sinai. UNEF's term expired that day.

Faced with certain Soviet veto of any renewal of UNEF's term, the Security Council instead agreed unanimously to a U.S.-Soviet plan to use an expanded United Nations Truce Supervision Organization (UNTSO) force in the area to monitor Israel's withdrawal.

UNTSO was an unarmed observer corps created by the Security Council. It had operated in the Sinai and other parts of the Middle East since 1948. It served at the discretion of the U.N. secretary general.

UNEF had been formed after the 1967 war and was the successor to a similar force stationed in the Sinai. UNEF served at the discretion of the Security Council.

After the Security Council decision, Israeli delegate Yehuda Blum reiterated his government's opposition to UNEF's replacement by UNTSO. He said American support of the scheme was a violation of President Carter's pledge at the signing of the Israeli-Egyptian treaty in March to put together "an acceptable alternative multinational force."

Israel insisted that UNTSO had neither the personnel nor the mandate to oversee fulfillment of the treaty. It noted that in the first annex of the pact, Egypt and Israel had agreed "to the redeployment of the United Nations Emergency Force" or an unspecified multinational force. Israel claimed that the Security Council's failure to renew UNEF's mandate gave Israel the right to invoke Carter's promise.

Israel further objected to the fact that since UNTSO served at the discretion of Secretary General Kurt Waldheim, he might bow to pressure in a crisis and pull out the force. The Israelis cited the case of U.N. Secretary General U Thant who, in 1967, had yielded to Egyptian demands that he withdraw a U.N. force from the Sinai, a decision that led to war.

Israel also opposed UNTSO because of the presence of Soviet officers on its staff. Israel insisted that any force in the Sinai be made up of nations with whom it had diplomatic relations.

The U.S. July 25 dismissed Israeli objections to UNTSO as "misconceptions." The State Department recalled that it was not UNTSO but a predecessor of the present-day UNEF that had been pulled out of the Sinai at Egypt's insistence.

The department pointed out that Waldheim had the authority to expand and adequately equip UNTSO to carry out the functions specified in the Israeli-Egyptian treaty. It said that Waldheim could not withdraw UNTSO without consulting the Security Council, but conceded that the U.S. could not veto a pullout of UNTSO forces.

Egyptian President Anwar Sadat, whose government approved the UNTSO force, July 24 said the Israeli-U.S. dispute over a force to be used in the Sinai was "a side issue."

Unarmed UNTSO troops had started to take up Sinai positions, it was reported Aug. 1.

The U.S. and Soviet contingents in UNTSO had left the force two or three weeks earlier, according to an UNTSO official.

The UNTSO force, however, was ultimately rejected by Egypt and Israel.

This decision was taken by Sadat and Begin at a meeting in Haifa Sept. 4–6.

A statement issued Sept. 5 said Begin and Sadat had agreed to joint Israeli-Egyptian patrols and observation posts.

In announcing the agreement on the Sinai, Sadat said, "If the Soviet Union wants to maneuver, well let's take the whole thing in our hands. And we took it."

An agreement was reached on the sale of Egyptian oil to Israel once Israel turned over the Alma fields in the Sinai to Egypt.

As a gesture of goodwill, Begin agreed to return Mount Sinai and surrounding territory more than two months ahead of the schedule outlined in the Israeli-Egyptian treaty, putting the area in Egyptian hands by Nov. 19.

Observer Agreement—The U.S., Egypt and Israel Sept. 19, 1979 reached a tentative agreement for monitoring the Israeli-Egyptian peace pact in the Sinai. The principal element of the plan provided for increased U.S. ground and air surveillance to augment Egyptian and Israel military patrols.

The accord followed two days of negotiations in Washington among Secretary of State Cyrus Vance, Egyptain Defense Minister Kamel Hassan Ali, Israeli Foreign Minister Moshe Dayan and other officials

The U.S. field mission, which had been operating an early warning system between Egyptian and Israeli lines in the Sinai since 1975, would have its term extended and its functions expanded. Original plans had called for the 200-man U.S. unit to be disbanded by early 1980.

Israeli-Egyptian Border Opened. The opening of the Israeli-Egyptian border and other steps to normalize relations were announced May 27, 1979 after talks between President Sadat and Premier Begin during an exchange of visits to El Arish and Beersheba. Secretary of State Cyrus Vance attended the meetings with Begin and Sadat in El Arish and then all three flew by helicopter to Beersheba for further talks and ceremonial speeches.

The three officials rode in an Egyptian plane from Beersheba over Tel Aviv to Cairo, circled the Egyptian capital and returned to a military airfield outside Beersheba. The flight inaugurated a new air corridor between the two countries that would be used for direct commercial flights.

The announcement of the open borders was made by Begin, who said, "Citizens of Egypt will be able to visit Israel; citizens of Israel will be able to visit Egypt."

Begin said that in return for Sadat's agreement on the borders, Israel would reciprocate by freeing a number of Palestinian "prisoners whose release will not impair Israel's security."

In a speech in Beersheba, Sadat said he looked forward to Israel's "veritable willingness to live in peace with all your neighbors, including the Palestinian people."

In a report to the Cabinet on his meetings with Sadat, Begin said May 28 that the Egyptian leader had turned down his request to permit Israeli settlers in Neot Sinai to continue cultivating a vegetable field near El Arish.

Begin stressed Israel's security needs in his address. Considering the terrorist activities of the PLO, this was "an absolute, inescapable necessity of life," he said.

Egypt-Israel Travel Accord—Israel and Egypt agreed June 6 to permit their citizens to travel freely between both countries. The accord, reached at the conclusion of talks between Foreign Minister Moshe Dayan and Premier Mustafa Khalil and other Egyptian officials, implemented the agreement on open borders.

Travel between the two countries would be allowed only by air or sea, not overland through the Sinai Peninsula. Khalil said the national airlines of Israel and Egypt would not provide direct air service between Cairo and Tel Aviv for some time. He said international airlines would be permitted to do so.

U.S. Envoy Renews Shuttle Mission. U.S. Middle East mediator Robert Strauss returned to Egypt and Israel Sept. 9–13 to receive briefings from President Anwar Sadat and Premier Menahem Begin on their talks in Haifa, Israel the previous week.

Commenting on his latest discussions with Sadat in Cairo Sept. 9, Strauss told newsmen the following day that the Egyptian leader had informed him that his country's peace negotiations with Israel were "so far down the road to success that we don't need to really worry any more about a breakdown." Despite anticipated differences with Israel "over the next several years," there would "never be a conflict between Israel and Egypt, and Sadat and Begin," Strauss said he was told by Sadat.

Before leaving for Washington Sept. 13, Strauss said his latest mission to Egypt and Israel had left him with the feeling of "certainty and inevitability that our search for peace will be successful."

Egypt Ends Boycott of Israel. The Egyptian People's Assembly (parliament) Feb. 5, 1980 voted overwhelmingly to end Egypt's participation in the Arab economic boycott of Israel. An Arab boycott law, in effect since 1955, formally imposed sanctions against Israel and companies that had dealings with it. Egypt had been observing an unofficial boycott before 1955.

Five members of the opposition Socialist Labor Party and one independent member abstained in the Assembly voting. About 250 of the body's 390 members attended the session.

Egypt, Israel Exchange Envoys. Egypt and Israel exchanged ambassadors Feb. 26 in another step toward normalization of relations between the two countries.

Eliahu Ben-Elissar, Israel's ambassador and former director general of Premier Menahem Begin's office, presented his credentials to Egyptian President Anwar Sadat in Cairo. Sadat said: "Today we are opening another new chapter in the history of our nation. It is a living symbol of our determination to live together in peace and harmony."

In a simultaneous ceremony in Jerusalem, Egyptian Ambassador Saad Mortada, a career diplomat, presented his credentials to Israeli President Yitzhak Navon. Citing "the difficulties that may lie in store," Mortada said he would "spare no effort to alleviate them . . . ."

On arriving from Cairo Feb. 24, Mortada had made clear that his presentation of credentials in Jerusalem would not imply Egyptian recognition of the city as Israel's capital but would be done merely because the Israeli president lived there.

Egypt had established its embassy in Tel Aviv Feb. 21 and Israel had set up its diplomatic mission in Cairo Feb. 18.

Two opposition parties in Egypt had objected to establishment of Israeli-Egyptian relations by flying large Palestinian flags from their Cairo offices Feb. 26. One of the two groups, the Union Progressive Party, urged that a million Palestinian flags be flown throughout Egypt, but there was little response. The government had denied the party permission to stage a protest march through Cairo to the presidential palace.

Egyptians opposed to diplomatic relations with Israel claimed that such ties should not be normalized until Israel withdrew from all Arab land, especially the eastern third of the Sinai, and agreed to a solution of the Palestinian controversy.

The exchange of Israeli and Egyptian ambassadors provoked a day-long protest in the West Bank and East Jerusalem. Shops and schools were closed in many towns.

Settlements Controversy

Israel Approves 2 New Settlements. The Israeli Cabinet April 22, 1979 approved the creation of two settlements on the West Bank—at Elon Moreh, just south of

Nablus, and at Shiloh, about 20 miles northwest of Jerusalem. The only dissenting vote was cast by Deputy Premier Yigal Yadin.

The U.S. State Department April 23 expressed opposition to the Israeli plans, reiterating the Carter Administration's view that Israeli settlements "in occupied territories [were] illegal and obstacles" to achieving peace in the Middle East. The department said that the Israelis had ignored warnings by U.S. Ambassador Samuel Lewis April 13 not to proceed with the two settlements.

The State Department recalled that Premier Menaham Begin had given President Carter a pledge at the Camp David summit in September 1978 not to establish settlements until negotiations were completed on Palestinian autonomy in the West Bank and Gaza Strip. Begin, however, claimed that he had only promised a three-month "freeze" on new settlements and that the deadline expired in December 1978.

The Cabinet June 3 gave final approval to the establishment of the Elon Moreh settlement. The vote was 8–5, with three abstentions, including Begin. Dissenters included Yigal Yadin, Defense Minister Ezer Weizman and Foreign Minister Moshe Dayan.

The June 3 vote was taken to reject an appeal by Yadin that the Cabinet reverse itself.

Yadin opposed the project on the ground that part of Elon Moreh's unused 200-acre site was privately owned by Arabs. Weizman June 4 signed an order formally requisitioning the land.

Begin, who was attending a meeting of his Herut Party, said after the vote: "There has never been an action more legal than settlement by Jews in all the territories of the land of Israel."

The U.S. June 4 expressed regret over the Israeli decision, saying it was "harmful to the peace process." The State Department said it was especially concerned because the move to establish the new settlement came at a time when negotiations had started on autonomy for the Arabs in the West Bank and Gaza Strip.

The Department and the White House reiterated the U.S. position that such settlements were illegal under international law, an argument disputed by Israel.

Israeli Ties to West Bank Cited. A Jordanian study circulated among other Arab states cited the deep economic ties that had developed between Israel and the occupied West Bank and Gaza Strip since 1967, the Washington Post reported May 3, 1979. The survey underscored Arab doubts of Israel's intentions to give up the territories.

The report contended that Israel had expropriated 27.3% of the West Bank's total area, primarily for Jewish settlements and military camps. By the start of 1979, sixty-eight settlements housing 90,000 people took up 6.3% of the land area of the West Bank and East Jerusalem.

Israel was expected to suffer a water shortage in 1979 of 265 million cubic meters, the report said. This would require it to tap the West Bank's water supply, which had a surplus of 700 cubic meters a year. Israel, according to Jordan's findings, had started to restrict Arab rights to pump water on the West Bank and required some Arab wells to supply Israeli settlements.

Israel's claim to the West Bank was reaffirmed by Premier Menaham Begin May 2. He said the border between Israel and the West Bank and Gaza Strip "no longer exists, it has vanished forever." He also said that Israel would not return the Golan Heights to Syria because without it there would be no security for Israel.

■ Israeli Agriculture Secretary Ariel Sharon, who headed a committee responsible for the settlements, May 30 urged a concerted drive to establish more Jewish communities in the West Bank and Gaza Strip. Without settlements, he said, Israel "might as well proclaim a Palestinian state and withdraw to the coastal plain, permitting the breakup of everything we have created in 30 years of war and 100 years of constructive settlement."

Current plans envisioned by Sharon: the building of a chain of urban communities north of Jerusalem and about 12 miles east of the so-called "green line," the demarcation line between Israel and the West Bank; the doubling of the number of settlements in the Jordan Valley to 50 from the current 25, and the establishment of seven settlements in the Rafah area southwest of Gaza.

■ Defense Minister Weizman declared May 31 that the West Bank and Gaza Strip were "parts of the land of Israel from historical, spiritual and, without a doubt, a defense point of view."

Begin Defends Settlements. Israeli Premier Menahem Begin June 11 defended his government's policy of establishing settlements in the West Bank and Gaza Strip. He denounced domestic and foreign critics of that policy as "following the evil path of the enemies of the Jewish people" and participating in a "campaign of incitement."

Begin said Israel had the right to build settlements in the occupied Arab territories "since this is our land." He pledged to implement the autonomy plan for its residents in accordance with the September 1978 Camp David agreement. He contended that the "true understanding" of the pact was that there would be "Jews and Arabs living together in Eretz Israel," or the land of Israel, "and security for Israel and all its citizens."

Begin described as inaccurate an editorial appearing in the June 10 issue of the New York Times, which said he was "building new settlements, as he promised he never would, on territory seized from the Arabs." In denying the editorial's accuracy, Begin repeated his claim that he had told President Carter at the Camp David meetings that Israel would suspend the building of settlements for three months of negotiations with Egypt. That deadline had ended Dec. 17, 1978, he said.

Begin also took issue with a statement June 10 by Zbigniew Brzezinski, Carter's national security adviser, that he was "very encouraged" by the large number of Israelis at a demonstration at Nablus protesting the nearby Israeli settlement of Elon Moreh. Work had been started on the project June 7 by members of Gush Emunim, the nationalist religious group. "In a democracy," Begin said, "not the minority but the majority decides, and foreign countries conduct relations with the legitimately elected government, not with groups of demonstrators or authors of opposition articles."

The demonstrators referred to by Brzezinski and Begin were members of Peace Now, an Israeli movement that said it advocated better relations between Jews and Arabs. Nearly 3,000 of its followers had gathered near Nablus June 9 to voice opposition to Elon Moreh.

Defense Minister Ezer Weizman addressed a smaller group of the Peace Now members outside Nablus June 10 and told them that the decision to build Elon Moreh was "irrevocable." As Weizman spoke to the protesters, Arabs in Nablus staged demonstrations of their own opposing the settlement. Shopkeepers closed their stores but were later forced to reopen them.

The foreign ministers of the nine European Community countries issued a statement in Paris June 18 assailing Israel's settlement policies and its stand on the Palestinians in the occupied territories. The ministers said Israel's position was harmful to peace.

Israeli Settlement Work Halted. The Israeli Supreme Court June 20 ordered suspension of construction of the controversial Elon Moreh settlement. The court gave the government one month to show why plans for the project should not be dropped entirely. (Four months later the court ordered the settlement removed.)

The court's issuance of a temporary injunction was in response to a suit by 17 Arab landowners in Nablus seeking to overturn the Israeli military government's order requisitioning Arab land for the new community.

Foreign Minister Moshe Dayan, who had voted against the Elon Moreh settlement, said June 18 that he did so because of the expropriation of Arab land in the area. However, he insisted that he supported every other settlement approved by the government.

The court Oct. 22 unanimously ordered the government to remove the settlement. It rejected a government assertion that Elon Moreh was established for military security reasons.

The court challenged the arguments of Lt. Gen. Rafael Eitan, chief of staff, noting that in previous testimony he had said the initiative for building Elon Moreh came from the government. The court said he had been asked for his opinion only after two Cabinet committees had approved the project.

The court held that the site of the project was chosen by the government for political reasons, that its action was in response "to the strong desire" of the ultraorthodox Gush Emunim to settle there.

The court's decision did not overturn its earlier rulings authorizing the government to requisition land from private owners for settlements that could be demonstrated as vital for military security, Israeli officials said.

West Bank Settlement Developments— The Israeli Supreme Court July 25 lifted a temporary ban against the establishment of a new Israeli civilian settlement near Modiin in the West Bank. Overruling Arab objections, the court accepted the Israeli military's contention that the settlement, to be known as Matityhau, was necessary for national security and that requisitioning of the land for its construction was legal.

In earlier action, the Supreme Court had issued an injunction July 24 temporarily stopping the military from going ahead with preliminary work on Efrat, a new West Bank settlement near Bethlehem. The decision was in favor of Arab farmers who complained that the military was taking over 50 acres of cultivated land for the settlement.

And on July 12, the Supreme Court had granted Arab landowners a temporary injunction stopping further work at a site expropriated for the expansion of an existing settlement near the Arab village of Salfit.

U.N. Asks Israel to Halt Settlements. The United Nations Security Council July 20 approved a resolution calling on Israel to halt the establishment of settlements in the Arab territories it occupied. The vote was 14–0, with the U.S. abstaining.

The Council's resolution was based on the findings of a three-member commission made up of Bolivia, Portugal and Zambia. The group had conducted a 10-day investigation, taking testimony from Arab witnesses and meeting with leaders in Egypt, Jordan, Lebanon and Syria and with Yasir Arafat, head of the Palestine Liberation Organization. The commission was barred by Israel from visiting occupied Arab lands.

The commission's report, made public July 14, said there were 133 Israeli settlements in occupied territory: 17 in and around Jerusalem, 62 in the West Bank, 29 in the Golan Heights area and 25 in the Gaza Strip and Sinai Peninsula.

The report accused Israel of carrying out policies that were "often coercive and

sometimes more subtle, which include the control of water resources, the seizure of private properties, the destruction of houses and the banishment of persons. . . ."

Israeli delegate Yehuda Blum July 18 denounced the report as "predictably one-sided and distorted." He accused Jordan of instigating the inquiry as part of its campaign to undermine the Israeli-Egyptian peace treaty. Jordan's complaint to the Security Council in March had prompted the investigation of Israel's settlement policies.

Land-Purchase Ban Ended. The Israeli Cabinet Sept. 16, 1979 abrogated a 1967 law barring Israeli citizens and businesses from purchasing Arab-owned land in the occupied West Bank and Gaza Strip. The move was condemned by the U.S. and Egypt.

Despite the lifting of the prohibition, there would be no change in the regulation barring an Israeli purchaser from remaining in the occupied zones for more than 24 hours without permission from Israeli military authorities, a Cabinet spokesman said. All land transactions also would require the approval of the Israeli military.

The Cabinet spokesman said the change in the law merely revoked a discriminatory ban against Jews that did not exist anywhere in the world except in Arab states that forbade the sale of land to non-Moslems.

The spokesman noted that Article 20 of Israel's 26-point Palestinian autonomy plan provided for the purchase by private Israeli citizens of Arab land. He pointed out, however, that Israel was not unilaterally invoking one article of the plan without the approval of Egypt in implementing their peace treaty.

The ban on the purchase of Arab lands had been instituted after the Israeli capture of the West Bank and Gaza Strip in the 1967 war. The law's purpose was to curb Jewish land speculation in the areas and to continue Jewish settlements in regions mapped out for security reasons.

Despite the new rulings, Arab landowners faced obstacles in openly selling their property. Jordanian law, enacted shortly after the Israeli occupation, made the sale of land to Jews a crime punishable by death. While it was unlikely that Jordan would be able to enforce this ruling, prospective sellers were said to fear possible death threats from the Palestine Liberation Organization.

The U.S. Sept. 18 said the new Israeli regulation appeared "contrary to the spirit and intent of the peace process." A State Department spokesman said: "What we regret in general are actions which make the negotiations in the peace process more difficult."

Egypt Sept. 17 had asserted that the lifting of the land-purchase ban "cast doubt on Israel's intention to respect its commitment at Camp David to recognize the rights of the Palestinian people."

Jordan called Israel's decision a confirmation of its policy of "creeping annexation" of the West Bank.

Israel Expands 7 Settlements. The Israeli Cabinet Oct. 14 voted unanimously to expand seven existing Israeli civilian settlements in the occupied West Bank but decided against seizing privately owned Arab land for that purpose.

About 1,000 acres (405 hectares) of publicly owned land were to be used for the expansion program. This was so-called "state land" owned by Jordan before the 1967 war. The Israeli government said this property included land that was not registered, although Palestinian Arabs might claim ownership.

The settlements, located in the vicinity of Jerusalem, Nablus and Hebron, were called Efrat, Ariel, Givon, Elkana, Beit Horon, Kedumin and Givat Hadasha.

During Cabinet debate, Foreign Minister Moshe Dayan had threatened to resign if the ministers approved the expropriation of Arab land for the settlements. Dayan, who had returned Oct. 11 from a meeting of Socialist leaders in Strasbourg, France, said that the government's settlement policy had undermined Israel's support in Western Europe.

The Israeli group, Peace Now, which favored a more conciliatory approach on the Palestinian issue, expressed fear that continued Israeli settlements in the occupied Arab territories might undermine Israel's peace treaty with Egypt.

Gush Emunim, an ultraorthodox religious group that advocated intensified settlement of the West Bank, complained that the Cabinet action did not go far enough.

The Egyptian Foreign Ministry Oct. 15 denounced the expanded settlement program as a "continuing obstruction of the establishment of a just and lasting peace in the Middle East."

The U.S. State Department Oct. 15 said it was encouraged by Israeli "restraint" in foregoing the seizure of private property. At the same time, the department said the U.S. remained concerned by "any settlement activity including the acquisition of land."

Hebron Settlement Approved. The Israeli Cabinet Feb. 10, 1980 approved in principle the right of Jews to resettle in Hebron, the exclusively Arab city in the West Bank.

Final approval would mark a radical departure from Israel's traditional practice of restricting Jewish settlements in the West Bank to vacant rural land, usually some distance from Arab cities.

The last Jewish settlement in Hebron was destroyed in Arab rioting in 1929. Residents of the Israeli outpost of Qiryat Arba, just outside Hebron, said 56 buildings in the city were still registered to Jewish families.

Hebron was held sacred by Jews and Moslems. The city was the site of the Jewish Tomb of the Patriarchs and Hebron had served as King David's capital for seven years before Jerusalem.

The Israeli Cabinet's decision on Hebron was in reaction to the fatal shooting Jan. 31 of a Jewish youth in the city's marketplace. A radical faction of the Palestine Liberation Organization took responsibility.

The U.S. Feb. 12 criticized the Israeli decision on Hebron, saying it could be "a step backwards in the peace process and could well have serious consequences" for the Israeli-Egyptian negotiations on autonomy for Arabs in the West Bank and Gaza Strip. The movement of Jews into Hebron, the State Department said, "raises a basic question of Israel's commitment to full autonomy."

Palestinian Autonomy Issue

Talks in Beersheba. Israel and Egypt started negotiations in Beersheba, Israel May 25, 1979 on autonomy for Palestinian

Arabs. U.S. Secretary of State Cyrus Vance attended the opening talks.

Continued differences were evidenced by the introductory statements of the delegates at the opening ceremonies.

Egyptian Defense Minister Kamel Hassan Ali, who spoke first, said "we are not here to determine the fate of the Palestinian people. Only they can do that." Ali then submitted additional Egyptian demands—the return of East Jerusalem to Arab rule, the condemnation of Israeli settlements in occupied Arab territories as illegal and recognition that Israeli laws or measures to alter the status of the disputed area "have no validity."

Speaking for the Israeli side, Information Minister Yosef Burg said his government believed that "the Palestinian Arabs should and must conduct their own daily lives for themselves and by themselves." However, "what must be understood," he said, "is that autonomy does not and cannot imply sovereignty. Israel will not agree and indeed totally rejects the establishment of a Palestinian state. It would be a mortal danger to Israel and a grave peril to the whole of the free world."

In his address, Vance called on Israel and Egypt to exercise "maximum restraint and farsightedness" in the negotiations, which were expected to last a year. "Today marks a milestone on the road to a comprehensive peace," he said.

Vance stressed the need for "general acceptance" of Israel's right "to live in peace and security" and "the legitimate rights of the Palestinians." He also said there must be a resolution of the problems of Palestinians "living outside the West Bank and Gaza Strip" in such countries as Lebanon and Syria. The secretary, after consultation with U.S. Embassy officials in Israel, dropped from his text a phrase that said the Palestinians in those countries "must have a means of political expression and fulfillment."

A member of Israel's negotiating team, Defense Minister Ezer Weizman, had quit the delegation May 17 in opposition to the government's plan for Palestinian self-rule. Foreign Minister Moshe Dayan also expressed reservations and asked to be dropped as a negotiator. Both men later rescinded their decision.

Weizman voiced his complaints to Premier Begin at a meeting of a ministerial committee that completed guidelines for the Israeli negotiators. The text of the plan adopted by the committee May 17 rejected a proposal submitted by the Defense Ministry earlier in May that called for greater Egyptian participation in the West Bank autonomy plan. Weizman also sought omission of the explicit rejection of a Palestinian state and Israel's claim to sovereignty of the occupied territories. Instead the committee plan called for Israel to demand control over security and defense matters, public land and water resources in the occupied areas, while ceding only administrative affairs to an elected Arab body that would derive its powers solely from the Israeli government.

The Israeli Cabinet's approval of the guidelines May 21 was accompanied by a statement saying that Weizman and Dayan had accepted the Cabinet's appeal to take part in the negotiations. The other members of the negotiating team were Agriculture Minister Ariel Sharon, Justice Minister Shmuel Tamir and Moshe Nissim, minister without portfolio.

(Visiting Egypt later for talks with President Sadat, Dayan reaffirmed at a Cairo news conference Israel's policy positions as stated by Premier Menahem Begin the previous day. Among these, Dayan said, were: "No Palestinian state in the West Bank and Gaza areas, no change in the status of Jerusalem as the undivided capital of Israel and no halt in the establishment by Israel of Jewish settlements in the West Bank and Gaza.")

Disputes on Autonomy Continue. Israel, Egypt and the U.S. held further talks June 11–12 in Alexandria and June 25–26 in Herzliya, Israel on self-rule for Arabs in the West Bank and Gaza Strip. Egypt and Israel agreed only on a timetable for future meetings.

The principal stumbling block remained Israeli opposition to an Egyptian proposal calling for acceptance of "bases and objectives" for eventual attainment of self-rule for the Arabs in the two territories. Israel insisted that the negotiations deal only with "practical ways and means" of establishing an Arab self-governing council in the West Bank and Gaza Strip.

■ Israeli Agriculture Minister Ariel Sharon, a member of his government's negotiating team, June 15 accused the

U.S. of "imperiling the peace achievements in the Middle East" by promoting the idea of establishing a Palestinian state in the West Bank and Gaza Strip. The U.S. stand was "far more extreme than Egypt's because of its interests in the Middle East, as it sees them," Sharon said.

A U.S. State Department spokesman countered by recalling President Carter's May 29 statement in which he had said, "We've never espoused an independent Palestinian state."

■ Israeli Defense Minister Ezer Weizman June 17 announced his resignation from the six-member Israeli negotiating team. The Cabinet June 24 formally accepted his request to quit. Officially Weizman's aides would only say that he found Israel's six-man negotiating group "too cumbersome." However, Weizman was known to have disagreed with the government's plan for Palestinian autonomy and with its West Bank settlement policies.

U.S. Envoy Enters Autonomy Talks. A suggestion by Robert Strauss, U.S. envoy to the Egyptian-Israeli peace talks, appeared to move the talks on Palestinian autonomy a step forward July 6. The Egyptian and Israeli representatives agreed to form two committees to discuss specific steps to grant autonomy to Palestinian Arabs on the West Bank and Gaza Strip.

Meeting in Alexandria, the Egyptians and Israelis agreed to set up one committee that would decide what form of government the West Bank and Gaza Strip Palestinians would have and how it would be elected. Another committee would decide what powers the Palestinian government would have.

Strauss hailed the decision as a move to come "to grips with the practical problems of implementing autonomy for the Palestinians." He said the form of government and its powers "have to be disposed of before you can move on to other related issues." He called the agreement a "breakthrough" that "demonstrated again that this process can work."

The decision to organize working groups on specific problems seemed to resolve the stalemate in the negotiations. At first, Egypt had demanded that both sides agree to a set of principles before moving on to specifics, while Israel wanted to negotiate the specific means of implementing autonomy.

Strauss said the other issues connected with autonomy—such as the set of principles and the status of East Jerusalem—could be discussed by other working groups.

Strauss attended the Egyptian-Israeli peace talks July 5–6 during his first Middle East trip July 1–8. His first stop was in Israel, where he spoke with Israeli Premier Menahem Begin July 2 and repeated U.S. objections to Israeli settlements on the West Bank.

Strauss flew over the West Bank July 3 in an Israeli helicopter to view several of the settlements. (After his return to the U.S. July 8, he said, "Even if [the settlements] do lend themselves toward Israeli security objectives, it has to be asked if that is sufficient compensation for what Israel loses on the peace process and in world opinion. My answer is no. It is not worth it.")

Strauss flew to Alexandria July 2 for a meeting with Egyptian President Anwar Sadat. After their talks, they expressed the hope that West Bank Palestinian delegates would eventually join the Egyptian-Israeli autonomy talks. Sadat told reporters that he felt October would be "a psychological deadline" for demonstrating progress in the talks. (October was the anniversary of the 1973 Arab-Israeli war.)

(President Carter had asked West German Chancellor Helmut Schmidt to put pressure on Israel to change its policy on West Bank settlements, a West German source reported July 9. The U.S. request reportedly was made during a meeting between Carter and Schmidt in Washington in June. The report said the U.S. was encouraging West Germany and other Western European nations to try to help the stalled Middle East peace process.)

Israel: U.S. Seeks Palestinian State. Israel said Aug. 1 that the U.S. had proposed the creation of a Palestinian state at the latest round of discussions on Palestinian autonomy held in Alexandria, Egypt July 29–31.

Israeli radio said that in the meetings with the Israeli and Egyptian delegations, the U.S. had proposed a legislative council to be established in addition to the administrative council agreed to by all sides at the 1978 Camp David summit. The legislative council, the Israelis argued, would, in effect, give the "autonomous" region of the West Bank and Gaza Strip all the powers of a state.

Israel raised further objections to American proposals that East Jerusalem be included in the autonomy discussions and that Palestinians living in refugee camps be permitted to vote in the autonomy elections.

Interior Minister Yosef Burg, Israel's chief negotiator at the talks, said Aug. 2 that "autonomy is less than sovereignty." He warned that "an autonomous Palestinian state will be a constant irredentist," seeking to expand at Israel's expense. "Because it would not be viable economically, it would have to rely on someone, and the nearest thing is a big power—Russia," Burg said.

Palestinian Vote Plan. Egypt, Israel and the U.S. agreed on the procedures for Palestinian autonomy at their fifth round of tripartite talks on the subject in Haifa, Israel Aug. 5–7, 1979.

The "Modalities of Elections" for Palestinians in the West Bank and Gaza Strip agreed to in a joint statement dealt with the following points: constituencies; conduct and limitations of campaigning and political expression; the voting system; voting eligibility and eligibility of candidates, and administration of free elections and supervision.

A three-nation working group was to meet in Alexandria, Egypt in two weeks to arrange details. (But the initial meeting, held Aug. 21, produced a deadlock. Israel insisted that autonomy be limited to administrative issues; Egypt demanded judicial, executive and political powers for the Palestinians. It took another month for a "breakthrough" to an agreement.)

At the Aug. 6 session, the Israelis rejected two American-inspired proposals raised by the Egyptians at the previous meeting in Alexandria July 29–31. They dealt with granting Arabs in East Jerusalem the right to vote in the autonomy elections and similar privileges for Palestinians living outside the West Bank and Gaza Strip.

The Americans and Egyptians did not raise their other controversial proposal, the one calling for the creation of a Palestinian legislative council in addition to the administration council agreed upon. Israel had objected on the ground that this would inevitably lead to establishment of an independent Palestinian state.

The head of the Egyptian delegation, Premier Mustafa Khalil, did raise a new question Aug. 6 regarding United Nations Security Council Resolution 242, the basic formula for a Middle East peace settlement. He suggested amendments to the resolution that would recognize the right of the Palestinians to determine their own future.

The U.S. and Egypt hoped that such an amendment would encourage the Palestine Liberation Organization to recognize the right of Israel to exist and thus make it eligible for a role in peace negotiations.

Interior Minister Yosef Burg, head of the Israeli delegation, pointed out that Resolution 242 was the framework behind the Israeli-Egyptian peace treaty and that any effort to alter it might force Israel to reconsider its treaty obligations.

Khalil explained Aug. 7 that his intention was not to amend Resolution 242 but to draw up a new resolution that would only "refer" to 242.

U.N. Delays Palestinian Vote. The United Nations Security Council Aug. 24 postponed a vote on a proposed resolution calling for "self-determination, national independence and sovereignty" for Palestinians. The decision to delay was taken in view of a certain U.S. veto.

The draft resolution, supported by Arab and other Third World countries, had been introduced at the start of Security Council debate Aug. 23. It had been approved Aug. 21 by the General Assembly's Committee on the Exercise of the Inalienable Rights of the Palestinian People.

In explaining the reason for not pressing for a vote on the resolution, Kuwaiti delegate Abdalla Yaccoub Bishara said: "We can't imagine [U.S.] Ambassador Andrew Young being blemished with a veto. We agreed to postpone the vote out of deference to him. My only concern was the enhancement of the status of Ambassador Young."

Young reaffirmed the U.S. position that the Palestinian issue would best be resolved through Egyptian-Israeli negotiations on Palestinian autonomy.

Israeli delegate Yehuda Blum later criticized Young's remarks, saying they were "totally uncalled for," "factually incorrect" and "morally misguided."

Opening Council debate Aug. 23, Egyptian delegate Ahmed Esmat Abdel Meguid gave surprising backing for the resolution. Meguid said, "Any new resolution would in fact constitute a confirmation and consecration of the legitimate rights of the Palestinian people which are addressed by the Camp David agreements."

Israeli delegate Blum objected to any change in Resolution 242, generally regarded as the basis for resolving the Middle East dispute. "Any tampering with it can only gravely jeopardize the current peace process—and this is precisely what the initiators of this debate want," Blum said.

PLO observer Zehdi Labib Terzi Aug. 21 had denounced the General Assembly committee's resolution. He said: "The wording does not satisfy us, the resolution does not satisfy the request of the General Assembly and our aspirations." He implied that the PLO had wanted the resolution to contain the words, "independent state."

Other Developments

U.N. Rejects Israeli-Egyptian Pact. The U.N. General Assembly Nov. 29, 1979 adopted a resolution declaring that the 1978 Israeli-Egyptian peace treaty had no validity as far as the Palestinian people were concerned. The vote was 75–33.

Nov. 29 had been proclaimed by the U.N. as International Day of Solidarity with the Palestinian People.

The U.S. was defeated in an attempt to make the resolution subject to a two-thirds majority. The Assembly also rejected an Egyptian proposal to soften the resolution.

U.S. delegate Richard W. Petree said the resolution did not "contribute to bringing Palestinian rights one day closer." The Assembly action, he said, "undermined the only viable means of reaching a peaceful settlement."

Israel Dec. 2 denounced the resolution, asserting that it was "adopted by a bloc of nations that automatically supports any proposal put forth by extremist Arab nations and the communist bloc."

Andrew Young Resigns in PLO Scandal. Andrew Young resigned Aug. 15, 1979 as U.S. ambassador to the U.N. in the wake of domestic and international controversy stemming from an unauthorized meeting he had held in July with a representative of the Palestine Liberation Organizaton. Young had been reprimanded by Secretary of State Cyrus Vance Aug. 14 for violating official U.S. Middle East policy that barred direct contacts with the PLO.

In a letter of resignation to President Carter, Young said of his meeting with the PLO official that it was "extremely embarrassing that my actions, however well-intentioned, may have hampered the peace process. In order to avoid any further complications, I would like to offer my resignation."

Informing newsmen of his decision at a press conference at the State Department in Washington, Young said Carter had not asked for his resignation.

Young said he did not approve of the U.S. government's refusal to recognize the PLO, "but I understand it." Noting that the PLO was gaining political and economic strength, he said "it is in nobody's interest to ignore these forces."

The State Department Aug. 15 acknowledged that Milton A. Wolf, U.S. ambassador to Austria, had also held unauthorized meetings in June and July with a PLO official in Vienna. But the department said Wolf was not reprimanded, rather "reminded" of U.S. policy.

The controversy had surfaced Aug. 13 in a State Department disclosure that Young had met July 26 with Zehdi Labib Terzi, the PLO's U.N. observer, at the New York home of Abdalla Yaccoub Bishara, the Kuwaiti delegate to the U.N. The department said Bishara had invited Young to discuss U.N. matters and that Terzi had "arrived unexpectedly" during the discussions. Young "did not know he was coming and, after observing social amenities, departed 15 minutes later."

The department, whose account was based on information given it by Young Aug. 11, denied that he had discussed official matters with Terzi.

The State Department questioned Young after Newsweek magazine had asked the department about the ambassador's reputed meeting with Terzi.

Vance's reprimand of Young followed an Israeli protest of the U.N. ambassador's meeting with Terzi. Israel was apprised of the meeting as a result of Young's account of the talks given to Yehuda Blum, Israel's ambassador the U.N.

In Vance's Aug. 14 criticism of Young, the secretary said through a spokesman: "In going to the apartment of the Kuwaiti permanent representative at [his] invitation, Ambassador Young knew that Terzi would probably be there.

"While there, they discussed the question of postponing the Security Council vote scheduled for July 31 on the Kuwaiti resolution [which dealt with a proposed change in Resolution 242 stating that the Palestinians had a right to an independent state].

"In holding this discussion with Terzi, Young acted on his own initiative and without authorization. Ambassador Young explained this situation to Ambassador Blum in New York."

The State Department's statement expressed regret that its Aug. 13 announcement on the Young-Terzi meeting "was incorrect."

The Israeli government's protest was filed in Washington and Jerusalem Aug. 14. Israeli Ambassador Ephraim Evron complained to Vance that the State Department's version of the affair issued Aug. 13 was inaccurate and said that Young had business dealings with Terzi, Israeli sources said.

In response to Vance's criticism of his diplomatic behavior, Young conceded Aug. 14 that he had acted on his own in meeting with Terzi. He insisted, however, that the discussions had been restricted to seeking a postponement of a Security Council debate on Palestinian rights. Young acknowledged that he had told the State Department Aug. 11 that his meeting with Terzi was inadvertent and consisted only of the exchange of social amenities. He said "that was not a lie, it was just not the whole truth."

Young said that later July 26 he gave Israeli Ambassador Blum a full account of his conversation with Terzi. Young said he decided on this action because he didn't want the Israelis "to blame the State Department for what I had done and which they might fit into a conspiracy theory. I didn't tell State because the less they knew, the less they would be responsible."

Blum said at a news conference Aug. 14 that when Young had told him about his meeting with Terzi, he replied that it "would be very difficult for the man in the street to accept that a meeting of this kind was purely accidental."

Blum also criticized the U.N. ambassador for having discussed Security Council matters with Terzi, charging that this was a violation of the 1975 U.S. pledge to avoid all contacts with the PLO.

Terzi upheld Young's original version of their meeting in statements Aug. 13 and 14. The PLO observer insisted that his discussion with Young was brief and casual because "Young refused to talk politics to me."

PLO Bars Compromise. The PLO Aug. 12 insisted that it would oppose any U.N. resolution that did not specifically recognize the right of the Palestinians to an independent state. It also played down reports of contacts between the U.S. and the PLO.

The PLO position was outlined at a two-day meeting in Damascus of its 57-member Palestine Central Council. A spokesman said, "The council decided to refuse any resolution that does not stipulate frankly on the need to establish an independent Palestinian state and make clear that the PLO is the sole and legitimate representative of the Palestinian people and clearly state our right to return [to Palestine] and self-determination."

At the opening of the conference Aug. 11, most of the speakers "were unanimous that what's being said about a dialogue between the United States and the PLO are only maneuvers aimed at clouding the Arab position and dividing the Arabs," the spokesman said. The PLO would "continue refusing such a dialogue as long as Washington refuses to recognize the PLO and the legitimate rights of our people."

Peace Prospects. The New York-based International Peace Academy sent a task force to the Middle East in March and April 1980 to gather data on peace prospects. It said in a report on this mission:

The "Third Middle East Task Force" was authorized by the Academy's governing Board to spend 6 weeks in Israel, the West Bank, Jordan, Syria, Lebanon, Egypt, Oman, and the United Arab Emirates. In addition, lengthy meetings were held with Arab League officials in Tunis and a wide spectrum of the PLO leadership. The Task Force consisted of John Edwin Mroz, Academy Executive Vice President and author of "Beyond Security: Private Perceptions Among Arabs and Israelis;" and Ira D. Wallach, a member of the Academy's Board of Directors and New York industrialist.

The following views were among those which emerged during private discussions with 124 governmental and non-governmental leaders in the Mideast, March 9–April 21, 1980.

1. It was generally believed by the Arabs and Israelis with whom the Task Force talked that the vast majority of the people of the other group favors an end to the Arab-Israeli conflict. Likewise they doubt that the leadership of their adversary equally seeks an immediate end to the conflict. Many feel that the major initiative for peace will come from the youth of the countries and from the military, the latter because of a deep-seated frustration over their inability to achieve a decisive military victory as a result of great power interference (examples given include 1956, 1967, and 1973).

2. A clear majority of the Israeli people with whom the Task Force spoke support an end to the current military occupation of most of the West Bank and Gaza (however, this often excludes Jerusalem). The crucial question is clearly how one reconciles the security needs of Israel and its neighbors with the exercise of Palestinian self-determination.

3. There is full agreement by all Arabs and Israelis with whom the Task Force spoke that the Middle East will know no peace until the Palestinian problem is solved in all its aspects. The Palestinian problem is seen as inextricably linked to dozens of other current or potential conflicts from the north of Africa to the Gulf. It is felt by many that settlement of this problem will tend to facilitate resolution of other regional problems.

4. There is full agreement among Arab policy and opinion leaders with whom the Task Force spoke, including the mainstream PLO leadership, that Israel is a permanent factor in the region and there is a noticeable absence of talk of militarily defeating Israel. The Task Force encountered persistent discussion in all quarters about the mechanics and specific benefits of a comprehensive settlement. The Arab view is that delay of a settlement for a period of years could again negatively change the Arab position on acceptance of Israel (the favorable change appears to have taken place between 1973 and 1976). Meanwhile strong private pressure upon the PLO to publicly recognize Israel's right to exist is coming from both West and East.

5. Most Israelis with whom the Task Force spoke believe that Israel is finding the military occupation of the West Bank and Gaza increasingly difficult to maintain. The Palestinians, including small children, are becoming openly rebellious and antagonistic. Incidents of mass civil disobedience and acts of violence are becoming more common and difficult to control. Fears of wider violence by extremist Arab (Moslem and Christian) and Jewish fringe groups is growing.

6. There is unanimous agreement by Arabs and Israelis alike that some third parties will play a major role in carrying out the transitional phases of a settlement. This could include monitoring buffer zones, inspection of demilitarized and limited armament areas, providing early warning information, plebiscite supervision, and the like.

7. The desire was generally expressed by most Arabs and Israelis of the need to limit Soviet military influence in the region, in which case it often followed that the United States military presence likewise should be restricted. The growing military presence of the Soviets and the Americans is a cause of private concern to most Arabs with whom the Task Force spoke; Israelis are likewise concerned about the Soviet presence. The confidence in the intentions and capabilities of both great powers has seriously eroded during the past year.

8. It is evident to the Task Force that security fears are deeply held by all of the parties (including the Palestinians for the security of a Palestinian state). All parties agree that a period of confidence-building will be necessary to allay these fears. There was some feeling that outside guarantees might be helpful, as part of a comprehensive settlement, possibly under Security Council auspices. Some Arab leaders, including the PLO, also hoped that a final settlement would include an agreement by the signatures to limit great power military presence in the region.

9. It was explained to the Task Force by many Arab leaders that communist parties in the region are considerably weaker today than in the 1940s.

10. Most Palestinians and other Arabs with whom the Task Force spoke (except in Egypt and Oman) do not see where the Camp David process is going. They fear that acceptance of Mr. Begin's "full autonomy" (which they claim is actually a limited autonomy designed to continue Israeli control over the military, water, and other critical areas) would amount to an acceptance of the perpetuation of the occupation. Based on extensive conversations with Jordanian officials, it appears unlikely that Jordan will participate in the autonomy talks under present circumstances.

The PLO, Syrian and other Arab leaders do not privately call for the renunciation of the Egyptian-Israeli Peace Treaty but for a freeze of the normalization process and pressure on Mr. Begin to change his policy on the occupied territories and self-determination. Most Israelis with whom the Task Force spoke agreed that some change of the status of the occupied territories would come with a change of government in Israel. However, many Arabs doubted whether a change of Israel's government would make a major difference in its policy.

• • •

Index